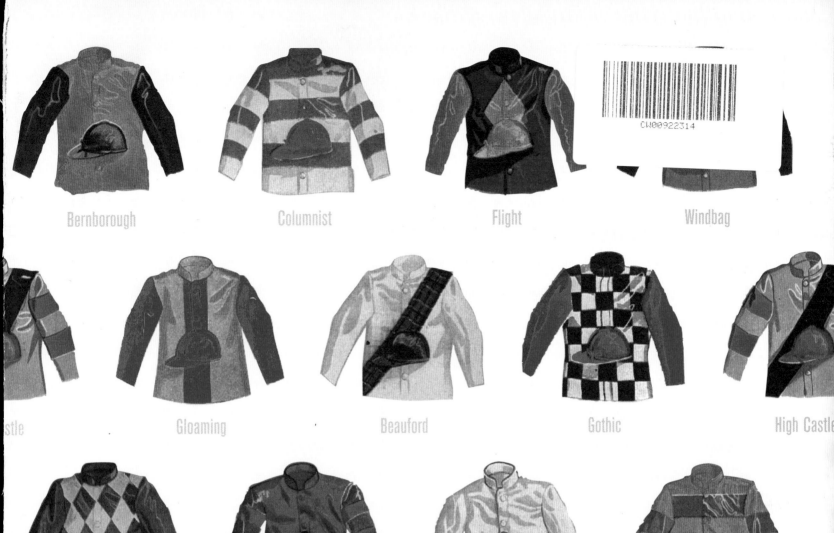

Bernborough

Columnist

Flight

Windbag

stle

Gloaming

Beauford

Gothic

High Castle

Amounis

Phar Lap

Phar Lap

Peter Pan

am

Carbine

Poitrel

Tranquil Star

Chatham

Heroic

Royal Gem

Bernborough

Columnist

They're RACING!

VIKING

They're RACING!

THE COMPLETE STORY OF AUSTRALIAN RACING

VIKING

CONTENTS

Viking
Penguin Books Australia Ltd
487 Maroondah Highway, PO Box 257
Ringwood, Victoria 3134, Australia
Penguin Books Ltd
Harmondsworth, Middlesex, England
Penguin Putnam Inc.
375 Hudson Street, New York, New York
10014, USA
Penguin Books Canada Limited
10 Alcorn Avenue, Toronto, Ontario, Canada
M4V 3B2
Penguin Books (N.Z.) Ltd
Cnr Rosedale and Airborne Roads, Albany,
Auckland, New Zealand
Penguin Books (South Africa) (Pty) Ltd
5 Watkins Street, Denver Ext 4, 2094, South
Africa

First published by Penguin Books Australia
Ltd 1999

10 9 8 7 6 5 4 3 2 1

Printed in Singapore by Tien Wah Press

National Library of Australia
Cataloguing-in-Publication data:

Hutchinson, Garrie, 1949– .
They're racing!: the complete story
of Australian racing.

Includes index.
ISBN 0 670 88502 9.

1. Horse racing – Australia – History.
2. Horse racing – New Zealand – History.
I. Ross, John, 1938–. II. Title.

798.400994

www.penguin.com.au

THEY'RE RACING!

Produced by:
Ross, Hutchinson & Associates
52 Cambridge Street
Collingwood 3066 Victoria
for Penguin Books Australia Limited

Editor: Garrie Hutchinson

Introduction and keynote essays:
Les Carlyon

Picture research: in association with
Australian Racing Museum

Special writers: Bill Casey, John Costello
(New Zealand), Charlie Frost, Andrew
Lemon, Ross McMullin, Peter Pierce,
John Ryan

Staff writers: David Austin, Damien
Cash, Ted Cavey, Margaret Geddes, Garrie
Hutchinson

Race results: Warwick Hobson.

Production editor: Peter Ascot

Editorial assistance: Donlevy Associates

Design: Philip Campbell Design

Cover photograph: Saintly, ridden by
Darren Beadman, wins the 1996
Melbourne Cup. By Ray Kennedy/*Age*

Special thanks: Narelle Symes, Australian
Racing Museum; Danny Curran, Racing
Victoria; Bruce Postle; Noel Pascoe; Geoff
Ampt; Jill Rymill at the Horseman's
Bookshop and Gallery of Armadale;
Marni Kelly and Andrea Stanley at Mitty's
of Queen Street; Mary-Anne Dibbs,
Thoroughbred Racing Board; Stephen
Howard and Paul Rovere at the *Age*; Bill
Brennan, Allport Library and Museum of
Fine Arts; Georgia Hale, Art Gallery of
South Australia; Kevin Leamon, State
Library of New South Wales; Anne Day;
Rachel Owens, National Library of
Australia; Jodie Murray, Tasmanian
Museum & Art Gallery; State Library of
Victoria: Phillip Carr and Open Access
team Peter Ajum, Don Baker, Graham
Barnett, Boris Bojovski, Annemarie
Carnell, Stella Copolla, Jacob Edmonson,
Xavier McMahon, Neil Munro, Anthony
Paine, Mahera Parry, Terri Rolfe, Steve
Shannon, Sandra Sindici, Ria Soemardjo
and Michael Thomas.

Photocredit abbreviations on captions:

Age	The *Age*
AJC	Australian Jockey Club
AL	Allport Library & Museum
ARM	Australian Racing Museum
AWM	Australian War Memorial
BP	Bruce Postle, Melbourne
CA	Craig Abraham, Melbourne
DA	David Austin, Melbourne
HWT	*Herald & Weekly Times*
ML	Mitchell Library – State Library of New South Wales, and Dixson Collection, Sydney
NP	Noel Pascoe, Brisbane
SLV	State Library of Victoria
TMAG	Tasmanian Museum & Art Gallery
VRC	Victoria Racing Club

Abbreviations used:

AJC	Australian Jockey Club
BATC	Brisbane Amateur Turf Club
CJC	Canterbury Jockey Club
f	furlong (approx. 200 metres)
gns	guineas (1 guinea = 21 shillings)
imp.	imported
nd	no date
SAJC	South Australian Jockey Club
STC	Sydney Turf Club
TCSA	Turf Club of South Australia
TTC	Tasmanian Turf Club
VJA	Victorian Jockeys Association
VRC	Victoria Racing Club
wfa	weight-for-age

Select bibliography:
Arrold, Tony ed., *Champions*, Sydney, 1980
——, *More Champions*, Sydney, 1983
Barrie, Douglas M., *The Australian
    Bloodhorse*, Sydney, 1956
——, *Turf Cavalcade,* Sydney, 1960
Cavanough, Maurice, *The Melbourne Cup,
    1861–1982*, Melbourne, 1983
Collins, J. J. & G. H. Thompson, *Harking
    Back – The Turf, Its Men and Memories*,
    Brisbane, 1924
Costello, John & Pat Finnegan, *Tapestry of
    Turf, The History of New Zealand
    Racing, 1840–1987*, Auckland, 1988
Freeman, Harold & Andrew Lemon, *The
    History of Australian Thoroughbred
    Racing, Volume One*, Melbourne, 1987,
    Volume Two, Melbourne, 1990
Griffiths, Samuel, *A Rolling Stone on the
    Turf*, Sydney, 1933
Haydon, Thomas, *Sporting Reminiscences*,
    London, 1898
Penton, Neville, *A Racing Heart*, Sydney,
    1987
Pierce, Peter (with Rhett Kirkwood),
    From Go to Whoa, Melbourne, 1994

The big heart of Australian RACING

Introduction by Les Carlyon

ASKED to nominate a figure who gets close to the spirit of Australian racing, one might, if feeling mischievous, come up with Les Boots, the baffling hoop from South Australia. For most of its players, racing is more often about losing than winning. Boots, who died in 1987, gave new meaning to the cliche 'having a bad trot'. In an 18-year career that began in 1929, Boots never rode a place-getter on the flat. Over the jumps, he system-atically broke most of the bones in his body and bled a lot. He had 39 rides for 40 falls. The numbers come up this way because he once remounted only to fail at the next jump. Before he left for the races, his wife would wrap his pyjamas in brown paper and put them in his Gladstone bag. That way there would be no delay when he arrived at the hospital.

Neville Penton wrote in *A Racing Heart* that racing elevates a chosen few and dumps its rejects into life's great tip. Which means that even though he was probably the greatest fall-guy in the history of racing anywhere, and a good bloke as well, Les can't qualify as a big player in the pageant that unfolds in this book. Most of the time this book is looking at what Damon Runyon called 'stick-outs': lasting suc-cesses in a sport where fame brushes so many, but often only for one ride or one season.

Yet, in one sense, Les Boots tells us much about the game. Racing, like just about everything else, is increasingly being run by corporate people. They don't talk about the sport but 'the industry'. And racing is a big industry: anything that turns over tens of bil-lions of dollars each year has to be. That, how-ever, is not why it touches our hearts, or why people write books about it. Packaging is a big industry but no one writes books about it. No one suggests a cardboard box be elevated to the pantheon of Australian heroes. No one suggests a cardboard box has character.

Joe Palmer, the American sports writer, once wrote that betting is maybe three-quar-ters of the reason people go to the track. In a lifetime of going to the track, I have never had anyone come up to me and say: 'God, I enjoyed watching the industry today.' At the end of a heady day at Rosehill or Fleming-ton, I have, however, had conversations with strangers in car parks and on trains, people who need to tell you that they'll never forget what they saw Octagonal do today or that Bart Cummings has to be smarter than Einstein and funnier than Groucho Marx. Money seems to have little to do with these conversations. When horses do wonderful things, they make people feel good; they wriggle their way into our hearts. This isn't the corporate way. Corporate people would never warm to Les Boots. He was, after all, a loser.

Anyway, if racing were just an industry, it would be vaguely rational. The business world likes good order. It runs on concepts such as yields and cost-effectiveness. Racing is not rational and seldom cost-effective. Why would a track rider who is paid peanuts climb back on a horse that has already pelted him off three times this week? Why would a train-er blunder out of bed at 3 a.m. to minister to a horse with two proppy legs, a lot of bad dis-position, and a flea of an owner who is always four months in arrears?

And if racing is an industry, this isn't the reason it matters. Racing is also a way of thinking and a way of living. It has its own language and its own humour. It is loaded with danger, physical and financial, and comes with the hint of a conspiracy. It doesn't build character but it does throw up characters and you'll meet some of its best in this book. In short, racing matters not because it's a big industry but because it's *interesting*.

And in Australia racing matters for at least two other reasons. It is part of the folklore, in a way it isn't in Europe or Asia. The United States has Walt Whitman and we have Banjo Paterson. And, second, racing here has always carried the whiff of democracy. Elsewhere in the world it is dominated by old money, fast money and Arab money. The public is let in to bet and to provide the crowd scenes. In Australia the crowd is allowed to own horses too. In Australia, a drover, if he flukes the right horse, can be bigger than a sheikh.

Back in 1910, a station hand who had a gift with horses began riding his mare Myrtle from Alice Springs to Adelaide, where he intended to look for work. He stopped at Jamestown, about 200 kilometres north of Adelaide, and entered Myrtle in a race. She won and a saga began. As a trainer, James Martin Cummings would later win the Melbourne Cup with Comic Court. And his son, James Bartholomew, born in 1927, would become the grand figure in Australian racing, not just this century but probably for all time. Bart Cummings is a stick-out, even though his rivals among the trainers are a formidable lot: Etienne de Mestre, James Scobie, John Tait, Walter Hickenbotham, Dick Bradfield, Maurice McCarten, Jack Holt, Fred Hoysted, Lou Robertson, Tommy Smith, Jack Denham, Colin Hayes and Lee Freedman, as well as several gifted people we tend to overlook.

Theo Green, for instance. The sweetest of men and now retired, Green is the finest trainer of jockeys we've seen: his apprentices include Darren Beadman, Malcolm Johnston, John Duggan and Ron Quinton. And what about Bob Hoysted? When it comes to keeping one horse happy, so that it keeps winning and winning, there's never been anyone like him. His magnificent obsessions have included Manikato, Rose of Kingston, River Rough, Love A Show, Sydeston and Scamanda. No trainer has more wit and wisdom than George Hanlon, who has won three Melbourne cups. He's our version of Lawrence 'Yogi' Berra, the New York baseballer who said: 'If you come to a fork in the road, take it.' Once after his horse had run like a centipede at a bush meeting, George offered a lopsided smile and intoned: 'Horses are only human.' Hanlon is one of the reasons racing is interesting.

Cummings' closest rivals are the late T. J. Smith and C. S. Hayes. TJ won the Sydney training premiership 33 years in a row. No one will ever do that again. TJ also changed the way racehorses look. His were all muscle and bone, lean and mean, full of protein and right in the head, and they came to win. The punter never had a better friend than TJ. Aside from his feats as a trainer, breeder and innovator, Colin Hayes is the best ambassador the sport has had. Articulate, kind-eyed and presidential, he made racing seem wholesome and no one had ever done that before

TJ, CS, Bart – between them, they won dozens of premierships and hundreds of classics. But one statistic sets Cummings apart from the others in the same way that Bradman's batting average sets him apart from Sobers and Hutton. Cummings has trained 10

Geoff Ampt's evocative view of Dunkeld races.

Melbourne Cup winners and five times produced the quinella. Since 1965, Cummings has averaged a Cup win almost every three years. And remember this: the Cup is a handicap – you can't win it, as the Dubai sheiks win the European classics, by spending fantastic sums on buying the best bloodlines. Cummings has won it with big geldings and tiny mares and skittish stallions, with cheap horses and expensive ones, good-lookers and boofheads, brilliant gallopers and plodders. He's won on wet tracks and dry, in good times and bad, as a 37-year-old and a 68-year-old. And the saga isn't over yet. Cummings is only 71. As he said a while back: 'I'm just getting the hang of this caper.'

He plans so carefully but makes it all

sound like nothing much. He never talks sports babble. In the mounting yard before a Melbourne Cup he gives the impression that he only turned up because he had nothing better to do.

When he was young, a doctor told him he could beat asthma and hay fever if he stayed away from horses. But horses like him, probably because he's kind and coaxing. Bob Charley, former chairman of the Australian Jockey Club, once summed him up perfectly in two sentences: 'If I were a horse, I'd like to be trained by Bart. He doesn't command horses; he psyches them.'

George Moore is the stick-out jockey – but there are other freaks One thinks of Frank Wootton, the Sydney kid who won a big race in Johannesburg as a nine-year-old before winning the English jockey's premiership in 1909 as a 16-year-old. And what about Jim Pike, who rode Phar Lap 30 times for 27 wins? Horses ran so sweetly for him. A compulsive gambler, he retired rich and in 1969 died poor, skin stretched like parchment, eyes haunted, a tenant in a block of Sydney flats he had once owned. He'd lost his job as a barman because he couldn't understand decimal currency.

George Moore is these days good fun to be around, especially when he's telling stories or doing T. J. Smith impersonations in falsetto ('Just jump him out and let him run'). When he was riding, Moore often seemed greatly put-upon, especially at trackwork. TJ liked him that way: he thought George rode better when he was angry and went out of his way to provoke him. Moore had it all. Some jockeys have vigour and attitude and some have style. Moore had the kind hands of Peter Cook, the balance of Pike and the will of Mick Dittman. He even looked special riding trackwork. One test in any sport is how the local heroes fare against the rest of the world. Moore won the Arc de Triomphe on St Crespin and the Epsom Derby on Royal Palace. He won around 120 group ones, but no Caulfield or Melbourne cups.

Rae 'Togo' Johnstone did his best work overseas. The kid from Newcastle left Sydney in 1931 slightly ahead of the stewards, settled in France, and won thousands of races in nine countries. He won three Epsom derbies and 36 European classics. Scobie Breasley is the eternal jockey. The boy from Wagga was apprenticed as a 12-year-old in 1926 and in 1957 won his first English jockey's premiership. After that, he won two Epsom Derbies and an Arc de Triomphe He also won five Caulfield Cups. Scobie never looked to be working. He knew where the post was and would appear, almost casually, at the death. Watch the film of him winning the 1964 Epsom Derby on Santa Claus. Scobie makes

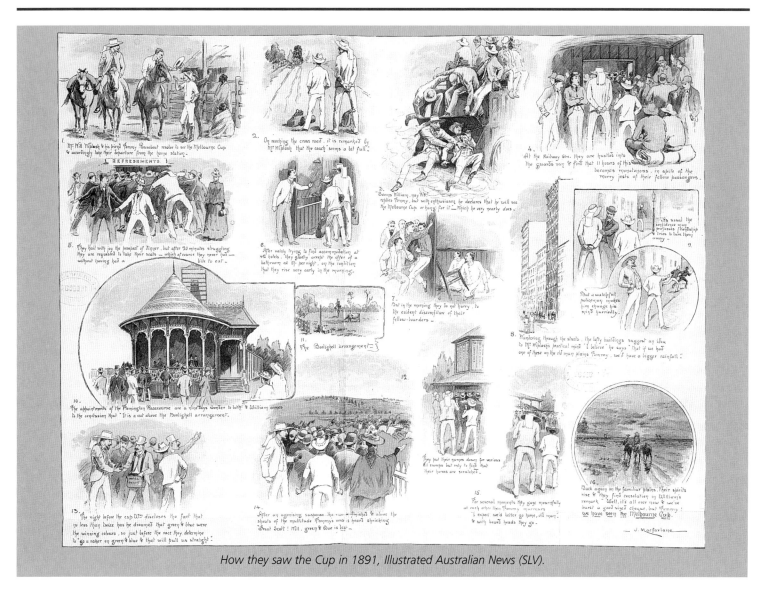

How they saw the Cup in 1891, Illustrated Australian News (SLV).

it look so simple – just a case of arriving at the right time.

Bill Williamson was also a joy to watch, mainly because of the lovely rhythm of his hands-and-heels riding. Neville Sellwood was pretty too. He won the Two Thousand Guineas at his first ride in England, then won the Epsom Derby on Larkspur. Most of us best remember him for his win on Tulloch in the 1957 Caulfield Cup. He gave the colt one dig in front of the old Guineas stand and the race was over.

Darbie Munro has to rate highly because of his ability to 'lift' horses. Roy Higgins was good at that too. He won around 2300 races, even though for most of his career there was (as he put it) a little fat man inside him trying to get out. His rides on Light Fingers in the 1965 Melbourne Cup and Star Shower in the 1979 Blue Diamond will live forever in the minds of all who saw them. He had the curious habit of riding a finish with his toes almost perpendicular to the ground. This isn't the way it's supposed to go but it worked for Roy. Mick Dittman has a style of his own too. The Enforcer is famous for his bustling, yet

he should be famous for his soft hands. He can look busy in a finish, messy even, but often his slashing whip isn't touching the horse. What Mick is good at is intimidation. He stands over the horse, telling him he wants to win, just as he stands over jockeys by telling them, with his body language, that he's going to get out of that pocket. From the stand, you can feel Mick's hunger, see everything he's trying to do.

When it comes to horses, there's no doubt Carbine is the most influential Australasia has produced. He was the shot that echoed around the world: his blood still runs in descendants of Northern Dancer, Nasrullah and Ribot. But was Carbine the best racehorse, better than Phar Lap? A fortnight in the career of Phar Lap tells you how good he was. On 25 October 1930, he won the Cox Plate by four lengths with his ears pricked. The following Saturday, he won the Mackinnon Stakes by three lengths with Pike looking back. The following Tuesday, carrying 62.5 kilograms he won the Melbourne Cup by three lengths. On Thursday, Oaks Day, he came back to a mile and strolled in by four

lengths in the Linlithgow. On the following Saturday, he took the Fisher Plate over a mile and a half with Pike sitting against him.

Tulloch might have been up there with Phar Lap if he hadn't missed his four-year-old season and half of the next with illness. As a three-year-old, he was arguably better than Phar Lap, winning 11 group ones and from 1400 to 2800 metres. He won the AJC St Leger by 20 lengths; the official margin between second and third was one furlong

There are lots of great ones and they are part of the folklore: Manikato, Bernborough, Kingston Town, Peter Pan, Rising Fast, Galilee, Shannon, Archer, Might And Power, Surround, Flight, Dulcify, Wakeful, Poseidon, Let's Elope, Malua, Ajax, Redcraze, Gunsynd, Vain, Todman, Light Fingers, Noholme, Heroic, Tobin Bronze, The Barb, Sky High, Leilani, Better Loosen Up, Wenona Girl – and more.

They're all in this book, part of the pageant, along with the fabled jockeys and trainers. And Les Boots is also there. Racing likes a winner, but it has a big heart too.

by Les Carlyon

Old Hector was the most successful stallion imported into New South Wales in the first 50 years.

 1813.

Racing Kalendar.

STEWARDS:

J. T. CAMPBELL, ESQ.   CAPTAIN GLENHOLME,
CAPTAIN COANE.

FIRST DAY,

Monday, August 16.—To start at One o'Clock.

A PLATE, Value FIFTY GUINEAS, given by the MEMBERS of the *SYDNEY RACE CLUB*, for HORSES of all AGES belonging to SUBSCRIBERS. The best of three two-mile Heats; carrying Weight for Age.

Three Years old	......7st. 4lbs.	Six Years old	......9st. 10lbs.
Four Years old	......8st.	Aged	......10st.
Five Years old	......8st. 12lbs.		

Horses Entered	Colour	Age	Weight carried. st. lbs	Riders.	Dress.	Owners.	Heats. 1 2 3 4
Pickle	Bay H.	3 yrs		John Fisher	blue jacket & black cap	Col. O'Connell	
Dungannon	Iron Gr	4 yrs		J. Bayliss	black and yellow	Capt Glenholm	
Cheviot	Grey	4 yrs		J. Reynolds	black cap & green jacket	Mr. Birch	
Castor	Grey G	aged		....Acton	pink & blue	Lt. Raymond	
Sarsnet	Ch. M.	3 yrs		——Field	yellow and black	Lieut. Wright	

In the beginning was Hector

When the First Fleet arrived in 1788 with one stallion, three mares and three colts chiefly of Arab stock aboard, horse racing was far from anyone's mind. The First Fleeters were charged with establishing a penal colony in which sporting entertainments had no place. As it was, the convict charged with looking after the horses neglected them, and they went bush. Some, but not all, were recovered.

Eight years later, 41 saddle horses – the progeny of Spanish jennets and the ancestors of the Australian working horse – arrived from the Cape of Good Hope. By 1800, there were 203 horses in the colony; by 1810, 1,114.

The first thoroughbred, a stallion named Rockingham, is thought to have arrived in New South Wales in 1799, but left no known progeny. One year later a number of Arab stallions were imported, and in 1806, Old Hector, the most successful of the early stallion imports, arrived.

By 1805 there was already a recognised race ground in the Windsor–Richmond area, and this first account in the *Sydney Gazette* on 5 April 1810 of a match race at Parramatta between the horses Parramatta and Belfast implies that many had gone before:

'The sport commenced with a race between the celebrated horse Parramatta and the b.h. [bay horse] Belfast which was won by the former. A trotting race succeeded, when the famous mare Miss Betty was victorious,

going over the ground in a style scarcely to be surpassed by some of the first trotters in England. On these matches, bets to a considerable amount were pending.'

The correspondent goes on to describe the cock fighting, footracing, wheelbarrow races and sack racing that followed.

The man behind the meeting was pardoned convict James Larra, innkeeper of the nearby Freemason's Arms.

Governor Lachlan Macquarie gave his blessing to the first official race meeting in 1810, and sanctioned race meetings were held for the next three years. In 1814, the 73rd Regiment was posted to India and the race meetings were banned by Macquarie, who declared he could not 'sanction any more meetings of this kind because of the serious scenes of fighting and rioting affrays between soldiers and inhabitants that made it necessary to confine the troops to barracks'.

Unofficial match races continued, and from May 1819, Governor Macquarie again allowed the official Hyde Park race meetings, though the grandeur of those early meetings was not repeated.

In 1821, Sir Thomas Brisbane took over from the generally more liberal Macquarie as Governor of New South Wales. He was charged with instigating the harsh recommendations of the Bigge Report and for the next four years, official race meetings were out of the question.

How a race was run

Due to the shortage of quality racehorses, the races were run in heats to provide spectators with a substantial day's racing. Three heats were usually run, regardless of the race's distance, with the best of three declared the winner. To start a race, the starter sitting mounted on a pony at the starting line would drop a flag. The horses lined up on the line in no particular order. About 220 metres from the finishing line, a pole called the distance pole was set in the straight. Horses that had not reached that pole when the winner crossed the line were declared 'distanced' and were not eligible to start in the next heat.

Many early races were 'sweepstakes' – a winner-takes-all system in which a set sum was paid to enter the race, and that sum went to the winner. Clubs added to the sweepstakes to make races more attractive.

A blind eye was turned by officialdom to what was considered the sport of gentlemen, the match races. These were head-to-head races between horses and riders. Some were the result of public challenges, issued in early days in the Government publication the *Sydney Gazette*. Road match races of up to 25 kilometres were also run, with spectators following the race on horseback or in carriages. In both cases, a lot of money was wagered on the result.

Part of Harold Freedman's giant mural depicting the cavalcade of Australian racing (VRC).

Horse business, Sydney Gazette, 15 Nov. 1826.

The Turf's native green: the first races at Hyde Park

The 73rd Regiment had replaced the New South Wales Corps in 1809 and, with the blessing of Governor Lachlan Macquarie, the horse-loving Colonel O'Connell decided to stage a race meeting as an entertainment for his troops.

The colonists threw themselves into the preparations; subscribers were found, dinners were held, a fundraising Bachelors' Ball was thrown, and the races were set for Monday, Wednesday and Friday, 15, 17 and 19 October 1810, with three plates of 50 guineas each, to be run alongside match, hack and pony races, foot races and other entertainments. The Governor granted government workers three days' leave to attend the races, trusting that they 'will conduct themselves in a sober, discreet and orderly manner'. Balls and other social events were arranged for the Tuesday and Thursday between the races.

Hyde Park, which was known then as the Common, was chosen as the site of the race track. Both the site in relation to the town and the surface of the track itself were judged unsuitable for an anti-clockwise track, so a 1¼-mile clockwise track was created. New South Wales, Queensland and Australian Capital Territory tracks still run clockwise, while the rest of Australia's tracks run the more conventional anti-clockwise.

Chase, a 6-y-o grey gelding owned by Captain Ritchie, declared himself an early champion of the colony by winning the first race of the meeting and the Ladies of the Colony Cup the following race day. In both cases, the races were open to horses of race subscribers only, and the winner was the best of three two-mile heats with weights set according to ages. Two-year-olds carried 6 st 2 lb; 3-y-o, 6 st 12 lb; 4-y-o, 8 st; 5-y-o, 8 st 8 lb; 6-y-o, 8 st 12 lb; and aged, 9 st.

The Purse on the final day was open to all horses, with Chase excepted because of his previous wins. Dr D'Arcy Wentworth's grey gelding Gig, who had already won a 3-mile match race for 60 guineas against Mr Broughton's black gelding Jerry on the first day, had a fall in the first heat of the Purse: 'occasioned by a dog crossing the course. The rider (Fisher) was too much hurt to recover himself in time to remount, but the horse was not much injured by his fall.' The Purse was won by Mr Benn's black horse Scratch, who was also startled by dogs during his second heat, but 'was however attended with no bad consequence, being far-ahead of his antagonist'.

The race meeting drew together the largest crowds the colony had ever experienced and was an unqualified success. It served many purposes. It was a great social get-together for the young colony, and as the *Sydney Gazette* remarked, racing was also 'conducive to the rising colony's interests' in that it would improve the breeding of the horses.

At the dinner on the last evening of the race meeting, Francis Williams, one of the Stewards, sang a song he had composed, which spoke for many present:

Whilst the turf's native green
Ever hallow'd has been,
And a contest more glorious enliven'd the scene;
When the high mettled Racer, proud, pampered, and gay,
Bore the meed of his prowess triumphant away.
These sports are confin'd to no climate or shores,
But regions remote shall new Patrons secure them,
Like the orb in the east which all nature adores,
They have dawn'd on our land, and 'tis ours to mature them!
No longer a waste,
As in rude ages past,
Shall our Turf be forsaken by Beauty and Taste.

Racing meeting at Petersham, c. 1844, by W. Scott (Mitchell Library).

Sydney horseracing is saved from oblivion

In the 1820s, two of New South Wales's richest men and competitors in the colony's growing social world, surgeon and landowner Sir John Jamison and the colony's naval officer Captain John Piper, got together and breathed new life into Sydney racing. In March 1825 horses belonging to Piper, Jamison and the colony's treasurer, William Balcombe, competed in a three-day meeting.

For the event, they established a new course on the eastern side of the Old South Head Road at Bellevue, opposite Piper's property. Spectators turned up when a second five-day meeting began only days later on St Patrick's Day.

The success and relative orderliness of these meetings enthused the colonists, who then met at Jamison's house in George Street and formed the Sydney Turf Club (sometimes called the Australian Turf Club). The club brought together wealthy free settlers, military officers and government officials, with Governor Brisbane as patron.

The club's first race meeting was held in April 1825. Running his first race – and winning it – was Mr Nash's Junius, who won the Town Plate of £50. Subsequent meetings were held at Bellevue and Hyde Park, but both courses were so poor that some owners refused to enter their horses. In 1826, the Sydney Turf Club built a new course at Camperdown, known as the Grose Farm Racecourse, and in that year Junius won the Brisbane Cup. Junius went on to prove himself a champion, winning the Brisbane Cup again in 1827, but the Grose Farm course met with no long-term enthusiasm. But it was politics, not courses, that proved the downfall of the STC.

Turf Club meeting is best in the colony to date

The Turf Club meeting on 11 and 13 April 1832 was considered by many to be the best in the colony to date. The *Sydney Morning Herald* of 16 April 1832 could scarcely contain its excitement:

'The much talked of "Sydney Races" commenced on Wednesday at Parramatta. The day was particularly fine, and with its early dawn, all was lively bustle and anxious preparation. The Race course was honoured by a fashionable assemblage of the fair – we seldom have seen on any public occasion, in this colony, so brilliant a display. So imposing and so numerous were the equipages; so multitudinous the equestrians; the arrangements so excellent; that our imagination carried us on to Ascot or Epsom … We observed his Excellency's carriage and four, containing the family of the Governor and part of the suite; indeed all the "haut ton" with 200 miles of Sydney were present: and we are happy to add that so excellent was the sport, and the horses so superior, that we predict our AUSTRALIAN RACES will soon vie with those of the mother country.'

The meeting had some lively spectators, as a second article reported: 'During the second day's races, about 40 women who had been taken out of the Factory to cut brooms, bolted from the overseers, and made to the course, where they were received with loud cheers. One of them was mounted on a horse behind a rider, and borne round in triumph. The others were liberally treated to brandy and ginger beer; they were, however, eventually secured, and remanded to their places of durance. Several men also escaped from gaol, and took a few hours recreation at the races; they were also retaken.'

View of the racecourse at Homebush, 1854.

Birth of the Australian Jockey Club

On 26 May 1840, a group of wealthy horseracing enthusiasts got together to arrange annual subscription races and find a new track. They called the temporary body they formed the Australian Race Committee. The site for the new course was on land at Homebush made available by W. C. Wentworth. The first meeting was held in March 1841, when the first Australian St Leger was won by Richard Rouse's Eleanor who beat three opponents and won the stake of 200 sovereigns along with a sweepstake of 10 sovereigns. (A first Australian Leger had been proposed for 1827, but had not been run.) The Metropolitan Cup was won by Mr Hall's Hercules. A crowd of 8000 attended and the Governor Sir George Gipps was present.

A successful spring meeting followed, and on 5 January 1842 the committee became the Australian Jockey Club. Homebush remained the headquarters of New South Wales horseracing until 1860 when the AJC and racing returned to the new Randwick course.

Governor Darling's revenge

The Sydney Turf Club held its first annual dinner in 1827, at which a cup donated by the club's first patron, the former Governor Brisbane, was presented. The colony's seventh governor and Brisbane's replacement, Ralph Darling, was already at war with the colony's press over efforts to restrain press freedom so it was not surprising that neither W. C. Wentworth nor his friend Robert Wardell, proprietors of the *Australian*, could resist sniping at the absent Darling during the Turf Club dinner.

Wentworth criticised the Governor in his speech, and a second diner, in speaking to a toast to 'Australian exports', suggested that Governor Darling 'be the first of them'.

Darling's revenge was not to ban horseracing. Instead he set out to destroy the Sydney Turf Club, resigning as patron and advising all government officers to do the same. Twenty-nine men left the club and in April 1828 they formed the Australian Racing and Jockey Club, with Darling as patron. Civil officers who chose to stay with the Sydney Turf Club found themselves out of a job. Sir John Jamison accepted the role of president of the new club and the ARJC staged it first meeting at Parramatta in October 1828.

The loser in the battle of the racing clubs was horse racing in general. The colony had too few quality racehorses to spread between two clubs, and though the ARJC meetings – dubbed the Party races by Wentworth – had smaller crowds, fewer entrants and less prizemoney than its opponent's, it was the STC that had disappeared altogether by 1834.

Work began on the preparation of a new racecourse at Randwick in 1832, known as the Sandy Course. Times were slow due to its sandy surface and, while racing thrived in rural NSW, the deterioration of the city courses meant there was no city racing at all during 1839 and 1840.

Police incidents: Monday. Henry Giblit, a lad about 14 years of age, was charged with decamping to the Races, where he was captured sporting his blunt like a 'lad of the Turf'. 'Four to one upon Chancellor,' shouted Mr Giblit, when the arm of a constable laid roughly upon his shoulder, closed his potato trap, and he was marched to Sydney. – 15 lashes for absconding.
Sydney Morning Herald, 23 April 1832

Final judgement: The first civil action on record in Australia concerned an 1832 match race between Henry Bayley's Velocipede and Hartley's Blacklock. The race judge had decided that Velocipede had won the match, and Hartley took the matter to court in protest. The magistrate confirmed the judge's decision.

Match races draw crowds: The Melbourne *Argus* recorded with some glee that the New South Wales Legislative Council was unable to find a quorum on the day of the private match between Sportsman and Cooramin at Homebush in October 1853.

The race, which prompted a rematch, was won by Sportsman, and, the *Argus* recorded, 'A very large sum of money changed hands on the event.' Courses were constructed on private land to exploit the popularity of the match races. One of the most successful during the 1840s was Thomas Shaw's course at Petersham. Shaw not only owned the local public house, he also charged admission to his course to all vehicles and saddle horses.

Strop stops: Strop, the New Zealand entrant in the 1860 Australian Champion Stakes (over three miles), staggered on his return to the saddling paddock and fell down and died. Lung congestion was said to be the cause of death, and he was buried just at the back of the Randwick winning post. At the same meeting, Archer won the Maiden Plate.

The first stud book: Horse breeding in Australia developed rapidly. At the first race meeting in 1810, very little was asked about a horse's ancestry; he was judged by speed alone. By 1825, the STC was able to rule that pure-bred horses be restricted to handicap races. Soon, breeders in New South Wales were feeling the need for a stud book after the fashion of the General Stud Book of England, and on 31 May 1843, the Australian Jockey Club announced their intention to collate one. Fowler Boyd Price's *The Stud Book of New South Wales* was published in 1859.

A party of gentlemen setting off from Sydney for the Homebush races, 1854.

Capt. John Piper

Captain John Piper's mare Miss Kitty ran, with no success, in the Ladies of the Colony Cup flat race at Sydney's first race meeting. The next year she contested a nine-mile trotting match race, and finished in 32 ½ minutes, only three seconds behind the winner. The stake? £50 and a dinner.

Piper arrived in New South Wales in February 1792, a member of the New South Wales Corps. In 1807, his bay stallion Young Northumberland, sired by the good stallion Northumberland, with his dam 'an excellent trotting mare of Captain Piper's' (Miss Kitty, perhaps?), was the first Australian-bred stallion advertised for duty.

Appointed Naval Officer to the colony in 1813, the following year he imported the thoroughbred stallion Wellington for breeding purposes. From 1816, he lived in splendour in Henrietta Villa, a mansion he built at what became the suburb of Point Piper.

Piper was exposed as incompetent by the incoming Governor Darling in 1825 and forced to retire from Government office in 1827. He retreated to Alloway Bank, near Bathurst. It was here he brought the famous Arab stallion Abdallah. The extravagant yet honourable man was a bad businessman, and his family was rescued more than once by his friend W. C. Wentworth.

He died aged 78, in 1851.

John Piper

Thomas Icely

Businessman, landowner and stock breeder, Thomas Icely was a success in just about everything he touched, and horse breeding was no exception. He arrived in New South Wales in 1820 and 12 years later, had established the Coombing Park Estate, near Carcoar, comprising about 26 000 acres.

Icely imported Manto, the first race mare, to Australia in 1825, and Cornelia was dropped within days of Manto's arrival. In writing *The Racehorse in Australia*, first published in 1922, Dr W. H. Lang takes Icely to task: 'Unfortunately, Mr Icely, unappreciative of the excellence and value of his importations, didn't keep anything like accurate records of his stud. He did not even take a note of the colour of his foals.' In Manto, Icely had the mare to which thousands of Australian racehorses can trace their origin.

Sir John Jamison

Sir John Jamison, 'the hospitable squire of Regentville', loved to stage race meetings at his grand manorial property near Penrith in the 1820s. The Irish-born physician was one of the colony's largest landholders and Chance and Benelong were among the quality horses he owned. He was a founder of the STC in 1825 and the first president of the Australian Racing and Jockey Club in 1828. He died in 1844, aged 68.

Henry John Rous

In the two years Henry John Rous, second son of the Earl of Stradbroke, was in Australia, he had a significant impact on Australian horseracing.

He arrived in Australia in command of the HMS *Rainbow* on a mapping voyage to Moreton Bay Island in 1827 and during his stay he was elected an honorary member to the Sydney Turf Club, then helped stage the Australian Racing and Jockey Club's first meeting in 1828.

But his lasting influence came from his desire to improve the bloodstock of the colonial horses. He imported the influential English stallions Emigrant and Theorem, and sent thoroughbred stock to Launceston in Van Diemen's Land. Emigrant became a famous sire at Charles Smith's stud.

Rous was recalled to India, and returned to Sydney in May 1828, with the thoroughbred mare Isis. He was granted land on the Molonglo plains (now Canberra).

On Rous's return to England in 1829 he devoted his life to the turf. He was elected steward of the English Jockey Club in 1838, he wrote *The Laws and Practice of Horse Racing*, published in 1866, and was an honorary handicapper for the English Jockey Club. He also created the weight-for-age scale that was adopted around the world and is still used, with only minor adaptations, today.

Rous's great-nephew George Stradbroke, third Earl of Stradbroke, was Governor of Victoria from 1921 to 1926.

Groom exercising horses near the sea, H. Aitken (ML).

'Honest John' Tait.

'Honest John' Tait – the king of Cups

Horse owner and trainer 'Honest John' Tait began his working life as a jeweller, and migrated with his family to Hobart from Scotland in 1837. By 1843 he was proprietor of the Albion Inn in Hartley, New South Wales, and in 1847 he moved on to the Black Bull Inn at Bathurst. The role of innkeeper suited him, his physical presence and boxing skills making him a match for troublemakers.

In 1847 Tait won the Homebush St Leger with Whalebone. In the years that followed, he bought a string of horses from breeders like Thomas Icely, hired the trainer Noah Beale and the jockey James Ashworth. Between 1851 and 1854 he won £2500 in stake money, winning races at Homebush, Bathurst, Parramatta and Penrith. He won two more St Legers and three Queen's Plates. He won a £1000-a-side match race at Homebush in 1854 when Sportsman beat John Earle's Cooramin. By then he was the licensee of the Commercial Hotel in Castlereagh Street, Sydney.

In 1855, Tait sold his horses and used his winnings to finance a trip to England, accompanied by the rider Ashworth. There he and Ashworth selected breeding stock for a stud farm he established in partnership with Alfred Cheeke at Mount Druitt on his return to Australia in 1857. In the early 1860s, Tait moved on to stables at Byron Lodge, Randwick.

John Tait was known for his honest dealings and the fine condition of his racehorses. He owned four Melbourne Cup winners, and the best of them, The Barb, won 17 races from 24 starts, including the AJC Derby and Melbourne Cup in 1866 and the Sydney Cup in 1868 and 1869.

The Fisher family

The Fisher family has the distinction of being pioneers of both South Australian and Victorian racing. In January 1838, 800 of South Australia's 2000 people attended the colony's first race meeting, held in front of James Hurtle Fisher's riverside property.

The first race was won by Fisher's horse Black Jack. In 1840, James Hurtle Fisher was elected the first mayor of Adelaide, and in 1860, as president of the Legislative Assembly, he became the first resident of South Australia to be knighted. He was also president of the South Australian Jockey Club. He imported many famous thoroughbreds, and owned the winner of the first official race held in South Australia.

His large family included sons Hurtle and Charles, who established the Lockleys Stud. The young Fishers moved with their horses to Victoria in 1863 and set up the influential Maribyrnong Stud. Among their many successes was the 1864 Melbourne Cup winner Lantern, one of their four Victorian Derby winners.

Hurtle Fisher.

Charles Smith

Charles Smith first came to prominence as the proprietor of George Street's Beefsteak Corner in Sydney. Smith was a wholesale butcher and cattle merchant who turned his hand to horses. He bought the historic Bungarribee, near Doonside, from Thomas Icely in 1832, and the stallions here included Steeltrap, Emigrant and Emancipation. In 1836 he bought the Abbotsbury estate, then Bayley Park, and finally the Clifton stud, near Windsor in New South Wales. At the time of his death in 1845, he was Australia's most successful breeder and owner. He raced only pure-bred stock, including the early champions Chester and Emancipation.

The Five Dock Grand Steeplechase, 1824, by E. Winstanley (ML).

Old Old Hector

In 1806 the bay Arab stallion Old Hector was brought to Sydney by the merchant Robert Campbell. Hector was sold to D'Arcy Wentworth, though in 1812 he was still at stud at the stables of Robert Campbell. In 1813, Hector stood at Sydney on Fridays and Saturdays and the rest of the week at Wentworth's Homebush property.

Old Hector's obituary was published in the *Sydney Gazette* following his death on 27 December 1823:

'A death took place this week which may be thought worthy of a place in our columns. That fine Arabian horse, Hector, the property of D. Wentworth Esq., died at his master's seat at Homebush on Saturday night last, worn out with debility and age – being between 31 and 32 years old. This noble animal was once the property of Colonel Wellesley (now the Duke of Wellington). By the then Colonel, Hector was taken from India to Europe, and from thence he returned to India in the stud of the Marquis Wellesley, brother to his Grace the Duke of Wellington. After his visit to Europe, it became the lot of the deceased to be thought worthy of the honor of a trip to New South Wales, so that his name might be handed down as having improved the then extremely poor equestrian race. Mr Merchant Campbell, of George Street, brought him to this colony many years since. It is well known that Hector is the progenitor of many excellent horses amongst us; that his breed is of the most serviceable kind.'

'Iron horse' Jorrocks

Known as the 'iron horse', Jorrocks ran over 100 races, winning more than 60, and placed in another 24. Foaled in 1833, he was running his best from 1846 to 1849, winning 31 of 32 starts while carrying at least 9 stone.

Jorrocks was bred on Henry Bayly's property near Mudgee in 1833, the progeny of two of the best horses of their time. His sire was Bayly's imported horse Whisker and the dam was Matilda, who was by Steeltrap. Like many racehorses of the day, he was broken in at the age of four, and spent time as a stockhorse.

Jorrocks was the Homebush master. He won most of the colony's major races including the Australian Plate (four times), the Metropolitan Stakes (three times) and the Cumberland Cup.

He was brought out of retirement at the age of 19 by yet another new owner and ran in the Metropolitan Handicap in October 1852. Jorrocks died in 1860.

Junius's Cup

Junius, owned by Andrew Nash, was Australia's first champion racehorse. He was foaled in 1819, sired by D'Arcy Wentworth's Hector and, according to racing historian Douglas Barrie, his dam was inbred to another Arab horse, Shark.

Andrew Nash, a non-subscriber to the Turf Club, owned the Woolpack Inn in Parramatta, formerly the Freemason's Arms, which he had bought in in 1821. Coincidentally, it was the inn outside which the famous match race was staged between Parramatta and Belfast in 1810. Nash had attempted to buy Junius as a foal, then bought him once he was raced.

By 1824 Junius had already won several match races and was looking a champion. He won his first race at the Sydney Turf Club's first meeting in 1825, and at the second Sydney Turf Club meeting in 1826 he won the first Brisbane Cup, then went on to win the Turf Club Plate the next day.

Junius won the Brisbane Cup again in 1827 and his jockey, James Spinks, increased his owner's challenge of 500 guineas to £1000 'to run three times around the Sydney course against any other horse in the colony'. There were no takers. In October Junius was 'by general consent' excluded from the Parramatta races. He died when Nash's Parramatta stables burned in 1831, and before long horses of pure Arab breeding were being outperformed by the offspring of the imported English thoroughbreds.

'What do you want for him?' by G. Lacy, in Sketches in Australia (nd, ML).

A 'stormy' Petrel

Ask anyone down south and they would tell you: the only reason Jorrocks beat the Victorian champion Petrel in the 1847 match race was because the sailing ship in which Petrel was transported hit rough weather, tossing him about in his crate in the hold. The horse was given no time to recover, and was well beaten.

Petrel's breeding was a mystery. Some said his sire was Rous's Emigrant, others claimed it was Steeltrap. In 1841, an overlander on his way from Sydney to Adelaide arrived at a station at the foot of the Grampians with two well-bred-looking mares, both in foal, suspected of having been stolen. He found work there, and a station overseer bought the two foals as two-year-olds for £36 the pair to work as stockhorses. It didn't take long for Petrel to gain a reputation. One day, legend has it, he ran down an emu in a mock hunt. Buangor squatter Colin Campbell swapped a mare worth £20 for him and he began his life as a racehorse.

Campbell rode Petrel in the first meeting of the Pyrenees Turf Club, winning easily, and following wins in Melbourne and Geelong he raffled him at the Royal Hotel in Collins Street, with 40 tickets at £5 each. The winner Mr Riddell, a socialite and later a member of the Legislative Assembly, threw the Grand Petrel Ball to celebrate, decorating the ballroom in Petrel's colours, with the outfit of his jockey, Sandy Ellis, known as 'Sandy the Butcher', on display. He then promptly sold the horse by auction at Kirk's Bazaar to Mr Borrodaile for 150 guineas.

Petrel was a dark chestnut, a fine-looking horse who was nevertheless described by some early in his career as too powerful and clumsy for a racer. He won the Melbourne Town Plate in 1845, 1846 and 1848 and the Geelong Town Plate four times between 1845 and 1849, then again as an 11-year-old in 1853. Petrel had many owners during his career, but he finished life in the possession of James Austin, 'roaming the flats by the homestead creek' until he died at the age of 25.

Veno: champion

On 3 October 1857, 40 000 spectators saw Victoria's grey mare Alice Hawthorn defeated by the Sydney champion Veno at Flemington, in a race described as 'a humiliation and a disgrace' by *Bell's Life of Victoria.*

Veno laid claim to the title of Australian champion in the 1850s. His sire was the locally bred Waverley; his dam Peri was from the half-Arab mare Aspic. Born in 1849, he improved with age. In 1857, he won 13 races from 15 starts, along with a second and third.

In Melbourne, Andrew Chirnside's Alice Hawthorn was beating all-comers and Chirnside challenged the Sydney-sider to a £1000-a-side match race. The race was run at Flemington over three miles and Veno won comfortably by about 2 lengths, in 6 minutes, 12 seconds. Later in the day, Veno took on Van Tromp in a second three-mile race, winning in an even faster time.

Fisher's Fisherman

Bred in England in 1853 and the winner of 69 races including two Ascot Gold Cups, the champion English stayer Fisherman was imported to South Australia by Hurtle Fisher in 1860 and was the foundation sire first at the Fisher family's Lockleys Stud in South Australia and then their Maribyrnong Stud in Victoria in 1863. He was a great sire and his offspring include Angler, Boatman, Fishhook, Maribyrnong, and Sylvia (dam of Goldsborough).

Victoria took it personally. It was an 'ignominious defeat' which the colony sought to avenge. The race and the fervent colonial parochialism it inspired contributed to the establishment of the Australian Champion Sweepstakes in 1859.

Benjamin Duttereau (1767–1851), New Town Racecourse 1830s (TMAG).

Under starter's orders in Hobart Town

Only nine years after Van Diemen's Land was first settled as a penal colony in 1804, match races were run at a course at New Town in Hobart Town. The horses competed for stakes ranging from £5 to £300 (an 1816 match between Mr W. Maum's black mare Beauty and J. Michell's roan horse Piper, easily won by Beauty) and among the regular spectators was Thomas Davey, the colony's Lieutenant Governor from 1813 to 1817. Known as 'Mad Tom', Davey was a racing enthusiast who shocked the establishment in New South Wales by drinking with convicts and choosing as his friends men Governor Macquarie considered 'low' and 'vulgar', not to mention 'of bad character'.

In 1817 Davey was replaced by Colonel William Sorell, a non-racing man who considered horseracing inappropriate to a penal colony, and the number of race meetings quickly decreased. Nevertheless Launceston staged a meeting on 22 March 1824, probably not the town's first.

The people of Van Diemen's Land found a Lieutenant Governor even less sympathetic to horseracing in George Arthur, who took over from Sorell in May 1924. By then Tasmanian racing was facing another more familiar problem: in spite of the lack of official enthusiasm, the free settlers had been importing some fine thoroughbreds to the colony, but these horses were spread between Hobart Town and Launceston. In 1826 the first Tasmanian Turf Club was established at Jericho, a town chosen because it was midway between the two settlements, and the first race meeting was set for April 1827 in the nearby town of Ross.

This middle course failed to please anyone and by March 1829 Launceston was again staging its own race meeting. In 1830, the Cornwall Turf Club was established to organise the Launceston meetings. On St Patrick's Day 1831, a three-day public race meeting began at New Town in Hobart Town, drawing a crowd of 2000. The Derwent St Leger was run for the first time the following year. Both Launceston and Hobart ran Town Plates as their major races, attracting competitors from both ends of the island.

In March 1847, the Tasmanian Turf Club was re-formed with the Governor Sir William Denison as patron. The club assumed responsibility for the 'running or training of horses at Hobart Town, Launceston, Campbell Town, or Oatland', in an attempt to 'better regulate racing in the Colony'. It also took on the creation and keeping of a Tasmanian Stud Book, with the view of refusing entry to TTC meetings to horses not registered. In spite of masses of newly drawn up regulations (or perhaps because of them), the TTC did no better than its predecessor and on 20 April 1859 yet another new racing body was born, the Tasmanian Jockey Club. In that same year, the Northern Tasmanian Turf Club was formed to look after the Launceston interests and, with the establishment of the first Tasmanian Turf Club in Launceston in 1860, the dream of a united racing industry was a thing of the past.

The great stallion Panic came to Tasmania as a two-year-old, by Frederick Woodhouse (ARM).

Charles Constantini's Racing man, 1855 (AL).

Tasmania's bold championship claim

'Tasmania now boldly put forward her claims to equal rank in the sporting federation, and though many of her own people laughed at the notion of a Champion Meeting coming off in our rather slow little island, so industrious a committee was organised, and so determined were they not to be pooh-poohed! out of their enterprise, that what was deemed a myth by most, soon turned out not only a substantial reality, but actually a more liberal inducement to the owners of racehorses than was even offered by their richer neighbours of Melbourne, or Sydney. Independently of the £500 for the great event, not less than £1200 was distributed on the program for minor races; and we are indeed proud to record that nearly £1500 was raised in public subscriptions, despite the cry of hard times, in the "tight little island", which has scornfully been termed a dustbowl.

'For once in the way, by-the-bye, this sorry satire is a verbal truth, for friends and

strangers must alike confess that no other colony has hitherto "put down the dust", as we have from our private pockets. In the other settlement, the established courses bring in so large a revenue that the public are scarcely called upon to contribute, except indirectly, but here it is quite "another pair of shoes", and any amount of praise is due to those who solicited subscriptions, and those who so readily paid them,' said the *Mercury*.

Sadly, the three-day meeting was postponed due to torrential rain, and the *Mercury* struggled to list the other entertainments offered by Hobart to its intercolonial visitors. The final day's racing coincided with Regatta Day and, since rowing was a far more popular sport in Hobart than horseracing, only a small crowd turned out. A reasonable crowd on the first day saw the Victorian six-year-old Mormon (who had run second to Archer in the first Melbourne Cup) defeat Shelalagh and Panic in the Champion Sweepstakes.

TURF TOPICS

First Arabs: Arab horses were imported to Van Diemen's Land from India when the colony was first settled, and among the first English thoroughbreds imported were Viscount in 1825 and Peter Fin in 1826. The Cressy Company (or Van Diemen's Land Company) imported Buffalo and Bolivar in 1826, Waterloo in 1828 along with other thoroughbreds, and then sponsored races for the progeny of these horses.

During his two-year stay in Australia from 1827, Henry John Rous, second son of the Earl of Stradbroke, sent imported English throughbred horses to a property he had bought near Launceston, and in 1832 Thomas Henty arrived in Launceston with thoroughbred horses which belonged to his son James. The Hentys advertised their horses at stud; Wanderer stood for six guineas and Little John for eight, the highest stud fee in the district. Charles Brown Hardwicke, a foundation member of the Tasmanian Turf Club in 1826, opened a horse market in Launceston in the 1830s.

Flemington racecourse from the Footscray side of Salt Water River, c. 1845 (Rex Nan Kivell Collection, National Library of Australia).

Racing down by the Salt Water River

While Melbourne's founding parties were still squabbling over who had got there first (was it John Fawkner or John Batman?), its new inhabitants – 984 male and 280 female at the end of 1837 – got on with enjoying themselves. The first official Melbourne race meeting was on 6 and 7 March, 1838, within three years of settlement.

The meeting was held at Sheoak Hill (later known as Batman's Hill), an area now mainly taken up by the Spencer Street railway station and yards with the starting post close to the existing North Melbourne railway station. The account of the race meeting in John Fawkner's *Melbourne Advertiser* reveals that Melburnians were already thinking big:

'Perhaps it may appear boastful in us, but we do maintain that the Melbourne race ground can scarcely be matched, taking it all in all; the course is on a level plain of large extent, and for about one third of its circle is surrounded by a gentle acclivity of some 20 to 50 feet, and it will thus afford a clear open view of the whole race to 50 000 people …'

And of the race meeting itself? After recounting an accident in which a mare was killed and the lucky jockey 'so free from injury, that he joined in hunting a pig (with its tail greased) on the following day', the *Melbourne Advertiser* concluded: 'It has scarcely ever in the colonies been our lot to witness a more orderly assemblage; joy beamed in every face and few accidents intervened to mar the harmony of the assembled people … not a cloud obscured the sky.'

In February the following year, a public meeting was called at the Lamb Inn and races were staged the following month. John Batman's Postboy won the hurdle race on the second day of the meeting, and the Melbourne Town Plate was won by Mountain Maid. In fact Mountain Maid – like Postboy, a winner in 1838 – won almost everything, which some of the large crowd felt detracted a little from the meeting.

The Melbourne race meeting quickly outgrew the near-perfect Sheoak Hill racecourse and a public meeting held at the Lamb Inn on 9 October 1839 called on newly elected race stewards to find a new course. Early in 1840, they selected a tract of swampy land alongside the Salt Water River (now the Maribyrnong), about four miles from the centre of the township, on which a match race had been successfully run between two mares owned by John Brown and John Highett.

The first races were held there on 3, 4 and 5 March 1840 and the geography of the course ensured that they were run anti-clockwise. Until 1859, the winning post was alongside the river bank in the vicinity of the existing mile and seven furlong barriers, and a grandstand was placed on the river bank, along with some makeshift booths. The dis-

tance from town was a problem for some, but otherwise the Melbourne Racecourse (it wasn't called Flemington until about 1857) was a great success.

The former VRC handicapper, Dr W. H. Lang, offered a colourful account of Flemington's early days in *Racehorses in Australia* (1922):

'In those early days everyone went to the races, and the route to and from the course was either by river-steamer or by road. The boats left the wharves at eleven o'clock and returned at sunset, and you may be sure there were hot times in the town o'nights after the races. Bands and Christy minstrels enlivened the voyage by water. Passengers on the trip home not infrequently toppled overboard, and one or two were actually drowned. Accidents by road were common. At one meeting alone [1850], three men were killed, two being run over by vehicles, and one by a runaway horse. Assaults were common, and fighting very popular.'

The racecourse was enclosed in 1850 after the Governor of New South Wales's deed which granted the 352 acres in trust as a public racecourse was finally ratified. Horsemen and vehicles were charged an entry fee, the entry for pedestrians remaining free. The course was changed to its present shape in time for the 1859 Australian Champion Sweepstakes meeting.

S. T. Gill (1818–80), Tattersalls Horse Bazaar (NLA).

Frederick Gosse (1838–84), Bourke St West in the Forenoon, 1864 (NLA).

Old guard v. new

In 1851, along with the discovery of gold in Victoria, came the establishment of the Victoria Turf Club, made up of the old guard of men who had already made their way in the colony. In 1854 the Victorian Parliament granted £200 as the purse for a Queen's Plate, and that year the Turf Club introduced a Spring racing meeting.

As the VTC gained in strength and financial clout, so the opposition to it grew. The club's disqualification of William Lang in 1855 was one cause of unrest. Lang, a member of the pastoralist family said to have originally had grazing rights on the crown land which became Flemington racecourse, had been disqualified at a country race meeting and was subsequently disqualified from racing by the VTC for five years. He disputed the original disqualification and successfully challenged the club's ruling in court.

In 1855 the Turf Club ran its first Victoria Derby, with stake money of £100 along with the entrance fee of £10 per horse. It was won by the chestnut Rose of May. The filly's owner H. N. Simson was a founding member of the Victoria Jockey Club, formed in 1856. The pastoralist and woolbroker Richard Goldborough was elected chairman.

The VJC's first meeting was a four-day affair in February 1857. (The Governor of Victoria had finally persuaded the course trustees – and members of the Turf Club – to give the Jockey Club access to the Melbourne Racecourse.) Winner of the Jockey Club Plate, a two-mile weight-for-age, was Thomas Chirnside's Alice Hawthorn.

One good thing came of the competitive nature of the clubs. Looking for a race to one-up its opposition, in 1861 the VTC came up with the Melbourne Cup.

The top end of the small dusty town v. the rest

The popularity of race meetings with the general public was a mixed blessing for the young gentlemen of the Port Phillip settlement. A degree of exclusivity was what they were seeking. They had already formed the fiercely elitist Melbourne Club, and so they formed the Port Phillip Turf Club along similar lines. The entrance fee was set at 50 guineas, and election to the club was by ballot, with the members reserving the right to reject in secret any applications of which they did not approve.

The Port Phillip Turf Club adopted rules for its first meeting held in mid-April 1841, including the stipulations that all horses would take their ages from 1 August and that jock-

eys could be disqualified for unfair riding. Depression, which blanketed the young Australian colonies during the 1840s, meant that the Port Phillip Turf Club's 1842 meeting was its last.

John Kirk, whose Kirk's Bazaar established in the early 1840s in Bourke Street West was Melbourne's first horse market, was one of those who kept horseracing afloat in Victoria during the hard times of the early 1840s. In 1843, Kirk, a racing steward, and his colleagues attracted 13 starters to the Trial Stakes – the largest field seen in a local race. Nevertheless, the prize for the 1843 Town Plate was only £40.

In 1845 James Henderson was elected

treasurer and secretary for the next annual races. According to the racing historian Andrew Lemon, Henderson was one of the most significant contributors to Victorian racing for the next 15 years during which 'he acted in various official capacities at most of the Melbourne race meetings'. He also acted as an official at the St Kilda Races held from 1847 to 1852. (Races were also held in Brighton during the 1840s.)

By 1847 the Town Plate purse was back to 100 sovereigns and for the first time the race attracted horses from outside Victoria. The race was won by James Austin's Bunyip, who defeated the local hero (and Plate winner in 1845, '46 and '48) Petrel.

Johnny Higgerson aboard Veno, who trounced Alice Hawthorn in the 'Championship of the turf of NSW and Victoria'.

The forgotten men of early racing

While the mounts beneath them are remembered, their bloodlines etched into history, all but a few of the jockeys who rode the horses in Australia's early years have been forgotten. Those that are more than a name on a race card tend to be the champions of their day, James Spinks, Sam Holmes, John Fisher – and those were killed, a solemn footnote to a race meeting. In those early years, jockeys were in great demand, due to their scarcity. Before the first Sydney race meeting, concern was expressed in the *Sydney Gazette* that the considerable weight of the riders would hamper the horses.

According to the *Sydney Morning Herald* obituary for John Fisher on 14 May 1832, 'the rider of Chase, Domino, Sampson, Carlow, Rob Roy and all the crack horses of the Australian turf in former days' was 99 when he died, which puts him at 75 for the first Sydney race meeting in 1810. While D'Arcy Wentworth's gentleman son W. C. Wentworth rode his horse Gig in a match race on the third day of that meeting, it was the English-born jockey to whom Wentworth entrusted his horse in the more important race, the Purse. Fisher had already had a win in the meeting on Chase.

The Victorian Jockeys Association was formed in March 1858 and 19 jockeys signed up at the first meeting, including the rider of Alice Hawthorn, Stephen Mahon, and the champion English-born Sydney rider Sam Holmes. The aim of the association was to look after jockeys in the case of accidents, which tended to be all too common. The clubs agreed on the need for a fee per race, but the poorly paid jockeys remained dependent on the generosity of the owners and vulnerable to the persuasive powers of the well-heeled bookmakers and punters.

One of Australia's first champion jockeys, John Higgerson was one of the few men in his era to earn his living from horseracing. Higgerson was born in 1810, the year of Australia's first race meeting, and started racing at the age of 17. He was the leading jockey for the successful Charles Smith stable during the 1830s, and the regular rider of Jorrocks.

In 1835, a punter offered Higgerson £50 to throw a race, promising him another £50 after he had lost it. Higgerson took the money, then went out and won the race. On returning to the mounting yard, he produced the notes and flourishing them high, he asked their owner to come forward, announcing to the assembled masses that the punter who had given him the money to throw the race had been a stranger.

Johnny Higgerson's name was synonymous with the Sydney champion Veno whom he trained and rode to victory in the famous match race with Alice Hawthorn for £2000 at Flemington in 1859. He had travelled south from Sydney with Veno and Cooramin. After winning on Veno, he rode Cooramin to victory in a match race with Tomboy for £200 a side and then saddled up again on Veno and won against the Geelong champion Van Tromp over three miles. He later bought Veno from his owner G. T. Rowe and continued to race him.

In the 1860s, he rode another champion, Tarragon, who won a series of races at Randwick. In 1866, Higgerson won the rerun of the VRC Champion Race at Flemington on Tarragon after he dead-heated with Volunteer. In the 1867 Sydney Cup, one of the nine-year-old Tarragon's last races, Higgerson fell, a fall put down variously to age, wasting, or exhaustion. Higgerson was 57 at the time.

Higgerson continued training after he gave up riding, and died at the age of 95 following a shooting accident at his home at Heathcote in New South Wales in 1905.

E. Winstanley, The stone wall at Five Dock, 1844 (ML).

Steeplechasing at Newtown, 1854.

Colonial jumping and steeplechasing

The Botany Steeplechase, the first steeplechase recorded in Australia, took place in Randwick on 25 August 1832. Starting on 'the Botany Road' (now Anzac Parade) and finishing near the Old South Head Road, the gruelling five-mile course was through steep scrub. Steeplechasing had social kudos in early Australia because of its connection to the hunt in England and Ireland. All but one (the winner, Thiefcatcher) of the seven starters were ridden by their gentlemen owners.

The steeplechase or hurdle race soon became a regular part of New South Wales racing. On 20 September 1836 the first Annual Sydney Hurdle race held at a course near Randwick had nine starters and was won by Whisker, ridden by Major England. The winner received £73. One of the last impromptu cross country steeplechases over open country took place near Sydney on 30 October 1854. It was raced over an unfenced course described as 'at Newtown' and billed as the Grand Metropolitan Steeplechase.

The first Batman Hill race meeting, in March 1838, included a Hunters' Stakes for gentlemen riders with four-foot-high jumps. That same year Tasmania staged its first hurdle race at Hobart's New Town course. The rules declared that horses would be disqualified for 'clouting', or knocking over hurdles, and as a consquence, there was no winner! In Brisbane, a two-mile hurdle and a Tally-Ho Stakes were included in the first race meeting at Cooper's Plains in 1843.

In 1844, a steeplechase called the Hawkesbury Stakes was held at Mr J. Abercrombie's Five Dock estate near Sydney, over three miles of countryside including stone walls, bricks, brush-top fences, fences and brooks. The winner, a roan gelding called Highflyer, went overlanding with cattle to South Australia and ran second in the first steeplechase held at Glen Osmond in 1846. Ridden by his owner C. B. Fisher, he won the Coppin Cup in Adelaide in 1850.

The practice of running a horse both on the flat and over jumps was not unusual. The Victorian champion Rob Roy won the 1844 Geelong race meeting's Town Plate of two heats over two miles and a distance, and the following day won the hurdle race which consisted of two laps of the course and ten jumps, each four feet high.

Steeplechasing and hurdling thrived in rural Victoria, perhaps because the colder Victorian winters came closer to the English climate. In March 1858, the first Warrnambool race meeting included a steeplechase won by Mr Bostock's Rambler and one year after its first meeting in 1857, the Western District town of Coleraine laid out a four-mile steeplechase around the town, boasting 42 fences, all of them natural hazards.

In 1859, the imported horse Panic was taken to Victoria by Henry Phillip after winning races in Tasmania, to stand at the Byron O'Lynn stud at Warrnambool. Panic sired Nimblefoot, but his major contribution was siring the winners of jumping races, including Sir Peter, Rhesus, Prodigious and Game – all GN winners.

TURF TOPICS

Joe Carter's winning ways: Joe Carter rode Flying Doe to victory in the second Victoria Derby at Flemington in 1856, his first successful Melbourne ride. Flying Doe headed Barbelle, with Sam Holmes on board, in the straight to win by a length and a half. The winning stake was £150, and the owner gave Carter £10 as his fee for the winning mount.

Carter had been apprenticed to the English trainers Boyce Brothers of Newmarket, at the cost of £100 to his parents, but before completing his indentures, he sailed for New South Wales where he was employed first as a labourer, building the railway line from Redfern to Parramatta. His first Australian ride was on a horse called

Socrates, who won a Maiden Plate at a Drapers' Meeting held at Homebush.

Carter won the Australian Cup three times and the VRC St Leger three times. He visited New Zealand regularly, and was paid a £100-a-year retainer by a Mr Harris for first call on his services. He also rode for John Tait, Etienne de Mestre and Hurtle Fisher.

S. A. Lindsay, *A bush race in Australia, Darling Downs* (Rex Nan Kivell Collection, NLA).

They're racing all round the bush

Racing spread quickly throughout rural Australia. By the late 1820s, annual meetings were held in Ross in Tasmania. In New South Wales, the first Liverpool races, held in October 1832 on the Throsby family's Glenfield estate, were followed the next July by races in Maitland in which horses named Pitch and Toss won principal events. In 1833, Captain John Piper organised the first meeting in the Bathurst area at the private course on his Alloway Bank estate.

In 1834, a race club was formed in Goulburn and the Illawarra Turf Club started with a meeting in Wollongong. In its second year, the Goulburn Club introduced an annual hurdle race. In these early years, it was usual for imported and thoroughbred horses to be penalised by extra weight. Most horses were run weight-for-age, with fillies carrying less.

At the 1834 Cumberland Turf Club's annual meeting at Campbelltown, the Sydney winner Mantrap was substituted for the little known Forrester, owned by Mr Howe, in the Members' Cup. The stewards discovered the ring-in after the decision had been declared, and were unable to alter the result. Mantrap was owned by a professional gambler who sold it to Howe just before the Cup meeting.

Racing in the form of match races was already popular in the Parramatta and Hawkesbury areas when Sydney held its first race meeting in 1810, with the Hawkesbury horse Scratch a popular winner of the Purse on the third day of the Sydney meeting. In 1841 the Hawkesbury Racing Club held its first race meeting at Windsor.

Match races continued their popularity, with first the *Sydney Gazette* and then *Bell's Life in Sydney* frequently used as the place in which to throw down the gauntlet. In *The History of Horse Racing*, the English racing historian Roger Longrigg claims that at least ten courses within 100 kilometres of Sydney were enclosed and charging admission for this purpose by 1837.

By 1850, racing had spread to 45 districts in the colony of New South Wales. As in Liverpool and Bathurst, many of the courses were private, established by wealthy landowners like the Macarthur family, who in 1855 laid out a course on Camden Park.

Some of the first country meetings in Victoria were private meetings modelled on the English point-to-point races, but the demand for public race meetings soon won the day. The Geelong Turf Club held its first

public race meeting in 1841, the Pyrenees Turf Club at Mount Emu near Beaufort was established in 1842, and several other country public clubs held meetings in the 1840s.

They took their racing seriously down Geelong way. In 1844, an enemy of Geelong horse owner John Highett attempted to cut out the tongue of Highett's 3-year-old filly Fancy, who was defeated for the 30 sovereign Town Plate by Rob Roy two weeks later. Fancy's preparation for the race was disturbed and she was unable to feed properly with her badly lacerated mouth.

By this time racing had spread throughout Tasmania, with race meetings held in Richmond, New Norfolk and Oatlands during the 1830s, and Bothwell, Campbell Town and Longford in the 1840s.

As settlers moved out into the rest of rural Australia, racecourses were among the first reserves settlers set aside in their new towns. In South Australia, early meetings at Penola and Apsley near the Victorian border each lasted a week. By the 1850s, racing had spread into rural Western Australia. There were meetings inland at York in the 1840s, and Bunbury held its first meeting in 1854, and Busselton two years later.

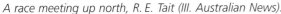

A race meeting up north, R. E. Tait (Ill. Australian News).

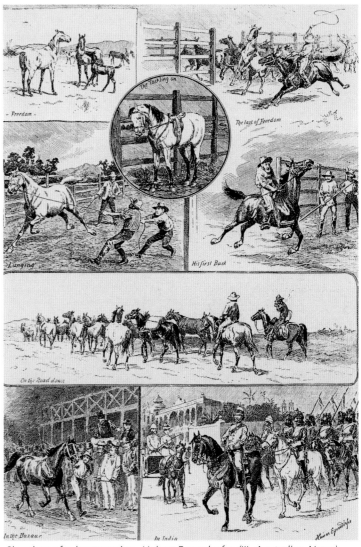

Sketches of a horsestation, Heiner Egersdorfer (Ill. Australian News).

TURF TOPICS

Romeo runs that extra lap: In 1845, on the third day of the Geelong Carnival, a five-mile match race was run between Mr Cunningham's The Lawyer and Henry Dewing's Romeo. The stake for the race was £100, and the horses were to run three laps. The Lawyer won comfortably by six lengths, despite the fact his price was out to 5/1 against Romeo. The punters were not pleased. On returning to scale, the riders were accused of not completing the three laps, and Dewing immediately remounted Romeo and took off for another lap. On his return to scale a second time, the stewards had to stand firm in the face of a popular acclaim that The Lawyer had not completed the distance.

According to the *Geelong Advertiser*: 'Such a scene we venture to say never occurred on a racecourse, and never will again. Even bets were given and taken with avidity upon a matter which had passed before the better's eyes only a few minutes before and upon a question which involved no other problem than simply counting to three.'

The matter was resolved when several people came forward saying they had timed the laps, which took between three and four minutes, and the race had totalled 11 minutes and 40 seconds. Both Dewing and Cunningham then protested to the stewards that they had been jostled.

Gold, gold, gold: With the huge population explosion prompted by the gold rushes in the 1850s, the demand for horseracing grew. The speculators were gamblers by nature and race clubs were formed and race meetings were held wherever gold was found in any quantity. In Victoria, early meetings were held at Bendigo, Ballarat and Ararat.

Gold discoveries in the Rockhampton area in Queensland led to the establishment of the Fitzroy Jockey Club in 1863. High stakes drew good racehorses north for the race meetings. At the first Fitzroy Jockey Club meeting, £800 in prize money was up for grabs. The bulk of it was won by T. Ryan's Traveller, a Randwick winner ridden by the Sydney jockey Sam Holmes. Race meetings had been held in Drayton (Toowoomba) in 1848 and Warwick in 1850, but it was the Grange at Ipswich that was the centre of racing in Queensland in its early years. In 1861, it played host to the Queensland Champion Sweepstakes, which was won by John Tait's Zoe from New South Wales. The Gayndah Jockey Club was another successful Queensland club formed in the 1860s.

First telegraphed results: Sydney was delighted to receive the message that NSW horse Veno had defeated the Victorian Alice Hawthorn in the 1859 Australian Champion Sweepstakes – the first result by telegraph.

Old and new: The great old horse Jorrocks died in 1860, and the great jockey and trainer James Scobie was born.

Founding the turf in Western Australia

The new Swan River colony was not the most hospitable place for thoroughbred horses, as James Henty discovered when he arrived in 1829. He brought with him four thoroughbred racehorses from the estate of a Sussex neighbour, the third Earl of Egremont, a famed British breeder. Three of the four survived the voyage, and two survived until 1831 when they (and the Henty family) were shipped to Van Diemen's Land. James Henty explained why in a letter to his friend, the Governor of Western Australia, Sir James Stirling:

'My thoroughbred horses are at present a heavy tax on me without affording me an adequate return, and until this Colony is farther advanced I propose keeping them in Van Diemen's Land where I am certain of obtaining for the services of horses sufficient (over and above the expenses) to purchase flocks of sheep annually.'

The first match race was run in Perth on 20 July 1829, near Fremantle, between ponies belonging to Governor Stirling and Lieutenant Preston. Another was recorded in 1834, and from 1835 races were regularly run as part of a sports day held on 1 June, Western

The horse named West Australia never raced down under. He won the Triple Crown in England in 1853 (NLA).

Australia's Anniversary (Foundation) Day. In 1836, a race meeting was held at Guildford which for many of the local aristocracy was considered the first 'real' race meeting in Western Australia because it included a race between (two) thoroughbreds.

'After dinner several appropriate toasts were given. Sir James [Stirling] proposed Mr Brockman's [one of the race meeting's organisers] health, as founder of the turf in this colony – a compliment that gentleman disclaimed, as the merit was due to his Excellency, who was the importer of the horses.'

Governor Stirling and William Locke Brockman were among the founders of the Western Australian Stud Club in 1838. In 1844 Brockman donated the Margeaux Cup, to be awarded to the winners of a race restricted to the progeny of his stallion Margeaux, who had been imported to the colony by Stirling.

In March 1848 the first race meeting was held at the Ascot Racecourse (the name Ascot came later), and the Western Australian Turf Club was formed in 1852. The Queen's Plate was made the feature race of the first WATC race meeting in April 1853. WATC rules were used for the subsequent race meetings at Fremantle, York and Bunbury.

Whalebone's race

The first hurdle race at Brisbane's New Farm in 1852 was won by Whalebone, not the thoroughbred champion of the same name, but a horse owned and ridden by a Mount Brisbane stockman, Larry Flannery. Whalebone had fallen at the water jump in his first round. The spectators took pity on Flannery, and they managed to yank Whalebone out of the ditch, leg Flannery up and send him on his way again. Meanwhile, on their second time round, the remainder of the field had baulked at the water jump. Whalebone cleared all the jumps on the second round and, as his competitors remained stalled at the jump, he finished alone and won.

Racing at Moreton Bay takes off

The Moreton Bay Racing Club had its headquarters at Cooper's Plains and the first race meeting on record was held there in July 1843, only one year after Queensland was opened up to general settlement. The primitive course was about six miles out of Brisbane, and was the venue for two meetings each year in the 1840s.

Meetings were held at New Farm from 1852 – often on a Sunday. Another course was built in South Brisbane, and race meetings drew as many as 30 000 from throughout the colony in these early days. The Queensland Turf Club was formed in August 1863 with a membership of 53. The first president was the son of the commander of the 73rd Regiment Colonel O'Connell, who had played a central role in introducing horseracing to Sydney in 1810. The younger Colonel (later Sir) Maurice O'Connell was president of the Legislative Council of Queensland.

The colony surveyor chose the site for Eagle Farm which was granted to the club by the government, and racing enthusiasts got together to clear the land. In its first incarnation, Eagle Farm was one and a half miles round. Later it was shortened to a little over a mile. A lagoon in the centre of the course ensured that on wet days the going was indeed heavy.

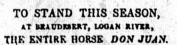

TO STAND THIS SEASON,
AT BEAUDESERT, LOGAN RIVER,
THE ENTIRE HORSE *DON JUAN.*

DON JUAN is a thorough-bred Horse, dark bay with black points; stands 15 hands 2 inches high, and for blood and bone is not to be excelled in the district.

He is got by *Mentor*, the property of Colin J. Mackenzie, Esq.; his dam *Haidee* by *Black Prince*. g. dam by *Mariner*, imported by Captain Lamb; g. g. dam by *Surveyor*, imported by T. Icely, Esq.

Terms—£2 10s. each Mare, and 3s. groomage.

A good paddock will be provided, but no responsibility incurred. The Mares to be removed on or before the 1st of January, prior to which payment must be made.

From the Moreton Bay Courier, 1847.

William Emery, Zoe, winner of Queensland champion race (Rex Nan Kirvell Collection, NLA).

Race course, Adelaide, Jan. 1840, by John Michael Skipper (NLA).

Black Jack comes up trumps in SA

The first race meeting in South Australia was held on a course in front of resident commissioner James Hurtle Fisher's house below Adelaide's West Terrace on 1 and 2 January 1838.

It was a fine affair – the program was printed on yellow silk and the jockeys, too, were resplendent in silks. Appropriately, Fisher's horse Black Jack won the first race in front of a crowd of almost 1000 people. Fisher's co-steward was Colonel William Light, the colony's surveyor-general.

The Turf Club of South Australia was formed following a second meeting in August 1838 but it lasted only two years, due to the depression which swept the colonies in the early 1840s.

The South Australian Jockey Club, formed first around 1850 but disbanded, was re-formed on 24 January 1856 at a meeting chaired by James Hurtle Fisher. In 1861 a meeting dissolved the club and again appointed a new committee designed to 'put racing in South Australia on a more satisfactory footing'.

The new meeting appointed Fisher as president and E. M. Bagot, the brother of the Victorian Racing Club's first secretary Robert Bagot, as secretary and treasurer.

Races were run on Adelaide parklands in an area which later became Victoria Park, and from 1857 at the Thebarton course.

Bagot, the SA engine

Edward Mead Bagot was a prominent owner and secretary of the SAJC from 1861 to 1869. Mark Gawen, the Stipendiary Steward of the Adelaide Racing Club in 1899, said of him: 'He was an "engine-like" personality in the affairs of the sport, a dominating presence, who, adopting the emblematic garb of the typical John Bull, wore it for all the years I can remember, and longer.

'His tremendously solid figure, with its leonine head, clothed in top boots and Bedford cord breeches, single-button Bliss tweed coat and broad, flat-brimmed 'topper', made a unique and imposing impression in the city streets, and his deep rolling voice commanded immediate attention.

'E. M. Bagot was a moving force of great potency in the racing world.'

S. T. Gill, Adelaide racecourse '45 (NLA).

Henry Redwood, 'father of the NZ turf'.

Racing seemed to be popular with all sections of New Zealand: Wairarapa in the 1850s.

The first Canterbury race meeting, held at Hagley Park in 1851, more than 10 years before Riccarton became New Zealand's first regular racetrack.

The formative years of New Zealand racing

Starting not long behind Australia in terms of organised racing – the Canterbury Jockey Club was formed 10 years before the Victoria Racing Club emerged from the ashes of its predecessors – New Zealand nevertheless relied heavily on its large neighbour across the Tasman for racing stock during the formative years.

Considering that Australians have dominated the buying bench at New Zealand thoroughbred sales since the 1950s, it is somewhat ironic that in the early years the traffic was mainly the other way.

Australia, and especially New South Wales, had already built up a sizeable thoroughbred population by the time the 1840 Treaty of Waitangi legitimised the birth of the infant colony named New Zealand.

That year coincided with the first recorded race meeting in Wellington at the Basin

Reserve. and with the arrival at Wellington wharf of a horse named Figaro, the first thoroughbred to be landed in New Zealand.

The latter occurrence was in its way as significant as the first. Early race meetings in the colony were got up either by the military or by settlers celebrating an anniversary of their settlement. In either case the equine competitors were non-thoroughbred riding hacks. That first Wellington meeting was an example, celebrating the province's first anniversary. The equine star of the show was a horse (non-thoroughbred, naturally) named Calmuc Tartar.

Figaro, a yearling colt when he arrived on the wharf at Wellington, was bred by Thomas Iceley, of Coorning, New South Wales. His purchaser was James Watt, a former Bathurst settler himself, who was to play an important role in New Zealand racing.

Perhaps his first such role was to ride a four-year-old Figaro to victory over Calmuc Tartar at the Wellington races of 1842 thus proving the superiority of the thoroughbred. Thirty years after bringing the first thoroughbred to New Zealand, James Watt was the first president of the Auckland Racing Club.

Figaro, on the other hand, while he had some influence as a sire and indeed sired the first fully New Zealand bred thoroughbred, Il Barbiere, was perhaps most notable as a sign of things to come.

Picnic races were jolly occasions and a dapple-grey half-bred mare could be more than competitive against a farmer's sturdy cob. But if you wanted to take the sport of racing seriously, you needed a thoroughbred.

Earlier recorders of New Zealand's racing history accorded the title 'Father of the New Zealand Turf' to Henry Redwood, an English

Ted Cutt, one of the early Canterbury trainers.

Pioneer W. O. Williams, also a man of the turf.

First Wanganui Jockey Club program, 1848.

Wanganui meeting in the 1880s, complete with dog carts.

Bullock drays at the Stoke course in Nelson in the 1860s.

migrant who settled first in Nelson and then in neighbouring Marlborough, the provinces at the top of New Zealand's South Island. Though not the first to import thoroughbreds, he was the most enthusiastic and determined of his era.

Redwood made his first modest imports from Australia – two mares and a colt – in 1851. The following year he brought out a larger shipment of thoroughbreds from New South Wales – eight mares, two colts and a stallion named Sir Hercules. And a year later Redwood imported, again from Australia, more than 30 thoroughbreds.

Singlehandedly he virtually doubled the colony's thoroughbred population in the space of less than three years.

By the end of the 1850s he had a huge lead on other racing owners in the quality and quantity of his racing stock. Sir Hercules stood in New Zealand for only five years but did much to improve the young breed. Sold back to Australia, he sired the champion The Barb and other good horses.

Most notable of the mares in that 1852 shipment were Flora McIvor and her daughters Flora and Zoe (both by Sir Hercules and both good race-mares at Nelson meetings).

The records indicate that Flora McIvor was 24 when she arrived in New Zealand yet, remarkably enough, she produced a further two filly foals (Io and Waimea) who accounted for most of the family's ongoing success in New Zealand breeding.

Remarkably, the 1850s were not out before Redwood made his first return raid on the Australian racing scene, enjoying notable success with Zoe, Zingara and Chevalier and selling all three in Australia.

Redwood waged several other campaigns in Australia, generally with success. But meanwhile the wider New Zealand scene was beginning to attract his attention.

The Nelson Jockey Club was formed in 1848 and remains the longest-lasting New Zealand racing club to race continuously from its formation (the Wanganui Jockey Club in the lower North Island was formed in the same year but was in recess for some years in the late 1860s).

And, rather than the already much larger centres of Christchurch, Wellington or Auckland, the little township of Nelson was the early centre of racing strength. The Canterbury Jockey Club was formed in 1854 and the Riccarton course (originally a three-

mile circuit) was ready for the first race meeting the following year.

Within 10 years the Canterbury Jockey Club was offering stake money of a level to tempt Henry Redwood and, despite having to travel his team hundreds of miles over rough tracks and unbridged rivers, he at first made the Christchurch owners look like beginners. In 1868 he set up stables in Christchurch, Chokebore Lodge, and put Edward Cutts in charge.

In partnership with James Watt, who had imported Figaro all those years earlier, Henry Redwood raced horses in Auckland (trained by George Cutts, Edward's brother) and with George Gatenby Stead in Christchurch, from the 1870s into the 1890s, when Stead bought out his elderly partner.

Henry Redwood died in 1907 aged 85, having seen New Zealand racing develop from mad scurries through fern and gully on half-bred horses to a nation-wide sport run by properly constituted clubs up and down the country, contested by thoroughbreds on nearly a hundred racecourses, and with a national controlling body operating and enforcing a standard set of rules.

by John Costello

A huge watercolour by George Rowe entitled Victoria race meeting near Sunbury, 1858. It was exhibited at the London Exhibition in 1862 (SLNSW).

More claret than gold when Flatcatcher

In May 1857, a rich vein of gold transformed an isolated mining camp in the shadow of the Grampians in western Victoria into a robust canvas city. When the Mount Ararat Advertiser *first appeared in August 1857, the city of Ararat boasted 16 hotels, six banks, numerous lawyers, two schools, five doctors, a horse mart, wine and spirit merchants and more than 30 000 people.*

And what did every burgeoning Australian rural township need? A race meeting, that's what, though the town at this time had no post office, no resident magistrate or court house, no gold receiver's office or escort, and a police force of ten.

Public meetings were held to appoint a committee and agree on the rules and the resident mining warden declared that he would not allow any mining claim to be jumped during race week.

On 15 December, the Advertiser *announced that Mr Orr's Flatcatcher had been entered to race on each day of the three-day meeting. Flatcatcher, who ran fifth in the first Melbourne Cup, had recently challenged the NSW champion Veno in a forthcoming intercolonial sweepstakes. It was a propitious beginning for the town's first race meeting, which the local newspaper reported with gusto:*

Our maiden meeting opened with a morning as bright as an English sunny June; and though a cooler breeze would have been an improvement, still little alteration could have been desired in the weather. We don't believe in cool winds and cloudy skies for holidays; nothing like a bright sunny day and a heat that makes you enjoy the furious number of drinks that one is obliged to imbibe.

At 12 o'clock the exodus from Ararat commenced, and the neighbourhood of the Camp was alive with our good folks hastening up to Green Hill; all sorts of traps were pressed into service, from Cobb & Co's four-horse conveyance for the nobs, at a crown, down to spring carts for the million, at eighteen pence … It is surprising how many started to walk, and how few reached the course by this means of locomotion; the traps picked them up like chickens pick up grubs, none seemed able to resist the tempting 'going down, sir,' of the drivers …

The arrangements of the booths, with the Grand Stand opposite the winning post, were admirably made … We were rather surprised to see such an amount of gambling being openly carried on; these temptations consisted of several roulette tables, over and under hazard, and other games of the same description. There were also some knock 'em downs, with ha'crowns for prizes, four throws at a shilling …

About one o'clock the business of the day commenced … Of seven horses entered for the first race, five came to the scratch. The non-appearance of Lady of the Lake caused some regret as she was decidedly the favourite. We heard of bets as little as three to two being taken about her. We believe she broke loose and met with some slight accident. Alpion was reported to have become lost in the bush.

At half-past one they formed in line, and were off in an instant, all but Don Juan, before Mr Chadwick, the starter, had even raised his whip. The jocks, however, not hearing his cry of back, ran the race out, and even the second time round they did not hear the shouts to them to stop. It was a good race; Arab Chief went away with a strong lead, and when half

finally raced for the Ararat Camp Cup

way round was six lengths ahead. At the stand he was beaten, the last round being a beautiful match between Wanderer and Don Juan, the former coming in first by about a length. Great disappointment was felt by some parties at its being declared a false start, but it evidently was so, as Neemo did not get away.

The Clerk of the Course should have rode and met them in the middle, and signed them to stop. Three only made their appearance at the second start, Creeping Tom having dried up and Don Juan being accidentally out of the way at the time of starting. The result was the same as in the previous race, Wanderer beating Neemo with greater ease than he had Don Juan …

Only two horses came to the post for the race of the day, the Publican's Purse, so it was declared a no race. The Spring Stakes and the Hack Race were run, with few surprises. Flatcatcher did not race.

Second Day – Wednesday, December 16

Tuesday was hot enough – quite, but today beat it entirely; it was a regular baker, and what rendered the heat more oppressive

was the dust which was much worse than on the previous day; however, the attendance was again first rate. We think there were hardly so many diggers present, but the Grand Stand was much fuller; indeed the township was perfectly cleared. The racing was very poor indeed … Another sell for the Town Plate under exactly similar circumstances as those of the Publican's Purse opened the day's proceedings. The public however were fully prepared for it and consequently took it very coolly …

Third Day – Thursday, December 17

In consequence of Flatcatcher starting, it was looked upon by most as the grand day. The attendance was, however, not much more numerous, if any. The day's sport opened with the Camp Cup, for which four showed, the 'crack', Warhawk, Coronet and Wanderer. Of course it was looked upon as a certainty, three and four to one being laid on Flatcatcher … but it was by no means such a certainty as people expected, the bleeding flanks of the grey gelding showing that Holmes had made the most of him … It was decidedly the best

race of the meeting and gave great satisfaction, the gallant grey being loudly cheered on his return to the weighing post …

The number present today is estimated at 8000.

The aptly named Blister noted: Claret Punch – How the deuce was it that there was such an astonishing run upon the claret punch alias sangaree? The barmen no sooner saw you approach the counter than they dabb'd you down a tumbler of the popular tipple without waiting an instant for your order. Is it a custom to drink nothing but claret at races? Well, I suppose it is. At all events they seemed to know best what was good for us; and I don't think the mixture did anybody any harm. One place they had an American tub of the largest size brim-full, and were ladling it out like smoke. A friend of mine imbibed 53 glasses to his own check, and was disgustingly sober when I last saw him: in fact nobody would get drunk; the very few men that had the few fights were as sober as judges.

Mount Ararat Advertiser, 18 December 1857

A competition was held for the best depiction of the tragedy. This painting is held at the Art Gallery of South Australia.

The wreck of the *Admella* ruins racing

The *Admella* was said to be one of the safest ships built. The 395-ton steamer, which ran between Adelaide and Melbourne, had been built in 1857 in Port Glasgow, Scotland, and designed specifically for passenger service between the Australian colonies. As well as dripping with luxury, she was laden with the newest safety features: watertight compartments, the latest in lifeboats. Those who boarded her at Port Adelaide on 5 August 1859 would have had no qualms about the voyage ahead.

The destination was Melbourne where, on 1 October 1859, the first Australian Champion Sweepstakes was to be held to find the fastest horse in the country. The *Admella* was transporting the South Australian entrants, Jupiter and The Barber, as well as South Australia's champion steeplechaser, The Shamrock, in the company of their owners, the well-known young horsemen, George and James Hurtle Fisher, and Benjamin Rochford, who was the business partner of their elder brother C. B. Fisher. Also on board was James Margarey, a wealthy flourmiller, who was returning to Melbourne with three stallions he had bought in Adelaide.

On board along with the 87 passengers and six racehorses was a crew of 26, and a cargo which included copper from the Kapunga mines and flour for the Victorian goldfields. The vessel was in the hands of Captain McEwan, a seaman with 30 years' experience.

The steamer had an uneventful trip until the early hours of Saturday, 6 August when, swaddled in fog, she approached Cape Northumberland. A small bump was all that was felt by those on board. Then moments later, the *Admella* was picked up by the swell and thrown on to the notorious Carpenter Rocks. The days that followed were the stuff of the worst of nightmares. Land was within sight, but the fierce current carried away those who tried to make it. Ships passed and failed to hear their cries. On the Sunday, two sailors managed to reach the shore, and 24 hours later, they notified the Cape Northumberland lighthouse keeper of the *Admella*'s plight. Two others to struggle ashore were the racehorses The Shamrock and The Barber.

Finally on Saturday 13 August, two men managed to get ropes to those that survived the gruelling week and winch them to safety over the tumultuous seas to the lifeboat of the whaler, the *Lady Bird*. Eighty-nine people had perished.

The Shamrock was found ashore but he had broken a leg and had to be destroyed. After a 10-day search The Barber was found –

all in one piece despite his adventure – in the scrub around Mount Gambier. From there, he travelled overland to Geelong, and then by train to Melbourne where he ran, as planned, in the Australian Champion Sweepstakes.

In the *Argus* of Monday 15 August 1859, survivor James Hutchison, chief mate, stated: 'The ship struck at about 4.30 a.m., and in less than 10 minutes she was in three pieces. About 40 people were clinging to the bow part for two days, when they were nearly all washed off and lost, with the exception of about 15, who were brought to the after part of the vessel by means of a rope. Some very harrowing scenes of separation occurred at this time …

'Each night carried off its victims. About 20 died on Tuesday night from cold; it was a bitter night. Deaths were so frequent as to lose all terrors to the survivors, who looked callously on … Margarey was most anxious of all to go ashore, and continually wishing to make attempts. He at last fell overboard by accident; and although he was kept up by a life buoy for a time, he at last sank about 300 yards from the wreck. Three days before, he gave a large warm coat to Rochford, which was the means of saving his and Hurtle Fisher's lives.'

Herbert Palmer, The Australian Champion Sweepstakes, 1859 (NLA).

Victoria wins the day in the Champion Sweepstakes

The race for the championship of the Australian colonies is over – witnessed by 35 000 people, and won by a Victorian horse. Flying Buck, when the prospects of Victorian pre-eminence were dubious, came to the rescue, saved the national reputation and achieved victory. He came as other horses have come – from whence he was least expected; of respectable pedigree, but unknown, he held a place in the rearward rank; he has, however, won, and henceforth will be famous. All that his competitors can complain of is his extreme ill-breeding in leaving them so far behind. New South Welshmen may sneer, Tasmanians look dismayed, and South Australians bewail over their 'Barber', but the laurels remain with Victoria. Having said so much, we will, before describing the race itself, endeavour to give some account of the features connected with it.

For days previous to the race, steamers from the neighbouring colonies and the seaboard of Victoria have been crowded with passengers; while from Ballarat and Dunolly, from Bendigo and the Ovens, they came in as great numbers as the conveyance available would contain.

From an early hour on Saturday morning Melbourne became the entrepôt of eager expectants of the sport from the suburban districts. By river, by road, by rail, in vehicles and on foot, they poured in thousands. Brighton the seaward, St Kilda the secluded, Prahran the spacious, Collingwood and Rich-mond the noisy, each contributed its quota. At 10 o'clock the streets leading to the Spencer St Railway terminus began to be traversed by continuous streams of people and within an hour afterwards the station was completely blocked … cab after cab rattled off along Flemington Road. Steady-going drays, filled with steadier people – furniture vans, going tandem – American waggons, four-in-hand – well-to-do citizens and their wives in decent traps – patricians in broughams, spreeish clerks in dashing turnouts, were all jostled, sworn at, and put in bodily terror by the invading swarm of cabs …

As time wore on, and thousands of whom we speak became concentrated in the vicinity of the racecourse, the coup d'oeil was magnificent – a sight such as has never been witnessed in Victoria, and which could only be obtained when Britons, true to their instincts, were bent on the enjoyment of that which to them is of all others the most engaging of entertainments – a horse race …

It was noticed as an especial feature in the 'events' of Saturday, that it was the first occasion of the kind at which respectable persons of all classes had turned out with their families for the purpose of a day's enjoyment. The prevailing good order and the respectability of the concourse was a general theme. Of course there was both drunkenness and disorder, but not to any great extent, and, apart from the immediate vicinity of the booths, there was little or none. In short, we venture to say, in spite of the League of Progress and stump orators, that no other city of the size of Melbourne in the world would have poured forth from the ranks of its population so large a number of persons bearing the evidence of the enjoyment of world comforts as appeared on the Racecourse on Saturday. If there was little splendour, there was less poverty; if not honoured by the presence of peers, it was not disgraced with the company of black-legs …

The result took everyone by surprise, as the winner had previously done nothing in public to justify any belief in his victory. When it is remembered, however, how much he has improved, and that he carried 52 lb. less weight than Zoe, who finished half-a-dozen lengths before the renowned Strop, the wonder becomes considerably less … A revision of the scale of weights therefore, in future national racing events becomes imperative, for it is quite clear that aged horses, who have done much work in their time, and are past their prime, cannot give away nearly 4 stone to youngsters, whose mile-gallops previously have only been play to them. Notwithstanding this, Victoria may be well proud of her champion, and in future contests, with so much good stock growing up, need not fear to re-enter the lists against all-comers. As the Winner cantered past the post, ten thousand hoarse voices shouted a welcome, and the cry was caught up and re-echoed on the distant hill.

Argus, 3 October 1859

A view of the Flemington Racecourse in 1861, with marquees, refreshment tents, a small grandstand. The race soon had Melbourne's interest.

The Cup: 'A mad idea, doomed to failure'

'Its effect would be to make any brumby bought out of a mob for thirty shillings the equal of the finest horse in the land. It is a mad idea, doomed to failure' said a newspaper of the concept of the Melbourne Cup. Rather than a race between the champion horses of the colonies at set weights, a Derby-like race (like the Australian Champion Sweepstakes which had proved popular as it rotated around the colonies in the late 1850s), the Melbourne Cup was to be a handicap race run over the long distance of two miles.

The Melbourne Cup was an effort by the Victoria Jockey Club to make its Spring meeting a success, which meeting was also part of the ongoing rivalry with the Victoria Turf Club. The VTC had, on Saturday, 3 November 1860, been successful with the Corporation Cup, a handicap for a purse of three sovereigns and a Cup valued at 50 sovereigns presented by the Mayor on behalf of the Corporation of the City of Melbourne. The Corporation Cup was won by Phoebe at a gaily bedizened Flemington.

The Melbourne Cup was dreamed up some time before 9 September 1861, which is the date the VJC met at the Albion Hotel in Bourke Street, Melbourne, and considered the propriety of giving £100 to be raced for

at the forthcoming Turf Club races in November. Reports of the meeting noted that business was 'very shady' and confined to double-event betting, with the Melbourne Cup as the second leg.

The idea of the Melbourne Cup is credited to a committeeman of the Victoria Turf Club, Captain Frederick Charles Standish.

Standish, born in Lancashire, England, in 1824, was a Captain in the Royal Artillery, and had a property in Yorkshire. It was said that 'no backer of horses was better known or more liked upon English racecourses' than Standish between 1848 and 1852. No wonder: in that year he had lost so much money that he was forced to depart for the colonies. After a time on the goldfields he was appointed Assistant Commissioner at Sandhurst (Bendigo) in 1854 and became Chief Commissioner of Police in Victoria in 1858. He held this position until 1880. A heavy drinker and bon vivant, and Chairman of the Victoria Racing Club 1881–3, Standish died in 1883 of cirrhosis of the liver.

On the next Monday, 16 September, business 'not only brisk but significant' was done at the Albion. Archer was in demand 'as most of the books are pretty full against him', and he started at 10/1.

Come to the Cup

At the end of October 1861 a notice appeared in the *Argus*:

THE VICTORIA TURF CLUB RACES. Entries were made, and acceptances declared, last evening at the Subscription Room at the Albion Hotel.

The Victorian Turf Club program for day one of their three-day meeting was:

THURSDAY, NOVEMBER 7.
To start at half past one o'clock:
THE MAIDEN PLATE of 50 sovs.; entry 3 sovs. – One mile and a half.
THE TWO-YEAR-OLD STAKES of 100 sovs.; entry 5 sovs. – Three-quarters of a mile.
THE MELBOURNE CUP of 20 sovs.; 10 sovs forfeit, or 5 sovs. If declared; with 200 sovs. Added by the Victoria Turf Club – Two miles.
The fourth and last race of the day, the THE HANDICAP HURDLE RACE.

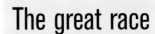

Trainer Etienne de Mestre and strapper Dave Power with the great Archer, dual Cup winner.

Archer sails to a win in Melbourne

Melbourne in 1861 was a prosperous city, still building on gold-given prosperity and increased population. Some 150 000 people lived there: it had independence from NSW, Victorian Rules football, gas lighting, clubs, reticulated water, a University – and great confidence. It had sent the Victorian Exploring Expedition under the command of Burke and Wills to walk to the Gulf. News that Burke and Wills had perished arrived a week before the first Melbourne Cup meeting, causing a great upwelling of emotion and grief. Much of Victoria's new reputation had been staked on the expedition, its tragic failure was a 'national' disturbance. Victoria needed something to celebrate. While the Melbourne Cup was not conceived as a great public festival, and the first meeting was overshadowed by the deaths of Burke and Wills, which kept crowds down, it almost immediately was taken to heart by the people.

Four thousand enthusiastic patrons attended Flemington Racecourse on the first Thursday (not Tuesday) in November 1861.

The night before the race a market was framed at the Albion Hotel. There was plenty of support for the local horse Mormon at 2/1, while NSW entry Archer eased to 8/1.

Horseshoe woven from Archer's tail hair by Theresa Haynes, about 1870 (ARM).

The traditional story goes that a month before the Cup, Dave Power, Etienne de Mestre's strapper, had led and ridden Archer the 560 miles from Braidwood/Nowra in NSW to Melbourne. The journey took more than five weeks. However, recent examination of the shipping lists makes it almost certain that Archer in fact came by ship.

Archer was trained by de Mestre, foaled on Mr T. J. Roberts' property, Exeter Farm, and owned by the estate of T. M. Royds. T. M. Royds died while riding in 1852.

De Mestre trained Archer in Melbourne from stables situated behind the Botanical Hotel in South Yarra, galloping him on the St Kilda Park.

De Mestre, though white-haired, was 29 in 1861 and owned a 1200-acre model training establishment on the Shoalhaven. It was rated the best private track in NSW.

He was born in Sydney in 1832, and won his first race at 15 on his own horse named Sweetheart at Bathurst. In the 1850s he established his stud, track and stable on his father's property at Terara at the mouth of the Shoalhaven River. Before Archer's consecutive wins in the first two Melbourne Cups, he had trained Veno, the winner of the first Intercolonial Challenge in 1857. He had many ups

The great race

But for the unfortunate accident the day would have been one of unmixed enjoyment, noted the *Age*. The unfortunate accident was that two of the 17 starters were killed during the running of the race.

The Cup was the third race on the four-race program. Of the 17 runners, Archer and Inheritor were from NSW. Twilight, an ill-mannered black mare, bolted from the start and ran a lap of the course. George Mason, the starter, in a long red coat and on a grey cob, waved a red flag and they jumped – turning into the straight soon after.

Flatcatcher was in the lead. Dispatch was pushed into a line of wooden stakes marking the running rail and did a somersault, breaking her back. Medora and Twilight fell over her, killing Medora. Twilight survived with deep cuts to the legs. Spectators cleared the track, and Joe Morrison the jockey was badly injured. In the run home, Johnny Cutts on Archer in de Mestre's all-black silk shirt sat tall in the saddle and won in a canter, by six lengths from Mormon.

ARCHER

and downs in business and in racing in the next 50 years, eventually winning five Cups. He died in 1916.

De Mestre treated Archer with Patrick Egan's Liniment after a slight injury incurred during training, and the horse's Irish farrier Egan shod Archer for the Cup with special lightweight racing plates. Egan is supposed to have said of the shoes, 'As dainty as a lady's dancing slippers they were, and it was the sight of me own four-leafed shamrock which brought him luck.'

Not everyone was convinced Archer was a sure thing. The *Argus* opined: 'Archer is a magnificent horse eye for eye but too limbering a galloper for our first class. He is in rare condition, apparently, and is full of enough of life to frighten those who have laid against him, but whether it is the reverse galloping on our course, or from other reasons, he cannot go our race today.'

The Melbourne Cup of 1862, by Frederick Woodhouse Senior (ARM). Woodhouse (1820–1909) was Australia's leading racehorse painter.

'One racing club must be formed at once'

The formation of the VRC (Victoria Racing Club) at Scott's Hotel on 9 March 1864 marked the end of years of mismanagement and squabbling. Since the Melbourne Race Club had staged the first meeting in 1838, four race clubs had vied for control of Melbourne racing.

At that first meeting in 1864 the gentlemen spoke plainly: 'The financial situation of the two existing metropolitan clubs is such that they should give way and make room for one racing club to be formed at once.' The Victoria Turf Club and the Victoria Jockey Club gave way and the VRC was formed with an interim committee that included the most influential men in Victorian racing of the day, among them Herbert Power, Henry Creswick, Captain Standish, and Hurtle Fisher.

The new club became the trustees of the Flemington Racecourse and inherited both the debts and the assets of the existing clubs. From the Victoria Turf Club, they inherited the already very successful Melbourne Cup, from the Victoria Jockey Club, the Oaks for three-year-old fillies and the Victoria Derby.

A surveyor by the name of Robert Cooper Bagot was appointed secretary of the VRC and remained in that position until his death in 1881. Not a racing man himself, Bagot was an able administrator who was devoted to the club and its well-being. Under his guidance, the Melbourne Cup grew from a promising event to Australia's principal horse race and a major sporting event. Bagot was instrumental in persuading the government to declare Melbourne Cup Day a half-holiday for public servants and bank officials from 1866.

Melbourne Cup 1865: Toryboy beats Panic.

Early Melbourne Cups

The 1862 Melbourne Cup saw a repeat of the 1861 Cup with Archer first, winning from Mormon. Archer carried 10 stone 2 pounds, but still ran five seconds faster than the previous year and was 10 lengths ahead of Mormon when he crossed the line. In 1863 a 'technicality' over Archer's entry prevented his running. Sydneysiders remain suspicious.

TURF TOPICS

Short reign: 1864 Melbourne Cup winner Hurtle Fisher's Lantern was killed soon after his Cup win in an accident in Ballarat.

Nobbled: The day before the Champagne Stakes of 1866, C. B. Fisher backed his Derby winner Angler £12 000 to £3000. That night someone broke into the stable and drove a piece of bone into Angler's foot, crippling him and causing him to be scratched. The race was won by Hurtle Fisher's Fishhook who was bred in Victoria in 1863 and had fetched the record Australian price as a yearling of 3600 guineas. Fishhook also won the AJC St Leger, the Sydney Cup, the VRC St Leger, the VRC Champion Stakes, and the Essendon Stakes. In 1866, Hurtle Fisher sold all his horses from his Maribyrnong Estate, realising 26 455 guineas for them.

Later he said: 'I've only been sorry for parting with them once, and that's ever since.'

Minus one third: The judge, J. D. Dougharty, refused to declare a third place-getter in the 1866 Melbourne Cup because John Tait's Falcon raced in yellow with a red cap, colours which had not been supplied to him. The following day the VRC declared Falcon third, but some bookmakers refused to pay out.

Dead heated exchange: The connections of Nimblefoot protested when Exile won the Ballarat Cup in 1867 for the second year in a row. Certainly Exile was first past the post, but he dropped dead after crossing the line and the owner of the second horse protested on the grounds that a winner had to be ridden back to scale. The stewards disagreed and Exile's win stood.

Toryboy, winner of the 1865 Melbourne Cup, painted by Samuel Knights (SLV).

Racing's classic beginnings

In 1862, the first Victorian Sires' Produce Stakes was won by James Wilson's Musidora and in 1864 Falcon won the first Adelaide Cup. The first Launceston Champion Cup in 1865 was won by the imported Panic.

The AJC's Australian Derby Stakes, the race that became the AJC Derby, was won by Alfred Cheeke's mare Clove on 2 September 1865. Mr Justice Cheeke went into partnership with John Tait in his first stud farm at Mount Druitt. The Australian Derby Stakes began life in 1861 as the Randwick Derby Stakes and was renamed by the AJC in 1865 when the sweepstakes fee was increased to 30 sovereigns each with 38 subscribers. This was all part of the AJC's effort to keep up with horseracing in Victoria which seemed to have cornered the market in classic races with high stakes at the time.

The Epsom Handicap was run for the first time on the same Saturday as the Derby. Twelve starters ran the mile which was won by Mr Chaafe's Dundee in 1 minute, 53 seconds. The stakes were £4 each, with an added 50 sovereigns.

On New Year's Day, 1866, the first VRC Grand National Steeplechase was won by Firetail. That same year the first Doncaster Handicap was won by Dundee; the first Sydney Cup by Yattendon; the first AJC Champagne Stakes for 2-year-olds was won by Fishhook; the first QTC Brisbane Cup by Forester, and Bylong won the first Great Metropolitan Stakes (the Metropolitan).

In 1867, Glencoe won the first AJC Produce Stakes (now the AJC Sires' Produce Stakes) and Yattendon won the first Craven Plate, a 1¼-mile weight-for-age race. The first Tattersall's Club Cup in 1867 was won by Bulgimbar, the year the first Queensland Derby Stakes was run at Gayndah.

Tim Whiffler, Tim Whiffler, Tim Whiffler

S. T. Gill's engraving of Tim Whiffler, 1867.

It's Tim Whiffler, by a head from Tim Whiffler. That could have been the story of the 1867 Melbourne Cup, but it wasn't. Tim Whiffler, dubbed Sydney Tim by the press, bred in New South Wales in 1862 and trained by Etienne de Mestre, did win the Cup. His namesake, dubbed Melbourne Tim but bred in South Australia in 1862 and owned by the Ballarat publican Walter Craig, finished fifth. A third Tim Whiffler was imported in 1871, just to confuse things even further.

One of Tarragon's sons who was called Tim Whiffler raced successfully in Perth during the 1870s. Oh, and the NSW Tim Whiffler sired a successful son in 1877 called – you guessed it – Tim Whiffler.

Sydney Tim duly won the 1867 Melbourne Cup, causing some ructions on the course as inventive punters claimed to have backed Sydney Tim when the bookies said they'd backed Melbourne Tim.

Melbourne Tim, a 50/1 shot, followed Sydney Tim 5/2f, Queen of Hearts, Exile and Glencoe home.

In 1877 Sydney Tim sired yet another Tim. This one, 'Kiwi' Tim, won the Great Northern Derby and several other races in New Zealand.

The VATC Amateur Challenge Cup, won by Mr E. Miller's Marquis, ridden by J Simpson (ARM).

Fast horses in old Australia

The fastest, most dangerous thing that you could do in early colonial Australia was to ride a racehorse in a horse race. The Australian population at that time was predominantly young, male and far removed from the civilised restraints of home. At the same time, horses had become an indispensable part of town and country life. For all of these reasons, horseracing was the great colonial sporting attraction and one that rapidly appeared wherever European settlement took hold in this country.

If tempted to launch into an analytical study of the social history of racing, we should not overlook its ancient appeal as a sport, harnessing man's will and energies to the grace, speed and athleticism of the horse. There is a human instinct to risk safety for exhilaration, sometimes for inner satisfaction, sometimes for kudos. Horseracing today is no longer the fastest sport, and with so many safeguards it is far less hazardous; but it is still high-speed and potentially lethal.

The competitions that did have a following in early Australia were adapted from Britain – rustic holiday sports of the running, jumping and throwing kind; field sports such as fishing, shooting and fox (or kangaroo) hunting; and the gambling sports which included prizefighting and horseracing itself.

Racing had other particular attractions in the colonial setting. It provided a good excuse for a carnival, for bringing people together from remote places. You could spread the events out over two or three days, and no one worried if the same horses ran several times. There was plenty of scope for drinking and eating. The whole thing was reasonably easy to organise and the rules were basic enough: the first horse home won. If you could find an elevated viewing spot nearby, then hundreds or even thousands of spectators could watch the action. It was an ideal medium for a wager.

In Britain, horseracing had a tradition of some hundreds of years, with royal and aristocratic support, but the sport was still evolving. Handicap events, for instance, were an innovation of the 1790s. English classic races such as the St Leger, the Derby and the Oaks appeared only a decade before the first settlement in Sydney Cove.

Right from the start there were two groups who set themselves up to organise horseraces. The first were prosperous men, the aspiring gentry, army officers and senior civil servants. To own a beautiful, fast horse, then as now, was a status symbol. To ride it to victory was an added glory. Organisers were conscious of a desire to graft British institutions onto life in Australia.

Sydney was a small town, and the 1820s and 1830s saw much jealousy, pettiness and politics in the business of organising races. Until 1825 committees drawn from interested persons ran meetings on an annual basis. Then several competing clubs came into existence. The one that endured was the Australian Race Committee which set out a course at Homebush in 1840; two years later

it reconstituted itself into the Australian Jockey Club and soon became the leading racing club in the colony, moving its headquarters in 1861 to Randwick.

The second group of racing organisers were entrepreneurs – those who saw that they could make money not so much from the sport but from those who followed it. In paddocks by Thomas Shaw's Woolpack Inn in the days when Petersham was an outer suburb, a privately promoted race meeting on the Boxing Day holiday in 1844 furnished handsome business for the pub-keeper.

Many condemned the growth of racing in any form. Moralists echoed the sentiments of the Rev. William Horton who lectured in Sydney in 1826 on the 'Evils of Horse Racing', including drunkenness, reckless gambling and even unwanted pregnancies!

This strident opposition to racing and gambling was at the heart of political debate about the sport for the next century and a half. It prompted racing clubs to cultivate respectability – to control gambling and crowd behaviour and to ally the sport with the rich and powerful. On the other side, curiously, an unacknowledged coalition of churchmen and bookmakers did much to delay the acceptance of the totalisator betting machine after its appearance in the 1870s.

It was in Melbourne – a town founded nearly 50 years after Sydney – that racing developed most rapidly from a sport into a business. They were racing in Melbourne within three years of the time that the first Europeans unloaded stores onto the banks of the Yarra. By 1840 the annual autumn race meeting was moved to the flats of the Maribyrnong River in a location that was later called Flemington.

In that brief pastoral era, racing was an occasional, once or twice-a-year event organised by amateurs, where owners tended to ride their own horses, and where the purpose was primarily social and recreational.

After the gold rushes in the 1850s, the climate changed: more people. more money, more demand for entertainment. Suddenly there was a new class of professional making or scrounging a living from the sport – horsebreeders, jockeys, journalists dispensing advice on how the meetings should be organised, tipsters, bookmakers offering to lay bets on which horses would win.

Edward Coleman was among the first public horse trainers in Melbourne, advertising in 1858 that he combined experience and modern science in the treatment of horses entrusted to his care. Kirk's Bazaar, a horse saleyard in Bourke Street, became the unofficial racing centre where deals were made and where bookmakers plied their trade. Rival turf clubs vied to run richer and classier meetings. More big race meetings resulted, soon in all of the seasons.

Higher stakes attracted better horses and bigger crowds. A much-anticipated match race between Sydney's Veno and Melbourne's Alice Hawthorn drew thousands to the racecourse in 1857. Even more witnessed the first Australian Champion Sweepstakes two years later. Horses came from all of the colonies.

Racing predated Federation by decades. This Champion Sweepstake was the beginning of an Australia-wide consciousness. The formula was copied over the next 10 years, promoted with varying success in places such as Ipswich, Launceston, Sydney, Ballarat and Wagga Wagga. From this time onwards, too, the results of big races in Melbourne and Sydney were noted around the continent. The Melbourne Cup emerged almost fully fledged in 1861, as an extremely rich handicap race worthy of interest in all the colonies.

Money to be reaped from racing gave rise to further classes of person dependent on the sport: officials, handicappers, club secretaries, stewards to see that the rules were observed, starters and judges. The 1860s saw the merger of two clubs to form the Victoria Racing Club. Its full-time secretary, Robert Bagot, made it his business to beautify the racecourse and promote racing. Bagot reinvented Flemington. He is credited with making the Melbourne Cup into an event worthy to be patronised by governors, visiting princes and finely-dressed ladies.

The Cup became a marvel. Crowds exceeding 80 000 travelled to Flemington in the 1870s and 1880s. If a self-appointed colonial elite had control of the principal clubs, the sport continued to be a great leveller, followed with an equal passion by the middle section of society who paid to enter the public enclosures and grandstands, and by the poor or thrifty who could go to the flat inside the racecourse free.

Organisational structures for bodies such as the AJC and VRC were copied around the colonies. By the end of the 1870s each colony had its principal racing club, except Queensland where distance and regional rivalries made this impossible. Country clubs paid allegiance to the principal clubs and ran their meetings along similar lines.

One development complicated the scene. Proprietary racecourses were originally an outgrowth of publicans' race meetings. Among the earliest was Croxton Park, attached to the grounds of a Melbourne suburban hotel in the 1860s. Their problem was in attracting quality fields and enforcing honest racing. Many such ventures failed. One of the first men to make a success of proprietary racing was W. S. Cox at his Moonee Valley racecourse, which he opened in 1883. Private

'The Career of a Racehorse' as seen in the Illustrated Australian News, 20 October 1884 (SLV).

courses included Rosehill, Canterbury, Warwick Farm, Epsom and Mentone.

In the final decade of the century this process was taken a step further. The establishment of pony-racing tracks on small circuits (at grounds such as Richmond in Melbourne, Rosebery in Sydney, and Albion Park in Brisbane) created a rift in the control of racing which was not repaired until pony racing was abolished well into the 20th century. Yet it was pony racing with its need for quick, orderly starts that supplied innovations such as the automatic starting barrier which was soon put into common use.

Racing was part of the British colonial experience. Racing was also strong in parts of the United States and was growing in importance in Europe. The difference in Australia was the extent to which the sport was practised and followed, and the degree to which it pervaded the popular consciousness.

In early Australia, racing had this great advantage. It was a time when men and women dealt with horses in their daily life, knew their good points and their bad, had an eye for a champion; a time when many, perhaps most, knew for themselves the sensation of taking a horse to the gallop and of feeling the wind in their hair.

by Andrew Lemon

Horses were useful in many ways: Patrick William Morony, Night raid on Bathurst (NLA).

Frank Mahony, As in days of old, 1892.

Bushranger Ben Hall and Troubadour

The bushrangers who terrorised the countryside during the 1850s and 60s were a particular hazard to the owners of champion racehorses. Horse stealing was one of their specialities, and they liked to choose the fastest and finest horses in the colonies as their own particular mounts. A post-mortem of the champion Troubadour, who was sired by Sir Hercules, revealed nine bullets in various parts of his body that had been meant for the bushranger Ben Hall.

Between February 1863 and April 1865, the Hall and Gilbert gangs stole 23 well-known and successful racehorses in the Central Western Tableland district of New South Wales. The thoroughbred racehorses provided both the explosive speed and the hardy endurance for rides of up to 200 kilometres a day which the bushrangers needed to evade capture.

Ben Hall stole Troubadour at least three times. On one occasion, he tied up the stable hands at Groggan station at Bland Plains in New South Wales and went to the homestead to tell the owner, Mr Chisholm, 'I've come for Troubadour.' No amount of pleading on Chisholm's behalf worked, and Hall also stole Union Jack, who had recently won the Champion Plate at the Wagga Wagga races.

In one notorious event near Carcoar, the Hall gang stole horses from the Coombing Park estate of Thomas Iceley, including one of Iceley's favourites and a fine grey which belonged to the sub-inspector of police, Davidson, who had been searching for the bushrangers in the area and left his horse in Icely's stables.

A contemporary account of a raid which followed indicated that at least one of the horses was immediately put to work: 'O'Meally rode Vomus [a well-performed racehorse stolen previously from Icely just after being retired to stud], John Vane Davidson's grey, and Gilbert a racehorse called Matheroo, stolen some 10 days since from Grant – three first-rate horses, and Edric says all in splendid condition.'

Hall and his gang were following the example of one of the earlier bushrangers, William Westwood, best known as Jackey Jackey. He terrorised the New South Wales Southern Tablelands districts in 1840, and stole from all the notable horse breeders in the area.

Because of the threat of horse 'duffing', as stealing was called, country race meetings caused the authorities headaches and champion racehorses attended under police guard. In May 1864, five quality horses were travelling from Cowra to take part in a race meeting near Young – Dick Turpin, Jemmy Martin, Duke of Athol, Hollyhock and Bergamot. The horses travelled together, and were stabled at Bong Bong's Koorawatha Inn, to break the journey.

In a spectacular show of force, three members of Ben Hall's gang fired between 25 and 30 shots in their attempt to steal the horses, but they had not counted on the Bathurst troopers who accompanied the party in plain clothes. They left empty-handed, and the horses made it to their destination and raced the following day. They were again heavily escorted on their return to Cowra.

The closeness of the bushrangers and the horseracing fraternity is illustrated in an account of the meeting between the South Australian trainer George Stanmore and his apprentice jockey (and later the trainer) Jim Hanford, and the Kelly Gang. Stanmore and Hanford used to travel overland together to meetings in northern Victoria and southern New South Wales.

'Early one morning, just when they had prepared breakfast in the open, both looked up and saw a gun being pointed at them from behind a tree. It was the Kelly gang, who had sights on the meal. Then, suddenly Ned Kelly shouted to Dan: "Don't shoot, it's Stannie and little Jim."'

Adam Lindsay Gordon over another obstacle. He rode a steeplechase treble at Flemington.

Adam Lindsay Gordon on Outlaw, 1863 (NLA).

Adam Lindsay Gordon's galloping rhymes

Poet, horseman and gentleman jockey, Adam Lindsay Gordon was sent to Australia at the age of 19 in 1852 by his wealthy Gloucestershire family. He joined the South Australian Mounted Police and was stationed in Penola, near Mount Gambier until he resigned in 1855 and took up horse breaking.

Steeplechasing was the first love of Gordon's life, and he was an exceptional horseman. On 10 October 1868 he won a treble of three-mile steeplechases in the one afternoon at Flemington. The *Australasian* gave an account of the first race:

'The favourite [The Babbler] sailed along in his usual lolloping style, and at the riverside his backers were put in a "funk" when he stuck Mr Gordon up at the fence there. He refused twice, but Mr G. forced him over the third time of asking, and he took it so slovenly that he came down on his nose, but his rider's fine horsemanship soon had him on his legs again.'

Gordon won the third race, the Selling Steeplechase, on Cadger, one of his favourite steeplechasers, and reluctantly accepted £40 for him. He needed the money. (In 'selling races' the owners sold the winning horse to the highest bidder, with, at most courses, any money over the specified selling price going to the race club.)

Gordon's courage and recklessness as a rider led to one legendary jump. While riding with friends in the Mount Gambier district, he jumped his horse Red Lancer over the fence which surrounded the Blue Lake, across a chasm of more than 12 metres, and over the

fence again on the other side. It was an extraordinary feat, and one misstep would have plunged Gordon and his horse into the lake more than 60 metres below.

Adam Lindsay Gordon's second love was poetry and his verse was published in local publications throughout the 1860s. In search of a more sustaining profession, he served briefly in the South Australian parliament, a position he gave up when he moved to Western Australia. He spent a few unfortunate months in Bunbury in 1866-7, where he saw his 5000 sheep reduced by at least one-third. He returned to the Mount Gambier area and published his first two volumes of poetry in 1867.

Later that year he rented Craig's livery stables in Ballarat and the following year he joined the Ballarat Troop of Light Horse. As his reputation as a rider and poet grew, his financial and emotional security diminished. His young daughter died, his wife left him temporarily and Craig's livery stables failed.

In 1869 he fell in the Grand National Steeplechase. In March 1870, after another serious fall in a steeplechase at Flemington from the horse Prince Rupert, he wrote to his friend John Riddoch, 'I am hurt inside somewhere.' As his depression deepened so did his financial concerns. On 23 June 1870 his *Bush Ballads and Galloping Rhymes* was published, and he was shown an enthusiastic review written by his fellow poet Henry Kendall. The following day he went to the beach at Brighton early in the morning and shot himself.

From **Hippodromania – The Race**

See, they come round the last turn careering,
 Already Tait's colours are struck,
And the green in the vanguard is steering,
 And the red's in the rear of the ruck!
Are the stripes in the shade doom'd to lie long?
 Do the blue stars on white skies wax dim?
Is it Tamworth or Smuggler? 'Tis Bylong
 That wins – either Bylong or Tim.

As the shell through the breach that is riven
 And sapp'd by the springing of mines,
As the bolt from the thunder-cloud driven,
 That levels the larches and pines,
Through yon mass parti-colour'd that dashes
 Goal-turn'd, clad in many-hued garb,
From rear to van, surges and flashes
 The yellow and black of The Barb.

Past The Fly, falling back on the right, and
 The Gull, giving way on the left,
Past Tamworth, who feels the whip smite, and
 Whose sides by the rowels are cleft;
Where Tim and the chestnut together
 Still bear of the battle the brunt,
As if eight stone twelve were a feather,
 He comes with a rush to the front.

Tim Whiffler may yet prove a Tartar,
 And Bylong's the horse that can stay,
But Kean is in trouble, and Carter
 Is hard on the satin-skinn'd bay;
And The Barb comes away unextended,
 Hard held, like a second Eclipse,
While behind, the hoof-thunder is blended
 With the whistling and crackling of whips.

The Barb was the champion horse of the 1860s, admired for his withering runs home (ARM).

The Barb was a black demon

In an era of many fine horses, including Tarragon, Zoe, Tim Whiffler, Strop and Fishhook, 'Honest John' Tait's The Barb was the best of all. Sired by Sir Hercules, from Fair Ellen, he won races by as much as 30 lengths and was the greatest of Tait's many champions.

The Barb was bred by George Lee in 1863 at Leeholme, near Bathurst. He was stolen from there by bushrangers as a foal and recovered. A bad-tempered horse, he was nicknamed 'The Black Demon' and threw his jockey and bolted at his first start at Homebush in 1860.

In 1866, he won the AJC Australian Derby Stakes, beating Bylong and Fishhook comfortably by two lengths. Six days later he beat Fishhook by three lengths in the AJC Spring Bruie Stakes. He won the 1866 Melbourne Cup – the first of John Tait's four Melbourne Cup wins – in the record time of 3:43, carrying 6 stone 11 pounds in front of a crowd of 12 000.

The Barb confirmed his champion status at the 1867 VRC New Year's Day meeting when he won the Champion Sweepstakes. With the exception of his stablemate Volunteer who ran second, he beat the field by more than 30 lengths.

He was unbeaten as a five-year-old in 1868. He won the Great Metropolitan Stakes, the Craven Plate, the Randwick Plate and the Port Phillip Stakes. He won the Sydney Cup twice, first in 1868 carrying 8 stone 12 pounds, and then again in 1869, carrying 10 stone 8 pounds – running the same time of 3 minutes 40 seconds. When The Barb ran in the 1869 Melbourne Cup, he carried 11 stone 8 pounds.

The Barb won 15 of his 23 races, and sired some winners and the sires Fitz Hercules and Tocal. His daughter Melodius was the dam of Carbine's champion son, Wallace. He was 25 years old when he died at stud at Mitta Mitta in 1889.

A collectors' card featuring Banker.

A good tip for Duke

The Duke of Edinburgh mounted a horse and went down to see the start of a race when he attended Flemington on New Year's Day in 1868. According to Samuel Griffiths in *A Rolling Stone on the Turf*, just as the starter George Watson was about to start the race, the Duke asked: 'Mr Watson, you know all about horses. What is going to win?'

Almost in the same breath came the reply: 'Off, you devils!' and 'Damn it man, judge for yourself. You know as much about 'em as I do.'

On Captain Standish expostulating with Watson for his uncouth manner, the starter went up to the Duke to apologise, but was met with: 'Oh, don't apologise, Mr Watson. I was to blame in speaking to you at a critical moment. Come and have a drink with me.'

Prince Albert's visit to Flemington prompted a rerun of the 1867 Victoria Derby. The 1867 winner, John Tait's Fireworks, managed to prove his mettle by winning the race a second time and then winning the race that followed it, the 1¾-mile Midsummer Handicap. To honour the Prince, the VRC arranged its first seven-race program. The feature race was the Duke of Edinburgh Stakes, a handicap run over a mile and a half.

The Duke also visited Morphettville in South Australia, which meant he missed watching the hurly-burly in the Doncaster at Randwick. Two hoops named Colley and Stanley whipped each other, as well as their mounts, down the straight and past the finishing post.

Hurtle Fisher's great English stallion Fisherman died in June 1865 at his Maribyrnong stud.

Frederick Woodhouse's painting of the first meeting of the VATC, Ballarat 1876 (ARM).

The gentlemen form a club

The Victorian Amateur Turf Club (VATC) was born at a long and convivial dinner hosted by the landowner and rider Norman Wilson at Craig's Hotel in Ballarat on 13 and 14 (it went on into the early hours of the morning) October 1875. The gentlemen wanted to increase the opportunities available to amateur horsemen like themselves. Amateurs like W. S. Cox, Norman Wilson, A. S. Chirnside and J. O. Inglis were among the leading cross country riders and their plan was to feature jumping races for amateur riders at the meetings.

The first VATC race meeting was held at the Ballarat Turf Club's Dowling Forest course on Friday, 26 March 1876. Five of the six races at the meeting were over jumps, with the feature race of the day The Victoria Gold Cup, a three-mile steeplechase won by Sailor, owned by Andrew Chirnside and ridden by his son Andrew S. Chirnside.

Next the amateur horsemen sought a course of their own. Horseraces had been held at Caulfield Racecourse since 1859, but other than the occasional meeting of the Melbourne Hunt Club, it had fallen into disuse.

Thomas Haydon in his book *Sporting Reminiscences* (1898) recalled Caulfield as it was in those days:

'Caulfield is now dubbed the "classic" heath; there was nothing classic about it in these days. A track had been cut on the heath, it is true, and it was marked out by white-washed poles, and the run-in was protected on either side by a few panels of post and race fencing. Cabs and vehicles of all sorts were ranged in line about the winning post, and these formed the only "Stands" available.'

The proprietor of the nearby Turf Club Hotel, John George Heywood, and George Watson, master of the Melbourne Hunt Club, were trustees of the course and they agreed to surrender it to the gentlemen of the VATC.

The VATC set about clearing the unruly track and employed W. O. 'Broady' Broad-bridge, a groundsman at Caulfield until his death in 1901. The secretary of the VRC, Robert Bagot (with the VRC's approval) supervised the building of the grandstand. The club held their first meeting there on 5 August 1876. Again the main race of the day was the three-mile steeplechase, The Victorian Cup, and again it was won by Sailor, ridden by A. S. Chirnside.

The VATC introduced more flat races into their programs and, with an eye to the success of the Melbourne Cup, they ran the first Caulfield Cup in 1879.

Peter St Albans, by F. Woodhouse (ARM).

Peter St Albans

Peter St Albans, a 13-year-old Aboriginal jockey, won the 1876 Melbourne Cup on Briseis for the St Albans stable when stable jockey Tom Hales failed to make the weight. St Albans, whose surname was really Bowden, was apprenticed to James Wilson and, at 12, had already won on Briseis in the Doncaster Handicap. During a successful riding career he won the 1880 VRC St Leger, the 1881 Sires' Produce, the Geelong Cup and the Ascot Vale Stakes. On giving up riding, he became a trainer. His most successful horse Forest King ran second in the 1891 Caulfield Cup.

TURF TOPICS

First Caulfield Cup: The first Caulfield Cup was run on Saturday 5 April 1879 on a day when the red dirt from the drought-ridden north of Victoria was swept into the city by a fierce blustery wind. The VATC had accepted 53 entries for the Cup with 22 final accepters. The race was won by Newminster, the 1876 Victoria Derby winner, by a neck from Levant, with Mountaineer a close third. Newminster was owned by Andrew Chirnside, who was a foundation member of the VATC.

Onkaparinga at Oakbank: On Easter Monday, 1876, four horses fought it out for the two mile Handicap Steeplechase at Oakbank in the Adelaide Hills, South Australia. Champion amateur rider Candy Harslet crossed the line first on Tormenter.

Don Juan wins the 1873 Melbourne Cup as told by Marcus Clarke in the Melbourne Herald, and shown in a contemporary lithograph (ARM).

The Cup told by camera (and the novelist)

The Australian novelist Marcus Clarke set newspaper readers talking with his Cup day coverage in 1873. Clarke wrote his lively eyewitness description of the race seated at his desk in the Herald office. He began the article with an elaborate description of a 'camera obscura' which he claimed enabled an illustrious gathering at the Herald to see the Cup (in colour!) as it was run at Flemington:

But the bell rings for the Great Race – we could see its motion though its metallic tones were inaudible, and the various moving groups concentrate themselves in one place, the stand. There is some delay, some flag waving and shifting of colours, and then, but let us here transcribe word for word the report which, with eyes fixed upon the picture before us, we dictated through a speaking tube to a shorthand writer.

Ah! Yes! They're off! Hamlet leads, with Exile and Priam close behind. The savage chestnut, ridden by the lad in green, bores to the front, Lapidist changes his leg and the white and crimson links Fitz Yattendon level with him in an instant. Wollamai, the light-weighted colt of jolly Cleland's is leading the field, but the pace is too good, and in five strides the yellow and black of deadly Arrow slides out of the ruck, and a great roar goes up from the Ring.

'Whose horse is that?' asks Cameron.

'Tait's!' replies Ellery.

The ruck lengthens out, and Branch drags Goyder out of his bath chair as the white nightcap of Don Juan emerges out of the mass of colour.

The rain of yesterday is beginning to tell. Lapidist falls but confident in the brave old blood, D'Estre's Horatio, funereally black, forces past Fitz Yattendon and struggles for the lead. Exile lags, Priam seems lame, the Arrow sweeps past them both in three tremendous strides.

'By ____,' cries a proprietor of the *Herald*, 'he'll never stay at that pace.'

But John Tait's stable is not given to shirking, and the horse that 'carries the pot' never slackens his stride for an instant. Horatio labors and Fitz Yattendon creeps up again.

The Lancer is neck and neck with Exile, and then as Dolphin runs through his horses the hopes of Pearson's faction rise. Two bookmakers hurry to the rails. The horses turn. We cannot see! Ah! does he carry nine stone nine for it – he does, and Dagworth is the cry!

Round the sweep they come, mud flying in showers. 'Dagworth! Dagworth! Horatio! The Arrow!'

Cameron swears in his excitement. Ellery grasps the left hand of the editor of the *Herald* until he roars again. The two Professors are speechless. The writer of this alone is calm, and as the diminutive field sweeps out of the range of the lens for a moment he reflects with a smile that he has put his money on Don Juan.

There is a roar from the ring! Hats fly, men strain over the rails, the Stand flashes white with suddenly turned faces! One can almost hear the shouts.

'Horatio! The Arrow! No, Don Juan! Horatio! Lapidist! Lapidist! Lapidist! h-h-h-h-h-h! s-s-s-s-sh! Don Juan has it, Don Juan!' Neck and neck. Whips cracking like pistol shots. The lean head of Dagworth glides past the saddle flap of Horatio. An effort! Another! Shouting, yelling, grassland slipping away under the feet like a dirty green ribband. It is all over. A tremendous roar (Don Juan canters in a winner of the Melbourne Cup).

Herald, 6 December 1873

News of the Cup winner reaches the punters of Billybung, Australian Sketcher (SLV).

Joe 'King of the Ring' Thompson

The bookmaker Joe Thompson enjoyed the title 'King of the Ring' and named a racehorse after himself. In an interview he gave on his return to Melbourne in 1903, he recalled his early years:

'In 1854, I was before the mast. I was an apprentice, but I did not like the life, so I hid myself in a cask for 36 hours, and I was landed (not as a first-class passenger) at Sandridge Pier. When they knocked the head off the cask, I jumped out. I made for the diggings, but, having no luck, I served before the mast again for three years. I worked my passage out from home again at the magnificent wage of one shilling a month. Three months later I found myself at Ararat. I got a little bit of gold, which enabled me to go on a racecourse, and from that day I have been on the course ... I am proud to say that I led the Australian ring legitimately for 30 years.'

Thompson.

Thompson had a close relationship with the trainer James Wilson who established the St Albans Stud near Geelong in 1872. As well as training Thompson's horses, Wilson and his stable were associated with a number of his coups as a bookmaker. Regardless, the partners were said to loathe each other and on one occasion they brawled in the Paddock at Flemington and were fined £50 each for disturbing the peace.

The most notorious of Thompson's winners was Don Juan, the 1873 Melbourne Cup winner, a five-year-old which Wilson ran as a four-year-old owned by William Johnstone. Thompson and Wilson had paid Johnstone £100 for the use of his name and backed the horse heavily at long odds. When bookmakers became aware of Thompson's connection, the odds narrowed and Don Juan started favourite and won easily in record time. The horse had been on the private sale list and had actually been bought for £500 only days before the Cup by J.O. Inglis. Thompson had managed to lease him back in time and after the win, he bought him back for £2000. He called his East Melbourne mansion Don Juan House. Thompson had earlier had a near miss with the Melbourne Cup when he sold a young Nimblefoot to the Ballarat publican Walter Craig. The gelding later won the 1870 Cup.

When Thompson was attacked by the *Argus* newspaper for his dual role of horse owner and bookmaker, he responded by naming one of his horses Argus Scandal.

Thompson didn't always win. He took a very public loss on the 1877 Melbourne Cup when Chester won and his owner and breeder, the New South Wales parliamentarian James White, won at least £20 000.

Mei Quong Tart with his horse Nobby.

Mei Quong Tart

Mei Quong Tart, Chinese merchant, racehorse owner and philanthropist, promoted a series of popular race meetings at Jembaicumbene in the 1870s. Most of the owners and jockeys were Chinese, working in the mines around Arulen and Braidwood, New South Wales.

Quong Tart came to Australia at the age of nine with an uncle. By the time he was 18, his success as a merchant and entrepreneur on the goldfields had made him rich. He moved to Sydney as a tea merchant and opened a number of successful tearooms.

Quong Tart was a keen racegoer who called his Ashfield home Gallop House. He crossed the cultural boundaries with ease and was a Freemason and Anglican. He represented Australia in an unofficial capacity on trips to China, mediated between Chinese and Europeans in Australia and campaigned for better conditions for Chinese coolies and against the import of opium. He died of pleurisy in 1903, aged 53.

Joe Thompson returned to work in England in 1889 and was among the first to introduce doubles betting to the English courses. He also teamed up with the celebrated actress Lillie Langtry in 1898 and together they raced the St Albans–bred Merman who won a string of number one races in Britain, netting them at least £100 000.

When Joe Thompson returned briefly to Melbourne in 1903, he was given a civic reception and feted by the press. He died in 1909, almost 71.

The steamship City of Melbourne in a gale: the scene on deck (Australasian Sketcher).

Gale losses

Etienne de Mestre's 1876 Melbourne Cup entry and race favourite Robin Hood, winner of the 1875 VRC Derby, Royal Park Stakes, Mares' Produce Stakes and the 1876 AJC St Leger, was one of nine horses, worth £20 000, to die when the steamship *City of Melbourne* ran into a heavy gale on its way from Sydney to Melbourne on 11 September 1886. The horses were returning from the AJC Spring meeting and two other Melbourne Cup entrants, Burgundy and Sovereign, also died in the tragedy.

A correspondent of the *Australasian Sketcher* was on board: 'The *City of Melbourne*, crammed with passengers and having on board 11 racehorses, comprising the flower of the Victorian studs, left Sydney at midnight on Saturday. On Sunday morning a strong southerly gale set in, and as the ship was not far from Jervis Bay, Joe Morrison [the trainer and leading jockey who was in charge of the horses] requested Captain Paddle to return, in order to save the lives of the valuable animals under his charge, but the captain determined to face the gale.

'Soon after passing Cape St George the vessel shipped a number of heavy seas, and the gale increased to a hurricane. The wheel was smashed and the binnacle washed away, the ship at the time going round like a top.

'The crew behaved splendidly, and rigged a temporary steering gear, and as some of the racehorses had fallen, the captain at last determined to return; but the weather being hazy and thick, he could not ascertain rightly where he was, and put the ship's head to sea.

'Then commenced the slaughter amongst the horses. Eros and Mr Evan's Gwendoline filly were about the first to succumb, being washed on to the deck, and killed. Poacher followed, then Burgundy was killed. Nemesis was thrown on to the deck, and was drowned where she lay; so was Sovereign, Etoile du Matin having also been killed. The greatest loss of all was Robin Hood, who fell under the other horses, and notwithstanding the efforts of Davis, Morrison and Harris, and the chief officer, he also was killed.'

Only two horses survived the turmoil: Redwood and a Chrysolite colt, which the dedicated Morrison kept alive by constant rubbing and doses of beer and gin. The colt was named Robinson Crusoe, and had a successful career as a racehorse and a sire.

Public suspicions were roused in relation to the disaster when Melbourne bookmakers presented skipper Captain Paddle with a purse in recognition of the part he played in the disaster – the death of the favourite had saved them thousands of pounds!

NIMBLEFOOT

Walter Craig's dream

When the 12/1 chance Nimblefoot won the 1870 Melbourne Cup, he was fulfilling a prophecy made by his former owner, the late Walter Craig, proprietor of Craig's Hotel in Ballarat.

The *Age* newspaper recounted the story on 11 November 1870, after the race had been postponed for a week after ten and a half inches of rain fell on Melbourne from the beginning of September.

'Several months ago Mr Craig died, but before his death he had a remarkable dream, which will assuredly be henceforward the most wonderful tradition of the Victorian turf. On the night before his death, Mr Craig dreamt that he saw Nimblefoot win the Melbourne Cup, carrying his well-known colour – violet – but with a piece of crepe on the sleeve, whereby he concluded that the event would take place after his death. "Nimblefoot will win the Melbourne Cup, but I shall never live to see it," said Mr Craig the next morning, and that very night he died. The prophecy was generally known at the time, and was published in the *Age* of Wednesday last. So that it is no "after the event" affair.'

Stamping out private racing in New Zealand

In New Zealand non-proprietary clubs were the norm from the outset and these moved as swiftly as possible, through combined action, to stamp out proprietary racing (where any group of characters could get together to organise a race meeting and split up the profits afterwards).

In 1876 the Canterbury Jockey Club, then the strongest racing organisation in the country, resolved to recognise only the Dunedin–Wellington, Auckland and Hawke's Bay clubs and to take no cognisance of any complaint or disqualification made by any other club unless it had been first referred to and confirmed by 'the Metropolitan Club of the Provincial District within which such club holds its meetings'. By this time there were a myriad of racing clubs up and down the country. In the southernmost provinces of Otago and Southland alone, where the gold mining boom was at its peak, there were 46 clubs south of the Waitaki River holding 73 days' racing! The end of the gold rush and the mid-1880s slump saw many of these Otago and Southland clubs into natural oblivion. But a number of other clubs – and not only in the Deep South – were proprietary affairs running notoriously 'shonky' meetings. They needed a nudge to aid their departure and the major racing clubs simply decreed in concert that horses (and their connections) which competed at unregistered meetings would be banned from meetings held under the auspices of the principal clubs. While the unreg-istered clubs had already departed by the time a national racing body, the New Zealand Racing Conference, was formed in the last decade of the 19th century, there were still 84 registered racing clubs, and virtually as many racecourses as the 20th century began.

Spencer Gollan: 1870s Hawke's Bay owner.

Fashions of the field, 1874

The ladies of Melbourne have always dressed up for the Cup (SLV).

The *Argus* reports: 'Those voluminous trains, with so many breadths of costly material in them, were not designed and fabricated to be hidden from critical, from envious, or from admiring eyes. Those extraordinary combinations of colour, those startling juxtapositions of pink and claret, of blue and yellow, of mauve and russet; those wonderful head-dresses, belonging to no order of architecture in particular, and built up of such indescribably fantastic fabrics; those cataracts of lace falling from the girdle to the hem of the robe; those variegated panels, so to speak, which remind you of the ornamental papers with which old-fashioned housewives ornament their empty grates during the summer months; those miraculous dresses which are so puffed and purfled … as to suggest that the wearer had been cased in a light paste and then baked, leaving the crust full of wrinkles and crinkles, bosses and corrugations; those amazing costumes, striped like a zebra's skin, or covered with horizontal bands, bends, bars, batons, fesses, or chevrons, like shields in heraldry; those corslets of one pronounced colour, sleeves of another, and substructure of a third; those glittering displays of metallic buttons, which only required to be a little more numerous to be mistaken for scale-armour; – all these things were not meant to be hidden from the public gaze.'

Kiwi bloodlines

The most significant early stallion in New Zealand breeding was Sir Hercules (by Cap-a-pie from Paraguay), bought from Australia like so many of New Zealand's early thoroughbreds by Henry Redwood.

Sir Hercules spent only five years in New Zealand before the Australians realised what they had let slip through their fingers and bought him back. In that relatively brief stint, however, he had a marked influence on the New Zealand breed, leaving a number of mares who did great service first as racemares and subsequently at stud. After returning to Australia, Sir Hercules left a champion in The Barb and numerous good gallopers, and was regarded as one of the outstanding 'colonial-bred' sires of the 19th century.

The next significant sire was Traducer, a stallion who, along with the splendid broodmare Mermaid, was almost put over the side on a long and arduous voyage from England.

Bred in England in 1857, Traducer must have inherited some of the bad temper for which his sire, The Libel, was noted. During his 18 years at stud in New Zealand he changed hands at least seven times and spent much of the 1860s in Wanganui serving half-bred or non-thoroughbred mares. Yet the quality of his few thoroughbred foals was such that he was returned to Canterbury and spent his last years seeing the best mares. The stock of Traducer won all the major races of the day, his best progeny being the champion mare Lurline (to his old shipmate Mermaid).

Many of the early mares imported to New Zealand, though undoubtedly thoroughbred, could not be traced to the General Stud Book. In some cases it was a failure to maintain records, in others it was because the mares, landed along the coast after dark, had no doubt been stolen in either New South Wales or South America.

One of the first imported mares who could be traced directly to the English Stud Book was Flora McIvor. Her foaling date was generally given as 1828, which made her 27 and 29 years old respectively when she produced two filly foals in New Zealand to Sir Hercules, Io and Waimea. Through those two mares the Flora McIvor family still thrives.

Those early New Zealand mares which could not be traced to the General Stud Book were described as 'Colonial' mares. Those who had a significant and continuing influence in New Zealand included Cutty Sark, Dudu, Gipsy, Josephine, Moth, Princess, Rosebud, Sappho, Sharkie, Woodstock and two of the most famous New Zealand 'dagger' families, those founded by Winnies (bred in 1878) and Yatterina (bred in 1865).

1870–1879 RESULTS

VICTORIA DERBY
1870 Florence, J. Tait, (J. Morrison), 3:0, Pyrrhus, Doubtful
1871 Miss Jessie, J. Wilson, (J. Wilson), 2:49, The Irish King, Formosa
1872 Loup Garou, (T. Brown), 2:46, King of the Road, Patriarch
1873 Lapidist, W. Filgate, (H. Grubb), 2:51, Mountaineer, Maid of Avenel
1874 Melbourne, J. Tait, (J. Ashworth), 2:46.5, Stockbridge, Scan Mag
1875 Robin Hood, E. de Mestre, (G. Donnelly), 2:48, Richmond, Sour Grapes colt
1876 Briseis, J. Wilson, (T. Hales), 2:43.25, Queen's Head, Sibyl
1877 Chester, E. de Mestre, (P. Pigott), 2:43, Pluto, First King
1878 Wellington, (M. Griffin), 2:47, Warlock, His Lordship
1879 Suwarrow, (R. Walker), 2:43, Belladrum, Rivalry

MELBOURNE CUP
1870 Nimblefoot, W. Lang, (J. Day), 3:37, Lapdog, Valentine
1871 The Pearl, J. Tait, (J. Cavanagh), 3:39, Romula, Irish King
1872 The Quack, J. Tait, (W. Enderson), 3:39, The Ace, Dagworth
1873 Don Juan, J. Wilson, (W. Wilson), 3:36, Dagworth, Horatio

1874 Haricot, S. Harding, (P. Pigott), 3:37.5, Protos, The Diver
1875 Wollomai, S. Moon, (R. Batty), 3:38, Richmond, Goldsborough
1876 Briseis, James Wilson, (P. St Albans), 3:36.5, Sibyl, Timothy
1877 Chester, E. de Mestre, (P. Pigott), 3:33.5, Savanaka, The Vagabond
1878 Calamia, E. de Mestre, (T. Brown), 3:35.75, Tom Kirk, Waxy
1879 Darriwell, W. Dakin, (S. Cracknell), 3:30.75, Sweetmeat, Suwarrow

SYDNEY CUP
1870 Barbelle, 3:43, The Earl & Bylong =
1871 Mermaid, 3:40, Little Dick, Romula
1872 The Prophet, 3:36.75, Hamlet, Barbelle
1873 Vixen, 3:40, Patriarch, The Ace
1874 Speculation, 3:39, Dagworth, Fugleman
1875 Imperial, 3:36, Reprieve, Lurline
1876 A.T., 3:37.7, Kingsborough, Neredah
1877 Kingfisher, 3:36.2, Viva, Spark
1878 Democrat, 3:33.5, Streatham, Macaroni

1879 Savanaka, 3:33.8, Chester, Bosworth

AJC DERBY
1870 Florence, J. Tait, (C. Stanley), 2:51, Pyrrhus, Challenger
1871 Javelin, (J. Kean), 2:47, The Prohpet, Hamlet
1872 Loup Garou, (T. Brown), 2:26.3, King of the Ring, Horatio
1873 Benvolio, (T. Brown), 2:48.5, Excelsior, Goldsborough
1874 Kingsborough, (W. Yeomans), 2:50, Melbourne, Neredah
1875 Richmond, (T. Hales), 2:45, Kingston Colt, Valentia
1876 Robinson Crusoe, (J. Morrison), 2:43.5, Tocal, the Cardinal
1877 Woodlands, (B. Colley), 2:49, Chester, Cap-a-Pie
1878 His Lordship, E. de Mestre, (J. Morrison), 2:55, Vulcan, Woodlawn
1879 Nellie, (B. Colley), 2:51.5, Falmouth, His Grace

CAULFIELD CUP
1879 Newminster, T. Wilson, (W. Yeomans), 2:45.5, Levant, Mountaineer

Karl Kahler's famous painting, The Lawn, Flemington, Cup day 1887 (VRC). Subscribers to the painting had their portraits included in it.

Malua, a versatile champion

Malua was one of the most versatile of champions, with wins in the 1884 Melbourne Cup and the 1888 Grand National Hurdle to his name. His other wins included both sprints and distance races.

He began life as a horse called Bagot owned by the Hon. Thomas Reibey, Premier of Tasmania, and bred by John Field in Tasmania by St Albans from Edella. As Bagot, he raced as a two-year-old with two wins and a second in his three races. On a move to the mainland, he raced as a three-year-old, and it was at the beginning of his four-year-old season that his name was changed to Malua by his new owner, J. O. Inglis, who rode him (carrying 73 kg) in his Grand National Hurdle win.

His efforts in the 1884 VRC Spring Carnival show his versatility: on the first day, he won the Melbourne Stakes (1¼ miles). Next, as the second top weight carrying 9 stone 9 pounds (61.5 kg) he won

Malua.

the Melbourne Cup in only .75 of a second off the record set the previous year. Malua carried 33 pounds more than the record holder. On Thursday he lost the sprint, the Flying Stakes, by a head, a gallant effort considering he conceded 37 pounds to the winner. He finished his carnival on the Saturday with a second in the VRC Canterbury Plate.

The races he won during his career included the Adelaide Cup, the Australian Cup, the VRC Yan Yean Stakes, the first Oakleigh Plate (1884), the VRC Spring Handicap, and the AJC Spring Stakes. He won over distances from five furlongs to three miles. In one of his final races, Malua went on to win the 1889 Geelong Gold Cup.

Malua was trained by Ike Foulsham who described him as the best horse he had anything to do with. Malua had light stud duties while racing and in 1886 he sired the 1891 Melbourne Cup winner Malvolio.

GRAND FLANEUR

Grand Flaneur – the unbeatable champion

Grand Flaneur, the 1880 Melbourne Cup winner, is Australian racing's only unbeaten champion. The son of Yattendon won all nine of his starts, eight of them as a three-year-old, including the AJC Derby, the AJC Mares' Produce Stakes, the Victoria Derby, the VRC Mares' Produce Stakes, the VRC St Leger Stakes, and the 2-mile VRC Town Plate (weight-for-age). In the Champion Stakes, his only rival, Progress, was two lengths back, with the rest of the field tailing off a distant 25 lengths or more behind.

In training for the AJC Autumn Carnival, Grand Flaneur broke down in the near foreleg and was immediately retired to stud. He was the leading Australian sire in 1895.

Striped-coated bookmakers in action at Flemington.

The new face of bookmaking

Up to the early 1880s, bookmakers at Australian racecourses came to you. The bookies would roam the course, challenging people to bets which they recorded in a note-book. Most wagers were taken on credit and little cash changed hands. Then in 1882, a 22-year-old Englishman, Robert Standish Siever, changed all that. First at Morphettville, then at Flemington, Siever stood with his clerk on the same 'pitch', calling out the odds and wearing a big bag containing money which enabled him to take cash, giving each cash punter a numbered ticket recording the horse's initials. In his first year as a bookmak-er, Siever won £70 000 and changed the face of bookmaking in Australia.

In his book *A Rolling Stone on the Turf*, Samuel Griffiths recounts: 'When Siever stood up to bet for the first time at Flemington, he had little cash but plenty of assurance. On the first race Siever laid far more against the winner than he was able to pay, but when the jubilant backers presented their tickets he airily told them to come up after the next race. He was too busy betting to pay them just then; and they took it like lambs. Some got paid after the second race, others had to wait. Then things began to come Siever's way, and he wound up the day a big winner. Everyone received payment,

Siever handing out the money in a lordly style. His name as a dashing cash bettor was made right then.'

In 1880 a large number of leading book-makers in Victoria broke away from the Tattersalls Club and formed the Victorian Club. The new club set about creating a new image for bookmakers, scrupulously screen-ing members and introducing strict rules. VRC Committee members were persuaded to join, including VRC chairman Captain Frederick Standish.

In 1882 the VRC Committee permitted bookmakers to work in the Saddling Pad-dock for a fee of £25 per year and agreed to endorse the disqualifications and other disci-plinary measures imposed on bookies by the Victorian Club committee. The VRC also allowed the Victorian Club to hold its own race meeting at Flemington and the Gov-ernor of Victoria accepted an invititation to attend.

Thomas Haydon noted this new social acceptance in his *Sporting Reminiscence*s: '… to spend a few hours of the evening at the Club Rooms became quite the vogue. Doctors, lawyers, barristers, and leading merchants were frequently found discussing – not always racing or sporting topics, but topics such as politics, parliamentary, hospital elections, etc.'

Tatts sweeps Sydney

On 30 April 1881, the publican George Adams ran the first public Tattersalls sweepstakes on the Sydney Cup, with 2000 tickets at £1 each, with first prize £900, second £600 and third £300. The sweep was drawn in Adams's hotel parlour. Adams's previous sweepstakes had been open only to the Tattersalls Club members who met at his Adams's Hotel in Pitt Street, Sydney.

In Melbourne similar sweeps were held by J. J. Miller, son-in-law of the racing identity Sam Cook, on the Melbourne Cup. Miller arranged a sweep on the first Champion Race in 1859 which was drawn at Melbourne's Bull and Mouth Hotel. By 1877 sweeps with prizes of £2000 were held on the Cup and Miller was reported to have made £5000 from his sweepstakes in 1882.

A manual tote at Awapuni, NZ, 1890s.

The tote sweeps NZ

In 1880 a primitive invention known as a totalisator made its first appearance at an Auckland race meeting. Criminal charges were laid against fly-by-night operators with an alleged penchant for changing the number of bets placed on a given horse after the race was under way.

In Christchurch, however, a Mr Ekberg had patented a totalisator apparatus based on the French pari-mutuel, which record-ed bets mechanically rather than by hand-writing on pieces of paper. This was used at the Canterbury races later in 1880 and met with general approval from the public. The following year (the Auckland Racing Club meanwhile having employed the totalisator on a more formal basis), the Gaming and Lotteries Act was introduced providing for the Colonial Secretary to issue permits for the use of the totalisator.

The bookmakers could at first have seen little threat in this betting form which initially permitted only win betting and, at most meetings, a £2 minimum which would have precluded the average working man from betting.

Racing was booming in the 1880s. How they saw the races, a Troedel & Co. print from the 1880s (Rex Nan Kivell Collection, NLA).

Proprietary racing was for private profit

Proprietary race meetings, staged by companies formed to generate a private profit rather than public clubs, burgeoned in the 1880s.

The first race at the new Moonee Valley course on 15 September 1883, a Maiden Plate, finished in a dead-heat between Eveline and Pyrette. It couldn't have been a better beginning for W. S. 'Sam' Cox who the previous year had taken out a seven-year lease on Feehan's Farm, some vacant land in a valley only six kilometres north of central Melbourne. Cox was seeking to improve on the race meetings he had conducted at Kensington Park in Melbourne from 1874, and in laying out Moonee Valley he provided fine accommodation for the general public and the latest in stables for the competing horses. He also brought in enough prize money to attract the finest horses to the course.

Sam Cox died two years after Moonee Valley's opening, and his son Archie took the

reins as secretary of the club.

Moonee Valley was Melbourne's most successful proprietary racing club. Other proprietary clubs in metropolitan and suburban Melbourne were the trotting track Elsternwick, Epsom, Mentone, Sandown (originally Oakleigh) Park, Aspendale and Maribyrnong (a second course established by W. S. Cox).

Canterbury Park (Canterbury) was the first proprietary racecourse in New South Wales, and it opened with a meeting on 19 January 1884. Officials from Randwick oversaw a fine day's racing on the 1200-metre course, with horses familiar from Randwick meetings. The owner and breeder and New South Wales parliamentarian James White was a patron of the new course. Canterbury's success prompted the establishment of several other clubs. The Rosehill Race Club spent close to £100 000 promoting the Rosehill course which was a part of John Macarthur's

original grant. They held their opening meeting on 18 April 1885, a day marred by torrential rains in the morning.

Warwick Farm near Liverpool began as the private racecourse of the racing enthusiast and stud owner William Forrester. The success of the other courses prompted Forrester to join a syndicate to form the Warwick Farm Race Club which held its first meeting on Saturday and Monday, 16 and 18 March, 1889. The first race was a 2-mile hurdle race won by Pell's Drilldool and the main race was the Warwick Farm Cup, won by S. Kennedy's Aberdeen.

Moorefield, named after one of its founders Peter Moore, was established in the 1880s, and meetings were held by the Moorefield Racing Club.

In NSW in the 1890s, some private courses and pony races outside the jurisdiction of the AJC continued to flourish – until legislation was passed in 1906.

The fatal accident in the 1885 Caulfield Cup, Illustrated Australian News (SLV).

Death at the Caulfield Cup

It has gone down in history as the worst accident in Australian racing history. In front of a crowd of 20 000, 16 of the 41 runners in the 1885 Caulfield Cup fell and 24-year-old jockey Donald Nicholson was killed.

The race was started by Thomas Watson, son of regular starter George Watson who was ill, and there were several false starts before the enormous field finally got away. According to turf historian Maurice Cavanough, two incidents combined to create the tragedy: 'The rider of Sardius went for a split which was not quite wide enough. His mount cannoned into Too Too. Further out, Tom Brown had his running taken by another horse. These three, Sardius, Too Too and Tom Brown, dipped to the track almost together.'

The resulting chaos was inevitable in a field of 41. In his *Sporting Reminiscences*, Thomas Haydon wrote: 'The scene that followed can more readily be imagined than described. For a time a perfect panic prevailed, as riderless horses, some almost mad with fear, and others maimed and limping, passed the Stand.

'Women shrieked and fainted, as one after another the injured jockeys were carried, some insensible, and some with broken limbs, to the casualty room, and the extent of the calamity could not be gauged for some time … I don't suppose such a disaster on a racecourse has ever before or since been witnessed. The jockeys and horses were hurled hither and thither in appalling confusion, and it was many months before the injured boys were able to ride again, and certainly many horses never raced afterwards.'

Nicholson, a popular lightweight jockey, was killed.

The remaining horses completed the race, with Grace Darling finishing first, Britisher second and the veteran Coriolanus third.

TURF TOPICS

Touts asleep on the job: J. L. Collins ('Orion') and G. H. Thompson recount in *Harking Back*: A good story is told of a happening in connection with an important QTC meeting at Eagle Farm in 1886, and which created much merriment in sporting circles when it leaked out. It concerns some would-be 'touts'.

A few hard-heads of the racing game of the time got wind of a trial which was to take place on the track early in the morning before the regular 'touts' would arrive.

They made up their minds to be in the secrets of it, and in the late hours of the night before they armed themselves with a pack of cards and a couple of bottles of whisky, and hied themselves off to Eagle Farm to a sheltered spot in the grandstand.

By the dim light of candles they played poker into the wee sma' hours of the morning, interspersing the game with a nip of the best Scotch.

As the hours of the morning wore on first one and then another dozed off, until they were all asleep.

One and all were dead to the world when, before the dawn had really broken, the horses were despatched on their trial.

The cuties were aroused from their slumbers only by the sounds of the horses galloping towards the finishing post.

Much to their disgust and amazement the trial had taken place, and all they saw was the finish, and in their half-asleep state they were even unable to discern the identity of the horses.

They returned to town none the wiser, but tired and sadder men.

Run-off for the 1880 Geelong Cup

A run-off decided the 1880 Geelong Cup. The field had been reduced to eight when the local St Albans stable scratched two runners, and Zambesi and Columbus crossed the line together in a record time of 3:35. The judge Valentine Griffith declared a dead-heat, with Lord Harry third.

The owner of Zambesi, Andrew Chirnside, offered to split the winnings with Columbus' owner E. A. Johnson-Boe. Chirnside only wanted the gold cup – he offered Johnson-Boe the stake money. Johnson Boe refused and a run-off was held two hours later.

Columbus, the 5/4 favourite, was leading past the post the first time with Zambesi making up ground, and the two were neck and neck as they entered the straight for the last time. With about 80 metres to go, Columbus hung out, taking Zambesi with him, and the horses finished with Columbus in front by a nose under the judge's box. Zambesi's jockey Sam Cracknell protested against the winner for jostling.

The handicapper's evidence led to the disqualification of Columbus and Zambesi was declared the winner. Tempers flared, and the trainer of Columbus Morris Griffin broke a picket from the fence and threatened to 'split someone's skull'. A brawl broke out. No one was severely injured, but Griffin's behaviour earned him a two-year disqualification.

Columbus and Zambesi dead-heat.

Tom Hales and other great jockeys of the late 19th century (ARM).

Tom Hales – supreme rider

Tom Hales was the top jockey during the 1870s and 80s. The English-born Hales rode the winners of seven Victoria Derbys, seven AJC St Legers, ten VRC St Legers, eight Australian Cups and won the 1880 Melbourne Cup on Grand Flaneur.

In 1888 Hales rode 11 winners at the VRC autumn meeting and between 1872 and his retirement in 1892, he had 1645 mounts for 495 wins, 326 seconds and 190

thirds, and won a total of £166 770 in stakes for grateful owners.

Ike Foulsham, the jockey who also had success as a trainer (he trained Malua), described Hales as 'a great rider who could ride at a boy's weight and not once in 50 times make the slightest error of judgement'. Hales retired a wealthy man. He established a stud called Halesville near Albury–Wodonga, where the stallion Lochiel stood.

Flemington Racecourse in the 1880s.

Adelaide races east

The Adelaide Cup was run at Flemington in May 1885, in a two-day meeting staged by the SATC in which rain caused the Cup to be postponed from Thursday to Saturday. The 3200-metre Cup, first run at Thebarton in 1864, was one of Australia's wealthiest races attracting some of the country's finest horses.

The radical move to Victoria was made in response to the banning of on-course betting in South Australia in 1883. The VRC secretary Henry Byron Moore offered Flemington as an alternative site.

On-course totalisator betting had been legalised in South Australia in 1879 after it was first used at a private meeting at Morphettville. It was introduced at SATC meetings, with the club deducting 10 per cent of the money wagered. In 1882 legislation limited the operator's deduction to five per cent, but the sum of money gambled continued to increase.

Morphettville, South Australia in 1888.

Profits for the race clubs grew, but so did public opposition and, in 1883, the *Totalisator Act* was repealed and all betting was banned. Horseracing was suspended in South Australia and due to the SATC's financial problems, Morphettville reverted to the Queensland Mortgage Company. In 1888 Morphettville was bought at auction for £14 000 by Tom Wigley, Sylvester Browne and R. Pell who offered it back to the SATC for the same amount when South Australian racing resumed.

Squires of the South Island

George Stead and Sir George Clifford.

The blue and gold colours of Sir George Clifford were carried to victory for the first time by a colt named Stonyhurst at Riccarton in 1884. Complete statistics for the 1880s no longer exist, but from 1897 to his death in 1930, Sir George won £181 258 on the turf. This eclipsed even such famous Australian owners of the era as E. E. D. Clarke and the Hon. James White.

The Clifford-bred horses excelled in New Zealand's feature two-year-old and classic events. From one broodmare alone, Madowla, Sir George bred the winners of the Dunedin McLean Stakes, Wellington Wellesley Stakes, Great Northern Foal Stakes and CJC Welcome stakes (twice each), the CJC Middle Park Plate (four times), the Champagne Stakes (seven times), the Great Northern Derby once and the New Zealand Derby twice.

George Stead headed the New Zealand owners' list six times during the 1890s and continued a marvellous success rate up to his death in 1908. An important factor in his success was his private trainer, Dick Mason, who had been accounted one of the best of the first crop of professional jockeys, and indisputably the best trainer of New Zealand's first 70-odd years of racing.

In his territory George Stead won the New Zealand Derby 13 times, the New Zealand Oaks nine times and the Canterbury Champagne Stakes for two-year-olds 16 times, including 10 years in succession.

Stead was also a tireless administrator: treasurer of the Canterbury Jockey Club for more than 30 years and chairman from the turn of the century. He was also involved in the formation of the New Zealand Racing Conference, and uniform nationwide rules.

TURF TOPICS

Dog day upsets: The 1881 Melbourne Cup was disrupted when a dog ran on to the track, bringing down the AJC Derby winner Wheatear. In an unrelated incident, Suwarrow fell, and his jockey George Dodd died from the injuries he sustained. To the bookmakers' delight, the Cup was won by the outsider, Sydney horse Zulu.

Big mis-stake: Stud master Etienne de Mestre, trainer of Veno and Archer, laid the biggest single bet ever chronicled in the colonies when he backed his horses Navigator and Gudarz for the 1882 Victoria Derby–Melbourne Cup double. Navigator won but Gudarz ran third and de Mestre was

ruined. In 1883 de Mestre's stud Terara was auctioned. A special race meeting was held at Randwick to raise money for him and he retired to a small farm called Garryowen near Moss Vale. De Mestre's youngest son, Leroy Leveson Laurent Joseph, is better remembered as the artist Roy de Maistre.

Women only: A record field of 43 lined up for the Ladies' Trophy, a handicap for two-year-olds and upwards, conducted by the VATC at Caulfield on 30 June 1883. The six-furlong race was won by Mrs Sanderson riding The Ghost in 2 minutes, 31 ½ seconds.

Trapped on the rail: Seventy people died when the mail train between Melbourne and

Sydney ran off the line outside Cootamundra due to flooding on 25 January 1885. Many of the passengers were sporting people bound for the Sydney races, among them several prominent bookmakers including Joe Thompson and Austin Saqui, who both survived.

Riotous assembly: Crowds rioted at the Eagle Farm races on 12 November 1887. After six false starts in the Sandgate Handicap, the frustrated starter let the horses go but the flag was not lowered correctly. When the handicap was declared a race, a riot began and police were called upon to restore order.

1880–1889 RESULTS

VICTORIA DERBY
1880 Grand Flaneur, T. Brown, (T. Hales), 2:44, Progress, Mulatto
1881 Darebin, W.F. Dakin, (E. Power), 2:41.5, Santa Claus, Commotion
1882 Navigator, E. de Mestre, (T. Hales), 2:41.5, Frying Pan, Segenhoe
1883 Martini-Henri, M. Fennelly, (Williamson), 2:39, Sardius, Hurricane
1884 Rufus, (M. O'Brien), 2:41.75, David, Bargo
1885 Nordenfeldt, T. Payten, (R. Ellis) 2:43.75, First Chester, Winchester
1886 Trident, T. Payten, (T. Hales), 2:39, Chesham, Aglaos
1887 The Australian Peer, (E. Gorry), 2:40, Abercorn/Niagara
1888 Ensign, T. Payten, (T. Hales), 2:45.5, Carbine, Melos
1889 Dreadnought. T. Payten, (T. Hales), 2:41, Richelieu, Rudolph
MELBOURNE CUP
1880 Grand Flaneur, T. Brown, (T. Hales), 3:34.75, Progress, Lord Burghley
1881 Zulu, T. Lamond, (J. Gough), 3:32.5, The Czar, Sweetmeat
1882 The Assyrian, J.E. Savill, (C. Hutchens), 3:40, Stockwell, Gudarz
1883 Martini-Henri, M. Fennelly, (J. Williamson), 3:30.3, First Water, Commotion
1884 Malua, I. Foulsham, (A. Robertson), 3:31.75, Commotion, Plausible
1885, Sheet Anchor, T. Wilson, (M. O'Brien), 3:29.5, Grace Darling, Trenton
1886 Arsenal, H. Rayner, (W. English), 3:31, Trenton, Silvermine

1887 Dunlop, J. Nicholson, (T. Sanders), 3:28.5, Silvermine, The Australian Peer,
1888 Mentor, W.S. Hickenbotham, (M. O'Brien), 3:30.75, Tradition, The Yeoman
1889 Bravo, T. Wilson, (J. Anwin), 3:32.5, Carbine, Melos
SYDNEY CUP
1880 Petrea, 3:37.5, Martindale, Strathearn
1881 Progress, 3:36.8, Strathearn, Wandering Jew
1882 Cumnamulla, 3:34, Sweet William, Rainbow
1883 Darebin, W.F. Dakin, 3:33.5, Mistaken, Willeroo
1884 Favo, 3:36, Empress, Sardonyx
1885 Normandy, 3:35, Velocipede, Lord of the Lake
1886 Cerise & Blue, 3:33.2, Silvermine, Britisher
1887 Frisco, 3:39.7, Kitawa, Tom Brown
1888 The Australian Peer, 3:32.5, Algeria, Acme
1889 Carbine, W. Hickenbotham, (M. O'Brien), 3:31, Melos, Abercorn
AJC DERBY
1880 Grand Flaneur, T. Brown, (T. Hales), 2:45.2, Trevallyn, Sapphire
1881 Wheatear, (W. Yeomans), 2:52, Sardonyx, The Gem
1882 Navigator, E. de Mestre, (T. Hales), 2:48.75, Segenhoe, Lord Loftus, Nicholas=
1883 Le Grand, (B. Colley), 2:46.5, Kingsdale, Copra

1884 Bargo, (T. Hales), 2:42.25, Tremando, Cairngorm
1885 Nordenfeldt, T. Payten, (R. Ellis), 2:47, Uralla, First Chester
1886 Trident, M. Fennelly, (T. Hales), 2:38, Blairgowrie, Kingfish
1887 Abercorn, T. Payten, (T. Hales), 2:39.5, Niagara, The Australian Peer
1888 Melos, (E. Power), 2:46, Volley, Lamond
1889 Singapore, (E. Huxley), 2:44, Rudolph, Sydney
CAULFIELD CUP
1880 Tom Kirk, I.T. Carslake, (R.Walker), 2:28.5, Robbie Burns, Timothy
1881 (Autumn) Blue Ribbon, H. Yeend, (R. Walker), 2:30, Robbie Burns, Aspen
1881 (Spring) Master Avenel, T. Ivory, (P. Pigott), 2:29.5, Pirate, Woodlands
1882 Little Jack, J. Wilson, (C. Moore), 2:41.5, Verdure, Gipsy Cooper
1883 Calma, P.T. Heywood, (M. O'Brien), 2:42, Stockdale, Anglesey
1884 Blink Bonny, T. Wilson, (G. Blair), 2:40.5, Lord Wilton, Vergy
1885 Grace Darling, J. Duffett, (J. Williams), 2:40, Britisher, Coriolanus
1886 Ben Bolt, P. Kelly, (M. O'Brien), 2:42, Silvermine, Britisher
1887 Oakleigh, T. Wilson, (E. Gorry), 2:41.75, Remus, Dunlop
1888 Chicago, E. McKenna, (J. Campbell), 2:38.25, Tradition, Bravo
1889 Boz, J. Cripps, (R. Ramage), 2:43.75, The Charmer, Bravo

A contemporary poster of Carbine, perhaps the greatest Cup winner ever. Mick O'Brien up.

Carbine the champion

There is one certainty about the Melbourne Cup: each year, the winner has to lick the other runners plus a ghost. The ghost appears as a yellow-bay stallion with a kind head and awful front legs. Back in 1914, when this horse was old and hidebound, they put him away with chloroform at Welbeck Abbey, near Nottingham, England. He was Carbine, and only his body died.

No horse was ever better named. For one thing, he was by Musket, who was sent to the Antipodes to sire coach horses. For another, Musket's breeder, the Earl of Glasgow, was so obsessed with improving the breed he refused to sell his failures. Instead, he shot them. He had wanted to shoot Musket, who was by Toxophilite, a bleeder, by Longbow, a roarer. God took the Earl before the Earl could take Musket.

On the first Tuesday of November in 1890, Carbine won the Melbourne Cup. In a sport that, as Mark Twain observed, is all about differences of opinion, it is at least conceded that Carbine remains the greatest Cup winner. He carried 66.5 kilograms, or 7 kilograms over weight-for-age, a record that will never be beaten because the Cup is now weighted as a quality handicap. He beat the biggest field ever, 39 runners. He won by two-and-a-half lengths, untouched. He won wearing a bar shoe holding together a split heel so rotten with infection it had to be opened and drained a few days later. And he set an Australasian time record of 3:28¼ that would last 15 years.

Yes, that's about 55 lengths slower than Tawriffic ran in 1989. But they don't use sheep to mow the grass at Flemington these days. They did in 1890; the flock left spidery tracks all over the course. Anyway, Carbine would have been great even without that Cup win. Consider a few of his other feats.

At the Flemington Autumn carnival of 1889, Carbine, then three, came out on the Saturday to run third of 21 in the Newmarket, a sprint. The following Tuesday, he went down by three-quarters of a length to Lochiel in the Australian Cup over 3600 metres. On the Thursday, Carbine easily won the Champion Stakes over 4800 metres. On the Saturday, Carbine won the first race, the All-aged Stakes over 1600 metres. He then returned to win the fifth, the 3200-metre Loch Plate. In a week, the bay had started five times, won three wfa events, two of them on the same day, and covered 14 400 metres.

At the Randwick carnival a month later, Carbine ran second to the fine stayer Abercorn over 2400 metres on the Monday. On the Wednesday, he won the Sydney Cup, carrying 57 kilograms, or 5.5 kilograms over wfa. Next day he went around twice. He won the All-Aged Stakes of 1600 metres, then the Cumberland Stakes of 3200 metres. They gave him Friday off. On Saturday he beat the best stayers of the day in the AJC Plate over 4800 metres, posting an Australasian time record. In those six days, he covered 15 200 metres.

At the Flemington Spring Carnival of the same year, Carbine, now four, and troubled by the split heel that would never heal so long as he raced, ran second to Bravo in the Cup. He went down by a length, carrying 63.5 kilograms to the winner's 54 kilograms. Two days later he came out in the Flying Stakes over 1400 metres – and won, even though his infected hoof was held together with thread, beeswax and a bar shoe.

At the 1890 Flemington Autumn carnival, Carbine again raced twice in a day, and again won the All-Aged and Loch Plate.

At the Randwick carnival a month later, he again won the All-Aged and Cumberland Plate on the same day. He also won his second Sydney Cup, carrying four kilograms over wfa. He started five times at that carnival, won every time, and clicked over another 15 200 metres in a week.

Makes Vo Rogue seem like a pansy, doesn't he? Actually, shades of the Rogue, Walter Hickenbotham, Carbine's trainer, decided to run the stallion unshod at the 1891 Randwick autumn meeting. Carbine was trying to win the All-Aged Cumberland Stakes double for the third year. He slipped and floundered on the long wet grass in the All-Aged and went down to Marvel. Carbine was plated for the Cumberland a couple of hours later – and won by seven lengths.

Here was the genuine freak. There have probably been only two others, Phar Lap and Tulloch. All three, of course, are known as 'Australasian wonder horses' – which is to say they were bred and raised in New Zealand.

Carbine was foaled near Auckland in 1885 and made $1302 (620 guineas) at the yearling sales, a good price considering his blood and his front legs.

Musket had cost only $1000 to land in New Zealand after failing to sell at auction at Kirk's Horse Bazaar in Melbourne. Mersey, Carbine's dam, was imported from England for $315. A chestnut, said to be small and common, she never raced.

As to conformation, there seem to be two Carbines – the one who was painted, and the one who was photographed. The paintings invariably show an elegant horse with strong black points, a kindly outlook, and most of his angles correct. Grania Poliness' book *Carbine*, published in 1985, contains photos of Carbine I have not seen elsewhere. They mostly show a horse who is too 'straight' in front – a little straight in the shoulder, long in the forearm, and with upright, stumpy pasterns. The yearling buyers of 1887 were obviously less fussy.

Carbine won his only five starts as a two-year-old in New Zealand before coming to Australia and being sold for $6300 to Donald Wallace, a Victorian MP and VRC committeeman who had ridden the Broken Hill silver boom of the 1880s. When Carbine retired, Wallace stood the horse at Bacchus Marsh. From his first mating, Carbine produced Wallace, who won the Victoria Derby and Sydney Cup and went on to sire the Melbourne Cup winners Kingsburgh and Patrobas.

After four seasons at stud, Carbine was sold for $27 300 to the Duke of Portland, who stood the great St Simon at Welbeck Abbey. St Simon was highly strung; the Duke thought the easygoing Carbine would be a good outcross for St Simon's mares. Carbine might never have left if Wallace had not lost heavily in the bank crashes of the 1890s. Still, by going to England, Carbine won the sort of immortality that was impossible for Phar Lap, a gelding, and denied to Tulloch, who was scorned at stud.

Carbine sired an Epsom Derby winner in Spearmint, but it was two of Spearmint's daughters who ensured that Carbine's name would live all over the world. Catnip, bought by the Italian genius Federico Tesio, became the granddam of Nearco, sire of Nasrullah. Plucky Leige produced the great American sires Sir Gallahad and Bull Dog. Carbine is in the blood of Northern Dancer, Ribot and Star Kingdom. A table in the Poliness book also shows him in the pedigrees of 51 of the Melbourne Cup winners between 1914 and 1984.

Some horse.

Some ghost.

by Les Carlyon

W. McSherry's Sydney Cup 1889. The line-up: Keith, Abercorn, Melos, Carbine (AJC).

Carbine beats a huge field and monstrous weight in the 1890 Melbourne Cup.

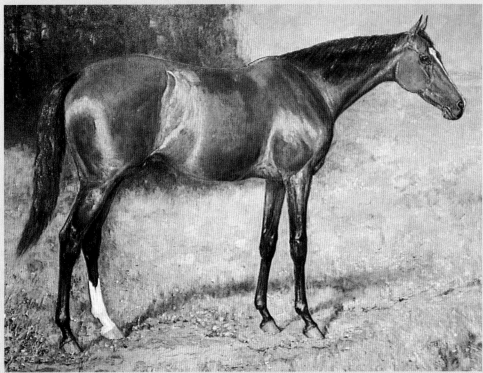

Carbine painted to look his best. He was nicknamed 'Old Jack' after Jack the giantkiller.

Sydney Cup, 1889, by W. McSherry. Carbine wins from Melos, Abercorn and Keith (AJC).

Musket, the powerful sire of Carbine.

An old punter reminisces …

H.C. Coghlan reminisces: Half an hour before the Cup of 1890, a friend bumped me gleefully in the crowded ring with:

'Just the man I want to see! I've got a good thing!'

'Too late, old chap. I'm done. A seat up above in the best thing for the Cup now.'

'I don't mean what you mean altogether. What do you fancy?'

I opened a pocket-book.

'There you are – Carbine, backed 11 times during the past few weeks, and Vengeance, Melos and Enuc once each.'

'Good! Now listen! You hear them laying Carbine 4 to 1. Well, a friend of mine has drawn him in a £10 000 sweep, and his brother is here laying a bit of it off at 6 to 1 – quietly, over behind the clock, to anyone introduced by a mutual friend. Will you have some of it?'

I hesitated, and he hurried me away to a bar. 'Well?'

'Lead me to it!'

We battled our way against the tide surging standwards. A gabbled introduction to a little, dapper, bearded person, and I handed over a ball of paper, part of my winnings on The Admiral's Derby three days before. The little man picked it into four £1 notes, each of which he handled as if testing elastic. 'Thank you, £24 to £4. Pay after the race if necessary.' And the records allege that 4 to 1 was Carbine's starting price in 1890! Parted from my pal by the crowd, I managed to get a good place on the stand-roof before the start. But I didn't see Carbine win. Half-way up the straight, he was so obviously giving the Sydney outsider, Highborn, all the difference between 10st 5lb and 6st 8lb, and donkey-licking him that I slipped away for a

good view of the return to scale of the great horse who was winning the Cup with the highest weight on record, in the largest field on record and in time that was then the actual best on record, and is so still when differences in weight are considered.

The champion came in through a tumult of cheering. On the steps of the members' pavilion, Donald Wallace stood, or, rather, danced, waving his grey tall hat above his greyer head and shouting: 'Come on, Old Jack; come on! Well done! Well done!'

The emotional use of the horse's stable name touched the crowd on a tender spot, and 'Old Jack' was called amid the cheering on all sides. Backers of other runners in the Cup and confirmed non-bettors, equally with those who had followed the colours of this old rosette, grasped the magnitude of a triumph that made the day the first of Cup Days, and they kept on being vociferous accordingly. The Church was in it, too. Here and there in the throng, twos and threes of the clergy made sedately jubilant noises and flung black hats aloft.

And the horse came in the gate and down the green lane, through all the tumult, the same old serene, imperturbable Carbine. For all the traces of effort he showed he might have been enjoying a spell in the paddock at Bacchus Marsh. When jockey Bob Ramage had removed the saddle and things, Donald Wallace came down to his horse, and, throwing an arm around his neck, laid his head lovingly upon him, while the late J. L. Purves, QC took Old Jack's head between his hands and kissed him on the nose. It was a rare picture of a rare day, but the illustrated journals were content to give us the usual photographs of 'The Finish' and 'Gowns on the Lawn'! – *Lone Hand*, 1 November 1907

TrustyMusket

Musket, originally brought to New Zealand to sire carriage and utility horses, was purchased to stand at the newly formed Glen Orchard Stud in Auckland when news of some promising progeny in England came through.

He was to prove an outstanding sire, a breed-shaper. His first mating with a thoroughbred mare, Sylvia, produced the first New Zealand-bred Melbourne Cup winner, Martini-Henri. Sadly Musket died just six years after his arrival in New Zealand, a month after Carbine, his greatest son, was born. But between Martini-Henri and Carbine he also left sons like Trenton, Nordenfeldt, Manton, Maxim: all high-class gallopers and (except Manton) significant sires.

Dan O'Brien

The Melbourne-born jockey Daniel O'Brien headed for New Zealand in the 1870s, and gained fame as the owner (relatively briefly) of Carbine. He became a regular campaigner on the NZ goldfields circuit, where money and grog flowed like water, and competed in footraces, hurdle races, flat races and saddle trots.

He was successful enough to buy the Racecourse Hotel at Riccarton, and had notable winners before Carbine with the likes of Tasman, Trenton, Rubina and Launceston. The 3000 guineas O'Brien was paid by Donald Wallace for Carbine after he had won seven races with him (including five straight in New Zealand as a two-year-old) was big money at the time – and a handsome return on the 620 guineas he paid for the colt as a yearling.

They're racing at Randwick

Randwick Racecourse, 1863.

The Australian Jockey Club began racing at Randwick in 1860 and set into the Australian Racing Calendar, in these first years, races now embedded in the tradition of the Australian Turf – the AJC Derby and Champagne Stakes, the Epsom, Doncaster and Metropolitan Handicaps and the Sydney Cup.

The racing rivalry between Sydney and Melbourne can be traced back to these years. Horses had been crossing the colonial borders to race in the rival city carnivals since the early intercolonial match races in the 1850s. The wealth of the goldfields led to the emergence of 'Marvellous Melbourne', and the Melbourne Cup, first raced in 1861, soon became the focus of colonial racing. Five years later the AJC introduced the Sydney Cup with a specially crafted gold cup of 150 sovereigns (at today's value about $15 000) and a great rivalry was born.

As if in answer to Etienne de Mestre taking back the first two Melbourne Cup trophies to New South Wales with his horse Archer, the Victorian-based C.B. Fisher brought Fishhook to Sydney to carry off the Sydney Cup at its second running in 1867. The fabled champion The Barb won the Melbourne Cup in 1866, and then the Sydney Cup in 1868 and 1869.

Border crossings like these brought crowds to the carnivals, and when Carbine came to Sydney in 1889 by train, he brought excited racegoers along with him. He won the Sydney Cup, then won it again in 1890, the year of his Melbourne Cup win. So it has gone on throughout our racing history.

Racing spread quickly throughout rural NSW and on the occasion of the colony's centenary in 1888, the *Sydney Morning Herald* reported 'that despite hot dry conditions in the colony no less than 66 [racing] features appear on the list for the Anniversary Celebration'. The problem was that all these various clubs – district clubs, St Patrick's clubs, hunt clubs, picnic clubs – could race under different rules. Some clubs framed the 'Bush Rules', while others advertised that they were racing under 'AJC Rules'. Still others raced 'under AJC Rules where Practical'. Goulburn, an early racing district where it was said a bushranger's horse might be found among the runners, raced under Bush Rules, 'not bothered by the irksome regulations decreed by the AJC'.

What was needed, said the *Australian Sportsman*, 'was for one Club to achieve the status and control exercised by the Jockey Club of England and for a publication to compile, record and circulate all information for the proper control of the sport'.

On 3 August 1900 the AJC took control of NSW racing and issued the *Australian Jockey Club Register*, which listed the raceclubs, officials, programs, prizes, fees and forfeits, disqualifications; the names and assumed names of owners, trainers, jockeys and apprentices, bookmakers and those suspended or warned off. Soon more than 100 clubs elected to race under these rules and the AJC was established as the principal club of NSW, with Randwick as 'headquarters'.

One consequence of the Register was the establishment of the proprietary race clubs – privately owned racecourses each with its own club and authority outside the ambit of the AJC. These were the Unregistered or Pony Clubs of Sydney. 'The ponies' were part of Sydney racing until their closure by the *Sydney Turf Club Act* of 1943.

It was at Randwick, however, that racing

history was formed. Bigger grandstands were built for the crowds who flocked to the city for the Easter and Spring Carnivals; 30 000 people saw the Randwick-trained Poseidon win the 1906 AJC Derby: 'all morning the roads resounded to the rattle and roar of race trams, along with cabs and drays bringing the biggest crowd ... Randwick looked like a giant ant heap.'

by John Ryan

1890–1899 RESULTS

VICTORIA DERBY
1890 The Admiral, S. Cook, (T. Hales), 2:46.75, Magic Circle, Gatling
1891 Strathmore, (H. Cusdin), 2:41.5, Stromboli, Oxide
1892 Camoola, T. Payten, (E. Huxley), 2:42, Meli, Jonathan
1893 Carnage, H. Munro, (J. Gough), 2:39, The Sailor Prince, Pounamu
1894 The Harvester, S. Cook, (C. Moore), 2:40.5, Malachite, Bonny Scotland
1895 Wallace, H. Munro, (J. Gough), 2:46, Osculator, Auria
1896 Newhaven, W. Hickenbotham, (H. Gardiner), 2:39.5, Resolute, Coil
1897 Amberite, W. Duggan, (M. Harris), 2:39.5, Aurum, Fleet Admiral
1898 Cocos, T. Payten, (W. Delaney), 2:41.5, Bobadil, Woodlark
1899 Merriwee, J. Wilson jnr, (V. Turner), 2:41.25, Dewey, Parthian

MELBOURNE CUP
1890 Carbine, W.S. Hickenbotham, (R. Ramage), 3:28.25, Highborn, Correze
1891 Malvolio, J. Redfearn, (G. Redfearn), 3:29.25, Sir William, Strathmore
1892 Glenloth, M. Carmody, (G. Robson), 3:36.25, Ronda, Penance
1893 Tarcoola, J. Cripps, (H. Cripps), 3:30.5, Carnage, Jeweller
1894 Patron, R. Bradfield, (H.G. Dawes), 3:31, Devon, Nada
1895 Auraria, J.H. Hill, (J. Stevenson), 3:29, Hova, Burrabari

1896 Newhaven, W.S. Hickenbotham, (J. Gardiner), 3:28.5, Bloodshot, The Skipper
1897 Gaulus, W. Forrester, (S. Callinan), 3:31, The Grafter, Aurum
1898 The Grafter, W. Forrester, (John Gough), 3:29.75, Wait-a-bit, Cocos

SYDNEY CUP
1890 Carbine, W. Hickenbotham, (M. O'Brien), 3:37, Mantilla, Muriel
1891 Highborn, 3:37.5, Greygown, Yowi
1892 Stromboli, 3:31.25, Oxide, Highborn
1893 Realm, 3:39, The Admiral, Camoola
1894 Lady Trenton, 3:34, The Trier, Nightingale
1895 Patroness, (H. Cook), 3:38.5, Quiver, Cobbity
1896 Wallace, H. Munro, (J. Gough), 3:31, Toreador, Trentham
1897 Tricolor, 3:31.5, Kallatina, Loch Leigh
1898 Merloolas, 3:31, Amberite, War God
1899 Diffidence, 3:31, Clarion, X Ray & Vocalist =

AJC DERBY
1890 Gibraltar, (T. Nerriker), 2:39, Gatling, Whimbrel
1891 Stromboli, (E. Huxley), 2:41, Oxide, Aster
1892 Camoola, (E. Huxley), 2:40, Arquebus, Blarney Stone

1893 Trenchant, (H. Gardiner), 2:54, Solanum, Delaware
1894 Bonnie Scotland, (W. Morrison), 2:44, Chesterman, Cobbity
1895 Bob Ray, (E. Huxley), 2:41, Onward, Mannilicher
1896 Charge, (M. Harris), 3:14, Coil, Sabretache
1897 Amberite, W. Duggan, (M. Harris), 2:45, Clarion, Metford
1898 Picture, (A. Delaney), 2:49, Lee Metford, Cocos
1899 Cranberry, (F. Fielder), 2:44.5, Kalingo, Reviver

CAULFIELD CUP
1890 Vengeance, A. Taylor, (P. McGowan), 2:38, Loyalstone, Enuc
1891 G'naroo, I. Foulsham, (W. Morrison), 2:36, Forest King, Clonard
1892 Paris, J. Monaghan, (C. Parker), 2:38.25, Yarran, Clonard
1893 Sainfoin, I.T. Carslake, (C. Ettridge), 2:38, Oxide, Moscow
1894 Paris, J. Allsop, (J. Fielder), 2:38, Devon, Bruin
1895 Waterfall, M. Thompson, (W. Delaney), 2:36.75, Trenchant, Quiver
1896 Cremorne, J. Allsop, (E. Huxley), 2:38.5, Straightfire, Le Var
1897 Amberite, W. Duggan, (M. Harris), 2:37, Parthenopaeus, Ayrshire
1898 Hymettus, P.T. Heywood, (N. Leek), 2:36.75, Massinissa, The Chief
1899 Dewey, T. Payetn, (L. Kuhn), 2:38.5, Gauleon, Ballistite

Tom Corrigan, with his magnificent mo: Troedel & Co. lithograph (NLA).

A. B. 'Banjo' Paterson dressed in racing silks, by Walter Syer (ML).

Tom Corrigan – never flinched from fence or wall

The Irish-born jockey Tom Corrigan was small, even for a jockey, and boasted a huge moustache. Acclaimed as the best cross country rider in Australia, he was regarded for his ability and horsemanship, rather than for any fancy riding style, and he was also much loved for his generosity.

Corrigan was apprenticed to a Warrnambool stable as a youngster, and rode in Melbourne for the first time at Flemington in 1867. He rode in the 1872 Melbourne Cup, but it was as a jumps rider that he excelled. From 1866 to his death in 1894, Corrigan won seven Grand Nationals: the VRC's Grand National Hurdle on Sir Peter, the Grand National Steeplechase on Great Western, Wymlet and Game, and the VATC's Grand National Steeplechase on Left Bower, Game and Sir Wilfred. At the first Grand National day in 1881, he won the Maiden Hurdle, and Maiden Steeple and the Grand National Hurdle race. From 788 rides, he had 238 wins, 135 seconds, and 95 thirds.

He teamed up with the Ballarat owner Martin Loughlin in 1877 and won many races for him. Corrigan was known for his integrity and Loughlin used to say: 'There is not enough money in Victoria to buy that boy.' He was also a heavy gambler, and in his autobiography *My Life on the Australian Turf*, the jockey and trainer James Scobie describes a race in which Corrigan allowed his horse to hang in on his, quoting Corrigan as saying: 'Don't enter a protest. I have a lot of money on Kangaroo [Corrigan's mount].' According to Scobie, 'Corrigan had wonderful "hands". He could ride a horse lighter over stiff obstacles than any man in the game, but at the finish of a race his skill wasn't quite so pronounced.'

Tommy Corrigan died as a result of a fall in the VRC Grand National Steeplechase at Caulfield on Saturday, 11 August 1894. He was riding Waiter, who fell at the fence near the mile-post. Corrigan died the following Monday morning. He was 40 years old. His funeral was one of the largest seen in Melbourne. The cortege of more than 250 vehicles left his Caulfield home for the Melbourne General Cemetery and was joined at Princes Bridge by 150 jockeys and trainers who marched in procession. Corrigan's green and white jacket and his boots rested on the coffin.

Tommy Corrigan

You talk of riders on the flat, of nerve and dash and pace!
Not one in fifty has the nerve to ride a steeplechase.
It's gay enough while horses pull and take their fences strong,
To rush a flyer to the front and bring the field along;
But what about the last half mile, with horses blown and beat –
When every jump means all you know to keep him on his feet!
When any slip means sudden death – with wife and child to keep,
It needs some pluck to draw the whip and flog him at the leap.
But Corrigan would ride them out by danger undismayed,
He never flinched from fence or wall, he never was afraid.

With easy seat and nerve of steel, light hand and cheery face,
He held the rushing horses back and made the sluggards race,
He gave the shirkers extra heart, he steadied down the rash,
He rode great clumsy, boring brutes and chanced the fatal smash,
He got the rushing Wymlet home that never jumped at all,
But clambered over every fence and clouted every wall;
But ah! you should have heard the cheers that shook the members' stand
Whenever Tommy Corrigan weighed out to ride Lone Hand!

They were, indeed, a splendid pair – the great upstanding horse,
The gamest jockey on his back that ever faced a course,
Though weight was big and pace was hot and jumps were stiff and tall,
'You follow Tommy Corrigan' was passed to one and all.
And every man in Ballarat raised all he could command
To put on Tommy Corrigan when riding old Lone Hand.

But now we'll keep his memory green while horsemen come and go,
We may not see his like again where silks and satins glow;
We'll drink to him in silence, boys, he's followed down the track
Where many a good man went before, but never one came back.
And let us hope in that far land, where shades of brave men reign,
That gallant Tommy Corrigan will ride Lone Hand again.

by 'Banjo' Paterson

Steeplechase jockeys: R. Batty, F. Hill, T. Corrigan, M. Lloyd, H. Chifsen and R. Bour (SLV).

The silks worn to Cup victory in 1889.

It's a dangerous game …

While Tom Corrigan's death was the most publicised death of a jockey in the 1890s, it was far from the only one. Within weeks of Corrigan's death, a second rider, Martin Bourke, was killed schooling horses over hurdles at Flemington. Riding was a perilous business, and young jockeys were killed in training sessions and race meetings, their deaths barely noticed by the racing public who showed far more concern and compassion for the death of a horse.

Banjo Paterson captured the disregard with which jockeys were held in *Only a Jockey* which he wrote on the death of the 14-year-old Richard Bennison who was killed while riding William Tell in track work.

Percy Strickland, 25, died in a fall in the Queensland Guineas on 11 August 1890. His memorial in the Toowong Cemetery reads: The turf which sorely needs/An honest race/Shall hold his memory/In a fond embrace.

The huge fields run in races totally disregarded the safety of both horse and rider. The Caulfield Cup field of 41 in 1885 resulted in a fall involving 16 horses and the death of Donald Nicholson. But this did not prevent the VATC accepting a Caulfield Cup field of 33 in 1898, which resulted in the death of the 13-year-old jockey James Flanagan, who died in the spectacular pile-up of seven horses. Flanagan was riding Robin Hood.

Nat Gould spells out some of the other realities facing jockeys in *On & Off the Turf in Australia* (1895):

An Australian jockey had not much chance of making a big fortune from riding fees alone; there are exceptions, but not many. An attempt was made by Mr W. W. Long, one of the members of the AJC Committee, to reduce the jockey's fee for a losing mount to a pound. I wrote strongly at the time against this, and so did others, and eventually the fee was fixed at £2 instead of £3. For a winning mount on the flat, a jockey receives £5. It is considerably more for hurdle and steeplechase riding.

When we consider the small number of mounts a jockey can get in a year, his income cannot be large. Thirty winning mounts is far above the average for a jockey in Australia in a season.

Jockeys are not allowed to bet, but they do bet, and heavily sometimes. It is a bad system, but it will never be avoided so long as a jockey cannot make a good income from riding fees alone. I have known of jockeys standing to win large stakes on races. They have told me the amount on several occasions.

It is a pernicious practice for an owner to put a jockey up and give him orders not to win, and yet this is done by men who ought to know better.

I once asked a popular jockey why he did not decline to ride a horse when he was given orders not to win.

'If I did I would never get another mount from him,' he answered, naming a well-known owner. 'Not only that, but he would influence other owners against me.'

Only a jockey

Out in the grey cheerless chill of the morning light,
Out on the track where the night shades still lurk;
Ere the first gleam of the sun god's returning light,
Round come the racehorses early at work.

Reefing and pulling and racing so readily,
Close sit the jockey-boys holding them hard,
'Steady the stallion there – canter him steadily,
Don't let him gallop so much as a yard.'

Fiercely he fights while others run wide of him,
Reefs at the bit that would hold him in thrall,
Plunges and bucks till the boy that's astride of him
Goes to the ground with a terrible fall.

'Stop him there! Block him there! Drive him in carefully,
Lead him about till he's quiet and cool.
Sound as a bell though he's blown himself fearfully,
Now let us pick up this poor little fool.

'Stunned? Oh, by Jove, I'm afraid it's a case with him;
Ride for the doctor! Keep bathing his head!
Send for a cart to go down to our place with him' –
No use! One long sigh and the little chap's dead.

by 'Banjo' Paterson

The betting ring at Flemington 1887, by Karl Kahler (VRC). The artist (standing with binoculars, directly above) included a self-portrait.

Nat Gould, on and off the turf in Australia

I was seated in a tramcar one morning when a particular friend of mine stepped in and sat down. Suddenly, without a word of warning, he jumped up and rushed out again.

I looked under the seat to see if a dog had been secreted there, and had gone for his calves, but there was nothing to cause alarm in that direction.

Much to my surprise I saw him come in at the other side of the tram and quietly sit down. 'What's the matter?' I asked. 'Too much whisky last night?'

'No,' he replied solemnly; 'it's race day, you know, and I got on the wrong side of the car. It's unlucky.'

Class distinctions are not so marked on Colonial racecourses as in England. There are no reserves for the Upper Ten, as at Ascot, Goodwood, Sandown, and other places. The VRC and the AJC, that is the Victoria Racing Club and the Australian Jockey Club, have reserves for their members, and on the Jockey Club Stand at Randwick ladies are not allowed, and the public can be admitted upon paying an extra five shillings – a privilege not availed of to any great extent.

Racing in the Sunny South is more of a pleasure than a business. Thousands of people are not cooped up in small rings, as though

they were so many sheep crowded into a pen. There is plenty of elbow room, and even on a Melbourne Cup Day at Flemington there is ample room for the ladies to promenade on the spacious lawn, although there are from fifty to eighty thousand people present on the course.

On training at Randwick:

There is nothing more exhilarating than to take a long walk in the early morning to the racecourse to see the horses do their work. In Australia especially this part of the day is best, because the sun is unpleasantly strong the greater portion of the day. Many pleasant hours I have spent both at Randwick and Flemington on the training track, when the dew is on the grass and the sun's rays give quite enough warmth to be pleasant.

The scene is Randwick, the time is about 5 a.m., or perhaps before.

A rapid walk along the Randwick Road brings us in sight of the famous course, and strings of thoroughbreds with their clothing on may be seen coming towards the entrance gates to do their morning gallop. How much depends upon those gallops only racing men know. The various boxes are all occupied by half past five, some at the Lower Randwick side, and others near the main entrance.

A few owners rattle up in their cabs, and the trainers come along either in buggies or on horseback.

There is a fair sprinkling of spectators, who have permission to be present, and also the representatives of the sporting press, whose business it is to give an account of the gallops in their various journals.

Reporting the work of horses is not looked upon as a degrading profession in Australia, and the men who chronicle the gallops are well up in their work, and treat all with fairness.

Timing horses in their work is the rule, and when the papers come out with the training notes in, the times registered for a mile, or whatever the distance of the gallop, are inserted.

I am not a great believer in the 'watch' on the track, although I do not think there is a trainer in Australia who does not time his horses in an important gallop. It is very different for a trainer, who knows the exact weights the horses have up, to time a gallop, to the ordinary looker-on who does not know the weights.

Australian trainers place a great reliance on the time test, and, judging by results, they appear to do very well on it.

Gould's best-selling non-fiction book.

Nat Gould in the 1890s.

Rosehill race card, 1896.

Nat Gould on gambling down under

The members of the ring in Australia are a respectable body of men, although an undesirable person is occasionally to be met with. Betting is inseparable from horse racing, and there are some heavy plungers on the Colonial turf. I am not a heavy bettor myself, and am none the worse off for it, although I must confess I cannot help having an occasional flutter when I fancy there is anything good on. If a young man, anxious to gamble on horse racing, asked me the best system to adopt, I should strongly advise him to systematically keep his money in his pocket and not bet at all.

The two principal clubs in Australia, I mean sporting clubs, are Tattersalls in Sydney and the Victorian Club in Melbourne. There are also clubs in Adelaide and Brisbane.

Sydney Tattersalls is one of the best appointed clubs of its kind in the world. The building cost a lot of money, and the main room, where the business is transacted, is a model of luxury … The Victorian Club in Melbourne is not so elaborate as that in Sydney, but it is adequate for all requirements, and during Cup week it is a busy place …

In Sydney there are scores of shops where double event betting takes place on all local events of any importance, and on every horse and pony meeting held during the week.

But to the ring and the men in it. First and foremost, the leader of the ring is Humphrey Oxenham, a man who has the goodwill of all classes.

Mr Oxenham has places of business in Sydney, Melbourne, and Brisbane; and in addition to his large bookmaking transaction

he now runs 'sweeps'. His name is known throughout Australasia, and a cheque signed Humphrey Oxenham would be acccepted as readily as coin in the realm. Mr Oxenham's ramifications extend from Thursday Island on the one hand to West Australia on the other, and all the intervening territory is represented on his books. Even from India, Fiji, and New Caledonia, money is sent for him to invest.

The year Malvolio won the Melbourne Cup (1891), Mr Oxenham lost £30 000 over the winner, and yet he had such an enormous amount of money in his book that he actually came out a winner on the race. Had an outsider won what a haul he would have made. Very liberal odds are laid by the ring over such races as the Caulfield and Melbourne Cups. A month before the Caulfield Cup race last year (1894), when Paris won, nearly 70 horses were quoted in Mr Oxenham's list of 50 to 1, and more than that number in the Melbourne Cup. When Glenloth won the Melbourne Cup in 1892, a 100 to 2 could have been had on the course. When Tarcoola won the following year I saw 40 to 1 laid against him; and when Patron won last year 33 to 1 could be had. When Carbine won it was a difficult matter to get money on at all, even at 4 or 5 to 1 in the ring; and I believe on the day of the race, in Sydney, some infatuated backers accepted 2 to 1 about his chance.

In 1893 Mr Oxenham had very large volumes on races. I saw in his book as much as £15 000 laid in a single wager over the Derby and Cup, and there were plenty of £10 000 and £5000 wagers. That year he laid what to

most men would have been a fortune against Carnage, and the colt ran second … There were wagers invested from the modest sov. to the 'merry monk' (£500).

Betting on the Melbourne Cup commences six months before the race, and an occasional wager is recorded before that. In addition to Mr Oxenham, there are many bookmakers with big volumes on this great race. Mr Jack Cohen, of Melbourne, lays in thousands; also Mr Alf Josephs, the leader of the Victorian ring. Mr Charles Westbrook makes a big book, and Paddy Burke is as genial a man as there is in the ring.

Nat Gould was born in Manchester in 1857, and worked as journalist before coming to Australia in 1884. He worked for a number of papers including the Brisbane *Telegraph*, and was editor of the *Bathurst Times*, but is best known for his racing writing for the long-gone Sydney sporting paper the *Referee*. He published the first of his celebrated racing novels under the pseudonym 'Verax' in the *Referee* shortly before he returned to England, where he spent the last 24 years of his life. Nat Gould died in 1919, and published his only book of non-fiction *On and Off the Turf in Australia* in 1895. He was prodigiously prolific in fiction – and lived on for his publishers until 1928 when the hoard of 26 novels left on his death were finally published. He sold more than 24 million books.

Inaugural Caulfield Cup winner Newminster was a successful St Albans stallion.

W. R. Wilson, the 'silver king' of St Albans.

The St Albans sweepstakes lottery

In March 1895, 'The Silver King' W. R. Wilson engaged George Adams to stage a sweepstakes lottery consisting of 125 000 £1 tickets in order to dispose of his prestigious St Albans Stud. It was every horse lover's dream: first prize was the 340-hectare St Albans estate, which included state of the art training stables, a 12-furlong training track and 13-furlong course. The stallions made up second to fifth prize, with Australia's most valuable sire Trenton leading the list. Then came the 19 racehorses – including as ninth prize, Wallace, with Wallace's dam Melodius right down the list as 68th prize, one of 57 broodmares. The 130th and last prize, after 400 sheep at 129th, was a carryall.

St Albans, just five kilometres from the centre of Geelong, was founded in 1873 by the breeder and trainer James Wilson. Melbourne Cup winners Don Juan and Briseis were from the St Albans Stud, and from 1878 to 1886 the annual St Albans yearling sales were a feature of the racing calendar.

In 1886, James Wilson was gored by a bull and nearly killed. He retired from training and his son James took over until the stud was sold later than year. It was bought by South Australian racing identity, John Crozier who, in 1890, sold it to W. R. (William Robert) Wilson. Wilson, who was no relation to the stud's founder, was a Port Pirie hotel keeper who had made his money through the mines in Broken Hill. He invested heavily in the stud, hired C. R. 'Leslie' Macdonald as manager and Hugh Munro as trainer, and during the 1890s headed the official Australian Owners' List four times.

His big wins included four Caulfield Guineas, three Victoria Derbys, VRC St Legers, VRC Australian Cups.

W. R. Wilson's reason for wanting to dispose of the stud is unknown. Rumour had it that he was under pressure from his 'stupendous mining interests in Western Australia'. What is known is that he changed his mind and at the last moment bought up thousands of tickets in the hope of winning St Albans back. He failed. A Seymour syndicate won the estate, though Wilson managed to win Bill of Portland (sixth prize and the first St Simon horse to come to Australia), the horses Pilatus and Merman and six of the broodmares. He then bought some of the unclaimed prizes, including Challenge for 500 guineas.

Wilson bought Wallace from his new owners, the Creswick syndicate, for £2500, on the condition that if Wallace won the Victorian Derby another £500 would be paid, and if he won the Melbourne Cup, Wilson would hand over an extra £1500.

The following year, W. R. Wilson bought back St Albans for £24 000. He offered £7000 for second prize, Trenton, but his bid was rejected. The estate remained in his possession until his death in 1900.

Wallace was one of the greatest sires Australia has known, producing the winners of 949 races worth £246 145 in stakes between 1900 and 1920. In his 22 years at stud, he was one of Australia's leading stallions 17 times.

Wallace was bred in Victoria in 1892 by W. R. Wilson, sired by Carbine in the first of his four Australian stud seasons. His dam Melodius can be traced back to the imported thoroughbred Fisherman. She was by Goldsborough, from Melody by The Barb, from Mermaid by Fisherman.

Raced by Wilson, Wallace won the VRC Flying Stakes (weight-for-age) as a two-year-old, and seven of 13 starts as a three-year-old, including the 1895 Victorian Derby and Fisher Plate and the 1896 Sydney Cup, which he won in record time carrying 4.5 kilograms over weight-for-age. He came third in his only start as a four-year-old, the VRC Caulfield Stakes in which he carried 10 stone.

His progeny include two Melbourne Cup winners, six Victorian Derby winners, winners of six VRC, four AJC and two South Australian St Legers, an AJC Derby winner, two South Australian Derby winners and six VRC Oaks winners. One of his many successful sons on the track was the stayer Trafalgar.

Wallace died at the age of 25 at Bundoora, Victoria in 1917. His influence as a sire survives through his daughters.

The starting barrier used at the Oakleigh pony track in 1893, pictured in use at Ascot.

Automatic starting barrier

The start of races was often chaotic. The horses were lined up at a line drawn on the course, with horses in huge fields sometimes lining up in two rows. False starts were common, and horses could run the complete race only to be told at the finishing post that they would have to take part in a rerun.

Jockeys were expected to make their horses toe the line, and on one occasion, a young jockey called Reuben Gray was unable to prevent his mount from walking over the line, and was fined £5.

Gray was forced to stay on at the course until he was able to find someone to lend him the money to pay the fine.

Subsequently Reuben's father Alexander Gray devised a superior starting method, which entailed a single-strand barrier that was raised at the start of the race. Gray's Barrier was tested at the AJC Metropolitan at Randwick in 1894 and the chairman of the AJC asked that it be installed at the six-furlong post during the meeting.

A similar barrier was trialled in 1893 at an Oakleigh pony track in Victoria and the VRC tested four different types of starting barriers in 1894, all of which had strands stretching the 175-foot width of the straight, and decided on one made by Johnstone and Gleeson. The VATC followed, and ordered machines for each starting point of the flat races, plus one for the training grounds.

Bad luck Trance: Trance, an early favourite in the 1892 Brisbane Cup, eased off in the betting on the day of the race. During the race her rider ran a second horse, Newbold, off the track and out of the running, then on leaving the straight the first time round, Trance was pulled to a standstill, and returned to the weighing-in enclosure. The mare was disqualified for life for a case of foul riding and pulling.

Trance was bought by a prominent owner-trainer, who had the disqualification lifted and took her to race in Victoria. There he was accused of running the mare as a ring-in for another of his horses which had won an unlikely double. He proved his innocence, but disposed of Trance.

Trance was then taken to England where she and her connections were outed for inconsistent running.

That's a first: The first King Island race meeting was staged on New Year's Day 1892, before a crowd of 11. The adult population of the island at the time was 15, four of whom were on lighthouse duty. The receipts of £11 for the day were paid partly in wallaby and kangaroo skins.

Cup controversy: In the 1893 Caulfield Cup, Tim Swiveller rushed down the outside and swerved in against leaders Oxide and Sainfoin. Tim Swiveller then ran on to win the race. A protest was lodged by the owner of Sainfoin, but it was dismissed. The owners appealed to the Commitee of the VRC, which overturned the ruling and the race went to the second placegetter Sainfoin. Outraged stewards argued that the committee had the right to overturn their decision only on an interpretation of the rules, not an interpretation of the facts.

Redleap, the greatest jumper of them all

Redleap, one of the greatest jumpers of all, started in only eight races, each time carrying a weight more outrageous than the last. Foaled in 1884, his dam was a Panic mare, his sire Denta. He was owned by Septimus Miller, trained by Humphrey Bellamy and ridden by the champion amateur jockey W. S. Cox, son of the founder of Moonee Valley.

Redleap won the VRC Grand National Hurdle in 1889 and 1892, the second time with 11 st 11lb; and the 1892 VRC Grand National Steeple, carrying a record 13 st 3 lb. Later that year, he won the VATC Australian Steeplechase, weighed down with 13 st 12 lb.

Cox's body weight was 8 st 12lb, so five stone dead weight was needed. An especially heavy saddle was used, which was on display at Cox's training stable in Ascot Vale Road, Flemington, until his death in 1912.

This last race was the only time the whip was used on Redleap. When coming into the gap in the course proper, Boulevard threatened to close in on Redleap, and Cox hit the champion once in order to get through first and avoid any trouble.

'He would stand off a long way from his fences,' Cox said of the champion, 'but he always got well over them.'

Martin Stainforth's evocative painting of Ibex defeating Wakeful in the 1902 VRC Flying Stakes.

Versatile Trafalgar – a good looker.

The first lady of the turf

Wakeful is the best racemare bred in Australia. Foaled in 1896, by Trenton from Insomnia, Wakeful's pedigree reached back to both Panic (imp.) and Fisherman (imp.) through her dam.

The First Lady of the Turf started her racing career as a four-year-old. She won the 1901 Oakleigh Plate by four lengths in her third start, the Newmarket in her fourth and the Doncaster in her fifth. From 44 races, she won 25, was second in 12, third in four and unplaced in three, for stakes of £16 690.

In 1901 she won the Caulfield Stakes, came a close second in the Caulfield Cup and ran fifth to her stablemate Revenue in the Melbourne Cup, carrying 8 st 10 lb (55.5 kg).

In 1902, she ran on all four days of the AJC's autumn racing meeting and was unbeaten. She won the Sydney Cup carrying 9.7 (60.5 kg). Her next races were three unbeaten starts in the AJC spring meeting.

In her final and possibly greatest race, she ran second in the 1903 Melbourne Cup as a seven-year-old carrying the top weight of 10 stone (63.5 kg). She lost by only ¾ head and conceded 48 pounds to Lord Cardigan with 6.9 (41.5 kg) who the following year won the Sydney Cup carrying 8.7.

Retired to stud, she produced 10 foals, including Blairgour, Baverstock (who sired David) and the 1918 Melbourne Cup winner Night Watch.

Grandson of a gun

Grandson of Carbine and son of the champion sire Wallace, the handsome Trafalgar was a great stayer who won 23 races (nine at his favourite distance of two miles) and stakes of £22 111. He had seven starts over the distance of three miles and won five and came third twice.

Born to the dam Grand Canary in 1905, Trafalgar's wins as a three-year-old included the VRC Flemington Spring Handicap, the AJC Randwick Autumn Stakes and the 1909 Sydney Cup. He was a seven-year-old when he won his last race, his fourth AJC Randwick Plate, in 1912.

In *Racehorses of Australia*, Dr W. H. Lang said of Trafalgar: 'He won at distances varying between nine furlongs and three miles, but the farther he went the better he liked it, and, strangely enough, he appeared to be gaining in speed as he grew older. And he never left an oat in his manger, and would clean up everything that was offered him, even when undergoing a course of physic, while his legs were of iron. I would not have liked to go into his box by myself, nor without his boy as his head. He was a sour old dog, and did not like to be disturbed in his castle. I have seen him "round" on his trainer and eject him without much ceremony from his box when in an ill humour.

'But I have no doubt that after he went out of training, and had liberty and not too much strapping, he became the mildest mannered horse that ever won a race or cut a rival's throat. I fear, however, that he is not a success at stud, although a sure foal-getter.'

Wakeful had a big heart: over-weighted for the 1903 Melbourne Cup, she lost narrowly.

Fashions on the field, Flemington 1906 (SLV).

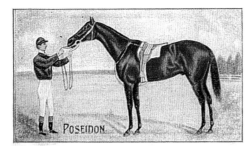

Poseidon – one of the greatest of his day.

Poseidon's 1906 Melbourne Cup

Poseidon first showed what he was made of in the AJC Derby in 1906. Called upon by his jockey Tom Clayton when the race leader turned into the straight, the three-year-old powered on to win by 4½ lengths.

In the next five weeks, Poseidon won the Victoria Derby, the Eclipse Stakes and the Caulfield and Melbourne Cups. He went on to win the VRC and AJC St Legers and in 1907 won the Caulfield Cup again. When he retired to stud as a six-year-old, he had won 19 of his 33 races and was one of the greatest racehorses of his day.

The brown colt, by Positano from Jacinth, was bought for 500 guineas at the 1905 yearling sales by trainer 'Ike' Earnshaw for 'U. R.

Robertson', the name under which Hugh Denison (later Sir Hugh) raced his horses.

After an uneventful career as a two-year-old, Poseidon won his first race as a three-year-old, the Tattersall's Club Welter. Backing him was the Chinese market gardener Jimmy Ah Poon, the horse's shrewdest supporter.

Nicknamed first 'Possumum' and then 'Louis the Possum' because of his mispronunciation of 'Poseidon', Ah Poon followed the colt throughout his extraordinary year as a three-year-old and was estimated to have won £35 000. Rather than gamble away his winnings, he disappeared from the racecourses and was said to have returned to China a wealthy man.

Tempe 'Nin' Hoysted on the grass outside the family home in Grey Street, Wangaratta.

She's another winning Hoysted

Tempe Hoysted's mare Eunice (Devon–Blue Eyes) won the Tally-Ho Welter at Moonee Valley on 1 July 1908.

Tempe 'Nin' Hoysted was the daughter of the Wangaratta owner–trainer Harry Hoysted, and brother of trainer Fred Hoysted who was the father of trainers Norman (Bon)

and Bob. When Nin's father died in 1906, she and her brother Henry (known in the racing fraternity as 'Tib') took charge of their father's racing stables. Tib moved from the family home when he married in 1908, leaving the care of the stableboys to Nin and a younger sister Daisy.

All in the family: Revenue, winner of the 1901 Melbourne Cup, was trained by Hugh Munro, father of Jim, who rode Cup winners Windbag (1925) and Statesman (1928) and Darby Munro, who rode Peter Pan (1934), Sirius (1944) and Russia (1946).

Too late: Lord Cardigan, winner of the 1903 Melbourne Cup, ruptured himself in his courageous run in the 1904 Melbourne Cup that won him second place to Acrasia and died the following Saturday. In the same race, the New Zealander favourite Wairiki fell and broke his shoulder. John Mayo, the owner of Lord Cardigan, had been offered £4000 for Lord Cardigan before he died.

The bookies win again: The 1904 Caulfield Cup was won by bookmaker John Wren's Murmur, with Sydney bookmaker Humphrey Oxenham's Acrasia second. Bookmaker Sol Green's Gladsome, the race favourite, was unplaced. Acrasia went on to win the 1904 Melbourne Cup.

Eight on the run: Lady Wallace won eight straight races in the 1905–06 season as a three-year-old: the VATC Guineas, Victoria Derby, VRC Oaks, AJC and VRC St Legers, VATC St George Stakes, VATC St Helliers Stakes, and the VRC All-Aged Stakes. She came third in the AJC Derby and won nine of her 13 three-year-old starts. At stud, Lady Wallace foaled the AJC Breeders' Plate and Derby winner, Cisco, and Balarang, the VATC Futurity Stakes winner.

Ladies' Rooms at last: In 1908 Sir James John Joynton Smith (later the publisher of Smith's Weekly) opened the Victoria Park racecourse at Zetland on land he had reclaimed. He declared it was the 'first course in Australia to cater for ladies in the provision of retiring rooms'.

Miss Gordon's winner: Alawa, winner of the 1908 VRC Derby, was owned by Miss M. Gordon, making it the first Derby winner owned by a woman.

John Wren branches out: In 1909 John Wren purchased Queensland's Albion Park racecourse from Wesley Castle.

Wakeful purchase: Wakeful was owned and raced by C. Leslie Macdonald, who had been the racing manager at W. R. Wilson's St Albans Stud. When the stud was dispersed on Wilson's death at the age of 50 in 1900, Macdonald made two memorable purchases: the four-year-old gelding Revenue for 725 guineas, and the unraced four-year-old Wakeful for 310 guineas.

Murmur won the Caulfield Cup, and £2500 for John Wren.

Wren was controversial on and off the track.

John Wren's world of racing

Whatever the enigmatic John Wren was, he was first of all a sportsman and a gambler, a Collingwood lad tough, working class, and Catholic. In the struggling inner suburbs of Melbourne in the late 19th century, sport was the King that rewarded battle before birthright. Sport bred winners and raised self-esteem. And betting on sport raised meagre incomes, if you were in luck – and John Wren was lucky, and smart enough not to waste his winnings.

As a 19-year-old boot factory apprentice in 1890, Wren grabbed the early long-odds on Carbine and raked in £180 on the Melbourne Cup. A run of later wins helped him multiply this bank many times, and he set himself up in the more lucrative and reliable pursuit of taking, rather than making, bets.

From 1893 to 1907 Wren allegedly cleared £20 000 a year running a totalisator in Collingwood. Its legality was questionable, but never properly tested. Superb defences, local support and deficient legislation made the tote almost impregnable to police raids, although it attracted vehement opposition from anti-gambling crusaders or 'wowsers'. Between 1903 and 1907 Wren also took bets at his City Tattersalls Club in Bourke Street. His major bookmaking rival was Sol Green, who ran the Melbourne Tattersalls Club in Royal Lane. There were other betting 'clubs' in central Melbourne and numerous gambling outlets in the suburbs.

Wren wisely closed his tote and City Tatts after the *Lotteries, Gaming and Betting Act* strengthened the law in January 1907. He then concentrated on racing, trotting, boxing and cycling promotion, and developed an empire of over 40 companies, with interests including newspapers, sports grounds, mining, theatres, distilleries, retailing, cosmetics, farming, property and oil.

On his way to becoming a millionaire, Wren crossed to the high side of the Yarra to live in the wealthy suburb of Kew, overlooking the Collingwood flats. In old age he was targeted as a 'capitalist' symbol by the communist writer Frank Hardy, whose novel *Power Without Glory* (1950) portrayed a corrupt character called John West whose story bore enough circumstantial resemblance to suggest that West was Wren.

The real John Wren was a smart operator who pulled strings in politics and business. But he didn't deserve Hardy's epic of disinformation which deliberately confused facts, like the Collingwood tote, with fabrications.

Wren became a serious owner of thoroughbreds around 1900, when he paid 500 guineas for a Bill of Portland colt and its dam Melodious. The colt, Melport, and a half-sister, Chansonette, raced for Wren in 1903–04 along with the equally well-bred colts Pilgrim's Father and Charlemagne. In April 1904, Wren paid £470 for a Positano–Morisca colt and named it Pius, presumably after the new Pope Pius X. Wren's faith might have been tested when Pius didn't win a race over the next two years.

Murmur was a 'most ordinary looking little horse' according to the *Australasian*, bought for £200 in Tasmania and gelded late in life. He lacked the long pedigree of Wren's other horses, but his sire Arsenal had won the 1886 Melbourne Cup. Murmur won at his first start for Wren in the Moonga Handicap at Caulfield in October 1903. He failed at his next eight, then galloped into racing history in the spring of 1904, when he took out the Balaclava Stakes, followed up with the Heatherlie Handicap, then clinched the Caulfield Cup by three lengths over Acrasia. Wren netted £51 000 after backing him in from 150/1 to 10/1.

Wren plunged on Murmur to win £35 000 in the 1904 Melbourne Cup, then lost heavily when the horse finished 24th to Acrasia. Wren bought the third place-getter, Blinker, for 1650 guineas in March 1905 and had at least a dozen horses in work by Sep-

Figure, W. Cook, won 1930 Oakleigh Plate.

John Wren's horse Pius never won a race.

The Tote, looking across Johnston Street.

Police guard the Tote during a raid.

tember, when the VRC suddenly announced it would no longer accept his entries. The VRC announcement, reported in the *Australasian* on 14 October 1905, said there was 'not the slightest imputation on him as regards the manner in which he had run his horses'.

Wren was banned primarily because of his involvement with betting clubs and totes. In an increasingly hostile environment for gambling, it was politically expedient for the racing industry to proclaim its purity by punishing a prominent backyard bookie. And, after all, Wren's off-course facilities stopped people going to the track, and racing clubs received no return from unlicensed book-making. The *Argus* noted on 29 September 1905 that it was also a 'rather remarkable' coincidence that the VRC banned Wren at the same time he was making an application for permission to open a racecourse at Eltham, where he proposed to run a £10 000 race (nearly double the Melbourne Cup prize money) every year.

The VRC soon found Wren was not easily stopped. He acquired three old Melbourne racetracks (Richmond, Fitzroy and Ascot) and moved into unregistered pony racing. This working-man's sport was tainted by crooks and criminal rackets, but Wren warned off 'Squizzy' Taylor, stopped bookies taking bets from jockeys and minors, and kicked out the welshers. He also introduced independent stewards.

The 'ponies' thrived under Wren's reforms and ample financial backing, so much so that in early 1908 the VRC was obliged to officially recognise pony racing.

Wren had taken over trotting in Victoria by 1908, when his Victorian Trotting Association was established.

Although Wren's Eltham plans were abandoned, he kept pressure on the VRC. In 1906

he made a standing offer of £25 000 a year to lease Flemington racecourse, which the Government declined. Later, when the Melbourne Cup was postponed in 1916 due to floods, Wren staged a rich Cup Day race at his nearby Ascot course.

To avoid opposition to proprietary or private ownership of racecourses, John Wren sold the freehold of Fitzroy, 75 per cent of Ascot, and the leasehold of Richmond to the non-profit VTRA in 1919. The deal was a time-payment arrangement whereby the properties could have reverted to Wren in the event of a default, but this did not occur. He adopted similar schemes elsewhere.

Wren eventually owned or leased six racecourses in the Brisbane area, including Doomben. He bought Albion Park for £31 000 in 1911, improved its facilities, then reaped up to £30 000 a year in returns before selling it to the BATC for £450 000 in 1923. Wren's arrangements were enormously profitable and monopolistic, but that did not make them inherently corrupt, despite such a conclusion being drawn by a Queensland Inquiry under A. E. Moore's antagonistic non-Labor government in 1930.

In Western Australia, Wren leased Belmont Park in 1912 and ran the course subject to WATC rules. His control in the West was possibly greater than this track alone. The fact remains his arrival coincided with dramatic improvements, not just in facilities. Wren fostered 'straighter racing,' a police representative told a WA Select Committee in 1915, because he significantly increased stakes, making owners and jockeys less susceptible to bribery.

In that year, long after the VRC ban was lifted, Wren's return to racing his own horses was signalled by Garlin, winner of the Doncaster Handicap and Chelmsford Stakes at Randwick, and fourth in the Caulfield and

Melbourne Cups. Wren donated the Doncaster prize money (£2125) to the Belgian Relief Fund (after making £28 000 on bets). He had splashed £400 among the poor of Collingwood following Murmur's Caulfield Cup win in 1904. It is easy to take a cynical view of these gestures, but if Wren was merely courting personal publicity he could have obtained better value for money.

By the early 1920s Wren had owned around 50 thoroughbreds. He almost held the great 1920 Melbourne Cup winner Poitrel, after instructing his agent, Jim Donohue, to buy the horse as a yearling in Sydney. Jockey Paddy Kelly later told the *Sporting Globe*: 'Donohue bought the horse, but the deal fell through because he thought the cost of transporting Poitrel to Melbourne was excessive.' Wren didn't complain. In 1921, after his horse The Rover won the Australian Cup at Flemington, he backed it to win over £100 000 in the Melbourne Cup. The plunge failed when The Rover went down by three-quarters of a length to Sister Olive.

His brilliant sprinter Figure was runner-up in the 1929 Newmarket Handicap and won the Oakleigh Plate in 1930. Wren's many fine horses in the 1920s and 1930s included Beedos, Biscay, Galenist, Kildennis, Kilroy, Kingsfield, Liberty Loan and Little Flower. His colt Pandect won the AJC Derby in 1940. Pure Fire took out the VRC and AJC Sires' Produce Stakes in 1952.

John Wren died in October 1953, a few weeks after watching Collingwood win the Victorian Football League premiership. Five days after Wren's death, a horse he owned won the VRC Maribyrnong Plate. Most of all, Wren loved winning. It was appropriate his passing was marked by the victory of his beloved football team, and an unbeaten colt called Fascinating.

by Damien Cash

A flag start at an early 20th century Grand National Steeplechase (ARM).

Grafter and Gentleman Jim

At a Newcastle race meeting on 20 April 1903, James 'Grafter' Kingsley's horse Gentleman Jim was running, carrying 10 st 9 lb. That was enough for most bookmakers to let his odds drift out, and it wasn't until they were hit by a huge amount of money that they sniffed a rat. When Gentleman Jim came home in style, one of the bookmakers confronted Kingsley as he made his way to the jockeys' room for the weigh-in. By the time Kingsley had brushed him aside, his jockey had weighed in 29 lb (13 kg) light. Can't be, blustered Kingsley, claiming that he had been there earlier when the jockey had weighed in at 10 st 9 lb. In fact 'Grafter' even went as far as to claim that he was outraged at the slur on his character, stamping down hard with his foot in a monstrous display of pique. The

jockey took to the scales again and weighed in correct weight.

The bookmakers knew they had been fleeced, but had to pay out. After the last race, the Newcastle stewards dismantled the scales and found a wire running through a hole in the floor. Outside they found a trap door which took them under the building and directly under the scales where they found a young boy huddled. It was his job to add lead to the wire on a signal – a stamp of the foot – from above. Gentleman Jim's other recent wins were investigated and more cubby holes were found beneath the scales in other Newcastle area racecourses.

The boy refused to implicate Kingsley, but Grafter and his jockey were disqualified for life.

The Kiwi raid of 1905

Few raiders have come near the success of New Zealand owner and his private trainer Richard 'Dick' Mason in the spring of 1905 in Sydney.

Noctuiform won the AJC Derby, with his stable-mate Sun God second. Sun God later won the New Stakes and Grantham Stakes. The Stead–Mason filly Isolt made a winning debut in the Spring Maiden and went on to add the Wycombe Stakes and Members

R. J. (Dick) Mason.

Handicap, while Nightfall won the Squatters Handicap and the Randwick Plate.

In four days the Stead horses won eight races, while Tod Hewitt, the stable horseman generally credited with introducing the crouch seat to Australian race riding, also won the Shorts Handicap on the crack Kiwi sprinter Machine Gun, and another New Zealand raider, Maniapoto, won the Metropolitan.

The 1908 Broken Hill bookies' strike

In 1908 the bookmakers responded to an increase in their licence fee by the Broken Hill Jockey Club by going on strike. According to Samuel Griffiths in *A Rolling Stone on the Turf*:

That evening the Trades Hall Council sat until nearly midnight – with crowds outside awaiting a decision – debating whether the race meeting should be declared 'black'. Eventually common sense prevailed and it was decided that unionists could please themselves whether they attended the races or not – a declaration of neutrality.

In the meantime, the BJC had not been idle. 'Tot' Hall, the leading lawyer of the town and chairman of the committee, volunteered to turn bookmaker on behalf of the club and enlist the services of other members. A rough and ready 'blind tote' had also been installed.

To the surprise and dismay of the 'strikers' there was an excellent attendance on the opening day of the meeting. The news that several amateur bookmakers were to bet on a practically unlimited scale – strike-breakers, the recalcitrant 'books' called them – proved a splendid attraction, with the miners expecting to find them easy marks.

At this time the 'tote' was illegal in New South Wales; but the contraption was called a 'blind bookmaker', and the sporting police also were suddenly afflicted with defective vision. 'Tot' Hall proved as able in his novel role as he had done at the bar.

All of the amateur bookmakers did a roaring business in more ways than one, and results favouring them greatly, the club reaped a rich harvest. That night the 'strikers' capitulated – wanted to don their satchels on the second day – but were politely told to go to blazes. It was the best and most profitable meeting the BJC had ever held.

Unpopular with punters – a welshing bookie.

Morphettville, SA, in the early 1900s.

A glorious grandstand at Ascot in Perth, WA, 1905. Inset: Tickets for Caulfield, 1900.

Phantom win

On 13 July, the last day of the 1906 Grand National meeting, a horse called Blue Jacket in the Footscray Steeplechase was backed in from 15/1 to 6/1 in Melbourne clubs and betting shops.

The clubs were notified of the race winners by a telegram sent from the Flemington racecourse to the Universal Press Agency which passed on the information. On this occasion, the telegram declared Blue Jacket the winner. Money had already been paid out when the second authentic telegram arrived, declaring Error the winner.

Blue Jacket had been scratched. Those who had stepped in fast enough made away with their winnings. The remainder of punters holding tickets for Blue Jacket were paid their stake money for the scratching. Two small fry (a punter and a telegram clerk) were arrested for their involvement. The major beneficiaries were not traced.

Wootton wins in England

Frank Wootton rode his first big winner in the Goldfields Cup, a major Johannesburg race, in 1903 when he was only nine years old. His father, New South Wales owner-trainer Dick Wootton, had set up base in South Africa after setting off around the world with his wife and sons Frank and Stanley, and the 1902 Metropolitan Handicap winner Queen of Sheba.

With his nine-year-old child on board, Dick Wootton's new horse Centurion understandably drifted out to 50/1, but won handsomely by two lengths.

Young Frank continued to ride winners for his father's stable in South Africa, and in 1906, the Woottons returned home for six months, before heading for England where Dick Wootton became the leading trainer in 1913, and Frank was a teenage sensation.

Frank won his first race in England at Folkestone in 1906 as a 13-year-old. At 14, he won the Cesarewitch Handicap at Newmarket on Demure, carrying 6 st 9 lb (42 kg). In 1907 he rode seven winners at the St Leger meeting at Doncaster and in 1909 at the age of 16, he became the first Australian jockey to win the English jockeys' premiership with 165 winners. He won it again for the next three years.

Frank Wootton rode on the flat in Britain from 1906 until 1913. He rode 882 winners, 705 seconds and 452 thirds.

He served in France during the First World War and on his return, due to his increased weight, he started riding over fences. In 1921 he was the leading winning jockey under National Hunt Rules with 61 wins. Falls and an increasing difficulty in making weights led to Wootton's retirement in 1924, and he rejoined his father who was again training in Australia. He died in 1940 at the age of 46.

1900–1909 RESULTS

VICTORIA DERBY
1900 Maltster, J. Scobie, (R. Lewis), 2:48, Kinglike, Barbarossa
1901 Hautvilliers, J. Scobie, (R. Lewis), 2:37, Grasspan, Haymaker
1902 Abundance, F. McGrath, (J. Barden), 2:36.25, Great Scot, Rienzi
1903 FJA, J. Scobie, (A. Richardson), 2:35.25, Sweet Nell, Belah
1904 Sylvanite, J. Scobie, (R. Lewis), 2:39, Lord Fitzroy, Billingsgate
1905 Lady Wallace, J. Burton, (F. Hickey), 2:40, Grama, The Infanta
1906 Poseidon, I. Earnshaw, (T. Clayton),2:40.5, Antonious, Booran
1907 Mountain King, J. Burton, (F. Hickey), 2:39, Peru, Welcome Trist
1908 Alawa, J. Scobie, (R. Lewis), 2:35.5, Parsee, Lord Nolan
1909 Prince Foote, F. McGrath, (D. McCarthy), 2:37, Danilo, Lord Foote
MELBOURNE CUP
1900 Clean Sweep, J. Scobie, (A. Richardson), 3:29, Malster, Alix
1901 Revenue, H. Munro, (F. Dunn), 3:30.5, San Fran, Khaki
1902 The Victory, R. Bradfield, (R. Lewis), 3:29, Vanity Fair, Abundance
1903 Lord Cardigan, A.E. Cornwell, (N. Godby), 3:29.25, Wakeful, Seaport
1904 Acrasia, A.E. Wills, (T. Clayton), 3:28.25, Lord Cardigan, Blinker
1905 Blue Spec, W. Hickenbotham, (F. Bullock), 3:27.5, Scot Free, Tartan
1906 Poseidon, I. Earnshaw, (T. Clayton), 3:31.25, Antonious, Proceed

1907 Apologue, I. Earnshaw, (W. Evans), 3:27.5, Mooltan, Mountain King
1908 Lord Nolan, E.A. Mayo, (J. Flynn), 3:28.75, Tuleroo, Delawere
1909 Prince Foote, F. McGrath, (W. McLachlan), 3:27.5, Alawa, Aberdeen
SYDNEY CUP
1900 La Carabine, 3:31.5, Severity, Ace of Diamonds
1901 San Fran, T. Payten, (A. Richardson), 3:32, Australian Colors, Wakeful
1902 Wakeful, Hugh Munro, (F. Dunn), 3:38, Acetine, Courada
1903 Street Arab, Harry Raynor, (F. Hickey), 3:31.75, Patronage, Bewitcher
1904 Lord Cardigan, A.E. Cornwell, (J. Barden), 3:31.75, Saida, Sweet Nell
1905 Tartan, (J. Rogers), 3:27, Tatterdemalion, Cherson
1906 Noreen, 3:29.5, Proceed, Bobadil
1907 Realm, 3:29, Proceed, Florance
1908 Dyed Garments, 3:34, Tartan, Ansentee
1909 Trafalgar, W. Hickenbotham, (W.H. Smith), 3:29.5, Unaarie, Didus
AJC DERBY
1900 Maltster, (R. Lewis),2:39, Hautboy, Hautesse
1901 Hautvilliers, (R. Lewis), 2:37.5, Caravel, Grasspan
1902 Abundance, (J. Barden), 2:45, Strata Florida, Free States
1903 Belah, (W. H. Smith), 2:39.75, Sweet Nell, Duke of Grafton

1904 Sylvanite, (R. Lewis), 2:37.25, Koopan
1905 Noctuiform, (L.H. Hewitt), 2:37.5, Sun God, Lady Wallace
1906 Poseidon, I. Earnshaw, (T. Clayton), 3:38, Collarit, Antonious
1907 Mountain King, (F. Hickey), 2:41.75, Welcome Trist, Peru
1908 Parsee, (T. Clayton), 2:38, Monabel, Mother Goose
1909 Prince Foote, F. McGrath, (D. McCarthy), 2:37.5, Patronatus, Danilo
CAULFIELD CUP
1900 Ingliston, J. Leek, (C. Cooper), 2:36.75, Mora, Alix
1901 Hymettus, P.T. Heywood, (W. Powell), 2:35.25, Wakeful, Flagship
1902 Lieutenant Bill, D. Harris, (W. Daniells), 2:36.75, Flagship, Vanity Fair
1903 Sweet Nell, J. Scobie, (A. Richardson), 2:35.25, The Idler, Flagship
1904 Murmur, F. Musgrave, (S.D. Fisher), 2:37.25, Acrasia, Emir
1905 Marvel Loch, T.F. Scully, (A. Hood), 2:35.75, Warroo, Torah
1906 Poseidon, I. Earnshaw, (T. Clayton), 2:34.75, Simoda, Booran
1907 Poseidon, I. Earnshaw, (T. Clayton), 2:35.5, Apologue, Welcome Jack
1908 Maranui, D. O'Brien, (W. McLachlan), 2:35.75, Tulkeroo, Iolaire
1909 Aborigine & Blue Book =, (W. McLachlan/M. Connell), 2:35, Pendil

The run home in the 1905 New Zealand Cup. The winner Noctuiform is in the centre of the track under the crouch of jockey Hewitt.

James Scobie: training is a business

James Scobie was unabashed about his aim when he started out as a trainer in the 1880s, declaring in his autobiography *My Life on the Australian Turf* (1929): 'It always had been my aim that, if I became a trainer, I would seek rich patrons, who could afford the expense and be prepared to go on with the business.'

Norman Wilson (then Master of the Ballarat Hounds for whom Scobie acted as huntsman), William Bailey and Andrew Chirnside were among the first to put their horses with him and, in 1892, he began his long association with Sir Rupert Clarke and his brother Ernest.

The association with Sir Rupert was a close one. Together with Bob Lewis, the jockey who worked with Scobie from 1895, they formed what was called 'Australia's most successful turf confederacy'. In his autobiography, Scobie attributes a lot of his success as a trainer to the jockey Lewis: 'He won Derbys, Legers, Cups, and races of all descriptions for me.'

Born in Ararat in 1860, James Scobie began his career as a cross country jockey in the Western District and started riding in Melbourne for the Ballarat trainer Robert Howie. He used his winnings as a jockey to buy out Howie's stables at Miner's Rest near Ballarat in 1882. During the 1880s, he was the great Tommy Corrigan's main rival and won the Caulfield Grand National Steeplechase (which became the Australian Steeplechase) in 1883 on Euchre and in 1887 on the champion Blue Mountain, and the 1888 VRC Grand National Steeplechase.

Scobie declared the 1903 spring the 'high water mark' of his training career. At Caulfield, he won the Debutant Stakes, Caulfield Guineas, Toorak Handicap, Gwyn Nursery and Caulfield Cup; at Flemington he won the Sires' Produce Stakes, Victoria Derby, Flying Stakes, Oaks Stakes, and Flemington Stakes.

In 1906 he became the non-resident manager of Ernest Clarke's Melton stud and in 1912, he moved to the Flemington stables, Pytchley Lodge.

Scobie's impressive list of winners includes four Melbourne Cup victors: Clean Sweep in 1900, King Ingoda (1922), Bitalli (1923) and Trivalve (1927).

He also won six VRC and three AJC Sires' Produce Stakes; two VRC, four AJC and seven SAJC St Legers; four Australian Cups, 12 VRC Ascot Vale Stakes, eight Victoria Derbys and five SA Derbys, the last in Adelaide at the age of 79, one year before his death in 1940.

James Scobie was a widely respected trainer, renowned for his ability to prepare stayers. In the 1923 Melbourne Cup his horse Bitalli started 4/1 favourite, though he had not been raced for more than three months.

Scobie recalled the story of Sweet Nell:

'In 1902 Sir Rupert said to me, "If it can be done, I want you to buy me a filly capable of winning the Oaks. My intention is to call her Sweet Nell."

'Classic winners do not "grow on every bush", and I had been set a tough task. Hoping for the best, I paid 400 gns. at the Randwick sales for a yearling filly by Haut-Brion – Novelette 11.

'Sir Rupert realised his ambition in the following spring. Sweet Nell led off by taking the Caulfield Guineas. Next came a Caulfield Cup victory.'

Of the Derby, Scobie writes: 'It was no race. Sweet Nell toyed with her rivals, and cantered home a length ahead of Pliable [her stablemate]. Possibly this is the only occasion on record of an Oaks winner having been supplied to order. Sir Rupert Clarke was a proud man indeed.'

American jockeys introduced the 'crouch seat' in the late 1890s. A newspaper illustrated the difference in style.

Introducing the monkey-on-a-stick seat

The adoption of the Tod Sloan seat or 'Sloaning' – crouching well up on the horse's neck with short reins – by Australian jockeys in the later 1890s and 1900s caused seconds to be slashed from race records.

For most jockeys it was a complete change in posture but a few had already adopted it instinctively.

Tot Flood, a successful lightweight Melbourne jockey, is described by racing author Samuel Griffiths as a jockey 'who quite naturally adopted "the monkey-on-the-stick" seat – as it was once derisively termed' in the early 1890s. James Barden, who in 1902 rode 16 winners from 20 rides at Randwick and Flemington in one month (he was unplaced only once), also rode in the crouch position.

The Sloan position was gradually adopted by all jockeys, though it took some time to spread through their ranks and gain total acceptance. The style was named after Tod Sloan, the American rider who introduced it in Europe and America before the turn of the century. Sloan rode 254 winners in Britain before he lost his licence in 1900 for associating with criminals.

Though it quickly gained acceptance among the jockeys, the new riding style met with some resistance from the racing public. An account in 1906 in the *Argus*, critical of a ride by the New Zealand jockey Leslie Hewitt, referred to him derogatorily as 'the New Zealand "Tod Sloan"'.

As late as 1924, the case against the crouch style was being put in the racing publication *Harking Back*, which declared: '… the present-day jockey had more the appearance of a tom-tit on a butcher's block than a rider capable of doing justice to the final finish of a good horse.'

It argued: 'One prominent trainer, who was a successful rider in the 80s, when good riders were numerous, was asked recently if the present style was advantageous in getting the most out of a horse in a race, and he gave an emphatic "No" to the question, and added, "How can the riders now do full justice to their mount with their knees almost stuck into their mouths?"

'Nature has built the horse on symmetrical lines and never intended that the whole load should be placed on the shoulders. The hind quarters, which are muscular, should take their share, so as to give the necessary quick propelling power and maintain the equilibrium of the animal … How can one lift a load if a grip cannot be got of it, and how can a horse be assisted in his final effort in a race if you cannot grip the saddle with your thighs and relieve him of a pound or two?'

The length of the stirrups and reins has varied with different generations of jockeys.

In an interview not long before his death in 1969, the champion jockey Jim Pike, the rider of Phar Lap, lamented the disappearance of short stirrup riders of the Tod Sloan style from Australian racing. He claimed that jockeys in the late 1960s seemed more like show riders, sitting well down in the saddle, riding with long reins and stirrups.

'They don't seem to realise the horse gets his speed from his hind legs and that if you lift your weight up from his loins and rest it against his shoulders he will go faster. You need good hands and balance, but it's a better way to ride than to sit up and flog your horse to death.'

The Ballarat Miner's Turf Club still flourished in 1912 – using the old-style poster and riding style (ARM).

Some notable jockeys of the golden age

Claude Andrews

A champion lightweight, Claude Andrews had three brothers who were also jockeys. He served an apprenticeship of three years with Dick Bradfield at Flemington, and three months after the indentures were signed he had his first public mount. He won his third ride, and then rode two other winners the same afternoon.

His first big win was on Eighteen Carat in the Hobart Cup. When 18-year-old Andrews won the Breeder's Plate on Cisco at the 1910 AJC Spring meeting, he received a fee of £200.

Cyril Bolton

Cyril Bolton was born in Dubbo in 1884. He defied his mother to become a jockey, and rode his first race as a schoolboy. Bolton left school to work on a property in the district, then went to Sydney and served as an apprentice to W. Duggan, trainer of the Caulfield Cup winner Amberite. During his three years as an apprentice, he rode track work only. On leaving Duggan, he went to

Cyril Bolton.

Queensland where within two years he topped the jockeys' list. He won four races in one afternoon at Eagle Farm. He moved to Victoria and in his first season finished second in the jockeys' premiership, topping it for the first time the next year. He became the leading jockey for W. S. Hickenbotham's Flemington stable and of the horses he rode he considered that Comedy King was the best.

Fred Burn

Fred Burn took over from Tommy Corrigan as the leading cross country rider. He began riding horses and ponies for his father at Queenscliff and at 13 worked for Carbine's owner Donald Wallace, who had stables at Queenscliff. He was apprenticed to Tom Kelly in Adelaide for three years and had success as a lightweight jockey on the flat. In 1886 he returned to Victoria and worked for 12 months with James Scobie at Dowling Forest. At the age of 18 he gave up riding altogether and, when he returned, it was to the jumping stable of Humphrey Bellamy at Caulfield. Burn introduced lying out on a horse's neck in jumping events. Approaching a fence, he gave his mount freedom of rein until coming down, when he took it up again.

Burn received an offer of £1000 from Baron de Rothschild to ride a season over fences in Europe but refused. He made £800 in the 1910 Grand National campaign and had success as a trainer with winners of the Australian Cup and an Australian Grand National. His son Tom had success as a jockey in England.

Fred Burn.

Walter P. Burn

Wally Burn was as successful as a lightweight jockey on the flat, as his older brother Fred was over jumps. In 1894 when he was 12½, he followed Fred to Adelaide to ride for the trainer Tom Kelly. He found early

success and returned to Melbourne, winning the Newmarket Handicap on the outsider Forest. He rode La Carabine to victory five out of the seven times he rode her and declared her his favourite horse. 'I never rode Wakeful, but, fit and well, I think that La Carabine would have beaten her any day over three miles,' he said. 'La Carabine would go anywhere you wanted her, and never failed to go as fast as she was asked. In the AJC Plate she made hacks of Merriwee and Parthian.'

The many races won by Burns included the Australian Cup, the Sydney Cup, the Adelaide Cup, the Hobart Cup, the Oakleigh Plate, the VRC Sires' Produce Stakes and the VRC St Leger.

Walter P. Burn.

Brownie Carslake

'Brownie' Carslake was among the first of the Australian jockeys to find success in England where he was renowned for his spectacular late runs. After being indentured to his father in Melbourne, he left Australia in 1906 and was successful in Europe before World War I, when he was interned by the Austrians. He escaped to Rumania disguised as a stoker on a steam engine. He was based in England between the wars and won a 2000 Guineas, two 1000 Guineas, and an Oaks along with three St Legers. At the age of 51 in 1938 in one week he came second in the Derby on Scottish Union and won the Doncaster and five other races. Jockeys in England and Europe were 'thought something of', he said, compared to Australia where they were 'looked upon as outsiders'. On his death in 1946, Carslake's ashes were scattered on the track at Newmarket.

Jack Chevalley

Born in Switzerland in 1875, John 'Jack' Chevalley grew up on a property on the Clarence River in New South Wales. He began riding at a Grafton stable, then went to Sydney for 15 months where he rode at pony meetings as well as in brush steeplechases, before he moved to Melbourne. After a year riding for Jack O'Brien at Mordialloc, ill-health caused his return to Sydney. He won his first VRC Grand National in 1902 on Bay Eagle, winning again in 1906 on Decoration in record time.

During his career, Chevalley had his right collar bone broken nine times, all but three ribs broken and suffered concussion several times.

William Evans

Bill Evans Snr had his first ride as a 16-year-old in the 1897 Rosehill Cup among a field of 43. After a false start, the race had to be rerun and two horses fell. This was one of only four public rides Evans had as an apprentice to the trainer James Monaghan at Randwick. His problem then was that he was too

Bill Evans.

light! He was a leading pony rider for five years, then spent a season riding in India. In 1907 he attracted the attention of W.S. Hickenbotham and rode winners for him in the Caulfield Guineas and the Caulfield Stakes during the VATC Spring meeting. He was then hired by the trainer Isaac Earnshaw and rode Apologue to victory in the 1907 Melbourne Cup, reducing by 19 lb to ride at 7 st 9 lb. On returning to scale, Evans collapsed unconscious and his body was placed on the scales and weight was declared before he was taken to the members' room where Sir Thomas Fitzgerald in the company of other doctors injected large quantities of strychnine and brought him around.

Evans tried his hand in England but was unplaced in the 1908 Derby, and had a successful season in India on his way back to Australia. His son Bill was India's premiership jockey 14 times from the 1930s on, and rode successfully in England until he retired in 1960. His grandson Bill (born in 1937) rode as an amateur from 1954 to 1962 and became a Sydney-based trainer.

Fred Hickey

Fred Hickey was a popular jockey whose run from the half-distance on Flavinius to win the 1910 Caulfield Cup was talked about for years. Hickey was born in Temora, New South Wales, and was apprenticed to the Randwick trainer John Allsop at the age of 17, weighing five stone. He won

Fred Hickey.

the 1903 Sydney Cup on Street Arab and in 1905 won the Derby and the Oaks at the VRC Spring meeting on Lady Wallace.

In 1907 he won the AJC and Victoria Derbys and both St Legers on Mountain King, the son of Wallace. In February 1908, Hickey rode Mountain King for a walk-over in the Loch Plate weight-for-age at Flemington, when no other owner would take the chestnut on. Hickey said: 'Mountain King was easily faster than Lady Wallace. He was the kind of horse that you meet once in a lifetime.'

James Pike

Jim Pike is best remembered for his 27 wins from 30 rides on Phar Lap. Pike was taller than most jockeys and was a skilful rider known for his balance and touch. He began as a stable boy in the Newcastle stables of Ernie Connors, who trained horses owned by Pike's uncle. On moving to Sydney, he worked briefly with the trainer J. W. Noud, and was then apprenticed to Bill Kelso as a 14-year-old. His first metropolitan success was in 1906 on Victoria Cross in the Liverpool Mile at Warwick Farm. In 1908, Pike went to England with Kelso, where Kelso intended to settle. Pike had already ridden 41 Australian winners, and during his brief stay in England he had 17 mounts and was placed on five. Kelso bought Son of the Marsh and returned with Pike to Sydney. Pike rode Trafalgar in his final victory at Randwick in 1912.

Pike's halcyon period as a rider began in the 1920s. Pike won his first and only Melbourne Cup on Phar Lap in 1930. His other classic wins included six VRC Derbys, three AJC Derbys, three VRC St Legers, two Caulfield Cups, and two W S Cox Plates. On his retirement as a rider, he tried his hand at training with no success.

Gregory Ross

Gregory Ross was a lightweight jockey born at Orbost in Gippsland, Victoria in 1886. He was apprenticed to the owner of Wakeful and the former manager of the St Albans stud, Leslie Macdonald at his Mordialloc stables for five years. Ross rode for Baron Oppenheim in Europe, following his victory on Dyed Garments in the Sydney Cup, but returned to Australia after a short time. He considered Wandin the best horse he had ever ridden, and attributed his success to 'some brains and good hands'.

Gregory Ross.

The Greens, looking every part the prosperous Edwardian family in 1904.

The philanthropic bookie

When asked how his luck was holding, bookie and racehorse owner Sol Green would reply: 'I lost last Saturday.' This was something, he said, that his customers wanted to hear. When his horse Comedy King won the 1910 Melbourne Cup, he varied that just a little, saying: 'On this day I did not lose.'

Sol Green, a cockney Jew, arrived in Australia in 1885 aged 17, 'broke to the wide'. At 20, he began his first book, but ended up pencilling for other bookies and returned briefly to England. In 1891 he returned to Australia, starting up as a bookie again, and this time he did not falter. With nerves of steel and a fine head for figures, he soon established himself as the biggest bookie in Australia, willing to lay bets of any size.

In an era when bookmakers liked to make a splash, Green wore the two blues of Oxford and Cambridge, with one side of his outfit a dark blue, the other light blue. Off-course, he ran Melbourne Tattersalls, a betting club in opposition to John Wren's City Tattersalls, both closed by the Government in 1905.

Sol Green is credited with introducing telegraphy betting to expand his doubles betting. With his catchcry 'Sufficent address – Sol Green, Melbourne', he was known throughout Australia. The telegraph system broke down with the weight of his business in 1912 when Piastre won the Melbourne Cup. Thousands of messages were not delivered until days after the race was run.

One of the biggest doubles ever laid was Sol Green's £100 000 to £1000 for Poseidon and Apologue for the 1907 Caulfield–Melbourne Cups which the agent for Sir Hugh Dennison, the Sydney Tattersalls Club chairman D. H. Smart, won. Green handed Smart a bank cheque for £100 000 the next morning and announced that he had still made a £20 000 profit on the carnival.

With the money he made as a bookmaker, Green invested extensively in property. He was also the owner and breeder of many fine racehorses, not least the 1910 Melbourne Cup winner and outstanding sire Comedy King, and dual Newmarket winner Gothic (1927 and 1928). At Shipley Estate (which he dispersed in 1918), he bred the 1914 Melbourne Cup winner Kingsburgh.

Green withdrew from racing as an owner in 1929, but maintained the splendid Underbank Stud near Bacchus Marsh. In his later years, he was renowned for his philanthropy. 'People born rich are apt to forget the existence of the poor' was a favourite saying of his. He set up the Sol Green Trust to establish housing for returned servicemen in Sandringham in 1943 with the gift of £50 000, he donated the profits from the sale of 20 yearlings to a Blanket Fund in England, and in 1947 not long before his death at the age of 79, he donated £50 000 to Melbourne's public hospitals.

A triptych of legends by Martin Stainforth: Cross Battery with Artilleryman at foot; Comedy King, Artilleryman's sire; Artilleryman.

Comedy King

In 1907 Sol Green imported the mare Tragedy Queen to Victoria while she was in foal to the English Derby winner Persimmon. The resulting black colt was Comedy King whom Green set to win the Melbourne Cup, which he did in 1910. He also won the VATC Futurity, the St George's Stakes, the Essendon Stakes, the All-Aged Stakes and the Autumn Stakes. He won only one race of 13 starts in the 1911–12 season at the age of five. In his second Melbourne Cup won by The Parisian in 1911, he ran a worthy fifth, carrying 9 st 7 lb.

In 1912 Sol Green retired Comedy King from racing and sold him to Norman Falkiner for 7300 guineas. He stood at Norman Falkiner's property Noorilim and proved to be an outstanding sire. From 1917–18 to 1927–28, he was among the top 10 Australian stallions, and was leading sire in 1919–20 and 1922–23. His progeny won stakes amounting to £327 553, and included the great Artilleryman in 1916.

Norman Lindsay at the races

Norman Lindsay's raceday observations for the magazine Lone Hand in 1907 (SLV).

RESULTS 1910–1918

VICTORIA DERBY
1910 Beverage, W. Kelso, (J. Pike), 2:37.25, Styria, Bobadea
1911 Wilari, W. Risby, (G. Lambert), 2:38.75, Cisco, Jacamar
1912 Wolawa, J. Scobie, (R. Lewis), 2:39.5, Cider, Perdita
1913 Beragoon, J.E. O'Brien, (J. Pike), 2:35.5, Radnor, Andelosia
1914 Carlita, J. Moore, (R. Lewis), 2:37.5, Aristaeus, Giru
1915 Patrobas, C. Wheeler, (W. Smart), 2:37, Cetigne, Westcourt
1916 Wolaroi, B. Quinn, (A. Wood), 2:42.5, Mehi King, Eastcourt
1917 Biplane, R.J. Mason, (B. Deeley), 2:35.25, Prince Viridis, Broken Glass
1918 Eusebius, C. Wheeler, (L. Franklin), 2:47.75, Outlook, Finmark
MELBOURNE CUP
1910 Comedy King, J. Lynch, (W. McLachlan), 3:37.75, Trafalgar, Apple Pie
1911 The Parisian, C. Wheeler, (R. Cameron), 3:27.75, Flavian, Didus
1912 Piastre, R. O'Connor, (A. Shanahan), 3:27.5, Hallowmas, Uncle Sam
1913 Posinatus, J. Chambers, (A. Shanahan), 3:31, Belove, Ulva's Isle
1914 Kingsburgh, I. Foulsham, (K.G. Meddick), 3:26, Sir Alwynton, Moonbria
1915 Patrobas, C. Wheeler, (R. Lewis), 3:38.5, Westcourt, Carlita

1916 Sasanof, M. Hobbs, (F. Foley), 3:27.75, Shepherd King, St Spasa
1917 Westcourt, J. Burton, (W. McLachlan), 3:26.75, Lingle, Wallace Isinglass
1918 Night Watch, R. Bradfield, (W. Duncan), 3:25.75, Kennaquhair, Gadabout
SYDNEY CUP
1910 Vavasor, 3:25.5, Daisy Chain, Jinnee
1911 Moorilla, 3:36.5, By Play, Eric
1912 Saxonite, 3:29, Jewelstone, Aurofodina
1913 Cadonia, 3:28.25, Cagou, Jacomar
1914 Lilyveil, 3:26.5, Multifoil, Belove
1915 Scotch Artillery, 3:36.5, Frasea, Onazer
1916 Prince Bardolph, 3:24.75, Green Cap, Scout Master
1917 The Fortune Hunter, 3:26, Harriet Graham, Court Jester
1918 Rebus, 3:26.25, Shadowland, Lanius
AJC DERBY
1910 Tanami, (W. Foulsham), 2:36.5, Bobodea, Beverage
1911 Cisco, (W. Osborne), 2:37.5, Jacamar, Ladies Man
1912 Cider, (P. Foley), 2:38, Harpist, Perdita

1913 Beragoon, (J. Pike), 2:35.75, Radnor, Ulva's Isle
1914 Mountain Knight, (W. McLachlan), 2:35.25, Woorak, Giru
1915 Cetigne, T.F. Scully, (A. Wood), 2:37, Wallace Isinglass, Westcourt
1916 Kilboy, (W. McLachlan), 2:39.75, Eastcourt, Colbert
1917 Biplane, (B. Deeley), 2:34.75, Bronzetti, Thrice
1918 Gloaming, R.J. Mason, (B. Deeley), 2:33.5, Finmark, Kilmoon
CAULFIELD CUP
1910 Flavinius, J. Siely, (F. Hickey), 2:34.5, Apple Pie, Britain
1911 Lady Medallist, J.W. Noud, (W. Barnett), 2:34.5, Flavian, Aurofodina
1912 Uncle Sam, M.P. Whitty, (G. Lambert), 2:34.25, Lady Medallist, Royal Scotch
1913 Aurifer, J. Siely, (W.H. Smith), 2:34, Anna Carlovna, Wassail
1914 Uncle Sam, M.P. Whitty, (J. Ettershank), 2:34.75, Rathlea, St Carwyne
1915 Lavendo, L. Robertson, (F. Dempsey), 2:34, William the Silent, Cyklon
1916 Shepherd King, C. Wheeler, (R. Lewis), 2:33.25, Amata, Sasanof
1917 Bronzetti, J. Smith, (F. Dempsey), 2:39.5, Chrome, Rael Lochin
1918 King Offa, R. Bradfield, (F. Bullock), 2:32, Night Watch, Chrome

Pompey Elliott's horse Darkie, Lieutenant J. D. Campbell up, France 1917 (AWM H15589).

Brigadier General H. E. 'Pompey' Elliott.

'Pompey' Elliott and racing in World War I

On 17 October 1914, with the first Victorian contingent of the Australian Imperial Force (AIF) about to sail away to war after two months' arduous training, a group of livewires from the 7th Battalion decided to spend their last full day on home soil at the Caulfield Cup. The identity of these temporary absconders became apparent at rollcall. On their return they were paraded before their redoubtable battalion commander 'Pompey' Elliott, and wondered what he had in store for them.

'Never before have I seen such an array of horse-lovers,' Elliott observed. 'I have never been attracted to horseraces, and much less to the duties a stable entails. I am glad to have discovered your attachment at so opportune a time, as it solves any difficulty associated with the care of the horses we are taking over with us. You can all expect to be called upon to act as horse batmen for the duration of the voyage.'

So these men had to take turns at mucking out the stables as the impressive convoy of ships proceeded across the Indian Ocean. On the first Tuesday in November, when they were off the coast of Western Australia, a wireless message notified them that Kingsburgh (a 20/1 chance, owned by well-known racing identity L. K. S. Mackinnon) had won the big race. Some could not help wondering how many of them would see another Melbourne Cup.

Throughout the conflict many Australian soldiers retained a keen interest in horseracing. Everyone in the AIF devoured news from home intently; racing enthusiasts followed the latest track tidings with particular zeal.

Australian horses were in demand during the war. About 40 000 of them were shipped overseas for the AIF, and more than twice as many were sent to India. If they could have been conveyed directly to the Western Front (which was impossible because of shipping difficulties), even more would have been sent. Among the AIF officers supervising the care of these horses was the famous horse balladeer Major A. B. 'Banjo' Paterson.

It was the fabled quality of Australia's horses that created the demand. 'The thoroughbred element in Australian remounts rendered them invaluable for operations in which stamina and the spark of spirit were needed,' explained the *Official History of Australia in the War.*

This equine excellence was most evident in the acclaimed AIF Light Horse units. Australia's lighthorsemen formed a strong bond with the horses that accompanied them through arduous and perilous experiences across the arid sands of Palestine, and felt the rupture of this close association keenly at the end of the war.

While these horses made a substantial contribution throughout the conflict, it was most dramatically exemplified by their mar-

vellous performance in the famous Beersheba stakes, the last grand cavalry charge ever made. In this astonishing exploit (which occurred, by appropriate coincidence, during Melbourne Cup week in 1917) horses and riders displayed the highest standards of courage and dash, endurance and grit. Even the Germans, observed the famous turf journalist 'Milroy' at the time, were acknowledging that Australia produces 'the best cavalry horse in the world'.

Not all the notable horses in the AIF were in the Light Horse. Throughout the war Pompey Elliott retained a famous big steed known as 'Darkie', whose remarkable powers became legendary. On parade Darkie was reputedly able to spot even infinitesimal infringements: he would routinely lead his rider directly to someone who hadn't shaved properly, or stop in front of some other unfortunate who was found to have a puttee out of place. At all times, in fact, Darkie was responding to directions – Pompey, an accomplished horseman, manipulated Darkie with a subtlety undetected by many of his men, and relished the notoriety his horse acquired in the process.

But Darkie was no mere ceremonial trickster. Elliott, the most famous fighting general in the AIF, was regularly to be found in advance positions. He sometimes conducted forward inspections on horseback – especially when transport by motor vehicle was

7th Battalion at Alexandria (AWM H15574).

The 5th Light Horse enthusiastic spectators at the Baalbek races, Syria 1918 (AWM H02558).

impossible in the Western Front mud – and Darkie was wounded more than once.

At the end of the war, when Elliott reluctantly had to relinquish his favourite quadruped before returning to Australia, he arranged for a leather label to be tied around Darkie's neck with a note outlining this war service and asking the purchaser to look after Darkie well. Subsequently Pompey was delighted to receive a letter of assurance from Darkie's new English owner that he was being treated kindly.

Back in Australia the continuation during the war of horseracing, together with certain other spectator sports, came under concerted challenge. Attending racetracks during the greatest war there had ever been was seen in some quarters as decidedly inappropriate, especially for fit adult males who were conspicuously refraining from enlisting, even though the AIF badly needed reinforcements. A New South Wales MP asserted that 'the attention of the people is being diverted and distracted daily to a sport which has no place in a time of war'.

In response, influential racing enthusiasts insisted their sport was much more than an attraction for idlers who were unable to recognise their responsibility to the nation in its critical hour of need. By providing an inherent incentive, racing's advocates claimed, it encouraged equine development of the highest quality and thereby contributed significantly to the war effort. The official VATC handicapper went so far as to contend in 1917 that 'the nation which comes out on top in the end is that one which possesses the best horse supply'. Devotees also pointed to the substantial contributions the racing clubs were making to war-related fundraising.

Racing's detractors managed to achieve some wartime reductions (mainly in relation to the number of meetings held at smaller clubs and tracks), but did not succeed in the kind of substantial cutbacks they avidly desired. Two years after Pompey Elliott and his battalion left Australia, for example, the 1916 spring carnival was as big an attraction as it ever was.

That year's Caulfield Cup was won by Shepherd King, a six-year-old maiden part-owned by a Victorian grazier who had been a partner decades earlier with none other than Pompey Elliott's father in an altogether different pursuit – goldmining in Western Australia during the 1890s.

Shepherd King was heavily fancied in the 1916 Melbourne Cup, but after incurring a 10-pound penalty for his inaugural win was narrowly defeated by lightly-weighted Sasonof. The King's gallant performances in the 1916 carnival constituted a training triumph for Charles Wheeler, but his satisfaction was marred by news that underlined the shadow hanging over everything at that time: his brother, an ex-jockey and trainer displaying gallantry in another sphere, had been killed on the battlefield.

That year's Melbourne Cup was only the second in the long history of the race to be postponed. It was a particularly wet spring, and not only in Melbourne – meetings in Sydney and Brisbane were cancelled. With Flemington saturated, it was decided on the eve of the traditional Cup Tuesday to hold the big race on the following Saturday instead. John Wren, ever astute, reacted by bringing forward the Ascot meeting he had scheduled for Wednesday in order to cater for deprived holiday racegoers, a shrewd manoeuvre which proved highly profitable.

In 1918, with the war about to end, the crowds attending the spring carnival were more festive than they had been for years. After dashing lead-up form King Offa, a tall, long-legged English import, was clearcut Caulfield Cup favourite, and won convincingly despite a pre-race injury scare which was overcome thanks in large measure to the insightful management of his trainer Dick Bradfield.

Just like that other well-credentialled and well-trained equine monarch two years earlier, King Offa as a result of that victory was given 10 extra pounds in the Melbourne Cup, started favourite nevertheless, but was unable to pull off the big double. Victory went to stablemate (and son of Wakeful) Night Watch, with 18-year-old Billy Duncan in the saddle.

The owners partied in style, but there was nothing posh about Duncan's celebration of his first big win: 'I took a couple of mates into town and bought them fish and chips. I was home in bed by 10 o'clock. Just as well – at four in the morning Mr Bradfield had me mucking out Night Watch's stable.'

by Ross McMullin

Artilleryman, painted by Martin Stainforth.

Artilleryman's dam, Cross Battery (Stainforth).

Bullock rode horses for a Steere (ARM).

The tragedy of Artilleryman

How good was the noble three-year-old Artilleryman? He took the answer to the grave a few months after thrashing 19 rivals in the 1919 Melbourne Cup, winning by six lengths in a record time of 3:24½.

The first Cup after the Great War attracted a crowd of 105 000. The prevailing gaiety, after four years of austerity, seemed to concern the *Argus*, which noted soberly: 'The desire for pleasure is more noticeable than the will to work.' And why not, after four years of Kaiser-inspired deprivation. Everyone seemed to have money, including some free-spending ex-servicemen.

The riddle of Artilleryman, who first showed signs of illness as a two-year-old, was solved only by a post-mortem, which revealed that he died of cancer of the lymphatic gland. The malady might explain his inconsistency in a short career that yielded 11 wins from 26 starts.

Two things were apparent from the day Artilleryman stepped into the sale ring. He was even more handsome than his sire, the 1910 Melbourne Cup winner Comedy King, and, fit and well, was an exceptional colt. After his Melbourne Cup win, the VRC handicapper, Dr Lang, said: 'I never saw a performance in my life to equal it.'

Artilleryman was bought for 1000 guineas as a yearling by wealthy Sydney retail magnate Sir Samuel Hordern at a dispersal sale of Mr Sol Green's Shipley stud in Victoria. The genial Sir Sam raced the horse in partnership with Melbourne identity Mr A.D. Murphy. He was prepared by Phillip Heywood, who trained privately at Orleigh Park near Dandenong, before switching to Flemington. Heywood won three Caulfield Cups with Calma and Hymettus (twice).

At two, Artilleryman performed indifferently, often showing signs of waywardness.

Nine starts produced only one win.

He returned to racing in the spring of 1919 and third-up won the Memsie Stakes at Caulfield. Two starts later, in the AJC Derby, he dead-heated for first with his great rival, Richmond Main, owned by Newcastle coal king John Brown, who raced his horses under the pseudonym 'J. Baron'.

In the Melbourne Cup, neither colt was expected to trouble Caulfield Cup winner Lucknow, the favourite at 6/1. Artilleryman, piloted by Bobby Lewis and carrying the 'hard-earned' of servicemen unable to resist an omen wager, in spite of the reminder of dark times in his name, was at 10/1.

Carrying weight-for-age (7.6) because of his AJC Derby dead-heat, Artilleryman was never further back than sixth. Given his head turning for home, the dashing brown colt swept to the most emphatic win since Newhaven also scored by six lengths in 1896. Richmond Main (11/1) headed the beaten division. Never had the colours of Sir Sam – grey with a red sash – been so popular. Heywood praised Lewis, saying: 'He managed Artilleryman to perfection.' It was Lewis's third cup win, after The Victory (1902) and Patrobus (1915).

Four days later, Artilleryman and Lewis made one act of the CB Fisher Plate at Flemington and the next autumn five more wins were forthcoming. Then, after starting at 12/1 on and being beaten by Millieme in the AJC St Leger, Artilleryman developed a big lump in his thigh. Signs of it had been there before but this time it didn't go down.

The colt was sent home and died at Bacchus Marsh on the same day his part-owner Mr Murphy died in Melbourne. Sir Sam continued to race horses but said his one great regret was that he never knew how good Artilleryman 'really was'.

The much-travelled horseman Frank Bullock bobbed up in Perth on Boxing Day 1919, to pilot the star chestnut colt Eurythmic (5/4 favourite) to a three-length win in the WATC Derby at Ascot.

It was Eurythmic's sixth win in 10 starts since making his debut for wealthy Western Australian owner Ernest Lee Steere in the spring of 1918.

Three days after his Derby success, Eurythmic (7/2) had a titanic battle with fellow three-year-old, the 20/1 outsider Rivose in the Perth Cup over two miles. The judge could not separate the pair, declaring the first dead-heat in the history of the race, first run in 1879.

Eurythmic rounded off his three-year-old career with three more wins from as many starts, the last in the WATC St Leger at the prohibitive odds of 12/1 on. It was time to head for Melbourne.

Eurythmic's ability came from his maternal side, since his sire Eudorous produced only one other notable performer, namely Eusebius. Eurythmic's dam was Bob Cherry, a granddaughter of the imported Bill Of Portland (by St Simon), a prolific sire of winners around the turn of the century. They included Merriwee, winner of the Victoria Derby and Melbourne Cup in 1899, and Maltster, the 1900 Victoria Derby winner who in turn sired two winners of the VRC classic – Alawa and Beverage.

Bullock moved to Germany, and won the jockeys' championship five times in six years. He went to England with the Kaiser's horse, Cyklon, before World War I and arranged for Cyklon to be sent to Australia. Cyklon raced well and sired the 1927 Melbourne Cup winner Trivalve.

Record-making mare Desert Gold bows out

Desert Gold, an owners', trainers' and punters' dream with 19 straight wins.

Desert Gold rears after tangling with the open strand barrier at Trentham, NZ, in 1919.

The grand New Zealand mare Desert Gold, who won 19 races straight on her home turf – an Australasian record – bowed out of racing in the Stead Memorial Cup at Canterbury (NZ) on 15 November 1919, at the age of seven.

Sadly, she ran a distant third, and last, behind Gloaming, beaten by nearly six lengths. It was Gloaming, three years her junior, who was to equal Desert Gold's feat of 19 wins on end. Desert Gold's winning streak lasted from May 1915 to April 1917. Her jockey in all 19 victories was J. O'Shea. Desert Gold met Gloaming four times and on each occasion had her colours lowered.

The Stead Cup was Desert Gold's 59th race start and 18th minor placing in a remarkable career that began in 1914 and yielded 36 wins for £23 133 in stake money. One of the champion mare's five unplaced runs was in the 1918 Melbourne Cup, won by Night Watch, in which she was burdened with equal topweight of 9st 6lb and ran eighth at 20/1. She conceded nearly three stone to the winner who carried 6.9. As a three-year-old in NZ, Desert Gold won the New Zealand Derby and Oaks, the Great Northern Derby and Oaks, and the St Leger.

Desert Gold had 10 races in Australia as a five and six-year-old, winning four weight-for-age events, two at Randwick and one each at Flemington and Caulfield, twice beating the well-performed Cetigne. Her clash with grand stayer Poitrel in the 1918 Spring Stakes at Randwick drew a huge crowd. Poitrel won by a short head.

Desert Gold was a good broodmare, though it was asking too much of her to produce her equal. One of her close descendants was Gold Rod, winner of the Epsom Handicap in 1937 and the Doncaster Handicap in 1939. Others were Gold Trail, whose many good wins numbered the 1934 Auckland Cup, and Rakanui, winner of 17 NZ races, including the Avondale Cup.

1919 RESULTS

VRC MELBOURNE CUP (2m)
Artilleryman, 7.6 (R Lewis) Trained by PT Heywood; 3:24.25; Richmond Main, Two Blues
AJC SYDNEY CUP (2m)
Ian Or, 6.10 (T McNamara) Trained by F Marsden; 3:31.5; Night Watch, Arch Marella
QTC BRISBANE CUP (2m)
Venerable, 8.13 (A Davis) 3:26.75; Everkeane, Had-I-Wist
SAJC ADELAIDE CUP (13-f)
Dependence, 7.8 (F Herbert) Trained by I Reid; 2:49; King Of The Sea, Wee Gun
WATC PERTH CUP (2m)
Dead-heat Eurythmic, 7.9 (F Bullock) and Rivose, 6.13 (F Robinson); Eurythmic trained by JJ Kelly, Rivose trained by J Jeffery; 3:25.8; Red Banner 3rd

VATC CAULFIELD CUP (12-f)
Lucknow, 8.6 (F Bullock) Trained by R Bradfield; 2:32; Night Watch, Chrome
VRC AUSTRALIAN CUP (2 ¼ m)
New Tipperary, 7.7 (R Lewis) Trained by J O'Hara; 3:59.25; Earlborn, Menin
AJC DERBY (12-f)
Dead-heat Artilleryman, 8.10 (G Harrison) and Richmond Main, 8.10 (A Wood); Artilleryman trained by PT Heywood; Richmond Main trained by F Marsden; 2:35; Millieme third
VRC VICTORIA DERBY (12-f)
Richmond Main (A Wood) Trained by F Marsden; 2:35.75; Artillieryman, Surveyor
AJC DONCASTER HANDICAP (1m)
Hem, 6.7 (T McNamara) Trained by M Thompson; 1:45.25; Greenstead, King's Word

VRC NEWMARKET HANDICAP (6-f)
Molly's Robe, 7.8 (P O'Neill) Trained by J Booth; 1:15; Sir Ibex, Greenstead
AJC SIRES' PRODUCE STAKES (7-f)
Millieme, 8.10 (K Bracken) Trained by W Kelso; 1:32.75; Sweet Rosaleen, Golden Desert
VRC SIRES' PRODUCE STAKES (6-f)
Lisnavane, 8.7 (F Bullock) Trained by J McCann; 1:18; Artilleryman, Bandurria
VRC GRAND NATIONAL STEEPLECHASE (3m 1-f)
Sir Prim, 11.0 (E Moon) Trained by P Padfield; 6:23; Cobram, Murrangong

Alex Thurgood: a big winner.

Melbourne's Epsom?

In 1919, the VRC decided it should have a feature mile race. Enter the £2000 Cantala Stakes, soon dubbed 'the Epsom of Melbourne'. The AJC Epsom Handicap has been around as long as Captain Cook, metaphorically speaking. Captain Cook, a son of New Warrior, won the second running of the famous AJC mile race at Randwick in the spring of 1871, cutting out the journey in 1:48.

Melbourne's premier open mile was the VATC Toorak Handicap (first run in 1881). The first running of the Cantala Stakes, formerly the Coburg Stakes, was on Derby day and attracted a good field. VRC vice-chairman Septimus Miller donated a neat gold cup valued at £100 to the winning owner. It was a coincidence that he was a former owner of Chal, the surprise winner at 25/1. Mr Miller, tiring of Chal, sold him to former football hero A. J. Thurgood for 350 guineas. Thurgood had a big win on his horse, said to be £33 000. Chal, a four-year-old grandson of Maltster, carried on 7.1 and was cheered home by bookmakers, who agreed with owners that the Cantala Stakes was a winner.

Dick Bradfield's 'trifecta'

The word 'trifecta' didn't get a guernsey in dictionaries (circa 1919). It came into racing parlance half a century later as a popular betting medium on the tote – for the lucky, big dividends for little outlay.

The Ascot Vale stable of trainer Dick Bradfield would have collected had the trifecta been around in 1919, for that year the 62-year-old saddled up the three placegetters in the Caulfield Cup – Lucknow (9/2), Night Watch (5/2 favourite) and Chrome, the value runner at 12/1.

It was the first time such a feat had been achieved. The year before Bradfield had trained the Caulfield–Melbourne Cup double with King Offa and Night Watch.

Bradfield's three runners in the 1919 Caulfield Cup – all aged six – were not the only fancies. The well-performed three-year-old Richmond Main, who had dead-heated for first with Artilleryman in the AJC Derby, and Eusebius were under double figure odds.

Lucknow was an English horse with no credentials other than his illustrious breeding. He was bred by King George V, who arranged the mating of Minoru, the English Derby winner owned by his father King Edward VII, and Amphora. Impressed by Lucknow's bloodlines, Melbourne owners Lionel Robinson and William Clark, known as 'The Firm', bought him after the Great War and shipped him to Australia.

Lucknow, a maiden, had his first outing in Australia in the Futurity Stakes in the autumn of 1919 and won comfortably.

When he resumed in the spring, he promptly won the Heatherlie Handicap at Caulfield. But his stablemate Night Watch, a son of the great racemare Wakeful, was favourite for the Caulfield Cup on the strength of wins in the 1918 Melbourne Cup and 1919 Williamstown Peace Cup.

Lucknow's jockey, the crack horseman Frank Bullock, who had won the race the year before on Bradfield's King Offa, would not have a bar of his mount being beaten. He put his career on the line, saying: 'If Lucknow gets beaten I'll never ride again.' When George Harrison, rider of Night Watch, learnt this, his riposte was forthright. 'Well, I'm afraid his riding days are over.'

Harrison wasn't far wrong. To the roars of the record crowd of 45 000, Lucknow and Night Watch had a stirring duel in the straight, Lucknow with a 5 lb weight advantage (8.6 to 8.11) getting home by a half-neck. Chrome was three-quarters of a length away in third place. Lucknow ran the 12 furlongs in a record 2:32.0.

For Bendigo-born Bradfield, one of the most highly regarded trainers in the business, it was his fifth major cup win in Melbourne. He had already won the Melbourne Cup with Patron, The Victory and, of course, Night Watch.

TURF TOPICS

Few trainers: A special Sydney-bound train left Melbourne on Saturday evening, October 4, to enable racegoers to see Monday's AJC Metropolitan. Only 28 passengers travelled north. As 80 had been guaranteed, the difference had to be met by the guarantors. The Metropolitan was won by the imported Rebus, whose owner Mr J. Lemon backed him to win £20 000. The flying Greenstead, bred in Victoria, lumped 9.13 to a brilliant win in The Shorts (6f).

A risky bet: The licensee of the Victoria Inn, George Ferns, was fined £30 or three months' imprisonment, in Williamstown Court in November 1919, for having the care and management of a common gaming house. Betting at the Steampacket Hotel, in Cole Street, also came under the notice of the court. Altogether, the Magistrate, Mr Knight, meted out fines totalling £105. William Kilty was fined £20 for street betting in Nelson Place and his wife, Isabella,

£5 for accepting small wagers at a confectionery shop in the same street.

Randwick to the rescue: A 'flu epidemic all but wiped out the AJC carnival in 1919. Facilities at Randwick racecourse were converted for use as an emergency hospital. Muslin masks had to be worn by citizens outdoors. All country racing was suspended. In one week in April, 230 deaths were reported in Sydney. The death toll throughout the country was 11 000.

Eurythmic's win in the 1920 Caulfield Cup made it 10 wins in a row. Ridden by Frank Dempsey, he started favourite at 6/4.

Eurythmic, the swinger from the west

Handsome chestnuts usually brought more than 310 guineas at the Randwick yearling sales in the early 1900s. Not so Eurythmic, knocked down for that modest sum in 1918 to an agent acting for wealthy West Australian pastoralist and chairman of the WATC, Ernest Lee Steere, later knighted.

By the less than notable sire Eudorous, the colt's only impediment turned out to be a 'swinging leg' – at full gallop his off foreleg moved in an arc, meaning his action sometimes endangered himself and horses around him, especially when he raced on the inside.

Named Eurythmic, a Greek word meaning harmonious rhythm, Lee Steere's purchase soon lived up to his name in WA, bounding to 10 wins as a two and three-year-old, nine of them at Ascot.

Soon after Eurythmic's fourth birthday it was time for him to try the big time in Melbourne, so he was shipped from Perth to far-off Mordialloc and the stables of Victoria's premier trainer, 41-year-old Jack Holt.

Holt, who had a wonderful eye for horses, soon established that Eurythmic needed little work to keep him in top trim. More important, he discovered that the aristocratic-looking WA champion became distressed if stabled in an inside box. So he built a special outside box for the star newcomer.

Eurythmic, who had some pretty fancy blood flowing through his veins – he traced back to St Simon and Carbine – had his first Melbourne run in the wfa Memsie Stakes in the spring of 1920. Track watchers, having noted Eurythmic's light preparation and curious action, gave him little chance. How little

they appreciated Holt's perspicacity. 'I'll lay 25/1 Arithmetic,' chortled one bookie to amused punters at Caulfield before the Memsie. The odds went begging. No one wanted a bar of 'the funny old leg-swinger from Perth', as one scribe called Eurythmic. There was no mirth after the Memsie; rather laments all-around of a golden opportunity lost. Carrying 9.7 and starting at the afore-mentioned 25/1, Eurythmic gave his 14 rivals a galloping lesson, scorching to victory by three lengths and cutting out the nine furlongs in a record 1:53 ½.

Eurythmic, with only 8.9, was immediately installed a hot favourite for the Caulfield Cup, which he duly won in impressive style even though he raced wide all the way because of his swinging leg. His decisive win at 6/4, the shortest priced winner in the history of the race, was greeted with great enthusiasm by the big Caulfield crowd, which also hailed the riding of young Frank

Dempsey, who dashed his mount to the front turning for home. The winning margin over runner-up Accrington, raced by Mr E.A. Underwood and carrying only 7.9, was a length and a half. Having won the Caulfield Cup on Lavendo (1915) and Bronzetti (1917), Dempsey, still only 21, became the first jockey to win the race three times.

Eurythmic's victory was his 10th in a row and earned Mr Lee Steere a cheque for $10 000, plus a handsome trophy for his mantelpiece. Next up Eurythmic won the wfa Melbourne Stakes on Derby day, then ran a gallant fourth to Poitrel in the Melbourne Cup. He just failed to see out the distance. He gained his revenge on Poitrel on the last day of the VRC spring carnival, defeating the Cup winner in the wfa CB Fisher Plate (12f). Eurythmic then went for a well-earned spell at Holt's stables, having won at six of his seven starts in Melbourne. There were a lot more wins in store for the WA swinger.

Seven of the best: Carbine, Trafalgar, Poitrel, Kennaquhair, David, Rivoli and Gloaming (ARM).

Only Archer and Carbine carried more weight to win a Melbourne Cup than Poitrel.

Unwanted Melbourne Cup winner

Poitrel qualifies on several counts as one of the best horses ever to look through a bridle in Australian turf history. He became the first horse in Australia to beat the mighty Kiwis Desert Gold and Gloaming, and lumped 10 stone to victory in the 1920 Melbourne Cup. Only Archer in 1862 and Carbine in 1890 carried more.

Yet the great-grandson of the formidable English sire St Simon was unwanted as a yearling, failing to reach the reserve of 300 guineas at the 1916 Sydney sales. True, Poitrel had a parrot mouth, which did not enhance his looks, but it did not stop him eating. Of more concern were his shelly (brittle) feet, which, when possible, were kept in dampish mud so that they would not crack. In winning the Melbourne Cup, he carried 14 nails in one shoe, so thin was the hoof.

At his third start as a three-year-old, the chunky chestnut, who was on the small side, won over 10 furlongs in open company at Randwick. That convinced trainer Harry Robinson and the owners, the Moses brothers, that here indeed was a stayer, a notion reinforced by Poitrel's four-length win over Kennaquhair in the three-mile AJC Craven Plate in May 1919. According to clockers, Poitrel ran the last half mile of that race in a particularly brisk 46 seconds.

At five and six, Poitrel strung together eight wins from 11 furlongs to three miles, hence his huge impost of 10 stone in the 1920 Melbourne Cup.

Poitrel had only two more runs after the Cup, going out on a winning note in the Rosehill Rawson Stakes in March 1921, dead-heating for first with Richmond Main. Including two dead-heats, Poitrel achieved 19 wins from 37 starts, yielding the Moses brothers a handsome dividend of $49 485.

Not bad for a horse shunned as a yearling.

1920 RESULTS

VRC MELBOURNE CUP (2m)
Poitrel, 10.0 ((K Bracken) Trained by H Robinson; 3:25.25; Erasmus, Queen Comedy

AJC SYDNEY CUP (2m)
Kennaquhair, 9.5 (A Wood) Trained by W Stringer; 3:22.75; Poitrel, Millieme

QTC BRISBANE CUP (2m)
Golden Sunset, 8.5 (L Walker) 3:26.25; Had-I-Wist, Impeyan

SAJC ADELAIDE CUP (13-f)
Wee Gun, 8.5 (J Hopwood) Trained by H Gregory; 2:53.75; Green Cap, Queen Comedy

VATC CAULFIELD CUP (12-f)
Eurythmic, 8.9 (F Dempsey) Trained by J Holt; 2:33.25; Accrington, Tangalooma

VRC AUSTRALIAN CUP (2 ¼m)
Macadam, 7.1 (J Mahoney) Trained by J Scobie; 3:57.75; Tenterfield, East Court

AJC DERBY (12-f)
Salitros, 8.10 (M Connell) Trained by F Williams; 2:32; Malurys, Erasmus

VRC VICTORIA DERBY (12-f)
Salitros (M Connell) Trained by F Williams; 2:37.75; Nautical, Syce Knight

AJC DONCASTER HANDICAP (1m)
Sydney Damsel, 8.4 (J Killorn) Trainer J Tomlinson; 1:37.75; Chrysolaus, Mount Frisco

VRC NEWMARKET HANDICAP (6-f)
Red Dome, 7.10 (J Mahoney) Trained by F Foulsham; 1:14.7; Gambler's Gold, Cetigne

AJC SIRES' PRODUCE STAKES (7-f)
Glenacre, 8.10 (M Connell) Trained by F Williams; 1:26.75; Erasmus, Skysail

VRC SIRES' PRODUCE STAKES (7-f)
Gossine Hatan, 8.7 (K Bracken) Trained by E Mayo; 1:29; Glenacre, Crimson

VRC GRAND NATIONAL STEEPLECHASE (3m 1-f)
Iolaus, 9.13 (H Thompson) Trained by N Godby; 6:15.7; Kinlark, Doiran

Jack Holt's house 'Lethe' at the Mordialloc training establishment in 1920.

The Wizard of Mordialloc

At 16, Michael John Holt left the Berwick postal department to train a team of six horses and ponies. Jack, as he became known, was the son of Irish migrants. He inherited his father's wit and way with horses, and his mother's goodness of heart.

By nature well mannered, he was fortunate to be befriended by the headmaster of Berwick Grammar School, Mr E. L. Vieusseux, who taught him the social graces, including a talent for billiards, that were to stand him in good stead in the rarefied atmosphere of well-to-do racehorse owners.

By 1910, aged 31, Jack Holt had won the respect of several patrons in the Berwick district. He trained at Beaconsfield, but the mountain soil there was too wet for his liking. So he rented stables at Epsom, where the firmer sandy going was appreciated by his team.

The move was to be permanent. Holt bought land at nearby Mordialloc, built a modest home and stables and entrusted a solicitor friend with £100 for the purchase of good quality furniture. It cost £96, Holt receiving £4 change. With that the young trainer sent for his sisters, Margaret and Catherine, to come and live with him, for the Holts had always been a close-knit family. The three lived in the same house for more than 40 years, the two sisters playing vital roles in the management and care of Victoria's top training establishment.

Holt began his metropolitan career with six horses, one of whom he owned. She was a mare called Carette, who gave Holt his first important success, winning the 1911 Standish

Handicap at Flemington at the nice odds of 12/1. She provided the foundation for the fortune Holt was to amass. He was often reminded of her, as he won the Standish no fewer than eight times.

Holt had several important strings to his training bow. He kept meticulous records and was a father and guardian to his apprentices, insisting they always be neatly dressed. Sympathy for horses was regarded as one of his secrets. He never turned them out to agistment farms. They spelled at his stables where he could keep an eye on them. If a horse put on too much weight, he was soon back in work. Hence Holt's capacity to win first-up with many of his charges, such as Eurythmic in the 1920 Memsie Stakes, a race the trainer was to win 11 times.

Hall Mark, for instance, was attached to a grey pony and they always travelled together, even to Sydney. The talented Nuffield was highly excitable, so was stabled in a box lined with rubber to protect him. Holt always examined his horses straight after training, testing by hand their wind and condition.

He insisted that his boys or track riders be on friendly terms with their horses. 'You are not dumb,' he would say. 'Talk to the horse.' Holt knew a horseman when he saw one; two of Melbourne's best jockeys, Frank Dempsey and Billy Duncan, did most of the stable riding early on.

The year 1920 was a watershed in the career of Holt, who won the first of 13 Victorian trainers' premierships in 1918–19 and was soon dubbed 'The Wizard of Mordialloc'.

Kennaquhair's big day

The Sydney Cup, while not enjoying the prestige of the Melbourne Cup, often attracted the best stayers in the Commonwealth. The 1920 running before a record crowd of 80 000 on a fine Easter Monday saw a clash between two Sydney staying titans, the top-weights Poitrel (9.9) and Kennaquhair (9.5), not forgetting the Victorian-trained Artilleryman (9.2), who had run away with the 1919 Melbourne Cup as a three-year-old.

Not before time, it was the turn of the five-year-old chestnut Kennaquhair to prevail in a cup. In 1918, he had been runner-up to Night Watch in the Melbourne Cup, conceding the winner a staggering 33 pounds (9.0 to 6.9), and he had won of the 1919 Metropolitan.

Poitrel was the public elect at 5/1 in the big race at Randwick in 1920, followed by Artilleryman and King of the Sea at 6/1, with Kennaquhair solid at 7s in a field of 20. In a daring move, jockey Albert Wood dashed Kennaquhair to the lead three furlongs from home and they made the turn into the long straight two lengths clear, with Poitrel making a move from well back. Kennaquhair hung on to down the fast-finishing Poitrel by a neck, with Millieme (8.3) two lengths away third. Artilleryman finished well back.

The winning time of 3:22¾ was an Australasian record, and the owners, Mr W. H. Borthwick and J. Laycock, received a gold cup.

Of concern to the AJC was the lack of amenities for the huge crowd, even though the public stand had recently been extended and other buildings and facilities improved. The totalisator, a new and popular betting medium, could not handle the immense traffic, with crushes forming at the windows.

A big crowd watches Beauford defeat Gloaming in the 1922 Spring Stakes at Randwick.

Gloaming and the golden era

In 1924 a racehorse called Gloaming returned from New Zealand to the scene of his birth – Victoria – to win the Melbourne Stakes (10f) at Flemington on Derby day. It was the only time Gloaming raced in Victoria. His other 56 wins in a career lasting from 1918 until 1925 (when he was nine) were achieved in New Zealand and in Sydney.

Turf romantics rightly claim that the 1920s was a golden era for Australasian racing. The rollcall of participants supports the notion. Along with Gloaming, examine this imposing field – Poitrel, Eurythmic, Beauford, Spearfelt, David, Heroic, Manfred, Windbag, the flying filly Valicare, Amounis, Trivalve, Limerick, Gothic and Nightmarch, not forgetting jumpers Fiscom, Mountain God and the mighty Roisel.

And who should step out for the first time in 1929 but a NZ-bred two-year-old by Night Raid out of Entreaty. His first four runs, all in Sydney, were unproductive. Indeed, he was unplaced in all four. The best was yet to come. His name was Phar Lap.

Guiding the fortunes of these champions were horsemen of the calibre of Frank Dempsey, Bill Duncan, Bobby Lewis, George Young, Bill McLachlan, Hughie Cairns, Frank Bullock, Jim Pike, Jimmy Munro and youngsters Harold Badger and Scobie Breasley. Household names among the ranks of trainers were James Scobie, Lou Robertson, Jack

Holt, Cecil Godby, Dick Bradfield, Frank McGrath and Vin O'Neill.

Following the end of hostilities in Europe in November 1918, good racing and economic prosperity were in the wind. Desert Gold, the undoubted champion at war's end,

Horse talk

In 1924 Gloaming was shipped home to New Zealand. While being led through the cheering crowd at the wharf, Gloaming looked anxiously for his travelling companion, Cupidon, annoyed at not being allowed to say goodbye. His shrill calls to his mate amused the crowd.

had retired. Gloaming, having brought to an end her record of 19 straight wins (in 1919), stepped into her shoes and in 1922 thrilled

Sydney racegoers with four titanic battles with Beauford, the pride of Newcastle.

Money flowed. Melbourne Cup prize-money soared to £13 288 in 1923. The jazz age ushered in a refreshing gayness ('gay' then meant spirited, carefree) as blue skies swept away the dark clouds of war. Sport became an outlet for all social classes and racing began to attract huge crowds.

No fewer than 109 701 people packed into Flemington to watch Poitrel win the 1920 Melbourne Cup. A staggering statistic considering the population of Melbourne was little more than 700 000. By 1926, the Cup Day crowd had risen to an astounding 126 000. That was Spearfelt's year. Cup Day had become a great carnival, drawing together folk from the remotest parts of Australia; in the words of one newspaperman 'a kaleidoscope of varied interest and scene, pervaded with good humor and cheerfulness'.

Good horses, better facilities (especially for the members), the proximity of Flemington to the city, and reliable train travel, not to mention the lure of a quick quid at the expense of rich bookies, combined to make racing popular the year round. It was one of life's enjoyable constants. The newspapers ran columns of fields, results and accounts of meetings, highlighting, of course, the numerous dignitaries who bowled up in their finery. For it was a time of pomp and ceremony. Rich owners were identified as sportsmen, a euphemism for all manner of pursuits, not all of them admirable. But battlers were not blackballed. Touts were always on the lookout for a good thing. Trainers often worked their horses in the dark, in secret, to escape the attention of the clockers.

Across the country, at big tracks and little bush tracks, townsfolk took to racing as eagerly as a horse to a good feed. At Easter, 1920, Randwick was strained to bursting point when a record crowd of 83 000 turned up to see grand stayers Kennaquhair and Poitrel fight out the Sydey Cup.

For every good looker who has brought a high price in the sale ring, such as Heroic, racing has thrown up a bargain. Bred at Melton Stud, Victoria, by Mr E. E. D. Clarke, Gloaming had just recovered from illness when offered for sale in Melbourne in 1917, so was not looking at his best. New Zealand owner/breeder Mr G. Greenwood had contacted his Melbourne agent and asked him to secure a cheap yearling. He got Gloaming for 230 guineas. Probably the bargain of the century, as the bay son of The Welkin out of Light won 57 races (46 in NZ and 11 in Australia) and £43 100. He was unplaced once, when the barrier strand became entangled around his neck.

by David Austin

John Wren had racetrack troubles in 1914, as his letter shows. The government eventually took over his track, and his ill-luck continued when his horse Rover (below) bolted before the 1919 Caulfield Cup (ARM).

Another year on, and Violoncello has a two-length win over Easingwold in the Cox Plate (SLV).

Sir Sam picks a winner

When Artilleryman died in 1920, his owner Sir Samuel Hordern went to England in search of another cup winner. He returned with Violoncello, a lightly raced six-year-old son of Valens owned by Mr Anthony de Rothschild.

It was Mr de Rothschild who came up with the melodious sounding name of Violoncello, whose dam had the misfortune to be called Catgut.

The fact that the son of Catgut was a half-brother to the 1916 AJC Metropolitan winner Quinologist impressed Sir Samuel, whose offer of 4000 guineas was accepted by Mr de Rothschild.

At his final start in England, in 1920, Violoncello won a mile welter at Newmarket with the steadier of 9.12. At his second start in Australia, he ran second to Beauford in the 1921 Hill Stakes at Rosehill.

Given 9.5 in the Metropolitan, the eight-year-old chestnut Violoncello instead went south for the Caulfield Cup, in which he had 8.13. By mid-September Violoncello was 4/1 favourite for the cup. By race day, which was wet, he had blown out to 16/1. The favourite at 7/2 was the Jack Holt–trained Tangalooma, who had finished third to stablemate Eurythmic the year before.

Violoncello, ridden by heavyweight jockey Bill Foulsham, gained the day by a half-length over the well-backed Purser, ridden by Billy Duncan, with Lionel Attwill third.

There was some confusion over Violoncello's name. In the Caulfield racebook it appeared as Violincello, but as the horse had been registered as Violoncello in England that was deemed to be his correct name.

TURF TOPICS

Nice little earner: In 1920–1 the coffers of the New South Wales Government were swelled to the tune of £602 794 – every penny of it from horseracing taxes. The breakdown was – stamp duty and tickets, £101 893; betting taxes from racing clubs, associations and bookmakers, £108 911; totalisator tax £274 171; and racecourse admission tax £117 819. The Treasurer, Mr McPherson, told the Legislative Assembly it was planned to raise an additional £80 000, 'a modest sum', from the racing clubs.

No penalty: It was decided that the winner of the Hotham Handicap would no longer be liable to a penalty for the Melbourne Cup. The Hotham had long been regarded as

a good guide to the Cup. The VRC was keen to encourage owners and trainers to run their horses in the Hotham as a final outing for the big race.

One a fortnight: Having won three races in a row at Flemington in the autumn, Eurythmic, aged four, went north and won three consecutive races at Randwick – the Autumn Stakes, Sydney Cup and Cumberland Stakes. By year's end he had won a total of 26 races.

Queensland coup: When Queensland owner Mr I. Freedman and his trainer, the veteran Bill Blacklock, left Brisbane with Gold Tie, the top sprinter in the north, they had designs on Australia's most famous sprint

race, the VRC Newmarket Handicap at Flemington. Gold Tie had excellent credentials, having won the 1918 and 1919 Stradbroke Handicap.

To the surprise and delight of connections, Gold Tie, the sturdy brown son of Maltster, won first-up in Melbourne, saluting in the prestigious Futurity Stakes at Caulfield at the attractive odds of 12/1. Gold Tie took charge entering the straight and held off 25/1 shot Whizz Bang by a half neck. Freedman and Blacklock left the course with £4200 in stake money and their winnings from the bookmakers. Gold Tie was unplaced in the Newmarket Handicap, won by the Jack Holt–trained Blue Cross.

Frank Dempsey, Eurythmic's regular rider, missed the Melbourne Cup through injury (ARM).

An easy ride for jockey Bob Lewis (ARM).

Filly's trainer has last laugh

The 1921 Melbourne Cup was a tale of two horses – the champion Eurythmic, who ran last, and the three-year-old chestnut filly Sister Olive, who won at 16/1.

Eurythmic, winner of 10 races in a row, including the Sydney Cup with 9.8, was asked to carry 10.5 – Carbine's weight. The popular elect at 5/1, luck deserted him when he needed it most.

Ridden by Sydney rider Bill McLachlan, replacing the injured Frank Dempsey, Eurythmic caught a barrier strand in his mouth at the start and nearly fell. He was last early on but made up ground steadily and was well placed four furlongs out. Soon after, however, he was involved in a scrimmage, in which he injured a fetlock joint. The big crowd was stunned when he faulted. He limped home in last place, his first unplaced run since the 1920 Cup. It seemed he was jinxed in the nation's biggest horserace.

Spelled, Eurythmic returned in the autumn and won the St George Stakes at Caulfield first-up. The 1921 Cup winner, Sister Olive, owned by Melbourne bookmaker F. W. Norman, began her career in brilliant fashion, winning the VRC Maribyrnong Trial Stakes for fillies at her first start. Her subsequent form and early outings as a three-year-old were lacklustre, but a good third to Purser in the 10-furlong Stand Handicap at Flemington raised the hopes of her quiet trainer Jack Williams, a former jockey.

Sister Olive, by the imported Red Dennis from Jubilee Queen, had the blood of Comedy King on her dam's side, and revealed a liking for more ground by running fourth in the Caulfield Cup.

With only 6.9 to carry in the big race, she was specked at 16/1. Her pilot Ernie O'Sullivan took her to the front soon after entering the straight and she held off John Wren's The Rover, by three-quarters of a length, to become the 17th mare to win.

Cup winner Sister Olive.

Fast Furious

The smart filly Furious, owned and bred by Victorian Ernest Clarke, became only the 11th of her sex to win the Victoria Derby. Starting favourite at 7/4, she did so with authority, being eased up by jockey Bob Lewis and defeating Bassi by three lengths, with the Melbourne Cup winner Sister Olive, third. Furious clocked race-record time of 2:35.

From the outset of her career, Furious, who was by Gloaming's sire, The Welkin, was outstanding. As a two-year-old, she had six starts in Sydney for four wins, including the AJC Sires and Champagne Stakes.

At three, she opened her winning account in the Rosehill Guineas, then finished second to Cupidon in the AJC Derby.

After winning the VRC classic, she was unplaced in the Melbourne Cup, but won the VRC Oaks two days later. The following autumn she won the VRC St Leger. At four, she ran third to Violoncello in the first WS Cox Plate.

Furious died of blood poisoning as a five-year-old, having won £20 222 in stakes.

1921 RESULTS

VRC MELBOURNE CUP
(2m) Sister Olive, 6.9 (E. O'Sullivan) Trained by J. Williams; 3:27.25; The Rover, Amazonia

AJC SYDNEY CUP
(2m) Eurythmic, 9.8 (F Dempsey) Trained by J Holt; 3:24.75; Arch Marella, Amazonia

QTC BRISBANE CUP
(2m) Impeyan, 7.7 (W Hill) 3:24; Snow Star, For My Lady

SAJC ADELAIDE CUP
(13-f) Sir Marco, 6.12 (B Rosen) Trained by R Burgess; 2:47.75; Bon Vue, Annexit

WATC PERTH CUP
(2m) (1 January 1921) Seigneur, 6.7 (G Morse) Trained by R Burns; 3:30.6; Earl Of Seafield; Jolly Cosy

WATC PERTH CUP
(2m) (31 December 1921) Earl Of Seafield, 7.4 (R Morley) Trained by T Tighe; 3:26.8; Queen Comedy, Gold Digger

VATC CAULFIELD CUP
(12-f) Violoncello, 8.13 (W Foulsham) Trained by CH Bryans; 2:35.75; Purser, Lionel Attwill

VRC AUSTRALIAN CUP
(2 ¼m) The Rover, 7.2 (V Sleigh) Trained by C Moore; 3:53.75; Democracy, Clever Jim

AJC DERBY
(12-f) Cupidon, 8.10 (G Young) Trained by R Mason; 2:33.75; Furious, Honey Bee

VRC VICTORIA DERBY
(12-f) Furious (R Lewis) Trained by F Marsden; 2:35; Bassi, Harvest King

AJC DONCASTER HANDICAP
(1m) Speciality, 7.5 (J Toohey) Trained by D Lewis; 1:37.5; Wish Wynne, Beauford

VRC NEWMARKET HANDICAP
(6-f) Blue Cross, 8.5 (G Harrison) Trained by J Holt; 1:14.5; Rostrum, Rathillet

AJC SIRES' PRODUCE STAKES
(7-f) Furious, 8.7 (WH McLachlan) Trained by F Marsden; 1:29; Isa, Woodville

VRC SIRES' PRODUCE STAKES
(7-f) Isa, 8.7 (R Lewis) Trained by J Scobie; 1:28.7; Antarian, Sefton

VRC GRAND NATIONAL STEEPLECHASE
(3m 1-f) Mountain God, 11.5 (S Reid) Trained by H Harrison; 6:12.5; Wooloo, Doiran

James Scobie on top in the twenties.

Lewis: began riding for Scobie in 1895 (ARM).

Scobie beats the handicapper

The magic of Ararat-born James Scobie, so evident throughout his long training career, manifested itself once again on Melbourne Cup day, 1922.

In the autumn of that year, a three-year-old who had raced with moderate success in South Australia was sent to his Ascot Vale stables.

The horse was King Ingoda, whose sire Comedy King kept on producing very good gallopers. Scobie took King Ingoda quietly, and the colt responded by winning the SAJC St Leger. Scobie did not produce him again until the VATC Congy Handicap, three weeks before the Melbourne Cup. But he had impressed Scobie in trials and he certainly gained favour with the public by winning the Hotham Handicap on Derby Day.

The Cup that year boasted a good field,

**1922
KING INGODA
A. WILSON
7st. 1lb.
Time: 3.28¼
32 STARTERS**
*wners: C. J. L. Dubois
and R. W. Bennett
2nd The Cypher
3rd Mufti*

Tich Wilson aboard 1922 Cup winner King Ingoda (ARM).

no fewer than six of the 32 runners having won various cups. It contained horses of the calibre of Purser, Whittier, David, Tangalooma and the top mare Furious. But King Ingoda, a four-year-old with only 7.1, was too good for them, though The Cypher, race favourite at 6/1, ran him to a head after Scobie's apprentice, the highly regarded Tich Wilson, had dashed King Ingoda, an 8/1 chance, to the lead at the distance.

Although he was just 20, Wilson had ridden more than 250 winners in only four years, a lot of them on pony tracks. King Ingoda was another example of a cheap buy. His part-owner, Mr C. L. Dubois, had bought the broodmare Ingoda, with a foal at foot, for 325 guineas when Sol Green sold his Shipley stud. King Ingoda won £9624 on Cup Day, a handsome return for his owner.

The name of Munro hit the headlines in a big way in 1922 when 17-year-old apprentice Jimmy Munro won the Sydney Cup on Prince Charles. Later, his younger brother Darby Munro would add lustre to the family name.

Jimmy Munro, born in 1905, was apprenticed to his father, Randwick trainer Hugh Munro, who prepared many top-class horses, including the 1901 Melbourne Cup winner Revenue. Racecaller Cyril Angles, who grew up in the same area as Jimmy Munro, rated him as the best jockey he ever saw.

The innovative Munro introduced a new element to race riding. Whereas jockeys of the day tended to save their mounts for the sprint home, Munro often used more daring tactics, speeding up his mounts in mid-race and 'stealing' victory from riders who felt duty bound to stick to instructions. Later, Darby Munro employed the same tactics successfully.

From 1920 until 1935 Jimmy Munro rode the best horses in the land – Phar Lap, Windbag, Amounis, Peter Pan, Valicare and Chatham. He once nominated Amounis, on whom he won the 1926 and 1928 Epsom Handicaps, as the best horse he had ridden.

Years later, Munro painted a much different picture to turf writer Fran O'Loghlen, naming German horse Alba as 'the best horse the world has ever seen. He stood alone.' Munro won the German Derby on Alba, owned by Baron Oppenheim.

Asked how Phar Lap, Peter Pan and Windbag compared to Alba, Munro replied emphatically: 'Phar Lap, or any of them, wouldn't be in it.' Who would finish second? 'Daylight,' said Munro.

Windbag and Munro in the 1925 Cup.

What of Windbag, winner of the 1925 Melbourne Cup? 'He was a good horse. He won the Cup nicely.'

Munro rode in Europe on occasions, but never on a permanent basis. He impressed the critics with his polished horsemanship.

Martin Stainforth's celebrated painting of the Spring Stakes at Randwick – the third of four fiercely contested match races (AJC).

Beauford v. Gloaming: clash of the titans

If a picture is worth a thousand words, Martin Stainforth's celebrated painting of Beauford defeating Gloaming rates a volume or two. It captures in vivid detail two of the mightiest gallopers in Australasia during the third of their four memorable clashes in Sydney in the spring of 1922.

Beauford, head up in victory, with Albert Wood sitting quietly as the post is reached … Gloaming, on the outside, head at full stretch, urged on by George Young, striving in vain to close the narrow gap. Victory for Beauford by a neck, giving him a 2–1 lead in four 'match races' that drew vast crowds in Sydney.

Gloaming, Victorian-bred and NZ-trained, met Beauford, the Newcastle champion, for the first time in the wfa Chelmsford Stakes (9f) at Randwick on 9 October. Their records were staggering. Gloaming, a compact seven-year-old bay gelding standing only 15.3 hands, had raced 48 times for 42 wins; Beauford, a big, powerful six year-old brown gelding, had raced 23 times for 14 wins.

Beauford, by Beau Soult, winner of the 1913 Rosehill Guineas, out of Blueford, was a great-grandson of St Simon. Bred by NSW pastoralist Mr W. H. Mackay, he was leased to Newcastle trainer Sid Killick for whom he won eight races, including the 1921 Epsom Handicap with 9.2. From the start of 1922, Beauford raced in Mr Mackay's colours.

Local punters pinned their faith in Beauford (10/9 on) in the Chelmsford and cheered home the local idol, who won by three-quarters of a length from Gloaming (2/1) with grand stayer David (50/1) third. Gloaming had dashed to the front on the turn but Beauford, chasing his ninth win on end, won nicely. Said Gloaming's trainer Dick Mason: 'Beauford is a truly great horse.'

Round two, a week later, was in the wfa Hill Stakes (1m) at Rosehill. This time Gloaming, with a 7 lb pull in the weights, prevailed by a length and a quarter in course record time of 1:38.25. Both were odds-on.

Enthralled racegoers had to wait two weeks for round three – the wfa Spring Stakes (12f) at Randwick, the race depicted by Stainforth. The crowd was so great it was impossible to move in the betting ring. Weights were level (9.3) and the crowd opted for Beauford (evens). Once again their judgment was vindicated. The local champion led into the straight and Gloaming, despite a valiant attempt, could not run him down.

It was evens each of two for the fourth and last clash in the time-honoured Craven Plate (10f), which attracted a mid-week crowd of more than 60 000 to Randwick. Soon after the start, Wood took Beauford to the lead but Young on Gloaming tracked him perfectly, being only a length behind on the turn. At the furlong they were together, then Gloaming surged ahead, swamping his rival by three lengths. To the roar of the huge crowd, Gloaming had levelled the score at 2–all, a fitting conclusion.

Beauford had 10 more starts, winning only one. Perhaps Gloaming had exhausted him. All up, the Newcastle hero had 37 starts for 17 wins, eight minor placings and more than £17 000 in stake money. He died at 23 on the property where he was born.

The iron-horse Gloaming went on his merry way, posting another 13 wins in Australia and New Zealand, bowing out with victory over another old rival, The Hawk, in a match race at Hawkes Bay in May 1925. That was his 57th win from 67 starts for earnings of £43 100. Gloaming was only once unplaced.

Above: Beauford. Right: His owner, W. H. Mackay, and G. D. Greenwood, owner of Gloaming.

The Victoria Derby winner's sash makes Whittier a touch fractious (SLV).

The Sydney Connection

Who inspired the WS Cox Plate? Answer: Sydney owners and trainers. They requested the inclusion of the weight-for-age event on Moonee Valley Cup day to give their best horses 'an outing' between the VATC and VRC carnivals.'

In those days, the last day of the four-day AJC spring carnival clashed with Caulfield Guineas day. The Sydney request was taken up by the Moonee Valley Racing Club, then under the chairmanship of Alister Clark.

The initial Cox Plate, worth a modest £1000 compared to the £2204 of the AJC's long-standing wfa race, the Craven Plate, produced a fine contest with no fewer than six Sydney runners, including topliners Violoncello and David, in the field of 14. Indeed, in keeping with subsequent events, the race, run over 9½ furlongs, had a Federal flavour with two runners from Western Australia and one

from South Australia.

Unfortunately Eurythmic had to be withdrawn because of a leg injury. In his absence, stablemate Tangalooma was favourite at 3/1 but he never flattered. Victory by the comfortable margin of a length-and-a-half went to Violoncello. All eyes then focused on Purser's win in the Moonee Valley Cup.

So successful was the Valley meeting that the following year a record crowd turned out in bright sunshine. All and sundry cheered the Cox Plate victory of the Jack Holt–trained Easingwold, denied success the year before. Easingwold (6/4 favourite) defeated two good gallopers in Whittier and Purser. Though the Moonee Valley Cup, won by Princess Mernda, commanded most interest, there was no doubt pulses were stirred to a greater extent by the second running of the Cox Plate.

Squizzy and the Caulfield fire: Next to a woman scorned, hell hath no fury like a crook thrown off a racecourse for being 'an undesirable'. Particularly if the undesirable was weight-for-age scoundrel Squizzy Taylor.

At Caulfield on Coongy Handicap day, 1922, Taylor, punter and urger, was ordered off the course by the racecourse supervisor, Mr E.J. Napthine, a former police detective. Taylor, the Little Napoleon of the Melbourne underworld, tried to see the committee, which was otherwise engaged. So he repaired to a public house where he partook heavily of strong drink and plotted his revenge.

Legend has it that at 4 a.m. on Caulfield Cup day, Taylor doused the course grandstand with petrol and set fire to it. Luckily, a suburban train driver at nearby Caulfield station noticed the flames and alerted the fire brigade.

If Taylor was the arsonist – no charges were laid – he did the VATC a favour as it had decided a month beforehand to demolish the wooden grandstand, which had become inadequate for crowds of 50 000-plus, and build a bigger one.

Not at sea this time: Pastoralist John S. Feehan was at sea returning from England, when his grand chaser Mountain God won the 1921 Grand National Steeplechase at Flemington. News was cabled to him aboard the RMS *Naldera*.

In 1922, Mr Feehan was at Flemington to see Mountain God, again ridden by New Zealand–born Stanley Reid, win for the second year running, the first to do so since Daimio in 1894–95. Mr Feehan was roundly congratulated.

Mountain God, burdened with 12.7, struck the second-last fence heavily, losing three lengths, but still won well to take his earnings to £6636. His first win was in a £5 hack race at Echuca.

1922 RESULTS

VRC MELBOURNE CUP (2m)
King Ingoda, 7.3 (A Wilson) Trained by J Scobie; 3:28.25; The Cypher, Mufti
AJC SYDNEY CUP (2m)
Prince Charles, 7.11 (J Munro) Trained by F Marsden; 3:26.25; Kashmir, Stare
QTC BRISBANE CUP (2m)
Grichka, 8.6 (A Wood) 3:26.25; Fairy Bob, Demeranthis
SAJC ADELAIDE CUP (13-f)
Repique, 7.11 (R Morley) Trained by P Timmens; 2:49.25; Socratea, Crusader
WATC PERTH CUP (2m)
Jolly Cosy, 8.7 (G Leonard) Trained by J O'Mara; 3:27.8; Scorpius, Poondarra

VATC CAULFIELD CUP (12-f)
Whittier, 6.13 (E Simmons) Trained by H McCalman; 2:32; Tangalooma, Purser
VRC AUSTRALIAN CUP (21/4m)
Harvest King, 7.10 (J Toohey) Trained by J McCann; 3:54; Sister Olive, Purser
MVRC WS COX PLATE (91/2-f)
Violoncello, 9.4 (J King) Trained by CH Bryans; 1:57.5; Easingwold, Furious
AJC DERBY (12-f)
Rivoli, 8.10 (P Brown) Trained by I Andrews; 2:35.5; Soorak, Caserta
VRC VICTORIA DERBY (12-f)
Whittier (P Brown) Trained by H McCalman; 2:34; Cliffdale, Anton King

AJC DONCASTER HANDICAP (1m)
Julia Grey, 8.12 (J Toohey) Trained by AE Thompson; 1:38; Sir Maitland, Tressady Queen
VRC NEWMARKET HANDICAP (6-f)
Rostrum, 7.8 (V Sleigh) Trained by EA Connolly; 1:14.5; Whiz Bang, Lisnavane
AJC SIRES' PRODUCE STAKES (7-f)
Soorak, 8.10 (J Pike) Trained by W Laidlaw; 1:28; Theory, Rosina
VRC SIRES' PRODUCE STAKES (7-f)
Scarlet, 8.7 (G Harrison) Trained by H Torr; 1:28.2; Caserta, Prince Tressady
VRC GRAND NATIONAL STEEPLECHASE (3m 1-f)
Mountain God, 12.7 (S Reid) Trained by H Harrison; 6:38.5; Resembler, Monrose

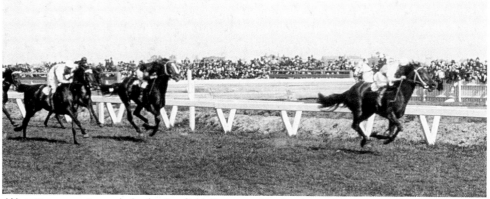

Wynette romps to a win in the Caufield Cup, carrying the tiny weight of 6.11 (SLV).

Spot of magic at Caulfield

Little-known South Australian mare Wynette was quoted at 100/1 in early charts on the 1923 Caulfield Cup. On race day she started second favourite at 5/1.

The Wynette story began in the autumn of '23 when Caulfield trainer Harry Torr was invited to Adelaide on holiday by his cousin Syd Torr, who owned Wynette, then a five-year-old. Harry saw Wynette run a couple of ordinary races in Adelaide but felt that she had some ability. He persuaded cousin Syd to send her to Melbourne.

Harry Torr's perspicacity was rewarded when Wynette easily won first-up, in the Heatherlie Handicap, six weeks before the cup. VATC handicapper J. H. Davis gulped. He had allotted Wynette only 6.11 in the Cup.

After a week of inclement weather, Cup Day dawned bright and sunny for the opening of the new grandstand, burnt down the year before. At the VATC annual meeting, retiring chairman George Woodforde was in a jovial mood, thanking those who had set the stand ablaze – the club collected on the insurance and had been saved the cost of demolition.

On Cup day, reported one scribe, '55 000 people made Caulfield the Mecca of their pilgrimage, pouring out to the racecourse in a seemingly endless stream of trains, trams, cabs, motor cars and char-a-bancs'.

Harry Torr, a licensed trainer since 1904 but neglected by the major events, gave the Wynette mount to his capable 20-year-old apprentice Ted Simmons, who had ridden the previous Caulfield Cup winner, Whittier.

From barrier no. 6, Simmons positioned Wynette beautifully all the way. Turning for home the six-year-old mare was running third. From there she soon assumed control, racing to victory by a length and three-quarters from the Jack Holt–trained Easingwold, who carried 9.1. Third was Yacamunda, the first 100/1 chance to run a place in the cup.

Wynette went on to greater fame, winning the 1924 Adelaide Cup with 9.2. Sadly, Simmons, who won his first race in 1921 at Ballarat, suffered a series of nasty falls in 1924, cutting short a promising career.

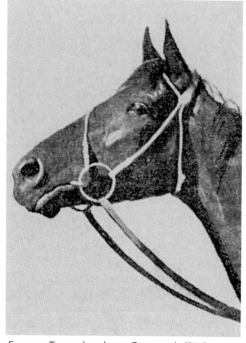

Frances Tressady – busy Cup week (SLV).

Filly's day out

A long-running police strike over the vexed question of promotion, or lack of it, threatened to disrupt the VRC Spring Carnival in 1923. Only 58 police, eight of them mounted, were on hand at Flemington instead of the usual 150. Despite this, the large Derby Day crowd was orderly.

Popular wins by Heroic (Maribyrnong Plate) and Rivoli (Melbourne Stakes) preceded the Victoria Derby, which was a triumph for the only filly in the race, Frances Tressady. She was only the 13th of her sex to win the VRC classic in 69 years. Ridden by Frank Dempsey, his first success in the race, she won by three-quarters of a length from Bobby Lewis's mount Drongo, one of racing's great losers.

TURF TOPICS

Owners' own: Wealthy owners Charles Kellow and Eric Connolly (also one of the country's biggest punters) turned two premier Melbourne sprint races – the Newmarket and Standish Handicaps – into their personal property in the early 1920s. Mr Kellow's Blue Cross, trained by Jack Holt, won the Standish in 1920–21 and the Newmarket in 1921, and Mr Connolly won back-to-back Newmarkets with Rostrum and Sunburst in 1922–23. Sunburst also saluted in the '23 Standish. Rostrum proved a dandy miler, winning the 1922 AJC Epsom.

Crowds flock to a spring meeting at Randwick in the 1920s (SLV).

Heroic, a sensible horse around the stables, was excitable on the racecourse .

A postcard of David, a racing bargain (DA).

The wayward wonder colt

Heroic, a striking looking chestnut by the English sire Valais, was a sensation from the time he was born in 1921. Knocked down to leading owner Jack Corteen for 1300 guineas at the 1923 Sydney yearling sales, he nearly didn't make it to the racecourse. An eye problem – 'recurring ophthalmia' – threatened to blind him. Luckily it was detected by a vet and treated successfully.

Bred by the Moses brothers (F. and W. A.) at Arrowfield stud in NSW, Heroic won the AJC Breeders' Plate at his first start, repaying his purchase price by almost double. Despite two notable hiccups, he then swept to five more wins as a two year-old, three of them in the Maribyrnong Plate and Ascot Vale Stakes at Flemington and the Champagne Stakes at Randwick.

But Heroic the hero, described by trainer Cecil Godby as one of the most sensible horses to pass through his hands, was prone to racetrack tantrums, a trait blamed on his breeding.

Wayward barrier behaviour cost Heroic any chance in the two-year-old classics, the VRC and AJC Sires' Produce Stakes, both over seven furlongs. Starting at 9/4 on, he ran second in the Flemington race but at Randwick he dug his heels in at the start and took off like a buckjumper despite the efforts of jockey Hughie Cairns. To the boos of the big Randwick crowd, Heroic, at even money, came in half a furlong behind the winner, Leslie Wallace. Four days later, he bolted home in the Champagne Stakes, ending his two-year-old days with six wins and more than £22 000 in winnings.

Heroic 'was rather intensely inbred', which may have explained his impatience at the barrier. Heroic's sire, Valais, and his dam, Chersonese, had the same grandsire, Cyllene.

David a Goliath

As stayers go, David was a Goliath, lumping big weights in big races and becoming Australia's best sire of hurdlers and steeplechasers.

In 1923 he carried 9.7 to victory in the Sydney Cup, a Herculean effort that earned him topweight of 9.10 in the Melbourne Cup. He was not equal to the task at Flemington, finishing 13th behind Bitalli.

David, foaled in 1917, had staying blood in his veins, his sire Baverstock being by Victoria Derby winner Maltster out of the great racemare Wakeful. Sold for 40 guineas as a yearling, he earned £32 110 for his owner, Mr O. R. Falkiner.

From 1940 to 1945, five of his progeny won the GN Hurdle at Flemington – Cheery Jack, Saul, Claudette, Zalmon and Bay David. Three of his sons won the GN Steeple – Santa Casa, Giant Killer and Quixotic.

1923 RESULTS

VRC MELBURNE CUP (2m)
Bitalli, 7.0 (A Wilson) Trained by J Scobie; 3:24.25; Rivoli, Accarak
AJC SYDNEY CUP (2m)
David, 9.7 (A Wood) Trained by W Booth; 3:26.5; Heir Apparent, Shillinglee
QTC BRISBANE CUP (2m)
Seremite, 8.4 (J Andrews) 3:35; Warwick Gun, Polardee
SAJC ADELAIDE CUP (13-f)
King Ingoda, 9.7 (A Wilson) Trained by J Scobie; 2:51.5; Chapparal, Mambray Lord
WATC PERTH CUP (2m)
(Not run in 1923)

VATC CAULFIELD CUP (12-f)
Wynette, 6.11 (E Simmons) Trained by HW Toor; 2:33; Easingwold, Yacamunda
VRC AUSTRALIAN CUP (21/4m)
Prince Cox, 7.13 (A Wilson) Trained by F Marsden; 3:56; Sir Andrew, Stalwart
MVRC WS COX PLATE (91/2-f)
Easingwold, 9.4 (G Harrison) Trained by J Holt; 1:57.2; Whittier, Purser
AJC DERBY (12-f)
Ballymena, 8.10 (M McCarten) Trained by FD Jones; 2:33.5; Shrapnel, King Carnival
VRC VICTORIA DERBY (12-f)
Frances Tressady (F Dempsey) Trained by W. Foulsham; 2:33.25; Drongo, Kenilcost

AJC DONCASTER HANDICAP (1m)
The Epicure, 8.2 (J Toohey) Trained by W Booth; 1:38; Duke Isinglass, Etive
VRC NEWMARKET HANDICAP (6-f)
Sunburst, 8.9 (G Harrison) Trained by EA Connolly; 1:12; Easingwold, All Serene
AJC SIRES' PRODUCE STAKES (7-f)
The Monk, 8.10 (G Harrison) Trained by CT Godby; 1:27; Call Bell, Rahiri
VRC SIRES' PRODUCE STAKES (7-f)
King Carnival, 8.10 (H Cairns) Trained by A Foulsham; 1:28.5; Frances Tressady, Coolah
VRC GRAND NATIONAL STEEPLECHASE (3m 1-f)
Kunjolio, 9.0 (D Glennon) Trained by E Whiley; 6:34.5; Wooloo, Monrose

Above, Purser romps home; below right, the Governor General presents the cup (Age).

The Purser sensation

Turning out of the straight in the 1924 Caulfield Cup, Purser, topweight with 9.5 and piloted by Gloaming's jockey George Young for the first time, was last of the 23 runners. Less than two minutes later, after sweeping around the field to win by 2½ lengths, Purser sparked one of the most sensational episodes in Australian turf history.

There was more than a whiff of foul play in the Caulfield air after the race. Purser, an eight-year-old, had been backed from 50/1 to 15/1 despite being declared a non-runner the day before the race. The race-day betting plunge on him sent a buzz around the ring, given the old fellow's inglorious ninth in the Coongy Handicap only three days beforehand when friendless at 33/1. In contrast, at his previous start, he had won the Sydney Handicap at Randwick, a warm favourite at 3/1.

After the Coongy, jockey Hughie Cairns had an eye full of mud and a mouthful of excuses for Purser, saying he had been anchored in the heavy going with his impost of 9.9.

Purser received an icy reception from the Cup crowd of 60 000 on his return to scale, in itself a turnabout for he was a popular horse. Bookmakers, in particular, howled in protest, having been taken to the cleaners as a result of a stable coup. Why, asked rank-and-file punters, had connections scratched The Monk, previously declared the stable elect? Why was Cairns, Purser's regular rider, replaced by Young, who had never ridden at Caulfield, even in a track trial?

Talk of sharp practice concerned trainer Cecil Godby, whose stable was noted for its plunges, especially on horses raced by Purser's owners, George Tye and Jack Corteen. As a result, Godby straight away wrote to the Melbourne papers explaining he had been negotiating to sell The Monk, a recent winner in Sydney, to an Indian sportsman. Terms were not agreed upon until cup eve, when Godby said he sent a cable to the new owner seeking permission to run The Monk in the cup. When permission was not forthcoming, the horse was scratched at 1.55 p.m. on race day. Godby, opined one paper, would have saved a lot of unpleasantness if he had mentioned this before, not after, the race.

On the Tuesday after the cup, VRC stewards opened a retrospective inquiry into Purser's run in the Coongy Handicap. Two days later Tye, Corteen, Godby, Purser and jockey Cairns were disqualified for 12 months from 23 October. No horse could meet its engagement if entered in the ownership of Tye or Corteen.

The two men owned 22 horses. Mr Corteen was the sole owner of the turf's latest star, Heroic. After wins in the AJC Derby and Caulfield Guineas, Heroic was odds-on for the Victoria Derby and 4/1 favourite for the Melbourne Cup. When all four disqualified persons lost their appeals, the VRC committee rejected Heroic's nomination for the Derby and the Cup, meaning pre-post punters did their money cold.

A distressed Mr Corteen put Heroic, who had won nine races for him, up for auction. He was knocked down to another notable owner, Charles Kellow, for a record 16 000 guineas. Mr Kellow sent him to Jack Holt, who did not race Heroic until early in 1925.

As for Purser, that was it for a gallant campaigner, who came up smiling spring, summer and autumn, and sometimes in the winter. Other than the Caulfield Cup, his 19 wins from 60 starts included the Moonee Valley Cup, the AJC All-Aged Stakes, and the Herbert Power Handicap in which he downed Eurythmic. The drama that followed the Caulfield Cup clouded Purser's achievement of carrying a record 9.5 to victory.

Purser was cleverly named. He was by Sea Prince from Paper Money. Pursers, of course, were officers on ocean liners, dispensing goodwill and comfort to passengers.

TURF TOPICS

Women come to blows: The unedifying spectacle of women trading punches provided an unusual diversion for lawn patrons after the running of the 1924 Cup. Rain was falling. Suddenly, the attention of portion of the crowd was turned from discussion of Backwood's win and the unpleasant change of weather by the sound of excited women's voices. Dissension developed among a party of five women and the argument was prosecuted with more than verbal effort. The contestants came to blows and hats were knocked off and trampled on the wet ground. Clothes were torn and a policeman who tried to restore order was belted by one of the belligerents. Eventually peace, or at any rate an armistice, broke out.

Wrong jockey: When Swordbin finished third in the Victoria Steeplechase at Flemington on Derby day, all seemed in order – but the horse had finished the race with a different jockey. The horse fell on the first lap, losing barrier jockey T. Butler, and was remounted by a bystander, who happened to be a jockey named S. T. Murphy.

Murphy reined in Swordbin after the horse had gone some distance, mounted him and completed the course. His action only became apparent at the weigh-in. Swordbin was disqualified and Murphy was hauled before the stewards for trying to mislead them. The race was won by King's High, who four days later won the steeplechase on Oaks Day.

Randwick, with (l–r) the St Leger, the Members, the Public and the Official Stands (SLV).

Scenes from the South Australian Jockey Club's spring meeting at Morphettville. At right, Derby winner Wycherley. The bottom picture shows the Derby riders waiting for their horses (SLV).

The splendour of the VRC spring meeting.

Doyen of racecallers, Ike Treloar.

Bob your head Charlie!

'They're racing.' This expression first hit the airwaves in 1924 when Arnold 'Ike' Treloar, in not-so-dulcet tones, called a Port Adelaide racing club program for radio station 5CL in Adelaide.

Treloar's love of racing began as a boy and blossomed when he won £100. A gift of a tenner from his mother was plonked on a 10/1 shot that won.

Clubs were slow to cotton on to the merit of broadcasts. Initially, Treloar called the races from outside the course, from a tree or temporary platform, sometimes in the rain. Clubs used every device to block his view, including large tarpaulins. At Oakbank, a lofty tree at a brewery gave him an eyrie's view of events.

Treloar's problems did not evaporate when he was accepted on-course. From his vantage point in open grandstands, the microphone picked up the roars and groans of the crowd. When the large hat of a high-society lady obstructed his view, the millinery was squashed over her face.

Treloar lacked the polish of later prac-titioners, but he was always colourful. 'They're goin' 'ead and 'ead,' he cried one day at Victoria Park as two runners settled down to fight out a race. As they hit the line, he bellowed: 'What you call it … that thing of Skinny Woods has just got up.' Everyone knew who had won.

One day at Gawler, a friend stood up in front of Treloar during a close finish. 'Bob your head, Charlie!' yelled Ike. Legend has it that a bloke called Charlie, crouched over a wireless in a country pub, took Treloar's advice and fell over.

Backwood, and (inset) trainer Dick Bradfield (ARM).

Drongo (at rear) after the Derby (SLV).

Bradfield's fourth Cup

Comedy King, owned by the flamboyant Sol Green, was the first imported horse to win the Melbourne Cup, in 1911. Name the second? It may seem uncharitable but Backwood was not regarded as being in the upper echelons of Cup winners, even though he cost his owners, Messrs W. Clarke, A. Hughes and E. L. Baillieu, the not inconsiderable sum of 2500 guineas.

Trained by Dick Bradfield, Backwood was fancied in the 1923 Cup, but finished only 10th. More indifferent form enabled him to get into the 1924 Cup with only 8.2, a postage stamp for a six-year-old entire.

Not for the first or last time, the Hotham Handicap on Derby day alerted punters to Backwood's Cup chances. He dead-heated for third behind the winner, Lilypond, and was backed from 12/1 to 8/1 for the big race. On the day, all vantage points were taken to observe horses and jockeys do battle.

Powerfully built with a claret-coloured coat, Backwood was not the most handsome individual. Nor was he anything more than a plodder. So jockey Bunty Brown allowed him plenty of time to settle down in the Cup. They made their long, steady run from the nine-furlong post and won the day by a head from the Moonee Valley Cup winner Stand By, ridden by Bobby Lewis. Third place went to the three-year-old Spearfelt, the 9/4 favourite, though initially Brown Rajah was semaphored as running third. The judge amended the placings after a number of people complained to the stewards.

After the Cup, it was agreed that full credit for Backwood's win must go to veteran Melbourne trainer Bradfield, a patient, well-respected man whose thoroughness with his charges was reflected in the neat and tidy appearance of his stable, which he seldom left. His methods paid off, for Backwood was his fourth Melbourne Cup winner, the others being Patron (1894), The Victory (1902) and Night Watch (1918). Bradfield was only 'a lad' of 27 when he saddled up Patron.

No, not a Drongo

A Drongo is a half-wit, a fool. The derisory term, part of our folklore, hails from the racetrack … from a horse called Drongo, who never won a race in 37 starts.

But he wasn't a complete no-hoper. He took on the best of company and on two occasions almost had the last laugh.

By imported stallion Lanius, who sired the 1924 Moonee Valley Cup winner Stand By, Drongo ran a sterling race in the 1923 Victoria Derby, going down to classy filly Frances Tressady by only three-quarters of a length.

Drongo twice lost by a neck – to King Pan in the 12-furlong Northcote Handicap at Flemington in March 1924 – the day a horse called Windbag ran second in the Ascot Vale Stakes – and to Wycherley in the SAJC Handicap (12f) in Adelaide in May 1925. He even ran in the 1924 Melbourne Cup, starting at 25/1 and finishing near the tail.

Drongo's 11 minor placings would have earned him close to $100 000 today.

1924 RESULTS

VRC MELBOURNE CUP (2m)
Backwood, 8.2 (P Brown) Trained by R Bradfield; 3:26.5; Stand By, Spearfelt
AJC SYDNEY CUP (2m)
Scarlet, 7.6 (J Crowe) Trained by W Booth; 3:28.25; Stony, King Of The Forest
QTC BRISBANE CUP (2m)
Balaton, 8.0 (J Toohey) 3:38.5; Seremite, Ardglen
SAJC ADELAIDE CUP (13-f)
Wynette, 9.2 (E Simmons) Trained by HW Torr; 2:45; Graculus, Buffline
WATC PERTH CUP (2m)
Lilypond, 7.10 (F Staker) Trained by J Jeffery; 3:27.4; Char, Feathernest

VATC CAULFIELD CUP (12-f)
Purser, 9.5 (G Young) Trained by CT Godby; 2:33; Feathernest, All Sunshine
VRC AUSTRALIAN CUP (2 1/4m)
Accarak, 7.8 (W Duncan) Trained by H McCalman; 3:53.25; Jackstaff, El Dorado
MVRC WS COX PLATE (9 ½-f)
The Night Patrol, 9.4 (G Young) Trained by J Scobie; 1:59.2; Whittier, Demades
AJC DERBY (12-f)
Heroic, 8.10 (H Cairns) Trained by CT Godby; 2:34.25; Nigger Minstrel, Spearfelt
VRC VICTORIA DERBY (12-f)
Spearfelt (G Young) Trained by V O'Neill; 2:35; Royal Charter, Versine

AJC DONCASTER HANDICAP (1m)
Whittier, 9.5 (F Dempsey) Trained by H McCalman; 1:36.5; Trimacre, The Monk
VRC NEWMARKET HANDICAP (6-f)
Quintus, 8.0 (J Munro) Trained by W Burke; 1:11.5; Blackadder, Una Carlos
AJC SIRES' PRODUCE STAKES (7-f)
Leslie Wallace, 8.10 (J Munro) Trained by SR Lamond; 1:25.5; Versine, Brimming
VRC SIRES' PRODUCE STAKES (7-f)
Arendal, 8.10 (W Duncan) Trained by F Foulsham; 1:27.2; Heroic, Olola
VRC GRAND NATIONAL STEEPLECHASE (3m 1-f)
Fleetstone, 11.12 (Mr C Grice) Trained by N Godby; 6:12; Haoma, Berribee

Byron Moore, VRC secretary for 45 years, created the style and substance that made Flemington a world-class racecourse (ARM).

Moore's Flemington – 'a place of beauty'

The Victoria Racing Club was fortunate to have Robert Bagot and Henry Byron Moore as its first two secretaries. Between them, they presided over the well-being of racing and Flemington for 65 years.

Byron Moore took over when Bagot died in 1881 and held office for 45 years. He retired in 1925, aged 86, and died a few weeks later. Even in his 80s, he was always at his desk at 7.30 a.m.

Like Bagot, Byron Moore was a surveyor. Both enriched the racing scene. Whereas Bagot was forthright, often brusque, Byron Moore, an Englishman by birth, was refined and always impeccably dressed.

To everyone's delight, Byron Moore spent the first few weeks in his new job sprucing up the VRC offices – new desks, ink wells etc.

Asked if the VRC would ever find a suitable replacement for Bagot, Chairman C. B. Fisher replied: 'I think we have found one. I really think we have.'

Before long Flemington had more stands, a vice-regal suite, a lavish press box in line with the judge's stand, and improved refreshment and toilet facilities. And roses, for Byron Moore was a gardener. And trees and shrubs on either side of the roadway leading to the course. And lower down, more trees to obscure the view of touts spying on track gallops. They sold their news to newspapers, to the annoyance of the committee. Needless to say, the press, barracking for the touts, criticised Byron Moore, until it was realised that the trees were deciduous, bearing no leaves for half the year. The shrewd secretary had used

nature to outfox his critics.

Byron Moore's vision, too grand in the eyes of some, was to 'ensure that Flemington remained unchallenged as the finest racecourse in Australia'. Only a sceptic could say he failed in his duty.

One of Moore's greatest initiatives was to attract women to the races, in the belief that where they went the men would follow. After overhearing two women complain that Cup Day was no place to wear one's best clothes, he called on the newspaper editors of the day to make Oaks Day a day of high fashion. His entrepreneurial skills worked brilliantly. In the space of two years, the Oaks became the fashion event of the year. The fashion stores and newspapers, through advertisements, did very nicely.

Windbag – ungainly, but the gamest horse to look through a bridle

Windbag, from the Kia Ora Stud, Scone (NSW), was bought by prominent New Zealand racing man Ian Duncan, whose commissioner paid 150 guineas for him at the 1923 Sydney sales.

First, Duncan was impressed by 'the rein and heart room of the colt'. A closer examination revealed less-than-perfect legs, so the quaintly named son of Magpie–Charleville was offered for sale. When the top bid was only 100 guineas, he was 'knocked down' to Bob Miller, brother of Kia Ora part-owner Percy Miller.

Bob Miller was reluctant to take him, but for the sake of the stud accepted the bay colt, and he was trained by former New Zea-

lander George Price.

In the spring of 1925, Windbag won four wfa races in Sydney, then journeyed south, running third in the Melbourne Stakes on Derby Day. Then came the Melbourne Cup.

Turning for home, there were only two horses in it, with Manfred (Frank Dempsey) leading Windbag (Jim Munro). A furlong out it was Manfred by a length but Windbag, despite his 9.2, slowly wore him down to win by a half-length in Australian record time of 3:22¾.

George Price said Windbag, whose disposition matched his ability, was the gamest horse that ever looked through a bridle. His name was on his old stall long after his death.

Billy Duncan, long-suffering jockey, aboard the difficult but brilliant Manfred (Age).

Manfred, cranky champion

Brilliant one day, an erratic no-hoper the next. That was Manfred, the enigmatic son of Valais who won 11 races and £28 830 in stake money for owner Ben Chaffey.

Manfred's most remarkable victory was in the 1925 AJC Derby. With Bill Duncan in the saddle, Manfred was 5/2 on favourite. When the big Randwick crowd cried 'they're off', they were – all except Manfred. The handsome bay just stood there. As turf writer Frank O'Loghlen noted: 'Manfred had a look around. In my opinion it was Manfred who woke up and took charge of the position.'

Manfred walked five or six steps, and then trotted. He sidled halfway across the track when the field had gone half a furlong.

Manfred gradually made up the ground. Turning for home Manfred, given his head, bounded home by a length and a half. At his next start, Manfred (11/4 on) stood flat-footed at the barrier in the Caulfield Guineas, taking no part. Frank Dempsey took over in the Cox Plate. Still cranky, Manfred almost knocked the field down before settling, but got the verdict by a short head. The crowd loved him despite his manners.

The return of Heroic

Chapter two of Heroic's colourful career, a sequel to the Purser case, began in February 1925 when he carried Charles Kellow's colours of green and gold for the first time. At 16 000 guineas, Heroic turned out to be a good investment for the motor car magnate. Now trained by Jack Holt, he won 12 more races. He won his first race for Mr Kellow in the Autumn Stakes at Randwick in April, 1925, then, reverting to his cantankerous days, played up at the barrier and was unplaced in the All-Aged Stakes, won by The Hawk.

One of Heroic's finest wins was in the 1926 Newmarket Handicap with 9.8. He proved his versatility by also taking the WS Cox Plate (9½f), the AJC Cumberland Stakes (14f) and the VRC King's Plate (2m).

Of the string of wfa races Heroic won, none rivalled his defeat of Gloaming in the 1924 Chelmsford Stakes at Randwick. The start before, Heroic was left at the barrier in the Warwick Stakes, so wary punters wanted no part of him in the Chelmsford. So what did Heroic do? He walloped Gloaming, the 10/9 on favourite, by a length and a half at 5/1.

Heroic ended his racing days at five, having won 21 of his 51 starts and earned £38 062. Chapter three then began – a distinguished stud career. He headed the Australian sires' list a record seven times and sired the likes of Hall Mark, Ajax, Nuffield and Hua.

1925 RESULTS

VRC MELBOURNE CUP (2m)
Windbag, 9.2 (J. Munro) Trained by G. Price; 3:22.25; Manfred, Pilliewinkie
AJC SYDNEY CUP (2m)
Lilypond, 9.0 (W Duncan) Trained by J Holt; 3:26.75; Windbag, Solidify
QTC BRISBANE CUP (2m)
Te Kara, 9.10 (J O'Shea) 3:26.5; Mountain Song, Alabama
SAJC ADELAIDE CUP (13-f)
Stralia, 6.10 (H Badger) Trained by H Morgan; 2:49.5; The Tyrant, Dependence
WATC PERTH CUP (2m)
(1 January 1925) Mercato, 7.6 (R Morley) Trained by T Tighe; Time: 3:27.2; Eracre, Char

WATC PERTH CUP (2m)
(30 December 1925) Great Applause, 6.11 (L Marrable) Trained by WD Atwell; 3:28.4; Prince MacDonald, Eracre
VATC CAULFIELD CUP (12-f)
Whittier, 9.0 (J Pike) Trained by H McCalman; 2:34; Raith, Lemina
VRC AUSTRALIAN CUP (2¼m)
Answer, 6.8 (P O'Meally) Trained by G Maher; 3:53.5; Accarak, Suomi
MVRC WS COX PLATE (9½-f)
Manfred, 7.11 (F Dempsey) Trained by H McCalman; 1:57; The Night Patrol, Pantheon
AJC DERBY (12-f)
Manfred, 8.10 (W Duncan) Trained by H McCalman; 2:35; Petunia, Tibbie

VRC VICTORIA DERBY (12-f)
Manfred (J Dempsey) Trained by H McCalman; 2:31.5; Belgamba, Hampden
AJC DONCASTER HANDICAP (1m)
Fujisan, 8.1 (G Harrison) Trained by C Hodson; 1:38.7; King Cyllene, All Sunshine
VRC NEWMARKET HANDICAP (6-f)
Valiard, 7.8 (R Marsden) Trained by F Marsden; 1:11.75; Adrift, Lausanne
AJC SIRES' PRODUCE STAKES (7-f)
Los Gatos, 8.7 (W Duncan) Trained by A Foulsham; 1:27.5; Poetaster, Yule Cake
VRC SIRES' PRODUCE STAKES (7-f)
Poetaster, 8.7 (A Cooper) Trained by G Maher; 1:25.7; Petunia, Manfred
VRC GRAND NATIONAL STEEPLECHASE (3m 1-f)
Dundalk, 10.6 (T Butler) Trained by S Reid; 6:22.5; Mailman, Palbi

A sketch of Valicare, a Sydney favourite.

Manfred: on his best behaviour.

A flying machine

Not many horses thrashed Windbag at weight-for-age. Valicare did so, by eight lengths, in the Rawson Stakes (9f) at Rosehill in 1926. But she was exceptional, the fastest and best of her sex since the mighty Wakeful.

The annihilation of Windbag was Valicare's sixth win from six starts, all as a three-year-old. The daughter of Valais, trained by Bayley Payten, was the darling of the Sydney race crowds, so much so that two weeks after she had beaten Windbag she was sent out at 5/4 on in the Doncaster Handicap at Randwick.

Competing against the best milers in the land, Valicare, ridden by Jimmy Munro, walloped them by 1½ lengths with 8.9 – 3 lb more than weight-for-age – in 1:37¾.

At her next start, four days later, she beat two good gallopers, Top Gallant and The Night Patrol, in the All-Aged Stakes at Randwick. It was time for a spell.

Valicare resumed in the wfa Warwick Stakes (1m) at Warwick Farm and for the first time in eight starts lost – by a short neck to her 'old' rival Windbag. Valicare was in front at the distance, with Windbag (9.12) wide on the track finishing straight and fast, to the roars of the crowd. At the post it was Windbag by a short neck.

Manfred behaves

Manfred, whose AJC Derby win in 1925 was still a talking point 12 months later, was up to his old antics at the start of 1926, ignoring the starter in both the St Leger Stakes and Essendon Stakes at Flemington.

Spelled, he left his bad manners in the paddock. When he resumed in the spring, he ran second to Heroic in the Memsie Stakes at Caulfield, then won the VRC October Stakes and VATC Caulfield Stakes.

With their fingers crossed, punters plunged heavily on Ben Chaffey's four-year-old in the Caulfield Cup, despite his impost of 9.6. At 5/4, he was the shortest-priced favourite in the history of the race.

And Manfred never gave his supporters a moment's worry, striding to the front a half-mile from home and winning nicely by a half-length from The Banker. In victory, Manfred set a weight-carrying record for a four-year-old and stamped himself as a champion, albeit an erratic one.

He missed the 1926 Melbourne Cup, in which he had 10.1, because of a leg injury suffered when he won the Melbourne Stakes on Derby Day. Manfred had two more starts, or non-starts, in 1927, being left at the post both times. Douglas Barrie wrote that of his 28 starts Manfred 'consented to win 11'. And £28 830 in stake money.

At stud, Manfred was a failure initially, then sired The Trump, winner of the 1937 Caulfield and Melbourne Cups.

1926 RESULTS

VRC MELBOURNE CUP (2m)
Spearfelt, 9.3 (H Cairns) Trained by V O'Neill; 3:22.25; Naos, Pantheon
AJC SYDNEY CUP (2m)
Murray King, 7.2 (S McNamara) Trained by G Price; 3:26; Caserta, Naos
QTC BRISBANE CUP (2m)
Piastoon, 8.4 (A Davis) 3:27; Sum King, In Petto
SAJC ADELAIDE CUP (13-f)
Spearer, 8.6 (A Reed) Trained by H Gymer; 2:47.5; Stralia, Caserta
WATC PERTH CUP (2m)
(Not run in 1926)

VATC CAULFIELD CUP (12-F)
Manfred, 9.6 (R Lewis) Trained by H McCalman; 2:32.5; The Banker, Royal Charter
VRC AUSTRALIAN CUP (2 ¼m)
Pilliewinkle, 9.6 (G Young) Trained by J Scobie; 3:51.75; Lemina, Valbee
MVRC WS COX PLATE (9½-f)
Heroic, 9.4 (H Cairns) Trained by J Holt; 1:58; Limerick, Metellus
AJC DERBY (12-f)
Rampion, 8.10 (S Cracknell) Trained by F Williams; 2:33; Limerick, Raron
VRC VICTORIA DERBY (12-f)
Rampion (S Cracknell) Trained by F Williams; 2:32.5; Thracian, Limerick

AJC DONCASTER HANDICAP (1m)
Valicare, 8.9 (J Munro) Trained by B Payten; 1:37.7; Valiant, Irish Prince
VRC NEWMARKET HANDICAP (6-f)
Heroic, 9.8 (H Cairns) Trained by J Holt; 1:11.75; Perspective, Fujisan
AJC SIRES' PRODUCE STAKES (7-f)
Cyden, 8.7 (A Wilson) Trained by J Scobie; 1:26.5; Lady Constance, Cromwell
VRC SIRES' PRODUCE STAKES (7-f)
Rampion, 8.10 (S Cracknell) Trained by F Williams; 1:25.5; Cyden, Cromwell
VRC GRAND NATIONAL STEEPLECHASE (3m 1-f)
Clan Robert, 11.8 (E Moon) Trained by H McCalman; 6:13.5; Namera, Epergne

Maurice McCarten (right) with trainer R. Sinclair (left) and owner G. W. Badman (Age).

Limerick, equine man's man

Jockey-turned-trainer Maurice McCarten was unequivocal – Limerick was the greatest horse he rode. Though for sheer speed, he plumbed for Ajax.

Limerick, by imported sire Limond out of Medley, was bred (and raced) by popular New Zealand turf identity Mr H. H. Knight, who lived south of Christchurch.

Limerick, unplaced at his first three starts as a two-year-old, came to Australia in 1926 and was placed in the AJC and Victoria Derbys, both won by Trivalve. He was also unplaced in Spearfelt's Melbourne Cup.

Limerick struck top form in 1927, winning 11 of his 16 starts. Trained by F. D. Jones,

he raced in hot weight-for-age company, beating Windbag in the Rosehill Rawson Stakes (9f), then downing Amounis in the Warwick Stakes (9f) and Gothic and Amounis in the Rosehill Hill Stakes (9f).

Other big wins included the AJC St Leger and the AJC Plate (2¼m). McCarten, who described Limerick as the equine equivalent of a 'man's man' – he didn't care for fuss – reckoned the horse's greatest win was in the 1928 King's Cup at Flemington with 9.5.

Limerick had shelly feet, so on occasions was a little lame, but the impediment didn't stop him from winning 28½ races (13 of them in a row) and £38729 in stake money.

Hot tip empties stand

Thanks to a careless smoker and a crack in the floor, the Guineas Stand at Caulfield was destroyed by fire on Oakleigh Plate day, 1927. A dropped cigarette butt found its way into the ceiling of the cloakroom. Soon drinkers in the long Guineas bar were smoked out. A new, bigger stand was built, but only half of it was available eight months later for the Caulfield Cup, which was won by 20/1 chance Textile. (pictures: ARM)

TURF TOPICS

Fourth time lucky: Having only his fourth ride in a race, Balmain-born apprentice Edgar Britt, aged 14, won on Gypsy King at Canterbury.

Lucky 13th: The Frank McGrath–trained Amounis, likened to Eurythmic for his powerful finishes, just got there in the 1927 WS Cox Plate, winning by a neck. It was his lucky 13th win.

Everyone's a winner: Cattle king Sir Sidney Kidman won the 1927 Moonee Valley Cup

with Silvius, and Manfred's owner Ben Chaffey led in the VRC Oaks winner Ninbela. VRC chairman L. K. S. Mackinnon won the Williamstown Cup with Star d'Or and Sol Green's fine sprinter Gothic won the VRC Newmarket Handicap.

Derby deeds: As a young horse, the well-performed Queenslander High Syce won the Queensland Derby. He won 21 races from 30 starts in his home state.

Top import: The imported Valais (Cicero –

Lily of the Valley) was the top sire in 1926–27, for the fourth year running, with 32 winners of 62 races and £86910 in stakes. Valais' chief winners were Heroic, Manfred, Valicare and Fujisan. Second was Magpie – 39; 76; £63514.

Squizzy's last stand: Squizzy Taylor, who was accused of starting the 1922 grandstand fire at Caulfield, was killed in a shootout with fellow Melbourne criminal Snowy Cutmore in 1927.

Bob Lewis gets Trivalve to the post.

Bob Lewis: starved, but triumphant (ARM).

Trivalve and Bob Lewis

For six days before the 1927 Melbourne Cup, top jockey Bob Lewis – a determined, wiry veteran of 49 – lived on water alone. He was hell-bent on getting down to 7.6 to ride the three-year-old chestnut Trivalve.

Trivalve was owned by well-known breeder Ernest E. D. Clarke, who kept the Cyklon–Trey colt because he had Carbine's blood on both sides of his pedigree. It was a wise decision. Trained by the incomparable James Scobie, Trivalve was one of the fancies for the Melbourne Cup on the strength of wins in the AJC and Victoria Derbys.

Courage was one quality Trivalve had in abundance, which he called on when downing 18 rivals in the AJC Derby at his first start as a three-year-old. Only the strong riding of Lewis, renowned for his wrists of steel, gained Trivalve the day by a neck from Winalot.

Trivalve had an easier time in the VRC classic, beating the nearest of his six rivals by three lengths. But he was not rated as a champion colt, hence his starting price of 6/1 in the Cup.

Once more his dogged spirit prevailed. With a furlong to go down the long Flemington straight, the 3/1 favourite Silvius grabbed the lead. Half a furlong out, Lewis popped the question to Trivalve and the colt, as usual, responded magnificently, going on to beat Silvius, owned by Sir Sidney Kidman, by a length. Sol Green's Son O'Mine flew home wide out to run third.

An exhausted Lewis slumped in the saddle after passing the post. But he soon recovered. Usually a dour little man, this time he smiled broadly and waved his cap to the delighted crowd of 101 000 on returning to scale.

Asked later if he was tired, Lewis said: 'Sure. Why wouldn't I be at my age after starving myself for six days?'

Trivalve gave Lewis his fourth Cup win, after Patrobas, Artilleryman and Backwood. For Ernest Clarke it was his first.

Trivalve, who came from obscurity, ended up back there. He won three races after the Cup, then lost all form and was retired to stud. None of his stock repeated his remarkable feats. Paradoxically, the winner of eight races from only 20 starts and £28 375 finished his days as a station sire in Central Australia. He died in the Northern Territory of snakebite.

The Kaiser's colt

It's a probable 6/5, as Damon Runyon would say, that Trivalve would not have been born but for World War I. His sire, the German horse Cyklon, was owned by Kaiser Wilhelm II. Before the war, the Kaiser sent Cyklon to race in England, where he won no fewer than six Maiden Plates. They were open to horses that had not won a race at the time of entry.

When war broke out, Cyklon was impounded. He was bought by Australian jockey Frank Dempsey, acting as an agent, from the Department of Fisheries. Some fish! Dempsey had ridden Cyklon in Germany and was impressed by the Spearmint colt.

Raced by South Australian Mrs Richard Hawker, Cyklon ran third in the 1915 Caulfield Cup and won the VATC St George Stakes and the Adelaide Cup (13f).

Silks worn by W. Scanlon on Textile in the 1927 Caulfield Cup, at the Australian Racing Museum, Caulfield Racecourse.

1927 RESULTS

VRC MELBOURNE CUP (2m)
Trivalve, 7.6 (R. Lewis) Trained by J Scobie; 3:24; Silvius, Son O'Mine
AJC SYDNEY CUP (2m)
Piastoon, 7.12 (S Davidson) Trained by E Fisher; 3:33.75; Limerick, Tibbie
QTC BRISBANE CUP (2m)
Kentle, 6.12 ((P Foley) 3:29.7; Coin Nut, Rawhetu
SAJC ADELAIDE CUP (13-f)
Three Kings, 8.3 (H Jones) Trained by F Godby; 2:45.5; Valbee, Au Fait
WATC PERTH CUP (2m)
(1 January 1927) Au Fait, 6.11 (J Miller) Trained by A Gosden; 3:26.2; Char, Maple

WATC PERTH CUP (2m)
(31 December 1927) Phoenix Park, 8.0 (L Marrable) Trained by JW McLarty; 3:25.75; Pica Pica, Spearage
VATC CAULFIELD CUP (12-f)
Textile, 8.3 (W Scanlon) Trained by EJ O'Dwyer; 2:32.5; Affirm, Star D'Or
VRC AUSTRALIAN CUP (2 ¼m)
Spearfelt, 9.13 (H Cairns) Trained by V O'Neill; 3:51.25; Naos, Pantheon
MVRC WS COX PLATE (9½-f)
Amounis, 9.1 (J Toohey) Trained by F McGrath; 2:00.5; Avant Courier, Gothic
AJC DERBY (12-f)
Trivalve, 8.10 (R Lewis) Trained by J Scobie; 2:33; Winalot, Black Duchess

VRC VICTORIA DERBY (12-f)
Trivalve (R Lewis) Trained by J Scobie; 2:33; Statesman, Avant Courier
AJC DONCASTER HANDICAP (1m)
Don Moon, 7.12 (K Daniels) Trained by R Baillie; 1:42; Horoscope, Garula
VRC NEWMARKET HANDICAP (6-f)
Gothic, 8.10 (A Reed) Trained by L Robertson; 1:12.5; Biskra, Chrystal
AJC SIRES' PRODUCE STAKES (7-f)
Royal Feast, 8.10 (M McCarten) Trained by R Sinclair; 1:32; Prime Don, The Wensum
VRC SIRES' PRODUCE STAKES (7-f)
Royal Feast, 8.10 (M McCarten) Trained by R Sinclair; 1:27.2; Trivalve, Sion
VRC GRAND NATIONAL STEEPLECHASE (3m 1-f)
Nyangay, 9.11 (F Leonard) Trained by H Myers; 6:18.5; Clan Robert, Namera

Gothic surges to win the Newmarket with style.

WITH COMPLIMENTS FROM

SOL. GREEN
MELBOURNE

Sol Green's calling card (ARM).

Kelso and Statesman

Patience is not always a virtue in racing. It was for veteran Sydney trainer Bill Kelso, who for years kept a mare called Marcelle at the famous Kia Ora Stud in NSW.

In 1925 Marcelle (by Martagon) had a chestnut foal at foot. An easy mover, he was to be called Statesman – an obvious but nonetheless imposing choice, since he was by the imported stallion Demosthenes. Students of history, of course, will recall that Demosthenes was a famous Athenian orator and statesman.

Statesman impressed jockey Jim Pike as a potential stayer in the 1927 AJC Derby. He was unplaced, then beat all but Trivalve in the Victoria Derby and ran an unlucky sixth in Trivalve's Melbourne Cup.

With Pike's assessment in mind, Kelso kept Statesman out of the firing line for most of 1928. In June, the rising four-year-old was given an impost of only 8.0 in the Melbourne Cup.

Statesman resumed racing in September, winning third up over 11 furlongs at Randwick. Then it was off to Melbourne where he ran fifth in the Cox Plate and a good third to Gothic and Amounis in the wfa Melbourne Stakes on Derby Day.

The latter turned out to be a winning trial, jockey Maurice McCarten telling Kelso that Statesman had stretched out well 'when the race was over'.

The words were prophetic. Statesman (7/2), ridden by Jim Munro, won the Cup by four lengths from Sol Green's colt Strephon (9/4 favourite), the Victoria Derby winner. It was the third year in a row that the wealthy Mr Green had owned a minor placegetter in the Cup.

Gothic's second Newmarket

Sprinter Gothic, renowned for his bulldog tenacity and prepared by the astute Lou Roberston, a neighbour of Jack Holt at Mordialloc, was responsible for one of the most amazing performances on the Victorian turf when he won the Newmarket Handicap for the second year running in 1928.

With less than two furlongs to go, reported the *Age*, jockey Jim Pike 'was in such dire trouble it seemed he would have to pull his mount up for fear of galloping on the heels of those in front of him'.

Gothic was reduced almost to a canter but miraculously an opening presented itself and the topweight, carrying the huge impost of 9.10, began what seemed to be a futile chase after the leaders, Thracian Belle and Chrystal.

'With set lips and determination in his heart, Pike called upon the 7/2 favourite for the effort. As if some of the rider's indomitable spirit had been transferred to him, Gothic answered the call and with long sweeping strides set off in pursuit.

'Amid tremendous excitement and encouraging cheers, Gothic caught Thracian Belle and forged ahead in the last few strides to win by a head. A well-earned ovation greeted horse and rider on return to scale.'

Gothic, foaled in England and imported to Australia by bookmaker Sol Green, shot to prominence in the autumn of 1927 when he won the Newmarket for the first time. Though a four year-old, it was only his seventh start. At five and six, he was in rare form, winning the 1928 VATC Futurity Stakes, a second Newmarket and seven wfa races, including the Memsie Stakes, CB Fisher Plate and William Reid Stakes.

Pike, who rode him more often than not, told Green after his second Newmarket win: 'I had £75 on him (at 5/2). If I'd had it, I would have put £10 000 on him.' Replied bookmaker Green: 'I'd like you to remember how I made my money. And got where I am today. It all came from mugs like you backing racehorses.'

Gothic won 14 races for Green and £20 430 in stake money.

1928 RESULTS

VRC MELBOURNE CUP (2m)
Statesman, 8.0 (J Munro) Trained by W Kelson; 3:23.25; Strephon, Demost
AJC SYDNEY CUP (2m)
Winalot, 8.2 (J Toohey) Trained by JW Cook; 3:32.25; Tangible, Strongbow
QTC BRISBANE CUP (2m)
Canning Queen, 7.9 (A Davis) 3:22.5; In Petto, Rhymond
SAJC ADELAIDE CUP (13-f)
Altimeter, 7.4 (A Wilson) Trained by H McCalman; 2:44; Benoni, Finsbury
WATC PERTH CUP (2m)
(Not run in 1928)

VATC CAULFIELD CUP (12-f)
Maple, 8.7 (W Duncan) Trained by J Holt; 2:33.25; Black Duchess, Gothic
VRC AUSTRALIAN CUP (2 ¼m)
Sea Money. 6.10 (J O'Brien) Trained by G Murrell; 3:53; Frilford, Kingun
MVRC WS COX PLATE (9 ½-f)
Highland, 9.1 (W Duncan) Trained by J Holt; 2:06.7; Ramulus, Fourth Hand
AJC DERBY (12-f)
Prince Humphrey, 8.10 (J Munro) Trained by J Jamieson; 2:32.75; Mollison, Oatendale
VRC VICTORIA DERBY (12-f)
Strephon (J Pike) Trained by L Robertson; 2:33; Yodelist, Balmerino

AJC DONCASTER HANDICAP (1m)
Simeon's Fort, 8.5 (W Duncan) Trained by MT McGrath; 1:45.2; Aorangi, Don Moon
VRC NEWMARKET HANDICAP (6-f)
Gothic, 9.10 (J Pike) Trained by L Robertson; 1:13.5; Thracian Belle, Chrystal
AJC SIRES' PRODUCE STAKES (7-f)
Mollison, 8.10 (J Daniels) Trained by F Foulsham; 1:32; Coercion, Ramulus
VRC SIRES' PRODUCE STAKES (7-f)
Mollison, 8.7 (J Daniels) Trained by F Foulsham; 1:26.7; Stanza, Staidan
VRC GRAND NATIONAL STEEPLECHASE (3m 1-f)
Namera, 10.1 (S Warner) Trained by N Turnbull; 6:11.5; Nyangay, Oral Treaty

George Lambert, The Tirranna Picnic Race Meeting, 1929 (University of Melbourne Art Collection, gift of the Russell & Mab Grimwade Bequest).

Queenslander a good buy for Mrs Buxton

On the opening day of the 1929 VATC Spring Carnival, Melbourne owner Mrs Rita Buxton had the distinction of winning the Caulfield Stakes with High Syce and the Toorak Handicap with Highland, winner of the Cox Plate the year before.

Both horses were trained by Jack Holt. Both were by the imported Highfield, who stood at Queensland's Canning Downs stud.

Mrs Buxton was only 28 but had been racing horses for seven years. On her 21st birthday a family friend had presented her with two racehorses.

Mrs Buxton's horses won good races for many years, but 1929 was a vintage year for her. Twelve months earlier, trainer Holt had contacted top turf journalist Bert Wolfe, then the chief steward in Queensland, for his opinion of High Syce, winner of 21 races as a two

and three-year-old in Brisbane – the Sires, Guineas, Derby and St Leger etc.

Wolfe gave High Syce the nod, cabling Holt: 'You could not buy any better.'

Holt had to fork out 4000 guineas for the horse, but Mrs Buxton more than got her money back.

High Syce, in the capable hands of Billy Duncan, started a hot favourite at 2/1 in the Caulfield Cup and, though drawn second from the outside in the field of 18, won as he liked by two lengths from Amounis. High Syce carried 9.4 and Amounis 9.5. First prize was £5000. It was Holt's second successive Caulfield Cup winner and third overall, after Eurythmic in 1920 and Maple in 1928.

Two weeks later High Syce won the Melbourne Stakes. The handicapper got the better of the five-year-old in the Melbourne

Cup, in which he finished fourth with 9.11. He had been penalised 10 lb for winning the Caulfield Cup.

Mrs Buxton was made a Dame of the British Empire in 1969 in recognition of her tireless work for St Vincent's Hospital for the best part of 50 years.

Mrs Rita Buxton with trainer Jack Holt.

1929 RESULTS

VRC MELBOURNE CUP (2m)
Nightmarch, 9.2 (R.Reed) Trained by A McAulay; 3:26.25; Paquito, Phar Lap
AJC SYDNEY CUP (2m)
Crucis, 7.5 (W Cook) Trained by D Lewis; 3:23.25; Paddie Eve, Kidaides
QTC BRISBANE CUP (2m)
In Petto, 7.13 ((H Horney) 3:23.5; Tradecraft, Sheila's Lad
SAJC ADELAIDE CUP (13-f)
Parallana, 6.11 (N Percival) Trained by E Williams; 2:49; Santa Theba, Glucose
WATC PERTH CUP (2m)
Jemidar, 7.0 (J Armanasco) Trained by V Pink; 3:25.5; Ductile, Exceeder

VATC CAULFIELD CUP (12-f)
High Syce, 9.4 (W Duncan) Trained by J Holt; 2:30.5; Amounis, Prince Viol
VRC AUSTRALIAN CUP (2 ¼m)
Some Quality, 7.5 (W Elliott) Trained by W Nolan; 3:55.25; Kidaides, Octember
MVRC WS COX PLATE (9 ½-f)
Nightmarch, 9.0 (R Reed) Trained by A McAulay; 2:01.5; Highland, Mollison
AJC DERBY (12-f)
Phar Lap, 8.10 (J Pike) Trained by H Telford; 2:31.25; Carradale, Honour
VRC VICTORIA DERBY (12-f)
Phar Lap (J Pike) Trained by H Telford; 2:32.25; Carradale, Taisho

AJC DONCASTER HANDICAP (1m)
Karuma, 8.4 (J Toohey) Trained by J Carey; 1:38; Sion, Loquacious
VRC NEWMARKET HANDICAP (6-f)
St Ardent, 7.4 (N Percival) Trained by H Gabell; 1:10.7; Figure, Violian
AJC SIRES' PRODUCE STAKES (7-f)
Honour, 8.10 (T Green) Trained by R Mason; 1:26.7; Comanche, Nedda
VRC SIRES' PRODUCE STAKES (7-f)
Nedda, 8.7 (J Munro) Trained by J Fielder; 1:26; Parkwood, Metaphor
VRC GRAND NATIONAL STEEPLECHASE (3m 1-f)
Sandhurst, 11.4 (A Fullarton) Trained by H Gabell; 6:6.7; Mosstrooper, Seafit

Mosstrooper jumps to fame and fortune

When Mosstrooper ran dashing fencer Sandhurst to a neck in the 1929 Grand National Steeplechase at Flemington, an unlikely new jumping star was born. Not forgetting a new racing expression that has stood the test of time – 'he (or she) jumped it like Mosstrooper'.

In the light of that winter's events, top-weight Sandhurst's effort in winning the GN Steeplechase in record time was remarkable enough, but to concede 26 lb to Mosstrooper made the effort all the more meritorious.

The next month, Mosstrooper entered the record books by becoming the fifth horse to win the Australian Hurdle and Australian Steeple, on successive Saturdays at Caulfield.

With a few notable exceptions, such as Redleap, Roisel and Les Paddington, steeple-chasers in those days, as now, usually stuck to chasing. Not so Mosstrooper, who seemed equally at home over the battens and fences, jumping anything in front of him like a stag. But it wasn't always thus.

Mosstrooper, a chestnut son of Kenil-worth, sire of top stayer Kennaquhair, started out in conventional fashion, on the flat. On breeding, he was regarded as a Derby prospect. But he was not blessed with speed, his 18 flat starts yielding only one placing. Along the way his despairing owner, Mr R. Turnbull, sold him for 200 guineas to horse-trader Gus Powell.

Mosstrooper began his jumping career in April 1928, in a brush steeple at Epsom. He ran a fair race and the following month, aged six, won his first race, over the brush at Bendigo. He then disgraced himself on a trip to Sydney, falling in two 'chases' at Randwick.

All credit for his rapid development went to Powell, who mostly sold horses to India. With jockey W. Murrell in the saddle, Mosstrooper, who was not a natural jumper, was schooled over hundreds of hurdles and big timber at Powell's agistment property at Dandenong. The two men perfected Mosstrooper's jumping, but when the gelding won a steeplechase at Moonee Valley in May 1929, there were suggestions that he was 'the only trier'.

There were no such accusations after the Australian Hurdle, which Mosstrooper won by five lengths. His pilot was the experienced H. Thompson, Murrell having incurred the displeasure of the stewards. Mosstrooper was second favourite at 4/1.

The Australian Steeple, in which he met Sandhurst, was a slightly closer affair, with Mosstrooper, favourite at 2/1, prevailing by three lengths. Unfortunately, Sandhurst failed to complete the course. A week later Sandhurst, by Baverstock (sire of David), won the August Steeplechase at Flemington with 12.12. Fullarton could not ride him, having suffered a broken collarbone in an earlier race.

Mosstrooper's win, worth £1500, took his earnings to £5460 – a handsome return on the 200 guineas Powell outlaid for him.

MOSSTROOPER

TURF TOPICS

Billy comes to the boil: Apprentice jockey Billy Cook, 19, landed his first big winner, Crucis, in the 1929 Sydney Cup.
Second fiddle: Prince Viol, a son of the first Cox Plate winner, Violoncello, won the Hobart Cup (12f), a race first run in 1875.
Last hurdle: New Zealand–born jockey Hughie Cairns, who won the 1926 Melbourne Cup on Spearfelt, was killed in a fall at Moonee Valley on 27 July 1929. His mount Quick Deal came to grief in the Gellibrand Hurdle race. For 20 years, Cairns rode successfully on the flat and over jumps.
Feast of racing: The VRC calendar listed 19 meetings for November, including the four days of the Cup carnival. There were nine mid-week country meetings – at Mildura, Sunbury, Mornington, Woodend, Cran-bourne, Gisborne, Kilmore and Bendigo (two days).
The money or the bag: On his return from Warwick Farm races, bookmaker Jas Borgan was held up by three masked men as he alighted from his motor car outside his villa in Waverley. The thieves took £70 in cash from his pockets but failed to see a bag containing £500 in the car.

A portrait of 'Big Red', Phar Lap with Jim Pike aboard, in David Davis's colours.

A Derby win: David Davis and Harry Telford.

Phar Lap walks in

It was only his third win in 12 starts, but New Zealand–bred gelding Phar Lap had the racing scribes reaching for superlatives in the autumn of 1929 when he won the AJC Derby at Randwick.

The giant son of Night Raid, his coat more red than chestnut, won by three-and-a-half lengths. It could have been 10. 'Walked in' was a popular description for his victory over Carradale, raced by Mr L.K.S. Mackinnon. 'He made them look like hacks' was the comment of another newsman.

At 5/4, Phar Lap was a hot favourite for the Derby on the strength of his three-length win in the Rosehill Guineas (9f). In hindsight, he was the bet of the century! But there were doubters on Derby day. After all, his record of two wins, one second and eight times unplaced was less than flattering.

In the Derby, the field bunched. Jim Pike then gave Phar Lap his head and before onlookers realised what had happened, the favourite was three lengths ahead entering the straight. Towards the end Pike sat up on his mount. Phar lap's time of 2:31¼ was a record. Ridden out, he would have lowered that considerably. Another highlight of Derby day was the win of Nightmarch, also a son of Night Raid, in the Epsom Handicap. Nightmarch also streeted his rivals.

Three weeks later, Phar Lap or 'Big Red' won the Victoria Derby in a canter.

The greatest duo

Jim Pike, a superb horseman, indeed an artist, had his first ride on Phar Lap in the AJC Derby. He was 36. Thus began one of racing's most famous associations, one that yielded 27 wins. Only once were they unplaced together.

Until Pike climbed into the saddle on Derby day, Phar Lap had had six different jockeys – H. Martin, F. Douglas, J. Baker, J. Simpson, J. Brown and Jimmy Munro. Munro rode him to victory in the Rosehill Guineas two weeks before the Derby.

Pike, a tall man for a jockey, was born in Newcastle in 1892. Aged 12 and weighing little more than four stone, he was taken on as a stablehand by local trainer Ernie Connors. Two years later he became apprenticed to W. Kelso in Sydney. The two, soon friends, went to England in 1908 where Pike made a good impression.

They stayed away a year. On his return, one of Pike's first big wins was on Pendil (7.1) in the 1909 Australian Cup. The first champion he was associated with was Trafalgar. In 1912, aged 20, he was entrusted to ride the handsome grandson of Carbine in his last five races, all in Sydney.

In the saddle, Pike had all the essential qualities – fine balance, strong wrists, and the touch of a pianist. A sound judge of pace, he seldom used the whip which he carried in his left hand. Like Phar, he had presence.

Making an idol

In January 1928, Australian trainer Harry Telford, a keen student of breeding since his boyhood days, was taken by the bloodlines of a yearling offered at the New Zealand sales at Trentham. The youngster was by Night Raid out of Entreaty.

Telford and his brother Hugh were born at Ballarat, and went to New Zealand as teenagers with their father. Hugh took up training and stayed in NZ. Harry, a jockey, became stable foreman for Gloaming's trainer Dick Mason, then returned to Australia and became a trainer.

Night Raid, whose dam Sentiment was a granddaughter of Carbine, had been a dud as a racehorse in England and was sold to Australia, and then to NZ breeder Mr A. F. Roberts, whose stud was at Timaru. There Night Raid served Entreaty, who traced back to St Simon. The result of the mating was Phar Lap. The big, gangling chestnut was the last foal offered at the Trentham sale and was knocked down to Hugh Telford, acting for his brother Harry, for 160 guineas.

But Harry was short of cash, so talked American owner David J. Davis into forking out the 160 guineas. When he saw his horse, a scrawny individual, in Sydney, Davis refused to pay the training fees, so Telford leased him until 1931.

Telford came up with the name Phar Lap, which is Sinhalese for lightning.

Handsome Amounis had 33 wins and 19 places from 79 starts.

Amounis and Billy Cook race for a Caulfield Cup win and a stakes record.

Amounis's biggest day

The 1930 Caulfield Cup attracted only 13 runners. True, the Depression had lowered spirits and bank balances, but the small field had more to do with the toing and froing of Phar Lap's lessee-trainer, Harry Telford, and the spectre of the giant horse himself.

After failing in the '29 Melbourne Cup, Phar Lap resumed in the autumn a more powerful individual, winning nine of his 10 races – one of them, the 2m King's Plate, at Flemington by 20 lengths. The collective winning margin in the nine victories was 59 lengths, an average of 6½.

Telford, a man of few words, finally spoke up on the Monday before the Caulfield Cup, scratching Phar Lap and costing a lot of punters their hard-earned. Phar Lap stayed in Sydney, winning five races in September and October. In four of them he downed Night-march, his conqueror in the '29 Melbourne Cup.

If the 1930 Caulfield Cup had the smallest field since 1880, when Tom Kirk beat 10 rivals, it had a grand topweight, namely eight-year-old Amounis, with 9.8. Six weeks before the cup he took on Phar Lap in the 1m AJC Warwick Stakes and won by a short head.

With young Billy Cook in the saddle, Amounis, favourite at 2/1, always had the Cup under control, finishing over the top of everything to win by a length-and-a-half from 15/1 chance Soulton. The £5500 Amounis earned made him the greatest stakewinner in Australasian history, with £48 197 compared to Gloaming's £43 100.

Amounis had only three more starts for a third. He ended a meritorious career with 33 wins and 19 placings from 79 starts.

Flamboyant punter Eric Connolly and a syndicate he organised pulled off a £200 000 betting coup when Amounis and Phar Lap won the 1930 Caulfield Cup–Melbourne Cup double.

Connolly's team included David Davis, owner of Phar Lap, jockey Jim Pike, trainer Harry Telford, who was guaranteed a sling, and spectacular woman punter Maude Vandenberg, a bookmaker's widow who was not afraid to slap £5000 on a horse she fancied.

Known as Madam X, she was a regular backer of Amounis, landing plenty of big bets on him – one of them £21 000 to £6000. Her association with Amounis stemmed from her son Ernie, who suggested to bookmaker Bill Pearson that he buy the gelding as a four-year-old. The price was 1800 guineas, a bargain.

Connolly, in between puffs of smoke (he was a chain smoker), masterminded a plan whereby Phar Lap was left in the Caulfield Cup until the last minute, frightening off most other owners.

In the meantime, Connolly and agents in Melbourne, Sydney, Brisbane and Adelaide backed the Amounis–Phar Lap double at odds of 20/1 and better.

When Telford announced Phar Lap's withdrawal from the Caulfield Cup five days before the race, Connolly smiled and unwrapped a fresh packet of cigarettes. Overnight the Amounis–Phar Lap double was slashed to 6/1.

The scratching of Phar Lap drew howls of protest from connections who had already withdrawn their horses and cleared the way for Amounis, a champion in his own right, to play his part and win – which he did despite carrying 9.8. He had only 12 rivals.

Madam X cleaned up £20 000 on Amounis, apart from her winnings on the double.

Years later, Sydney racing journalist Bert Lillye wrote that bookmakers all over Australia went broke when Amounis and Phar Lap took the double. 'They still remember it as one of the most calamitous days for bookmakers in the history of Australian racing,' he said.

BONG BONG (N.S.W.) PICNIC RACE CLUB'S MEETING, JANUARY 16 AND 17.
(S. J. Hood photo.)

Miss McLarty's Kinaird winning the Bong Bong Cup.

All pleased with the favourite's victory.

Misses Helen Monro, Shirley Dent, and Gloria Terry.

Miss Mona McLarty, whose horse, Kinaird, won the Cup.

Around the stables.

Miss Betty Grace's picnic party.

Style away from the big city: the pictures from the Bong Bong races, NSW (SLV).

TURF TOPICS

Outjumps them: The mighty Mosstrooper went on his merry way in the winter of 1930, winning the Grand National Hurdle, Grand National Steeple and the Australian Hurdle.

Famous father: Shadow King, a five-year-old son of Comedy King, stamped himself as an above-average stayer with a narrow win in the Moonee Valley Cup (11½f), the day Phar Lap won the Cox Plate at 7/1 on. Ten days later Shadow King finished third to Phar Lap in the Melbourne Cup.

So close: Gloaming and Desert Gold both won 19 races straight, a record Phar Lap would have smashed had he nosed ahead of old rival Amounis in the AJC Warwick Stakes in September, 1930, his first start as a four-year-old. Amounis won by a short head. Going into that race, Phar Lap had won nine on the trot. After it he won 14 in a row – 23 wins and a second in 24 starts.

Thanks, kids: Due to the exploits of Nightmarch and Phar Lap, Night Raid topped the sires' list in 1929–30, with four of his progeny winning 27 races and £96,718 in earnings.

Hail Hall: Hall Mark, a smallish son of Heroic out of the Cyklon mare Hero-winkie, was foaled at Tarwyn Park stud, part of the Thompson empire in the Widden Valley. The breeder was Mr C. B. Kellow, who leased Heroic to the Thompsons.

Outed after win: The Sydney press were critical of Melbourne trainer Paddy Quinlan for choosing to give the mount on Cragford in the 1930 AJC Metropolitan to 16-year-old apprentice Scobie Breasley. Cragford duly won, but Breasley was suspended for two months for crossing to the rails too sharply. Breasley said years later, 'It seemed hard to me. The stewards were for ever on my neck and I picked up a lot of suspensions.'

1930 RESULTS

VRC MELBOURNE CUP (2m)
Phar Lap, 9.12 (J Pike) Trained by H Telford; 3:27.25; Second Wind, Shadow King
AJC SYDNEY CUP (2m)
Gwilliam G, 7.0 (J Simpson) Trained by W Ross; 3:22.5; Royal Smile, Soulton
QTC BRISBANE CUP (2m)
Trainer, 8.4 (M McCarten) 3:27; Mintman, Sir Ribble
SAJC ADELAIDE CUP (13-f)
Temptation, 6.10 (R Evans) Trained by J Scobie; 2:46.5; Nadean, Kirrkie
WATC PERTH CUP (2m)
Coolbarro, 8.0 (R Morley) Trained by JJ Kelly; 3:25.75; Abergwain, Flying Miss

VATC CAULFIELD CUP (12-f)
Amounis, 9.8 (W Cook) Trained by Frank McGrath; 2:34.25; Soulton, Alcman
VRC AUSTRALIAN CUP (2 ¼m)
Nadean, 7.5 (A Wilson) Trained by W Brodie; 3:50.5; Kidaides, Leadlight
MVRC WS COX PLATE (9 ½-f)
Phar Lap, 8.11 (J Pike) Trained by H Telford; 1:59.2; Tregilla, Mollison
AJC DERBY (12-f)
Tregilla, 8.10 (E Bartle) Trained by C Battye; 2:3.2; Veilmond, Balloon King
VRC VICTORIA DERBY (12-f)
Balloon King (J Pike) Trained by RD O'Donnell; 2:33.5; Veilmond, Miss Arrow

AJC DONCASTER HANDICAP (1m)
Venetian Lady, 8.5 (D Munro) Trained by EF Walker; 1:37; High Disdain, Raisin
VRC NEWMARKET HANDICAP (6-f)
Greenline, 10.2 (J Pike) Trained by J Barden; 1:12.2; Birdcage, Wise Force
AJC SIRES' PRODUCE STAKES (7-f)
The Doctor's Orders, 8.10 (W Cook) Trained by J Scobie; 1:25; Veilmond, Balloon King
VRC SIRES' PRODUCE STAKES (7-f)
Thurlstone, 8.10 (A Reed) Trained by A Mulcahy; 1:26.25; The Doctor's Orders, Kaftan
VRC GRAND NATIONAL STEEPLECHASE (3m 1-f)
Mosstrooper, 11.10 (R Harris) Trained by G Powell; 6:28.5; Namera, Glentronie

Phar Lap, carrying the big weight of 9.12, goes easily to the line to win the Melbourne Cup by three lengths (Age).

Phar Lap shot at before the big race

It was midnight, nine hours after Jim Pike had won the Victoria Derby for the third year running, on Balloon King. All was quiet under a moonlit sky as the horse float backed gently into Joe Cripps' stable yard at Caulfield. Bags filled with hay, to soften the sound of hooves, lay on the ground. Under the watchful eye of armed police, a massive chestnut horse and a grey pony were loaded on to the float. Tommy Woodcock climbed into the seat next to the driver, Stan Boyden.

Phar Lap, the raging hot favourite for the Melbourne Cup, the talk of the equine world, indeed the nation, was being spirited away to Guy Raymond's St Albans Stud, at Geelong, 45 miles south-west of Melbourne, out of the reach of evil-doers until Tuesday – Cup Day. It was the considerate Raymond who had suggested the ploy.

On Derby morning gunmen had tried to shoot Phar Lap after he had worked at Caulfield racecourse. On the return trip to Scripps' stable through the streets of Caulfield, devoted attendant Woodcock, leading Phar Lap from his grey pony, noticed a large car parked in Glenhuntly Road. A suspicious Woodcock took a different route and shielded Phar Lap with himself and his pony. The car turned and gave chase. A man in the back seat thrust a shotgun through the open window and fired. The pellets missed, spraying a wall. A frightened Phar Lap reared. The police were called in.

With so much money riding on Phar Lap in the Melbourne Cup, particularly in doubles with Amounis, winner of the Caulfield Cup, it was no wonder that scoundrels, probably acting for those who would lose the most, should try to harm the 'Red Terror'.

On Derby afternoon, with two armed police for company, Phar Lap, under the watchful eye of owner-trainer Harry Telford, arrived in the mounting yard at Flemington in preparation for his final hit-out in the wfa Melbourne Stakes (10f). The week before he had won the WS Cox Plate by four lengths – his 20th win from 32 starts. He won the Melbourne Stakes almost as easily, by three lengths at the prohibitive odds of 5/1 on. By now he was odds-on for the Melbourne Cup.

After a quiet Sunday and Monday at St Albans Stud, Phar Lap left for Flemington on Tuesday morning with a police escort. He arrived at the course safe and sound in overcast weather.

In 1890, after Carbine had won the Melbourne Cup, the scribes predicted that Australian racing would not see his equal again. Wrong. Piloted as usual by Jim Pike, Phar Lap treated his 9.12, not to mention his 14 rivals, with contempt in the Cup, winning by three lengths from a pretty handy stayer in Second Wind (50/1), with another good performer, Shadow King (50/1), third. The winning margin would have been greater had Pike not eased down the champion over the last half furlong.

Pike, usually a man of few words, was lavish in his praise of Phar Lap, saying: 'He is a wonderful horse. I gave him his head only once and he won like the champion he is. He is able to do anything you ask him.' The fact that the track on Cup day was on the heavy side had no effect on the big horse. The crowd, though, was down, coming in at 72 358, the smallest since 1916.

One hard-luck story was related by jockey Billy Cook, who rode the 'above average' three-year-old Veilmond. Years later Cook told turf writer Bill Ahern that he was hit in the face by a flying racing plate about six furlongs from home, just after Veilmond had responded so well to his urgings that 'I gave myself a chance of beating the big fellow, even though I could see he was going like a winner. We'll never know.'

After being hit, Cook said he rode blind for a few moments. 'When I came to I was last. It was hard to say what Phar Lap had in reserve.' Veilmond finished fifth, five lengths behind the winner.

Two days after the Cup, on Oaks Day, Phar Lap (7/1 on) donkey-licked Mollison by four lengths in the Linlithgow Stakes and, on the final day, there was polite laughter when he romped home in the CB Fisher Plate.

In the space of eight days, Phar Lap had earned £12 229. His record stood at 24 wins, two seconds and two thirds from 36 starts.

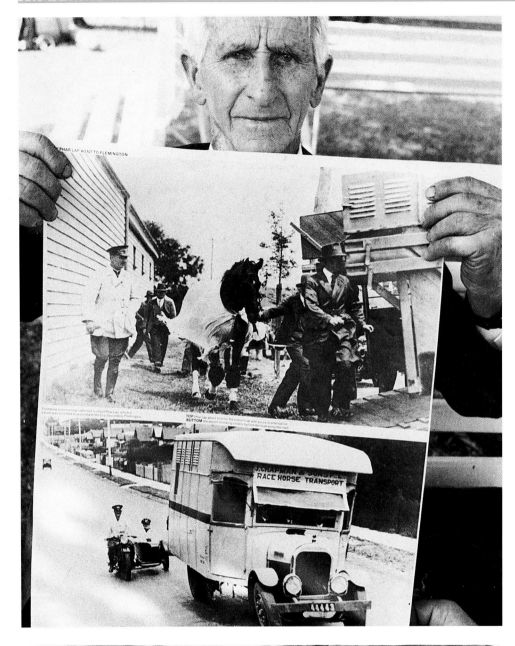

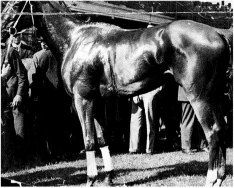

Left: The photos held by Tommy Woodcock show the drama of Cup day 1930, after a shot had been fired at Phar Lap (Age). The top picture shows float driver Stan Boyden, Tommy (partly obscured) and a police escort collecting Phar Lap from his St Albans Stud hideout at Geelong. In the bottom picture the horse's transport truck, with escort, arrives at the track. Top right: Phar Lap on show in the mounting yard. Below, left: the race card; and right: heading for the start with Jim Pike.

The Phar Lap phenomenon

'Probably the best and certainly the best-advertised horse Australia has ever seen' – this was the cool judgement of the racing columnist in Sydney's *Bulletin* magazine in the week following Phar Lap's premature, tragic death in California in April 1932.

Phar Lap was not the first horse to become an Australian hero. Horses now all but forgotten – names such as Jorrocks and Veno and Alice Hawthorn – were once idols of the turf and drew crowds by the thousands and tens of thousands to racecourses in days long gone, when Victoria and New South Wales were raw colonies. Time erases most of the memories, even of the stars. Grown men wept when the brave mare Wakeful, under a

horses won the best races on offer. Both set records that still amaze. Both horses had presence, speed, endurance, versatility and a capacity to demoralise their opponents. They had courage. For their rare failures there were legitimate excuses, and both atoned with astonishing performances.

When Carbine won the Melbourne Cup on a perfect November day in 1890 carrying a record weight against a record field in record time, the daily newspaper the *Argus* said that men leapt and shouted; women screamed with delight.

Unlike Phar Lap, who was gelded before his racing career began, Carbine went to the stud first in Victoria, then in England. He pro-

or super humans. He is the only horse there, except perhaps the colt from Old Regret.

Phar Lap deserved all the accolades that were heaped upon him. He was indeed a wonder horse, a Big Red if you can define chestnut that far, and so a Red Terror to those who competed against him.

A heart as big as Phar Lap's has become an Australian cliche to set beside Ned Kelly's gameness. Any sportsman who shows extra courage can be given the tag. A spirited come-back in the pool is headlined 'A Fish called Phar Lap'. Simon Poidevin is dubbed the 'Phar Lap of Rugby'. Peter Porter wrote a beautiful poem, much anthologised since, inspired by the sad yet stunning vision of

A rare shot of the champ in blinkers (ARM).

The ancient craft of taxidermy at work on Australia's sacred animal (Age).

crushing weight, went to the front four furlongs from home in the 1903 Melbourne Cup, only to be caught in the last seconds of the race by a three-year-old carrying six stone eight. Yet Wakeful's name is no longer a household word.

Carbine alone stands in the way of Phar Lap's claim to be the greatest. He is the reason for the *Bulletin* writer's 'probably'. As with Phar Lap, likewise born in New Zealand, Carbine made his way into the affections of the people – not just racegoers and gamblers – by his achievements and, yes, by his character. Those two horses raced 40 years apart. Little can be decided in comparing their performances. Carbine had 43 starts for 33 wins and was only once unplaced.

Phar Lap, after winning just one of his first nine juvenile starts, had a further 42 starts for a further 36 wins and five placings. Both

duced sons and daughters who became champions and progenitors of champions across the world.

Among them was Spearmint, who won an English Derby and sired a winner of this great race in his turn. Spearmint was also a grandsire of Night Raid, Phar Lap's sire; so Carbine was Phar Lap's great-great-grandfather. This pedigree was one reason why Phar Lap's trainer, Harry Telford, was attracted to the young horse in the beginning and bought him cheaply on behalf of an American owner at the New Zealand yearling sales. Surely there is no greater horse to have raced on the Australian turf than Carbine.

Yet it is Phar Lap who remains on the pedestal: an enduring hero standing in the select company of those who have a place in what is often called the Australian legend. The others in that hall of fame were humans

Phar Lap preserved in a glass case at Melbourne's Museum, a credit to the art of an American taxidermist.

It was true, as the *Bulletin* man had said, that Phar Lap was the best-advertised horse Australia had ever seen, to that time at least. But without great substance to Phar Lap's achievements the legend could not have been sustained.

His was a rapid rise to glory. Before September 1929 he was described as 'an obscure fellow', gangly and rangy. Then he ran a slashing fourth in the weight-for-age Warwick Stakes. Suddenly he and his personality began to be noticed. He transformed into an 'upstanding chestnut' and newspaper readers learned that the horse was so docile that he would come trotting over to Telford, his trainer, at the whistle. He won the Rosehill Guineas with brilliance, and drew a crowd of 78 000 – much larger than expected – to Randwick to see him win the AJC Derby. A month later, in Melbourne for the spring carnival he caused – as one paper said – 'almost as big a stir in the Flemington birdcage as the Prince of Wales did on the occasion of his visit'.

From obscurity until the urns of his death was a bare two-and-a-half years. In the interval were those three dozen wins which included, after the two Derbys, all the great weight-for-age races at Randwick, Rosehill, Caulfield, Flemington and Moonee Valley, and the coveted King's Cup at Morphettville. Sometimes he won by 20 lengths, sometimes by 10. Seldom were his victories close. Usually he was unbackable. His greatest moments were his 1930 Melbourne Cup, his rare narrow win under a large penalty weight in the 1931 Futurity at Caulfield and his last

over from silent movies in 1929 and 1930, drawing huge crowds to cinemas. Here they saw news footage and documentary films of Phar Lap's exploits. He was a photogenic animal. The newsreel brought the Melbourne Cup to an Australia-wide cinema audience within hours of the event itself. The only people who saw Carbine race were the thousands who went to the racecourses. Phar Lap's exploits 40 years later were seen by millions.

Economic depression had brought severe unemployment and financial hardship to Australia even in the time when Phar Lap was coming to prominence. It was a time when Australians were grateful for heroes and there were fewer distractions. Sport, even racing, was essentially a leisure time occupation, a diversion on Saturday afternoons and holidays. It has become a commonplace to observe that this wonderful horse, like the

country location. A win in Australia's greatest race, and the only horse to achieve it at odds-on. Disputes and intrigue involving the owner, the trainer and the powerful racing clubs. A sea voyage to America to show his ability internationally. A triumph in winning at his first overseas start. And then the death – sudden, mysterious, unexplained to our fullest satisfaction, the horse's head cradled in Woodcock's loving arms.

That great heart of Phar Lap has been on display in the Science Museum in Canberra: his skeleton went to Wellington, New Zealand. But it is the stuffed hide belonging to the Museum in Melbourne that allows obeisance to continue. Since its arrival in 1933 it has always been the Museum's most popular exhibit. Once, in 1980, it was paraded in its glass case, like a Spanish Madonna on a feast day, through the city at Cup time and

Phar Lap as a work of art by Eric Thake (NGV).

Phar Lap parades, mysteriously illuminated in the dark, on a last trip to Flemington (Age).

win of all against top international competition in what was billed as the richest race in the world, run on a dirt track in Mexico in a gambling heaven or hell called Agua Caliente.

Phar Lap's physical attributes and his achievements on the racecourse made him a champion. Other factors made the legend: the time and place in which he raced, and the frail and all-too-human people who were carried for a time in the slipstream of his success. In his story there were heroes and villains, dark deeds, perseverance, greed, good luck and sad misfortune; and there were the storytellers.

He lived in a time when new forms of storytelling were having their effect. Newspapers were able to print bigger and clearer action pictures. Tabloids such as Melbourne's *Sun News-Pictorial* were creatures of the 1920s. Talking films were taking

young Don Bradman and the daring aviator Charles Kingsford-Smith, helped to raise the spirits of their countrymen and women. It added relish to the satisfaction to know that a battler had selected an unwanted yearling in the sales and then humbled the wealthiest men in the land, and their expensive thoroughbreds.

There were other elements to the story, priceless to mythologising. Phar Lap was despised at first sight by the owner for whom the trainer was acting (and an American, to boot). An incredible bond of affection between the horse and his gentle young strapper – a failed jockey, Tommy Woodcock. Gangsters, crooks and big time illegal gamblers. A callous gun-shot attack foiled because of the selfless intervention of the strapper. Cloak and dagger tactics to protect him. Concealment, as with Newminster, at a secret

was taken for a last visit to Flemington, but it is too fragile now for such exertions.

If we romance Phar Lap, who can blame us? He symbolises those moments when sport elevates the spirit and words struggle to describe the sensation. A writer on the long-defunct *Sportsman* put it this way: 'Those who had the great good fortune to be there on Tuesday can never forget it, even if they live to be a hundred. It stirred the very soul, it lifted us for a spell to a height that only the best impulses can rise to … It is this sort of thing that at the time puts the genuine sportsman above the ordinary mortal. Such moments are worth living for, and worth remembering after they have passed.'

Mind you, he was writing about Wakeful in 1903, and of how gallantly she tried, but failed, to win the Melbourne Cup.

by Andrew Lemon

The barrier strand is up and the field charges away for the 1931 Melbourne Cup.

White Nose carries the day (Age).

White Nose's Cup: Phar Lap not up to it

The depression cast a pall over affairs, and almost everyone took a beating in 1931 – even the idol of the racetrack, Phar Lap.

First prize in the 1931 Melbourne Cup was slashed from £9429 to £5200, pickings were lean for pre-post bookmakers, and race crowds dropped, though 82352 paid their way into Flemington on Cup Day in anticipation of seeing Phar Lap beat Carbine's weight-carrying record of 10.5. The 1930 winner was burdened with 10.10 – 12 lb more than the 9.12 he carried to a comfortable victory 12 months before.

Phar Lap went in with a series of weight-for-age wins behind him – the most recent being the Cox Plate and the Melbourne Stakes, both for the second year running.

But jockey Jim Pike sounded a warning after the Melbourne Stakes on Derby day. He told joint owners Harry Telford and David Davis that Phar Lap had 'struggled all the way'. He advised against a Cup run, saying that in his view the horse could not win. Telford wanted to withdraw Phar Lap. Davis did not. A veterinary report said the race would not harm him.

Nevertheless, the champion's price drifted from 6/4 to 3/1. He finished eighth, Pike refusing to knock him about when he realised the horse could not win.

The race went to the lightly weighted White Nose (6.12), ridden by Neville Percival and raced by South Australian grazier H. P. McLachlan. Second, two lengths away, was Shadow King, by now six, and having his third start in the race. He finished third in 1930.

White Nose, a five-year-old entire, had won the Hotham Handicap on Derby Day, his first win since his two-year-old days, and started at 8/1 in the Cup after being at bolter's odds on Derby eve. The most distinguishing thing about him were the colours he carried – the McLachlan tartan with a white sash and cap. Two weeks after the Cup, White Nose failed in the Williamstown Cup with 8.0.

As for Phar Lap, he returned to the place of his birth, New Zealand, for a spell, while plans were finalised for him to race in the US.

Left at the post

If Manfred could do it, so could Phar Lap – in trumps! The most astonishing win of Phar Lap's career was in the 1931 Futurity Stakes (7f) at Caulfield. Carrying the maximum weight (10.3), he stood flat-footed at the start, as Manfred had in the 1925 AJC Derby. When the Futurity field settled down, Phar Lap was 40 lengths behind the tearaway leader, Taurus. Jockey Jim Pike took the only route possible on the four-year-old, around the outside of the entire field. Approaching the home turn, Mystic Peak had dashed clear but Phar Lap with giant strides grabbed him on the line to win by a neck at 2/1 on. Pike said afterwards: 'I wondered why his heart didn't burst.'

Three starts later Phar Lap had his colours lowered by the good performer Waterline, by a neck, in the CM Lloyd Stakes at Flemington, ending a run of 14 straight wins. There were rumours Phar Lap had been off his feed.

All up in 1931, Phar Lap had 14 starts for 12 wins and one second. At his other start he was unplaced in the Melbourne Cup, his last start in Australia.

TURF TOPICS

Top Kiwi: New Zealand–bred Ammon Ra, sold privately to Australian interests after winning his first two races in NZ, won seven races in 1931, including the AJC Sires' Produce Stakes, the AJC Derby and the Caulfield Guineas. His regular rider was Maurice McCarten. Ammon Ra was by Limond, the sire of Limerick.

Geldings barred: The AJC Derby wins of Phar Lap (1929) and Ammon Ra (1931) resulted in geldings being barred from classics run by the premier clubs. Though grand for breeders, some undistinguished colts won the big races. Geldings were readmitted in 1957.

Back-to-back wins: In 1885, young Sydney rider Frank McGrath almost lost his life in a horrific 16-horse fall in the Caulfield Cup.

In 1930, McGrath a trainer for 30 years, won the race with the popular Amounis. In 1931 he won it for the second year running with the lightly weighted Denis Boy, an Irish import with 7.0. A year later Denis Boy won the AJC Metropolitan with 8.6

Rival to books: The tote operated at Caulfield for the first time on Memsie Stakes Day, 1931. The first winner Clarity (5/4 favourite) paid 11/6 for a win for a five shilling investment.

Curtain call: Sandown and Aspendale courses closed in Melbourne. Epsom and Mentone were each granted an extra meeting.

Flat outing: Great jumper Mosstrooper, carrying the postage stamp weight of 7.3, ran unplaced in the Australian Cup (2¼m) at Flemington. Carry On, a son of Magpie, won from White Nose.

Hard times: Added prize money for the four-day AJC Spring Carnival was £25 000, a reduction of £15 000 on the 1930 figure.

Rising star: Chatham, a three-year-old son of Windbag, having only his second start, won his first race, over seven furlongs at Rosehill. Taken to Melbourne he finished second in the Cox Plate (to Phar Lap), second in the Victoria Derby, and won the Linlithgow Stakes.

Six Derbys: Jim Pike won the Victoria Derby for the fourth year in a row, on Johnnie Jason. It was his sixth win overall, the others being Beverage, Beragoon, Strephon, Phar Lap and Balloon King.

Ring-in exposed by Sherlock Holmes

The Sydney ferry is a revealing way to travel to work, not just for the views. One Monday morning on his way to work, the keeper of the Australian Stud book and Registrar of Racehorses, former Victorian Loddon Yuille, was fascinated by a newspaper account of a heavy plunge on horse called Gagoola in the Rothsay Trial Stakes at Flemington.

Gagoola, with whom Loddon was not familiar, had been backed from 33/1 to 6/4. Unfortunately for those involved, who stood to win £30 000, it was beaten into second place by a horse called Stephanite. With that, the connections fled the racecourse, not bothering about the £60 prize money. Talk of a ring-in swept racing circles.

At work, Yuille established that Gagoola was a three-year-old chestnut colt bred by H. J. Forrester at Moree and had been registered on 11 May 1931.

At Yuille's request the VRC investigated the case but, for the time being, found nothing untoward. The horse they inspected, how-

ever, was not Gagoola, who was elsewhere.

Yuille told author Clive Inglis he was far from satisfied and had received information that Gagoola, alias Simba, was about to travel to Sydney by train. A 'reliable man' was at the station when the train arrived but he was unable to establish anything. The horse was so well rugged up that not a hair was showing, and he was spirited away to Mulgoa. Yuille and his Dr Watsons gave chase but all they found were the charred remains of a horse in a creek. Gagoola was never seen again.

One of the people involved in the ring-in, a bit of a rough diamond, was disqualified for five years by the VRC. He expected a heftier term. When the penalty was announced he said he could have kissed the VRC Chairman, Mr L.K.S. Mackinnon, who observed 'What an escape'.

Simba, it seems, came from NZ but was not registered in Australia. Inglis was confident 'officialdom' knew of his whereabouts so that he was never produced again, as Gagoola, or any other horse.

The genuine Gagoola, or a spurious Simba?

1931 RESULTS

VRC MELBOURNE CUP (2m)
White Nose, 6.12 (N Percival) Trained by E. Hatwell; 3:26; Shadow King, Concentrate
AJC SYDNEY CUP (2m)
The Dimmer, 7.12 (E Bartle) Trained by C Barden; 3:35.25; Alcman, Donald
QTC BRISBANE CUP (2m)
Royal Smile, 8.0 (T Brown) 3:26.5; Rowladdie, Inducement
SAJC ADELAIDE CUP (13-f)
Suzumi, 7.5 (R Medhurst) Trained by I Reid; 2:45.2; Bridoon, Greek Gift
WATC PERTH CUP (2m)
The Dimmer, 8.0 (A Cooper) Trained by C Barden; 3:29.75; Serbury, Knight Commander

VATC CAULFIELD CUP (12-f)
Denis Boy, 7.0 (A Knox) Trained by F McGrath; 2:31.5; Prince Dayton, First Acre
VRC AUSTRALIAN CUP (2 ¼m)
Carry On, 7.3 (W Duncan) Trained by G Price; 3:53.5; White Nose, St Mary
MVRC WS COX PLATE (9 ½-f)
Phar Lap, 9.4 (J Pike) Trained by H Telford; 2:01.5; Chatham, Johnnie Jason
AJC DERBY (12-f)
Ammon Ra, 8.10 (M McCarten) Trained by J Jamieson; 2:34.7; Johnnie Jason, Koomeela
VRC VICTORIA DERBY (12-f)
Johnnie Jason (J Pike) Trained by C Unwin; 2:33.75; Chatham, Viol D'Amour

AJC DONCASTER HANDICAP (1m)
Sir Christopher, 8.5 (J Munro) Trained by R Cashman; 1:37; Mollison, Casque d'Or
VRC NEWMARKET HANDICAP (6-f)
Parkwood, 8.13 (F Hannan) Trained by F Musgrave; 1:13.5; Waterline, Mollison
AJC SIRES' PRODUCE STAKES (7-f)
Ammon Ra, 8.10 (M McCarten) Trained by J Jamieson; 1:25.5; Johnnie Jason, Gallantic
VRC SIRES' PRODUCE STAKES (7-f)
Mulcra, 8.10 (W Brady) Trained by C Goodfellow; 1:26.75; Bold Bid, Auto Pay
VRC GRAND NATIONAL STEEPLECHASE (3m 1-f)
Rakwool, 11.7 (R Inkson) Trained by FW Hoysted; 6:35; Kentle, Bestman

Tommy Woodcock, trainer in US. Insets: Tommy's stable passes (ARM). Above: Precious cargo.

Phar Lap after the Agua Caliente Hcp.

Phar Lap romps home in Agua Caliente

The American PR machine swung into action on two fronts – politics and racing – early in 1932. While the Democrats championed their presidential candidate, the charismatic Franklin Delano Roosevelt, newspapers across the country were fed glowing accounts of Phar Lap's deeds on his arrival in New Mexico for the $US58800 Agua Caliente Handicap over 10 furlongs.

Though hailed by the Agua Caliente Jockey Club as 'The Red Terror from the Antipodes', Phar Lap was a mystery horse to American racegoers.

He had not raced for more than four months, since failing in the 1931 Melbourne Cup, and his early work consisted mostly of jogging and walking for lengthy periods. American trainers were aghast at the seeming lightness of Phar Lap's eight-week preparation. In truth, part-owner David Davis, out to clean up financially, instructed trainer Tommy Woodcock not to allow Phar Lap to show his best in public. Woodcock was filling in for Phar Lap's regular trainer Harry Telford, who remained in Australia.

One thing was sure. Phar Lap looked a picture of health on a diet of Australian and NZ food, and water from a Mexican spring that Woodcock bought for $1 a five-gallon jar. Bill Elliott, substituting for Jim Pike who declined to make the trip, also won plaudits for his fine seat in the saddle and his accomplished riding in 10 races since arriving in America.

Come race day, 20 March, a record crowd of 50000 flocked to the Agua Caliente course, where the 15-event card kicked off at 10.20 a.m. An hour before the race, steady support for Phar Lap, topweight with 9.3 in

the 11-horse field, saw his price firm to 7/5 for the win and evens the place. By post time he had tightened to 6/5, a clear favourite.

The 13th running of the Agua Caliente Handicap, the start of which was delayed for 10 minutes because of unruly barrier behaviour by one of the runners, turned out to be 'a romp' for the Australian champion. Hats were thrown in the air as Phar Lap passed the post, winner by two lengths from Reveille Boy in record time of 2:2⅖.

The police were unable to hold the enthusiastic crowd as they rushed to the track to get a better look at the champion. Phar Lap, as calm as ever, took it all in his stride. He was then paraded in front of the judge's stand while a horseshoe of flowers was placed around his neck. Newspaper and cinema cameras played constantly.

After the race owner Davis announced: 'Phar Lap showed he is a champion. He will go after other rich American stakes.'

Melbourne *Herald* racing writer Bert Wolfe cabled: 'Every newspaper of any consequence in America is printing stories of the success of "The Big Train" from the Antipodes. They are saying Phar Lap and his connections made American jockeys and trainers look like suckers. They are lauding Woodcock to the skies for his cleverness, Elliott is being described as the Tod Sloan of Australia and owners are being advised to send to Australia for a shipload of trainers and jockeys.'

Phar Lap's win, his 36th, was worth $US50050 and took his earnings to $332250, second in the world to Sun Beau's $366744.

Woodcock revealed the following day that Phar Lap had suffered a bruised leg at the presentation. He stumbled down some steps

near the terrace while objecting to a wreath of flowers being placed around his neck. As a result, it was announced Phar Lap would not race again at dusty Agua Caliente. Instead he would travel 600 miles north to Ed Parry's training establishment near San Francisco and prepare for more engagements.

After Phar Lap's astonishing victory, a smiling Woodcock remarked that his primary interest was in proving that a horse could travel 10000 miles and be trained by the Australian method to win a great race under unfamiliar running conditions on a dirt track. 'Phar Lap was in better condition than at any time of his life, even when he won the Melbourne Cup,' Woodcock said.

TURF TOPICS

Fallen trooper: Mosstrooper, carrying 12.9, had one of his infrequent falls in the 1932 Australian Steeple, which was won by Bang Bang.

New star: Chatham proved himself a champion middle-distance horse by winning the AJC Epsom Handicap (1m), the AJC Craven Plate (10f) and the WS Cox Plate (9½f) in the space of three weeks in October 1932.

Shrinking odds: In June 1932, odds of 4000/1 were on offer about Rogilla and Peter Pan winning the Caulfield–Melbourne Cups double. By early October, odds of 50/1 were freely taken on the strength of Peter Pan's win in the AJC Derby and Rogilla's second to Denis Boy in the AJC Metropolitan.

Tommy Woodcock leads Phar Lap and Billy Elliott out at Agua Caliente. Inset: souvenir (ARM).   *New shoes in New Mexico.*

Death of Phar Lap in America stuns nation

The grave news was cabled around the world from San Francisco on 5 April 1932 – Phar Lap was dead. It must be a hoax, some said.

That ray of hope, however thoughtless, was scotched by reports that moments after the death had been confirmed, trainer Tommy Woodcock, Phar Lap's faithful attendant and friend, 'gave way completely and wept unrestrainedly after throwing his arms around the neck of the gelding'.

Friends and Mrs David Davis, wife of the part-owner, had to drag Woodcock away from the horse and the stable at the stock farm of wealthy sportsman Ed Perry.

One US paper, the *New York Sun*, published this poem –
'Where the thoroughbred immortal
Graze in pasture ever green
And steeds of song and story
Feel the touch of hands unseen
There's a whinny in the distance
And a pawing at the gate
As the big, stout-hearted Phar Lap
Joins the Legions of the Great.'

Less than a month after winning the rich Agua Caliente Handicap and becoming the most famous horse in the world, Phar Lap, the idol of three countries, – Australia, New Zealand and now America – was struck down in his prime, aged five. Whole nations don't mourn for racehorses. They did for Phar Lap. In New Zealand, where he was born, big crowds gathered outside newspaper offices.

Tributes flowed. So did questions. What had killed the five year-old gelding? Was it a simple case of colic, as first reported? Fears that he was poisoned circulated. If so, why?

Certainly the illness was sudden. Two days before his death Phar Lap was operated upon for a sore hoof. He seemed in good shape to begin his preparation for big races ahead at Arlington Park, Chicago.

Phar Lap died at 2.20 p.m. That morning Woodcock, who slept only a few feet away from the thoroughbred, entered the horse's stall upon wakening to find the animal lying down. Alarmed, he summoned vet Bill Nielsen, who called in other veterinary surgeons. They worked on Phar Lap all morning.

The symptoms with which the horse was stricken developed so quickly the vets were unable to counteract them.

Owner David Davis, who was flying from Los Angeles at the time of Phar Lap's death, arrived the next day and, though distressed, immediately ordered an investigation. He admitted the long trip from Australia might have weakened Phar Lap's constitution.

Several theories for Phar Lap's death were forthcoming, one being that it was caused by a small amount of green feed which was part of his customary diet. Those in charge of Phar Lap said he was allowed to nibble at a tuft of grass while exercising in an adjoining field. Vets expressed the belief that a bit of alfalfa, or some barley sodden with dew, brought on the colic that caused death.

Melbourne *Herald* racing reporter Bert Wolfe spoke to Dr Nielsen hours after the autopsy. Nielsen said the horse had died as the result of an irritant poison.

'I saw the lining of his stomach and I know what it means when the lining is eaten away,' Nielsen said.

1932 RESULTS

VRC MELBOURNE CUP (2m)
Peter Pan, 7.6 (W Duncan) Trained by F McGrath; 3:23.25; Yarramba, Shadow King
AJC SYDNEY CUP (2m)
Johnnie Jason, 8.4 (R Wilson) Trained by C Unwin; 3:32; Admiral drake, Veilmond
QTC BRISBANE CUP (2m)
St Valorey, 8.10 (W Duncan) 3:24.75; Terry Tone, Pamboona
SAJC ADELAIDE CUP (13-f)
Romany Rye, 7.8 (A Wilson) Trained by J Cripps jnr; 2:46; Income, Vertigern
WATC PERTH CUP (2m) (1 January 1932)
Bonny Note, 7.0 (P Bell) Trained by JJ Kelly; 3:29.75; Adeline's March, Camarina
VATC CAULFIELD CUP (12-f)
Rogilla, 7.12 (G Robinson) Trained by L Haigh; 2:34.25; Segati, Top Hole

WATC PERTH CUP (2m) (31 December 1932)
Alienist, 7.3 (J Corry) Trained by M Hennessy; 3:26.25; Adeline's March, Olympian
VRC AUSTRALIAN CUP (2 ¼m)
Madstar, 7.3 (R Medhurst) Trained by R Sinclair; 3:52.75; Mira Donna, Blatherskite
MVRC WS COX PLATE (9 ½-f)
Chatham, 9.0 (J Munro) Trained by F Williams; 2:02.7; Voil d'Amour, Johnnie Jason
AJC DERBY (12-f)
Peter Pan, 8.10 (J Pike) Trained by F McGrath; 2:34; Oro, Kuvera
VRC VICTORIA DERBY (12-f)
Liberal (J Munro) Trained by F Foulsham; 2:34.25; Gaine Carrington, Top Hole

AJC DONCASTER HANDICAP (1m)
Jacko, 6.10 (D Lightfoot) Trained by S Lamond; 1:37.25; Legislator, Tom Pinch
VRC NEWMARKET HANDICAP (6-f)
Lady Linden, 8.4 (W Cook) Trained by W Playford; 1:12; Winooka, Greenline
AJC SIRES' PRODUCE STAKES (7-f)
Kuvera, 8.10 (M McCarten) Trained by G Price; 1:25.5; Vauntry, Turbine
VRC SIRES' PRODUCE STAKES (7-f)
Kuvera, 8.10 (M McCarten) Trained by G Price; 1:24.5; Vauntry, Closing Time
VRC GRAND NATIONAL STEEPLECHASE (3m 1-f)
Precocious, 9.8 (T Lynch) Trained by Ms D Sheil; 6:18; Nauru, Mosstrooper

Who killed Phar Lap?

There are few solid facts about the death of Phar Lap. The evidence is a tease; it confuses and contradicts. And most of the witnesses are dead.

One of the best sources is thus Isobel Carter's *Phar Lap*, published by Lansdowne in 1964 when many of the witnesses were still living. The book is cool, painstaking and concerned to be fair. Carter worked for the Melbourne *Herald* until her death. She was a first-rate reporter, particularly of courts. In other words, she would have been wrong for current affairs TV.

Phar Lap, probably the best Australian racehorse ever, and hero to the lost age of the Depression and Ardath cork tips, died about midday on Tuesday, 5 April 1932. The gelding died in the barn of a racing establishment at Menlo Park, south of San Francisco. The following facts about the death have not been questioned.

Woodcock went to the horse before 5 a.m. Phar Lap seemed sick. Bill Nielsen, invariably referred to as the veterinarian accompanying the Australian party, found the horse's temperature close to normal (100.4° F). Woodcock and Nielsen thought the horse might have colic. Nielsen gave him a drench. So far as one can discover, what this contained has never been disclosed. It was probably a purgative.

By mid-morning, the chestnut's temperature had risen to 102. Woodcock says in Jan Wositzky's *Tommy Woodcock* that the horse was now in 'dreadful pain'. His belly was distended and he wanted to go down. He did not, however, show other symptoms of colic, such as sweating, anxious looks at his flanks, or violent fits.

Nielsen left to find a vet, Dr Carl Masoero, who worked at the nearby Tanforan Racecourse. According to Woodcock's account, Phar Lap shortly afterwards began to squeal with pain. Then he 'haemorrhaged terrible all over me and just dropped down dead'.

We know that Phar Lap had been grazing on lucerne at the farm for some 13 days. We know that about five days before the horse's death, trees on the property had been sprayed with lead arsenate to kill caterpillars.

We do not know whether Phar Lap was being fed arsenic as a tonic in the form of Fowler's Solution. He could have been, but this – of itself – would not necessarily prove anything. Many horses in the 1930s were given Fowler's, as were show cattle. Every farm had some arsenic somewhere. It was used as a worm drench and as a dip for sheep. The drug was not then in disrepute, although

veterinary texts warned that it accumulated in the organs of horses and could cause inflammation.

Phar Lap's corpse – or parts of it – was subjected to four examinations. None could be called conclusive.

First, Nielsen and Masoero performed a post-mortem a few hours after Phar Lap's death. Nielsen was not a 'vet' as we now understand the term. He was registered under an old Act that allowed on the veterinarians' register those who had demonstrated their skills in treating horses. Nielsen's skills are unquestioned, but he was not a university graduate.

Anyway, this autopsy found the horse's intestines to be red and raw; there was inflammation in the stomach and colon, and the horse was full of gas. Masoero said – and this

Stuart Reid's sketch for his famous 1931 painting of Phar Lap was donated to the Australian Racing Museum at Caulfield Racecourse by the late Tommy Woodcock.

is important – there was no obstruction in the digestive system, as there often is in cases of colic.

Second, the US Food and Drug Administration began an investigation the next day. The Department was looking for arsenic: it wanted the substance outlawed as an insecticide.

Its investigation found arsenic present in leaves from the trees that had been sprayed, in grass and lucerne that had been sprayed, in grass and lucerne that Phar Lap had grazed on, in grass pulled for Phar Lap, and in the horse's lungs and liver. But – and this is the crucial part here – the arsenic was not in quantities likely to kill the horse.

Third, on the following day, the Thursday, Nielsen stored as many of the horse's organs as would fit in a refrigerator. David Davis, the

horse's co-owner, had already donated Phar Lap's heart to the Institute of Anatomy, Canberra, and Nielsen put it in a jar. The hide was taken. What was left of the horse went into the ground. This was a frightful mistake, but Woodcock and Nielsen could not have foreseen the controversy that would rage for the rest of the century.

Fourth, Davis commissioned his own autopsy. Pathologists headed by Dr Karl Meyer from the University of California began work on the Saturday. Meyer immediately complained about the missing organs. He concluded that some disturbance in the large intestine or stomach was the cause of death. His toxicologist tested the organs for arsenic – and found not a trace.

Meyer finally issued a statement. It said, 'An enormous accumulation of gas in the stomach and intestines' probably killed the horse. It went on: '… lead arsenate, which was found in very small quantities in the body of the horse, and in the feed, may be responsible for the irritation of the intestinal tract.' Where did Meyer get the arsenic from? His own toxicologist had found none.

The riddle deepens. Twelve years later, one of Meyer's team talked of an 'impaction' a foot long in the intestines. Masoero was the only one to have seen all the organs and he said there was no impaction.

The serious evidence ends here. The rest is gossip. It is hard to believe that Woodcock fed bad grain, as some Americans suggested. What about the paddock lucerne? Some animals react to it. There is no conclusive evidence that it bothered Phar Lap. Some said Phar Lap was poisoned by gangsters. Why? And with what? Again, no evidence. Some said Phar Lap was worn out from thirty-six wins in Australia and one in Mexico. Again, no evidence.

Vets, looking at the serious evidence half a century later, say Phar Lap could have died from tympanites, a bloat-like condition. Others, like Percy Sykes, talk of colitis X, a disease of uncertain cause (hence the letter 'X') characterised by an inflamed colon and, eventually, a haemorrhage in its wall.

Who really knows? Phar Lap may be one of Australia's peculiar heroes, up there in the pantheon somewhere between Les Darcy and Gallipoli, but he was still a racehorse. Racehorses die all the time, and sometimes we cannot work out why.

What we do know is that there is nothing to suggest that Woodcock accidentally killed the horse or was negligent with him.

by Les Carlyon

Peter Pan's striking Melbourne Cup win

Heavy clouds hung over Flemington on Melbourne Cup day 1932, but the winner, a showy colt called Peter Pan, brightened everyone's day. As did Sir Charles Kingsford Smith by flying over the course in his famous monoplane, the Southern Cross.

It seemed inconceivable that the void created by the death of Phar Lap would be filled so soon. But with the splendid timing that was to mark his career, along came Peter Pan, in the words of Frank O'Loghlen a 'personality horse … a tall, light chestnut with a silver mane and tail, one of the most distinctive individuals of the turf in 50 years'.

Looks alone, of course, don't win races. Importantly, Peter Pan was a gritty galloper with 'extraordinary courage'. It was this quality that shone through in the Melbourne Cup after a stirring struggle with Yarramba, the Moonee Valley Cup winner.

Peter Pan almost lost his footing when jockey Bill Duncan went for an opening five furlongs from home. After stumbling, his stablemate Denis Boy (H. Skidmore) cannoned into him. This had the effect of putting Peter Pan back on his feet.

Peter Pan was seventh on the home turn, and destined, it seemed, for no better than a minor placing when the lightly weighted Yarramba (7.3) burst clear in the straight. However, with Duncan riding vigorously, Peter Pan, the top fancy at 4/1, finished with a paralysing burst to catch Yarramba (20/1) a few yards from the post and win by a neck in the good time of 3:23¼, only a half-second outside the record. Third, two lengths away, was old reliable Shadow King, placed for the third time in a year.

Andy Knox, rider of Yarramba, thought he had the race won until Peter Pan, the horse he feared, ranged up alongside him. 'Yarramba gave everything he had,' said Knox. 'Fifty yards out I gave him his last cut with the whip. I knew we were under.' For 32-year-old Duncan it was his second Melbourne Cup winner. He won on Night Watch in 1918.

Of Peter Pan's win, Duncan said: 'This is the best horse I have ridden. Peter Pan should have won by a dozen lengths. Even Phar Lap could not have overcome the difficulties he encountered.'

Peter Pan's Cup win, the 21st by a three-year-old, was immensely popular with the crowd of 84 480, not only because he was favourite as a result of his Melbourne Stakes win on Derby Day and unlucky fourth in Rogilla's Caulfield Cup. His bulldog tenacity was also applauded by one and all from men

Peter Pan's strength and showy looks are on display in this picture, with Andy Knox the rider.

in top hats and caps to women who covered their chiffon frocks with fur coats that could be removed should the sun shine.

'Another Phar Lap – Racegoers' impression of Peter Pan' said the *Age* headline, heralding the dawn of a new star having only his seventh race start (for five wins).

Peter Pan, by Pantheon (third in the 1926 Melbourne Cup) from Alwina, was bred by Rodney Dangar, whose Baroona estate was near Singleton in NSW. Dangar had bought Alwina (by St Alwynne) for 200 guineas as a yearling and retained her for breeding.

Her foal, a good-looking, leggy fellow, so impressed Dangar that he decided to race him himself. Veteran Frank McGrath, who had prepared Amounis, took on the training.

Peter Pan had his first start in a two-year-

old handicap at Randwick on 14 May 1932. He was unplaced and not long after ran a nail into his foot, which became seriously infected. It was not until August that he had his next race in a three-year-old novice at Warwick Farm. He dead-heated for first with Babili, after which McGrath told Dangar: 'I think we have a good horse on our hands.' Indeed. Two starts later, in a meteoric rise, Peter Pan won the AJC Derby with Jim Pike in the saddle for the first time. Then it was off to Melbourne and fame.

His Cup win was McGrath's second. He had won with Prince Foote back in 1909. Peter Pan was spelled after the Melbourne Cup. He returned to racing in March 1933, winning first-up in the City Tattersalls Randwick Stakes (wfa) over a mile.

L. K. S. Mackinnon (V.).

Ben Chaffey (V.).

S. A. Rawdon (V.).

Les. Hilton (V.).

F. E. Shillabeer (V.).

E. L. and C. Baillieu (V.

J. P. Arthur (V.).

George Woodforde (V.).

Agar Wynne (V.).

J. S. Feehan (V.).

R. INKSON, in colours of E. Y. Sheil (V.).

T. M. Burke (V.).

A. S. Chirnside

J. I. Winter-Irving (V.).

H. A. Currie (V.).

Mrs. L. R. Buxton (V.).

H. N. Leonard (V.).

Clive Leonard (V.).

R. C. Power (V.).

P. G. Hay (V.).

C. C. Stephen (N.S.W.).

J. E. Brien (N.S.

E. Moss (N.S.W.).

Sir Hugh Denison (N.S.W.).

Otway R. Falkiner (N.S.W.).

Sir Samuel Hordern (N.S.W.).

F. Smithden (N.S.W.).

P. H. Osborne (N.S.W.).

R. C. Allen (N.S.W.).

W. T. Brunton (N.S.

Robert Miller (N.S.W.).

R. E. H. Hope (S.A.).

C. L. J. Dubois (S.A.).

H. P. McLachlan (S.A.).

Sir Sidney Kidman (S.A.).

Harry Lewis (S.A.).

Alan McFarlane (S.A.).

C. L. Moorhou (S.

F. R. Mortlock (S.A.).

H. J. Winten (Q.).

D. A. Winten (Q.).

R. J. Winten (Q.).

Mrs. A. H. Whittingham (Q.).

B. de Burgh Persse (Q.).

W. Glasson (Q

E. L. Ramsay (Q.).

James Clark (Q.).

I. J. Moore (Q.).

A. B. Nagel (Q.)

L. HYNES, in colours of J. Fahey (N.S.W.)

J. P. O'Hara (W.A.).

Dr. T. Ambrose (W.A.).

J. H. S. Barnes (Q.).

fatt (V.)   James Wilson (V.)   J. M. Niall (V.)

Philip Russell (V.)   E. E. D. Clarke (V.)

R. Turnbull (V.)

M. S. Cooper (V.),

MacLeod (V.)   G. M. Davis (V.)   P. T. Heywood (V.)

W. DUNCAN, in colours of C. B. Kellow (V.).

J. Fell (V.)   A. T. Creswick (V.)   F. W. Kitchen (V.)

A. G. Hunter (V.)

fatt (N.S.W.)   J. S. Brunton (N.S.W.)   C. C. Sheath (N.S.W.)

Miss Una Clift (N.S.W.)

A. W. Thompson (N.S.W.)   H. S. Thompson (N.S.W.)

A. P. Wade (N.S.W.)   Mr. Constable (N.S.W.)

oses (N.S.W.).   Hunter White (N.S.W.)

Sir James Murdoch (N.S.W.)

C. W. L. Murchison (N.S.W.)

D. U. Seaton (N.S.W.),

T. C. Trautwein (N.S.W.)

J. J. Leahy (N.S.W.)   W. B. Carr (S.A.)

tter (S.A.).   T. H. McKay (S.A.).   T. S. Ryder (S.A.)

F. A. Tennant (S.A.)   S. Torr (S.A.)   F. W. Whyte (S.A.)

J. M. Cummings (S.A.),

C. A. Morris (Q.).

O'Shea (Q.).   E. Lee Steere (W.A.)

L. V. O'Hara (Q.).

H. E. Vaill (W.A.)   W. J. Winterbottom (W.A.)

W. H. Vincent (W.A.).

T. Lyons (T.).

R. Bunbury (A.).

D. E. Grant (W.A.).   W. McKenzie Grant

J. PIKE, in colours of S. Green (V.).

G. H. Cann (T.)   A. F. A. O'Connor (T.)

W. L. Southerwood (T.)   E. W. Freeland (T.)

Sprint winner

Waltzing Lily evoked memories of the flying Valicare with four superlative sprint wins in 1933. Though starting at 20/1, she certainly brightened up proceedings at Flemington on Newmarket Handicap Day, when a sultry morning gave way to afternoon downpours. Mackintoshes and brollies were much in evidence.

Those who braved the elements included the English cricket team, play in its match against Victoria having been washed out. All and sundry applauded Waltzing Lily, a three-year-old filly who was asked to carry 8.9 – 4 lb more than weight-for-age – in the dash up the straight six. Not since Molly's Robe in 1919 had a three-year-old filly won the Newmarket and she had only 7.8.

Waltzing Lily had earned her weight with wins in the Standish Handicap and William Reid Stakes at the start of the year. And once again, in the Newmarket, she displayed rare speed and courage, pitted as she was against two formidable adversaries in Chatham and Winooka. With two furlongs to go, half of the 22 starters were seemingly in a line across the track. Finally, it got down to a battle between Waltzing Lily (J. O'Brien) in the centre of the track and Jacko (H. Skidmore) on the grandstand side. The filly gained the day by a head, confirming her status as a superior sprinter. In the winter she again showed a liking for the straight-six, winning the Lawn Handicap.

As a four-year-old in 1933, Waltzing Lily won the Memsie Stakes and finished third to Rogilla in the Cox Plate. In 1934, she took the VATC Futurity Stakes with 9.10.

Retired to stud in 1935, she produced the 1953 VRC Oaks winner Waltzing Lady.

At the distance in the W. S. Cox Plate at Moonee Valley, on October 28, 1933. Waltzing Lily (E. Baxter), on the outside, Dermid (W. Cook) in the centre, and Chatham (J. E. Pike) on the rails, are racing in perfect line, with Break Up (E. Preston) immediately behind. Rogilla, who is not in the picture, came with a brilliant run and won from Dermid and Waltzing Lily, with Chatham next.

Inside the furlong at the Cox Plate it's all Waltzing Lily, Dermid and Chatham – but Rogilla won.

Chatham, king of the milers

The high-quality colt Hall Mark seldom played second fiddle to any fellow thoroughbred but he did so on AJC Derby day at Randwick in the spring of 1933.

No sooner had Darby Munro kicked him home a clear winner in the classic, landing some nice wagers at 2/1 for the confident Jack Holt stable, than one of Jim Pike's favourites, Chatham, made light of 9.10 to repeat his 1932 win in the Epsom Handicap.

Though forced to concede a stone or more to his 18 rivals, Chatham, a five-year-old son of the Melbourne Cup winner Windbag, was regarded as the horse to beat. He had won the Epsom the year before with 8.13 and three weight-for-age races since resuming. The prospect of rain-affected going saw his price drift to 3/1 by race morning but, when it became apparent the track was not as bad as anticipated, the fielders were set upon by confident punters.

As a result Chatham went to the post a warm favourite at 5/4. With Pike riding confidently, he gathered in the leader Whittingham inside the final furlong and held off long-shot Regal Son (7.7) to win by a length. Two days later Regal Son landed a fortune in bets when he won the AJC Metropolitan.

The second Epsom was Chatham's 13th win and one of his best. But he still had 11 more wins – and his greatest – to come.

Discussing the bay horse Pike said:

'Chatham was really great at a mile, whether at wfa or in a handicap. On top of the ground he could muster dazzling speed; in the mud he was still a champion – just like Peter Pan. Chatham had tiny feet – "goat's feet" we used to call them – but he could plough through the mud. I wouldn't say Chatham was the greatest miler ever, but if it were possible to line them all up – Gloaming, Heroic, Ajax, Amounis – it would be a great race. Chatham would compare with the best of them.'

Maurice McCarten, who rode many topliners, said 'You could not rate Chatham too highly. He was a great weight carrier and a marvellous handicapper. Records prove it: 24 wins (one a dead-heat) from 47 starts.'

Chatham was bred by Percy Miller at Kia Ora Stud in NSW. His dam, Myosotis, was by The Welkin, sire of Gloaming, so Chatham had speed as well as endurance. As a three-year-old, however, he had a problem, developing a 'whistle' while galloping. It was subsequently revealed he had a weakness in the bloodstream and kidneys, rather than a wind infirmity. The treatment involved blood-letting, a course of tonics, and a spell in the country.

After only one win from seven starts in the autumn of 1932, he swept all before him when he resumed, winning the Epsom, WS Cox Plate and four other races in the spring of 1932.

TURF TOPICS

Still winning: Sydney gelding Rogilla, the 1932 Caulfield Cup winner, had notable successes in 1933, including the Sydney Cup, WS Cox Plate and CB Fisher Plate.

Fined a fiver: Maurice McCarten, one of the few Sydney jockeys riding on the last day of the VRC Spring Carnival, rode four winners – Blixten (Batman Stakes), Cavalcade (Flemington Stakes), Oro (VRC Handicap) and Queen Helen (Ottawa Stakes). McCarten was fined £5 for excessive use of the spur on Oro.

Fast flight: A newsreel film of Hall Mark's Melbourne Cup win was flown by Sir Charles Kingsford Smith from Essendon to Sydney where that night it was shown at the Regent Theatre.

Hall Mark takes the pain

Hall Mark was not a big colt, not built to take a buffeting. But there was no doubting his courage and ability to gallop, as he proved in narrowly winning the 1933 Melbourne Cup.

Twenty-four hours before the race, he was long odds to run because of a cracked heel on the off hind leg.

The trouble was noticed on Saturday evening after the son of Heroic – with Victoria Derby honours thick upon him following a five-length victory – had returned to Jack Holt's Mordialloc stables. Hall Mark was in considerable pain and Holt called in veterinary surgeon S. O. Wood.

By Monday, Cup eve, little Hall Mark, winner of the AJC Derby as well as the Victorian classic, had improved. With the blessing of owner Charles Kellow, Hall Mark was floated to Flemington on Cup Day.

The vets subjected the colt's damaged heel to a thorough overhaul. Finally, they declared 'it was worth the risk'. Kellow, satisfied with their assessment, declared to the onlookers: 'Hall Mark will be a runner.'

Punters rallied to the cause. Though under a cloud and reported by some as scarcely able to walk, Hall Mark was backed from 5/1 to 5/2 equal favouritism with Rogilla.

When the barrier's strands went up, Hall

Mark, with 20-year-old Sydney apprentice Jack O'Sullivan in the saddle, was 4/1. The slow early pace – the first mile took 1:48½ – helped Hall Mark settle in a forward position. Turning for home, he was sixth. Soon after he made a dash to the front, streaking to a two-length lead. But the challenges came thick and fast, especially from 33/1 pop Shadow King, who had been held up for a run.

The finish was as stirring as they come. 'Onlookers were hysterical,' said the *Age*. With 40 yards to go, Hall Mark was less than a length in front. On the post, it was Hall Mark by a head from Shadow King (Scobie Breasley), with Topical and Caulfield Cup winner Gaine Carrington dead-heating for third, a head away. Rogilla was never in it.

Blood was oozing freely from Hall Mark's heel as he returned to scale. The crack in the heel had opened wider. After the race, grateful backers eager to heap praise upon the winner sought him out, only to find stall 66 deserted. Hall Mark, his heel patched up, was on his way to Holt's Mordialloc stable.

A jubilant O'Sullivan said that two furlongs out Hall Mark was going to win easily, but the colt seemed lame over the last 20 yards and eased up. 'I was never so relieved in my life when I reached the winning post,' O'Sullivan said. 'But poor little Hall Mark. He was a cot case.'

Hall Mark of breeding

Charles Kellow bought more than a champion racehorse when he outlaid a record 16 000 guineas for Heroic at the dispersal sale that followed the Purser case. Heroic turned out to be a grand stallion, topping the sires' list seven years in a row from 1932–33 to 1938–39, when he broke a leg running around in a paddock.

Kellow was described by jockey Jack O'Sullivan as a 'colossus of a man, a man with a charming personality'. He was also a horseman and a cyclist. And he was exceedingly rich, having made his pile out of automobiles.

When Heroic was retired in 1927 after winning 21 races, he stayed in Kellow's hands and went to Herbert Thompson's Tarwyn Park stud at Rylstone in NSW.

Heroic's first champion was Hall Mark. Foaled in 1930, he was out of Herowinkie, whose grandsire was Spearmint (by Carbine). Hall Mark was so named because of Kellow's association with fellow racing enthusiast Sir Samuel Hordern. They had landed a £100 000 plunge when Heroic and Pilliewinkie won the Newmarket-Australian Cup double in 1926. Kellow thought the Heroic colt would be the hall-mark of friendship and breeding.

Hall Mark, a diminutive yet compact chestnut colt, had his first run, aged two, in the VATC Debutant Stakes at Caulfield in October 1932. He was unplaced. Wins in the AJC Sires and Champagne Stakes heralded a momentous year in 1933, when he won eight races, including the AJC and Victoria Derbys and the Melbourne Cup.

TURF TOPICS

Top jockeys: Bill Duncan (47½ wins) topped the Victorian jockeys' list in 1932–33, followed by J. O'Brien (39), H. Skidmore (28) and H. Badger (26½). For the first time, Fred Hoysted, trainer of the mighty Redditch, was Victoria's leading trainer with 25½ wins. On the list were Vin Ryan (18) and Hall Mark's trainer Jack Holt (17½). In Sydney, Amounis's trainer Frank McGrath was top mentor with 24½ wins. In Adelaide, R. Medhurst was the top jockey with 25 wins, while G. V. Bates was the leading trainer, with 14 victories.

No jumps: The Cracksman was runner-up to Redditch in the GN Steeplechase at Flemington, after winning a Steeplechasers' flat race over two miles the week before.

They're racing: By means of a number of amplifiers installed in the members' stand, all races were broadcast at Flemington on GN Hurdle Day, particularly for the benefit of patrons on the flat where facilities were less favourable than those in the paddock and on the hill. The move followed the successful broadcasting of races at Williamstown.

Evils of the punt! On Cup Day, the Salvation Army held a service in the City Temple in Melbourne, protesting against the gambling spirit and the setting aside of a day for the running of the Cup. A procession of about 300 warriors of the cross, with two bands, marched along Swanston Street and Collins Street to the Temple, where Commissioner Maxwell said gambling was a 'national evil'.

Tale of two hustlers: In Sydney, the day before a July hurdle race at Moorefield, jockey W. Aldridge was approached by a hustler to lose the race. Aldridge declined and informed the AJC of the matter. Aldridge's mount won. It was called Hustler!

Knee pull: Ted Webster, rider of Blematic, was found guilty of grabbing hold of the knee of rival jockey J. L. Meagher on Iskander in the second Warook Highweight at Moonee Valley on 28 January 1933. Webster also seized Iskander's tail at the start. Webster, a cross country rider, was disqualified for 12 months. Stewards in those days did not acquaint racegoers with details of such offences, just that Webster had deliberately interfered with Iskander.

Winooka no Palooka

When Winooka thrashed 16 rivals in the AJC Doncaster Handicap in the autumn of 1933, his connections decided to take him to America. They reckoned their classy sprinter had no future outside weight-for-age races, which offered no big money as betting mediums.

Owned by Sydney bookmakers A. J. Matthews and W. A. McDonald and trained by Mick Polson, Winooka (favourite at 3/1) lumped 9.13 to victory in the big Randwick mile and cut out the journey in a slashing 1:35¾, an Australasian record. Heading the beaten brigade, a length and a half astern, was Jacko, the previous year's winner.

With Jim Pike in the saddle as usual, the win was Winooka's ninth, including the VATC Futurity Stakes. After the Doncaster, two wfa wins followed.

In May, the four year-old bay son of Windbag–Kanooka sailed for America.

Winooka received a good press on landing in San Francisco. The memory of Phar Lap's win in New Mexico was still vivid. Winooka's first run was in a $10 000 match race at Tanforan near the Golden Gate. He went as fast as necessary, easily beating Hawaiian sprinter Hueu. The party then travelled 1000 miles to Seattle where Winooka developed a bad cold and nearly died. So Winooka, carrying Australia's hopes, went to Laurel racecourse for an international race. Unfortunately the track was a bog and Winooka came in last to hoots and jeers, mostly aimed at Naylor.

Under a headline "Twas a Orful Shame', newspaper columnist W. Wilson Wingate wrote a poem, in which Winooka was described as a 'Palooka'. Wingate soon had to eat his words. On a dry track at Pimlico, Winooka thrashed many of the horses that had beaten him at Laurel. Back in Australia in 1934-35, six-year-old Winooka had six more races. His last race was in the Doncaster Handicap. Sadly, he broke down.

Racing's most popular loser

When it came to looks, Shadow King was not in the same picture book as his sire, the striking stallion Comedy King. And, unlike his father, Shadow King never won the Melbourne Cup.

But he did everything but, running in six and being placed four times in a row – third to Phar Lap in 1930, second to White Nose (1931), third to Peter Pan (1932) and second to Hall Mark (1933). The closest the popular bay gelding came to winning the Cup was in 1933, when he went down by a head to the courageous Hall Mark.

Scobie Breasley, who rode Shadow King in 1933, said years later: 'Jim Pike, one of the greatest jockeys I rode against, was the culprit. He brought his mount Gaine Carrington right round the outside of the field, then tried to cut in towards the rail. The rest of us were left in as heap.

'When old Shadow King saw some daylight he simply flew and was catching Hall Mark hand over fist in the last half furlong.

'We would have won in just one more stride and you will still find people who were at Flemington that day to tell you that we did win. But of course there was no photo-finish.'

This was typical of Breasley's luck in the Cup, a race he was never able to win.

Shadow King, of course, won his share of races, including the 1930 Moonee Valley Cup and the 1933 Herbert Power Handicap and Williamstown Cup.

He always attracted a crowd of well-wishers outside his stall.

His heroic Cup efforts led to the phrase 'as unlucky as Shadow King'.

At the age of 10, Shadow King (8.2) was given the honour of leading the field out for the 1935 Melbourne Cup. He came in fourth at 100/1 – showing a clean pair of well-worn hooves to two of his former conquerors, Hall Mark (9.6) and Peter Pan (10.6).

He ended his days as a police horse.

Lough Neagh, idol of Queensland

For sheer versatility, one of Australia's greatest gallopers was the Queenslander Lough Neagh, owned and trained by Tim Brosnan. A chestnut gelding by the 1916 Queensland Cup winner Bachelor's Persse, Lough Neagh won 32 races – handicaps from five furlongs to two miles and wfa races from six furlongs to two miles.

Foaled in 1928, Lough Neagh was a star from the outset. At two he won the QTC Sires' Produce Stakes and at three the Queensland Guineas and Derby and an open flying with 9.1.

The robust gelding travelled frequently to Sydney, winning the Rawson Stakes and Chipping Norton Stakes three times. He beat Peter Pan in the 1936 Rawson Stakes.

At five, Lough Neagh, by then the idol of Brisbane racegoers and a great favourite with Sydney crowds as well, carried 9.4 to victory in the 1934 Doomben Newmarket, the richest sprint in Australia.

In 1935, he twice defied the Brisbane handicapper by winning open sprints with 9.6 and 9.9.

A year later, aged seven, he silenced those critics who said he couldn't stay by winning the Brisbane Cup with 9.3.

In all, Lough Neagh had 127 races in eight seasons for 32 wins, 23 seconds and 21 thirds for £19 871 in stake money. More often than not he was ridden by Frank Shean.

Redditch won 14 races but was killed as a result of a fall in the 1935 Grand National Steeple.

Redditch jumps onto scene

When exciting fencer Redditch won the 1933 Grand National Steeplechase at Flemington with the steadier of 12.3 he never once put 'toe to timber' – so clean and momentous was his jumping.

Prepared at Mentone by 50 year-old Fred Hoysted, the state's premier trainer in 1932–33, Redditch made light of his big burden and smashed the race record, running the three miles and one furlong in 6 minutes, 5 seconds, lowering Sandhurst's time by 3¾ seconds.

Redditch, expertly piloted by R. Inkson, defeated The Cracksman by eight lengths, with grand old campaigner Mosstrooper, the 1930 winner, third.

A month later, Redditch, starting favourite at even money and carrying 12.13,

again showed a clean pair of hooves to eight rivals in the Australian Steeplechase. Jumping splendidly and displaying rare pace on the flat, he downed the gallant Mosstrooper (11.11). Three lengths was the winning margin in favour of the younger Redditch, at six a relative baby compared to old Mosstrooper, a greybeard of 12. Redditch's win was worth £1100 and took his winnings past £5000.

More than one scribe rated Redditch's effort in the national steeple as greater than that of the once incomparable Redleap, who won with a stone more (13.3) in 1892. Redditch's time was 40¾ seconds faster, which it was felt turned the scales in his favour.

But Redditch paid dearly for his success. A week after winning the Australian Steeple,

he was asked to carry a crushing 13.7 in the August Steeple at Flemington and crashed heavily after striking one of the formidable log fences. His jockey R. Inkson suffered concussion and was on the critical list for days. There were howls of protest, horse lovers decrying the cruel nature of the fences and the huge weights Redditch had to carry.

After winning the Australian Steeplechase for the second year in a row in 1934, again with 12.13, he crashed in the 1935 GN Steeple and had to be destroyed. His death raised an outcry and led to the timber fences being replaced by brush obstacles.

Redditch, who had stamina (through Carbine) and speed in his bloodlines, was bred in 1927 by World War I Army captain, Colin Chisholm, who had been bequeathed a stallion by his uncle.

Chisholm set up his own stud in NSW and bought Sister Olive's sire Red Dennis and several mares, one of which was Kenilworth Queen (by Kenilworth, sire of Mosstrooper).

Redditch, the second foal of Red Dennis–Kenilworth Queen, was bought for 75 guineas at the 1929 Sydney yearling sales by Loddon Yuille, keeper of the Australian Stud Book. Early on, Yuille leased the colt to W. J. Wood, brother of veterinary surgeons S. O. and E. N. Wood.

After a couple of runs in Sydney, Redditch was transferred to Hoysted's stable at Mentone. He showed pace for flat racing, his grand-dam Punkah having been a half sister to the speedy Headwind, winner of the 1919 Standish Handicap.

But Redditch did not show quite enough toe so it was decided to try him over hurdles. When his owner died in 1931, the executors of his estate exercised their option to race the bay gelding.

As a four-year-old in 1932, Redditch ran third with 11.0 in the GN Hurdle and in season 1932–33 it was decided to confine him to the big timber – post and rail fences. While this certainly was his forte – he won numerous chases – having to jump such unforgiving obstacles led to his demise.

1933 RESULTS

VRC MELBOURNE CUP (2m)
Hall Mark, 7.8 (J O'Sullivan) Trained by J Holt; 3:27.25; Shadow King, Topical & Gaine Carrington
AJC SYDNEY CUP (2m)
Rogilla, 8.10 (G Robinson) Trained by L Haigh; 3:23; Nord, Gippsland
QTC BRISBANE CUP (2m)
Herolage, 7.10 (E Conquest) 3:25.25; Bachelor's Advice, Poy Patrol
SAJC ADELAIDE CUP (13-f)
Infirmiere, 7.4 (S Kite) Trained by R Matson; 2:46; Eastern Star, Glenvarloch
WATC PERTH CUP (2m)
Cueesun, 7.0 (A Johnson) Trained by D McDonald; 3:33; Balindallock, Prince Paladin

VATC CAULFIELD CUP (12-f)
Gaine Carrington, 8.13 (J Pike) Trained by CT Godby; 2:28.5; Jimmie Boy, Oro
VRC AUSTRALIAN CUP (2¼m)
Topical, 7.8 (A Knox) Trained by W Kelso; 3:52.5; Flail, Eastern Chief
MVRC WS COX PLATE (9 ½-f)
Rogilla, 9.4 (D Munro) Trained by L Haigh; 1:58.5; Dermid, Waltzing Lily
AJC DERBY (12-f)
Hall Mark, 8.10 (D Munro) Trained by J Holt; 2:37.5; Deputy Ruler, Blixten
VRC VICTORIA DERBY (12-f)
Hall Mark (D Munro) Trained by J Holt; 2:31.25; Palphar, Miramond
AJC DONCASTER HANDICAP (1m)
Winooka, 9.13 (J Pike) Trained by M Polson; 1:35.7; Jacko, Parkwood

BTC DOOMBEN '10 000' (6-f)
(First run 1933) Wallun, 7.2 (H Hayes) Trained by E Smith; 1:12.5; Closing Time, Noel Soldat
VRC NEWMARKET HANDICAP (6-f)
Waltzing Lily, 8.9 (J O'Brien) Trained by S Smith; 1:13.25; Jacko, Ibrano
AJC SIRES' PRODUCE STAKES (7-f)
Hall Mark, 8.10 (W Duncan) Trained by J Holt; 1:24; Maid Of Orleans, Golden Hair
VRC SIRES' PRODUCE STAKES (7-f)
L'Elite, 8.10 (A Knox) Trained by H Freedman; 1:26.5; Heroic Lass, Shakuni
VRC GRAND NATIONAL STEEPLECHASE (3m 1-f)
Redditch, 12.3 (R Inkson) Trained by FW Hoysted; 6:5; The Cracksman, Mosstrooper

Writing about racing

Australian literature of the turf can boast of no Dick Francis, although the English master gave the nod to our greatest race when he made the Melbourne Cup the backdrop to skulduggery in his thriller *In the Frame* (1976). The most prolific of all racing novelists – Nat Gould – began his working career in Australia. A regular contributor to the Sydney sporting paper the *Referee*, Gould serialised his first novel, *The Double Event*, there in 1891, under the pseudonym 'Verax'.

Novelist Nat Gould.

Adapted for the stage in 1893, the play highlighted the running of the Melbourne Cup. Even after Gould's return to England in 1895, many of his novels had Australian racecourse settings – Flemington, Randwick, and even Coolgardie, for the Miners' Cup (1896). Gould's most important work was *On and Off the Turf in Australia* (1895). The book was memorable especially for its account of the champion Carbine, both on the track and on the occasion of his being shipped to England, where he would stand as a highly successful sire.

Novelists of the Australian turf have been relatively few. Before Gould, Marcus Clarke had been ridiculed for allowing a stallion to win the Oaks in his novel *Long Odds* (1869). Clarke's revenge was to borrow from his novel for the description that he wrote for the *Herald* of the 1873 Cup, won by Don Juan. When, in Tasma's novel *Uncle Piper of Piper's Hill* (1889), George Piper's horse Casserole runs second at Flemington, his punishment is to have his debt annulled on penalty of marriage to his cousin.

Marcus Clarke

In the 20th century, one notable racing novel was written in a prisoner-of-war camp; another in a gaol. Ian Sabey's *Of the Thunder of Hooves* (eventually published in 1982) was completed in 1943 while he was a prisoner of the Germans. The book relates how the aptly named bush horse Mountain Rogue wins the Great Eastern Steeplechase at Oakbank, on protest. Less sentimentally resolved is *The Last Gamble* (1974), by 'John Goodwood', in which a desperate punter touches his firm's till and risks all on a seven-race card at Randwick.

Wilda Moxham's *The Apprentice* (1969) prefers the happy ending. A reformed juvenile criminal cum jockey, Rufe Dale, teams up with the broken down champion galloper Pancho, seeing him back to form and fitness to win – of course – the Melbourne Cup. The racing action is altogether grittier in Frank Hardy's *Power Without Glory* (1950), where race-fixing is one of the nefarious pursuits of John Wren. A turf lover, Hardy collaborated with the champion and controversial jockey Athol Mulley to produce a selection of racing yarns, *The Needy and the Greedy* (1975). Hardy also wrote a novel about mad gamblers, ill-luck and welshing bookmakers, tartly titled *The Four-Legged Lottery* (1958), and replete with an epigraph from Egon Kisch.

Arthur Upfield turned aside from Boney awhile to seize an opportunity he could not resist to write *The Great Melbourne Cup Mystery*, a novel which was serialised in the *Herald* in 1932. There are scenes in Sydney racing stables in Patrick White's *The Tree of Man* (1995) – not so surprising when one recalls that his father raced horses of his own. Gerard Murnane's first novel, *Tamarisk Row* (1974), depicts a young boy's fascination with racing. No contemporary Australian novelist is such a fan of the horse sports as Murnane, who has lectured on English expression to the VRC's school for apprentice jockeys.

As Lord John Roxton says to young Ned Malone in Arthur Conan Doyle's novel, *The Lost World* (1912): 'Hope you know your Gordon, for he's the poet of the horse and the gun and the man that handles both.' And so Adam Lindsay Gordon has been remembered. Besides such perennial favourites as the verse yarn 'How We Beat the Favourite', Gordon was also an accomplished jockey. No one has equalled his feat of riding three steeplechase winners on a single day, as he did with Babbler, Viking and Cadger on 10 October 1868 at Flemington. Gordon shot himself on 24 June 1870 at Brighton, on the day of the publication of his volume of verse

Horseman and poet Adam Lindsay Gordon.

entitled *Bush Ballads and Galloping Rhymes.*

It was once complained of Henry Lawson that there was not a horse to be seen in all his verse. That charge could scarcely be levelled at his contemporary A. B. 'Banjo' Paterson, who not only celebrated 'the colt from old Regret' and the prowess of crack bush horsemen, but wrote a number of racing poems, including 'How the Favourite Beat Us' (ironically reversing Gordon's title) and 'Father Riley's Horse'. Paterson also wrote the racing novel *The Shearer's Colt* (1936) and his Great War service saw him as an officer in charge of supplying cavalry remounts in the Middle East.

Among punting professors (no fraternity they), Vincent Buckley was the best poet, and perhaps the only one since Paterson to take a serious, loving and informed interest in the turf. In the poem 'Kilmore Races', for instance, he writes of how 'Horses fret too and balance./Mounted, they shy under/the twin poles fringed with wattle'. 'In the loose box, horse' catches the physical grace and nervous energy of the thoroughbred. Both poems were collected in *Golden Builders* (1976).

Some of the finest writing about racing in Australia has been fugitive. Few pieces by racing journalists have been reprinted. Bert Lillye, chief racing writer for the *Sydney Morning Herald* when he retired in 1984, compiled a collection of anecdotes, *Backstage of Racing*. Before they can be literary stylists, turf writers have to be judges of form, tipsters and even detectives, as was Bert Wolfe ('Cardigan') when he exposed the Erbie/Redlock ring-in. Some are given more licence to show their creative flair, as Les Carlyon has been in his columns in the *Age*. There he has written of the sinew and spirit of racing, the bravery and beauty of the animals at the heart of the sport.

by Peter Pierce

A hostile welcome waits for the perennial punter in this drawing by Percy Leason.

A post-Cup tale

I 'ad the money in me 'and!
Fair dinkum! Right there, by the stand.
   I tole me wife at breakfus' time,
    Straight out: 'Trivalve,' I sez, 'is prime.
'Trivalve,' I sez. An', all the week,
I swear there's no one 'eard me speak
   Another 'orse's name. Why, look,
   I 'ad the oil straight from a Book
On Sund'y at me cousin's place
When we was torkin' of the race.
   'Trivalve,' 'e sez. "Is chance is grand.'
   I 'ad the money in me 'and!

Fair in me 'and I 'ad the dough!
An' then a man 'as got to go –
   Wot? Tough? Look, if I 'adn't met
   Jim Smith (I ain't forgave 'im yet)
'E takes an' grabs me by the coat.
'Trivalve?' 'e sez. 'Ar, turn it up!
'Ow could 'e win a flamin' Cup?'
Of course, I thort 'e muster knoo,
'Im livin' near a trainer, too.

Right 'ere, like that, fair in me fist
I 'ad the notes! An' then I missed –
   Missed like a mug fair on the knock
Becos 'is naggin' done me block.
'That airy goat?' 'e sez. "E's crook!'
Fair knocked me back, 'e did. An' look,
   I 'ad the money in me 'and!
   Fair in me paw! An', un'erstand,
Sixes at least I coulder got –
Thirty to five, an' made a pot.
Today I mighter been reel rich –
Rollin' in dough! Instid o' which,
'Ere's me – Aw! Don't it beat the band?
I 'AD THE MONEY IN ME 'AND!
Put me clean off, that's wot 'e did …
Say, could yeh len' us 'arf a quid?

by C. J. Dennis

How we backed the favourite

'Sure thing,' said the grocer; 'as far as I know, sir,
This horse, Peter Pan, is the safest of certs.'
'I see by the paper,' commended the draper,
'He's tipped and he carries my whole weight of shirts.'
The butcher said, 'Well, now, it's easy to tell now
There's nothing else in it except Peter Pan.'
And so said the baker, the barman, bookmaker,
The old lady char and the saveloy man.

'You stick to my tip, man,' admonished the grip-man,
'Play up Peter Pan; he's a stayer with speed.'
And the newspaper vendor, the ancient road mender,
And even the cop at the corner agreed.
The barber said, 'Win it? There's nothing else in it.

I backed Peter Pan with the last that I had.'
'Too right,' said the hitman. 'The horse is a gift, man.'
The old jobbing gardener said, 'Peter Pan, lad!'

I know naught of racing. The task I was facing,
It filled me with pain and unreasoning dread.
They all seemed so certain. And yet a dark curtain
Of doubt dulled my mind … But I must keep my head!
I went to the races, and I watched all their faces.
I saw Peter Pan's; there was little he lacked.
And as he seemed willing, I plonked on my shilling
And triumphed! And that's how the favourite was backed.

by C. J. Dennis

Chatham going 'the Sydney way'. Two of his 24 wins were in the Cox Plate.

Chatham's finest hour

Chatham's win with 10.4 in the 1934 Doncaster was rated by jockey Jim Pike as one of the three finest performances with which he was associated. The others were Phar Lap's Futurity win with 10.3 and Gothic's second Newmarket with 9.10.

Though he won the 1932 and 1933 Epsom Handicaps on Chatham, Pike said his Doncaster win was his greatest. Not only because he equalled Marvel's weight-carrying record that had stood since 1892, but because the opposition, which included Rogilla, was first rate and, most of all, because he missed the start on a track affected by half an inch of overnight rain. Conditions were so bad that trainer Fred Williams regretted taking Chatham to Randwick.

Yet this wonderful miler, in the expert hands of Pike, overcame all obstacles to win by half a head from 33/1 chance Golden Wings (9.6).

Said Pike: 'I didn't give Chatham a thousand-to-one chance when he was left several lengths but when he did get going he developed terrific speed and wouldn't give in in a battling finish.' The time of 1:40½ was admirable given the conditions.

Chatham's win at 6/1 in the mud was hailed by the crowd of 44 500 – down 3100 on the previous year. Even those who had backed Rogilla into 6/4 favouritism and saw him run fourth after missing the start too, were appreciative of Chatham's heroic effort.

After the prolonged ovation had died away, jockey A.E. Ellis, who rode Golden Wings, said: 'Fancy coming all the way from New Zealand and bumping a horse like Chatham. He's the greatest miler I've seen.'

Four days later Chatham was back at Randwick to win the mile All-Aged Stakes at wfa. Three days after that he skipped over six furlongs in 1:11¾, winning the CW Cropper Plate (wfa), also at Randwick.

With 19½ wins to his credit, Chatham was then spelled, resuming as a six-year-old in the spring of '34. His last campaign yielded four more wins, including a second Cox Plate, in which he downed Hall Mark and Rogilla. He failed in his attempt to win a third Epsom, the handicapper getting the better of him with 10.9. Pike eased him down when he realised he couldn't win, so those pundits who thought he was finished were kicking themselves a week later when, back at weight-for-age, Chatham, at a generous 8/1, won the 10-furlong AJC Craven Plate for the third time, beating the hot favourite Peter Pan by three-quarters of a length, with Rogilla third.

Peter Pan gave Chatham four lengths start at the turn. Not even Phar Lap could have done that to Chatham when he was at his best.

Chatham's last race was in the Melbourne Stakes, won by Peter Pan, on Victoria Derby day, 1934. He was unplaced, ending a career that no racegoer who saw him ever forgot.

At stud, Chatham produced Sydney Cup winner Craigie, Stradbroke winner High Rank and the good stayer Chatspa, winner of three ARC Birthday Cups.

Les the likeable loser

When Woodlace relegated the mighty Redditch to second place in the 1934 GN Steeple by three lengths, no one cheered louder than jockey Les Boots.

Boots, a cove straight from a C.J. Dennis tale – a loser with a sense of humour ('I've done me dash') – had ridden Woodlace in many schools over the jumps.

But Alex Ful-larton, not Boots, was entrusted with the mount on GN day for the soundest of reasons. Boots had a habit of falling off when it mattered … every time.

Boots often rode in jumps in Adelaide, with no success. Known as 'Autumn Leaves' because he was always falling, he had 39 rides over the obstacles and never once completed the course. He fell 40 times, once remounting and falling at the very next fence.

Boots, apprenticed to Harry Butler at Glenelg, had his first ride over the jumps at Cheltenham in 1929. Les and his mount Umtalia 'parted company' at the first fence.

Boots was no more successful on the flat, never riding a placegetter.

'You could say the Umtalia ride was not a good start to my career. I sort of came off after the first jump and broke my collarbone,' he said with a smile.

'I'm not kidding when I tell you that the nurses at the Adelaide Hospital used to check out the fields for the races and if they saw I had an engagement they'd get my usual bed ready in advance.

'I was in the saddle for about 18 years and I reckon I spent 12 of them in hospital.'

When Butler was preparing 'chaser Woodlace for the winter of '34, Boots rode the gelding in his schools and never once came off. 'I used to ride half a dozen horses in work two or three times a week and not fall, but when it came to the real thing I just couldn't stay on.'

Peter Pan in better weather, and his famous orange and green colours.

Watch us win, said Darby

And Peter Pan did. Not surprisingly Darby Munro, rider of 58½ winners in Sydney in 1933-34 and hailed as one of the best young jockeys in the land, sized up the situation brilliantly. A couple of inches of rain was not going to stop the 23-year-old horseman winning the 1934 Melbourne Cup on Peter Pan, even though the horse had the grandstand on his back (9.10) on a quagmire track.

Quoted at 4/1 for the Cup on Saturday night, he had blown out to 14/1 by starting time on Tuesday. After a break in the weather at midday, which lured thousands to the racecourse, heavy clouds once again hung over Flemington as veteran Sydney trainer Frank McGrath legged Munro into the saddle.

'I'm glad I'm not riding him,' McGrath had told Munro beforehand. 'I'm afraid the rain has beaten us.'

Munro, as calm as Peter Pan himself, replied that all was not lost.

'Don't think I'm mad if you see me wide out,' he said. 'The going is better out from the rails. In a two-miler it doesn't matter much if you never get to the fence. More than 10 furlongs is dead straight running. The biggest risk is trouble in the last half-mile and I'll try to miss that.

And there was more. 'Whatever chance he had before the rain, he still has. They all have to go through it and I think his No. 22 barrier (the extreme outside) is much better than No. 1. Watch us win this.'

When it happened the drenched crowd of 94 512, plus the 10 000 or so on the Footscray Hill, loved it. Thanks to Peter Pan, what threatened to be a total washout as a spectacle turned out to be a meritorious affair.

TURF TOPICS

Wrong post: Apprentice Jack Brown provided a sensation in the Doomben Newmarket (6f) in 1934, a year after the course opened. Riding there for the first time, he thought a stewards' stand halfway down the straight was the winning post. So when his mount, the 50/1 pop Cuban Song was in front passing the stand, Brown eased him. Champion Lough Neagh (3/1) and Whittingham (11/4 fav.) raced past him to finish 1–2. Cuban Song came in third. Lough Neagh's jockey Ted Tanwan was a hero for more reasons than one. He was badly wounded in World War I but recovered and became one of Queensland's top riders.

Little Perc on the punt: On the eve of the Melbourne Cup, Perc Galea, a 14-year-old milk boy in the King's Cross area of Sydney, was given a Cup tip by one of his customers, owner Rodney Dangar. 'Back my horse Peter Pan,' said Dangar. Galea duly had 2/6 each way on Peter Pan, who won at 14/1. Having cleaned up, Galea was on the road to bigger things!

In the money: At the VRC Spring Carnival, trainer cum big punter Bill Tindall built a bank of £100 into £115 000 when three of his horses – Sculpture, Nellie's Tip and Perfumery – won on Derby day. Two months later he was broke – again.

Treble farewell: Apprentice Edgar Britt, 21, who rode Winooka in America in 1933, had his first major success in Australia in 1934, winning the Sydney Cup on Broad Arrow. It was his third win of the day, the others being Mafoota and Turbulent. The following year Britt rode for the Maharajah of Baroda in India.

Fullarton at Oakbank

Oakbank in the Adelaide Hills was overflowing, as was the car park, on Easter Monday, when a record crowd of more than 50 000 saw the Victorian combination of Kenjin and Alex Fullarton win the Great Eastern Steeplechase in grand style.

The attendance was several thousand higher than the 1928 record. Perhaps the fact that bookmakers were operating for the first time in 40 years had something to do with the resurgence of interest. Certainly the tote figures were down, with the machine handling £33 838 compared with £43 068 the year before.

Only six of the 16 starters completed the gruelling 3¼-mile journey. Of the beaten brigade, Tasmanian hope Salonia was never prominent. The long confinement on the steamer from Hobart no doubt affected him.

Fullarton, a consummate horseman, was at his best on Kenjin, the popular elect at 2/1. A splendid jumper, Kenjin defeated Woodlace by 10 lengths in the 59th running

of the race. Fullarton, 24, was twice leading apprentice in Victoria, winning the inaugural King's Cup at Flemington in 1927 on Spear Maiden, trained by his master Bill Leyshon.

However, increasing weight forced him to switch to cross-country riding, and he achieved instant success.

Kenjin's victory was Fullarton's third major win. His first was on Sandhurst in the 1929 GN Steeple and his second on Polygonum in the 1932 GN Hurdle, both at Flemington.

Three months after the Great Eastern, Fullarton won the Grand National Steeple for the first time on the aforementioned Woodlace, who won by three lengths.

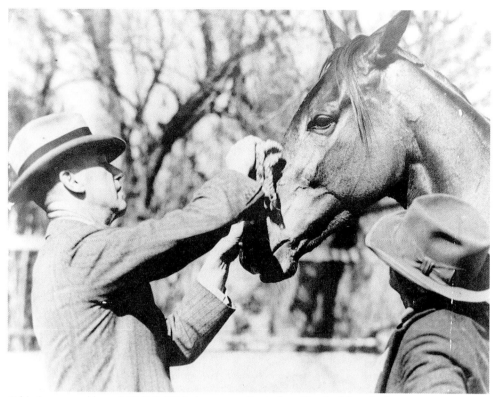

Erbie is exposed by vet W. R. B. Wakeham as guilty trainer Charlie Prince looks on.

Erbie, king of the ring-ins

No one knows how many races Erbie won. Unofficially that is. Officially he saluted 23 times from the late 1920s on, mostly on NSW country tracks. Four of the wins were at Rosehill and Canterbury. He was ridden by such crack horsemen as Ted Bartle and Billy Cook.

As a ring-in, Erbie won at least four races, probably more. His double-life was exposed in South Australia in 1934. The famous Erbie case had its beginnings at Murray Bridge in July when a Victorian horse called Redlock, trained by one Charlie Prince, was entered for the Trial Stakes. Redlock's form was indifferent; he was one of the bottom weights.

While bookmakers ruminated whether Garibaldi or Spearcombe should be favourite for the race, Prince and his cohorts stood quietly by. In places odds of 8/1, even 10/1,

were offered about Redlock. Money then poured into the ring. At the close of operations, 5/2 was accepted. Some fielders refused to lay the gelding. Redlock duly won easily, showing unaccustomed early pace. Prince and his team of punters collected £1500.

Acting on a tip, stewards interviewed Prince about Redlock. Prince produced a rough receipt as evidence that he had bought the horse legally for £30.

Enter racing journalist Bert Wolfe of the Melbourne *Herald*. He was familiar with the real Redlock and sniffed a conspiracy. When he learnt that Redlock was to race again soon at Kadina (also in South Australia), he travelled to the town. Once again Redlock bolted in, by 12 lengths.

Wolfe, writing under the pseudonym of Cardigan, was puzzled by Redlock's dramatic

improvement. With Prince's permission, Wolfe examined Redlock at Kadina and found the remains of some surplus dye. It was known that Erbie had a white blaze. Redlock did not.

Wolfe then exposed the ring-in, writing in the *Herald*: 'I'm satisfied that the horse which raced at Kadina on Saturday is not Redlock but is Erbie. He is a gelding with many names. Last year he raced at Holbrook (NSW) as Duke Bombita. On November 28 last year he won in sensational manner at Kilmore (Victoria) as Chrybean, and now he has reappeared as Redlock.

'I know Erbie's characteristics and markings. He still has his heavy tail and the half white sock on his near hind leg – but this time he hasn't a blaze down his face and his brands are different. How these changes have come about I cannot know. But despite his new face the gelding is Erbie, who won many good races in Sydney under big weights in good company.'

Wolfe's scoop got the VRC cracking. In no time, the real Redlock was discovered in a paddock near Sunbury in Victoria. In South Australia, detectives impounded Erbie, alias Redlock. With owner-trainer Prince looking on, veterinary surgeon W. Wakeham washed the horse's face, revealing a white blaze. Erbie was unfazed. Perhaps he had grown tired of impersonating others. He was himself again but was disqualified from racing again.

As for Prince, he was jailed for two years for fraud and disqualified from the turf for life. Twenty years later an amnesty was granted to mark a visit by Queen Elizabeth II. A man said to have masterminded the ring-ins was said to have sailed to England. He was not pursued.

Postscript: In July 1931, Erbie (aged 5) and Redlock (4) ran on the same day at Rosehill. Erbie, carrying 7.11 and with Billy Cook in the saddle, won the Flying Handicap (6f). Redlock (7.1) was unplaced in a maiden.

Erbie had his last race under his own name at Kembla Grange (NSW) in September 1933. Carrying 10.3, he ran second. Ten months later he stepped out at Murray Bridge as Redlock.

1934 RESULTS

VRC MELBOURNE CUP (2m)
Peter Pan, 9.10 (D Munro) Trained by F McGrath; 3:40.5; Sarcherie, La Trobe
AJC SYDNEY CUP (2m)
Broad Arrow, 7.1 (E Britt) Trained by W McGee; 3:28; Gippsland, Limarch
QTC BRISBANE CUP (2m)
St Valorey, 8.7 (M McCarten) 3:22.75; Soft Step, Arboreal
SAJC ADELAIDE CUP (13-f)
Sir Roseland, 6.13 (F Godby) Trained by F Matson; 2:46; St Mary, Bajardo
WATC PERTH CUP (2m) (Not run in 1934)
VATC CAULFIELD CUP (12-f)
Journal, 7.13 (A Knox) Trained by JT Cush; 2:29.5; Farndale, Sir Simper

VRC AUSTRALIAN CUP (2¼m)
Heroic Chief, 8.5 (M McCarten) Trained by H Leek; 3:55.25; Peter Jackson, Gippsland
MVRC WS COX PLATE (9 ½-f)
Chatham, 9.4 (S Davidson) Trained by F Williams; 2:03; Hall Mark, Rogilla
AJC DERBY (12-f)
Theo, 8.10 (M McCarten) Trained by F Williams; 2:32.7; Silver King, Dark Sky
VRC VICTORIA DERBY (12-f)
Theo (M McCarten) Trained by F Williams; 2:35.75; Sylvandale, Hyperion
AJC DONCASTER HANDICAP (1m)
Chatham, 10.4 (J Pike) Trained by F Williams; 1:40.5; Golden Wings, Whittingham

BTC DOOMBEN '10 000' (6-f)
Lough Neagh, 9.4 (E Tanwan) Trained by T Brosnan; 1:12.5; Whittingham, Cuban Song
VRC NEWMARKET HANDICAP (6-f)
Foursome, 8.13 (E Baxter) Trained by J Sing; 1:11; Dame Moab, Jacko
AJC SIRES' PRODUCE STAKES (7-f)
Dark Sky, 8.10 (D Munro) Trained by F Musgrave; 1:29.2; Myra Tip, Subsidy
VRC SIRES' PRODUCE STAKES (7-f)
Sir John, 8.10 (M McCarten) Trained by G Price; 1:26.5; Pasha, Dark Sky
VRC GRAND NATIONAL STEEPLECHASE (3m 1-f)
Woodlace, 9.12 (A Fullarton) Trained by H Butler; 6:11.5; Redditch, Copperfield

At the jump, and a wall of horses set off for the 1935 Melbourne Cup (Age).

Kiwis scoop pool in spring

The combination of trainer Lou Robertson and jockey Keith Voitre, both former New Zealanders, made history at the 1935 VRC Spring Carnival.

They became the first duo to win the carnival's three major races in the one year – the Victoria Derby with Feldspar, the Melbourne Cup (Marabou) and the Oaks Stakes (Nalda, owned by Sol Green). For good measure they also won the WS Cox Plate with Garrio, a race in which Feldspar ran third.

At 54, the wily Robertson, who prepared his team at Mordialloc, had earned the respect of all racing folk with his ability to condition horses. Robertson, born in 1881, took out a trainer's licence in Australia in 1908 after coming across from NZ with a trotter named Almont. His first major galloping win was with Wingarara (whom he owned) in the 1912 GN Hurdle at Flemington. He won the 1915 Caulfield Cup with Lavendo and trained Sol Green's mighty sprinter Gothic, winner of two Newmarkets.

But the plums of the VRC Spring Carnival had eluded him, though Naos and Strephon, both owned by Green, had finished second in the 1926 and 1928 Melbourne Cups.

But for Robertson's persistence, Marabou, a good-looking bay by English middle-distance horse Marconigram, might have been sold after his failure as a three-year-old in Peter Pan's Cup win in 1934. Marabou's owners, pastoralists J. Fell and T. Hogan, were not convinced he would improve with age. He did – winning the Cup at the handy price of 33/1.

Happy days & records

As the horses paraded for the 1935 Caulfield Cup, a band treated the assembly to a rousing rendition of the fox-trot 'Back to the Happy Days'. Not since the pre-depression days had such a huge, carefree crowd graced 'The Heath'.

Indeed, it was a day of records. The attendance of 60 500 exceeded the record of 58 676 set in 1929, all previous tote figures were smashed and the three-year-old Palfresco, in winning the Caulfield Cup, broke the Australasian record for 12 furlongs, clocking 2:27¾. His time was a half-second inside Gaine Carrington's race record established in 1933 and would last until 1957 when Tulloch stopped the watch at 2:26.9.

To many, of course, Palfresco's win did not signal the return of happy days because he started at 20/1, consigning the 4/1 favourite, Marabou, to third place.

All those folk in the new grandstand obtained a splendid view of affairs as the 24 runners left the mounting yard in program order, passing the judge's box on their way to the track.

On his form, Palfresco, a smallish brown colt by Son O'Mine from Little Millie, had every right to be 20/1. His early three-year-old form was less than flattering. But unbeknown to the public, he ran some outstanding track gallops at Caulfield in the

week before the Cup and was backed in from 50/1.

Turning for home, Palfresco hit the front, three wide. Proving himself a genuine stayer, he fairly bounded away, defeating Hot Shot by a length and a half.

Palfresco, who was bred at Sol Green's Underbank Stud, Bacchus Marsh, was raced on lease by Caulfield tobacconist and hairdresser Sam Kent, who collected £4500. Barber's shops were notorious places where the 'good oil' was given gratis with a haircut and shave. Needless to say, Sam Kent's shop did brisk business the week after the cup.

A fortnight later, Palfresco, the favourite, was injured when unplaced in the Victoria Derby and the following winter, in a court case, the owner, Mrs Alice Garland, sought to restrain Kent from putting Palfresco back into work without veterinary attention.

Champion of the dead-heats

It was a popular view that Rogilla, whose racing days ended in 1935, was the 'picnics horse' that won the Caulfield Cup (1932) and the Sydney Cup in 1933.

Newcastle lessee-trainer Les Haigh said the story that Rogilla was intended for picnic racing had no foundation. It was, he suggested, a good line of fiction from the pen of a romantic scribe.

What was true of Rogilla was that he was involved in five dead-heats – and he made them all with tenacious finishes. Said Haigh: 'He had a devastating run but equal to that was his courage. He was a real bulldog.'

One of his most memorable dead-heats was to come from behind Chatham and share the prize with the great miler in the Tramway Handicap.

Not surprisingly, Rogilla's last win, in the 1935 AJC Warwick Stakes at Warwick Farm, resulted in a dead-heat for first with Silver King.

Rogilla was in his eighth year. The chestnut gelding had five more starts for three placings, bowing out after 70 races, which yielded 26 wins, including those five dead-heats. He won more than £20 000 in prize money.

L. K. S. Mackinnon (left) with Lord Forster.

The R.I.P. Stakes

Within the space of two weeks in 1935, Melbourne racing lost two prominent administrators. Arthur Vaughan Hiskens died at his Moonee Ponds home on 10 August and, on 22 August, Lauchlan Kenneth Scobie Mackinnon died at his South Yarra residence.

At the time of his death Hiskens, aged 72, was secretary of two metropolitan racing clubs, Moonee Valley and the VATC. He was also connected with the Royal Agricultural Society. Hiskens is remembered each winter with the running of Moonee Valley's most prestigious jumping race, the AV Hiskens Steeplechase.

Scottish-born Lauchlan Mackinnon, known throughout his career as 'LKS', was chairman of the VRC from 1915 until his death, aged 73. He was a senior partner in the legal firm, Blake and Riggall.

The son of a clergyman, he was born on the Isle of Skye, Scotland, on Christmas Day, 1861. He came to Melbourne as a qualified lawyer in 1884 and soon became involved in racing in his new home. He joined the VRC in 1889 and, in 1906, stood for the VRC committee. Mackinnon owned many good horses, most notably Kingsburgh, winner of the 1914 Melbourne Cup. After his death, the Melbourne Stakes, run on Derby day, was renamed the LKS Mackinnon Stakes.

Redditch tumbles, destroyed

Tragedy marred the 1935 Grand National Steeple at Flemington, Australia's champion fencer Redditch having to be destroyed. He fractured a thigh after falling at the logs, the third of the stand treble.

Carrying the maximum weight of 12.7, Redditch, ridden by Alex Fullarton, was in a forward position when he came down. His owner, A. L. Yuille, had made the trip from Sydney to see him run.

After clearing the stone wall with a tremendous bound, Redditch struck the next fence with great force and fell heavily. He was swinging his off hind leg when he rose and it was apparent he would have to be put down.

Trained by Fred Hoysted, Redditch won the Australian Steeplechase in 1933–34 and the Grand National in 1933. The 1935 GN Steeple was won by Riawena, owned by VRC chairman, L. K. S. Mackinnon.

The death of Redditch and the resultant outburst against the severity of the Flemington fences, prompted R. M. Cuthbertson, an owner of jumpers, to write to the *Age* in defence of the course.

While deploring the loss of Redditch, he said it would be unfair to use the unfortunate accident as a reason for drastic alterations to the obstacles.

'We have very definite veterinary opinion that this horse was killed, not as a result of striking the fence, but through having been struck by the hoofs of another runner.

'It would be a thousand pities to alter the character of the best steeplechase course in Australia and convert it into a brush course for squibs.'

Cuthbertson called on the VRC to consider enlightened recommendations before any hasty decision was reached.

As a result of Redditch's death, the steeplechase fences at Flemington were soon altered to brush only. The first chase over the new fences was held on Cup Day, 1935.

VRC MELBOURNE CUP (2m)
Marabou, 7.11 (K Voitre) Trained L Robertson; 3:23.25; Sarcherie, Sylvandale
AJC SYDNEY CUP (2m)
Akuna, 7.0 (H Hanley) Trained by D Lewis; 3:27.75; Dark Chief, Sylvandale
QTC BRISBANE CUP (2m)
Rivalli, 9.3 (E Tanwan) Trained by 3:25.25; Glen's Spear, Pandion
SAJC ADELAIDE CUP (13-f)
Mellion, 7.10 (G Mules) Trained by CH Wood; 2:45; Sir Roseland, Supervalve
WATC PERTH CUP (2m)
Cueesun, 8.2 (S Dodd) Trained by TJ Stratton; 3:28; Dilemma, Game Pie
VATC CAULFIELD CUP (12-f)
Palfresco, 7.1 (N Percival) Trained by C Brown; 2:27.75; Hot Shot, Marabou

VRC AUSTRALIAN CUP (2¼m)
Sylvandale, 8.3 (J Pratt) Trained by F Williams; 3:51; La Trobe, Flail
MVRC WS COX PLATE (9½-f)
Garrio, 7.11 (K Voitre) Trained by L Robertson; 1:58.5; Hall Mark, Feldspar
AJC DERBY (12-f)
Dead-heat Allunga, 8.10 (D Munro) and Homer, 8.10 (A Knox); Allunga trained by
J Munro and Homer trained by G Price; 2:33.75; Buzzard King third
VRC VICTORIA DERBY (12-f)
Feldspar (K Voitre) Trained by L Robertson; 2:31.75; Allunga, Garrio
AJC DONCASTER HANDICAP (1m)
Hall Mark, 9.8 (K Voitre) Trained by J Holt; 1:37.5; High, Silver King

BTC DOOMBEN '10 000' (6-f)
Pamelus, 8.13 (B Tebb) Trained by H Duke; 1:11.7; Regular Bachelor, Thalwyn
VRC NEWMARKET HANDICAP (6-f)
Count Ito, 8.3 (K Voitre) Trained by PB Quinlan; 1:12.5; Melason, Closing Time
AJC SIRES' PRODUCE STAKES (7-f)
Young Idea, 8.10 (J Pratt) Trained by F Foulsham; 1:25.7; Garrio, Legatee
VRC SIRES' PRODUCE STAKES (7-f)
Young Idea, 8.10 (H Skidmore) Trained by F Foulsham; 1:26.5; Homer, Palfresco
VRC GRAND NATIONAL STEEPLECHASE (3m 1-f)
Riawena, 9.13 (L Healey) Trained by W McInnis; 6:34; Pactolus, Oldhome

A SPORT BREATHLESS MOMENT

OSSIE PHILLIPS

Nº4

One of the biggest upsets ever in the Melbourne Cup occurred in 1936 when Wotan, starting at 100 to 1, came with an amazing burst to win by a head from the unlucky Silver Standard who had been beaten a few weeks before in the Caulfield Cup by the long-priced North Wind. As his priced showed, Wotan wasn't considered a possible chance and he was a great result for the bookmakers.

Ossie Phillips, the Victorian jockey who rode Wotan to victory in the 1936 Melbourne Cup. Phillips said after the race that he had been confident of winning even when he was nearly last in the early stages.

3. By the time they reached the 2½ furlong mark, Young Crusader had gone through to take the lead, and so there was a ready-made pacemaker.

4. At this stage Mala, Hot Shot and the eventual winner, Wotan, were tailing the field, a long way back.

5. At the mile, Young Crusader led by 15 lengths and Wotan was last, a position he still held near the six.

6. Young Crusader now began to shorten stride. He had expended all his energy and now the others were closing on him, had him beaten.

1. They're off! The cry went up from the crowd as the field was away to an excellent start.

2. Entering the course proper Queen of Song seemed to be the leader from Dark Chief and Young Crusader.

7. Then with a furlong to go Silver Standard was in front looking a winner, but Wotan was moving forward.

8. Hard-ridden by Phillips, Wotan gathered in Silver Standard, won by a head going away. It was a sensational finishing burst.

All the excitement of the Melbourne Cup is captured in an artist's version of the race in Sporting Life.

Wotan a bolter of lightning at dream odds

New Zealander Wotan travelled first-class to Australia for the 1936 Melbourne Cup and repaid his owners handsomely by winning the big race at 100/1, only the second horse to succeed at three-figure odds. The first 100/1 winner was The Pearl in 1871.

The Wotan story never fails to astonish turf historians. How could a poorly performed horse suddenly sprout wings and demolish a useful field of stayers in record time of 3:21¼?

Wotan had one thing in his favour – breeding. On this score it could be said he 'left' his rivals for dead. His dam, Left (by four times New Zealand Cup winner Martian), also produced Gaine Carrington, winner of the 1933 Caulfield Cup and Peter Jackson, winner of the 1933 Moonee Valley Cup. His sire was the imported Siegfried.

Wotan was raced by three New Zealand brothers, Tom, Bill and Ray Smith, who were dairy farmers at Mangawaka.

They bought Left, who was no great shakes as a racehorse, for about £50 as a broodmare. Wotan was her third foal. He won at his only start as a two-year-old in 1934. Shipped to Sydney for the 1935 AJC Derby, Wotan ran poorly. Early in 1936 he failed in NZ hack races. He was offered for sale but there were no takers.

Having entered him for the Melbourne Cup, the Smiths asked top Kiwi trainer Jack Fryer to include him in his team for Melbourne. Fryer was reluctant but said if Wotan showed late winter form he would change his mind.

At his first start as a four-year-old, Wotan ran fourth in a mile hack race. The following day he won a similar race with 8.8.

The owners fluked a box for Wotan on the liner *Mariposa*, which made a smooth crossing to Sydney. Wotan travelled to Melbourne by train. His arrival cracked it for one paragraph in the Melbourne *Herald*. He was written off as a Cup chance after finishing a distant last to Young Idea in the Cox Plate.

The Smiths did not engage a Cup jockey until the morning of the race. The lucky postilion was Ossie Phillips, lately back from a successful season in the Far East. Passing the mile post, Wotan, carrying only 7.11, was last, a half furlong behind the tearaway leader Young Crusader. From that point, Wotan began a sustained run that carried him to victory by a neck from the unlucky Silver Standard. Third, a length and a quarter away, was Balkan Prince. The 3/1 favourite Talking came seventh.

One punter who profited from Wotan's win was well-known Sydney businessman John Woolcott Forbes, who had two bets of £1000 to £5. Why? He liked Wotan's breeding. 'Staying could be his game.' Indeed.

An ill wind for punters

When the north wind blows on Melbourne's racetracks, the only haven is the bar. It was so after the bolter Northwind had won the 1936 Caulfield Cup. It was a time to drown one's sorrows, for he started at 66/1, though loyal followers of top young Melbourne jockey Harold Badger would have been celebrating.

It was 27-year-old Badger's first major win. He was soon to become associated with Ajax, on whom he won 30 races.

As for Northwind, a five-year-old son of Melbourne Cup winner Windbag, he turned out to be the best of an ordinary lot of stayers, the possible exception being the AJC Derby winner Talking. No horse was deemed worthy of carrying 9.0 or more. The topweight was the Queenslander Pamelus with 8.13. He was unplaced.

Northwind was bred by A. G. Hunter at his Northwood Park stud. Small for a yearling, he realised only 110 guineas at auction, the buyer being G. Farrow. In time he grew into a strong individual but his form was moderate in moderate company. He did not lack opportunities. At four, in season 1935–36, he had no fewer than 20 starts, winning rarely

Colonel Cohen, Northwind's owner.

and never looking likely to earn a huge pay cheque for his connections.

A month before the '36 Caulfield Cup, successful Caulfield trainer Cecil Godby, of Purser fame, saw Northwind rattle home to run second in a race at Ascot. That effort resulted in a change of ownership. A client of Godby, the prominent Melburnian Colonel Harold Cohen, had asked the trainer to buy him a horse worthy of sporting his colours in the Caulfield Cup. That horse turned out to be Northwind. Colonel Cohen, who had commanded the 6th Brigade Artillery of the AIF in World War I, wore many hats. He was the MLC for Melbourne South Province (which included Caulfield), a solicitor and chairman of Carlton and United Breweries.

Northwind had his first run for the Colonel in the Herbert Power Handicap and finished second last. Northwind was a 200/1 chance for the cup. Followers of the Godby stable snapped up the odds, probably more out of loyalty than prescience.

The astute Godby, mindful of Northwind's Ascot run, told Badger to let the gelding drop out and make one run in the straight. Badger followed instructions to the letter. Northwind, carrying only 7.6, finished over the top of Silver Standard and AJC Derby winner Talking. It was Godby's third Caulfield Cup win, after Purser (1924) and New Zealander Gaine Carrington (1933).

Northwind did little after his cup win but, thanks to Godby, Colonel Cohen was the toast of his constituency on Cup Day '36.

Badger rode to two Caulfield Cup wins, the second on Columnist, but was destined never to win a Melbourne Cup despite 17 tries in a 30-year career.

Harold Badger weighs in.

Pike quits: Champion jockey Jim Pike, who rode Phar Lap to 27 wins and also piloted such greats as Heroic, Gothic, Manfred, Chatham, Hall Mark, Amounis and Peter Pan, retired at the age of 43 because of illness caused by years of wasting and starving himself. As riders go, he was a heavyweight. Pike failed as a trainer. A gaunt figure, he faded from the racing scene. Gambling got the better of him. He once owned 12 houses in Sydney and lived in a mansion in Centennial Park. When he died in 1969, he was renting a flat in Bondi. He had formerly owned the entire block.

SA is King: Adelaide first hosted the King's Cup in 1930. The winner was Phar Lap, ridden by Jim Pike. When the race returned to Morphettville in 1936, the winner was Victorian galloper Doncaster, ridden by W. Cox.

Last winner: Victorian jockey Bobby Lewis, aged 58, rode his last winner, Lilirene, at Caulfield in 1936. The ninth child of a Welsh miner, he was born at Clunes and won his first race there in 1892. He won four Melbourne Cups – The Victory (1902), Patrobas (1915), Artilleryman (1919) and Trivalve (1927). Trivalve was trained by James Scobie, with whom Lewis had a long association. In a career lasting 48 years, Lewis was suspended only once. He retired in 1938 and advised many young jockeys.

Rain stops GN: Pooley Bridge's win in the Mia Mia Hurdle at Moonee Valley on MV Cup day 1935 heralded the start of a brilliant 12 months. He won the 1936 VRC Grand National Hurdle with 11.3 and the Australian Hurdle with 12.5. The GN Hurdle was run on a Tuesday, heavy rain forcing a three-day postponement.

Young star: The Jack Holt–trained Young Idea, aged four, added two more notches to his considerable record by winning the Caulfield Stakes and WS Cox Plate in successive weeks in 1936. As a two-year-old, the son of Constant Son won the AJC Sires and AJC Champagne Stakes and the VRC Sires. At three he won the Caulfield Guineas. His Cox Plate win was Holt's fourth in the race.

Good buy: Talking, sold for a handsome £19 000 virtually on the eve of the Victoria Derby, promptly won the race for his new owner, A. E. Cooper. After starting 6/4 favourite, Talking was untroubled to win by two lengths from the unlucky New Zealander Mala.

A panorama of the Oakbank Racetrack, home of the Grand Eastern Steeple, during the centenary year of South Australia.

At Oakbank for the centenary celebrations.

The car park is full as racegoers gather at the Oakbank race meeting.

A collection of Sydney racing identities, as seen by cartoonist Frith.

1936 RESULTS

VRC MELBOURNE CUP (2m)
Wotan, 7.11 (O Philips) Trained by J Fryer; 3:21.25; Silver Standard, Balkan Prince

AJC SYDNEY CUP (2m)
Contact, 8.4 (M McCarten) Trained by D Lewis; 3:23.75; Egmont, Spear Prince

QTC BRISBANE CUP (2m)
Lough Neagh, 9.3 (F Shean) 3:25.75; Spear Prince, First Buzzard

SAJC ADELAIDE CUP (13-f)
Cape York, 7.1 (N Percival) Trained by M Whelan; 2:51.5; Highardo, Alfange

WATC PERTH CUP (2m)
Picaro, 7.0 (N Hutchinson) Trained by J Robinson; 3:29.25; Staunch, Yaringa

VATC CAULFIELD CUP (12-f)
Northwind, 7.6 (H Badger) Trained by CT Godby; 2:28.75; Silver Standard, Talking

VRC AUSTRALIAN CUP (2 ¼m)
Amalia, 8.3 (H Bastian) Trained by H Gregory; 3:56; Highardo, Hot Shot

MVRC WS COX PLATE (9 ½-f)
Young Idea, 9.0 (H Skidmore) Trained by J Holt; 2:01; Mala, Shakespeare

AJC DERBY (12-f)
Talking, 8.10 (A Knox) Trained by A Papworth; 2:32.5; Mala, Gold Rod

VRC VICTORIA DERBY (12-f)
Talking (A Knox) Trained by A Papworth; 2:33; Mala, Beechworth

AJC DONCASTER HANDICAP (1m)
Cuddle, 9.4 (M McCarten) Trained by G Price; 1:38; Cabalist, Barak

BTC DOOMBEN '10 000' (6-f)
High Benia, 7.3 (K Jeffers) Trained by R Rogers; 1:12; High Speech, Verdun

VRC NEWMARKET HANDICAP (6-f)
Regular Bachelor, 8.11 (E Tanwan) Trained by R Trihey; 1:11; Valiant Chief, Cardinal

AJC SIRES' PRODUCE STAKES (7-f)
Gold Rod, 8.10 (M McCarten) Trained by G Price; 1:25.75; Fidelity, Siren

VRC SIRES' PRODUCE STAKES (7-f)
Gold Rod, 8.10 (J Pratt) Trained by G Price; 1:24.5; Fidelity, Boongarry

VRC GRAND NATIONAL STEEPLECHASE (3m 1-f)
Santa Casa, 9.1 (J Regan) Trained by J Devine; 6:27.75; Draconic, Woodlace

Soon after the start of the 1939 Melbourne Cup with more than a circuit of Flemington still lying ahead (Age).

The Trump trumps them in both Cups

The saying 'she's apples' took on an equine flavour when The Trump won the 1937 Caulfield Cup. The race had to be delayed four days until Wednesday because of a spring deluge, which Melbourne delights in turning on from time to time.

Had the event been run on the Saturday, as scheduled, The Trump might not have started. Usually a good doer, he went off his feed after winning the mile Toorak Handicap the week before. This setback rocked his owner, the popular sportsman and punter Darcy Eccles.

Trainer Stan Reid, a former successful cross country jockey who rode the mighty Mountain God to successive wins in the 1921 and 1922 GN Steeple, and his stablehands tempted The Trump with all manner of morsels from thistles to greens, but to no avail. Eventually apples, by the bagful, did the trick, aided by the weather.

Restored to good health by race day, The Trump, piloted by Ashley Reed, won the Caulfield Cup by a half-neck, defeating the Sydney stayer Sir Regent. The victory earned him the full penalty of 10 lb for the Melbourne Cup, taking his weight to 8.5.

No horse had won the Cups' double since Poseidon in 1906 and, despite The Trump's win in the LKS Mackinnon Stakes on Derby Day, he was only equal favourite for the Melbourne Cup with Sir Regent and Hua at 11/2.

The Trump was equal to the task. In winning his sixth race in a row, he finished with typical bulldog spirit to down 40/1-chance Willie Win by a half-length, with perennial placegetter Sarcherie third.

But for the combination of Eccles and Reid, The Trump might not have enjoyed such success. The son of Manfred, who cost Eccles 200 guineas as a yearling, had all man-

ner of leg problems as a young horse but Reid was able to rectify them with outstanding results. The Trump's six wins in the spring of 1937 netted Eccles something in the vicinity of £200 000 in bets, most of which was gambled away. In that spell, the gelding won £14 000 in stake money.

The Trump derived his name from World War I German flying ace 'The Red Baron', known by Australian troops as 'The Trump'. The baron's Christian name was Manfred.

Four days after his Cup win, The Trump was unplaced in the CB Fisher Plate. He pulled up lame and was never the same horse again. He ended his days on the Murray River property of Eccles' brother and served as an obliging hack for children in the neighbourhood.

Ajax at nice odds

Ajax, a good-looking son of Heroic, had his first race start in the Holiday Stakes (5½f) at Caulfield on January 16. Ridden by Harold Badger, he won by three-quarters of a length at 12/1.

That was the last time he started at such fancy odds. He had 12 starts in 1937 for eight wins, three seconds and once unplaced. He

ended his two-year-old days with wins in the AJC Sires' Produce Stakes and AJC Champagne Stakes at Randwick.

As an early three-year-old, he took the Rosehill Guineas and Caulfield Guineas. He finished second in both the AJC and Victoria Derbys, to Avenger then Hua, suggesting a disliking for too much distance. But Hua beat him by only a half-head in the Flemington classic.

TURF TOPICS

Last and first: Young Victorian jockey Bill Williamson rode his first winner, Lilirene, the horse that gave Bobby Lewis his last winner. Lewis taught Williamson, his great-nephew, the art of horsemanship. He did a brilliant job.

Ups and downs: Cross country jockey Frank Dummett, who broke his collarbones 19 times in a long and successful career, won the first of three VRC Grand National Steeplechases, on Last End.

At last: Gallant mare Sarcherie, second in the 1935 and 1936 Melbourne Cups, showed her versatility by winning the 1937 AJC Doncaster Handicap (1m) in slick time, 1:35½. Later in the year, she ran third to The Trump in the Melbourne Cup

Nice trio: Gold Rod, a son of Chief Ruler, ruled supreme in three big races in 1937 – the VATC Futurity Stakes, and the AJC Epsom Handicap and AJC St Leger. Maurice McCarten piloted him.

Bad fall: Queensland jockey Bustling Billy Briscoe, so named because haste was his caper on race day, suffered a horrendous fall from a horse called Monalba at Albion Park in Brisbane. Coming to the tight first turn, Monalba crashed through a tin fence on the outside of the track. Horse and rider, complete with three pieces of corrugated iron, ended up in someone's back yard. Monalba collapsed and Briscoe suffered a fractured skull, putting him on the sidelines for months.

Character is born: Mel 'The Shoe' Schumacher first saw the light of day in 1937. Raised on a dairy farm at Boonah in Queensland, he rode a pony to school and became one of Australia's most colourful and controversial jockeys.

Final Trump call: The 1937 Melbourne Cup was The Trump's last win. Knee problems saw the end of his great winning streak, and he finished last in the next two Melbourne Cups.

1937 RESULTS

VRC MELBOURNE CUP (2m)
The Trump, 8.5 (A Reed) Trained by SW Reid; 3:21.25; Willie Win, Sarcherie
AJC SYDNEY CUP (2m)
Mestoravon, 7.3 (J Duncan) Trained by R Cashman; 3:21.75; Sir Ross, Oro
QTC BRISBANE CUP (2m)
Glen's Spear, 8.0 (T Spencer) 3:23; Tapestry, The Buzzard
SAJC ADELAIDE CUP (13-f)
Doncaster, 8.11 (A Breasley) Trained by FW Hoysted; 2:43.5; Highardo, Mutable
WATC PERTH CUP (2m)
Manolive, 7.12 (H Whitbread) Trained by JE Hay; 3:25.25; Panto, Mariner
VATC CAULFIELD CUP (12-f)
The Trump, 7.12 (A Reed) Trained by SW Reid; 2:28.75; Sir Regent, Donaster

VRC AUSTRALIAN CUP (2¼m)
Mutable, 7.3 (H Morris) Trained by W Smart; 3:51; Pooley Bridge, Demotic
MVRC WS COX PLATE (9½-f)
Young Idea, 9.4 (D Munro) Trained by J Holt; 1:58.5; Court Craft, Charles Fox
AJC DERBY (12-f)
Avenger, 8.10 (E Bartle) Trained by J Holt; 2:36.5; Ajax, Hua
VRC VICTORIA DERBY (12-f)
Hua (R Wilson) Trained by J Scobie; 2:32.75; Ajax, Avenger
AJC DONCASTER HANDICAP (1m)
Sarcherie, 8.10 (R Maxwell) Trained by M Webster; 1:35.5; Silver Rose, Evening Mist
BTC DOOMBEN '10000' (6-f)
Gay Chou, 8.3 (W Cook) Trained by J Cook; 1:12.25; Manresa, King Merlin

VRC NEWMARKET HANDICAP (6-f)
Aurie's Star (M McCarten) Trained by J Doyle; 1:11.2; Pamelus, Regular Bachelor
AJC SIRES' PRODUCE STAKES (7-f)
Ajax, 8.10 (M McCarten) Trained by F Musgrave; 1:23.5; Caesar, Nightguard
VRC SIRES' PRODUCE STAKES (7-f)
Hua, 8.10 (F Dempsey) Trained by J Scobie; 1:24.5; Caesar, Nightguard
VRC GRAND NATIONAL STEEPLECHASE (3m 1-f)
Last End, 10.2 (F Dummett) Trained by J Brett; 6:8.25; Seymour, Montargis

A beautiful win for a horse said to be ugly – Mrs Jamieson's Catalogue.

Sir Keith Murdoch, Lord Huntingfield and Sir John Latham at the Cup.

Kiwi Cup winner trained by Granny

Male chauvinism was alive and well in Victorian racing circles in the 1930s. It surfaced when the plain-looking New Zealander Catalogue, at eight the oldest horse in the race, won the 1938 Melbourne Cup.

Catalogue was owned by a widow, Mrs A. ('Tui') Jamieson, a keen racing enthusiast and world traveller who believed that if Wotan could win the Melbourne Cup – she won £1000 on him in 1936 – she could find a horse to repeat the dose.

Her logic was sound. Taking a line through Wotan, she reckoned that moderate staying form in NZ could develop into winning form in Australia.

At the presentation after Catalogue's easy win at 25/1, the Governor-General, Lord Gowrie, said to Mrs Jamieson, as he handed her the gold cup: 'I am told you are only the second woman to own a Melbourne Cup winner on the day.'

Replied Mrs Jamieson, who didn't mix her words: 'Maybe I am, but another woman, Mrs Allan McDonald (known as Granny), should be standing here with me, as the first woman to train a Melbourne Cup winner. She got him ready.'

Indeed, Granny McDonald, the daughter of successful NZ cross country jockey-turned-trainer Jack Maher, had trained Catalogue for five years. But on her arrival in Melbourne, the VRC knocked back her credentials from the New Zealand Racing Conference. In those unenlightened days, the VRC rules stip-

ulated that a woman could not hold a trainer's licence, ride track work or in a race or act as strapper. Of course, their money in other facets of the Sport of Kings was quite acceptable.

The upshot, as related by turf historian Bill Ahern, was that Granny's husband, Allan, was granted a permit by the VRC to train Catalogue.

Even then there was no certainty Catalogue would run in the Cup. An irate Mrs Jamieson wanted to scratch him.

The presentation to 'Tui' Jamieson.

'I was mad,' she said. 'The VRC committee was quite prepared to allow women as owners, take their money at the gate, but allow them to train … ?

'I told Granny we would scratch him but she would not hear of it. She said the rule was there and had to be obeyed.'

The trip to Melbourne became a certainty when, in August 1938, Catalogue won the

Winter Cup at Riccarton. McDonald felt Catalogue could be improved and was close enough to wfa standard, having finished a close second to Melbourne wfa winner Nightly as a three-year-old.

Said Jamieson: 'Granny reckoned the horse was good value at 100/1, so I had a bit each-way on him.'

On arrival in Melbourne, Catalogue did not do well initially, but his appetite picked up and he ran well enough against stars such as Ajax and Young Idea in the Cox Plate, to lift the spirits of his connections.

Jockey Frank Shean was impressed with Catalogue's early turn of speed and courage and was happy to ride him in the Cup, believing him to be on the improve.

Shean piloted Catalogue perfectly, taking advantage of the slow pace and giving him his head a mile from home. Catalogue stretched out merrily in front and, turning for home, was well clear. Before an official crowd of 95 681, he cruised to victory by three lengths from Bourbon, with Ortelle's Star third. First prize was £7200. The race was not run to suit the stayers, whose number included the 5/1 favourite Royal Chief, also a New Zealander.

Even though Catalogue started at 25/1, much longer odds were on offer before Derby Day, and not all bookmakers cleaned up. One punter who did nicely was previous owner Ted Barnes. And well-known Melbourne racing man Jack Heaney had one bet of £5000 to £100.

TURF TOPICS

Back-to-back: Heroic sired his second successive Victoria Derby winner when Nuffield took the 1938 classic. Hua had won it in 1937. Nuffield was raced by Heroic's owner, Charles Kellow. Heroic also sired the 1933 winner Hall Mark.

Two killed: Melbourne lightweight rider Ray Wilson and local horseman Stan Kite were killed in a five-horse pile-up in a sprint race on Adelaide Cup day.

Look out! High Caste, one of the turf's most durable customers, stepped out for the first time, in New Zealand, and won two races from three starts at Ellerslie. Next port of call was Melbourne.

13 straight: Carrying 9.0 – 3 lb over weight-for-age, Ajax won the VRC Newmarket (6f) in the autumn after downing two good gallopers, Hua and El Golea, in the VATC Futurity Stakes (7f). The Newmarket was the second of 13 straight wins Ajax recorded in 1938, mostly in wfa events.

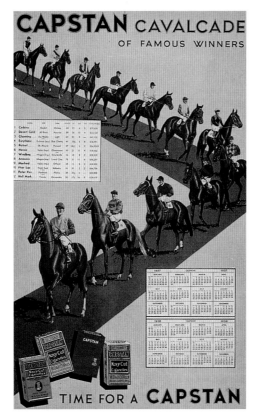

A cavalcade of winners for Capstan.

Keith Voitre killed

Top New Zealand jockey Keith Voitre, who came to Victoria in 1934 and was an instant success, was killed in a race fall at Moonee Valley in September 1938. He was 25.

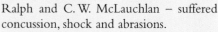

He suffered a fractured skull and other injuries in a four-horse pile-up in the Budgeree Handicap. He died in St Vincent's Hospital. The three other jockeys involved in the fall – apprentices Bill Williamson, Stan Ralph and C. W. McLauchlan – suffered concussion, shock and abrasions.

The tragedy occurred when McLauchlan's mount, Pilot, stumbled near the three-furlong pole as the field bunched. Frill Prince, ridden by Voitre, crashed into Pilot, throwing Voitre heavily to the ground. The mounts of Williamson and Ralph also came down.

Voitre, from Palmerston North, was lured to Victoria by fellow Kiwi, the successful trainer Lou Robertson. In 1935, in the space of 12 days, they combined to win the Cox Plate (Garrio), Victoria Derby (Feldspar), Melbourne Cup (Marabou) and VRC Oaks (Nalda). It was the first time the four major races had been won by the same duo. In 1935, Voitre also won the VRC Newmarket on Count Ito, the AJC Doncaster on Hall Mark and the AJC Epsom on Synagogue.

Voitre, who lived in Preston, had his first ride in Victoria on 31 October 1934, when he won at Kyneton on Limbohn. In September 1936, he suffered a fractured leg in a fall, also at Moonee Valley. He was out of action for 12 months but was soon back to his best form. He rode more than 100 winners in one season in New Zealand.

Sun shines on potent Queenslanders

Queenslanders, with the help of an English sire bearing a less than complimentary name, made one act of the 1938 Caulfield Cup.

The aptly named winner Buzalong was bred by Queensland studmaster J. G. McDougall, owned and trained by A. Leftwich from Kingaroy and ridden by Queensland-born jockey Frank Shean, by then riding in Sydney.

As for the breeding, Buzalong was by The Buzzard, formerly The Bastard. When imported to Australia, the name offended the racing authorities, hence the change.

The Buzzard, by Carbine's grandson Spion Kop, turned out to be a grand dad, subsequently siring two Melbourne Cup winners, Old Rowley (1940) and Rainbird (1945) and a second Caulfield Cup winner in Basha Felika (1951). The Buzzard was Australia's leading sire in 1946–47 and 1949–50.

Buzalong cost Leftwich only 110 guineas, a bargain considering the Caulfield Cup was his 11th win and took his earnings to almost £9000. He raced in Ipswich and Brisbane up to the age of three, then moved to Sydney where he became a consistent winner of good quality races. As a five-year-old gelding he was 11/2 favourite for the Caulfield Cup on the strength of his second in the AJC Metropolitan.

Buzalong led into the straight and won by two lengths. For Shean, who had been having a bad trot, it was a good year. He also won the AJC Epsom, Williamstown Cup and Melbourne Cup (on Catalogue).

1938 RESULTS

VRC MELBOURNE CUP (2m)
Catalogue, 8.4 (F Shean) Trained by A W McDonald; 3:26.25; Bourbon, Ortelle's Star
AJC SYDNEY CUP (2m)
L'Aiglon, 6.8 (A Harvey) Trained by D Lewis; 3:23; Apollo, Young Crusader
QTC BRISBANE CUP (2m)
Spear Chief, 8.3 (M McCarten) Princess Rivoli, Spearbleu
SAJC ADELAIDE CUP (13-f)
Dartford, 8.5 (W Elliot) Trained by J Harvey; 2:48.5; Silent Tip, Grecian Princess
WATC PERTH CUP (2m) (1 January 1938)
Maikai, 7.11 (JJ Kelly) Trained by JJ Kelly; 3:26.25; Tetbury, Footmark
WATC PERTH CUP (2m) (31 December 1938)
Gay Balkan (E Treffone) Trained by JJ Kelly; 3:30.75; Tetbury, Dark David

VATC CAULFIELD CUP (12-f)
Buzalong, 8.6 (F Shean) Trained by A Leftwich; 2:29.75; St Constant, Marauder
VRC AUSTRALIAN CUP (2¼m)
Marauder, 7.4 (J O'Sullivan) Trained by W Burke; 3:47.2; Old Rowley, Pooley Bridge
MVRC WS COX PLATE (9 ½-f)
Ajax, 9.0 (H Badger) Trained by F Musgrave; 1:56.7; Royal Chief, Young Idea
AJC DERBY (12-f)
Nuffield, 8.10 (D Munro) Trained by J Holt; 2:32; Aeolus, Respirator
VRC VICTORIA DERBY (12-f)
Nuffield (D Munro) Trained by J Holt; 2:34; Tempest, Adios
AJC DONCASTER HANDICAP (1m)
Hamurah, 7.9 (P Hickey) Trained by W Henderson; 1:37.5; King's Head, Buzalong

BTC DOOMBEN '10 000' (6-f)
Hamurah, 8.12 (C Heath) Trained by W Henderson; 1:14.25; Bahwing, Spear Chief
VRC NEWMARKET HANDICAP (6-f)
Ajax, 9.0 (H Badger) Trained by F Musgrave; 1:11.5; Ena, El Golea
AJC SIRES' PRODUCE STAKES (7-f)
Nuffield, 8.10 (H Badger) Trained by J Holt; Fort Regal, Pandava; 1:25.25
VRC SIRES' PRODUCE STAKES (7-f)
Nuffield, 8.10 (R Wilson) Trained by J Holt; 1:26; Destiny Bay, Lady Montague
VRC GRAND NATIONAL STEEPLECHASE (3m 1-f)
Green Cape, 9.9 (F Dummett) Trained by W Burke; 6:8; Deckard, Grantley

Bookmaking – from the Silver King to the TAB

When horseracing became a spectator sport the modern bookmaker was born. As the 19th century passed, match races, where gentlemen owners would bet with each other, gave way to meetings run by clubs on enclosed tracks you had to pay to enter. One of these enclosed tracks in Melbourne was named Flemington where, in 1861, 4000 people turned up to watch the first Melbourne Cup. Twenty-nine years later, 100 000 crammed the course to see Carbine's Cup. The measure of the popularity of horse-racing was the growth of these city racing clubs, catering for both the colonial gentry and the urban masses, whose increasing wages and leisure time transformed horseracing into a mass recreation.

Thoroughbreds, ponies, trotters, grey-hounds: by the end of the 19th century there were plenty of opportunities for people to bet. In these circumstances how could book-ies do anything but prosper?

Nobody knows who Australia's first bookmaker was but the modern bookie, recognisable by his stand, his black bag, his clerk and his patter, arrived in Australia in 1882 from England in the person of Robert Standish Siever. Siever was the first to claim a 'pitch', write bets on tickets and bet in cash with all comers. With all the scorn of the innovator, he described local bookies as lumberers, who would 'run about the course in search of an up-country squatter and lay him a double this-and-the-next much under the legitimate price'.

Paintings of the big racecourses in the 1880s show the bookies Siever describes, distinguishable from their clients only by the small pocket books in which they recorded their bets. Yet the fundamentals of bookmaking remained the same. Like the lumberers, Siever would search out information on the prospects of a horse. Then he would survey the public form and set his book, shouting the odds: short prices on those he reckoned had the best chance and longer prices on the rest. (Much later bookies adopted the book-ies' board so punters could see the odds about

Calculating the odds on a bush meeting can be a lonely business (Age).

their fancy at a glance; calling the odds then became an art instead of a necessity.) Depending on how much money he held, Siever would shorten or lengthen a horse's odds. If a horse were plunged he would 'lay off', betting on the plunged horse with other book-ies. If it won he would use his winnings to cover his losses.

And he followed the same routine every race, hoping to come out in front at the end of the day.

Picture Flemington on Carbine's big day. In the Paddock stand the leviathans like Joe Thompson or 'The Count' (E. N. Abrahams), heavy-bearded, dressed in top hat and tails, flash perhaps but respectable. Some 'rails bookies' are taking 'on the nod' credit bets from Victoria Racing Club members. Down past the winning post is the Hill. Here a sec-ond rank of bookie is taking smaller bets from a second class of punters. There in 1890 is the 22-year-old Sol Green, on his way to fame and fortune. The real colour, though, is inside the course, on 'the Flat'. Here we find the 'Masher King', the 'Silver King' and dozens of others. Splendid in their many-coloured coats, their silver spangled bags, atop their boxes and under their own flags, they called the odds for the shilling pieces of the mass of working-class patrons out for their day at the races.

Such was the social milieu of late 19th century bookmaking. Ambitious and success-ful bookies like Sol Green could climb from the Flat to the Hill, then graduate to the

Paddock, paying the Club substantially for the privilege.

But this was the thoroughbred racing world. There was another rank of bookmaker in the on-course hierarchy, the bookies at that raffish world of *fin de siècle* horseracing, the pony tracks. Far beyond the pale for the aris-tocrats of the thoroughbred clubs, the pri-vately owned pony clubs took their horses from anywhere, and likewise their owners, trainers, jockeys and bookmakers (the pony clubs were the first port of call for those dis-qualified from the thoroughbreds). The names of the pony courses are now long forgotten; Ascot in Melbourne, one of many 'clubs' owned by John Wren, Moorfield in Sydney and Kensington Park in Perth, which went by the well-merited sobriquet of Robbery Park. And there were many more.

Late in the century clubs big and small, thoroughbred and pony, all began to cast off their amateur status and hire professional judges, starters and stipendiary stewards, and they also began licensing bookies. Hitherto any con-man who could pay an entry fee could stake out a 'pitch' and start calling the odds, so the VRC, in 1882, and others soon after, imposed a license fee, first on Paddock bookies, then on those on the Hill. On the Flat it took a little longer. In 1906 a Flemington Flat bookie, Donald McLeod, became overcommitted. He fled, was chased, caught, beaten, fell on his face and died. The bookies working on the Flat were registered soon after.

The bags, ready to be slammed at day's end.

Places like the Flemington Flat did not last long into the new century. Punters began to avail themselves of the better facilities and more generous bookies in better stands, so clubs closed these cheap stands down. Their bookies, the true descendants of the traditions of the 19th century Flats, either graduated to 'Silver Rings' in better appointed stands, moved on or disappeared.

Every bookmaker wants to stand where the big money is, but even the biggest must go where the races are. In the early 20th century Big Joe Thompson used to leave Melbourne to bet 'up country'. The Sydney old-timer Arthur Sing once recalled that bookies in the Great Depression had to work courses all over the state and in all types of racing: thoroughbreds, ponies, trotters and dogs. As the century passed many bookies began to specialise. Some went exclusively to the newer kind of racing like the trots, and others to the greyhounds. As pony racing was abolished or withered away those bookies either withered with it or, more likely, took another, even more unrespectable option: 'the SP'.

Bookmakers have always thought of themselves as part businessmen, part sportsmen, and their business needs and social ambitions led them to set up their own private clubs. After many years of settling with clients on the footpaths outside certain hotels, Sydney and Melbourne bookies set up Tattersalls clubs late in the 19th century, safe places where they could socialise, gamble and do business, and bookies in other cities soon followed. That famous pre–Melbourne Cup ritual, the Calling of the Card, has taken place at the Victoria Club in Melbourne for virtually a hundred years. And it was there, in April 1976, that some cool customers arrived at settling time and relieved the assembled members of several million dollars, in what became known as the Great Melbourne Bookie Robbery. Years later the Club moved to the Rialto building and settling was transferred to high-security premises at the races.

Bookmakers haven't always been a fixture at all Australian racetracks. Of doubtful legality in South Australia, police removed them from racecourses in 1893 and they were not allowed back until 1933. In 1932 Tasmania legislated to permit bookies on and off Tasmanian courses. In Queensland and Western Australia bookies were technically illegal but were never prosecuted. Many bookies feared the introduction of the on-course tote and tried to persuade governments not to introduce it (some governments introduced the tote specifically to get rid of bookies). Yet others welcomed it for the financial advantages it gave to clubs, and hence their own fortunes. Bookies lobbied against the taxes that governments imposed

Writing a ticket in the 1970s (Age).

on them and have continued to complain about them ever since. In pursuit of their interests and in defence of their occupation, they always appealed to an older image of themselves. As the Sydney bookie Jack Shaw told an ABC debate in 1949, racing would always need 'the bookmaker with red blood in his veins'. But would it? It was always equally possible that bookmakers needed racing more than racing needed bookies.

In 1977 the Sydney bookmaker, Big Bill Waterhouse, told an interviewer, 'The racecourse is the first thing affected in hard times.' It has been hard times for the racing industry

ever since and bookmaking has declined with the industry. The odd spectacular plunge notwithstanding, bookies now say there hasn't been much big money about since the 1980s recession and what there is, is shared in a highly competitive gambling market. In 1972 racing took nearly 90 per cent of the money Victorians spent on gambling; in 1996 it was just 20 per cent.

In 1986 there were more than 500 bookies in Victoria, yet in 1994 there were only 267 members of the Victorian Bookmakers' Association. In Perth the decline has been just as spectacular. In July 1982 there were 150 bookies registered by the Betting Control Board. In 1998 there were just 60. Perth bookies have been hit so badly that some years ago their local Tattersalls Club amalgamated with the Perth Bowling Club.

The future looks anything but rosy for the profession of bookmaking. Racing clubs haven't found the key to increased patronage. That golden goose, the TAB, which racing clubs reluctantly embraced in the 1960s, keeps racing afloat but on-course bookies need new sources of income. They got it in Victoria in early 1993 when they were allowed access to off-course money. David Cox, one Victorian bookie, said in 1996 that by 1998, 90 per cent of bookies' business would be off-course. Off-course is where the money is. Off-course is probably where the future of bookmaking lies, taking bets from that ever-increasing body of punters who want to bet from their homes.

by Charlie Fox

Flemington on Cup day is bookmaking heaven, and an unusual sight in the rest of the world.

Rivette, ridden by Teddy Preston, returns to the Flemington enclosure after winning the Cup.

A special edition of the 'pink paper'.

Bamber the battler & a mare called Rivette

Harry Bamber was a small man, tanned and wrinkled by years of outdoor work. You might not have noticed him in a crowd, but Australia saluted him on Melbourne Cup Day 1939 when his gallant mare Rivette won the first of the wartime Cups.

The front page of the *Age* in Melbourne on Wednesday, 8 November, having broken with tradition, carried seven paragraphs in large type as well as the usual classified advertisements.

With Hitler's war eight weeks old, four paragraphs forecast a German offensive in Belgium and Holland. The other three were devoted to Bamber's Rivette, only the third horse after Poseidon (1906) and The Trump (1937) to win the Caulfield–Melbourne Cups double and the first mare to do so.

The democratic nature of racing took a bow in 1939, the year the Sport of Kings singled out a 46-year-old battler called Harry Bamber. Melburnian Bamber, the son of a Williamstown blacksmith, learnt his trade at an early age in his father's shop.

At the outbreak of the Great War, Bamber joined the 13th Light Horse. In his four years abroad, he learnt much about veterinary care, which made him a good man in a crisis.

After the war he returned to Scoresby and, with his brother Edmund, bought for 200 guineas a mare called Riverside, a descendent of Carbine.

When Bamber registered her with the VRC, her name was changed to Riv and she became a top performer, twice winning the Ascot 1000, the Melbourne Cup for ponies.

In 1928, Bamber left Scoresby to train his team at Caulfield but times were hard and the depression years found him milking cows for one pound a week at Clyde in Victoria. A bonus was that he was able to keep Riv, now his own, on the farm. Aged 10, Riv was retired to stud. Bamber was keen to breed from her. But he was short of cash and could not afford a fashionable sire. Bloodstock agent Billy Cox suggested Ronsard, a sire of some good sprinters whose fee was 20 guineas.

Bamber acquired the 20 guineas on Melbourne Cup Day, 1932 after backing the Cup winner Peter Pan on the advice of the top colt's trainer Frank McGrath. The result of the Ronsard–Riv mating was a smallish bay filly named Rivette.

To put it mildly Rivette did not flatter early on. She first raced as a three-year-old and was winless. As a four-year-old, however, she won three races from eight starts. Bamber set her for the 1938 Caulfield Cup but plans were abandoned when she cut a leg artery playing in a sand roll. She lost a lot of blood but 'vet' Bamber saved the day and stitched the wound. When Rivette resumed in June, 1939, she gave Bamber heart by flashing home to run third in a Caulfield welter. Overnight Rivette became favourite for the Caulfield Cup after she finished a close second in the Herbert Power Handicap (12f).

She carried 8.8, 20lb more than her Cup weight of 7.2.

Ridden by Ted Preston, who replaced injured apprentice Jack Purtell, Rivette showed great courage in the Caulfield Cup, overcoming a severe bump at the half-mile post to beat the good stayer Maikai by three-quarters of a length, earning Bamber £5000. Said a smiling Preston: 'I didn't know how good she was. I almost gave up hope.'

Penalised the full 10 lb for the Melbourne Cup, Rivette with 7.9 was the popular choice with small punters and went to the post a 5/1 favourite in the big two-miler at Flemington.

For once it seemed luck was with her. In a rough race, she escaped interference. When Preston dashed her to the front on the home turn, it seemed a matter of how far. Suddenly, however, there was a roar from the crowd of 93 000 as the riderless Ortelle's Star, who had dumped jockey Frank de Valle early in the race, ranged up beside her. Preston 'talked' Ortelle's Star into keeping a straight course and averted danger.

Ortelle's Star was first past the post from Rivette with a half-length to Maikai.

Harry Bamber, a generous man, shared his two-Cups windfall of £12 000 with 'battling licensees and biters' and made donations to charities.

A richer owner would have won a fortune on Rivette in 1939. But Bamber was thankful for the £1500 he collected from bookmaker Sol Green.

The amazing moment when Spear Chief at 33/1 beats 1/40 certainty Ajax.

Ajax defeat shocks turf world

The defeat of Ajax by Spear Chief in the Rosehill Rawson Stakes (9f) in March 1939 ranked as one of the greatest sensations of the Australasian turf. Sent out favourite at the nominal quote of 1/40, Ajax was regarded as unbeatable. His only opponents were Spear Chief, whom Ajax had beaten decisively at Caulfield in February, and Allunga, regarded as not forward enough to do himself justice.

But 'the impossible' happened. So Ajax, with 18 consecutive wins to his credit, lost when least expected and failed to equal the Australasian record of 19 straight wins shared by Desert Gold and Gloaming.

After Ajax's inexplicable defeat, there were cheers for his vanquisher, Spear Chief (ridden by Maurice McCarten), consternation among the connections of Ajax and deep regret felt by lovers of the real galloper.

Ajax's jockey, Harold Badger, was criticised in some quarters for not making more use of the horse's speed, his critics saying he should have slipped away from his two rivals. In fairness, Badger rode an admirable race. Realising that Ajax was having his first race as a four-year-old on a Sydney track, and therefore going the reverse way, he allowed Allunga to run along with him to the turn. Badger was using the Sydney galloper to keep Ajax on the rails. Unfortunately, when Badger called on Ajax for the effort that would carry him to his 19th win there was no response.

Revealing form that was previously unsuspected of him, Spear Chief drew level with Ajax and, doing better than the champion, went on to win by a half length. Allunga (Darby Munro) was third, a length and a quarter away.

Some punters were aghast at Ajax's defeat, especially the fellow who laid £900 to £30 on him. Spear Chief and Allunga both started at 33/1. Spear Chief paid only 19/9 for a win.

Ajax's winning streak of 18 began in the VRC Linlithgow Stakes (1m, wfa) at Flemington on Oaks day, 4 November 1937. Five days beforehand he had run second to Hua, beaten by a head, in the Victoria Derby.

Spelled after the Linlithgow, he returned in the autumn of 1938 and won the VATC Futurity Stakes first-up. Then came his famous Newmarket win. He had five starts that autumn for five wins. He resumed in August, winning the WRC Underwood Stakes, his first start as a four-year-old. Eight starts in the spring of '38 yielded another eight wins, including the Mackinnon Stakes, Cox Plate and another Linlithgow.

After three months in the paddock he got away to a flying start in 1939, winning four races in Melbourne – the VATC St George Stakes, the Futurity, the King's Plate and the CM Lloyd Stakes. He had not been beaten for 15 months, 16 of his 18 wins being recorded in Melbourne, the other two in Sydney. Badger piloted him in 17 of those wins, Ted Bartle in the other.

As it turned out, Ajax clearly had an off day in the Rawson Stakes, for at his next start, two weeks later in the AJC All-Aged Plate at Randwick, he won easily, beating the good galloper Gold Rod, winner of the 1937 Epsom.

Before being retired to stud at the age of six, Ajax had another 15 starts for 10 wins, three seconds and two thirds. In total he had 46 starts for 36 wins and nine placings. His one unplaced run was at his third start, in the VRC Sires' Produce Stakes in 1937.

Ajax had the remarkable record of winning five major races three times apiece – the VATC Futurity and Memsie Stakes, the WRC Underwood Stakes, the AJC All-Aged Stakes and the CW Cropper Plate.

At stud, he sired the 1945 AJC and Victoria Derby winner, Magnificent, and the 1947 AJC Epsom winner Achilles. He later went to stud in America.

1939 RESULTS

VRC MELBOURNE CUP (2m)
Rivette, 7.9 (E Preston) Trained by H Bamber; 3:27; Maikai, Pantler
AJC SYDNEY CUP (2m)
Mosaic, 8.2 (E Bartle) Trained by JH Abbs; 3:21.5; L'Aiglon, Malagigi
QTC BRISBANE CUP (2m)
Spear Chief, 9.7 (M McCarten) 3:19.7; Six-Fifty, L'Aiglon.
SAJC ADELAIDE CUP (13-f)
Son Of Aurous, 7.9 (H Olsen) Trained by F Doran; 2:46; Tempest, Rotex
WATC PERTH CUP (2m)
Tomito, 8.0 (E Wright) Trained by J Robinson; 3:28.5; True Flight, Meadow Line
VATC CAULFIELD CUP (12-f)
Rivette, 7.2 (E Preston) Trained by H Bamber; 2:29.25; Maikai, Respirator

VRC AUSTRALIAN CUP (2¼m)
Pageant, 7.8 (R Bailey) Trained by FW Hoysted; 3:52; Dark David, Ortelle's Star
MVRC WS COX PLATE (9½-f)
Mosaic, 9.0 (D Munro) Trained by JH Abbs; 1:56.5; Gold Salute, Reading
AJC DERBY (12-f)
Reading, 8.10 (D Munro) Trained by J Cush; 2:34; High Caste, Wilson
VRC VICTORIA DERBY (12-f)
Reading (D Munro) Trained by J Cush; 2:33; High Caste, Dashing Cavalier
AJC DONCASTER HANDICAP (1m)
Gold Rod, 9.2 (M McCarten) Trained by G Price; 1:37; Korimaka, St Constant

BTC DOOMBEN '10 000' (6-f)
Micawber, 8.1 (F Shean) Trained by WJ Shean; 1:12.25; The Albatross, Brisbane River
VRC NEWMARKET HANDICAP (6-f)
El Golea, 8.12 (N Creighton) Trained by H Freedman; 1:11.7; Aurie's Star, Kanuri
AJC SIRES' PRODUCE STAKES (7-f)
Reading, 8.10 (D Munro) Trained by J Cush; 1:25.25; High Caste, Cardinal Puff
VRC SIRES' PRODUCE STAKES)
High Caste, 8.10 (E Bartle) Trained by J Jamieson; 1:26.7; Zonda, Aurania
VRC GRAND NATIONAL STEEPLECHASE (3m 1-f)
Giant Killer, 10.11 (R Watts) Trained by W Burke; 6:15.75; Turf Boy, Wakerife

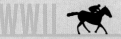

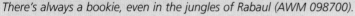

There's always a bookie, even in the jungles of Rabaul (AWM 098700).　*A digger explains the Cup odds: New Guinea, 1943 (AWM 060489).*

Hitler backs a loser – they're still racing

The day Ajax won his second Memsie Stakes at Caulfield — at a prohibitive 12/1 on – the Prime Minister, Robert Menzies, warned Australia that the odds about peace were not good. War threatened in Europe because of the aggression of an Austrian corporal intoxicated with power.

The following day, on Sunday, September 3, having postponed a public address at Colac and returned to Melbourne, Mr Menzies told the nation the grave news on the wireless, nationwide. Australia was at war.

On the racing front it was business as usual in the short term, then on a reduced basis, many tracks being commandeered by the army for training purposes. Caulfield racecourse was one. It was occupied for four years from 1940, the Caulfield Cup being run at Flemington from 1940 until 1943.

In South Australia, racing was abandoned in 1942–43. Oakbank, home of the Great Eastern Steeple, became a military base. In Brisbane, which was only a whiff of cordite away from the Kokoda Trail, major racetracks were closed from 1942 until war's end. The Brisbane Cup, first run in 1879, was abandoned from 1942 to 1946.

In Sydney, Warwick Farm was taken over by the army. Facilities at Randwick suffered because of the movement of troops and trucks across the tracks. Up to 1945, the AJC contributed £110 000 to the war effort. In Western Australia, there was one city meeting a fortnight.

The first city race run during World War II was the Durham Trial Hurdle at Ascot in Melbourne on 5 September. The winner was Orange Bitters owned by W. J. T. Clarke. The same day it was announced that New Zealander Catalogue, the 1938 Melbourne

Cup winner, might not be able to 'defend' his crown because of a shortage of shipping space. Ships were needed for troops and guns, not horses. Somehow Catalogue made it, but was unplaced.

Five days into the war, Melburnians took Mr Menzies at his word. He had encouraged Australians to 'carry on as usual'. A crowd of 47 200 rolled up at Caulfield to see champion Kiwi colt High Caste win the Caulfield Guineas, his ninth win in Australia. But the atmosphere was subdued. With a forecast of rain spot on, women racegoers wore warm coats and furs. A week later 67 500 people, some already in uniform, saw Rivette win the Caulfield Cup. For the first time at Caulfield tote figures topped £100 000, reaching £103 972. The VATC profits were earmarked for the Red Cross and War Funds.

The war put the international spotlight on the Melbourne Cup. Thanks to the BBC, Old Rowley's win at 100/1 in 1940 was broadcast to members of the AIF stationed in Britain. The broadcast was arranged by the officer commanding the Australian forces there, Major-General Wynter.

To most soldiers in Britain the horses in the cup were merely phantom names but a bookie soon materialised in each mess. For the soldiers, every punter's dream came true. Betting was available on credit. One battalion Cup sweep was organised by the padre.

As usual, the bookies cleaned up, thanks to a Queensland-bred bolter whose sire, The Buzzard, was originally called The Bastard. The expression no doubt surfaced as Old Rowley (ridden by Andy Knox) passed the post first ahead of Darby Munro's mount, the unlucky Maikai.

At Flemington itself, soldiers, airmen and

sailors were admitted free. More than 78 000 paid, swelling the crowd to more than 100 000. The tote turned over £127 376, a record for any course in Victoria.

Though horseracing continued to flourish, the debate whether it should continue hotted up as hostilies increased. New Prime Minister John Curtin, who took office in October 1941, banned mid-week racing, but gave the green light to meetings on a limited basis. 'Low key' to conform with the national austerity program was the message, 'some relaxation and entertainment for those who had the regulation half-day holiday on Saturdays'.

Rich folk and the less well-off rallied to the war effort. Wealthy owner and punter Sol Green sold 20 yearlings and donated the proceeds to England for blankets for the poor. In Perth, Eurythmic's owner, grazier Ernest Lee Steere, donated to War Funds the trophies won by his champion in the Caulfield and Sydney Cups. The cups were melted down at the Perth mint.

Of the one million Australians who joined up, racing provided its share; owners, trainers, jockeys, stablehands, farriers etc. Many riders and apprentices were engaged in wartime industries. Older trainers, deprived of sufficient labour, did the work of two men. Many bookmakers devoted themselves to war comforts, growing vegetables etc. Racing clubs cut staff to skeleton proportions.

Erudite young WA trainer Abe Jordan served in the Middle East with the 2/11 AIF battalion. On discharge, he put his deferred pay to good use, buying a horse called Oredanus who won 12 races. In Queensland, Corporal Neville Sellwood, who would ride two Melbourne Cup winners, served in an

The forces turn out in force to watch Colonus win the 1942 Melbourne Cup (Age).

TURF TOPICS

'Training' together: In September 1939 a knock-about jockey cum trainer called Tommy Smith, in his early 20s, boarded a Melbourne-bound train at Wagga with two horses prepared by Matt Sawyer. On the same train was a 16-year-old Queensland hoop called George Moore. They met. Both were broke. In Melbourne, the brash Smith told Moore and others: 'I'll train the Derby winner and you'll ride him.' Most laughed. As usual, Smith was right. In 1957 Tulloch won the AJC and Victoria Derbys, ridden by Moore.

Binoc-off: Binoculars were in short supply, so civilians were asked to surrender their field glasses for use by the armed forces. One day at Flemington a well-known 'fence' who had seen better days handed to the VRC a box containing four pairs of top-class 'glasses'. No questions were asked.

Toy soldier: Newcomer George Moore saddled his first big winner Expressman in the 1940 Doomben Newmarket, and served for three years with the First Army Employment Corps. At 6½ stone wringing wet, he described himself as the worst soldier Australia had produced. 'You couldn't see me for my uniform'. Returning home on leave one day, a busload of people broke into laughter when they saw him, after which the family dog tried to bite him.

'Hoofing' a ride: In November 1942, Canberra banned the carriage of racehorses by road for more than 25 miles. A permit was required for longer journeys. The move followed reports that NSW horses 'hitch-hiked' rides to Albury, then were placed on other floats for the trip to Melbourne.

Cup field runneth over: The Caulfield Cup was run in two divisions at Flemington in 1943 after the VATC received 47 acceptors. Each division was worth £3600, plus a £100 war bond. Bookmakers took bets on a unique double, the 'two Caulfield Cups'. Few punters collected. Saint Warden, a 100/1 shot from WA, won the first division and Skipton (14/1) the second. Skipton had a liking for Flemington, having won the 1941 Melbourne Cup.

Death knell of privates: In NSW, the war spelt the death knell of proprietary racing. Four financially troubled tracks (Ascot, Moorefield, Victoria Park and Rosebery) went out of business.

---

army postal unit at Townsville. He was allowed to ride track work each morning and take mounts at country Cluden, which had three meetings a month. Australian and American soldiers knew a horseman when they saw one. So did the bookies. 'Even-money Sellwood' was their familiar cry.

In Sydney, Darby Munro was a private in the Army Service Corps. One of his daily tasks was to pick up rubbish at the Sydney Showgrounds where he was stationed and load it on to a dray. Come Monday, fellow troops would boo him if he had been beaten on a favourite on the Saturday.

With the war at Australia's front door in December 1941, racing went into survival mode. Petrol rationing put the brakes on cars and horse floats. Oats, barley and hay were in short supply. Nags showed more rib than usual. Out-of-work stablehands joined up. Public transport was curtailed. Country tracks closed, places such as Pakenham, Mornington and Yarra Glen. Brisbane was hit hardest, Eagle Farm and Doomben being closed.

In a wise move, meetings up north were transferred to Albion Park, known as The Creek. Servicemen and women flocked there as families headed south with their children. A horse called Auction became a hero at The Creek, winning the 1942 Doomben Newmarket with 10.2.

For racegoers, horrid front-page news came out of Canberra in mid-1942. Mr Curtin announced that each calendar month there would be one Saturday without racing, nationwide. Howls of protest went unheeded.

Not only humans had to pay a sacrifice to help the war effort. It also applied to the horses. The number in training had to be reduced. The first raceless Saturday in Sydney saw punters betting on yacht races. Pubs ran out of beer. For those still left in racing, the first Saturday was given over to essential war work and repairing racing establishments. Twelve months later, in September 1943, the Curtin Government lifted the restriction. To widespread joy, every Saturday was race day.

With no mid-week racing, the Melbourne Cup carnival was reduced to two days, seven races apiece, on the second and third Saturday in November. The Derby was run on the second Saturday, the Oaks and Cup a week later. The first Saturday Cup was in 1942, the winner being 33/1 chance Colonus, raced by Melbourne businessman L. O. Menck.

There was much jubilation in Melbourne when Caulfield (The Heath) reopened for the Australian Steeplechase meeting in the winter of 1944. The Heath was looking tired but racegoers and bookies greeted each other tearfully.

With the guns silent, the Cup returned to the first Tuesday in November in 1945. The popular winner was Rainbird ridden by the popular ex-soldier Billy Cook. A jubilant day had a sad note. The familiar figure of old Shadow King, the grand stayer turned police horse, was missing. He had died during the year. A little headstone at the police depot at Bundoora marked his grave.

by David Austin

Silks and satins of 1941: Darby Munro, back row at left, and Billy Cook, third from left, 2nd row.

Billy Cook on 1941 Cup winner, Skipton.

Wrong horse shot

Gunshots were fired on the racing front six days before the 1940 Melbourne Cup. The target was the hot Cup favourite Beau Vite, winner of the AJC Metropolitan and conqueror of Ajax in the Cox Plate.

After the Cox Plate, police contacted the horse's owner, Ralph Stewart, warning him of threats to get the horse. Jockey Ted McMenamin had received an anonymous letter saying Beau Vite would be prevented from winning the Cup 'one way or another'. The usually stoic jockey had restless nights.

The Wednesday night before the Cup gunmen entered Beau Vite's stable in Glenhuntly. But they hit the wrong horse, namely the 1939 Newmarket winner El Golea, who looked like Beau Vite.

The villains, who were never apprehended, bored a hole in a stable wall and, using a small-calibre rifle, fired shots, thinking Beau Vite was in their sights. Poor El Golea had bullets removed from his near-hind thigh and off-hock.

After that close shave, Beau Vite, a highly performed Kiwi-bred stayer, was guarded night and day, especially at Flemington, which he visited twice in the ensuing days, first to win the LKS Mackinnon Stakes at 4/6 on Derby day. On Cup Day, with McMenamin in the saddle and the bookmakers offering only 7/4, he was escorted on to the course proper by police. Despite being cramped for room in the straight, Beau Vite's performance was disappointing. He ran fourth behind Old Rowley. McMenamin said the weight of 9.7 told on the four-year-old in the end. On Boxing Day, back in New Zealand, Beau Vite won the Auckland Cup, the 20th of his 31 wins.

Gift horse's Cup win

Skipton, named after the picturesque village near Ballarat, brought joy and more than a few bob to the Western District of Victoria by winning the Victoria Derby–Melbourne Cup double in 1941, the last three-year-old to do so. Missing from both races was his owner, Mrs J. J. Kitson, wife of a Hamilton publican. She listened to them on the wireless.

Why? She believed her presence would put a hoodoo on her horse. The only time she had seen him race that spring, in the Caulfield Guineas, he had been beaten.

On Cup Day, her excited daughter Morva received the trophy from Lady Dugan, wife of the Governor. Alongside him were trainer, former Kiwi Jack Fryer, and jockey Bill Cook, who rode the Marabou colt splendidly.

Mrs Kitson said from her Hamilton hotel: 'Everyone seemed to be here this afternoon and seemed to have a good win. That makes me happier still, for the people here are first-class.' It did not concern her that Skipton carried No. 13 saddlecloth, said to be unlucky.

Luck was on her side the day her husband bought the Marabou–Cupidity colt at the Melbourne yearling sales. Kitson had backed Marabou when he won the 1935 Melbourne Cup and liked his chestnut son, foaled in 1938. Kitson had gone to the sales with a friend after unsuccessfully scouring Melbourne's shops for a birthday present for his wife. Now for 250 guineas he had one, a well-built, exuberant baby who would win £15 042/10/-.

Solomons unwise

Melbourne racecaller Harry Solomons of 3XY was in need of some cash in December, 1939. The punt was treating him harshly; he owed the wrong sort of people big money. Solomons and his associates hatched a plan, which went into operation on the last race at Ascot, a Welter timed for 5.05 p.m.

The landlines of fellow callers Jim Carroll (ABC), Eric Welch (3DB) and Fred Tupper (3AW) were to be cut, leaving them talking into fresh air. Listeners switching to 3XY would hear Solomons waffling on about horses playing up at the barrier while the race was run. Mention of one horse in particular, Scobie Breasley's mount Buoyancy, was the signal for SP bookmakers to be hit for as much as possible, all of it on Buoyancy. That done, Solomons would do a phantom call, with Buoyancy, of course, winning. By now backed in 6/1.

But there was a hitch. A prearranged donnybrook below the broadcasting position got so out of hand that Solomons' colleagues had to go downstairs to break it up.

As a result, one racecaller hit the airwaves with: 'They're off' before the landlines were cut. Unaware of the foul-up, Solomons went ahead and called the race.

In the resultant confusion, the three stations put off the air were bombarded with queries, protests about what had happened in 'the last'. How come 3XY had broadcast it?

Solomons was subsequently sentenced to six months' jail for conspiracy. His cohorts escaped scot free. Whether any of them collected is unknown. As for Solomons, he dropped off the scene probably due to a lack of buoyancy.

1940–45 RESULTS

1940 RESULTS
VRC MELBOURNE CUP (2m)
Old Rowley, 7.12 (A Knox) Trained by J Scully; 2:26; Maikai, Tidal Wave
AJC SYDNEY CUP (2m)
Mosaic, 9.1 (D Munro) Trained by JH Abbs; 3:25.5; Royal Chief, Maikai
QTC BRISBANE CUP (2m)
Tragopan, 8.2 (B Sinclair) 3:25.5; Overdraft, Spear Vale
SAJC ADELAIDE CUP (13-f)
Apostrophe, 7.6 (R Medhurst) Trained by J Brett; 2:44.7; Lady Kidston, Saint Warden
WATC PERTH CUP (2m) (Not run in 1940)
VATC CAULFIELD CUP (12-f)
Beaulivre, 7.2 (E Preston) Trained by G Price; 2:29; Gladynev, Historian
VRC AUSTRALIAN CUP (2¼m)
Indignity, 7.7 (H Hanley) Trained by J Brett; 3:51.25; Morvren, Companion
MVRC WS COX PLATE (9½-f)
Beau Vite, 9.0 (E McMenamin) Trained by Frank McGrath; 1:575; Ajax, Beaulivre
AJC DERBY (12-f)
Pandect, 8.10 (W Cook) Trained by F McGrath; 2:37; Lucrative, Sun Valley
VRC VICTORIA DERBY (12-f)
Lucrative (M McCarten) Trained by H Freedman; 2:32; Tranquil Star, Dark Felt
AJC DONCASTER HANDICAP (1m)
Mildura, 8.8 (D Munro) Trained by G Price; 1:36.7; Beaulivre, El Golea
BTC DOOMBEN '10 000' (6-f)
Expressman, 7.2 (G Moore) Trained by W Bougoure; 1:10.5; Beaulivre, Vergure
VRC NEWMARKET HANDICAP (6-f)
Mildura, 8.0 (E Bartle) Trained by G Price; 1:13.2; Hilton, Chatsbury
AJC SIRES' PRODUCE STAKES (7-f)
Lucrative, 8.10 (M McCarten) Trained by H Freedman; 1:25.25; Pandect, Trueness
VRC SIRES' PRODUCE STAKES (7-f)
Trueness, 8.7 (E Bartle) Trained by B Payten; 1:25.7; Lucrative, Halifax
VRC GRAND NATIONAL STEEPLECHASE (3m 1-f)
Blackford, 10.3 (L Meenan) Trained by H Gabell; 6:5; Man Of Ayr, Brightello

1941 RESULTS
VRC MELBOURNE CUP (2m)
Skipton, 7.7 (W Cook) Trained by J Fryer; 3:23.75; Son of Auros, Beau Vite
AJC SYDNEY CUP (2m)
Lucrative, 8.2 (M McCarten) Trained by H Freedman; 3:20.75; Hope, Pandect
QTC BRISBANE CUP (2m)
Lady Buzzard, 7.4 (N Percival) 3:25; Tragopan, Abspear
SAJC ADELAIDE CUP (13-f)
Yodvara, 8.1 (R Elder) Trained by C Whitfield; 2:46.5; Prince Ariel, Indignity
WATC PERTH CUP (2m)
Fernridge, 7.13 (E Hodgson) Trained by A Hampton; 3:24.25; Yodvara, Jiggle
VATC CAULFIELD CUP (12-f)
Velocity, 8.3 (J Purtell) Trained by SB Ferguson; 2:29.5; Reading, Evergreen
VRC AUSTRALIAN CUP (2¼m)
Saul, 8.2 (M McCarten) Trained by D McRae; 3:50.5; Apostrophe, dead-heat third Tidal Wave and Velocity
MVRC WS COX PLATE (9½-f)
Beau Vite, 9.4 (D Munro) Trained by F McGrath; 1:58.2; Tranquil Star, Laureate
AJC DERBY (12-f)
Laureate, 8.10 (M McCarten) Trained by H Freedman; 2:32; Galliard, Chatham's Choice
VRC VICTORIA DERBY (12-f)
Skipton (N Creighton) Trained by J Fryer; 2:34.5; Laureate, High Road
AJC DONCASTER HANDICAP (1m)
Mildura, 9.3 (E McMenamin) Trained by G Price; 1:35.2; Rimveil, Evergreen
BTC DOOMBEN '10 000' (6-f)
High Rank, 7.8 (R Maddock) Trained by C Pile; 1:12.25; Rimveil, Monash Star
VRC NEWMARKET HANDICAP (6-f)
All Veil, 7.13 (H Badger) Trained by H Wolters; 1:10.7; Phoines, Zonda
AJC SIRES' PRODUCE STAKES (7-f)
Yaralla, 8.10 (E McMenamin) Trained by F Cush; 1:23.7; All Love, Prince
VRC SIRES' PRODUCE STAKES (7-f)
All Love, 8.7 (E Bartle) Trained by J Cush; 1:26.2; Primavera, Status Quo
VRC GRAND NATIONAL STEEPLECHASE (3m 1-f)
National Debt, 10.10 (G Kenny) Trained by F Dougall; 6.6.5; Brightello, Sachem

1942 RESULTS
VRC MELBOURNE CUP (2m)
Colonus, 7.2 (h McCloud) Trained by F Manning; 3:33.25; Ohoncion, Heart's Desire
AJC SYDNEY CUP (2m)
Veiled Threat, 8.1 (R Parsons) Trained by JM Mitchell; 3:25.5; Velocity, Beau Vite
QTC BRISBANE CUP (2m) (Race abandoned during World War Two, 1942–5)
SAJC ADELAIDE CUP (13-f) (Race abandoned during World War Two, 1942–3)
WATC PERTH CUP (2m) (1 January 1942)
Ragtime, 7.5 (E Parnham) Trained by J Light; 3:28, Rimutaka, Hestia
WATC PERTH CUP (2m) (26 December 1942)
Temple Chief, 7.12 (F Wright) Trained by F Foley; 3:27.5; Tropics, Pantheist

VATC CAULFIELD CUP (12-f)
Tranquil Star, 8.12 (A Breasley) Trained by R Cameron; 2:32.75; Heart's Desire, El Golea
VRC AUSTRALIAN CUP (2¼m)
Wise Counsel, 7.1 (W Beresford) Trained by R Cameron; 3:56; Togo, Mercury Bay
MVRC WS COX PLATE (9½-f)
Tranquil Star, 8.13 (K Smith) Trained by R Cameron; 2:00.7; Pandect, Leahere
AJC DERBY (12-f)
Main topic, 8.10 (D Munro) Trained by MT McGrath; 2:31.5; Hall Stand, Grand Prodigy
VRC VICTORIA DERBY (12-f)
Great Britain (W Cook) Trained by H Freedman; 2:31.75; dead-heat second Amazed and Illyrian
AJC DONCASTER HANDICAP (8½-f)
Tuhitarata, 7.10 (H Badger) Trained by W Gander; 1:45.25; Arahura, Evergreen
BTC DOOMBEN '10 000' (7-f)
Auction, 10.12 (T Spencer) Trained by R Wall; 1:28.5; High Rank, Bahford
VRC NEWMARKET HANDICAP (6-f)
Kelos, 7.12 (R Heather) Trained by H Wolters; 1:11.2; Fur Trader, Beaulivre
AJC SIRES' PRODUCE STAKES (7-f)
Hall Stand, 8.10 (W Cook) Trained by F Allotta; 1:27.7; Hesione, Angel
VRC SIRES' PRODUCE STAKES (7-f)
Regency, 8.10 (W Box) Trained by H Hilton; 1:26.2; Hesione, Blue Valley
VRC GRAND NATIONAL STEEPLECHASE (3m 1-f)
Parentena, 9.3 (F Dummett) Trained by S Murphy; 6:15; Victory March, Winterset

Admirers young and older for Tranquil Star.

1943 RESULTS
VRC MELBOURNE CUP (2m)
Dark Felt, 8.4 (V Hartney) Trained by R Webster; 3:23.25; Counsel, Claudette
AJC SYDNEY CUP (2m)
Abspear, 8.9 (D Munro) Trained by E Hush; 3:26; Wellesley, Moodarewa
QTC BRISBANE CUP (2m) (Race abandoned during World War Two, 1942–45)
SAJC ADELAIDE CUP (13-f) (Race abandoned during World War Two, 1942–43)
WATC PERTH CUP (2m) (Not run in 1943)
VATC CAULFIELD CUP (12-f)
Saint Warden, 7.3 (H White) Trained by J Nicholson; 2:30.75; Heart's Desire, Simmering
VRC AUSTRALIAN CUP (2m and 1½-f)
Taramoa, 7.2 (H Morris) Trained by F McKay; 3:47; Pandini, Frill King
MVRC WS COX PLATE (10-f)
Amana, 9.0 (A Dewhirst) Trained by RJ Shaw; 2:03.7; Sun Valley, Precept
AJC DERBY (12-f)
Moorland, 8.10 (E Bartle) Trained by R Lamond jnr; 2:37.7; Flight, Mayfowl
VRC VICTORIA DERBY (12-f)
Precept (E Preston) Trained by J Pengilly; 2:34.25; Valentino, Lawrence
AJC DONCASTER HANDICAP (1m)
Kingsdale, 8.9 (E McMenamin) Trained by L O'Sullivan; 1:36.5; Magi, Merrimba

BTC DOOMBEN '10 000' (7-f)
The Image, 8.2 (W Hill) Trained by C Pile; 1:29; High Rank, Ahto
VRC NEWMARKET HANDICAP (6-f)
Denko, 7.9 (C Sanderson) Trained by F Godby; 1:12; Burberry, Zonda
AJC SIRES' PRODUCE STAKES (7-f)
Mayfowl, 8.10 (E McMenamin) Trained by M Webster; 1:25; Flight, War Eagle
VRC SIRES' PRODUCE STAKES (7-f)
Simmering, 8.7 (J Neale) Trained by L Robertson; 1:25.5; Sirius, Scottish Mist
VRC GRAND NATIONAL STEEPLECHASE (3m 1-f)
Victory March, 10.13 (G Godfrey) Trained by D Zealley; 6:2; Highland March, Jack Farr

1944 RESULTS
VRC MELBOURNE CUP (2m)
Sirius, 8.5 (D Munro) Trained by E Fisher; 3:24.5; Peter, Cellini
AJC SYDNEY CUP (2m)
Veiled Threat, 8.13 (D Munro) Trained by JM Mitchell; 3:27; Mayfowl, Grand Fils
QTC BRISBANE CUP (2m) (Race abandoned during World War Two, 1942–5)
SAJC ADELAIDE CUP (13-f)
Chief Watchman, 8.10 (H Bastian) Trained by HG Porter; 2:49; Blue Valley, Nagambie
WATC PERTH CUP (2m)
Loyalist, 7.4 (A Ayres) Trained by T Tighe; 3:26; Smithie, Sydney James
VATC CAULFIELD CUP (12-f)
Counsel, 8.12 (A Breasley) Trained by R Webster; 2:29.5; Lawrence, Huntingdale
VRC AUSTRALIAN CUP (2m and 1½-f)
Similar, 7.9 (C Sanderson) Trained by F Godby; 3:48.5; Liberal Knight, Saul
MVRC WS COX PLATE (10-f)
Tranquil Star, 8.13 (A. Breasley) Trained R Cameron; 2:06.7; Lawrence, Tea Cake
AJC DERBY (12-f)
Tea Rose, 8.5 (H Darke) Trained by AG Anderson; 2:33.5; Removal, Prince Verity
VRC VICTORIA DERBY (12-f)
San Martin (A Breasley) Trained by L Robertson; 2:33.5; New Yorker, Bootle
AJC DONCASTER HANDICAP (1m)
Goose Boy, 8.2 (F Shean) Trained by N Dewsbury; 1:36, Flight, Easter Time
BTC DOOMBEN '10 000' (6-f)
Gold Force, 7.11 (E Parsons) Trained by A Clarke; 1:27.7; The Image, Bahtheon
VRC NEWMARKET HANDICAP (6-f)
Orteli, 8.8 (H Mornement) Trained by H Cousens; 1:12.75; Lilette, Distinction
AJC SIRES' PRODUCE STAKES (7-f)
Shannon, 8.10 (F Shean) Trained by P Riddle; 1:25; Tea Rose, Bravo
VRC SIRES' PRODUCE STAKES (7-f)
Delina, 8.7 (W Williamson) Trained by L Robertson; 1:26; San Martin, Kintore
VRC GRAND NATIONAL STEEPLECHASE (3m 1-f)
Highway King, 9.2 (W Johnson) Trained by J Mackie; 6:5.25; Parentena, Winterset

1945 RESULTS
VRC MELBOURNE CUP (2m)
Rainbird, 7.7 (W Cook) Trained by S Evans; 3:24.25; Silver Link, Leonard
AJC SYDNEY CUP (2m)
Craigie, 8.4 (J Duncan) Trained by G Douch; 3:25.5; Russia, Flight
QTC BRISBANE CUP (2m) (Race abandoned during World War Two, 1942–5)
SAJC ADELAIDE CUP (2m)
Blankenburg, 8.1 (H Olsen) Trained by H Bailey; 3:26.5; King Opera, Silurian
WATC PERTH CUP (2m)
Gay Parade, 7.10 (J Duggan) Trained by R Burns; 3:26; Smithie, Earl Mond
VATC CAULFIELD CUP (12-f)
St Fairy, 9.0 (A Breasley) Trained by T Lewis; 2:29.5; Rainbird, Punctilla
VRC AUSTRALIAN CUP (2m and 1½-f)
Spectre, 7.0 (R Hutchinson) Trained by CT Godby; 3:49; Similar, Philander
MVRC WS COX PLATE (10-f)
Flight, 8.13 (J O'Sullivan) Trained by F Nowland; 2:08.7; Don Pedro, Russia
AJC DERBY (12-f)
Magnificent, 8.10 (R Heather) Trained by A Croall; 2:36.7; Guiding Light, Cavalaro
VRC VICTORIA DERBY (12-f)
Magnificent (J O'Sullivan) Trained by A Croall; 2:33; Don Pedro, Attley
AJC DONCASTER HANDICAP (1m)
Abbeville, 8.5 (G Bougoure) Trained by TM McGrath; 1:40.2; Enthuse, Barnsley
BTC DOOMBEN '10 000' (6-f)
Port Raider, 7.6 (R Maddock) Trained by A Tindall; 1:28; Repshot, Maa Leesh
VRC NEWMARKET HANDICAP (6-f)
Three Wheeler, 8.2 (W Williamson) Trained by L Robertson; 1:12.5; Wonder Bird, Simmering
AJC SIRES' PRODUCE STAKES (7-f)
Magnificent, 8.10 (F Delaney) Trained by A Croall; 1:23.7; Lucky Stream, Courtship
VRC SIRES' PRODUCE STAKES (7-f)
Nestor, 8.10 (J Crilley) Trained by E Willmott; 1:28.5; Don Pedro, Lincoln
VRC GRAND NATIONAL STEEPLECHASE (3m 1-f)
Quixotic, 9.5 (J Cunningham) Trained by D McRae; 6:18.5; Parentena, Victory March

The mighty Bernborough goes to the post to win the Melbourne Stakes at Flemington.

The Toowoomba Tornado

The story of Bernborough and his rise to fame, lumping huge weights to heart-stopping wins, was out of the pages of a Nat Gould yarn. The most exciting galloper since Phar Lap, he gave racing the fillip it needed in the first year after World War II. His finishing bursts from well back in the field had punters roaring. Not even Phar Lap attracted such consistently large crowds. In 1946 alone, he won 13 topnotch races in succession

Foaled in 1939 at Dalby in Queensland, 'Bernie', or the 'Toowoomba Tornado' as he became known, was by Emborough from the 20-year-old broodmare, Bern Maid. Until he was six, he was only able to race at Toowoomba. His first owner, Frank Bach, had been involved in a 'ring-in' and was persona non grata with the Queensland Turf Club.

After winning four races as a two-year-old at Toowoomba, Bernborough was taken to Sydney, but the Australian Jockey Club declined his nomination because of ownership queries. So it was back to Toowoomba, where he won six more races before his new owner, Andrew Hawden, sickened by his horse having to carry 10.12 and more, decided to sell him. Rising six, Bernborough was at an age when most stallions are contemplating their love life. Not Bernie. He had some headline grabbing to do.

Sydney nightclub owner Azzalin Romano bought Bernborough for 2600 guineas and gave him to 54-year-old Harry Plant to train at Randwick.

The 'Toowoomba Tornado' had his first Sydney start at Canterbury on 8 December 1945. He ran fourth and jockey Noel McGrowdie was promptly sacked by Romano in favour of dashing Athol Mulley, Sydney's premier jockey.

Two weeks later, Bernborough won the Villiers Stakes at Randwick by five lengths at 3/1. Such handsome odds were seldom available again, as Bernborough and Mulley went about winning 15 races in succession. Three of Bernborough's most amazing wins were with 9.13 in the VRC Newmarket Handicap (6f), with 10.5 in the Doomben Ten Thousand (7f less 93yds) and, a week later, with a staggering 10.11 in the Doomben Cup (11f less 22yds).

Bernborough's powerful Newmarket win up the straight six at Flemington almost defied belief. In 18th place with a furlong-and-a-half to go, he mowed down the field to win by a neck, running the final furlong in a breathtaking 10 seconds.

It was in the Caulfield Stakes, in October 1946, that Bernborough (8/1 on) took his winning sequence to 15, beating handy galloper Columnist. The following week a record crowd of 107 167 somehow squeezed into Caulfield racecourse to see him run in the Caulfield Cup. Backed to 7/4 favouritism despite his impost of 10.10, Bernborough was cheered all the way to the post. Stunned racegoers saw him finish fifth. This time it was Mulley's turn to be sacked.

Azzalin the dazzlin'

Azzalin Romano, owner of Bernborough for one glorious year, had two passions — night clubs and racehorses. He dressed snappily, smoked Churchillian cigars, bet heavily and entertained lavishly. Born in northern Italy he started his working life as a hotel page boy, and became head waiter at the Savoy in London before moving to Sydney and launching Romano's cafe in York Street in 1927 and then the ritzy Romano's nightclub a decade later. With its lavish floor shows, a menu boasting 310 dishes and glamorous decor, it soon became a mecca for the famous and infamous. Romano skirted the prohibitive liquor laws of the time by showing lavish hospitality to major figures in the Police Department.

Romano was not popular for selling the horse to stud in the USA but he visited him at the property of film tycoon Louis B. Mayer. He declared the horse to be 'living like a prince.' It was a judgement based on experience.

The lucky owner, Azzalin Romano.

TURF TOPICS

Camera tells no lies: Racing history was made at Canterbury on 16 March 1946, when the Sydney Turf Club used a camera for race finishes, and starting stalls for two races. Jockeys agreed the starting stalls gave their mounts a cleaner start. The judge gave the camera full marks, no doubt mindful of punters' protests over 'wrong results'.

The most famous 'wrong result' occurred in the 1933 Melbourne Cup in which Hall Mark got the nod over Scobie Breasley's mount Shadow King. Breasley reckoned his mount won and many punters agreed, but Hall Mark's owners got the gold cup.

The Woman in Black

Bernborough's fan club stretched from Cairns to Broome, via Randwick and Flemington. One of his staunchest followers, who put her money on the line, was dubbed 'The Woman in Black'. Her name was Pauline Taks, a migrant from Estonia and the keeper of an 'establishment' at Sydney's infamous King's Cross.

She took a shine to Bernborough the day he won the Villiers Stakes and bet on him in every race. On Caulfield Cup Day 1946, she extracted her winnings, £6000, from her handbag and plonked the lot on Bernborough at 6/4. When her favourite was beaten, she complained of a headache and left the course. The Woman in Black was 'stone, motherless hearts-of-oak'.

Moment of tragedy. Bernborough, left, breaks down while Flight scoots to a six-length victory.

Tragedy at Flemington

When Bernborough stepped out in the WLKS Mackinnon Stakes at Flemington on Derby day 1946, he was set to become Australia's greatest stakes winner within a calendar year. And first prize of £1400 would all but catapult him into the top 20 all-time earners. His Caulfield Cup failure had not dimmed his popularity.

Alas, it wasn't to be. With new jockey Bill Briscoe in the saddle, the champion broke down three furlongs from home just as he was about to put champion mare Flight to the test.

The crowd of 71 000 was so concerned with Bernborough's condition that more people watched him than Flight's six-length victory. Some racegoers wept as Briscoe dismounted.

Bernborough's near-front leg hung limply. Horse and jockey were forlorn figures as officials and vets sped towards them. The crowd feared the usual end for a racehorse with a broken leg, a bullet to the brain behind a hessian screen.

Though obviously in great pain, Bernborough was as game as ever, and tried to put weight on his damaged leg, which turned out to be a displaced sesamoid, as he limped away to the float that took him to Caulfield.

The next morning, veterinary surgeon G. Heslop told anxious reporters that Bernborough had had 'a good night and is doing very satisfactorily. He is an extremely good patient and we are certain that he can be saved.' Hundreds of get-well cards were sent to him.

Indeed, Bernborough was patched up and went to stud in America after a drama-packed career that saw him win 26 times from 37 starts for earnings of £25 504 – enough to buy two waterfront homes in Sydney. The day he left Sydney, a big crowd farewelled him at the wharf.

A gem of a horse

In the brouhaha that followed Bernborough's 1946 Caulfield Cup defeat, the victory of Royal Gem, himself a dandy galloper, was almost overlooked.

Owned by South Australian businessman George Badman, Royal Gem had been a top two-year-old, winning the Ascot Vales Stakes at Flemington. At three, he deadheated for first with Attley in the Caulfield Guineas and won SA's premier sprint, the Goodwood Handicap.

By English sire Dhoti out of VRC Oaks winner French Gem, Royal Gem was small early, but grew into a robust individual. His Toorak Handicap win just one week before the Caulfield Cup was his 15th win from 24 starts.

Despite such success, Royal Gem was unwanted in the Cup at 33/1, all eyes (more than 107 000 pairs of them) and money being on the 7/4 favourite, Bernborough.

Bernborough was well back until the turn, and was twice held up in the straight, but Royal Gem, ridden by Reg Heather, had a good run. He was second turning for home; Bernborough was 12th in a field of 27.

Carrying 9.0 – weight-for-age for a four-year-old – Royal Gem gained the day by a neck from Columnist, winning £5000 for Badman. Bernborough finished fifth, four lengths behind.

On retirement – after 23 wins from 51 starts – Royal Gem went to stud in America, where he sired Dark Star, the 1953 Kentucky Derby winner.

Darby Munro and Russia after the Cup.

I did it my way

Going to the barrier for the start of the 1946 Melbourne Cup, Sydney jockey Darby Munro had a good look around him from the saddle of Russia, who was required to carry topweight of 9.0 in a big field of 35. Munro, who had won the Cup on Peter Pan (1934) and Sirius (1944), was less than impressed with his rivals. He had ridden a few of them.

His instructions from trainer/part-owner Ted Hush were to nurse Russia early, then make up ground. Munro decided that was a sure-fire way to lose, with tired plodders likely to impede his progress.

So, when the field jumped, Munro took Russia forward. As Munro had predicted, the poor quality of the field soon revealed itself. He took Russia to the lead at the top of the straight and they romped home at 16/1 in equal race record time of 3:21.25.

Spam, spam, spam – what does it mean?

Wrong Cup, Jack

Stablehand Jack Collins had a dream in 1946. A horse named Spam thundered down the straight to win the Melbourne Cup. But Jack had never heard of a horse named Spam, and put the dream down to the fevered excesses of food and drink. Until, that is, the Cup nominations. Lo and behold, an English horse named Spam was on its way.

The horse performed well in some lead-up races. Come Cup Day, Collins and his friends figured, Spam would be ready. The mighty plunge went in. But no! On the hard track in that hot, dry spring, Spam came in eighth. Lo and behold, Jack and his mates were stony broke.

Then it pelted with rain and the grounds softened. Ten days later Spam romped home in the Werribee Cup at 10/1. Right dream, wrong race!

TURF TOPICS

Punters' friend: It sometimes pays to follow the top jockeys. Nearing the end of the 1945–46 season, Scobie Breasley, well clear on the Victorian jockeys' list with 41 winners, was showing a profit on a level stake. For each £1 bet on Breasley's 170 mounts, punters were showing a profit of £7. Not much, it seemed, but multiplied by 100 it represented the price of a nice suburban house. On average, Breasley was placed every second time he was legged into the saddle. By far the most profitable rider was Sydney's Billy Cook. In two trips to Melbourne in 1946, he had 32 mounts and returned a profit of 62 units.

Number one: In 1946, Sydney mare Flight joined her great female rival Tranquil Star as a two-time winner of the WS Cox Plate. Flight also won in 1944. Sold for only 60 guineas as a yearling, Flight, a granddaughter of Heroic, went on to win 24 races from 65 starts and, with £31 185, become Australasia's highest stake-winning mare.

Day out for Hoysted: Henry Frederick (Tib) Hoysted, whose younger brother F. W. Hoysted achieved fame in Melbourne, trained the card on Albury Cup Day, 4 May 1946. His son Hal was strapper. Five of the six winners were ridden by Bill Williamson, later no. 1 rider for F. W. (Father) Hoysted.

Darby hooted unfairly

The brilliant middle-distance horse Shannon was best remembered for a race he lost – the 1946 AJC Epsom Handicap at Randwick.

Darby Munro was roundly hooted after Shannon, hot favourite at 5/4 on, almost pulled off the impossible in his bid to win the glamour mile race for the second year in a row.

Left a third of a furlong at the start, Shannon, lumping 9.8, failed by a half-head to catch the winner, Blue Legend. Shannon was in front a stride or two past the post.

Instead of being hostile to Munro, the crowd should have cheered him, for Shannon was being led to the line by a clerk of the course when the field was released. The starter, his eyes on a couple of unruly horses, did not notice Shannon's predicament and later apologised for his error.

Two days later Shannon shattered the Australasian mile record, clocking 1:34¾ and downing top mare Flight by six lengths in the George Main Stakes at Randwick. Game punters who had lost their shirts in the Epsom had to take 3/1 on about Shannon. At his next start Shannon won the King's Cup, again downing Flight.

A bay horse by Midstream, Shannon cost only 350 guineas as a yearling. In 1947, he was sold to W. J. Smith for £27 300 following the death of his owner–trainer Peter Riddle. Shannon had four runs in Australia for Smith, winning twice. He was then sold to America for £52 000, and won four races, including the Hollywood Gold Cup (10f) and the Albany Golden Gate Handicap (10f) in equal world record time of 1:59.8.

In Australia, Shannon won 14 of his 25 starts. His total earnings in Australia and America were £84 908 – a record for an Australian horse. At stud in Kentucky, Shannon sired the winners of more than $A4 million.

Unfortunately, Shannon never matched strides with Bernborough.

Winterset jumps to the lead in the 1946 Great Eastern Steeplechase.

Ossie Porter (centre) was soon to take flight.

Racing returns to Oakbank

It was fitting that Winterset, the greatest jumper of his time, should run in the 1946 Great Eastern Steeplechase (3 ¼ miles), the year it returned to its historic home at Oakbank (SA) after an absence of five years.

The race, abandoned in 1942–43 as a wartime measure, was run at Victoria Park in 1944–45 and at Morphettville in 1945.

In 1946, Winterset (Son O'Mine – Winter's Dream) was the titleholder, having won the famous race in 1945 at Morphettville with the steadier of 12.10 after a great struggle with old rival Lime Rock, the 1944 winner. The margin in favour of Winterset, ridden as usual by Laurie Meenan, was two lengths. Both horses were cheered by the crowd of 50 000.

A crowd of 75 000 welcomed the meeting's return to Oakbank. Winterset, now nine, and Lime Rock again matched strides in '46, but this time both went under, the winner

being Ajester. Lime Rock was a close second with old Winterset 40 lengths away third.

Meenan rode in the Great Eastern many times. In 1941, he thought his mount Dark David was feeling his weight. What he didn't know was that a fellow jockey, K. G. Parris, had grabbed hold of Dark David's tail. Parris was rubbed out for six months.

Meenan and Winterset enjoyed many grand wins, none better than the 1945 Hopetoun Steeple (2m) at Flemington with a massive 13.0. It was Winterset's third consecutive win in the race and his 13th overall. A crowd of more than 50 000, many of them in uniform, cheered the pair to victory.

The following month Winterset, carrying 12.7, fell in the Grand National Steeple, won by Quixotic. Winterset, trained by Des McCormick, was placed in the GN Steeple in 1942 and 1944. Meenan won the GN Steeple twice, on Blackford and David's Star.

Poor owners

Ossie Porter, a wealthy Melbourne shoe-maker, emerged as one of Australia's biggest gamblers in the 1940s, punting more than £250 000 a year on horses. He raced many top gallopers, including 1945 Caulfield Cup winner St Fairy. Porter was renowned for his generosity. After a win, he paid his factory workers a bonus, and he handed out cash to his employees on the course.

But all was not well on the racing scene immediately after World War II. In 1946, at the annual meeting of the Victorian Owners' Association, Porter, a vice-president, and fellow owners complained about the 'paucity of stake money at some city meetings and the absence of mid-week racing'. Mr Porter said there should be a revision of stakes in the Melbourne metropolitan area. He referred in particular to the Epsom meeting on 23 March, at which the highest stake was £700 and the hurdle race was worth only £300.

One breeder said his return from sales of £28 000 amounted to only £3000 after taxes. The high cost of feed, still scarce in the post-war years, also came under notice.

Another major concern in racing was off-course bookmakers, who paid no taxes and robbed the industry of valuable turnover. All kinds of undesirables set themselves up as SP bookies, including a policeman in Terang in country Victoria, who ended up in the court next door to his police station.

1946 RESULTS

VRC MELBOURNE CUP (2m)
Russia, 9.0 (D Munro) Trained by E Hush; 3:21.25; On Target, Carey

AJC SYDNEY CUP (2m)
Cordale, 7.7 (G Moore) Trained by G Ray; 3:28.5; Swan River, Russia

QTC BRISBANE CUP (re-named Victory Cup, run at 12-f)
Good Idea, 8.6 (H Badger) 2: 31; Chaytor, Swan River

SAJC ADELAIDE CUP (2m)
Little Tich, 7.7 (E Preston) Trained by I Reid; 3:31; Neutron, Beau Cheval

WATC PERTH CUP (2m)
Maddington, 7.0 (J Marshall) Trained by E Hodgson; 3:23.75; Gold Patois, Lord Treat

VATC CAULFIELD CUP (12-f)
Royal Gem, 9.0 (R Heather) Trained by GR Jesser; 2:30.25; Columnist, Two Grand

VRC AUSTRALIAN CUP (2m and 1 ½-f)
Knockarlow, 7.7 (J Purtell) Trained by T Woodcock; 3:48.2; Silurian, Oatcake

MVRC WS COX PLATE (10-f)
Flight, 8.13 (J O'Sullivan) Trained by F Nowland; 2:05; Star Act, Magnificent

MVRC WS COX PLATE (10-f)
Leonard, 9.0 (W Briscoe) Trained by L Robertson; 2:06; Monmouth, Cotham

AJC DERBY (12-f)
Concerto, 8.10 (W Cook) Trained by D Lewis; 2:34.5; Flying Duke, Monogram

VRC VICTORIA DERBY (12-f)
Prince Standard, 8.10 (W Briscoe) Trained by D Lewis; 2:33; Tribunal, Proctor

AJC DONCASTER HANDICAP (1m)
Blue Legend, 7.5 (J Duncan) Trained by R Abbott; 1:40; Abbeville, Sajakeda

BTC DOOMBEN '10 000' (7-f less 93 yards)
Bernborough, 10.5 (A Mulley) Trained by H Plant; 1:18.7; Cragsman, Puffham

VRC NEWMARKET HANDICAP (6-f)
Bernborough, 9.13 (A Mulley) Trained by H Plant; 1:12.75; Four Freedoms, Reperio

AJC SIRES' PRODUCE STAKES (7-f)
Flying Duke, 8.10 (D Munro) Trained by M McCarten; 1:27.7; Vigaro, Euryalus

VRC SIRES' PRODUCE STAKES (7-f)
Bol Beau, 8.10 (F De Valle) Trained by D Judd; 1:27.2; Chaperone, Minion

VRC GRAND NATIONAL STEEPLECHASE (3m 1-f)
High Flash, 9.7 (E Wilson) Trained by D Zealley; 6:12.25; Tente, Quixotic

Former jockey, 'Last Race' Dempsey, took over as chief starter at Moonee Valley in 1948.

Gentleman Jack's big win

Jack Purtell may have lacked the polish of Scobie Breasley and the grace of Bill Cook, but no one doubted his vigour, judgement of pace or devil to take narrow openings. Few matched his courtesy on and off the course – hence the sobriquet 'Gentleman Jack'.

Purtell, who had a struggle to reach the top, realised an ambition when he piloted Hiraji to victory in the 1947 Melbourne Cup. It came 11 years after his first ride in a race, one he would rather forget. An unruly mare called DerringDo dumped him at the barrier before a race at Ballarat. He remounted, completed the course, albeit at the tail of the field, and set about mastering his profession under the guidance of trainer Ted Temby. But winning did not come easily. He once rode 72 consecutive losers.

Purtell, Victoria's premier jockey in 1946–47 with 43 wins, had to call on all his skill to land Hiraji, whose saddle slipped 10 furlongs from home. Hiraji hit the front with a furlong to go and Purtell's coolness enabled the grey son of Nizami to hold off 11/2 favourite Fresh Boy, ridden by 16-year-old apprentice Brian Eames.

Hiraji, who started at 12/1 despite his second to Frank Packer's good galloper Columnist in the Caulfield Cup, became the first grey since Toryboy in 1865 to win the Cup.

TJ makes a mark

When it came to hardship, Tommy Smith, son of a timber teamster from Goolgowi in western NSW, had seen it all. To eke out a living in the 1930s, young Tommy tried his hand at rabbit-trapping, running bets for an SP bookie, riding in country races, breaking in horses and working as a stableboy for a Melbourne trainer. He had little formal education.

Smith's talent with horses fired his ambition to become a trainer and, in 1941, aged 21, he obtained a licence from the AJC. An ex-buckjumper called Bragger was Smith's early meal-ticket, winning eight races in Sydney, Newcastle and Wagga from 1942 to 1946.

Well-placed bets and the £4300 in stake money that Bragger earned, enabled Smith to acquire a modest stable in Sydney and buy a fancy suit or two. When Ajixa won the Gimcrack Stakes at Randwick in 1942, Smith's voice could be heard above the roar of the crowd.

At the other end of the training spectrum, the urbane and fashionably dressed Jack Holt, known as 'The Wizard of Mordialloc', was coming to the end of a distinguished career that has seen him win 13 Victorian trainers' premierships. When Chanak (H. Badger) won the 1947 Cox Plate, he

T. J. Smith, apprentice.

gave the 68-year-old Holt a record seventh win in the MV race. Holt, born in 1879, won the 1933 Melbourne Cup with Hall Mark and trained Heroic, winner of 21 races and one of Australia's most successful sires.

1947 RESULTS

VRC MELBOURNE CUP (2m)
Hiraji, 7.11 (J Purtell) Trained by J McCurley; 3:28; Fresh Boy, Red Fury
AJC SYDNEY CUP (2m)
Proctor, 7.10 (W Briscoe) Trained by D Lewis; 3:27.5; Rainbird, Spam
QTC BRISBANE CUP (2m)
Blue Boots, 7.5 (N McGrowdie) 3:22; Russia, Rimfire
SAJC ADELAIDE CUP (2m)
Beau Cheval, 8.8 (R Medhurst) Trained by GA McDonald; 3:23.5; Blankenburg, The Monk
WATC PERTH CUP (2m and 11 yds)
Sydney James, 7.2 (G Davies) Trained by R Burns; 3:22.5; Nullabung, Easewold
VATC CAULFIELD CUP (12-f)
Columnist, 9.0 (H Badger) Trained by M McCarten; 2:28.25; Hiraji, Fresh Boy

VRC AUSTRALIAN CUP (2m and 1½-f)
Sydney James, 7.3 (W Beresford) Trained by R Burns; 3:50.25; Field Balloon, Ellipsis
MVRC WS COX PLATE (10-f)
Chanak, 7.12 (H Badger) Trained by J Holt; 2:05; Attley, Sweet Chime
AJC DERBY (12-f)
Valiant Crown, 8.10 (N McGrowdie) Trained by A Doyle; 2:35; Conductor, Sovereign
VRC VICTORIA DERBY (12-f)
Beau Gem, 8.10 (D Munro) Tained by GR Jesser; 2:30.5; Chanak, Conductor
AJC DONCASTER HANDICAP (1m)
Blue Legend, 8.11 (H Badger) Trained by R Abbott; 1:41.7; Crusader, Wellington
BTC DOOMBEN '10 000' (7-f less 93 yds)
High Strung, 7.4 (N McGrowdie) Trained by W Neilson; 1:17.2; France, Hiraji

VRC NEWMARKET HANDICAP (6-f)
Gay Queen, 7.10 (H Badger) Trained by F Hoysted; 1:15.5; Reperio, Four Freedoms
AJC SIRES' PRODUCE STAKES (7-f)
Temeraire, 8.10 (W Cook) Trained by F Cush; 1:29.7; Deep Sea, The Groom
VRC SIRES' PRODUCE STAKES (7-f)
Chanak, 8.10 (A Breasley) Trained by J Holt; 1:29.2; Cronides, Sovereign
VRC GRAND NATIONAL STEEPLECHASE (3m 1-f)
Formidable, 9.4 (C Bickham) Trained by J Bence; 6:6.5; Parentena, Satellite

Birchip Boy has last laugh in the Cup

There were ripples of laughter in the jockeys' room before the 1948 Melbourne Cup. All eyes focused on fresh-faced apprentice Ray Neville as he dressed for his first ride in the big race. Making the weight of 7.2 was the least of his problems. Everything else was too big. The waistband of his jodhpurs had to be taken in, the sleeves of his white and blue silks rolled up and pinned, freeing up his hands, which had steered home one winner.

There was no laughter after the race. Birchip-born Neville, one day short of his 16th birthday and having only his ninth race ride, landed 80/1 chance Rimfire (No. 25) the narrowest of winners over Sydney Cup victor Dark Marne (12/1), ridden by craggy-faced Sydney veteran Jack Thompson, in a record time of 3:21.0.

The two horses were locked together crossing the line – Rimfire on the outside, the tiny, crouched figure of Neville, all red cap, seemingly no match for Thompson (The Professor), who was up in the irons, whip in the right hand extracting every last ounce of drive from Sydney Cup winner Dark Marne, always a fighter. But the post was too close. Another triumph for David over Goliath.

The judge for the first time had recourse to a photo finish. He needed it. But his decision in favour of Rimfire, by a half head, caused widespread controversy. A group of Sydney punters near the post booed. The result angered Thompson, a less than loquacious man. He said angrily that the camera was out of alignment. 'If I never won that race then I have never won any race.'

The result stunned young Neville, not to mention the crowd of 109 077, which had backed Harold Badger's mount Howe to 7/4 favouritism on the strength of his unlucky second to Red Fury in the Caulfield Cup and victories in the Moonee Valley Cup and Hotham Handicap (with 9.12).

Howe broke down and ran fifth, just behind Comic Court. Most punters had never heard of young Neville, who had gained his riding permit only two months before the Cup. His one winner, Lincoln, was trained by his master, Lou Robertson.

Neville learned from Robertson at 4 a.m. on Cup Day that he had the ride on outsider Rimfire. Several other riders had knocked back the mount. After telling Neville the news, Robertson told him to go about his chores quickly and clean his gear.

Sporting a boyish grin as wide as the

Look at the smile on the kid! 15-year-old Ray Neville can't stop.

Flemington straight, Neville was so elated after the race that he went through the presentation ceremony automatically. Later he shyly answered questions. 'I went to the front on the turn and from there on rode my hardest to the post. I was so excited halfway down the straight that I hardly realised Dark Marne was so close.'

After the race Rimfire was sore but not as sore as the punters who lost £500 000 on Howe. The bookies cleaned up and then some.

That evening Neville returned to Robertson's Aspendale establishment the way he had come, with stable hope Westralian, the 1947 WA Derby winner who failed in the Cup. That night Neville supped on steak and eggs before going off to Wirth's Circus to be presented with a gold-mounted whip.

The teenager's big family did not have time to make the trip to Flemington from Birchip in the Mallee. With friends they listened to the race on the wireless.

Rimfire, aged six, was owned by VRC committeeman Guy Raymond, who bred the Enfield gelding at his St Albans Stud near Geelong. He had leased the horse to Mrs Doll Clayton, of Sydney. It expired in April 1948, and Mrs Clayton did not exercise her option to buy Rimfire for 1500 guineas. Rimfire had damaged a leg when running third to Blue Boots and Russia in the 1947 Brisbane Cup and there were some doubts whether he would stand another preparation. But Raymond was confident he would.

Rimfire nearly didn't make it to the post. He was lame after failing in the Hotham Handicap on Derby day, but trainer Stan Boyden begged Raymond not to scratch the horse. Boyden's vigil, applying constant cold compresses to Rimfire's fore fetlock joints, did the trick.

Boyden had come to the attention of Raymond back in 1930. Boyden drove the float that spirited Phar Lap away to St Albans after a shooting scare. Raymond said of Boyden: 'His long battle to get Rimfire to the post deserved success.'

Increasing weight soon forced Neville to turn to jumps riding, and he rode for several more years. He also became a builder.

However, in his short riding career he won a Melbourne Cup, a feat denied great riders such as Scobie Breasley, Badger, George Moore and Jack Thompson, who also finished second on Silver Link in 1945 and on Monte Carlo in 1958.

SPORTING LIFE'S GALLERY
OF FAMOUS HORSES

Above: Carbon Copy. Inset: The 1948 VRC members' badge.

Carbon Copy's year

Two champion colts graced the turf in 1948–49. They were Carbon Copy and Comic Court. As three-year-olds they clashed eight times, Carbon Copy taking the honours 5–3. He won nine races that season, earning a record £29 197 until the end of his three-year-old career.

Carbon Copy (Helios–Havers), a descendant of Hyperion and Windbag, was bred by the Silk Brothers at their Glen Devon Stud, Werribee, Victoria. Des McCormick, who had great success with jumpers, was the trainer. Scobie Breasley rode him in eight of his 14 career wins.

Comic Court (Powerscourt–Witty Maid) was bred in South Australia and trained by Jim Cummings, father of Cups King, Bart Cummings.

Demon Darb outed

Home-town decision was the cry that followed the disqualification of three prominent Sydney racing folk – jockey Darby Munro, trainer Dan Lewis and owner Frank Spurway – after Vagabond had been beaten by the good galloper Ellerslie in the Burwood Handicap on Caulfield Cup day.

All three were disqualified for two years for not having allowed Vagabond, second favourite at 5/1, to run on its merits.

Race caller Fred Tupper of 3AW went in to bat for Munro, telling the inquiry Munro was wielding the whip turning for home. Vagabond's connections submitted that the horse was not at home with the Melbourne way of going; indeed, that the horse was something of a rogue. Subsequently, at a nine-hour hearing, the VRC committee upheld the appeals of Lewis and Spurway but dismissed Munro's.

Lewis and Spurway said they were satisfied with Munro's handling of Vagabond. Munro, 35, went on to ride until 1955, but the ban seriously interrupted his career.

Too much coffee: Frontal Attack hit the Sydney headlines for the wrong reasons in 1948. After winning a race in May, a swab taken from it proved positive to caffeine, a stimulant. The finding was announced by pioneer AJC analyst Jean Kimble, who had been in the job only a year. Frontal Attack's trainer R. Denham was outed for life, but his licence was restored in 1951.

What a month! Newcastle-born jockey Rae (Togo) Johnstone hit the big time overseas in June 1948, winning seven major races in England, France and Ireland. He won the English Derby at Epsom and the Grand Prix de Paris (at Longchamp) on My Love, the Irish Derby on Nathoo and three races in England.

War crowds: During the six years that service personnel were admitted free to Moonee Valley, 355 430 took up the privilege – an average of 3100 a meeting.

Top rider retires: Harold Badger, top Victorian jockey for the sixth time in 1947–48 with 46 winners, retired after the 1948 spring carnival.

More wins: Royal Gem, winner of the 1946 Caulfield Cup in which Bernborough's winning streak came to a controversial end, continued his good form in '48, winning in successive weeks the VATC Futurity Stakes and the VRC Newmarket (6f).

Clash of the titans: Carbon Copy beat Comic Court in the AJC Derby and Cox Plate. Comic Court beat Carbon Copy in the Victoria Derby and the VRC St Leger.

NZ breeders organise: Ken Austin, a former Australian auctioneer who had settled in NZ and founded the Inglewood Stud in Canterbury, became the inaugural President of the NZ Thoroughbred Breeders Association in 1948, recognising the tremendous increase in yearling sales since the first sale 21 years before.

1948 RESULTS

VRC MELBOURNE CUP (2m)
Rimfire, 7.2 (R Neville) Trained by S Boyden; 3:21; Dark Marne, Saxony
AJC SYDNEY CUP (2m)
Dark Marne, 8.3 (J Thompson) Trained by D Burke; 3:26.25; Columnist, Lungi
QTC BRISBANE CUP (2m)
Sicarda, 7.10 (P Morgan) 3:24.7; Dark Marne, Fly Bird
SAJC ADELAIDE CUP (2m)
Sanctus, 8.1 (A Breasley) Trained by J (Jerry) Moloney; 3:25; The Monk, Stenelaus
WATC PERTH CUP (2m and 11 yds)
Kingscote, 7.5 (A Ayres) Trained by H Campbell; 3:24; Royal Pageant, Repulse
VATC CAULFIELD CUP (12-f)
Red Fury, 7.10 (W Briscoe) Trained by J Flannery; 2:32; Howe, De La Salle

VRC AUSTRALIAN CUP (2m and 1 ½f)
Bannerette, 8.4 (D Graetz) Trained by F Hendricksen; 3:45; Few Words, Sanctus
MVRC WS COX PLATE (10-f)
Carbon Copy, 7.12 (H Badger) Trained by D McCormick; 2:04.2; Phoibos, Beau Gem
AJC DERBY (12-f)
Carbon Copy, 8.10 (A Breasley) Trained by D McCormick; 2:33.5; Vagabond, Foxzami
VRC VICTORIA DERBY (12-f)
Comic Court, 8.10 (O Phillips) Trained by JM Cummings; 2:35.25; Foxzami, Carbon Copy
AJC DONCASTER HANDICAP (1m)
The Diver, 7.12 (G Moore) Trained by T Brosnan; 1:38.75; Fine Fettle, Murray Stream
BTC DOOMBEN '10 000' (7-f less 93 yds)
Murray Stream, 9.4 (N Best) Trained by G Brown; 1:18.7; Radstock, Nestor

VRC NEWMARKET HANDICAP (6-f)
Royal Gem, 9.9 (H Patching) Trained by G Jesser; 1:11.5; St Razzle, Fine Fettle
AJC SIRES' PRODUCE STAKES (7-f)
Riptide, 8.10 (G Moore) Trained by A Croall; 1:27; Dynamite, Bengal
VRC SIRES' PRODUCE STAKES (7-f)
Ungar, 8.10 (H Badger) Trained by FW Hoysted; 1:25.7; Comic Court, Blessing
VRC GRAND NATIONAL STEEPLECHASE (3m 1-f)
Tente, 10.13 (K Denham) Trained by G Bewsher; 6:7.75; Wangaratta, Nantilla

Lightweight jockey Noel Eastwood pilots Lincoln home in the Caulfield Cup.

The Magician does the trick

When two-year-old Lincoln won at Caulfield at his third start in 1945, a *Sporting Globe* scribe predicted he would go places. By successful English sire Manitoba, Lincoln fetched 1400 guineas as a yearling and straight away looked the goods, beating a smart field in Caulfield's 2nd Alma Stakes and running third in the Sires' Produce Stakes.

But that early promise withered. Lincoln failed first as a stayer, which he was bred to be, his dam Lipstick being by Spearhead (a grandson of Carbine and sire of Spearfelt).

Switched to sprinting by his owner A. H. Griffiths and trainer Lou Robertson, Lincoln fared even more abysmally, finishing last of 23 runners in the Oakleigh Plate.

Two wins in four years was not paying the feed bills. As a last resort, Griffiths asked Robertson to give Lincoln, by now a gelding and rising seven, another shot at staying. Lincoln had always been a good track worker, a side of his make-up that Robertson reckoned would eventually manifest itself on race day.

The Malvina Welter at Caulfield on 27 July saw the rebirth of Lincoln the distance horse. Robertson, known as The Magician, told jockey Ray Neville not to use his spurs or hit Lincoln behind the saddle. It worked. Lincoln ran second to Derrymore and continued to show improved form. It was decided to push on to the Caulfield Cup, in which Lincoln had only 6.10.

But a jockey not much heavier than a dinner plate would have to be found. Enter 19-year-old NZ apprentice Noel Eastwood, with six winners from 20 or so rides. At 4 ft 8 in, he barely cast a shadow. He weighed 5.8.

With Eastwood in the saddle, Lincoln ran an encouraging fourth in the Toorak Handicap on Guineas Day. The following week, before the Cup, Robertson told Eastwood 'no spurs, let the horse settle, then bring him home strongly'.

Four furlongs from home, Lincoln was 15th in a field of 21. In the straight, the 12/1 chance finished powerfully, overhauling St Razzle and the 7/4 favourite Comic Court close to home and winning by a half-length.

Lincoln carried the colours worn by top stayer and wfa performer Lawrence, who finished a close second to Counsel in the 1944 Caulfield Cup. So Griffiths finally got a cup, but he didn't back Lincoln.

Eastwood, a droll young man, said it was the best win of his career. Meanwhile the scribe who forecast big things for Lincoln was vindicated. But, as with Griffiths and Robertson, his patience had been sorely tested. For Robertson it was his second Cup win, 34 years after his first with Lavendo in 1915.

1949 RESULTS

VRC MELBOURNE CUP (2m)
Foxzami, 8.8 (W Fellows) Trained by D Lewis; 3:28.25; Hoyle, Benvolo
AJC SYDNEY CUP (2m)
Carbon Copy, 8.5 (A Breasley) Trained by D McCormick; 3:23.5; Vagabond, Benvolo
QTC BRISBANE CUP (2m)
Sanctus 8.2 (A Breasley) Trained by T Lewis; 3:24, Dark Marne, Moneith
SAJC ADELAIDE CUP (2m)
Colin, 7.12 (W Williamson) Trained by R Roach; 3:23; Hoyle, Sunfire
WATC PERTH CUP (2m and 11 yds) (1 January 1949)
Gurkha, 7.0 (F Treen) Trained by F McAuliffe; 3:24; Black Law, Prince Brian
WATC PERTH CUP (2m and 11 yds) (31 December 1949)
Beau Vasse, 7.0 (B Boyle) Trained by FW Banks; 3:28; Leofred, Dhostar

VATC CAULFIELD CUP (12-f)
Lincoln, 6.10 (N Eastwood) Trained by L Robertson; 2:36.25; St Razzle, Comic Court
VRC AUSTRALIAN CUP (2m and 1½-f)
New Cashmere, 7.13 (G Bougoure) Trained by P Burke; 3:43.5; Saxonian, Golden Gem
MVRC WS COX PLATE (10-f)
Delta, 7.11 (N Sellwood) Trained by M McCarten; 2:04.7; Comic Court, Persist
AJC DERBY (12-f)
Playboy, 8.10 (G Moore) Trained by TJ Smith; 2:34; Delta, Dickens
VRC VICTORIA DERBY (12-f)
Delta, 8.10 (N Sellwood) Trained by M McCarten; 2:32.75; dead-heat second Dickens and King's Coin

AJC DONCASTER HANDICAP (1m)
Bernbrook, 8.4 (N Sellwood) Trained by H Plant; 1:36.2; Vagabond, Mortar
BTC DOOMBEN '10 000' (7-f less 93 yds)
Ungar, 8.2 (W Williamson) Trained by FW Hoysted; 1:18; Lucky Ring, Prince Monash
VRC NEWMARKET HANDICAP (6-f)
Reperio, 8.11 (B Eames) Trained by P Fergus; 1:13.5; San Domenico, Sentiment
AJC SIRES' PRODUCE STAKES (7-f)
Field Boy, 8.10 (E Briscoe) Trained by ED Lawson; 1:25.2; Lady Pirouette, Crag Son
VRC SIRES' PRODUCE STAKES (7-f)
Iron Duke, 8.10 (W Williamson) Trained by L Robertson; 1:26.7; St Comedy, Adela
VRC GRAND NATIONAL STEEPLECHASE (3m 1-f)
David Star, 11.10 (L Meenan) Trained by M Nichols; 6:4.2; Shot By, Briar

Betting off-course? 'SP', of course!

In 1953 the Perth weekly newspaper the *Western Mail* sent some reporters and photographers on a journey around the suburbs in search of a particular kind of vice. It published the results and the photos under the banner headline 'Street betting is sordid, blatant and evil'. It was certainly blatant, but whether it was also sordid and evil was more a matter of the *Mail*'s prejudices. For most Australians most of the time, it was a harmless service provided by enterprising bookmakers to people who wanted a bet but who wouldn't or couldn't go to the races.

In 1953 off-course betting, or 'the SP' as it was colloquially known, had long been an institution in Australia, an integral part of racing. It had also become one of Australia's longest and hottest political issues.

The earliest SP or 'starting price' bookies were probably on-course operators who, in the late 19th century, bet from their town offices. Racing clubs, who have always regarded the SP as a rival for the gamblers' money, quickly banned anyone who dabbled in both, and parliaments soon followed. Prompted by evangelical Christians, women's groups and racing clubs, parliaments outlawed most forms of gambling but soon all the capitals were overrun with SP bookies. Some, such as John Wren, bet from ingeniously concealed 'totes'; others bet openly from tobacconist shops. The biggest had 'stringers,' who took bets in pubs, factories, offices, clubs and homes. The smallest bet from a pub front or a street corner.

The greatest boon to SP bookies, though, was the telephone, which many began to use in the 1930s. They could now bet with anybody, anywhere, and anytime, as long as their clients had a phone and could get credit. They could lay off more easily and they could get on-course information faster. In the 1980s and 90s mobile phones made things even simpler. The telephone changed the SP in other ways too. SP traditionally offered punters just one price, the price at which a horse started the race, because bookies could not get pre-race, on-course fluctuations. Another advantage was that bookies could set themselves up in states with less stringent laws. So in the 1980s, when Victorian police clamped down hard, Victorian SP bookies moved to NSW; when in the 1990s NSW got tougher they moved to Queensland. The Internet promises to make things easier still.

There are three main reasons for the longevity of SP betting. The first is that people want to be able to bet without going to the races, the second is the determination and

ingenuity of the SP bookies and the third is the inadequacy of the laws. Many SP bookies played games of cat and mouse with the police, using 'cockatoos' to warn against raids and 'dummies' to 'take the rap' if police evaded the 'cockatoos'.

Some jurisdictions opted for control, raiding SP operations on a roster with the occasional blitz, but many police felt that off-course betting was harmless, and wondered why it should be targeted when on-course betting was apparently legal.

Control was sometimes mistaken for corruption, although Tony Fitzgerald's inquiries

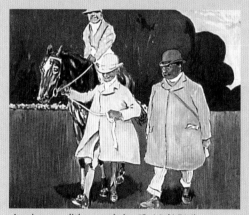
A winner – lithograph by 'S. J.' (ARM).

A loser – lithograph by 'S. J.' (ARM).

into the Queensland Police Force in the late 1980s left no doubt that some police were corrupt. In the 1959 Royal Commission into off-course betting in Victoria, Counsel assisting estimated that 60 per cent of the squad charged with enforcing the laws were corrupt. Was Pat Healy, the Perth SP king, talking about corruption or control when he told an inquiry in Perth that the 'police used to come and have a cup of tea and tell me I had to go off and I went'?

SP bookies added the raids to their gripes and fines into their costs. They had plenty of these because they suffered from the disad-

vantage of not being at the racecourse. SP bookies needed scratchings and results to run their books (they got the fields, opening and starting price from the papers or from press agencies set up to provide racing information), and the clubs tried to keep these to themselves. So, before clubs allowed radio broadcasts, SP bookies would subsidise radio stations to call races from outside the course.

Before radio they used the telegraph for results and before the telegraph they used armies of small boys as runners. Later, the phone enabled them to get betting fluctuations, so they could lay off and lay bets on-course to reduce odds or refuse bets. Where clubs removed the phones, 'scouts' took information outside the course, phoned it in, then went back inside. When clubs refused to let them back in, bookies sent small armies of men into the courses who would leave one at a time, phone in, then go home.

By the 1930s the influence of the anti-gambling lobby had faded; witness the licensing of off-course betting in South Australia and Tasmania. Bookies elsewhere seized the opportunity, organised and lobbied for legalisation. Only in Western Australia were they legalised, and that was for only four short years in the 1950s. Subsequently, state governments all adopted the off-course totalisator, hoping fervently that SP betting would disappear. It didn't.

On Pat Healy's last conviction in 1970 his lawyer told the magistrate that Healy 'did it really for something to do'. And in the Fine Cotton sting in 1987 most money went on SP networks around the country and even overseas.

SP betting has recently undergone a change of image. It used to be called colourful. Nowadays it is more likely described as criminal. Yet, although SP bookies are engaged in crime because they break the law, they are not universally regarded as 'real criminals', although several official inquiries have found that some SP bookmakers, particularly in NSW, have links to organised crime. One well-known former Sydney SP, George Freeman, always scoffed at this idea.

SP bookies have fought off many challenges to their existence but if governments give all Australia's on-course bookmakers access to off-course money then this may mean the end of the SP. It would be ironic indeed if at the end of the 20th century we could once again say about off-course betting that it was carried on by on-course bookies betting from their offices in town.

by Charlie Fox

Comic Court holds a class field at bay and wins the Melbourne Cup in record time.

A popular, versatile turf hero

Question: In a Melbourne Cup studded with class horses, why would a 25/1 outsider receive a tumultuous ovation after humbling the rest of the field?

Answer: Because the winner of that 1950 Cup was Comic Court, one of the most popular, honest and consistent horses in Australian turf history.

It was a performance that left most spectators stunned. Comic Court had been forsaken in the betting because he was 'doubtful' at the two miles of the Cup, unplaced the two previous years, had been well beaten in the Caulfield Cup and had the steadier of 9.5 to cope with. Yet, with seven furlongs to run, here was his 11th-hour-appointed jockey Pat Glennon sending him to the lead after holding him for the first mile. This, surely, was suicidal madness.

But the magnificent brown stallion never looked like faltering as he held his three-lengths lead down the long straight. His great rival Chicquita ran her usual gallant race to run second, but Comic Court had not only won in race record time but had completed the last six furlongs in 1:12½ – the same time a straight-six winner had taken earlier.

When the time was signalled the crowd went even wilder. Comic Court, seemingly sensing the adulation, tossed his head several times in acknowledgement as he returned to the mounting yard. Comic Court's win was a triumph for trainer Jim Cummings, who had also bred the horse. The strapper that day was his son, Bart Cummings.

Comic Court will also be remembered for the great rivalry with Chicquita. Chicquita had been the most brilliant of three-year-olds, making a clean sweep of the four principal fillies' races in Melbourne, including the VRC Oaks of 1949.

But Comic Court proved to be her nemesis from 1950. She ran second to him in the St George Stakes and Alister Clark Stakes and again in the Mackinnon Stakes and Melbourne Cup. In all, in the eight races they both contested, Comic Court won six with Chicquita second on each of those occasions.

Following his record first-up run in the William Reid Stakes nearly three months after the Cup, Comic Court won four consecutive wfa races, then ran third in the Sydney Cup, conceding 16 kg to the winner, Bankstream. He was then retired to stud. The best known of his progeny was Comicquita, the result of his mating with rival Chicquita.

Grey Boots and Arthur Ward.

'Non-stayer' stays

The 'non-stayer' Grey Boots raced into history when he stylishly won the 1950 Caulfield Cup. He became the first grey horse to win the Cup in its 70-year history.

Despite excellent lead-up form, Grey Boots started in the cup at the luxury odds of 7/1 (he was still favourite) in a wide betting race because it was believed he was purely a sprinter-miler. Certainly he had not won beyond a mile before the Caulfield Cup and was, in fact, descended from the English sprint champion The Tetrarch.

But Grey Boots was a horse that improved with age – and distance. A moderate performer early, he surprised by winning the 1950 Doncaster at 25/1. He came south and won the Toorak Handicap, gaining the services of Neville Sellwood for the Caulfield Cup. The Cup was considered beyond his stamina but he proved his critics wrong by beating the mighty mare Chicquita by three-quarters of a length. Grey Boots in fact went on to become a prominent weight-for-age horse, winning the CM Lloyd Stakes, the Rawson and Caulfield Stakes, and the CF Orr Stakes of 1952.

Another way to start at Doomben (NP).

Racecaller Tom Foley flanked by trainers Fred Best (l) and Athol Strong (r) (NP).

Just no stopping Rim Boy

Nothing, it seemed, could stop Rim Boy winning the Doomben Ten Thousand of 1950.

Not his stature, even though he was the tiniest and plainest horse – he was called the mouse – to win a race for many years.

Not his lowly beginnings – he had run in a hack race at Warwick as a youngster, travelling widely around the southern districts of Queensland.

And not the fact that it took more than a week to get him to Brisbane by float from Newcastle due to the disastrous NSW floods.

Even severe interference in the straight during the running of the Ten Thousand – his rider had to stop him and pull him around other horses – could not prevent his winning. Rim Boy simply had too much class.

In fact, this win was his 11th from 13 starts and his owners, NSW sportsmen A. Baker and E. Simpson, were always confident. In one bet alone they took £20 000 to £3000 with one bookmaker. Not so confident was Rim Boy's trainer Ray Cashman, who was quoted as saying, pre-race, that the cost of taking the horse to Brisbane caused by paying people to pull the float out of bogs was probably more than the horse was worth.

TURF TOPICS

The professional Pat Glennon: By winning the Cup in such dashing style on Comic Court, Glennon, who was a last-minute engagement, was the talk of the turf, and his career was subsequently followed closely. In July 1950 he made headlines when he recorded five wins from five mounts on the opening day of the Broken Hill racing carnival. Glennon won a second Melbourne Cup on Macdougal in 1959.

Johnny wasn't amused: Crack US jockey Johnny Longden rode at Caulfield on 8 April with his best result a second. Four days later Longden landed The Groom in the rich All-Aged Stakes at Randwick. The big crowd gave Longden a prolonged reception. The Sydney *Daily Telegraph* suggested the race had been rigged to allow Longden to win. Longden was affronted, saying he might not ride in Australia again.

Truly a champion: In the Champagne Stakes at Randwick, True Course carried a 10 lb penalty after her win in the AJC Sires' Produce, and was at the tail of the field on the heavy track But she accelerated so quickly that Bill Williamson was pulling her up on the post to win by 1¼ lengths.

Good Kiwi idea: A referendum in 1949 overwhelmingly supported off-course betting, but bookmakers failed in their quest to be legally reinstated after being banned in 1920. The new Totalisator Agency Board held its first meeting in 1950, two agencies opened in 1951, and by 1952 26 branches and 135 agencies were open. Turnover mushroomed from £3 827 803 in 1952 to £19 470 425 in 1954.

Mainbrace's one run loss: Mainbrace won his last six races in 1949–50 as a two-year-old, the best in NZ, but was beaten first-up the next season. He went on to win his next 15 in succession, just short of the great 19-win sequences of Desert Gold and Gloaming.

A flying start thanks to a faulty Randwick barrier gives Chief Mohican his only 1950 win (NP).

1950 RESULTS

VRC MELBOURNE CUP (2m)
Comic Court, 9.5 (P Glennon) Trained by JM Cummings; 3:19.5; Chicquita, Morse Code

AJC SYDNEY CUP (2m)
Sir Falcon, 7.13 (J Thompson) Trained by J Mitchell; 3:26.75; Hurry Up, Hoyle

QTC BRISBANE CUP (2m)
Silver Buzz, 7.1 (N McGrowdie) Trained by J Miller; 3:28.5; Benvolo, Spellman

SAJC ADELAIDE CUP (2m)
Peerless Fox, 7.12 (E Preston) Trained by C Manley; 3:23; King Comedy, Portage

WATC PERTH CUP (2m and 11 yds)
Azennis, 7.2 (P Knuckey) Trained by AG Smith; 3:26.25; Jovial Lad, Resound

VATC CAULFIELD CUP (12-f)
Grey Boots, 7.13 (N Sellwood) Trained by HV Cooper; 2:31; Chicquita, Saxony

VRC AUSTRALIAN CUP (2m and 1½-f)
Bold John, 7.10 (R Hutchinson) Trained by T Lewis; 3:42.7, Lady Vara, Henley

MVRC WS COX PLATE (10-f)
Alister, 7.11 (J Purtell) Trained by H Wolters; 2:06.2; Iron Duke, Bhutan

AJC DERBY (12-f)
Alister, 8.10 (R Heather) Trained by H Wolters; 2:32.2; Rumyle, True Course

VRC VICTORIA DERBY (12-f)
Alister, 8.10 (R Heather) Trained by J Wolters; 2:35.75; Midway, Londonderry

AJC DONCASTER HANDICAP (1m)
Grey Boots, 7.7 (R Selkrig) Trained by H Cooper; 1:38.2; Achilles, Buzmak

BTC DOOMBEN '10 000' (7-f less 93 yds)
Rim Boy, 7.11 (B Smith) Trained by R Cashman; 1:17.7; Radstock, Heroic Sovereign

VRC NEWMARKET HANDICAP (6-f)
High Jip, 7.7 (T Unkovich) Trained by R Trihey; 1:11; Carnage, Gay Saint

AJC SIRES' PRODUCE STAKES (7-f)
True Course, 8.8 (W Williamson) Trained by FW Hoysted; 1:27.7; Even Flow, Ragazza

VRC SIRES' PRODUCE STAKES (7-f)
True Course, 8.7 (W Williamson) Trained by FW Hoysted; 1:24.5; Flying Halo, Free Speech

VRC GRAND NATIONAL STEEPLECHASE (3m 1-f)
Parilla's Pride, 11.4 (R Watts) Trained by J Wheeler; 6:15.25; Jung Bahadur, Faunus

Delta goes strongly to the line to win the 1951 Melbourne Cup by three-quarters of a length.

Hydrogen – fifth winner for Munro.

Delta – deserved greatness

Sometimes it all comes together at the top level of racing. Delta should have been a champion – and was. His owner Adolph Basser should have enjoyed racing success – and did. And the pair (along with trainer Maurice McCarten) deserved to win the 1951 Melbourne Cup – and fate obliged.

Unlike his owner, Delta was anything but the classic rags to riches story. He was fashionably bred, looked every inch a racehorse and there was keen competition when he was first put up for sale. He went for the substantial price of 2600 guineas. Mr (later Sir) Adolph Basser, the successful bidder, was a wealthy jeweller.

Delta was an inspired buy. The brown colt had four starts for two wins as a two-year-old then at three won the Cox Plate, the Victoria Derby and the VRC St Leger.

Delta did not come up to expectations as a four-year-old and was sent for a long spell by McCarten. He missed the autumn of 1951 but the spring of that year belonged to him. After a brilliant Sydney campaign, he went to Melbourne where he won the Mackinnon Stakes from Akbar. Because of the depth of the Melbourne Cup field and his big lump of 9.5, Delta started at 10/1.

After a hard run, Delta shot to the lead near the post and won by three-quarters of a length over Akbar.

Akbar's defeat resulted in one of the turf's hard-luck stories. That horse's jockey, H. Wiggins, had been promised by the owner the complete first prize if he won. He had gone so close. Neville Sellwood's luck was right in – owner Besser presented him with a Rolls-Royce for winning on Delta.

Race crowds and Darby Munro

When the brilliant Hydrogen took out the Victoria Derby of 1951 jockey Darby Munro delightedly accepted the plaudits of the crowd. Munro deserved the applause since it was his fifth win in the classic and no jockey had been so harshly judged throughout his career as 'Demon Darb'.

Born David Hugh Munro in Melbourne in 1913, Darby established himself as a top jockey after being credentialled to his brother John.

He became well known for his association with champions of the turf – the first being Hall Mark, on which he took the AJC and Victoria Derbys of 1933. The following year he scored a dashing Melbourne Cup win on the great Peter Pan, whom Munro took wide through muddy going to win at 14/1 by three lengths. Munro later won the Cup on Sirius in 1944 and on Russia in 1946.

It was also in 1946 that Munro was the target for one of the most vicious demonstrations seen on an Australian racetrack when he was blamed (wrongly) for Shannon missing the start and losing the Epsom of that year. In 1948 Munro's careered was halted when he was suspended for two years for his ride on Vagabond in the Burwood Handicap on Caulfield Cup Day.

He bounced back to win the 1951 Derby and other good races and later rode in the United States and France before retiring in 1955 to become a trainer. He died in 1966.

Brisbane hoops Birrer & 'Whooper' Stephens.

Stephens hits the deck at Albion Park (NP).

Jack Purtell was both a leading jockey and a media celebrity in Melbourne.

Jack Purtell, jockey and gent

A race crowd had rarely seen the usually imperturbable Jack Purtell so obviously delighted. Purtell was smiling broadly as he trotted his mount back to scale and his elation lifted the ovation to a new pitch.

The scene was at Moonee Valley in January 1951 and racegoers had been treated to seeing Comic Court in arguably his greatest performance, even considering his mighty Melbourne Cup win the previous November. At this his first start since the Cup, Comic Court, the supreme stayer, had just smashed the six-furlong track record in the William Reid Stakes beating Flying Halo on the line. Comic Court had been last at the half-mile, still in the last three on the turn, been baulked in the straight yet had produced a withering finish to snatch victory and break the record.

For Purtell this was as sweet as it got. He had forsaken Comic Court in the Melbourne Cup, preferring the Cox Plate and Derby winner Alister and had thus presented Pat Glennon with a Melbourne Cup on a true champion. Alister had been unplaced.

But now Purtell was savouring victory on the horse he was to describe as the best he ever rode. And that took in some mighty gallopers in one of the most illustrious riding careers of the Australian turf.

Jack Purtell was born in 1921 in the Melbourne suburb of Carlton and from his earliest days as an apprentice was destined for racing fame and eminence – for his ability, his prominent nose and his gentlemanly demeanour. His first big race win was on Velocity in the 1941 Caulfield Cup and in 1949 he won the first of seven Melbourne jockeys' premierships.

Despite his rejection of Comic Court in the 1950 Melbourne Cup (all the more surprising since he rode that horse in 19 of his 21 wins), Purtell won Australia's greatest race three times and the Cox Plate, the richest weight-for-age race, on four occasions. When he won the Cup on Rising Fast in 1954 it gave him the perfect record of three wins from as many starts on the horse since they had also combined to win the Cox Plate and the Mackinnon. Purtell would also have ridden the great mare Rivette in his dual Cups wins in 1939 but a serious fall had sidelined him.

Purtell rode with distinction overseas during the mid-1960s, winning both the English Oaks and the Irish Oaks. He retired on his return to Australia where his superlative record – apart from his winning triumphs he was only once suspended as a senior jockey – saw him appointed a stipendiary steward by the Victoria Racing Club. He retired to Queensland's Gold Coast in 1981.

TURF TOPICS

A trophy to trash? The trophy for a winner of Commonwealth Jubilee Handicap at Flemington in 1951 was called 'The Thing' after the popular song of the same name. The trophy was said to cause horses to bolt, women to blanch, strong men to turn away and children to faint. 'The Thing' was a silver column standing on a wooden base with four gold-coloured women arching backwards as they held the flames of victory.

What price a dead-heat? A two-horse race at Seymour, Victoria, in December ended in a dead-heat. One jockey then protested against the other but the protest was thrown out. The dead-heaters were Garnet and Snow Valley.

A Queensland quinella: Basha Felika (his owners believed it was Arabic for fast lightning) spearheaded a Queensland triumph when he won the 1951 Caulfield Cup. Basha Felika and the runner-up Blue Vest were both by the great Queensland sire The Buzzard.

Truly a Ladies' Day: Oaks day at Flemington is known as Ladies' Day. The 1951 race was won by Lady Havers. She had joint owners, Mrs T. Newton and Mrs G. K. Silk. Lady Havers was the first Oaks winner to be owned by a woman since Mrs M. L. Falkiner's Folly Queen won in 1917.

Wellington dead heat: Three years after the introduction of the photo finish in NZ, Almora and Prawns dead-heated for first, the first in 31 years.

Honourable winner: The Hon. (later Sir) Stanley Goosman, Minister of Works in the NZ government, topped the owners list in 1950–51 with a record £35 955.

Wandering winner: Wandering Ways won the Auckland Easter Handicap with a great performance with 9 stone 11 pounds over weight-for-age.

1951 RESULTS

VRC MELBOURNE CUP (2m)
Delta, 9.5 (N Sellwood) Trained by M McCarten; 3:24.25; Akbar, Double Bank
AJC SYDNEY CUP (2m)
Bankstream, 7.0 (N McGrowdie) Trained by V Thompson; 3:22; Freedom, Comic Court
QTC BRISBANE CUP (2m)
Prince O' Fairies, 8.7 (G Bougoure) Trained by T Lewis; 3:23.5; Bankstream, Naispear
SAJC ADELAIDE CUP (2m)
Peerless Fox, 8.9 (E Preston) Trained by C Manley; 3:30; Cambridge, Star Monarch
WATC PERTH CUP (2m and 11 yds) (Not run in 1951)
VATC CAULFIELD CUP (12-f)
Basha Felika, 7.13 (N Sellwood) Trained by E Fisher; 2:30; Blue Vest, Davey Jones
VRC AUSTRALIAN CUP (2m and 1½-f)
Bold Belle, 7.0 (WA Smith) Trained by P Fergus; 3:43.25; Land Tax, Purdey

MVRC WS COX PLATE (10-f)
Bronton, 7.11 (J Purtell) Trained by R Sinclair; 2:05.5; Hydrogen, Iron Duke
AJC DERBY (12-f)
Channel Rise, 8.10 (B Smith) Trained by W Chaffe jnr; 2:33.7; Montana, Trizami
VRC VICTORIA DERBY (12-f)
Hydrogen, 8.10 (D Munro) Trained by E Hush; 2:31; Shoreham, Bronton
AJC DONCASTER HANDICAP (1m)
Oversight, 7.13 (J Thompson) Trained by F Dalton; 1:36.2; Davey Jones, Great World
BTC DOOMBEN '10 000' (7-f less 93 yds)
Coniston, 7.2 (N McGrowdie) Trained by H Plant; 1:18.7; Deep Sea, Davey Jones
VRC NEWMARKET HANDICAP (6-f)
Carnage, 8.4 (S Martin) Trained by J Besanko; 1:11.7; Comedy Prince, Flying Halo

AJC SIRES' PRODUCE STAKES (7-f)
Ocean Bound, 8.10 (W Cook) Trained by M McCarten; 1:26; Free Rule, Hydrogen
VRC SIRES' PRODUCE STAKES (7-f)
Usage, 8.10 (W Williamson) Trained by FW Hoysted; 1:26.2; Beau Silhouette, Memory Inn
VRC GRAND NATIONAL STEEPLECHASE (3m 1-f)
Llandrillo, 9.9 (K Wilson) Trained by J Moloney; 6:19.25; Grey Morn, Jung Bahadur

The view from the flat at Caulfield at the finish of the Caulfield Cup (Age).

'Ugly duckling' wins Cup

Sydney owners Alan Lewis and Sir Sydney Snow were lukewarm about an ugly duckling of a colt at the yearling sales of 1950. They liked his breeding but his plain looks deterred them. The colt was Peshawar, whose ability belied his looks and who brilliantly won the 1952 Caulfield Cup.

Peshawar's first start for trainer Paddy Quinlan resulted in a dashing victory in the wfa Memsie Stakes at Caulfield.

Master jockey Scobie Breasley was going for his fifth Caulfield Cup win when he piloted the race favourite Peshawar from barrier 13. And the pair combined for a memorable win, as Peshawar ran wide and made short work of his rivals, winning by a length and a half.

Among those unhappy with Peshawar's win were the doubles bookmakers who had laid him with every horse that had even a remote chance in the Melbourne Cup.

When the most popular second leg, Dalray, won the two-miler the payouts amounted to a huge figure.

Between rides at Albion Park: renowned 'Creek' jockey Bronco Conquest bottom right (NP).

Runaway favourites: Bookmakers were winners when most of the fancied starters ran off the course 5½ furlongs from home in the sensational VRC Grand National Steeplechase of 1952.

Seconds before, the prospects of fancied runners Hefty Loon, Granya and Japaddy looked undeniable as they bowled along in front and seemed certain to fight out the finish. However, in a flash Granya appeared to stop and then make a dive off the track, toward where horses came on to the steeple grass for schooling. He took Hefty Loon and Japaddy with him and Bindarra and Dynamic followed.

Suddenly, the plodders Faunus, Bronze Laddie and Jung Bahadur were contesting the finish. Faunus, the 25/1 chance and one of the main bookies' hopes, came away to win clearly. Bronze Laddie (7/1) hung on for second and another 25/1 chance (Nelangie) got up for third.

Punters were far from happy but jockeys of the wayward horses claimed they were the victims of circumstances beyond their control, with Granya's rider Harry Toomer saying in disgust: 'My mount took a dive for the gap, knocked down the temporary hurdle and ran off the course proper.' Lamented leading jumps jockey Brian Smith, who was on Hefty Loon: 'I had no hope of remaining on the track. Granya ran me off.'

They hadn't told the horse: Local knowledge almost cost 11-year-old Peter Blank the Summer Handicap at Warrnambool, Victoria, in January. Peter Blank seemed set for a comfortable win but the winning post had been shifted half a furlong down the track and Peter Blank, who knew every inch of the track, began to pull up at the old location. Sixteen-year-old apprentice N. Dickens rode him desperately with hands and heels, and the old fellow kept going long enough to win by half a neck. It was Peter Blank's 32nd win in 89 starts.

Stand does double burn: Racegoers witnessed the second leg of a rare double at the New Year's Day meeting at Flemington in 1952. The 70-year-old Hill Stand, which had been partly burnt out four years previously, caught fire again and was ablaze for more than an hour.

Strong blood: Top European mare Cinna never stood in NZ, but Balloch, top sire of 1951–52, her fifth son, won the sires' premiership ending the 11-year reign of Foxbridge. The other sons were Gay Shield, Beau Pere, Mr Standfast and Dink.

He carried the weight of unpopular owner

New Zealander Dalray's memorable Melbourne Cup win in 1952 has been compared with Phar Lap's triumph of 1930. Dalray's allotted weight of 9.8 was within 4 lb of Phar Lap's and to that time no other four-year-old had been asked to carry more. It was a mammoth assignment, representing 8 lb above weight-for-age.

But Dalray, although not considered in the same street as Phar Lap, had earned the weight. His New Zealand record was outstanding and his Australian form in the autumn and spring of 1952, culminating in great wins in the Metropolitan and the Mackinnon Stakes leading up to the Cup, was impeccable.

In fact, the greatest handicap to his winning, or indeed running, was his volatile owner Mr Cyril Neville whose unpopularity was probably unprecedented. Neville had been lucky to get Dalray in the first place. The horse had been knocked down to an American circus owner who demurred when he noticed a cut on the yearling's fetlock. Trainer C. C. McCarthy then persuaded Neville to take on the youngster.

Neville was volubly unhappy with each weight penalty that Dalray earned and continually insisted that a Melbourne Cup start was in doubt. However, bookmakers, who

Dalray's owner Cyril Neville shows the Cup to the crowd, watched by trainer C. C. McCarthy, jockey Bill Williamson, the Governor-General William McKell and Lady McKell.

invariably correctly forecast starters and non-starters in major races, were adamant a Cup run was certain because of heavy backing for Dalray from well-informed punters.

Dalray's first Melbourne run was on Derby Day and he could scarcely been more impressive when he accounted for Caulfield Cup winner Peshawar and the well-performed Bronton in the Mackinnon (although he had to withstand a protest from Peshawar's rider). In the previous week Cyril Neville was again in the headlines when he announced he was sacking Dalray's regular rider, New Zealander Keith Nuttall, in favour of Bill Williamson. Indeed, Nuttall had been changing into his silks before the Mackinnon when Williamson arrived. Nuttall was given his marching orders and left the course in high dudgeon.

Came Cup Day and Dalray was there to take in his place in the field of 30 starters with Williamson on board and with doubles bookmakers staring at huge losses if he won. Punters, unfazed by the huge weight, sent him out 5/1 favourite and Dalray did not let them down. Near the tail of the field early, he improved to sixth on the turn and had the

top fancies covered. However, the 200/1 outsider Welkin Sun dashed to the front with two furlongs to run and, carrying only 7.12, looked like pulling off the biggest boilover in Cup history.

However, Dalray's immense class told. He surged on relentlessly, caught Welkin Sun with 50 yards to go and came away to win by three-quarters of a length. The big crowd gave horse and jockey an enthusiastic reception. However, at the presentation ceremony Cyril Neville was pointedly ignored by the public he had treated with disdain. Neville was estimated to have won the then-huge sum of £50 000 in bets with Dalray's win.

Neville excitedly told everyone who would listen that Dalray would race in England or America following the Cup victory but the horse was back in Australia for the autumn of 1953 and won the Queen's Plate at Flemington. Injury ended his career and he later went to stud where he sired top horses including dual Metropolitan winner Tails and Sydney Cup winner Grand Garry.

Nothing fancy – the judges' box, Randwick.

Trainer Maurice McCarten and champ Delta.

VRC MELBOURNE CUP (2m)
Dalray, 9.8 (W Williamson) Trained by C Neville; 3:23.25; Welkin Sun, Reformed
AJC SYDNEY CUP (2m)
Opulent, 7.1 (N McGrowdie) Trained by JL Munro; 3:37.25; Dalray, Taressa
QTC BRISBANE CUP (2m)
Putoko, 7.0 (P Burkhardt) Trained by M McCarten; 3:27.25; Jan, Catchfree
SAJC ADELAIDE CUP (2m)
Aldershot, 7.12 (J Thompson) Trained by A Macdonald; 3:25.75; Winston's Gift, Double Blank
WATC PERTH CUP (2m and 11 yds)
Avarna, 7.3 (F Treen) Trained by WA Purvis; 3:26.75; Kingsman, Beau Scot
VATC CAULFIELD CUP (12-f)
Peshawar, 8.2 (A Breasley) Trained by PB Quinlan; 2:30.25; King Amana, Durham

VRC AUSTRALIAN CUP (2m and 1½-f)
Murray Glen, 7.6 (B Shaw) Trained by CT Godby; 3:53.5; Catchfree, Precedent
MVRC WS COX PLATE (10-f)
Hydrogen, 9.0 (D Munro) Trained by E Hush; 2:04.5; Ellerslie, Advocate
AJC DERBY (12-f)
Deep River, 8.10 (N Sellwood) Trained by M McCarten; 2:38.2; Flywood, Prince Dakhill
VRC VICTORIA DERBY (12-f)
Advocate, 8.10 (A Breasley) Trained by F Allotta; 2:30; Top Level, Gallant Archer
AJC DONCASTER HANDICAP (1m)
Prelate, 7.0 (R Reed) Trained by J Donohoe; 1:39; Iron Duke, Desert Warrior
BTC DOOMBEN '10 000' (7-f less 93 yds)
Highlea, 7.2 (N McGrowdie) Trained by H Plant; 1:17.5; Mr Standby, True Leader

VRC NEWMARKET HANDICAP (6-f)
Cromwell, 8.4 (A Ward) Trained by D Judd; 1:11.7; Joyance, San Domenico
AJC SIRES' PRODUCE STAKES (7-f)
Pure Fire, 8.10 (W Williamson) Trained by FW Hoysted; 1:27.7; Deep River, Ocean Spray
VRC SIRES' PRODUCE STAKES (7-f)
Pure Fire, 8.10 (W Williamson) Trained by FW Hoysted; 1:25.2; Deep River, Crevasse
VRC GRAND NATIONAL STEEPLECHASE (3m 1-f)
Faunus, 11.0 (A Moon) Trained by R Low; 6:13.75; Bronze Laddie, Nelangie

They sometimes have a lot of trouble starting in Brisbane!

Doc Baker in a precarious position at Doomben's 7-furlong start (NP).

The starter, Kelly (left), clears the scene at Doomben (NP).

The 5-furlong rope start at Eagle Farm was an early '50s highlight (NP).

Another victim of the rope start at Eagle Farm (NP).

TURF TOPICS

Glorious uncertainty: The atmosphere was electric before the running of the Ercildoune Stakes at Flemington in March 1953. The match race of the year – Dalray versus Hydrogen – was about to take place. Dalray had shown by his Melbourne Cup win with 9.8 that he was a champion, while Hydrogen had won the past two Cox Plates.

Dalray was backed to start at 10/9 on with Hydrogen 10/9 against. Other betting was Aldershot at 10/1 and Free Kick at 66s.

The stage was set for – a fiasco!

Before an amazed crowd, Aldershot went to the front soon after turning out of the straight – and stayed there. Setting a fast pace,

he simply stole the race and strolled in by 10 lengths. In his defence, Bill Williamson's mount Dalray pulled up lame after apparently striking himself during the race. Of course, Darby Munro on Hydrogen wasn't aware of the injury.

Double trifecta: The same three horses filled the placings in both the Caulfield and Melbourne Cups, albeit in different order.

The Caulfield Cup went to the New Zealander My Hero, a horse who could stay and was in fact noted for his flying finishes. Second was Wodalla at 14/1 and third was Most Regal at 25/1.

But in the Melbourne Cup, Jack Purtell

was at his mercurial best on Wodalla, and followed the favourite Hydrogen throughout the race to be handy at the finish.

Most Regal dashed clear, but Wodalla came at him strongly and held on to win, with My Hero surging home for third.

Salute the Queen: Takanini apprentice Dave O'Sullivan won the Auckland Railway Handicap on the little Foxbridge mare Te Awa, and became the first apprentice to salute the Queen.

It was the first time a reigning monarch had visited New Zealand, much less Ellerslie, as Queen Elizabeth II and her husband took in the day's racing.

The judge awarded the race to the horse, Sir Isfahan, but it was the dog that came in first in this race in Cheltenham, SA, in January 1953. The dog had joined in the race with only 25m to go, but it was no mean victory. In February Sir Isfahan ran second in the Oakleigh Plate.

The AJC holds a swab inquiry. Professor Shaw (in box, extreme left) is under cross-examination.

TURF TOPICS

Sensations in the Oakleigh Plate: The 1953 Oakleigh Plate was one of the most sensational ever run. It was won by Winlake over the favourite Sir Isfahan in a hard-fought finish. But Sir Isfahan, who was the subject of a huge betting plunge, was kicked at the start and was clearly lame behind the barrier. A veterinary inspection cleared him to run.

When the field lined up several horses were stirred up. They twisted and turned in the stalls and the start was delayed for 13 minutes. When the race got under way Eidolon broke a leg at the turn. The horse was subsequently destroyed.

Despite his setback at the start Sir Isfahan looked likely to land the plunge when he drew clear in the 5½-furlong event, but Winlake ran him down. There was a plunge on a horse called Patna who started a short-priced favourite but beat only one runner home.

King of weight-for-age: Hydrogen, who became Australia's highest stakewinner in the 1950s, relished weight-for-age races. He won back-to-back WS Cox Plates – and only Kingston Town has a better record in the race.

1953 was a vintage year for Hydrogen, who won the Alister Clark Stakes at Moonee Valley, then went to Brisbane where he scored in the PJ O'Shea Stakes and the Brisbane Cup. Back in his home town of Sydney for the early spring races, he won the Hill Stakes (beating odds-on favourite Tarien) and was second to Carioca in the Metropolitan.

Sent to Melbourne, he took his second Cox Plate, then won the Mackinnon Stakes on Derby Day. The following year bleeding attacks began to plague his career and he retired having won 26 of 60 starts.

On his retirement he'd won a record $119 000 in stake money.

1953 RESULTS

VRC MELBOURNE CUP (2m)
Wodalla, 8.4 (J Purtell) Trained by R Sinclair; 3:23.25; Most Regal, My Hero
AJC SYDNEY CUP (2m)
Carioca, 8.9 (W Cook) Trained by PC Hoysted; 3:22.5; Advocate, Friendly Feeling
QTC BRISBANE CUP (2m)
Hydrogen, 8.9 (W Williamson) Trained by E Hush; 3:22; Welkin Sun, Maynard
SAJC ADELAIDE CUP (2m)
Royal Pageant, 7.13 (W Pyers) Trained by K Lafferty; 3:24.75; Calaton, Rousvaross
WATC PERTH CUP (2m and 11 yds)
Raconteur, 7.12 (E Treffone) Trained by FE Spencer; 3:24.5; Jewel Time, Coronate
VATC CAULFIELD CUP (12-f)
My Hero, 8.7 (N Eastwood) Trained by OF Watson; 2:28.75; Wodalla, Most Regal

VRC AUSTRALIAN CUP (2m and 1 ½-f)
Arbroath (R Hutchinson) Trained by T Lewis; 3:44.2; Welkin Sun, Royal Radiant
MVRC WS COX PLATE (10-f)
Hydrogen, 9.4 (W Williamson) Trained by E Hush; 2:05.2; Prince Morvi, Cromis
AJC DERBY (12-f)
Prince Morvi, 8.10 (N Sellwood) Trained by E Fellows jnr; 2:31.2; Electro, High Forest
VRC VICTORIA DERBY (12-f)
Prince Morvi, 8.10 (N Sellwood) Trained by E Fellows jnr; 2:31.5; Cromis, Townsville
AJC DONCASTER HANDICAP (1m)
Triclinium, 7.4 (H Welch) Trained by D Lewis; 1:35.2; Iroquois, Mardi Tout
BTC DOOMBEN '10 000' (7-f less 93 yds)
True Leader, 8.4 (G Moore) Trained by M Laidlaw; 1:17.5; Coniston, Karendi

VRC NEWMARKET HANDICAP (6-f)
Cultured, 7.11 (S Cassidy) Trained by F Allotta; 1:11.7; Tarien, Winlake
AJC SIRES' PRODUCE STAKES (7-f)
Royal Stream, 8.10 (W Cook) Trained by F Cush; 1:24.5; Prince Cortauld, Seacraft
VRC SIRES' PRODUCE STAKES (7-f)
Surang, 8.7 (R Hutchinson) Trained by T Murdoch; 1:24.5; Cromis, Love To All
VRC GRAND NATIONAL STEEPLECHASE (3m 1-f)
Japaddy, 11.2 (R Hall) Trained by F Wilson; 6:5.75; Don sion, Accentuate

So close to double double

Not only did the great Rising Fast win the Caulfield Cup–Cox Plate– Melbourne Cup treble of 1954, he established a winning sequence of top races unlikely to be matched. In the spring of that year he won in succession the Turnbull Stakes, the Caulfield Stakes, the Caulfield Cup, the Cox Plate, the Mackinnon Stakes, the Melbourne Cup, then the Fisher Plate on the final day of the Flemington carnival.

Rising Fast's stirring Cup triumph.

Rising Fast might have stood atop the pinnacle of greatness had he been able to win the Melbourne Cup again the following year. He had scored a brilliant back-to-back victory in the Caulfield Cup and was 2/1 favourite to complete the double-double. He failed – but only in the most unlucky of circumstances.

Rising Fast was bred in New Zealand but did all his top-level racing in Australia after his owner fell out with NZ racing officialdom. The owner, Mr Leicester Spring, bought Rising Fast as a yearling for only 325 guineas and although it was his first racehorse purchase he chose advisedly.

Not that Rising Fast showed much ability as a young horse.

Rising Fast began his Australian career,

under the care of New Zealander Ivan Tucker, in Brisbane. In the spring of 1954, after demonstrating his ability by winning at Eagle Farm, he was sent to Melbourne where racegoers were treated to some of the turf's greatest performances.

Rising Fast's first win was in the Feehan Stakes but he was then beaten at odds-on (by Flying Halo) in the Underwood. However, he was not to taste defeat again that year and his unparalleled sequence of wins began with Bill Williamson, his regular jockey.

However, there was a sensation before the Caulfield which saw a dramatic switch of jockey. Williamson came down in the event preceding the Cup, suffered severe injuries and was rushed to hospital. Trainer Tucker had to find a substitute fast – and did so in the jockeys' room. Arthur Ward had been left without a mount when Engraver had been scratched. He was understandably delighted to jump on the favourite but had to use all his vigour to land Rising Fast a winner after taking him to the front on the turn.

Rising Fast's magnificent performance earned him the maximum 10 lb penalty for the Melbourne Cup and owner Spring responded by hinting that the champion might not start in the Melbourne Cup.

But it was not a serious threat, particularly when Rising Fast demolished a top field (including Hydrogen, Prince Delville, Pride of Egypt and King Boru) in the Cox Plate. His jockey by now was Jack Purtell, who then won on him in the Mackinnon Stakes.

Rising Fast by now was the idol of the people and went to the post a 5/2 Melbourne Cup favourite. He hit the lead on straightening and was simply too strong in the run to the post, giving Jack Purtell successive Melbourne Cup wins. The deafening reception he received was the public's way of saluting a great horse, and a great jockey.

Rising Fast: controversial at home.

What if …

Had young Queen Elizabeth not visited the Antipodes in 1953–54, the New Zealand-bred galloper Rising Fast might never have become an Australian icon.

Set for the Royal Auckland Cup of 1953 as a four-year-old, Rising Fast ran badly and was ridden atrociously in a lead-up race, the Te Awamutu Cup. Trainer Jack Winder and apprentice rider R. P. Salisbury were each suspended for a month.

Owner Leicester Spring sent Rising Fast to Winder's uncle, Alf, and the bay won the wfa Queen Elizabeth Stakes at Paeora to a hostile reception. Spring believed that this was a factor in what subsequently happened. On appeal, the Waikato committee increased Winder's suspension to 12 months, Salisbury's to three and disqualified Rising Fast for 12 months. The committee also charged Spring with being a party to not racing Rising Fast on his merits.

In February 1954, Spring was exonerated; in March the horse's disqualification was lifted. But the Auckland and Wellington Cups had long been run. Spring felt that 'officialdom' had been out to prevent his horse from contesting the Auckland Cup for fear of a hostile demonstration in front of the Queen. Rising Fast never raced in his homeland again.

Maurice McCarten's gelding Belmont Park won two Rosehill races within 34 minutes.

Horses hurdle fallen riders before the turn at Albion Park in the early 1950s (NP).

Carioca regularly smashed time records, including a world record for 7 ½ furlongs.

Carioca rewrote the records

Carioca was frequently described as Australia's best racehorse in the early part of 1954. He probably deserved the title until Rising Fast burst onto the scene. Certainly Carioca was a headline stealer. He regularly smashed time records and was one of the favourite horses of crack jockey Billy Cook who won 16 races on him.

Carioca would have capped a great career had he been able to win the Epsom in 1954 as he seemed certain to do. The previous Saturday he had figured in an amazing win in a seven-furlong race at Rosehill that was talked about for years.

In the Railway Highweight Carioca had missed the start by five lengths and been last most of the way. Then, under the big weight of 9.7, he finished with a paralysing burst to grab victory on the line and, incredibly, establish a new race record of 1.23 ¾.

But, again with the impost of 9.7 and with his propensity for coming from well back in the field, the Epsom proved beyond him – he finished fast for third. Thereafter, Carioca's star dimmed, although he was able to win twice as a seven-year-old.

However, his record speaks for itself. As a five-year-old he set up a winning sequence of seven victories in good races and broke three records on the way. In 1953 his big wins included the Sydney Cup and the Metropolitan Handicap, in which he had to beat another champion, Hydrogen.

Turned out after an unplaced run in the Cox Plate, he resumed with a win in the STC Club Stakes, clocking a world-record time of 1:30 for the 7 ½ furlongs. He was retired to stud in 1955.

Formidable partners

It was the finest of performances but was it a world record? The partnership of trainer Maurice McCarten and jockey Neville Sellwood won five races on the program at Randwick in January 1954. Racing experts with international experience said they could not remember any other partnership in the world achieving such a feat. Two years earlier they had won four races in one afternoon at Randwick and finished third on another runner.

TURF TOPICS

Ring-in case sequel: The notorious Erbie/Redlock ring-in had its sequel in March 1954 when former trainer Charles Prince had his life disqualification lifted. The SAJC, which had disqualified Prince, lifted the ban as an amnesty gesture to mark the visit of the Queen.

Prince, then 60, had been the trainer of both Erbie and Redlock in the 1930s. Under the name of Redlock, Erbie won a race at Murray Bridge, South Australia, then another run by the Kadina and Wallaroo Racing Club, also in SA.

1954 RESULTS

VRC MELBOURNE CUP (2m)
Rising Fast, 9.5 (J Purtell) Trained by IJ Tucker; 3:23; Hellion, Gay Helios
AJC SYDNEY CUP (2m)
Gold Scheme, 8.7 (N Sellwood) Trained by LJ Ellis; 3:21.75; Double Blank, Priory
QTC BRISBANE CUP (2m)
Lancaster, 8.8 (D Munro) Trained by PW Kennedy; 3:21.5; Lord Forrest, Kowhata
SAJC ADELAIDE CUP (2m)
Spearfolio, 7.11 (N Sellwood) Trained by H Cousens; 3:27; Engraver, Beau Regis
WATC PERTH CUP (2m and 11 yds)
Beau Scot, 7.13 (P Knuckey) Trained by N Armanasco; 3:29, Mercavy, Night Porter
VATC CAULFIELD CUP (12-f)
Rising Fast, 8.10 (A Ward) Trained by IJ Tucker; 2:30; Electro, Advocate

VRC AUSTRALIAN CUP (2m and 1½-f)
Sunish, 8.9 (W Williamson) Trained by W Allan; 3:43.25; Royal Radiant, Captain Hunter
MVRC WS COX PLATE (10-f)
Rising Fast, 9.4 (J Purtell) Trained by IJ Tucker; 2:03.8; Prince Delville, Pride of Egypt
AJC DERBY (12-f)
Prince Delville, 8.10 (R Selkrig) Trained by S Lamond; 2:33; Telyar, Eight Bells
VRC VICTORIA DERBY (12-f)
Pride of Egypt, 8.10 (W Cook) Trained by E Hush; 2:32.5; King Boru, Telyar
AJC DONCASTER HANDICAP (1m)
Karendi, 8.4 (W Camer) Trained by J Green; 1:36; Triclinium, Carioca

BTC DOOMBEN '10000' (7-f less 93 yds)
Nagpuni, 7.12 (W Wade) Trained by L Quinlan; 1:19.5; Rapid River, Lord Bosworth
VRC NEWMARKET HANDICAP (6-f)
Birdwood, 8.4 (N McGrowdie) Trained by S Lawrence; 1:11.7; Beach Chief, Tarien
AJC SIRES' PRODUCE STAKES (7-f)
Lindbergh, 8.10 (D Munro) Trained by H Darwon; 1:24.7; King Boru, Castle Moat
VRC SIRES' PRODUCE STAKES (7-f)
Acramitis, 8.10 (R Heather) Trained by J Mulcahy; 1:24; Indian Empire, Spritsail
VRC GRAND NATIONAL STEEPLECHASE (3m 1-f)
Fearless Chief, 9.5 (T Jones) Trained by L Meenan; 6:11; Teedum, Boanerges

Jack Purtell on the big and handsome Rising Fast after winning the 1954 Melbourne Cup.

TJ and Toparoa.

Rising Fast and 'Father' Fred

Both the stayer Rising Fast and the veteran trainer Fred 'Father' Hoysted had distinguished racing careers behind them when they came together in 1955. Rising Fast had set the racing world alight with his magnificent sequence of victories – including the Caulfield Cup, Cox Plate and Melbourne Cup – the previous year and Hoysted had for decades reigned as one of Australia's greatest trainers.

Rising Fast's owner Mr Leicester Spring sent the horse to Hoysted when Ivan Tucker was suspended over the positive swab of one of his charges in New Zealand. What Hoysted could not know was that the horse had barely survived a horror sea trip across the Tasman on his return to Australia from a spell in New Zealand. Rising Fast had been neglected and poorly fed and was only a shadow of himself when Hoysted began his autumn preparation. Not surprisingly, he failed in all starts except a farcical two-horse race, the Carbine Stakes, at Flemington.

Consequently, Rising Fast went into the 1955 Caulfield Cup a sentimental rather than actual favourite, although as post time neared his price firmed from 7/1 to 11/2. Certainly, he looked his old self and was the Rising Fast of old as the horses paraded. His barrier draw of 17 obviously would not help with his heavy weight but this year he was ridden by Bill Williamson, one of the calmest jockeys ever to sit in a saddle. Williamson was patience

personified and he gradually moved Rising Fast through the field until the home turn when he called on the champion for a finishing surge. Rising Fast, responding magnificently, easily passed the leader and favourite Maniana and coasted home by three lengths from Ray Ribbon and Historic Era.

Rising Fast had equalled the performance of the great Poseidon who had won two Caulfield Cups (in 1906-7) and a Melbourne Cup (1906) but had not been able to complete the double. The question Australia was asking was, of course: Could Rising Fast do it and thus become a true legend of the turf?

History records that Rising Fast failed – but no horse went closer to achieving the greatest of racing triumphs. Drama and controversy surrounded his Cup defeat by the aged gelding Toparoa who bored out and interfered with Rising Fast in the straight to such an extent that his jockey Neville Sellwood was subsequently suspended for two months. If not the interference then it was the weight that stopped Rising Fast: he had conceded Toparoa 34 lb (or 15.5 kg).

As some consolation, Rising Fast won the Fisher Plate at Flemington. He came back the following year, won the Blamey and the Orr Stakes but when he suffered a bleeding attack it was obvious his best days were behind him. Leicester Spring then retired his champion to New Zealand but not before Rising Fast was given an emotional farewell.

TJ's triumph

Rising Fast's valiant effort to just miss in the 1955 Melbourne Cup partly obscured the considerable training feat achieved by T. J. Smith in landing Toparoa that year's winner.

Toparoa was, after all, an aged gelding, had done most of his early racing in hack class and in several seasons had won only four events in New Zealand. But connections believed Toparoa had a depth of talent that only needed developing. His New Zealand trainer Joe Bromby recommended that Smith take the horse. Smith brought him along the way he did best and set him for the 1955 Metropolitan–Melbourne Cup double. Of course, the light weights Topara was allotted in keeping with his ordinary record did not hinder his chances.

Came the Metropolitan and Toparoa almost realised the first part of the plan, when second to Beaupa. So, penalty-free, Toparoa lined up in the Melbourne Cup with Neville Sellwood aboard and carrying the featherweight of 7.8.

In a Melbourne Cup recognised as one of the roughest in its history, Rising Fast was knocked to the rear of the field where Toparoa, always a slow starter, was biding his time. Sellwood gradually manoeuvred Toparoa through the field. When Toparoa hit the lead at the top of the straight, Rising Fast came after him and looked likely to win. Toparoa caused him more interference but held off the champion.

A thundering good scandal

The Thundering Legion case of 1955 ranks with the most sensational turf scandals – right down to the 'sting-in-the-tail' result of the relevant race.

The race was the 9-furlong 1st Clarendon Transition Handicap set down to be run at Morphettville, South Australia on 21 May 1955. Engaged in the field but originally never in betting contention was the poorly performed Thundering Legion, most recent form 0-0-0 and badly drawn in barrier 18 in a field of 22. Even his opening price of 33/1 looked to be skinny odds.

However, suddenly there was a flood and then a torrent of money for the horse, that saw his price tumble to 3/1. Chief stipe Fred Everest moved quickly and confronted rider Bill Attrill in the jockeys' room. Attrill denied any knowledge of batteries, but the plot came unstuck when Everest snatched Attrill's whip and received a shock to his right arm. The stipe then looked around for a replacement jockey, picking lightweight Des Coleman.

If Thundering Legion had run true to form the case might have just been another racecourse scandal. But he ran like a horse possessed and accelerated like lightning when Coleman applied his standard whip. Coleman said later of Thundering Legion, 'It was as if he really was battery-charged.'

Thundering Legion lasted by a head to win the race in a hectic finish. The successful punters took their winnings and jockey Atrill and trainer Conway met their fate. Attrill was disqualified for 10 years and Conway for life, though this was later reduced to 10 years. Attrill later admitted to using batteries on other mounts.

A specialist

The talented and durable Flying Halo received the recognition he deserved when he won his third William Reid Stakes in 1955. It was a proud record (he had run second and fourth in two other years) and was only surpassed by Manikato in the 1980s.

Flying Halo, then a seven-year-old, had to lump 9.7 on a heavy track to achieve his third Reid victory but having the services of Jack Purtell helped. The horse was conceding the leader 12 lengths at the half-mile and Purtell had to weave him through the field. Flying Halo finished fast to just snatch victory. (Even so he was lucky – Kemet looked certain to win but his jockey cramped! [see Turf Topic].

Flying Halo first came under notice by running second in the Standish Handicap on New Year's Day 1952, then won the race the following year. He won the Underwood Stakes of 1953 and 1954.

Jockey was really stiff! If ever a horse should have won a race it was Kemet in the 1955 William Reid Stakes. Kemet was in front well down the straight when jockey Norman Powell went to pull the whip to make certain of victory. But he couldn't move. Cramp had gripped his stomach.

Meanwhile, Flying Halo was looming, carrying 9.6 on the heavy track. Kemet had only 7.12 and surely would have 'lifted' with even a little encouragement. However, with Powell frozen, Flying Halo scored in a photo finish.

Prince ruled at wfa: The exceptional weight-for-age galloper Prince Cortauld was perhaps the main beneficiary of Rising Fast's lapse of form as he took time to recover from a debilitating sea voyage in 1955. Trained at Randwick by Maurice McCarten, Prince Cortauld had talent and great will-to-win, and at one stage had won 15 of 21 starts. He won the Orr and Blamey Stakes of 1955, took out the Futurity with 10.6 (65.5 kg), then beat Rising Fast in the Queen Elizabeth Stakes at Flemington. Back in Sydney he defeated Rising Fast and Carioca in the Autumn Stakes and later that year again beat Rising Fast, this time in the Caulfield Stakes.

Mother was a carthorse: There was nothing aristocratic about the breeding of 1955 Australian Steeplechase winner Cyrette. His dam, a Melita Man mare, was not only a social outcast but, according to Cyrette's owner, Mr Cyril Pritchard, she never started in a race and was last heard of pulling a baker's cart around Bendigo.

But his mother would have been proud of Cyrette. He was ranked one of the turf's greatest steeplechasers after his all-the-way win in the Australian Steeple at Caulfield – his fourth win in succession. He won the race by 15 lengths with a further 35 to the third horse.

1955 RESULTS

VRC MELBOURNE CUP (2m)
Toparoa, 7.8 (N Sellwood) Trained by TJ Smith 3:28.25; Rising Fast, Sir William
AJC SYDNEY CUP (2m)
Talisman, 7.4 (S Cassidy) Trained by CB Hasler; 3:29.5; Finito, Beaupa
QTC BRISBANE CUP (2m)
The Wash, 7.12 (J Purtell) Trained by WJ Shean; 3:23.2; Finito, Milwaukee II
SAJC ADELAIDE CUP (2m)
Storm Glow, 7.0 (R Hall) Trained by JM Cummings; 3:29; Al Crusa, Chatford
WATC PERTH CUP (2m and 11 yds) (1 January 1955)
Lenarc, 8.2 (C Tulloch) Trained by W Purvis; 3:29; Beau Scot, Priandy
WATC PERTH CUP (2m and 11 yds) (31 December 1955)
Yabaroo, 7.4 (H McCloud) Trained by J Collinson; 3:25.5; Dominic, Rexaldo

VATC CAULFIELD CUP (12-f)
Rising Fast, 9.10 (W Williamson) Trained by FW Hoysted; 2:29.25; Ray Ribbon, Historic Era
VRC AUSTRALIAN CUP (2m and 1½-f)
Hellion, 8.8 (W Cook) Trained by W Foster; 3:53.25; Dunsinane, Royal Sirius
MVRC WS COX PLATE (10-f)
Kingster, 7.11 (W Camer) Trained by J Green; 2:04.4; Caranna, Sailor's Guide
AJC DERBY (12-f)
Caranna, 8.10 (A Mulley) Trained by T Hush; 2:33.75; Gay Ranick, Prince Dante
VRC VICTORIA DERBY (12-f)
Sailor's Guide, 8.10 (N Sellwood) Trained by G Daniel; 2:31.75; Arlunya, Caranna
AJC DONCASTER HANDICAP (1m)
Fire Dust, 7.10 (N McGrowdie) Trained by G Brown; 1:39; Count Roussel, Prince Morvi

BTC DOOMBEN '10 000' (7-f less 93 yds)
Apple Bay, 7.2 (F Leman) Trained by TJ Smith; 1:18; Plato, True Leader
VRC NEWMARKET HANDICAP (6-f)
Swynphilos, 7.7 (B Gilders) Trained by J Moloney; 1:11.5; Great Saint, Diecast
AJC SIRES' PRODUCE STAKES (7-f)
Kingster, 8.10 (W Camer) Trained by J Green; 1:26.5; Knave, Sir Newton
VRC SIRES' PRODUCE STAKES (7-f)
Knave, 8.10 (M McCarten) Trained by N Sellwood; 1:24.2; Chetnik, Magic Nib
VRC GRAND NATIONAL STEEPLECHASE (3m 1-f)
Blue Lagoon, 10.4 (W Miller) Trained by D Turner; 6:9.5; Bold Flare, The Drum

The riderless Better Boy passes the post first, but Redcraze wins the Caulfield Cup.

Sir Chester Manifold and Sir Dallas Brooks.

Redcraze carries record to victory

Redcraze's Caulfield Cup win was the momentous achievement of a great year of racing. Not only did he beat a field of the highest quality (including Evening Peal and Baystone who were to go on and win Melbourne Cups) but he carried the record weight of 9.13 (63 kg) on a track that had been deluged with rain the previous week.

Redcraze, New Zealand–bred and magnificently proportioned, began his racing career under Syd Brown, who had charge of his Cups campaign in 1955. The following year Redcraze went to Sydney trainer T. J. Smith – with immediate success. After winning the O'Shea Stakes and the Brisbane Cup, Redcraze had to be immediately spelled

due to hoof problems.

He returned in September with a fourth in the Chelmsford Stakes after which he was lame and Smith had him fitted with a special set of bar shoes. Redcraze never looked back.

Redcraze had earned his substantial impost in the Caulfield Cup. Race followers sent the horse out 9/4 favourite. They were privileged to see that unforgettable performance as Redcraze, with only two of the 16 other runners behind him at the half mile, was called on by jockey Arthur Ward nearing the home turn. Within 200 metres, Redcraze had circled the field and, into the straight, had only Emphatic and Evening Peal in front of him (except for the riderless Better Boy).

He careered past them and went on to win by an official margin of four lengths, with Evening Peal second and Prince Delville getting up for third.

A delighted T. J. Smith wouldn't hear of Redcraze being beaten in the Melbourne Cup, but Evening Peal at last had her revenge, thanks largely to the handicapper asking the Caulfield Cup winner to shoulder another 4 lb (making his weight 10.3) over the two miles. He went so close, losing by only half a neck to an excellent mare who carried just 8.0. The only other Melbourne Cup runners to carry more than 10.0 into a place were Mormon, Commotion and the mighty Carbine, who won the 1890 Cup with 10.5.

A classic decade in NZ

The 1950s in New Zealand came in on a three-year-old crop of real quality – Beaumaris, Sweet Spray and Tudor Prince in 1949–50 – and carried on with four high-class colts in the next five seasons. These were Mainbrace, Dalray, Somerset Fair and Syntax.

Syntax, a medium-sized chestnut colt of great quality, earned £19 105 as a three-year-old, making his owner–trainer Stan Walker leading owner and his sire, Count Rendered, champion sire with only three crops racing.

Walker took Syntax to Australia as a four-year-old, but he was beaten twice by the NZ sprinter El Khobar, became very ill and went back to New Zealand, his four-year-old career wasted.

As a five-year-old, Syntax returned to Australia, to Fred Hoysted's Melbourne stable, and was well backed in the 1957 Melbourne Cup after four wfa victories – but broke down making his run and finished fourth. It was his last race.

Redcraze goes out to record one of his many great wins. He won 32 from 84 starts.

A long neck. Sailor's Guide keeps his record in the Craiglee Stakes.

'Sailor' stuck his neck out

Sailor's Guide had one of the most unusual records in Australian racing. Seven of his nine wins had been by a neck or less while his richest prize – the Sydney Cup in the autumn – was won by half a head.

The 'Sailor's' record read:

Flemington Princess Handicap, ½ neck; Flemington Burleigh Handicap, 2 lengths; Flemington Victoria Derby, neck; Caulfield Woodruff Handicap, ½ neck; St Leger Stakes, 2 lengths; Flemington Queen Elizabeth Stakes, neck; AJC St Leger, short head; Randwick Sydney Cup, ½ head; Flemington Craiglee Stakes, head.

After his 1956 Craiglee win Sailor's Guide showed his class by beating Rising Fast in the Pentathlon Stakes (a VATC Olympic Games commemorative event), then by defeating Redcraze in the CB Fisher Plate. Rising Fast overshadowed him in the autumn, but in the spring Sailor's Guide again won the Craiglee, was third in the Caulfield Cup and won the Mackinnon Stakes.

He defeated Prince Darius and Tulloch (narrowly) the following year in the Queen Elizabeth Stakes and later went to the United States where he won – on protest – the Washington International at Laurel.

Not my fault

Their action was unprecedented but the top jockeys had had enough. They objected to a censure of them by stewards after the running of the 1956 LKS Mackinnon Stakes.

The censure followed a farcical running of the important race in which outsider Sir William, ridden by Pat Glennon, 'stole' the event by dashing well clear – and staying there – while the best weight-for-ages horses in the country, Redcraze, Rising Fast and Ray Ribbon, waited … and waited.

When they finally made their moves it was too late and Sir William, who at one stage had led by 25 lengths, defeated Redcraze by four lengths with Ray Ribbon another three lengths away.

So what should have been a thrilling contest between great horses was a fiasco and the large crowd reacted predictably by lining the mounting yard, hurling abuse at the jockeys and demanding official action.

Stewards then called on riders including Arthur Ward (aboard the odds-on Redcraze), Bill Williamson (on the unplaced Rising Fast) and Jack Purtell (Ray Ribbon) for an explanation and all said they had been instructed to ride their own races and did not want to lead or carry the field up to Sir William.

The stewards found that the jockeys had ridden ill-judged races and they were severely censured for the tactics they employed. Then Purtell, Williamson and Ward took the almost unheard-of step of informing the stewards they objected to being censured. The chairman of stewards informed them they had the right of appeal but the jockeys felt they had made their point.

Fond Fast farewell

Sentiment does not play too big a part in racing but the people's farewell to champion Rising Fast in 1956 was charged with emotion. Stepping on to the Moonee Valley track – scene of some of his rich race wins – Rising Fast, ridden by Bill Williamson and accompanied by the Shetland pony who was his constant stable companion, led out the field for the Williamstown Cup. While the band played the Maori's Farewell and amid deafening applause, Rising Fast paraded past the stands, then turned and galloped the length of the straight to the winning post. Right on the line, he ducked his head, a trait he had displayed throughout his racing career. As the retired champion left the track racegoers raised their hats in tribute and trainer 'Father' Fred Hoysted openly wept.

Hoysted and Rising Fast.

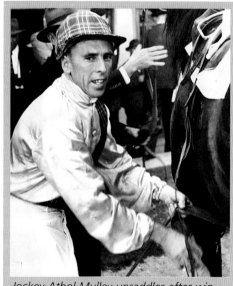

Jockey Athol Mulley unsaddles after winning the Newmarket Hcp on Kingster.

Can't separate them: Pandie Sun, Ark Royal and Fighting Force in the Hotham Handicap.

Triple dead-heat a first

Australasian turf history was made in the Hotham Handicap of 1956 when the camera-finish showed a triple dead-heat for first between Pandie Sun, Ark Royal and Fighting Force.

The big crowd gave vent to its excitement as the three desperately ridden horses fought head and head to the winning post. Then there was an expectant hush during the wait for the film of the finish to be sent down from the camera tower to the judge's box. Finally, came a deafening roar with the official announcement that the picture showed a triple dead-heat. The three horses then walked back abreast to the weighing enclosure.

The print, depicting Pandie Sun (Bill Williamson) on the rails, Ark Royal (Reg Heather) in the centre and Fighting Force (Jack Purtell) on the outside, was reproduced in newspapers throughout the world. It was believed the world's only similar camera finish was in New York in 1944.

During the 1980s two further triple dead-heats were recorded in Australian races – the first at Townsville in June 1985 when Angular, Apollo's Flame and Plenty of Spirit hit the line together, then at Stony Creek (Victoria) in January 1987 when Chester Field, Fast Seal and Mr Spectre saluted.

There were other reports of triple dead-heats before photo-finish cameras were installed with perhaps the most famous being that in the 10-furlong Moorefield (NSW) Handicap. A rerun (then the most usual way of deciding the race) resulted in another triple dead-heat!

Probably the most freakish finish of all was at Toowoomba (Queensland) on 2 June 1897, when it is recorded that four runners, Cornet, Blutcher, Minster Belle and Lord Roseberry, dead-heated in the Shorts Handicap over six furlongs.

The mirror image only confirmed the news.

Turmoil … and television: Melbourne was in the grip of Olympic fever when the Games were scheduled to begin but for months the Victoria Racing Club was in turmoil over the timing of the Melbourne Cup. The Club first decided to move the Cup to November 17, the Saturday before the Games' opening, following requests from the Olympic Council and the Premier, Mr Henry Bolte.

Controversy followed. Traditionalists were outraged. Then the Olympic Games organising committee asked for a return to the first Tuesday in November because accommodation in Melbourne would be booked out. Finally, it was agreed to revert to the traditional date and stage a special event at Flemington on 17 November – the Olympic Year Cup over 14 furlongs. The race was won by Pandie Sun from Arabil and Fighting Force and HSV-7 televised a race meeting live for the first time in Australia.

Apple Bay in upset: The only horse punters wanted in the Oakleigh Plate of 1956 was Apple Bay. A colossal betting plunge saw him start 10/9 favourite while the next horse in the betting was 9/1. At one stage bookmakers offered '10/1 bar one'.

However, fortunes were lost when 33/1 outsider Lucky Stride, ridden by Sydney's Noel McGrowdie, collared Apple Bay in the straight to win by a half-length. Lucky Stride had run fourth the previous year. Apple Bay went on to run third in the 1956 Newmarket.

Tas takes a record: Forty-four-year-old jockey Tas Wood created an Elwick record when he rode the winners of five of the seven races at the Hobart Turf Club meeting in December 1956. His mounts in the other two races finished second and fourth. His victories included the feature race, the HTC Cup, on Culver Lad.

1956 RESULTS

VRC MELBOURNE CUP (2m)
Evening Peal, 8.0, (F Fodmore) Trained by ED Lawson; 3:19.25; Redcraze, Caranna
AJC SYDNEY CUP (2m)
Sailor's Guide, 8.2 (N Sellwood) Trained by G Daniel; 3:30.4; Beaupa, Miss High Caste
QTC BRISBANE CUP (2m)
Redcraze, 9.0 (A Ward) Trained by TJ Smith; 3:22; Caranna, Beaupa
SAJC ADELAIDE CUP (2m)
Pushover, 8.10 (R Hutchinson) Trained by JP Lewis; 3:31.8; Rialkon, Storm Glow
WATC PERTH CUP (2m and 11 yds) (Not run in 1956)
VATC CAULFIELD CUP (12-f) Redcraze, 9.13
(A Ward) Trained by TJ Smith; 2:33.75; Evening Peal, Prince Delville

VRC AUSTRALIAN CUP (2m and 1 ½-f)
Pushover, 8.2 (R Hutchinson) Trained by JP Lewis; 3:41.5; Oxley, Acquilla
MVRC WS COX PLATE (10-f)
Ray Ribbon, 9.4 (J Purtell) Trained by GS Barr; 2:04.9; Rising Fast, Caranna
AJC DERBY (12-f)
Monte Carlo, 8.10 (J Thompson) Trained by F Dalton; 2:31.3; Bernfield, Harnham Hill
VRC VICTORIA DERBY (12-f)
Monte Carlo, 8.10 (J Thompson) Trained by F Dalton; 2:34.5; Summalu, Olympic Fire
AJC DONCASTER HANDICAP (1m)
Slogan II, 7.8 (J Thompson) Trained by F Dalton; 1:38.2; King's Fair, Decisive
BTC DOOMBEN '10 000' (7-f less 93 yds)
El Khobar, 8.4 (N Sellwood) Trained by R Roden; 1:18.2; Criollo, Teranyan

VRC NEWMARKET HANDICAP (6-f)
Kingster, 8.8 (A Mulley) Trained by J Green; 1:11.7; Copper Year, Apple Bay
AJC SIRES' PRODUCE STAKES (7-f)
Gay Sierra, 8.10 (A Ward) Trained by M Anderson; 1:27.3; Gay Lover, Starover
VRC SIRES' PRODUCE STAKES (7-f)
Starover, 8.10 (A Mulley) Trained by J Green; 1:25; Moonsun, Count Olin
VRC GRAND NATIONAL STEEPLECHASE (3m 1-f)
The Settler, 9.6 (E Anderson) Trained by E Jenkins; 6:12.25; Marten, Aussie Bear

Todman sprinted to racing immortality as the first winner of the Golden Slipper Stakes.

Todman had speed to burn

Explosive power. Many horses exhibit it. Todman exemplified it.

Todman ranks as the most sensational of Australian sprinters. His record speaks for itself but it was his sheer explosiveness that set him apart. He smashed time records in six of his 10 wins and broke the hearts of his rivals with sheer speed.

Todman was the son of the imported sire Star Kingdom and began the success story of the Star Kingdom link that was to make such a mark on the Australian breeding industry. Owned by Mr Stanley Wooton and trained by Maurice McCarten, Todman was small in size but very much a pocket dynamo with a gigantic stride.

McCarten set him for the inaugural Golden Slipper Stakes. Todman started at 6/1 on and won by eight lengths. Neville Sellwood, who was to be the champion's only race rider, was ecstatic. He said: 'There couldn't be another youngster like this fellow. I have ridden in England and America and I have never seen the likes of him. Todman is the greatest two-year-old I have ridden. Probably the greatest horse of any age I have ridden.'

So Todman, it seemed, would prove invincible. Taking his next race, the AJC Sires' Produce Stakes, seemed a formality. Racegoers flocked to Randwick to see the 'wonder colt of the century' demolish another field of two-year-olds. Again he started at

odds of 6/1 on.

But this time there was a difference. The Sires was a furlong longer than the Slipper and Tulloch was in the field. It was a boilover. Todman, having displayed his customary early speed, was under the whip a furlong and a half from home and Tulloch, ridden by a surprised George Moore, raced past him to win easily. The crowd was stunned.

Todman had his revenge four days later in the Champagne when, back in distance, his blistering speed gave Tulloch no chance. He shattered the race record in the fastest six furlongs by a two-year-old at Randwick – 1:10.

In the spring of 1957 Todman broke down badly in the STC Hill Stakes. The injury was diagnosed as a fractured sesamoid bone in his off hind leg, necessitating a major operation. Todman was off the scene for two years.

On 12 December 1959 he resumed his career in the STC Flying Handicap over six furlongs at Canterbury. Devoted followers backed him into odds-on favouritism and Todman did not let them down. To the roar of the crowd he burst from the barrier and not only led all the way but recorded a new race and course record. Taken to Melbourne he won the Lightning and Futurity Stakes.

It was decided to retire Todman while in good health and he joined his sire Star Kingdom at the Baramul Stud. In all he sired 32 individual stakes winners.

Golden race born

Sydney Turf Club committeeman George Ryder had a vision of a great race for two-year-olds – and followed his dream through to the inaugural running of the Golden Slipper Stakes in 1957.

Ryder said: 'The Sydney Turf Club needed a special race of its own. The Australian Jockey Club had all the big races, and we had nothing. I came up with the idea of the Golden Slipper Stakes as the richest prize for two-year-olds in Australia.'

Ryder was a self-made wealthy businessman who had come into racing after buying a horse for £100 and naming it Jan after his daughter.

George Ryder.

He bought Woodlands Stud in 1946 and from it launched into thoroughbred breeding by importing first-rate stallions and mares from Europe. Ryder sold Woodlands Stud in 1971, then bought Kia Ora Stud at Scone, standing top stallions of the day.

The Slipper became a great race, and by the mid-1990s it topped $2 million in prize money and became the richest two-year-old race in the world. Consequently, its prestige is unparalleled, and because of the stud value many winners are now retired early.

While Todman was a magnificent first winner in 1957, it was not the start for the Slipper that George Ryder and his staunch supporters would have wished. Hopes for a keenly contested race were dashed by Todman's dominance. He started at 6/1 on (it was 10/1 bar one with the bookmakers) and he won as he liked by eight lengths.

The first six winners of the Slipper were Sydney-trained and the first five were sired by Star Kingdom. It is a race where winning runs in the family – Todman produced Eskimo Prince and Sweet Embrace while Vain got Sir Dapper and Inspired.

Star Kingdom (left) and Todman (right).

Noel McGrowdie boots Straight Draw home in the Melbourne Cup ahead of Prince Darius.

Aussies at Ascot: Ron Hutchinson, Scobie Breasley, George Moore, Bill Collins, Garnet Bougoure, Bill WIlliamson.

Straight Draw's lucky win

Even allowing for the glorious uncertainty of racing, Tulloch would surely have won the 1957 Melbourne Cup. By any measure he had the race in his keeping. But … he had to be in it to win it. Trainer T. J. Smith wanted him to run but, in one of the most debated controversies in turf history, his owner, Mr Ern Haley, decreed: 'I love horses too much to run a three-year-old, any three-year-old, not only Tulloch, in the Melbourne Cup. I will not risk breaking the colt's heart.'

Despite Haley's convictions, there is not a scintilla of evidence to suggest that Tulloch would not have careered away with the greatest event on the racing calendar just as he had in other major races of the spring, including the Caulfield Cup.

Whether Haley was right and whether even a convincing win might have jeopardised the colt's future career will never be known. Certainly, no three-year-old had won the Cup since 1941 when Skipton beat a field reduced and weakened by war, and just as certainly many three-year-olds seemed to falter after failing in the Melbourne Cup.

So the 1957 Cup field lined up without

Cup jockey Noel McGrowdie.

Tulloch, and a relatively lacklustre field it was. Redcraze, who had been a magnificent performer throughout his career and who had won the Cox Plate, had his chance the previous year but was sent out favourite nevertheless. Second in the betting was Monte Carlo at 6/1 and third fancy was the Metropolitan winner Straight Draw, who might have been top pick had he not recorded an unlucky sixth in the Hotham Handicap. Also there was the endlessly unlucky three-year-old Prince Darius, whom Tulloch had consistently beaten by many lengths.

Straight Draw's jockey was Noel McGrowdie, who took the Cup by the throat. He had his mount prominent throughout and sent him to the lead before the furlong peg. He had to use all his vigour when Prince Darius challenged strongly but Straight Draw responded to win by a neck. Of course, Prince Darius' narrow defeat only confirmed the mortgage Tulloch would have had on the Cup had he started.

Tulloch went on to win the Fisher Plate easily on the final day of the VRC Carnival, then a week later took out the Queensland Derby starting at 16/1 on.

Scobie did us proud

Champion jockey Scobie Breasley headed the jockeys' list in England in 1957. He was the first Australian in 45 years to achieve the feat. Breasley never won a Melbourne Cup, but he did win nearly everything else.

TURF TOPICS

Jockey's day out: Sydney rider Arthur Ward dominated Newmarket day. He won the four top races – Sires on Tulloch, Newmarket on Kings Fair, St Leger on Summalu and Queen's Cup on Redcraze.
Bolter with a difference: There was a bolter with a difference at the Sydney Cup meeting of 1957. Gold Stakes twice charged through the crowd on the flat after breaking through the barrier and bolting. The horse threw jockey Athol Mulley and bolted for five kilometres.
Trans-Tasman battle: The 1957 Wellington Cup was memorable for a home-stretch battle between Aussie Neville Sellwood, on Cardigan, and New Zealand's 11-time champion Bill Broughton on Sombrero. Sombrero got there by half a head from Cardigan.

1957 RESULTS

VRC MELBOURNE CUP (2m)
Straight Draw, 8.5 (N McGrowdie) Trained by JM Mitchell; 3:24.25; Prince Darius, Pandie Sun
AJC SYDNEY CUP (2m)
Electro, 8.8 (D Weir) Trained by JA Haigh; 3:22.4; Aqua Boy, Sombrero
QTC BRISBANE CUP (2m)
Cambridge, 7.9 (N Sellwood) Trained by J Mitchell; 3:21.5; Sombrero, MacDougal
SAJC ADELAIDE CUP (2m)
Borgia, 7.9 (D Coleman) Trained by HG Heagney; 3:29.3; Thaumus, Newstone
WATC PERTH CUP (2m and 11 yds)
Elmsfield, 7.11 (F Moore) Trained by J Wall; 3:27, Fairetha, Fair Remarc
VATC CAULFIELD CUP (12-f)
Tulloch, 7.8 (N Sellwood) Trained by TJ Smith; 2:26.9; Mac's Amber, Sailor's Guide

VRC AUSTRALIAN CUP (2m and 1½-f)
Miss High Caste, 7.8 (N McGrowdie) Trained by A Lopes; 3:475; Beaupa, Lourdale
MVRC WS COX PLATE (10-f)
Redcraze, 9.4 (G Moore) Trained by TJ Smith; 2:05.5; Prince Darius, Pandie Sun
AJC DERBY (12-f)
Tulloch, 8.10 (G Moore) Trained by TJ Smith; 2:29.1; Prince Darius, Turkestan
VRC VICTORIA DERBY (12-f)
Tulloch, 8.10 (G Moore) Trained by TJ Smith; 2:33.5; Prince Darius, Tuki
AJC DONCASTER HANDICAP (1m)
Slogan II, 7.12 (J Thompson) Trained by F Dalton; 1:37.3; Mac's Amber, Fire Dust
BTC DOOMBEN '10 000' (7-f less 93 yds)
Teranyan, 8.4 (G Moore) Trained by L O'Sullivan; 1:17.9; New Joy, Mandingos

VRC NEWMARKET HANDICAP (6-f)
King's Fair, 9.1 (A Ward) Trained by J Mitchell; 1:10; Third Dimension, Copper Year
AJC SIRES' PRODUCE STAKES (7-f)
Tulloch, 8.10 (G Moore) Trained by TJ Smith; 1:25.2; Todman, Prince Darius
VRC SIRES' PRODUCE STAKES (7-f)
Tulloch, 8.10 (A Ward) Trained by TJ Smith; 1:27; Ace High, Gay Saba
VRC GRAND NATIONAL STEEPLECHASE (3m 1-f)
Pedro's Pride, 11.12 (L Moore) Trained by E Miller; 6:6.7; Blacksmith, Akanriver
STC GOLDEN SLIPPER STAKES (6-f)
Todman, 8.7 (N Sellwood) Trained by M McCarten; 1:11.4; Flying Kurana, Concert Star

Tulloch – TJ's tremendous champion

Tulloch – a yearling bargain at 750 guineas.

Above: Tulloch, surely the greatest three-year-old. Right: Tulloch's connections (l–r) T. J. Smith, Evelyn Haley, George Moore and Evelyn Haley Jnr.

Tulloch was a racing phenomenon. It was not only that he won, but the way he won. And when he didn't win he was placed every time but once. He was the epitome of class in a racehorse – the quality that sets racing apart from other sports and brings thousands to the track to bask in it and to see it with their own eyes.

Champions like Tulloch are different. He wasn't bred to be a champion. And with his pronounced sway-back and small stature he didn't look like a champion. He didn't even have the temperament that people would like to think befits a champion – he was ill-tempered and belligerent. And he couldn't pass on his great ability to his progeny since he was a failure at stud.

But what he could do was race – like possibly no other and in feature event after feature event he blitzed horses that were near-champions themselves – Sailor's Guide, Todman, Prince Darius, Dhaulagiri, Lord. It was a great era in Australian racing.

Tulloch was bought by trainer T. J. Smith at the 1965 New Zealand sales. He was one of 17 yearlings purchased and the last to be accepted by stable patrons. His sway-back had deterred most but octogenarian grazier Mr Ern Haley liked his other features and took the bay colt, naming him Tulloch after his mother's birthplace in Scotland.

Tulloch proved a quality two-year-old and won three of his five starts in 1956. In 1957 he began to demonstrate his invincibility over a distance by stunning racegoers with victory over Todman in the 7-furlong Sires' Produce Stakes at Randwick only to be eclipsed by Todman's explosive speed in the (then) 6 furlongs of the Champagne Stakes five days later. However, Tulloch was to go on and become the first horse to win the Sires' Produce Stakes in three states.

But it was from August 1957 until April 1958 that Tulloch strode to legendary status. Nothing could match him as he took the Warwick Farm Stakes, the Rosehill Guineas and the AJC Derby. On to Melbourne, where he effortlessly won the Caulfield Guineas and trainer Smith declared him a certainty for the Caulfield Cup.

And despite the fact that no three-year-old had won the cup for 22 years, bookmakers agreed. For the first time in the history of the race they installed a horse at odds-on. It was looked upon as Tulloch's greatest test.

What followed was one of the most memorable victories of the turf. Tulloch, ridden for the first time by Neville Sellwood because George Moore could not make the weight, was never going to lose. Despite the fast pace throughout, Tulloch cruised toward the lead nearing the home turn. On straightening, Sellwood let him go and the colt's sheer power overwhelmed the leaders in a

few strides. He won easing up in race record time. The ovation was thunderous.

Tulloch was hailed as the greatest since Phar Lap but the drama that was to develop into racing's greatest controversy was just beginning. Although he was entered for the Melbourne Cup (and trainer Smith said that even with the maximum penalty for the colt, the race was a foregone conclusion) owner Haley declared his opposition to running three-year-olds in the race for fear of breaking their heart. Argument raged throughout Australia about whether the horse should or should not run but, despite Smith's urgings, Haley's will prevailed and on 20 October 1957 the horse was scratched from the Melbourne Cup – a race he surely would have won.

Tulloch – at 10/1 on – easily won the Victoria Derby on the opening day of the Cup Carnival, beating Prince Darius by eight lengths. Prince Darius went on to run a gallant second in the Melbourne Cup, confirming Tulloch's mortgage on the race had he run. For good measure, Tulloch won the Fisher Plate from Sailor's Guide on the final day of the Cup Carnival (at 8/1 on), then took out the Queensland Derby (at 16/1 on). At that stage of his career the indomitable colt had a record of 15 wins, including the three Derbys, and six seconds from 21 starts.

Spelled, Tulloch resumed in February

T. J. Smith gazes fondly at his swayback money-spinner.

George Moore, happy with his mount.

1958 when finally luck went the way of Prince Darius who defeated the champion in the St George Stakes at Caulfield. Then came the Queen Elizabeth Stakes, to be run at Flemington in the presence of the Queen Mother and featuring the best three horses in Australia – Tulloch, Prince Darius and Sailor's Guide.

The race lived up to every expectation with the three horses thundering down the Flemington straight locked together. The camera gave the race to Sailor's Guide from Prince Darius with Tulloch third.

But Tulloch was now at his peak and won his next six races as the legend continued to grow. Then tragedy struck – a stomach illness that had him scouring whenever he was put into work saw him forced out of racing for nearly two years. Only patience and skilled veterinary care enabled him to return to full health.

But could he attain his former greatness? Tulloch left no doubt about his recovery when he came back in the 1960 Queen's Plate. The top-class galloper Lord was his main rival and they staged a two-horse war over Flemington's final furlong before Tulloch triumphed by a short half-head – and returned to the most emotion-charged reception in racing history.

So Tulloch was back and continued his winning onslaught with more victories in Sydney, then two seconds before a win in the Craven Stakes. Tulloch was then sent south where – at last – he would contest the Melbourne Cup.

But first came Australia's greatest weight-for-age race – the Cox Plate – against a crackerjack field including the exceptional three-year-old Sky High and Victorian champion Dhaulagiri. Tulloch, although drawing barrier 15 and racing on the tricky Moonee Valley circuit for the first time, won brilliantly from Dhaulagiri. Sky High was unplaced. The time was a new Australasian record.

When the champion easily took the Mackinnon Stakes on Derby Day it really appeared the Melbourne Cup would be at his mercy despite his crushing weight of 10.1 against 31 other runners. Smith would not hear of his being beaten and he went to the post 3/1 favourite.

Tulloch lost – but no horse set the task he was by jockey Neville Sellwood could have won. Tulloch, restrained by Sellwood, was 50 lengths from the leaders with six furlongs to run. When allowed full rein, Tulloch passed 11 horses in the straight and made up 46 lengths to finish seventh. It was to be his only unplaced run.

Tulloch was a champion to the end. He won in Adelaide and was second in the 1961 Sydney Cup. His farewell race was the 1961 Brisbane Cup which he won under 9.12 and again emotions overflowed. Tulloch's earnings totalled a (then) mammoth £220 247 – and he had been bought for a mere 750 guineas. If Tulloch was not the greatest of all time – and many believe he was – he was certainly the best of the modern era. He died on his owner's property on 30 June 1969.

by Ted Cavey

Alan Lambert captures the style of Neville Sellwood on Tulloch in the Fisher Plate, 1960 (DA).

Wiggle gets a wriggle on to win the Stradbroke Handicap at Eagle Farm.

The mighty Sailor's Guide.

Wiggle stars, young jockeys triumph

Nothing seemed more certain – surely Tulloch would dominate racing throughout 1958. It was true that he had not made a winning start but he could not have gone much closer to achieving victory in the St George Stakes (beaten at last by Prince Darius) and in the Queen Elizabeth Stakes (defeated narrowly by Sailor's Guide and Prince Darius in the most stirring of finishes).

But with these runs behind him Tulloch then won his next six starts culminating with a triumph in the Randwick version of the Queen Elizabeth Stakes on 12 April 1958. Then came the shattering news that he had contracted the stomach virus that was to strip two years off his racing life.

With Tulloch – and Todman – off the scene, racing took an entirely different complexion Not that racing is without stars for long. In Sydney, a two-year-old filly with the catchy name of Wiggle was taking all before her. She won four races in a row, including the Champagne Stakes (her sire was not nominated for the Golden Slipper) before travelling north to Brisbane and winning again, at Doomben.

The filly, trained by Ron Shirtliff, was lucky to be racing at all. She had nearly died after becoming entangled in barbed wire as a yearling. She had been named Wiggle by her owner who compared her walk to Marilyn Monroe's famous wiggle in *The Seven Year Itch* but it was galloping for which the horse achieved fame. Her next start resulted in a sixth in the Lightning Stakes at Eagle Farm. Then came one of the most astonishing victories in modern racing. Wiggle took on the older sprinters in the Group One Stradbroke Handicap and beat them to become the first two-year-old winner in nearly 50 years. The headlines labelled her 'The Wonder Filly'.

Wiggle completed a magnificent 1958 by winning the Hobartville Stakes, the Caulfield Guineas, the Edward Manifold and the Linlithgow Stakes. She was to win more good races in 1959, including the Kewney Stakes at Flemington and the Alister Clark Stakes at Moonee Valley before being leased to American interests. She showed her class in the United States by winning six races and breaking two time records.

Sailor's Guide just gets home in the 1958 Queen Elizabeth Stakes at Flemington.

A right royal race

The Queen Mother was at Flemington in 1958 to see the running of the Queen Elizabeth Stakes – and what a race she saw. The event was billed as the race of the year with Tulloch, Sailor's Guide and Prince Darius expected to dominate the field.

And so they did. The three fought out a thrill-packed finish with Bill Williamson on Sailor's Guide riding desperately to hold off first Tulloch and then Prince Darius. The judge called for a photo and gave the verdict to Sailor's Guide over Prince Darius and Tulloch.

Arthur Ward on Prince Darius lodged a protest against the winner. A lengthy hearing followed before it was announced that Sailor's Guide had retained the race.

Buzzie got home in the Inkerman Hcp.

Lou gets Buzzied

'It's been so long, oh! so long' said veteran jockey Lou Francis after he won the Inkerman Handicap aboard Buzzie at Caulfield. Buzzie pinched the race from favourite Pushover. 'It was good to see the winning post looming up again,' he said.

It was his first winner in 10 years, the last being Lord Cavil at Mentone in 1947. Francis had been riding for over 25 years.

Snappers line up for the parade before the 1958 Melbourne Cup.

The bridesmaid Prince

There is every chance Prince Darius would have ranked as an immortal of the turf had he not been so unfortunate as to emerge in the same year as Todman and Tulloch. Not for nothing did he become known as 'Tulloch's Shadow'. He ran second to the champion no fewer than seven times.

Initially, Tulloch beat him in the Canonbury Stakes and he was then third in Todman's first race. Next, he was third to Tulloch and Todman in the Sires' Produce Stakes. A string of seconds to Tulloch followed (including the AJC and Victoria Derbys) but while Tulloch was scratched from the 1957 Melbourne Cup, Prince Darius ran and was beaten by only a neck by Straight Draw.

Prince Darius exacted some revenge over Tulloch by beating him in the St George Stakes of 1958 and again finished in front of him in the Queen Elizabeth Stakes. Prince Darius might still have achieved greatness had he won the 1958 Cox Plate, but he was again second – to another champion in Redcraze.

However, Prince Darius was not solely the bridesmaid. He won a total of 13 races, including two Chelmsford and two Craven Plates, a Colin Stephen Stakes and a City Tattersalls Cup.

TURF TOPICS

Jockey with a future (1): Roy Higgins was still very much a bush rider in 1958 but he made headlines when he had his first city ride, at Moonee Valley. The reason for the interest: Riverina-based Higgins had ridden more winners that season than most of Australia's top riders.

Jockey with a future (2): Pin-up apprentice Geoff Lane served notice of future stardom when he landed five winners at Moonee Valley in December, 1958. Lane was already one of the most popular jockeys in turf history. The crowd gave him a sustained ovation and women racegoers rushed to the scales enclosure to cheer him as he returned.

Skyline's sustained speed: Illness – similar to that suffered by Tulloch – robbed Skyline of the chance of being one of the great racehorses of the century. Skyline was the first horse to win both the Golden Slipper (of 6 furlongs) and the AJC Derby (of 12 furlongs). But it was the way he won that was so exhilarating.

In the 1958 Slipper Skyline was given little chance against the odds-on favourite Misting and started at 25/1. Skyline was one of those rare horses that could keep going at the same fast pace all the way in a race. He was there when Misting weakened and drew away to beat him by a length-and-a-quarter.

In the 1958 Derby Skyline set a new record of 2:28.8, three tenths of a second faster than Tulloch's previous best, and the fastest derby ever run in Australia.

Family affairs: On 4 January, the Hoysteds trained five winners at Moonee Valley – 'Father' Fred, his son N. D. 'Bon' and his nephews Hal and Merv all had winners, with Bon getting a double. A fortnight later, again at Moonee Valley, the family did it again – five winners were shared by Fred with a treble and Bon with a double.

Tulloch has an early morning work-out before a small crowd.

1958 RESULTS

VRC MELBOURNE CUP (2m)
Baystone, 8.9 (M Schumacher) Trained by J Green; 3:21.25; Monte Carlo, Red Pine

AJC SYDNEY CUP (2m)
Straight Draw, 8.13 (N McGrowdie) Trained by JM Mitchell; 3:22; Caranna, Pushover

QTC BRISBANE CUP (2m)
Timor, 8.6 (F Treen) Trained by A Armanasco; 3:20.9; Baystone, Caranna

SAJC ADELAIDE CUP (2m)
Star Aim, 7.5 (T Hoppo) Trained by GA Reid; 3:34; Straight Flight, Watch Out

WATC PERTH CUP (2m and 11 yds)
Fairetha, 7.11 (J Wilson) Trained by AH Jordan; 3:28.25; Tribal Ring, Rendition

VATC CAULFIELD CUP (12-f)
Sir Blink, 7.5 (A Yeomans) Trained by J Godby; 2:28.8; Pandie Sun, Humber Hawk

VRC AUSTRALIAN CUP (2m and 1½-f)
Dream Son, 7.5 (A Yeomans) Trained by H Dale; 3:44.75; Andonnia, Humber Hawk

MVRC WS COX PLATE (10-f)
Yeman, 9.4 (L Whittle) Trained by H Wiggins; 2:16.4; Stormy Passage, Master Rane

AJC DERBY (12-f)
Skyline, 8.10 (M Schumacher) Trained by J Green; 2:28.8; Sir Blink, Prince Kerdieil

VRC VICTORIA DERBY (12-f)
Sir Blink, 8.10 (W Williamson) Trained by J Godby; 2:30.5; Master Rane, But Beautiful

AJC DONCASTER HANDICAP (1m)
Grenoble, 8.5 (N McGrowdie) Trained by F Lewis; 1:35.2; Teranyan, Theodric

BTC DOOMBEN '10000' (7-f less 93 yds)
Grey Ghost, 7.6 (C Kelly) Trained by JW Barker; 1:18.2; Troy, New Joy

VRC NEWMARKET HANDICAP (6-f)
My Hour, 8.9 (W Pyers) Trained by G Jesser; 1:12; New Spec, Zareeba

AJC SIRES' PRODUCE STAKES (7-f)
Man Of Iron, 8.10 (G Moore) Trained by H Plant; 1:24.2; Nilento, Skyline

VRC SIRES' PRODUCE STAKES (7-f)
Misting, 8.10 (A Ward) Trained by V Ryan; 1:25.7; Nilento, Man Of Iron

VRC GRAND NATIONAL STEEPLECHASE (3m 1-f)
Redfield, 10.8 (R Lindsay) Trained by H Myers; 6:7; Penang, Pedro's Pride

STC GOLDEN SLIPPER STAKES (6-f)
Skyline, 8.7 (A Mulley) Trained by J Green; 1:12.7; Misting, Magic Kingdom

Jockeys of 1959, photographed before the 9th Invitation Stakes at Caulfield: Back row from left: R. Hutchinson, W. WIlliamson, R. Maddock, N. Sellwood, G. Lane, W. Pyers, J. Thomspon, J. Johnson, J. Purtell. Front row: R. Selkrig, E. Cox, R. Yeomans, M. Wrigley, G. Podmore, K. Markham.

How 'Hutchy' missed a Cup winner

Ron Hutchinson deservedly ranks with the greats of Australian jockeys. His record was outstanding – premier Melbourne jockey, prolific feature race winner, success at the highest level in Europe …

But by 1959 Hutchinson, who won the Sydney Cup while still an apprentice in 1945, had not ridden a Melbourne Cup winner and it was his desperate desire for this achievement that cost him that year's victory.

Hutchinson seemed well placed as Cup Day neared, as he had the mount on the strong stayer Macdougal, who had won the Brisbane Cup, then the Metropolitan Handicap. But Macdougal became ill on the train trip to Melbourne, then injured a leg during a training gallop at Moonee Valley. Consequently, his chances of a Cup start began to look forlorn.

Naturally, Hutchinson despaired of Macdougal's Cup hopes and accepted the ride on the South Australian stayer Trellios.

Of course, forecasting the future in racing is always hazardous. Macdougal threw off his injury and began working brilliantly.

Came opening day of the Melbourne Cup Carnival and Hutchinson was scheduled to ride both horses in separate Cup preludes – the Mackinnon Stakes and the Hotham Handicap. Trellios won the Mackinnon and Hutchinson confirmed he would ride him in the Cup. However, he then rode Macdougal into second place in the Hotham and, perplexed, said after the race: 'I am convinced Macdougal's run was a better Cup trial than the win by Trellios.'

He was right. Macdougal won the Cup with Pat Glennon in the saddle.

Battling mare

Everything went right when the mare Regal Wench won the Caulfield Cup of 1959. She was the epitome of a battling horse who had one day of glory because it all came together for her and her connections.

Her early form was indifferent, which resulted in her being allotted the featherweight of 6.12 for the cup.

Her jockey was the unfashionable Trevor Dyer – a shy, former country boy light enough for her weight range. Her future amounted to nothing after the Caulfield Cup – she was unplaced in the following Melbourne, Sydney and Brisbane Cups.

But on the day she triumphed. Dyer rode her superbly, Sir Blink (the previous year's winner), who should have won the race, suffered severe interference, and in the end her light weight was the telling factor.

Last race for 'Last-Race Billy'

Punters had a special affection for jockey Billy Cook who retired from the saddle in July 1959. The affection, inspired through their pockets, was largely because of Cook's famous habit of landing the last winner of the day, particularly at Randwick. He had long been known as 'Last-Race Billy'.

Cook began his career after learning about horses while delivering meat by cart. His first big-race winner was Crucis in the Sydney Cup of 1929 and from then on

Cook achieved almost everything possible for a jockey.

He won two Melbourne Cups (on the three-year-old Skipton in 1941 and Rainbird in 1945), a Caulfield Cup (on Amounis in 1930), rode successfully overseas, and won 16 races including another Sydney Cup on his favourite horse Carioca who he said rekindled his interest in racing. In 1939–40, Cook set the longstanding Sydney riding record of 124 winners and three dead-heats in taking the first of four jockeys' premierships. Cook's son Peter later duplicated his father's feat of riding two Melbourne Cup winners. Billy Cook died in 1985.

All eyes on Fine and Dandy.

Two fine gallopers

Fine and Dandy – winner of the 1959 Golden Slipper – was an exceptional young sprinter who went on to become one of Australia's top milers. In fact, his best wins, the Slipper and the 1963 Doncaster, were four years apart. In between Fine and Dandy won the 1961 Doncaster.

Interestingly, one of the horses Fine and Dandy beat in the 1959 Slipper was Todman's full brother Noholme, who was to go on to have a magnificent year.

Noholme made amends for his Slipper defeat by winning the Champagne Stakes and then coming back in the spring to win the Epsom in 1:34.9 – the fastest time run by a three-year-old for a mile in Australia. Noholme was also the first three-year-old to win the race in the 20th century.

Sent to Melbourne, Noholme was narrowly beaten in the Caulfield Guineas but stamped himself as a champion by winning the Cox Plate by four lengths – again in record time. He then took out the Linlithgow Stakes and the CB Fisher Plate.

Noholme later had an outstanding career at stud in America where, among other successes, he produced the then world record of 24 individual two-year-old winners.

Sir Frank Packer and Neville Sellwood.

Martello mishap

The 'grey streak', Martello Towers, burst onto the Australian racing scene in 1959 with exciting victories in the Hobartville Stakes, Canterbury Guineas, Rosehill Guineas and AJC Derby.

He thus became the first three-year-old to win the four races and was the first grey in history to win the Derby.

Martello Towers was hailed as the likely star of the spring when he was sent to Melbourne. He was surprisingly beaten out of a place in the Caulfield Guineas but still went into the Victoria Derby a 10/9 favourite.

However, he was injured at the barrier and limped home last. The big crowd vented their anger at both Martello Tower's failure and the winner Travel Boy who had failed in the Cox Plate the previous Saturday when 5/2 favourite.

TURF TOPICS

Deadpan Bill fires: In October 1959 Bill Williamson became the first jockey in more than 100 years to ride five winners in one day at Flemington … but poker-faced Bill still didn't crack a smile. Even when punters in the crowd called 'Come on, Bill, give us a smile', he only touched his cap. The deadpan expression was the trademark of the champion jockey who was also known as 'Wearie Willie'.

A long-shot double: A Deniliquin grazier who made a special trip to Flemington races in August 1959 laid claim to a unique sporting double – riding a winner at Moonee Valley races and playing League (Australian Rules) football in the same afternoon.

He was Mr Cyril Gove, who rode as an amateur, won the first race on the Moonee Valley program on 30 September 1911, then changed clothes and dashed off to East Melbourne to play on the wing with Essendon in a Victorian Football League semi-final.

Lord of Caulfield: The grand galloper Lord confirmed his liking for the Caulfield track when he won his second Caulfield Stakes in 1959. He was to go on and dead-heat for first in the race the following year and was on his way to winning the Memsie Stakes at the track for four successive years.

Tragedy for jumps jockey: There was no better cross country jockey in Australia than Brian Smith – his record over the obstacles was magnificent. As well as winning almost every feature jumping race on the calendar, he once rode the 'card' – the treble of jumps events one day at Flemington. Smith retired in 1954 but after incurring business losses returned to the saddle and rode as well as ever. But tragedy struck in 1959 when he suffered shocking head injuries in a fall at Geelong.

1959 RESULTS

VRC MELBOURNE CUP (2m)
Macdougal, 8.11 (P Glennon) Trained by RW Roden; 3:23; Nethergold, White Hills

AJC SYDNEY CUP (2m)
On Line, 7.13 (B Howlett) Trained by F McGrath; 3:30.9; Foxmara, Bardshah

QTC BRISBANE CUP (2m)
MacDougal, 7.11 (R Hutchinson) Trained by R Roden; 3:22.4; Grand Garry, Baystone

SAJC ADELAIDE CUP (2m)
Mac, 7.12 (B Quinlan) Trained by Al Munro; 3:24; Stormy Passage, Morloc

WATC PERTH CUP (2m and 11 yds)
Fairetha, 8.7 (J Wilson) Trained by AH Jordan; 3:28; Zaica, Friar's Luck

VATC CAULFIELD CUP(12-f)
Regal Wench, 7.0 (T Dyer) Trained by WJ Murrell; 2:28.7; Sir Blink, Trellios

VRC AUSTRALIAN CUP (2m and 1½-f)
Gaybao, 8.0 (N Sellwood) Trained by O Lynch; 3:53; Regal Wench, Sir Akron

MVRC WS COX PLATE (10-f)
Noholme, 7.11 (N Sellwood) Trained by M McCarten; 2:02.7; Grand Jury, Prince Lea

AJC DERBY (12-f)
Martello Towers, 8.10 (G Podmore) Trained by ED Lawson; 2:32.4; Travel Boy, Polo Prince

VRC VICTORIA DERBY (12-f)
Travel Boy, 8.10 (R Selkrig) Trained by TJ Smith; 2:34; Ringleader, Roman Reveller

AJC DONCASTER HANDICAP (1m)
Tudor Hill, 8.11 (G Howard) Trained by N Francis; 1:36.3; On Guard, Book Link

BTC DOOMBEN '10 000' (7-f less 93 yds)
Second Earl, 8.6 (A Tindall) Trained by W Clifton; 1:17.8; Blue Dart, Squander Lad

VRC NEWMARKET HANDICAP (6-f)
Gold stakes, 9.6 (R Hutchinson) Trained by J Green; 1:13; Lady Cortauld, Tudor Hill

AJC SIRES' PRODUCE STAKES (7-f)
Fine And Dandy, 8.10 (G Podmore) Trained by H Plant; 1:24.6; Travel Boy, Ramazan

VRC SIRES' PRODUCE STAKES (7-f)
Travel Boy, 8.10 (N Sellwood) Trained by TJ Smith; 1:28.5; Prince Lea, Snow Flower

VRC GRAND NATIONAL STEEPLECHASE (3m 1-f)
Irish Sun, 10.0 (B Smith) Trained by H Myers; 5:58.5; Tranquil Glow, Count Con

STC GOLDEN SLIPPER STAKES (6-f)
Fine And Dandy, 8.7 (J Thompson) Trained by H Plant; 1:12.8; Akimbo, Morning Star

The packed field passes the stands for the first time in the Centenary Cup.

Tulloch fails in Centenary Melbourne Cup

If the 100th running of the Melbourne Cup could have been scripted to perfection, there would have been one result – Tulloch, the horse deserving to be ranked with Carbine and Phar Lap, would have won amid unprecedented fanfare.

In addition, Tulloch's victory would have topped off the Centenary Melbourne Cup, the preparations for which the VRC had spared no expense. And Tulloch was not just the sentimental favourite. He had earned top place in the betting with a stunning comeback from illness – any doubts had been obliterated by his winning the Cox Plate, Australia's richest weight-for-age race, 10 days earlier with his usual authority. For good measure he had just as easily taken the Mackinnon Stakes on Derby Day. Despite his burden of 10.1, the Cup looked to be at his mercy.

Certainly, that was the belief of most of Australia right until the 32-horse field jumped away on that first Tuesday in November. Minutes later, it was a different matter. In a ride that has been trenchantly criticised, jockey Neville Sellwood held Tulloch up for so long that the champion faced an impossible task to win from so far back in the field. As it was, he made up an astonishing 46 lengths in the final six furlongs to finish seventh. For the first and only time in his eminent career, he was unplaced.

So a fairytale finish to the Centenary Cup – the Cup for which Flemington had been altered and transformed and which was to be the showpiece of a carnival named 'The Festival of Fashions, Flowers & Favourites' – was not to be. Instead of the thunderous ovation that would have been accorded a Tulloch victory, the winner that year returned to the quietest reception in memory. And far from being a favourite or near-favourite, she was a neglected 50/1 outsider.

In truth, the winning mare, New Zealand Hi Jinx, would have been the last horse a scriptwriter would have chosen to spearhead the celebrated event. She had been labelled 'the ugliest thoroughbred in the field of 32 horses'; she had failed ignominiously in the Caulfield Cup; she had been so shockingly injured as a two-year-old she had been saved only for her stud value; connections gave her no chance of beating Tulloch – and she did not win another race after the Cup.

So race-followers understandably ignored Hi Jinx. So how did she – how could she – join the immortals of the turf and win the 1960 Melbourne Cup? Well, in retrospect there were some factors in her favour. After the Caulfield Cup she had run an exceptional race in the Moonee Valley Cup, finishing second to the highly rated Mac in fast time; she had obviously 'peaked' at precisely the right time; she had to carry only 7.10 compared with Tulloch's 10.1, and she had the services of the highly capable lightweight jockey W. A. Smith, a Victorian who had ridden in New Zealand for the previous five years.

It could also be that Smith's great ride won the race. He said later: 'Somewhere around the nine-furlong post I was behind a wall of horses and wondering how I was going to get out. Then one moved out and left a gap for me. I pushed up inside five or six horses and got up behind Valerius. I followed him then, and he was ridden a treat by Jack Thompson. I followed him to the home turn, then pulled out. I was confident a furlong and a half out that Hi Jinx would win.'

Meanwhile, second favourite Ilumquh, with Bill Williamson aboard, had been hopelessly pocketed until well into the straight. Seeing daylight, he flew and was in front just past the post. But, at the judge, Hi Jinx got the verdict by a half-neck from Howsie (Jack Purtell) and Ilumquh. Purtell was urged to protest but declined. However, he said later: 'I couldn't use my whip to full advantage and that might have made a little bit of difference, but I felt he was giving everything.'

The hard luck stories flew thick and fast – Sellwood said Tulloch had been sluggish from the start and that he had held him up because he thought the weight would beat him if he didn't – but all that really mattered was that Hi Jinx had won.

W. A. Smith and Hi Jinx.

Sky High easily beats Wenona Girl in the Golden Slipper Stakes at Rosehill.

The 'Sky' was the limit

In a widely quoted interview, the 'Prince of Punters' Perce Galea once counselled adherents with the rhetorical question: 'Why take 6/4 about a mongrel (mid-week) when you can take 6/4 about a Sky High on a Saturday?' If Galea wanted to name a champion of an era he could have made no better choice than the magnificent son of Star Kingdom who took all before him as a three-year-old in 1960.

When Sky High won the Golden Slipper that year it was simply the beginning of a career characterised by toughness and a resolute will-to-win. Sky High was a brilliant sprinter, winning two Lightning Stakes. His trainer, Jack Green, wanted him to be a stayer. Consequently, he became the only Slipper winner to run in a Melbourne Cup. (He was unplaced.) But in the years after the Slipper Sky High went on to break more records than the brilliant Todman, win as many races as the mighty Manikato and stage memorable racetrack duels with the great horses of the era – Wenona Girl, Aquanita, Fine and Dandy and Dhauligiri among them.

Sky High was partnered in his Golden Slipper win by Athol 'George' Mulley who once described him as 'a bugger of a horse'.

Mulley also said: 'The first thing you learned about Sky High was to grab a handful of mane as soon as you jumped on his back. He would rear up, wheel around, do anything to try and throw you. He wasn't savage but he was headstrong. Still, you can forgive a horse when he raced like Sky High.'

In the spring following the Slipper, doubts about Sky High's future emerged when he failed to win in six starts but he showed his ability by leading all the way in the 1960 Victoria Derby and then just failed to beat Aquanita in the George Adams Handicap.

Sky High's record after that was impeccable as he went on to win top races at most distances – and in exceptional times. His 10 victories as a four-year-old included the Epsom, the Rawson Stakes and the Chipping Norton Stakes.

As a five-year-old his eight wins included another Rawson Stakes, the Canterbury Stakes, and the Warwick Farm Stakes. The one chink in his armour was the tricky circuit at Moonee Valley where he was never happy yet still managed a courageous third in the 1961 Cox Plate. He later went to stud in Australia and the United States.

TURF TOPICS

Lady liked it wet: If ever a filly dominated a spring carnival, it was the Arthur Smerdon–trained Lady Sybil in 1960. Lady Sybil liked wet tracks and got them in abundance that year. She thrashed Misty View by six lengths in the Berwick Handicap. With young Roy Higgins aboard, she beat Samson in the Moonee Valley Stakes.

Then came a stunning victory in the Edward Manifold Stakes when, ridden this time by Geoff Lane, she won by 10 lengths. Lady Sybil beat the mighty Sky High in the Caulfield Guineas, starting 9/4 favourite with Higgins again in the saddle, and winning by three lengths.

Wenona Girl ended her winning run in the Thousand Guineas, but Lady Sybil had her revenge in the VRC Oaks. She led all the way to beat Smokeview with Wenona Girl third.

Summer mares stay: It started with Foglia D'Oro, who sneaked away to a big lead in the 1959 New Zealand Cup and hung on to win. It continued when Marie Brizard, a little bay mare from Te Aroha, won the Auckland Cup on New Year's Day 1960. And a remarkable clean sweep by mares of New Zealand's Big Three staying races was completed when Dave Arnott, Marie Brizard's trainer, lined up stablemate Jalna to win the 1960 Wellington Cup. In the 1960s a fourth two-mile handicap was run in New Zealand, the Autumn Handicap at Trentham in March. And in 1960 it was won by Ma Cherie – of course, she was another mare.

Dan Lewis dies: Eccentric NZ-born trainer Dan Lewis, died. He kept goats in his stable because he thought they kept disease away from his horses. He trained five Sydney Cup winners, two Metropolitans and two Derbys.

1960 RESULTS

VRC MELBOURNE CUP (2m)
Hi Jinx, 7.10 (WA Smith) Trained by TH Knoeles; 3:23.25; Howais, Ilumguh
AJC SYDNEY CUP (2m)
Grand Garry, 8.8 (N Sellwood) Trained by TJ Smith; 3:30.7; Valerius, Melroy
QTC BRISBANE CUP (2m)
Valerius, 8.12 (J Thompson) Trained by F Dalton; 3:21.2; Essayist, Dow Street
SAJC ADELAIDE CUP (2m)
Lourdale, 7.3 (K Ford) Trained by R Dini; 3:35.8; San Pasqual, Trellios
WATC PERTH CUP (2m and 11 yds)
Rendition, 7.7 (R Oliver) Trained by RH Treffone; 3:28.2; Brown Express, Cunderdin
VATC CAULFIELD CUP (12-f)
Ilumguh, 8.0 (W Williamson) Trained by E Rophia; 2:27.9; Dhaulagiri, Mac

VRC AUSTRALIAN CUP (2m and 1 ½-f)
Illoura, 7.7 (F Treen) Trained by W Preston; 3:43; dead-heat second Joss Sticks and Prince Dahorney
MVRC WS COX PLATE (10-f)
Tulloch, 7.11 (N Sellwood) Trained by TJ Smith; 2:01.1; Dhaulagiri, Persian Lyric
AJC DERBY (12-f)
Persian Lyric, 8.10 (A Mulley) Trained by J Cook; 2:30.6; Le Storm, Sky High
VRC VICTORIA DERBY (12-f)
Sky High, 8.10 (N Sellwood) Trained by J Green; 2:32; Persian Lyric, Myzami
AJC DONCASTER HANDICAP (1m)
Tudor Hill, 9.0 (G Howard) Trained by N Francis; 1:35; In Love, Prince Lea
BTC DOOMBEN '10 000' (7-f less 93 yds)
In Love, 8.11 (N Sellwood) Trained by F Allotta; 1:18.4; Queen Of The May, Second Earl

VRC NEWMARKET HANDICAP (6-f)
Correct, 7.7 (L Harbridge) Trained by GM Hanlon; 1:11.2; Anonyme, Merry Polly
AJC SIRES' PRODUCE STAKES (7-f)
Wenona Girl, 8.8 (N Sellwood) Trained by M McCarten; 1:24.4; Persian Lyric, Sky High
VRC SIRES' PRODUCE STAKES (7-f)
Wenona Girl, 8.7 (N Sellwood) Trained by M McCarten; 1:24.7; Dalby, Impulsive
VRC GRAND NATIONAL STEEPLECHASE (3m 1-f)
Blacksmith, 9.2 (L Knaggs) Trained by R Fisher; 5:59.7; Mudeet, Lord Toby
STC GOLDEN SLIPPER STAKES (6-f)
Sky High, 8.7 (A Mulley) Trained by J Green; 1:11.9; Wenona Girl, Impulsive

Above: The phones are running hot. Right: Day one at High Street, Reservoir, Victoria.

The TAB transforms racing

The 11th of March 1961 was the date that changed the face of racing in Australia forever. On that day legal off-course betting became a reality in this country when the Victorian TAB opened 13 agencies in Melbourne and country centres. This long-awaited event was to have far-reaching ramifications for racing and indeed for society itself – effects that are still being felt as racing attendances at all but major meetings decline while gambling revenues continue to grow.

In 1961, illegal off-course betting was widespread in Victoria (and throughout Australia) and had been since the days depicted so romantically but accurately in Frank Hardy's novel *Power Without Glory* about John West's Carringbush tote. For decades, SP (starting price) betting had been rife in pubs, back lanes and, really, any appropriately vacant premises.

The trouble was, of course, that while punters bet on races at Flemington, Caulfield,

Greg Taylor places a bet.

Moonee Valley and other tracks now closed, the racing industry received none of the money being so enthusiastically exchanged. Crime and corruption proliferated. The era might have had its romantic side – 'cockatoos' posted to watch for police, Keystone Cops–style raids, gambling being lambasted from the pulpits – but the social problems that resulted and the extent of the turnover by illegal bookies finally forced the Victorian government to act.

A study was made of the off-course betting system that had been set up in New Zealand; then a Royal Commission was convened with submissions being heard from 15 October 1958 to 18 December that year. Evidence was given that turnover by illegal bookmakers was as high as $324 million a year – revenue going begging that any government would have been derelict to ignore, but the other side of the issue was that the demand was obviously there. Many people enjoyed having a small financial interest on a horse but were unable or unwilling to attend a race meeting for the privilege.

Legalised off-course betting was championed by the chairman of the Victoria Racing Club, Sir Chester Manifold, who campaigned for it tirelessly. His powers of persuasion won through. Subsequently, legislation was passed to form a Totalisator Agency Board (Sir Chester became the first chairman) whose agenda was to establish agencies where cash betting facilities would be available in an atmosphere similar to a bank – sombre and sober. The intent was to provide a service for punters without encouraging the spread of gambling. Hence, there would be no live broadcasts of races and winning dividends were not to be broadcast until after the last race was completed. There was certainly to be no attraction for people to loiter on or near the premises and it was also stipulated that

agencies were not to be situated near schools or churches.

The early agencies were primitive by today's standards. Punters called their bets to clerks who laboriously wrote each bet manually. Queues of patient punters often extended on to footpaths. At first, betting was confined to win and/or place. It was not until the following year – on 14 April 1962 – that exotic betting was introduced in the form of a daily double.

Soon most suburbs and country centres had TAB agencies. SP bookmaking lingered for some years but as patronage of the TAB escalated it all but disappeared. Naturally, even on-course bookmakers – considered a vital, colourful part of Australian racing – suffered financially as the success of the TAB grew.

And grow it did. As the years passed computerised machines replaced manual ticket markers, expanded exotic betting – quinellas, trios, trifectas, quadrellas, even mystery bets – flourished, and sophisticated marketing drives – the Lucky Shop among them – urged gambling-loving Australians to embrace the TAB as never before. In the meantime, legal bookmakers launched spasmodic campaigns to convince people they would get better returns pitting themselves against the man rather than the machine.

Not surprisingly, TAB turnover, materially assisted by telephone betting, mounted year by year as antiquated betting restrictions at agencies were gradually lifted – to the point where agencies became what earlier state governments had vowed they never would – modern-day betting shops.

Through it all, punters continued as they have for centuries, taking the losses due to poor judgement, form reversals, bad luck in running and plain slow horses with the thrill of occasional collects.

Mel Schumacher's mount Blue Era (inside) and Summer Fair race for the line in the AJC Derby.

The fateful leg-pull was clearly seen head-on.

'I know when someone's pulling my leg,' says jockey

Sensational happenings aren't rare in horse racing, since jockeys have to make split-second decisions that mean the difference between winning and losing. But the 'leg-pull' incident involving a gifted young jockey Mel Schumacher goes down in Australian racing annals as the most extraordinary of all.

Schumacher, 24, and already a Melbourne Cup–winning jockey, paid dearly. He was disqualified for life, although the sentence was reduced on appeal to 10 years.

It was Schumacher's desperate will to win that provoked the incident. The race was the AJC Derby at Randwick. Schumacher was aboard Blue Era, which had been solidly backed in to 11/2, while veteran jockey Tommy Hill was riding the 7/1 chance Summer Fair. With 100 metres to run, Blue Era and Summer Fair had forged ahead of the favourite King Brian and were locked in a head-and-head battle.

Within a dozen strides of the post, Summer Fair hit the front narrowly, but Blue Era fought back, came again and the horses hit the line together.

A verdict was impossible to the naked eye but the camera gave the race to Blue Era – and Schumacher's superior strength in the finish appeared to have triumphed.

But as the horses returned to scale it was obvious all was not well. Tommy Hill, whose face was described as looking like a thunderstorm about to erupt, called out: 'Protest! Protest!' Barely able to contain himself in the stewards' room, he said: 'Schumacher grabbed my leg and held on to it for 50 yards.'

Schumacher, described as looking at his most innocent, called the allegation 'preposterous' and added: 'My fellow did lay in a bit but I did not hold Hill by the leg.' But Hill was furiously adamant. 'I'm a man of 34 and I know when somebody is holding my leg,' he said.

The head-on camera verified Hill's claim. The film clearly showed Schumacher extending his left arm and grabbing Hill's leg at the 100-yards mark. He had held on tightly for the next 50 yards, then released his grip. Then as the horses were about to reach the post he had again grabbed Hill's leg, levering his mount forward while restraining Summer Fair. Blue Era had snatched the race but the victory was short-lived. The protest was, of course, upheld.

Then another sensation. The AJC stewards took the unusual step of announcing over the public address system that Schumacher was disqualified for life immediately and could not even fulfil his riding engagements for the day.

Schumacher showed his great talent when he returned to the saddle after serving 5½ years. Based in Brisbane, he won the QTC Grand Prix on Lord Randolph in 1975 and the Doomben One Hundred Thousand on Charlton Boy in 1975.

The chief steward conducts a search for batteries before the start of a Doomben race (NP).

The blooming of Lord Fury

Rags-to-riches stories abound in the history of the Australian turf but few match the rise of a poorly performed Sydney welter horse who came from obscurity to be the star of the 1961 Cups Carnival. The horse was called Lord Fury – a name two months before the Cups few in even his home state had heard of, let alone racing adherents in Melbourne.

The four-year-old was a late bloomer. After plodding performances in nondescript Saturday-class races in Sydney, Lord Fury came out and won the Group 2 Hill Stakes run at Rosehill in September. It was a solid performance but widely regarded as one of those racing aberrations. However, when at his next start he was a fast-finishing third in the Epsom behind the champion miler Sky High, bookmakers began to look at Lord Fury with new respect. His new-found ability was confirmed when he won the Colin Stephen Stakes by a meritorious 12 lengths.

Suddenly, it seemed Lord Fury was a weight-for-age horse but his previous form had been so lacklustre he had been given a healthy 20 lb under the WFA scale for the Caulfield Cup, giving him the luxury weight of 7.8. His owner, Mr Norm Cohen, could hardly believe his good fortune and was understandably confident that Lord Fury would walk-in on Cup Day.

As it turned out, only the talented Summer Fair (of leg-pull incident fame) came between Lord Fury and Caulfield Cup triumph. But it was a great race. Weight of money meant Lord Fury started the popular elect but the sentimental favourite was the popular local horse Dhaulagiri, trained by Brian Courtney and ridden by the 'golden boy' Geoff Lane. But Summer Fair, ridden by the hugely successful lightweight, W. A. Smith, won by a length and a half. So the spotlight swung back to Summer Fair. However, the colt developed a splint and was not to race again as a three-year-old. So, with the Caulfield Cup winner out, Lord Fury was a strong fancy for the Melbourne Cup, but then confounded everyone by running an inglorious last in the Mackinnon Stakes on Derby Day.

But, as happens frequently, Mackinnon form can be deceiving, particularly when assessing the performance of class horses over handicappers. Relishing being back on the luxury weight of only 7.7, Lord Fury led the Melbourne Cup field from the start and was never going to lose. Five lengths clear at the turn, he careered down the long straight under a tight hold to win in the record-equalling time of 3:19½. Grand Print was second and the gallant Dhaulagiri third. As always in racing there was the lucky and the luckless. Jockey Ray Selkrig had an armchair ride to win the Cup but only got the mount when Bernie Howlett was disqualified for having caused interference in the Caulfield Cup.

Hollywood George

It was in June 1961 that Sydney racing authorities finally took action to curtail the racetrack career of flamboyant punter George Edser. The man who had been labelled 'Hollywood George' was banned by the Australian Jockey Club committee from owning or having an interest in any racehorse in New South Wales. Then he was officially warned off all racecourses as an undesirable person, which meant he could not step on to any racecourse in the world.

Edser had been a professional punter since he was 16 and regularly hit the headlines with his spectacular betting. During the 1950s he had sold everything he owned and bet £22 000 on Prince Marni at Rosehill. He collected when Prince Marni – which firmed from 4/7 to 2/9 – won a three-horse race by a lip. A few years later Edser won $100 000 when Tudor Hill took out a Doncaster.

The warning off did not stop Edser, who continued his betting plunges. He was frequently pictured watching the races from elevated vantage points outside the tracks. Five years after the AJC acted against him, Edser's Vaucluse home was raided by police who found his garage stacked with stolen liquor. Edser later pleaded guilty to receiving stolen goods and was told by a judge he was lucky to escape a jail term. In 1979 Edser, then 61, finally had his ban lifted by the AJC and Hollywood George was again back in action on Sydney racetracks.

1961 RESULTS

VRC MELBOURNE CUP (2m)
Lord Fy, 7.8 (R Selkrig) Trained by FB Lewis; 3:19.25; Grand Print, Dhaulagiri
AJC SYDNEY CUP (2m)
Sharply, 7.9 (B Howlett) Trained by WJ Elliott; 3:24.9; Tulloch, Rimyll
QTC BRISBANE CUP (2m)
Tulloch, 9.12 (G Moore) Trained by TJ Smith; 3:22.7; Sharply, Drumcondra
SAJC ADELAIDE CUP (2m)
Far Away Places, 7.3 (D Coleman) Trained by W Tait; 3:26.4; Torlete, Overproof
WATC PERTH CUP (2m)
England's Dust, 8.10 (M Lea) Trained by A Bowden; 3:25.25; Thompson's Bay, Kilfinane
VATC CAULFIELD CUP(12-f)
Summer Fair, 7.7 (WA Smith) Trained by LJ O'Sullivan; 2:28; Lord Fy, Dhaulagiri

VRC AUSTRALIAN CUP (2m and 1½-f)
Dream King, 7.11 (M Schumacher) Trained by M Barnes; 3:41.5; Chatoul, Contador
MVRC WS COX PLATE (10-f)
Dhaulagiri, 9.4 (G Lane) Trained by B Courtney; 2:04.8; New Statesman, Sky High
AJC DERBY (12-f)
Summer Fair, 8.10 (T Hill) Trained by L O'Sullivan; 2:32.2; Blue Era, King Brian
VRC VICTORIA DERBY (12-f)
New Statesman, 8.10 (G Lane) Trained by B Courtney; 2:30.75; Blue Era, Sometime
AJC DONCASTER HANDICAP (1m)
Fine And Dandy, 8.10 (K Smith) Trained by H Plant; 1:34.2; Friar's Peak, Sky High
BTC DOOMBEN '10 000' (7-f less 93 yds)
Aquanita, 9.0 (M Schumacher) Trained by R Shaw; 1:17.7; Prince Lea, Goldent

VRC NEWMARKET HANDICAP (6-f)
Correct, 8.1 (N Sellwood) Trained by GM Hanlon; 1:11; Gabonia, My Peak
AJC SIRES' PRODUCE STAKES (7-f)
Young Brolga, 8.10 (D Weir) Trained by M McCarten; 1:22.8; Commanding, Magic Night
VRC SIRES' PRODUCE STAKES (7-f)
Emblem, 8.7 (N Sellwood) Trained by R Roden; 1:24.75; Indian Summer, Heir Apparent
VRC GRAND NATIONAL STEEPLECHASE (3m 1-f)
Odd Boots, 9.0 (A Hollands) Trained by H Myers; 6:20.5; Mudeet, Struan Mist
STC GOLDEN SLIPPER STAKES (6-f)
Magic Night, 8.0 (M Schumacher) Trained by H Plant; 1:11.9; Young Brolga, Commanding

A crowd of enthusiastic punters watches the Doomben Ten Thousand in 1967 (BP).

Urgers, emus, gorillas and Angora goats

The language of racing is the language of desperates, of the clerisy of punters; by turns it is arcane and blunt, ornate and droll. Its sources are instructively various. General slang has been appropriated by the racecourse and taken on peculiar inflections. Thus 'mug punter' (meaning punter) has a poignant resonance, while 'mug' is mere disparagement. Then there is slang specific to the track and to its illegal off-course corollaries, betting shops. An 'emu' is an inveterate scrounger, a collector of betting tickets which he or she hopes may be 'live'. A 'cockatoo' was the office of look-out for the SP bookmaker, a vocation that the TAB made redundant and that pliable police ensured was never too strenuous.

The technical vocabulary of gambling is a mystery to outsiders, who ruin big race days for regular punters by asking what 'all-up' or 'quinella' or 'double' means. Racing slang is a language that these tyros will never learn to speak, or understand. Not that it all belongs to an earlier time, fondly preserved in the shared speech of ageing punters. As Barry Humphries invented slang (as in the majestic but now anachronistic simile for inebriation: 'as full as two race trains') and then gave it to the Australian people as if it had always been theirs, so racecallers in particular have by their own inventive flashes of wit enriched the language.

The most 'colourful' callers – Ken Howard and Bert Bryant – working in the glory days of racing radio, were willing to 'talk through their kicks' like punters, rather than pontificate as mouthpieces for the racing industry. Howard's signature for a certainty in running – 'London to a brick on' – did not save him from calling both the Epsom and Derby photo finishes wrong on the same day in 1968. Bryant spoke of horses labouring at the rear of the field 'seeing more tails than Hoffman', or so far behind that they would be in after dark and need the services of a 'black tracker with a hurricane lamp' to get them home.

Bryant and Howard refreshed the Australian vernacular. Their comic performances were far from the flabby euphuism of some latter-day commentators, who speak of good horses as 'equine marvels', of the jockey's whip as the 'shillelagh' when 'persuader' would do. There is one strand of neologism in the language of racing which has insinuated itself in the guise of technical explanation. But when we hear or read of an 'autumn horse' (because it keeps failing in the spring) or of horses 'jarring up' (because the track is faster than they like) we are – after all – only in the most familiar racing domain of all: the excuse.

Some of the most memorable racing language is in the optative mood. When an 'urger' (he who makes a living by tipping unwary punters any number of different horses in a race and then seeks a sling from the winner) assures one that this horse is a 'bank-teller's job' beware. Decoded, this means that it is such a good thing that a bank-teller could steal funds on Friday, invest them on Saturday, keep the profit and return the rest on Monday. But things may not go to plan. The hapless jockey might find himself 'snookered' or – improbably – might 'ride the horse too well'. And still lose. Worse, the horse may have been 'hooked' or have run in a 'boat race', a rigged event with only one trier. Besides the sound of ripped betting tickets, punters will swear to have heard 'the swishing of oars'.

Once bookies 'welshed' or 'scaled' (returning stake money and an IOU – this led to 'Big Mick' McLeod being beaten to death on Grand National Steeplechase day in 1906). Now they are quietly disappearing. Some racing language rejoices in being esoteric, at least when money is at issue. Thus a 'gizzard' is the guts of a 'monkey' (that is, $250 of $500), a 'gorilla' is $1000, or twice the size of a monkey. Slang drifts away from the track as well as on to it. Once there were 'horses for courses', Doomben specialists like Chief de Beers; now the phrase also refers to the capricious policy of the Australian cricket selectors. Racing slang changes meaning in other ways. The 'get-out race', the final chance to redeem the ruins of a day on the punt, was traditionally the last in Perth; now it is likely to be the concluding event on the card of the night meeting at Toowoomba.

And, of course, slang often rhymes: 'Angora' (goat) for tote; 'drum' for running a place (from 'drum and mace'); 'El Golea' (after the good racehorse who survived an attempted nobbling by shotgun) for a well-merited or desperately needed refreshment; 'goose's neck' for a promised form of payment that cannot be regarded as altogether reliable; 'Oxford scholar' for one of the kinds of racecourse currency. The other is the tip.

The language of racing conjures a world of unquenchable hope, while at the same time revealing the malign workings of fortune from which no one is immune. Jockeys 'pull the wrong rein' by passing up the ride on a horse that subsequently wins; punters are all too frequently 'flyblown'; horses 'cop a prat' or go 'via the Cape'; the 'rent bet' fails to deliver and the 'steed' (a shabby genteelism better avoided) that 'the dogs are barking' turns out to be a 'cat'. The language of racing is therefore, in large part, the richly inventive means by which mugs and desperates, urgers and touts, cope with the nature of racing.

by Peter Pierce

Jockey Les Coles, New Zealand 'pea king' James Wattie and trainer A. McGregor are all smiles.

So easy for Even Stevens

New Zealand horses had been taking out the rich Cups in Australia for so long it was no longer big news when another did so in 1962. No, it was the consummate ease with which dual winner Even Stevens captured the events that was the big story. Even Stevens was so superior he won as he liked.

He was in danger of being balloted out of the Caulfield Cup in which he had only 7.8. He was lucky; four late scratchings due to the heavy track let him into the race – if race it can be called. The ease of Even Stevens's win even surprised jockey Les Coles who said after the event he was certain of winning at every stage of the Cup. Even Stevens simply moved through the field and gathered in the two leaders while still on the bit.

On Melbourne Cup Day, Even Stevens went into the big two-miler a 3/1 favourite.

The VRC handicapper had given Even Stevens the maximum penalty of 10 lb after the Caulfield Cup, but it hadn't been the light weight that had won it. It was sheer ability. So the Melbourne Cup was a virtual repeat of the Caulfield Cup. In second place was the sentimental favourite, Comicquita.

Even Stevens went on to take out the weight-for-age CB Fisher Plate on the final day of the Melbourne Cup Carnival – once more winning by a space – then, amazingly, went home to New Zealand and continued racing without a spell. He won his first race and was narrowly beaten in two others. His owner, wealthy frozen foods manufacturer Sir James Wattie, then leased Even Stevens to the Queen Mother but the horse never raced for her. He fractured a sesamoid bone in training and was retired to stud.

Above: A publicity shot for the Spring Racing Carnival, featuring Miss Australia 1962, Patricia Reschke.

Below: The Victorian Tourist Authority's poster of a jockey without a horse attracted visitors to the Melbourne Cup meeting. The jockey was Geoff Lane.

Naughty Aquanita, fierce stallion from the West

Aquanita, one of the best thoroughbreds to come out of Western Australia, was not a horse to be trifled with. Handsome, but big and belligerent, he would savage other horses when the mood took him. But he was all class, a great weight carrier and 1962 was his big year.

In the autumn he lumped 55.5 kg to take out the Futurity, beating Anonyme, then in the Spring won the Cox Plate, the Turnbull Stakes and the Mackinnon Stakes beating Sky High and New Statesman. Aquanita could sprint – as shown by his Newmarket fourth – and stay. His third in the 1962 Melbourne Cup underscored his great versatility. He was retired to stud after leg problems ended his racing career.

SEE YOU AT THE

MELBOURNE CUP

VICTORIA AUSTRALIA

The great Neville Sellwood.

Sellwood with trainer Maurice McCarten.

Death on the racetrack

On 7 November 1962 the racing world was shocked by the news that top jockey Neville Sellwood was dead. Sellwood, who was 39, died from internal injuries received in a race fall in France. His mount, named Lucky Seven, had fallen and rolled on him. Thus ended the life and career of one of Australia's most outstanding and successful horsemen.

Neville Sellwood was born to be a jockey. His father, Charlie Sellwood, was himself a retired jockey and his mother a capable horsewoman. Sellwood served a successful apprenticeship in Brisbane, battled for some time as a senior jockey, then in 1949 won the Sydney premiership.

In the following 13 years Sellwood rode 1700 winners, including two Melbourne Cups (on Delta and Toparoa), three Caulfield Cups (on Grey Boots, Basha Felika and Tulloch), three Sydney Cups (on Gold Scheme, Sailor's Guide and Grand Garry), a Brisbane Cup (on Cambridge) and an Adelaide Cup (on Spear-

folio). Few of Sydney's big races eluded him and he won five Victoria Derbys at Flemington.

Sellwood was associated with many greats of the Australian turf including Todman on whom he won the inaugural Golden Slipper in 1957. However, it was his ride on Tulloch in the 1960 Melbourne Cup for which he was most criticised. Sellwood rode an ill-judged race by restraining Tulloch near the rear of the field, setting the champion an impossible task with his heavy weight. Tulloch finished seventh.

Sellwood frequently rode overseas and always with marked success. Earlier in 1962 he accepted a riding contract in France but had intended to return home to ride in that year's Melbourne Cup. However, he cancelled the trip because he was leading the French jockeys' premiership and decided to stay to cement the title.

TURF TOPICS

Le Filou top breed: Te Rapa trainer Ray Cotter achieved the pinnacle of his career at the Auckland carnival of 1961–62. On Boxing Day he saddled the Le Filou colt Cracksman to win the Great Northern Derby, and on New Year's Day he won the Auckland Cup with another of the Le Filou breed, the 65/1 shot Floutulla. Cracksman was ridden by the ex-Australian Les Coles, Floutulla by the lightweight David Raklander.

Goosman's tenth: When Sir Stanley Goosman headed the New Zealand winning owners' list in 1961–62, for the 10th and last time since he first topped the list in 1946, he could look back on a career honours board few owners could match. His horses won two Auckland Cups, four Great Northern Derbys, seven Great Northern St Legers, two NZ Derbys and four Great Northern Guineas.

Even Stevens starts: The Pakuranga Hunt meeting at Ellerslie NZ has an open-class 1600m named the Jellicoe Handicap. In 1962 it went to a flaxen-maned chestnut named Even Stevens on his way to glory in the Melbourne Cup and CB Fisher Plate.

Woman scorned: The AJC denied Betty Lane a trainer's licence for 'headquarters' so she upped sticks, and set up in Dubbo with an unraced horse named Delville Chief. She later won the Western Districts Racing Association trainers' premiership three times. The AJC relented 20 years later, granting her a No. 1 licence in 1982. Maureen Riley was the first woman licensed by the AJC – in 1961.

Last call: Cyril Angles, a pioneer racecaller, died in July. Angles was unsuccessfully prosecuted by a racing club in 1938 for broadcasting from outside the track.

1962 RESULTS

VRC MELBOURNE CUP (2m)
Even Stevens, 8.5 (L Coles) Trained by A McGregor; 3:21.4; Comicquita, Aquanita
AJC SYDNEY CUP (2m)
Grand Print, 8.8 (R Higgins) Trained by J Besanko; 3:33.7; River Seine, Dhaulagiri
QTC BRISBANE CUP (2m)
Kamikaze, 7.12 (W Taylor) Trained by H Riley; 3:21.7; Rural Loch, Dhaulagiri
SAJC ADELAIDE CUP (2m)
Cheong Sam, 8.3 (J Johnson) Trained by CS Hayes; 3:23.8; Sometime, Far Away Places
WATC PERTH CUP (2m)
Royal Khora, 7.2 (WA Smith) Trained by D Clark; 3:22, Little Empire, Ghost Town
VATC CAULFIELD CUP (12-f)
Even Stevens, 7.8 (L Coles) Trained by A McGregor; 2:34.1; Mamburdi, Cheong Sam

VRC AUSTRALIAN CUP (2m and 1 ½-f)
Welkin Prince, 7.8 (WA Smith) Trained by G Murphy; 3:45; Lucky Fred, Overproof
MVRC WS COX PLATE (10-f)
Aquanita, 9.4 (F Moore) Trained by RJ Shaw; 2:04.3; Grand Print, New Statesman
AJC DERBY (12-f)
Summer Prince, 8.10 (G Moore) Trained by TJ Smith; 2:29.2; Bogan Road, King Roto
VRC VICTORIA DERBY (12-f)
Coppelius, 8.10 (G Lane) Trained by B Courtney; 2:31.5; Bright Blend, Summer Prince
AJC DONCASTER HANDICAP (1m)
Te Poi, 7.5 (J Thompson) Trained by R Dickerson; 1:40.5; Prince Regoli, Emboss
BTC DOOMBEN '10 000' (7-f less 93 yds)
Red Smoke, 7.5 (W Welburn) Trained by N Larson; 1:18; Friar's Peak, Kilshery

VRC NEWMARKET HANDICAP (6-f)
Victorious, 8.2 (WA Smith) Trained by T Lewis; 1:11.2; Muirfield, Gabonia
AJC SIRES' PRODUCE STAKES (7-f)
Bogan Road, 8.10 (A Gallagher) Trained by J Montgomery; 1:25.9; Grammar Lad, Birthday Card
VRC SIRES' PRODUCE STAKES (7-f)
Jan's Image, 8.7 (G Moore) Trained by TJ Smith; 1:25.5; Bright Blend, Agra
VRC GRAND NATIONAL STEEPLECHASE (3m 1-f)
Prince Chantry, 9.4 R Cook) Trained by T Hughes; 6:1; Red Braid, I Spy
STC GOLDEN SLIPPER STAKES (6-f)
Birthday Card, 8.0 (R Greenwood) Trained by R Ferris; 1:11.4; Proud Miss, Grammar Lad

Pago Pago full of running as he goes to the line in the Golden Slipper at Randwick.

Gatum Gatum, 5; owner Malcolm Reid, 83.

Pago Pago humbles the best

How good was the South Australian wonder horse Pago Pago? Was he the best two-year-old Australia has produced? Many who recall his performances give a resounding 'yes' to that question.

The plain-looking but powerfully built colt is best remembered for breaking the monopoly of New South Wales horses on the Golden Slipper Stakes in 1963, after humbling the best two-year-olds in Victoria. Unfortunately, the Slipper was his last race. What he might have achieved had he not been sold to American interests can only be guessed at.

Certainly his short career, culminating in the Golden Slipper, was spectacular. The son of Matrice–Pompilia, Pago Pago was reported to be something special when brought from Adelaide to contest the six-furlong Merson Cooper Stakes at Caulfield on 2 March 1963.

His rivals that day were the exceptional two-year-olds Munich and Persian Opera. Pago Pago was backed into 6/4 favouritism and the trio rounded the home turn together. Straightening up, Pago Pago's jockey Billy Pyers said 'go' and the colt exploded away, winning by four lengths from Munich and Persian Opera with the Caulfield five-furlongs record-holder Kildarlin in fourth place.

The large crowd was stunned into silence, but they erupted a minute later when Pago Pago's time was semaphored – 1 minute 9.8 seconds. Not only was this a new race record but it was the fastest six furlongs run by a two-year-old in Australia. Previously, Todman (at Randwick) and All Love (at Flemington) had shared the record standing at 1 minute 10 seconds.

Pago Pago took out the VRC Sires' Produce Stakes at Flemington before going to Sydney for the Slipper where he was to be opposed to the outstanding local two-year-old Time and Tide. For the first time in the seven-year history of the race, the Golden Slipper had to be postponed because of torrential rain.

The new date was set for the following Wednesday but the track was a near-quagmire. Pago Pago had never raced anti-clockwise and had never encountered a heavy track. This was certainly his greatest test.

Pago Pago showed his class by giving Time and Tide, ridden by George Moore, a start – and a beating. The fact that he failed to handle the home turn and then raced wide made no difference to the result. The time of 1:15.5 was an indication of the state of the track rather than Pago Pago's ability. Time and Tide, incidentally, finished fourth in the Slipper but went on to record a brilliant three-year-old sprinting career.

Although Pago Pago was sold to American interests (for a record price for a two-year-old) for racing and breeding purposes, he did not race again. He failed to stand up to training on dirt surfaces and was retired to stud. Given limited opportunities because his bloodlines were unknown in America, he was still an outstanding success and later returned to Australia to stand at Robert Holmes à Court's Heytesbury Stud in Western Australia.

Jim Johnson shines

The Melbourne Spring Carnival of 1963 saw the departure of one top South Australian jockey and the 'arrival' of another. The superb horsemanship and infectious personality of the red-haired Billy Pyers was soon to be lost to overseas (although many, including racecaller Bert Bryant, wondered why, since Pyers was enjoying huge success in Australia).

Pyers had indeed been an ornament to Australian racing and was to ride with great distinction in Europe in the years ahead.

Jim Johnson was brought to Melbourne to ride Gatum Gatum in the Melbourne Cup. His victory led him to settle in Melbourne where he forged an illustrious career – and endured considerable controversy over his vigorous wielding of the whip.

Johnson received frequent warnings from stewards, particularly about applying the whip forward of the saddle. But Johnson was a favourite with punters because he did everything in his power to win races.

And win races he did. In the 1966–67 season he disrupted Roy Higgins' sequence as leading Melbourne jockey when he rode 63 winners. Johnson won three Melbourne Cups (on Gatum Gatum, then on Rain Lover in 1968–9). Besides Rain Lover, his most famous association was with the champion Tobin Bronze on whom he won the 1966 and 1967 Cox Plates and the 1967 Caulfield Cup.

Gatum Gatum, lightly weighted at 7.12, easily holds the field at bay in the Melbourne Cup.

Great Sensation wins a Wellington Cup.

South Australian winners

It was to be a vintage racing year for South Australia. Pago Pago won the Golden Slipper in Sydney in the autumn, but few would have guessed that both the big cups in Melbourne would go to SA later in the year.

Many doubted whether Sometime, a Summertime–Nereid colt, would ever win a major race despite his undoubted staying ability. He struck a purple patch in the spring of 1963, winning the Caulfield Cup.

From his earliest racing days, Sometime was regarded as an unlucky horse. As a three-year-old he ran good races in major events without winning. Frustrating as his performances were, jockey Billy Pyers never lost faith. His patience and that of the horse's connections was rewarded in the spring of 1963 when Sometime recorded a string of victories in lead-up races to the Caulfield Cup.

Sent out a 5/2 favourite in the cup, Sometime scored the easiest of wins aided by a masterly ride by Pyers. The horse literally cantered over the line to win by four lengths from Gatum Gatum and Grand Print. In fact, the ease of the win made him all the rage for the Melbourne Cup but doubts crept in when he again failed to salute in the Cox Plate (third) and in the Mackinnon on Derby Day (second). Consequently, punters began looking elsewhere, but not at Gatum Gatum, the Caulfield Cup runner-up.

So, Adelaide-owned and trained Gatum Gatum went into the Melbourne Cup virtually friendless. Even his Moonee Valley Cup jockey Les Coles, of Even Stevens fame, 'sacked' him and chose instead the better-performed Conference.

Gatum Gatum's connections then sent an SOS to Adelaide for jockey Jim Johnson, who had notched wins on the horse earlier in his career. And if Johnson's unorthodox riding style (back straight and whip flourishing) surprised racegoers, his effectiveness soon became apparent. In the Cup, Johnson had the lightly weighted Gatum Gatum (only 7.12) near the lead all the way, avoiding several scrimmages behind, and dashed him clear in the straight. Gatum Gatum had no trouble holding the higher-weighted Ilumquh and Grand Print and won by a length.

A Great Sensation

When Tommy Smith visited new Zealand for the 1960 Wellington Cup and yearling sales, the story goes that he was looking for a Kiwi stayer who might be a Melbourne Cup chance, and was told that a South Island galloper named Great Sensation might be available.

Told the horse would be an eight-year-old when the Melbourne Cup was run, TJ decided that was too old. After watching Jalna win the Wellington Cup from Sparkler and Great Sensation, he bought Sparkler.

Great Sensation was to win the next three Wellington Cups at eight, nine and 10 years respectively. His third and final cup win was the proof of Great Sensation's class; his main rival this time, and favoured to beat the old-timer, was Stipulate.

This was 1963, the year of Even Stevens' unbeaten spring campaign, including the Caulfield and Melbourne Cups, across the Tasman. Stipulate, who had earlier won the New Zealand Cup at Riccarton, met Even Stevens and soundly beat him in the Auckland Cup. Trainer Colin Jillings was by no means alone in believing that no horse, a 10-year-old Great Sensation included, could give Stipulate five years, weight and a beating in the Wellington Cup. Wrong. It was Great Sensation, with 9 st 7 lb (60.5 kg) against Stipulate's 9 st 3 lb, by a length and a half.

1963 RESULTS

VRC MELBOURNE CUP (2m)
Gatum Gatum, 7.12 (J Johnson) Trained by HG Heagney; 3:21.1; Ilumquh, Grand Print
AJC SYDNEY CUP (2m)
Maidenhead, 7.4 (WA Smith) Trained by K Cantrell; 3:33.1; The Dip, Kamikaze
QTC BRISBANE CUP (2m)
Campo, 7.5 (P Gumbleton) Trained by B Courtney; 3:22.8, Piper's son, River Seine
SAJC ADELAIDE CUP (2m)
Woolstar, 7.9 (A May) Trained by M Williams; 3:22, Sometime, Delville
WATC PERTH CUP (2m)
Bay Count, 7.6 (F Treen) Trained by F McAuliffe; 3:24; Dorbella, Rack And Ruin
VATC CAULFIELD CUP (12-f)
Sometime, 8.11 (W Pyers) Trained by LJ Patterson; 2:28.1; Gatum Gatum, Grand Print

VRC AUSTRALIAN CUP (2m)
Welkin Prince, 7.11 (L Coles) Trained by G Murphy; 2:56.4; Aladdin's Lamp, Alpensea
MVRC WS COX PLATE (10-f)
Summer Regent, 9.4 (J Riordan) Trained by RT Cotter; 2:06.2; Taua, Sometime
AJC DERBY (12-f)
Summer Fiesta, 8.10 (G Moore) Trained by TJ Smith; 2:32.3; Castanea, Para Inn
VRC VICTORIA DERBY (12-f)
Craftsman, 8.10 (P Hyland) Trained by A White; 2:30.4; Sir Dane, Future
AJC DONCASTER HANDICAP (1m)
Fine And Dandy, 8.12 (W Pyers) Trained by H Plant; 1:35, Our Cobber, Merthyr
BTC DOOMBEN '10 000' (7-f less 93 yds)
Tipperary star, 7.13 (C O'Neill) Trained by B Byrnes; 1:17.1; Lure, Mac's Pick
VRC NEWMARKET HANDICAP (6-f)
Our Cobber, 8.0 (B Gilders) Trained by N Brown; 1:10.3; Kilshery, Rashlore

AJC SIRES' PRODUCE STAKES (7-f)
Time and Tide, 8.10 (G Moore) Trained by H Plant; 1:25.4; Sunset Hue, Heirloom
VRC SIRES' PRODUCE STAKES (7-f)
Pago Pago, 8.10 (W Pyers) Trained by T Jenner; 1:25; Persian Opera, Rose Of Silver
VRC GRAND NATIONAL STEEPLECHASE (3m 1-f)
Sir Cameron, 9.4 (F Grenfell) Trained by R Benson; 6:16.3; Devon Boy, Foaming Sea
STC GOLDEN SLIPPER STAKES (6-f)
Pago Pago, 8.7 (W Pyers) Trained by TA Jenner; 1:15.5; Rosie Sun, Ripa

Athol Mulley on Eskimo Prince.

Princely Perc Galea congratulates Mulley after the Golden Slipper.

Perce Galea: the prince of punters

There never were scenes on a racetrack like those at Rosehill when Eskimo Prince won the Golden Slipper Stakes of 1964. For perhaps the first and only time the crowd's adulation was directed more to the winning owner than the victorious horse. And that was because the owner was 'The Prince of Punters', Perce Galea.

This was Galea's finest moment in racing – his beloved colt had won the big one, he had wagered hugely and collected, and the trophy presentations had almost been drowned out by the crowd chanting 'Three cheers for Perce'.

Overwhelmed, Galea made his way to the committee rooms for the traditional drinks as winning owner. As he mounted the steps to the rooms, punters called 'Good on you, Perce' and Galea responded by throwing handfuls of banknotes to the crowd. A near riot ensued.

Thus was the colour and panache of Percival John Galea, who began his reign as Prince of Punters by first making a fortune as boss of several of Sydney's biggest illegal casinos, then by winning a Sydney lottery, which he built on with mammoth betting sprees.

A dapper dresser and a fitness fanatic, he bought and raced a string of horses, naming them to fit his image – Social Prince, Prince of Fashion, Indian Prince, Glory Prince, Cultured Prince. But his favourite, and most successful, was Eskimo Prince.

When, as a four-year-old, Eskimo Prince put in two unplaced runs after winning the Hill Stakes, he was sold to American interests who subsequently discovered the horse had only one good lung and a throat valve that was paralysed. In retrospect, his racetrack performances were remarkable.

Meanwhile, Perce Galea's leviathan betting plunges continued. One day he needed to borrow a bag to carry his winnings from a track in Brisbane and, at the other end of the spectrum, he lost today's equivalent of more than $1 million when Eskimo Prince was beaten in the Stradbroke Handicap.

But the strain of his big betting told and Galea's life was constantly under threat from severe heart attacks. During one bedside interview in his hospital ward, Galea gave his well-publicised betting philosophy which included such axioms as: Have a big bank; have a go, particularly when you're winning, and follow the money. His list of don'ts included: Don't chase your losses by doubling up; don't bet at mid-week meetings; don't bet on heavy tracks; and, above all, don't bet on tips.

Galea finally succumbed to his third massive heart attack and died in a Sydney hospital in August 1977, leaving an estate worth more than $400 000.

A staggering Cup run

The biggest mystery of the 1964 Melbourne Cup was: what happened to the 3/1 favourite Sir Dane? While Polo Prince was again reinforcing the dominance of New Zealand stayers by forging to victory, Sir Dane had 'the staggers' at the rear of the field.

Immediately after dismounting, jockey Roy Higgins was asked by stewards for an explanation. Higgins said that after a perfect run Sir Dane 'collapsed' under him six furlongs from home. He later added: 'The Sir Dane I rode today was not the Sir Dane that finished so brilliantly to win the Cox Plate and Mackinnon Stakes. I couldn't believe I was on the same horse. He wobbled and staggered and was not able to go a yard.' The stewards reported after the meeting that a veterinary examination found Sir Dane to be 'normal in every respect'.

The most likely explanation was that Sir Dane, a brilliant middle-distance horse, simply was not a true stayer, since he had also failed in the Caulfield Cup. Certainly, he took no ill effect from the Cup runs. In 1965 he won the Blamey and the Futurity.

John Stocker salutes after winning the Cup.

Jim Johnson eases up aboard Yangtze after winning the Memsie Stakes at Caulfield.

Yangtze flows to a silent win at Caulfield

The three-year-old colt Yangtze reserved his place in Australia's racing history by becoming the first horse to lead all the way in a Caulfield Cup. His win that October day in 1964 mystified racegoers, principally because they had to watch the Cup in silence – the

Polo Prince swabbed after Melbourne Cup.

course loudspeaker system broke before the race started.

Yangtze had won the Caulfield Guineas the week before but, in assessing Caulfield Cup prospects, little notice was taken of that, although it had been an excellent front-running performance. But there were many older and supposedly superior horses in the Cup who had better form to justify higher consideration – including the weight-for-age star of the spring Sir Dane to be ridden by Roy Higgins. The cup was to be run on a heavy track and the field jumped without the usual course broadcaster's build-up and description. So when Yangtze, with unknown 19-year-old apprentice John Stocker in the saddle, took the lead from the jump there was an eerie silence, punctuated by occasional cries of: 'Who's the horse in front?'

Through the binoculars it was obvious that although Yangtze was in front, Stocker

didn't want him there. The jockey kept glancing to his right hoping another runner would take the lead. Nothing did, and in the home straight Yangtze was still there with most racegoers not knowing which horse he was. At last the challenges came – first Contempler, then the other three-year-old Royal Sovereign. But under Stocker's hard riding Yangtze held them all. Favourite Sir Dane could finish only ninth.

Yangtze thus became the first three-year-old to win the Caulfield Cup since Sir Blink in 1958 and Stocker the first winning apprentice since Alan Yeomans on Sir Blink. Yangtze was to go on and prove a worthy winner, running fourth in the following year's Melbourne Cup and winning the Mackinnon Stakes and St George Stakes of 1965. John Stocker became a top jockey and repeated his all-the-way Caulfield Cup win of 1964 in 1976 on How Now.

1964 RESULTS

VRC MELBOURNE CUP (2m)
Polo Prince, 8.3 (R Taylor) Trained by J Carter; 3:19.6; Elkayel, Welltown
AJC SYDNEY CUP (2m)
Zinga Lee, 8.7 (D Royle) Trained by WJ McNabb; 3:23.3; Summer Regent, River Seine
QTC BRISBANE CUP (2m)
Fair Patton, 7.11 (R Selkrig) Trained by V Thompson Snr; 3:23.7; Bore Head, Piper's Son
SAJC ADELAIDE CUP (2m)
Jamagne, 7.7 (G Pretty) Trained by HH Lehmann; 3:24; Londoner, Hunting Horn
WATC PERTH CUP (2m)
Resolution, 7.13 (F Treen) Trained by AH Jordan; 3:23.25; Cygnet Star, Light Cargo
VATC CAULFIELD CUP (12-f)
Yangtze, 7.4 (J Stocker) Trained by R Dini; 2:34.2; Royal Sovereign, Elkayel

VRC AUSTRALIAN CUP (10-f)
Grand Print, 8.11 (P Hyland) Trained by J Besanko; 2:1.3; Zinga Lee, Future
MVRC WS COX PLATE (10-f)
Sir Dane, 9.0 (R Higgins) Trained by RJ Shaw; 2:03.9; Contempler, Nicopolis
AJC DERBY (12-f)
Royal Sovereign, 8.10 (R Selkrig) Trained by J Page; 2:33.5; Strauss, Park Lane
VRC VICTORIA DERBY (12-f)
Royal Sovereign, 8.10 (R Selkrig) Trained by JB Page; 2:28.2; Strauss, Captain Blue
AJC DONCASTER HANDICAP (1m)
Persian Puzzle, 8.7 (H Molloy) Trained by S Haydon; 1:35.1; Papilio, Florida Keys
BTC DOOMBEN '10,000 (7-f less 93 yds)
The Tempest, 7.12 (W Camer) Trained by TJ Smith; 1:22.2; Cele's Image, Rashlore
VRC NEWMARKET HANDICAP (6-f)
Rashlore, 8.0 (P Hyland) Trained by AE Elkington; 1:10.1; Ripa, Nicopolis

AJC SIRES' PRODUCE STAKES (7-f)
Eskimo Prince, 8.10 (A Mulley) Trained by C Rolls; 1:24.2; Park Lane, Strauss
VRC SIRES' PRODUCE STAKES (7-f)
Boeing Boy, 8.10 (J Wakker) Trained by P Burke; 1:23.8; Park Lane, Star Of Heaven
VRC GRAND NATIONAL STEEPLECHASE (3m 1-f)
Sir Cameron, 10.3 (L Thompson) Trained by R Benson; 6:7; Hadley Wood, Davon Boy
STC GOLDEN SLIPPER STAKES (6-f)
Eskimo Prince, 8.7 (A Mulley) Trained by C Rolls; 1:11.9; Farnworth, Star Of Heaven

'Cups King' Cummings starts his run

James Bartholomew (Bart) Cummings was already a highly regarded, if still young, trainer before the spring of 1965. But his recognition was largely confined to Adelaide. No one could have predicted the impact Cummings and his charges would have on Australian racing during and after the Spring Carnival of that year.

What racing followers did know was that Cummings had a potential champion in his stable well before the Caulfield and Melbourne Cups. The undersized mare Light Fingers already had the most imposing of records. She had won the triple crown for fillies at Flemington – the Manifold, Wakeful and Oaks Stakes – the previous year and had returned in autumn to complete the classic double by winning the AJC Oaks at Randwick. She had also served notice of her future greatness by not having missed a place by the end of her three-year-old season.

Light Fingers' record spoke for itself but when she was allotted 8.4 in the Melbourne Cup it meant she had more weight than any mare had successfully carried to victory in the race.

Even so, many felt she was well up to the task, but bad luck began to dog her campaign. After proving she was all class by downing Nicopolis in the mile weight-for-age Craiglee Stakes and being installed as favourite for the Caulfield Cup, she suffered a viral disease and had to be rested.

Then in the Caulfield Stakes she clipped the heels of Winfreux, still managed to finish third but ricked a shoulder as she stumbled. Cummings was forced to scratch her from the Caulfield Cup.

Meanwhile, the spotlight swung back to one of Cummings' other quality stayers, Ziema, who ran second in the rough-house Caulfield Cup. And as Ziema firmed in Melbourne Cup betting, Light Fingers drifted out of calculations.

But Cummings still had faith in the stout-hearted mare, as did jockey Roy Higgins who affectionately referred to her as 'my little filly' (even though she was now a mare). Light Fingers ran a creditable third in the LKS Mackinnon Stakes on the Saturday before the Melbourne Cup and Higgins implied strongly on television that he had nursed the mare in the race, presumably with the Melbourne Cup in the forefront of his mind.

Light Fingers took no harm from her Mackinnon run and lined up for the Melbourne Cup. But could she really be expected to win considering her small stature, her huge weight and her extremely chequered

An even start as the Melbourne Cup of 1965 carries the hopes of Australia.

Early in the race, the outside barrier horses are still working their way into the field.

preparation of only five conditioning runs for the most gruelling race of all?

In an eventful race in which three fancied horses fell – including the well-fancied Matloch and Caulfield Cup winner Bore Head – Light Fingers and Ziema swept to the front to stage one of the most stirring finishes in Cup history.

In a stride-for-stride tussle with jockeys Higgins and John Miller riding feverishly, the horses went to the line locked together. Only the camera could decide the finish – Light Fingers by centimetres from her stablemate. The little mare's gallant heart had pulled her through.

Runner-up Ziema certainly was not disgraced but his second placing capped a heartbreaking spring for connections since it meant that Ziema had run second in the Caulfield, Moonee Valley and Melbourne Cups – all to different horses!

But not only had Light Fingers won the Cup, she had catapulted Bart Cummings into the big league. The man soon to be known as the Cups King had arrived with the first of many-to-come Cup quinellas. Australian racing was never to be the same again.

The Melbourne Cup was very much in young Bart's blood. Fifteen years earlier he had been part of the winning action when his father, Jim Cummings, prepared Comic Court to win the 1950 Cup. Bart was the strapper and attendant for Comic Court that day. He was exhilarated when their horse won the Cup in record time and resolved that he would train a Melbourne Cup winner one day.

Shocking Shrimp

It took more than great horses and a memorable training feat to put Australian racing on the front pages of world newspapers in 1965. It took a willowy London model called Jean Shrimpton, known as The Shrimp, who had been flown to Melbourne to be a judge of the Fashions on the Field contest.

But when The Shrimp appeared in the Flemington Members' Enclosure wearing a sleeveless mini-length shift without stockings, gloves or hat it was too much for the elegantly dressed matronly traditionalists she was meant to mingle with.

The outcry reverberated around the world, with one Fleet Street newspaper immediately flying out a journalist team to cover Miss Shrimpton's progress through the Spring Carnival.

Fashions on the Field, which had been introduced to lift racing's profile in the spring of 1962, had been trenchantly criticised by some racing purists, but the world-wide publicity gained for the Melbourne Cup carnival three years later was of inestimable value.

But fashion had been part of the spring racing scene for over one hundred years, though not always so controversial.

All eyes are on the Shrimp.

A huge crowd on opening day at Sandown.

Sandown chaos

It was the opportunity to be part of racing history that led to the chaos that marked the opening of Melbourne's Sandown Park racecourse on 19 June 1965.

Certainly, the opening of a new racecourse is an event rare enough to cause interest, but racing administrators were caught totally by surprise by the public's response to Sandown's unveiling. In fact, the crowd of 52 379 was bigger than at any Saturday race meeting in Victoria except Caulfield Cup Day – and the scenes of crowd chaos were unprecedented.

Even before most entered the course, bedlam prevailed on the roads. Traffic choked the Princes Highway between the suburbs of Oakleigh and Springvale and a journey that should have taken minutes lengthened into hours.

Indeed, the traffic jam altered the course of racing history. Jockey Brian Gaw should have ridden the winner of the first flat race at the new track – Work of Art at 33/1. Gaw was hopelessly caught in the traffic and arrived about a minute too late to take the mount. Stewards had substituted Bob Durey for Work of Art. Even when racegoers did get into the new course, tempers became ever more frayed. A power failure stopped the on-course totalisator and supplies of food and racebooks quickly ran out.

TURF TOPICS

Excuses, excuses: Victorian trainer Charlie Waymouth once calculated there were 187 ways a horse could be beaten in a race. A classic excuse was that of Red William, winner of the 1965 Moonee Valley and Sandown Cups. When he lost, connections said he suffered from equine ochlophobia, the horse version of fear of crowds.
Gigantic impact: Sub-fertile after an early infection, Gigantic sired Empyreus, top earner of 1964–65. Empyreus had 11 wins for the season, including the New Zealand Stallion and Great Northern St Legers.

Truly a star: Star Affair showed great potential by beating Citius (later an Oakleigh Plate and Doncaster winner) in the Merson Cooper Stakes at Caulfield, and was then beaten into second place by the sheer speed of Reisling in the Golden Slipper.

But in the spring, Star Affair came into his own, winning the Moonee Valley Stakes, then beating Tobin Bronze (who would win the Victoria Derby) in the Caulfield Guineas. Next, Star Affair beat Winfreux after a great struggle in the Cox Plate, then topped it off winning the Linlithgow Stakes.

1965 RESULTS

VRC MELBOURNE CUP (2m)
Light Fingers, 8.4 (R Higgins) Trained by JB Cummings; 3:21.1; Ziema, Midlander
AJC SYDNEY CUP (2m)
River Seine, 8.7 (G Podmore) Trained by N Prendergast; 3:25.1; Blue Shaun, Bon Filou
QTC BRISBANE CUP (2m)
Fair Patton, 8.8 (A Mulley) Trained by TJ Smith; 3:24.1; Ampass, Marco Khan
SAJC ADELAIDE CUP (2m)
Hunting Horn, 8.3 (A May) Trained by L Patterson; 3:23.5; The Dip, Jamagne
WATC PERTH CUP (2m)
Fair's Print, 7.10 (P O'Loghlen) Trained by AH Jordan; 3:22; Rack And Ruin, Royal Coral
VATC CAULFIELD CUP (12-f)
Bore Head, 8.9 (F Clarke) Trained by R Dillon; 2:28.3; Ziema, Craftsman

VRC AUSTRALIAN CUP (10-f)
Craftsman, 8.13 (P Hyland) Trained by AR White; 2:2.4; Gay Filou, Amusement Park
MVRC WS COX PLATE (10-f)
Star Affair, 7.11 (P Hyland) Trained by A Armanasco; 2:02; Winfreux, Yangtze
AJC DERBY (12-f)
Prince Grant, 8.10 (R Dawkins) Trained by TJ Smith; 2:29.9; Conclave, Shoreacres
VRC VICTORIA DERBY (12-f)
Tobin Bronze, 8.10 (N Mifflin) Trained by G Heagney; 2:34; Midlander, Diocletian
AJC DONCASTER HANDICAP (1m)
Time And Tide, 9.4 (D Lake) Trained by H Plant; 1:37; Our Fun, Ripa
BTC DOOMBEN '10 000' (7-f less 93 yds)
Winfreux, 8.2 (WA Smith) Trained by C Wilson; 1:18.9; dead-heat second Todwana and Arcadus

VRC NEWMARKET HANDICAP (6-f)
Ripa, 8.10 (D Lake) Trained by B Conaghan; 1:9.6; Time And Tide, Marmion
AJC SIRES' PRODUCE STAKES (7-f)
Peace Council, 8.10 (G Moore) Trained by TJ Smith; 1:25.9; Gay Gauntlet, Diocletian
VRC SIRES' PRODUCE STAKES (7-f)
Citius, 8.7 (I Saunders) Trained by T Murrell; 1:24.9; Glensharold, Peace Council
VRC GRAND NATIONAL STEEPLECHASE (3m 1-f)
Royal Rennie, 9.5 (T McGinley) Trained by A McClements; 6:1.1; Remount, Lagos
STC GOLDEN SLIPPER STAKES (6-f)
Reisling, 8.0 (L Billett) Trained by J Norman; 1:11.1; Star Affair, Citius

John Miller has all his troubles behind him as he brings Galilee back to scale.

Galilee's owner, Max Bailey, with his wife.

Galilee, the best horse since Tulloch

Two definite conclusions could be drawn from the 1966 Melbourne Spring Carnival: first, Bart Cummings was on the way to an illustrious training career; and second, his stayer Galilee was the best horse since Tulloch. When Galilee stormed down the Flemington straight to leave Light Fingers standing and again quinella the Melbourne Cup for Cummings, history was made.

Cummings became the first trainer to quinella successive Cups and Galilee emerged as the first horse since The Trump in 1937 to win the Toorak Handicap, the Caulfield Cup and the Melbourne Cup. The win was also a triumph for former West Australian jockey John Miller, who the previous year was second in the Moonee Valley, Caulfield and Melbourne Cups on Ziema.

It's said the only certain thing about luck is that it will change. Miller's fortunes certainly did. He would never have achieved his victories if Roy Higgins, as first rider for the

Cummings stable, had chosen to ride Galilee in his spring campaign. Higgins instead selected Ziema – a decision that backfired when that horse went lame and had to be scratched from the 1966 Cups.

Cummings proved with Galilee that he was not only a great trainer but an exceptional judge of horseflesh. He chose Galilee at the New Zealand yearling sales despite the fact that the horse was pigeon-toed. While this fault might have deterred other trainers (and almost certainly did), Cummings saw a lot to like in the horse's overall make-up and bought him for Ziema's part-owner, Adelaide builder Max Bailey.

Cummings brought Galilee along quietly, but by the spring of 1966, the gelding had done well enough to be in contention for the Caulfield Cup, at least. This was confirmed in spades when Galilee came from last down the side to sweep around the field and blitz a top field in the Toorak Handicap.

The simple reason why Galilee was not then all the rage for the Caulfield Cup was the presence of the great people's horse Tobin Bronze, who had justified his short-priced favouritism with outstanding victories in the lead-up wfa races. And while Tobin Bronze started in the red (the shortest-priced favourite since Tulloch), Galilee promptly drifted from 6/1 to start at 14/1. Galilee repeated his Toorak performance, again unleashing his trademark finish to win comprehensively. Tobin Bronze was unplaced.

So Galilee was the horse of the moment, but controversy was to follow. In his final run before the Melbourne Cup, in the Mackinnon Stakes, Galilee's withering finish failed to eventuate as Miller appeared to sit quietly while Tobin Bronze careered away with the race. Miller's ride did not impress the VRC stewards and he and owner Bailey were called to an inquiry. Another racing sensation on the very eve on the Melbourne Cup was unfolding.

Miller, strongly pleading his innocence, survived disqualification when stewards found no evidence of malpractice but he was warned to exercise more vigour in future. Rarely has a jockey been more relieved by a stewards' verdict. Meanwhile, the Mackinnon run had taken a little of the shine off Galilee, and the sentimental favourite was Cummings' great mare Light Fingers, who was back from injury and attempting to become the first mare to win two Melbourne Cups.

But her gallantry was not enough to hold off Galilee's surging finish in the big race. It was certainly no disgrace to go down to another champion.

Tobin Bronze beats local representative Proud Land at Santa Anita in California.

Mick Mallyon pictured aboard Altai Khan, but he said if Leilani could cook he would marry her.

Colourful Mick Mallyon

There have been better jockeys than Ronald 'Mick' Mallyon but few more colourful and controversial.

Mallyon was described by a leading turf writer as being 'straight from the pen of Banjo Paterson', such was his original turn of phrase and memorable quotes. But his prowess as a jockey was also considerable, particularly riding at Caulfield where he landed three Caulfield Cups.

However, it was in January 1966 that Mallyon first made national racing headlines when he was charged with not allowing the hot favourite Maritana to race on its merits in the 2nd Argyle Handicap at Moonee Valley. Mallyon was disqualified for three years.

However, Mallyon returned to racing glory in 1968 when he piloted Bunratty Castle to victory in the Caulfield Cup. His other Caulfield Cup winners were Gay Icarus in 1971 and Leilani in 1974. After Leilani's win he told the crowd: 'You'd have to travel the length and breadth of Australia to find a nicer filly … if she could cook I'd marry her.'

His greatest disappointment (after the disqualification) was to lose on protest the 1979 AJC Derby on Stylish Century. The pair atoned the following week by winning the Sydney Cup by seven lengths. 'Winning on that little cove gave me the greatest satisfaction of my life,' Mallyon said.

Injuries and frequent suspensions dotted his career. On his retirement in 1987 Mallyon was asked to relate his most humorous incident in racing.

He replied: 'I remember riding at Cranbourne one day and we got to about the half-mile and I was in fourth or fifth spot and this jockey rode up next to me and said: "Can you give me your whip?" and I said, "I'm still travelling alright myself buddy," and he said: "I've just dropped mine and I'm going for a good quid here." At the top of the straight I was stuffed and he was still beside me so I gave him the whip, but as it turned out he finished second.'

TURF TOPICS

A shotgun protest: Racegoers at Flemington in February 1966 were puzzled by a delay at the start of the Fulham Hurdle. A sensational incident was unfolding there. Walter Hoysted, a son of the famous trainer 'Father' Fred Hoysted, had bailed up the starter with a shotgun. He was protesting against the whipping of horses and demanding a promise that no whips be allowed in the hurdle race. He demonstrated he was serious by discharging the gun.

Police arrived and after receiving a guarantee that whips would be banned (a pledge not honoured), Hoysted surrendered. He was sentenced to a month's jail.

Class handicapper: Craftsman established himself as one of the turf's top performers when he won both the Australian Cup and the Queen Elizabeth Stakes for the second year in 1966. Perhaps the best son of the great sire Better Boy, Craftsman capped his three-year-old campaign by beating Sir Dane and Future in the 1963 Victoria Derby. He went on to record 17 more victories, most of them at the highest level. His best run may well have been in a race he did not win – the 1965 Caulfield Cup. Backed from 12/1 to 7/1, Craftsman was going like a winner when he almost fell at the five-furlong mark.

Straight to the line: Talented sprinter Bowl King had speed to burn but he threw away numerous races through his chronic tendency to veer off the track when going like a winner. However, when Bowl King brilliantly won the 1966 Newmarket Handicap, he had no choice but to race truly. He drew the outside of the straight six and raced down the grandstand rail. In fact, in contrast to 'nightmare' rides around turns, jockey Jim Johnson had an armchair sit. Bowl King beat the Peace Council.

1966 RESULTS

VRC MELBOURNE CUP (2m)
Galilee, 8.13 (J Miller) Trained by JB Cummings; 3:21.9; Light Fingers, Duo
AJC SYDNEY CUP (2m)
Prince Grant, 8.2 (G Moore) Trained by TJ Smith; 3:24; High Principle, Gin And Bitters
QTC BRISBANE CUP (2m)
Apa, 8.2 (R McCarthy) Trained by M Seal; 3:28.7; Tea Biscuit, Fulmen
SAJC ADELAIDE CUP (2m)
Prince Camillo, 7.5 (P Gumbleton) Trained by WT Fisher; 3:29.7; Fulmen, Sir Wynyard
WATC PERTH CUP (2m)
Royal Coral, 8.6 (G Webster) Trained by F McAuliffe; 3:22; Carol's Choice, Friendly
VATC CAULFIELD CUP (12-f)
Galilee, 8.7 (J Miller) Trained by JB Cummings; 2:27.8; Gala Crest, Pharaon

VRC AUSTRALIAN CUP (10-f)
Craftsman, 9.5 (P Hyland) Trained by AR White; 2:2.1; Vignoble, Beau Guard
MVRC WS COX PLATE (10-f)
Tobin Bronze, 9.0 (J Johnson) Trained by HG Heagney; 2:07.2; Winfreux, Light Fingers
AJC DERBY (12-f)
El Gordo, 8.10 (N Campton) Trained by L O'Sullivan; 2.34.5; Garcon, Mystic Glen
VRC VICTORIA DERBY (12-f)
Khalif, 8.10 (R Higgins) Trained by D Judd; 2:30.2; Pharaon, Sunhaven
AJC DONCASTER HANDICAP (1m)
Citius, 8.8 (G Moore) Trained by W Murrell; 1:34.8; Castanea, Bowl King
BTC DOOMBEN '10 000' (7-f less 93 yds)
Pterylaw, 7.12 (P Gumbleton) Trained by ND Hoysted; 1:18.1; Maritana, Citius

VRC NEWMARKET HANDICAP (6-f)
Bowl King, 8.8 (J Johnson) Trained by A Lopes; 1:9.6; Peace Council, Citius
AJC SIRES' PRODUCE STAKES (7-f)
Prince Max, 8.10 (C Clare) Trained by C Papworth; 1:24.3; Academy Star, Le Bull
VRC SIRES' PRODUCE STAKES (7-f)
Storm Queen, 8.7 (R Higgins) Trained by JB Cummings; 1:25.4; Legal Boy, Very Merry
VRC GRAND NATIONAL STEEPLECHASE (3m 1-f)
McEwan, 9.12 (T McGinley) Trained by O Gardner; 6:1.9; Malleur, El Carum
STC GOLDEN SLIPPER STAKES (6-f)
Storm Queen, 8.0 (R Higgins) Trained by JB Cummings; 1:12.9; Academy Star, Very Merry

They were calling from the treetops

Race calling in the early days was a hazardous business. Callers could fall out of a tree, step off a tower, tumble over a balcony – all in the line of work. And if you were Ken Howard, you even ran the risk of being shot.

During the 1920s and 30s, only the ABC had permission to broadcast from the racecourses, and those lucky callers, among them Jim Carroll (Victoria), Keith Noud (Queensland) and Keith Gollan (Western Australia), had only the crowds, the weather and the horses to contend with.

The racecallers for commercial radio stations were barred from the racecourses by the racing clubs, and so they called from various ingenious vantage points outside the tracks. In his book *London to a Brick On*, racecaller and writer Steve Cairns documented some of these: a Moreton Bay fig opposite Warwick Farm (Cyril Angles for 2KY), a boxroom beneath the gables of the Pioneer Hotel in Ballarat Road opposite Flemington (Fred Tupper for 3AW), the turret of a building in Alison Road opposite the Randwick course (Mick Ferry for 2FC), a tower erected in a fowl yard overlooking Canterbury (Lachie Melville for 2UE), the balcony of the Presentation Convent, Neerim Road, Caulfield (both 3AW's Fred Tupper and Eric Welch for 3DB).

Race broadcasts began in 1924 when Ike Treloar called a Port Adelaide meeting for 5CL and became the first man in the world to call a full race meeting. A former trainer's foreman, Mick Ferry began broadcasting Randwick for 2FC in 1925, the same year Bill Priestley, a racing journalist with the *Sporting Globe*, became the first man to broadcast the Melbourne Cup, bringing Windbag's triumph to an unprecedented number of punters.

The racing clubs believed that race calls would lead to an increase in the SP bookie's profits and a decrease in racing attendances, and their opposition to the commercial broadcasters created situations which bordered on farce. Cyril Angles placed a chair on top of a table on the back of a truck and stood on that to broadcast the Rosehill races. In an effort to keep Angles out, the Victoria Park Race Club erected a tall timber fence around its track. In response, Angles, working by then for 2UW, had a huge wooden tower built in the front yard of a house in Dowling Street, which was adjacent to the course, and broadcast from that.

In 1936 the Victoria Park Race Club sued 2UW and after a protracted court case, a 1937 High Court judgement ruled in favour

A pioneer caller, Eric Welch, shows the ropes to the 'apprentice' Bill Collins.

Lachie Melville at Grafton, 1950.

Jack Gorman on duty at Hawkesdale in 1959.

of the radio station. Not all race clubs relented overnight. In 1940, the Victorian provincial club Pakenham banned 3XY from broadcasting its Cup meeting, and after 3XY's Ken Howard broadcast the next meeting successfully from the roof of a house near the Pakenham railway station, the Pakenham secretary Michael Bourke bought the building. In the ensuing strife, Howard was rumoured

to have been shot at and he eventually took the situation to its ultimate absurdity by hiring a hot-air balloon and broadcasting the races from 30 feet above the course.

Eventually the racing clubs came to recognise the contribution of the race calls to the popularity of horseracing, and life – while still hectic and stressful – was comparatively easy for the racecallers who followed.

Some legends of the call

Joe Brown

When the ABC's Joe Brown retired in 1981 after a career of 37 years, he was something of a national institution.

Brown had joined the ABC as a part-time racecaller in Hobart in 1944 at the age of 25, and in 1947 won the coveted full-time position of racecaller in Melbourne on the retirement of Jim Carroll.

Joe Brown had a precise and confident delivery. In his first Melbourne Cup call in 1948, Rimfire and Dark Marne battled it out down the straight and for first time the photo-finish was called on to decide the winner. Brown declared: 'I think Rimfire might have just beaten Dark Marne.' He was the only broadcaster to predict the result.

He was awarded the MBE following his final call on 6 June 1981, which was relayed interstate by the commercial stations 3UZ and 3DB as well as the ABC. He had called 33 Melbourne Cups, and was the Melbourne course commentator for 26 years.

Joe Brown: precise, confident.

Bert Bryant

Bert Bryant took over from Tom Moon as 3UZ's chief racecaller in 1949, and added a larrikin humour to race calling which won 3UZ top ratings for all but the first two years of his 27-year-career.

Originally from Dubbo, Bryant served his time on the New South Wales country race circuit before breaking into the metropolitan league. He quickly became sporting editor after joining 3UZ and for many years his race calls were broadcast throughout Australia on the Macquarie network's 48 stations. His flamboyant calls were full of expressions like 'covering more ground than Burke and Wills' (running wide), 'going like last week's pay' (running way out in front), 'hanging on like granny's tooth' (hanging on) and 'late for school' (running at the rear of the field).

Bryant's race calling career was cut short in 1977 by illness, but he continued the popular Turf Talk until 3UZ gave away racing in 1983. He then retired from radio to represent the bloodstock agent Harry Lawson. Bryant died in 1991 at 64.

Flamboyant Bert Bryant.

Bill Collins

The son of a Gippsland trainer and bookmaker and cousin of the jockey Scobie Breasley, Bill Collins began his metropolitan calling career as an offsider to Bert Bryant at 3UZ. After only six months of playing second fiddle, he was hired by 3DB on the retirement of Eric Welch, and became Bert Bryant's biggest rival.

Bill Collins was dubbed 'The Accurate One' in a station promotion and it was a nickname he earned through his calm and careful calling. He was also the recipient of the Order of Australia.

Outside the racecourse, Bill Collins was what was called 'an all-round entertainer' - he sang, he danced, he compered. In his early days with 3DB he was a member of the cast of 'The Happy Show' and when television arrived and HSV7 began its long-running variety show 'Sunnyside Up' in 1958, he was a founding member of the cast.

The last race Bill Collins called was on 3UZ (3DB had recently given up racing) on Easter Saturday 1988. He died in 1997 at the age of 69.

Ken Howard: 'It's London to a brick on.'

Ken Howard

Ken Howard began his colourful career dodging bullets for 3XY in Melbourne, but it was in postwar Sydney, first with 2UE and then from 1959 with the Macquarie Network's 2GB, that he became a legend. He believed that racecallers should entertain as well as impart information, and his 'it's London to a brick on' (to affirm his declaration of the winner) was just one of his expressions to enter the racing language. Others include 'travelling via the Cape' (running wide), 'pulling the persuader' (reaching for the whip), and 'salutes the judge' (passing the winning post).

Howard called 32 Melbourne Cups, starting with The Trump's win in 1937. Racecaller Geoff Mahoney attributes to Howard the first use of a racecaller's stand in Australia. He had one made after seeing it used by a racecaller in a Hollywood movie. He retired at the end of 1973, and the last race at Randwick was called the Farewell Handicap in his honour. He died in 1976, aged 62.

Bill Collins: 'The Accurate One'.

Bart Cummings supervising Red Handed and stablemate Fulman, with an interested entourage.

Vintage year for 'the big reds'

It was to be another vintage year for Bart Cummings. The great Galilee won the Sydney Cup in the autumn for him and Red Handed snatched victory on the line to give the trainer his third Melbourne Cup in succession – a feat never before achieved.

Galilee's Sydney Cup win justified his 'champion' accolade – he carried the huge burden of 9.7 yet strolled in by six lengths. And at 6/4 on he was the shortest-priced favourite in the history of the race. Red Handed's win, while meritorious, was another story. He probably should never have beaten the second placegetter, the New Zealander Red Crest.

From the beginning, Red Handed was an unlikely Cups candidate, despite his good bloodlines – by Le Filou from the Red Mars mare, Red Light. Even allowing for his attraction to the breed, Cummings might not have shown much interest in him at the New Zealand yearling sales because, among other faults, he was described as having a head like a violin case.

But some months before the sale a dinner party had been held in the home of Adelaide businessman Mr F. W. Clarke. During the evening, Mr Clarke and two of his guests decided they would buy a racehorse. 'Perhaps we'll win a Melbourne Cup,' they joked. But each prospective owner knew it was unlikely, since they wanted a 'cheap' buy and put a ceiling of $1600 on the price.

While something of an ugly duckling, at least Red Handed's price was right. Cummings bought him for only a little more than the $1600 ceiling. He then put him into cotton wool and did not race him until well into his three-year-old season. He quickly found that Red Handed's ability belied his looks. The gelding put together a string of wins, stamping himself as a stayer of great promise in the process. Then, in October 1966 his career almost ended when he fell in the Geelong Cup and fractured a small bone in his hock. He did not return until 1967.

Now his career really blossomed. He won a sprint first-up, was second in a 2000-metre event, then took on a huge step-up in class by contesting the Toorak Handicap. He raced magnificently to beat all but the great Tobin Bronze. After another excellent run in the Mackinnon Stakes on Derby Day, the 'cheap' horse bought for a bargain price was suddenly equal favourite for the Melbourne Cup.

Cummings had timed Red Handed's campaign to perfection. But all looked lost when Red Crest came at him in the straight and put his head in front, only to see Higgins 'lift' Red Handed on the line.

Red Crest's trainer Jack Winder and jockey Ron Taylor were staying at Tommy Woodcock's premises. Red Crest, a well-performed stayer in New Zealand, had tender feet, and had been brought to Melbourne in the hope of finding a soft track on Cup Day. But despite watering, the track was expected to be flint-like. Woodcock said when Cup Day came around they were so depressed by the track they gave the horse no chance.

But nothing could detract from the winning trio. Higgins paid tribute to Cummings, saying he thought Red Handed was beaten but 'then I remembered who trained the horse and, believe me, that took us both to the winning post'.

TURF TOPICS

Versatile Eiffel Tower: Eiffel Tower was good enough to win the Wellington Cup on the flat, the Grand National Hurdle at Riccarton twice and the Great Northern Steeplechase at Ellerslie.

His win in the 1967 Great Northern was extraordinary. Ridden by his trainer, Bill Hillis, Eiffel Tower jumped the water jump at such an angle that he ran off Kumai, his main rival, and himself wound up between the stand double, the two fences more or less alongside the water jump which were to be jumped the next time round.

Eiffel Tower must have lost 50 lengths by the time Hillis had tacked on to the rest of the field, yet he picked them up one by one over the next two rounds. Then he had to survive a home-stretch battle with the veteran chaser Ringlock before getting there by half a length.

Not so Terrific: Dr Alex McGregor Grant, near the end of his 23-year reign as president of the Auckland Racing Club, would have loved to win his club's feature event, the two-mile Auckland Cup, with his handsome entire four-year-old Terrific on New Year's Day 1967.

The party-pooper was a Takanini chestnut named Royal Sheen, whose youthful jockey tracked Terrific all the way from the seven furlongs and then got his mount up by a nose. The young jockey was David Peake, now with six premierships to his credit and the 2000-winner mark within his sights.

Terrific, incidentally, had run unplaced in the Melbourne Cup when below his best, run second in the Auckland Cup, run a close and luckless fifth in the Wellington Cup and, in his fourth two-mile outing for the season, romped home in the HR Chalmers Handicap at Trentham in the autumn.

Potent Pakistan: Breeding history is littered with examples of stallions who made a promising start at stud but did not carry on with it. Pakistan II, however, whose first progeny hit the racetracks in 1966–67, began his stud career brilliantly and just kept going.

In that first crop he had eight individual winners of 17 races (making him the leading sire of two-year-olds overall in New Zealand), and he continued to produce the most versatile and genuine progeny (topping the sires' list with just three crops racing) until his sadly premature death at the age of 14 years.

Tobin Bronze – the people's champion

There is nothing in racing like a tumultuous reception for an idolised horse that has just won a big race at the amphitheatre that is Moonee Valley racecourse.

Tobin Bronze, the strikingly handsome chestnut stallion who swept all before him in the spring of 1967, was such a horse. And the reception he and jockey Jim Johnson received after their victory in the WS Cox Plate that year was unmatched in turf history.

Tobin Bronze was unquestionably the best of the progeny of Arctic Explorer, the imported English stallion brought to Australia to stand at Stockwell Stud, Victoria. His dam was Amarco who won the VRC Oaks in 1957. Trained by Grahame Heagney for Adelaide owners, metal dealers A. D. C and W. E. Brown, Tobin Bronze stamped himself as a horse of great potential by winning four starts as a two-year-old – potential realised when he won the Victoria Derby the following year.

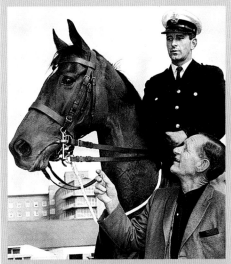

Trainer Norm Creighton is emotional as he hands over his beloved horse Samson for new duties with the police.

But the people really began to idolise Tobin Bronze when he won four weight-for-age races in the spring of 1966.

To atone for his defeat at odds-on in the Caulfield Cup, Tobin Bronze had a magnificent autumn in Melbourne, then went to Sydney to win the Doncaster Handicap and the All-Aged Stakes. But bad luck loomed. Tobin Bronze contracted a virus which affected his liver, and he did not recover until well into September – surely too late to play a hand in the major races coming up. But his first run – in a 1200-metre sprint at Moonee Valley – saw bookmakers slash his price to 5/4 on. With Geoff Lane up Tobin Bronze cantered in. By now, the idolatry had reached new heights.

The stage was now set for the Caulfield Cup, but he faced a mammoth task considering his lightest of preparations plus his weight, a burdensome 9.10 – only the great Redcraze had carried more to victory in the race. Then, with his fans counting the days to the Cup, it was announced Tobin Bronze had been sold to two Americans who announced he would pursue a career in the United States. The price was not officially disclosed, but it was a record to that time. The good news was that Tobin Bronze would run in the Caulfield Cup and Cox Plate before he left Australia.

Given his weight and chequered preparation, Tobin Bronze opened at 7/1 with bookmakers but the horse's following was such that this price fell to 5/1. In yet another rough-house Caulfield Cup in which several horses lost their chances, Jim Johnson this time avoided trouble, settled the chestnut beautifully, then set him alight with 600 metres to go. In the heart-stopping finish Tobin Bronze prevailed by a neck – and the sustained reception by the huge crowd shook the Caulfield stands.

With the Cox Plate the following Saturday to be the champion's last run in Australia, the small Valley track was filled to capacity. Bookmakers were not so generous this time and installed Tobin Bronze as 6/1 on favourite for the greatest weight-for-age race in Australasia. But the crowd had come to say farewell, not to bet on him, and when he gallantly fought off Terrific in the straight to win by a length, the thunderous ovation began. But in triumph there was sadness. Many in the crowd wept unashamedly and Jim Johnson later said he was close to tears himself.

Tobin Bronze was rushed to America where he ran a creditable third in the Laurel International against many of the top horses in the world.

Felipe Ysmael and his family assemble at Caulfield.

Felipe the Filipino Fireball

He was called the Filipino Fireball – and he certainly set betting rings alight in the 1960s. His name was Felipe Ysmael, although he preferred to be known as 'The Babe'. His foray into Australian racing was spectacular and exhilarating before ending in disqualification in 1968.

Ysmael hit the headlines in heady fashion when he placed a mammoth bet on champion Tobin Bronze in the Toorak Handicap the previous year. He was reputed to have been losing $90 000 (a huge loss then, when the average wage was less than $100). Ysmael's agent stepped up to leviathan bookmaker Bill Waterhouse and challenged him to a bet of '$96 000 to $60 000 Tobin Bronze'. Waterhouse took the bet. Tobin Bronze won convincingly and Ysmael was up $6000 overall.

From that time Ysmael was rarely out of the news. He set up his own stable of fashionably bred horses on a picturesque property in the Dandenong Ranges east of Melbourne. Security was described as being like that of a fortress. And although his horses won a string of good races (including Always There's triumph in the 1968 Victoria Derby) it was his betting that rocked racing circles.

For example, in January 1968 he set the well-primed Red Diver for an Australia-wide betting plunge. His trainer, Charlie Waymouth, knew he had a sprinter of exceptional ability and was convinced the horse would

win, but even he was staggered by the amount Ysmael and his agents bet on the colt. Red Diver, ridden by the noted 'money rider' Kevin Mitchell, bolted in and Ysmael reportedly won $250 000 in Melbourne and Sydney. Other sensational plunges followed. On 1 May 1968 Ysmael created turf history when he backed two-year-old Silver Strike to win $100 000 in a maiden race at Newcastle for which the first stake was a mere $350.

The gigantic betting sprees went on throughout the year. Ysmael took the losses with the wins but his time was running out. In December 1968 the performance of his horse Follow Me was the subject of an inquiry by Moonee Valley stewards. Ysmael had $13 000 on the horse but it was alleged someone at his stable laid out $21 000 on the second favourite Dalthing. Follow Me finished 11th in a field of 13 with the race being won by High Calibre.

Follow Me's jockey, George Hope, was charged with riding 'in such a manner as not to permit the colt to run on its merits'. Despite evidence brought by Ysmael that Follow Me had suffered a heart block before the race, he, Hope and trainer Waymouth were disqualified in January 1969 for two years. Although Ysmael later spent several more years in Australia, his racing career was effectively over. He died of a heart attack in the Philippines in 1984.

Fileur – perennial bridesmaid: Toward the end of the 1968 Spring Carnival, acclaimed race-caller Bill Collins said during a television racing panel: 'Gee, what a great horse Fileur would have been if Rain Lover hadn't been around.' His words were true – and prophetic. The Colin Hayes–trained Fileur is remembered as one of the best horses never to achieve racing glory. When Rain Lover beat him in the 1968 Melbourne Cup, it was a repeat result of the Mackinnon Stakes three days earlier. The previous Saturday Fileur had been beaten in the Cox Plate, running second to Rajah Sahib. In all, Rain Lover was to defeat Fileur six times before revenge came.

Bill's big year: Bill Skelton had a big year in 1966, when he joined the 1000-winner club a few months ahead of Grenville Hughes. But 1967–68 was even more notable; the likeable Skelton, known to his public as Bustling Bill, not only won his sixth premiership but broke Keith Voitre's 35-year-old record of 123 wins in a season. Bill Skelton made it with just one win to spare.

Baggy Hillis ducks: Top hurdles horseman Brian 'Baggy' Hillis, some notable feats still ahead of him in that department, turned to training in the mid-1960s and quickly enjoyed success. With a three-year-old named Nausori, he realised that his good one was up against a very good one in Ben Lomond, and ducked him in the second half of the season to take on two important open miles instead. Nausori won the Ellerslie version of the George Adams outright – and dead-heated with fellow Takanini galloper Bywon in the Wellington George Adams.

Tough filly: She went down in her preliminary like a cat on hot bricks, but Takanini filly Mayo Gold was as tough as they came. Trained by Ray Wallace for an expatriate County Mayo man, Frank Conway, Mayo Gold lined up 17 times as a two-year-old for eight wins and a string of placings. Furthermore, despite this testing first-season campaign, she also reached good form at three and four years

Thanks, Jack: At Randwick, young apprentice Ron Quinton had a filly stumble beneath him. Old hand Jack Thompson leaned over and took Ron's weight, allowing the filly to regain her balance. Quinton would have fallen without Thompson's helping hand, he later told the stewards.

Rain Lover rains on Cummings' parade

Everyone, it seemed, expected Bart Cummings to win the 1968 Melbourne Cup, particularly since he had taken out the three previous Cups and again had a strong representation (three exceptional stayers) lining up. Certainly, no one could have anticipated the result – all Cummings' runners unplaced and a horse prepared by a newly licensed trainer winning the race by a record-equalling eight lengths.

That horse was Rain Lover, who was to go on to racing immortality by winning again in 1969 – a remarkable feat since many had considered he was not a genuine two-miler. So for once Bart Cummings was pushed into the background and the fledgling trainer, former horse breaker Mick Robins, was the toast of racing. But the trainer who should have been taking centre stage was Adelaide's Grahame Heagney, who had both the Caulfield Cup winner Bunratty Castle and Rain Lover in his stable but he decided to answer an SOS from

Tobin Bronze's new owners in the United States, and the two stayers went to other trainers.

Robins might have been inexperienced but he prepared Rain Lover to perfection, guiding him expertly through the spring lead-up races and culminating with a win in the LKS Mackinnon Stakes on the Saturday before the Cup. Even so, the spotlight was still very much on the Cummings horses, particularly Galilee who was making great progress in his comeback campaign after being badly injured in the Sydney Cup. But Cummings also had excellent chances with the mare Lowland and Arctic Coast.

Consequently, on Cup Day these two representatives of Cummings were sent out equal favourites at 6/1. Next in the order came Galilee, Rain Lover and Prominence at 7/1 with the betting indicating the perceived evenness of the field. But the chances of many horses were ruined soon after the jump and

Jim Johnson on Rain Lover.

the race was marred by scrimmages and a fall. Many described this Cup as the roughest yet run. But Jim Johnson on Rain Lover was able to avoid the trouble, secure a handy position and loom up to the leaders approaching the turn. Once into the straight Johnson said 'go' and Rain Lover careered away like a sprinter just joining the race.

12/1 shot Bunratty Castle with Mick Mallyon aboard wins the Caulfield Cup.

Maritana gallops home in the Liston Stakes at Sandown, defeating favourite Winfreux.

Glamour jockey Geoff Lane wins the Victoria Derby on Always There.

1968 RESULTS

VRC MELBOURNE CUP (2m)
Rain Lover, 8.2 (J Johnson) Trained by ML Robins; 3:19.1; Fleur, Fans
AJC SYDNEY CUP (2m)
General Command, 9.3 (G Moore) Trained by W Wilson; 3:26.4; Prominence, Padtheway
QTC BRISBANE CUP (2m)
Prominence, 7.10 (WA Smith) Trained by N Creighton; 3:18.6; Swift Peter, Booberella
SAJC ADELAIDE CUP (2m)
Rain Lover, 7.4 (J Letts) Trained by HG Heagney; 3:31; Debhel Boy, Arctic Coast
WATC PERTH CUP (2m)
Lintonmarc (B Ryan) Trained by E Parnham; 3:23; Rock Drill, Hilney
VATC CAULFIELD CUP (12-f)
Bunratty Castle, 7.13 (R Mallyon) Trained by K Wynne; 2:29.7; Future, Arctic Coast

VRC AUSTRALIAN CUP (10-f)
Arctic Coast, 7.7 (M Goreham) Trained by JB Cummings; 2:2.3; Yootha, Nanna Tale
MVRC WS COX PLATE (10-f)
Rajah Sahib, 7.11 (G Moore) Trained by TW Hill; 2:04.8; Fileur, Crewman
AJC DERBY (12-f)
Wilton Park, 8.10 (H Cope) Trained by M Anderson; 2:31.2; Royal Account, Always There
VRC VICTORIA DERBY (12-f)
Always There, 8.10 (G Lane) Trained by C Waymouth; 2:31; Vanishing, Crewman
AJC DONCASTER HANDICAP (1m)
Unpainted, 8.10 (S Spinks) Trained by TJ Smith; 1:34.7; Cabochon, Shakedown
BTC DOOMBEN '10 000' (7-f less 93 yds)
Gay Gauntlet, 8.2 (R McCarthy) Trained by T O'Leary; 1:19.6; Academy Star, Dual Control

VRC NEWMARKET HANDICAP (6-f)
Manihi, 8.1 (H White) Trained by T Jenner; 1:10.1; Nebo Road, Begonia Belle
AJC SIRES' PRODUCE STAKES (7-f)
Black Onyx, 8.10 (K Langby) Trained by TJ Smith; 1:23.1; Cottonon, Alfalfa
VRC SIRES' PRODUCE STAKES (7-f)
Flying Fable, 8.7 (M Schumacher) Trained by TJ Smith; 1:24.9; Crewman, Alfalfa
VRC GRAND NATIONAL STEEPLECHASE (3m 1-f)
McEwen, 10.13 (T McGinley) Trained by O Gardner; 5:58.2; Sir Cameron, Delville Boy
STC GOLDEN SLIPPER STAKES (6-f)
Royal Parma, 8.7 (N Campton) Trained by J Daniels; 1:11.9; Alfalfa, Flying Fable

Big Philou sensation

There never was a racehorse so enmeshed in controversy as the quality stayer Big Philou. In fact, controversy continually clouded his great ability. He is remembered not so much for his performances but for the 1969 pre-Melbourne Cup doping scandal that remains unsolved to this day.

Big Philou started equal favourite in the Caulfield Cup and was always going to figure in the finish. However, just as he was about to make his run on the inside, the Sydney-trained Nausori was moved across to the rails by jockey Des Lake. Roy Higgins was forced to check Big Philou and for the last 100 metres to the post Big Philou appeared to be badly unbalanced. However, he gradually wore Nausori down to fail by a neck.

Higgins' ensuing protest caused a sensation. When stewards announced after a 20-minute hearing that the protest had been upheld, the course was in uproar. If only for this event alone (only the second successful winning protest in Cup history) Big Philou would never be forgotten.

But the Caulfield Cup protest win was merely a prelude to the drama set to unfold just before the Melbourne Cup 10 days later. The 85 600 people who attended the Cup that day could never forget that moment 39 minutes before the scheduled start. At precisely 2.01 p.m., the warning siren sounded and the course broadcaster announced that Big Philou had been withdrawn by order of the stewards. Flemington was abuzz.

Top jockey Roy Higgins had won the Maroona Handicap on Via, before the horse decided to head for the roses and ditch him on the return to scale.

In truth, the 1969 Cup didn't need the extra drama. Rain Lover, carrying 9.7 compared to 8.2 in the previous year's victory, was ridden to perfection by Jim Johnson who had him in front in the straight as he had in 1968. This time the weight told and Rain Lover could not break clear. But still he was able to hold off every challenge. Then as they surged towards the post, the lightly weighted Alsop, carrying only 7.7, reached and headed him. Rain Lover, under Johnson's desperate riding, displayed indomitable courage to come again and snatch victory on the line. Rain Lover had become the first horse since Archer in 1861 and 1862 to win successive Melbourne Cups.

It was one of the greatest of wins but what, racegoers were asking, had happened to Big Philou? As the countdown to the Cup neared, Big Philou was noticed to be visibly distressed and scouring uncontrollably in his stall. Cummings, thinking the horse had developed a virus, asked for and was given permission to take him to his stables nearby. The stewards' machinery for testing a horse in these circumstances was set in motion. Seven days later, the analyst's report revealed that Big Philou, the horse backed for so much money to win the Melbourne Cup, had been nobbled with the purgative Danthron. There has never been a bigger sensation in the history of Australian racing.

An intensive inquiry was begun. Impatient with lack of progress, Big Philou's owner Charles Gawith offered a reward of $5000 for information leading to the conviction of the nobbler or nobblers. Despite lengthy sittings, Victoria Racing Club stewards made little progress and the investigation was handed over to police. Three months later there appeared to be a breakthrough – it was announced that a former strapper in the Cummings stable, Leslie Lewis, was being sought for questioning.

It was found that Lewis had flown to New Zealand, entering under an assumed name. Subsequently deported by the New Zealand Government, he was charged on his return with conspiracy with an unknown person or persons to administer a purgative to Big Philou with intent to cheat and defraud. He was later acquitted of the charge.

Meanwhile, the cause of the scandal, Big Philou, recovered from the nobbling and went on to win good races, including the famous 'match race' against Rain Lover.

The very volatile Charles Gawith

By all accounts, the Honourable Charles Sherwin Gawith was a man to be reckoned with. He became widely known as a businessman, philanthropist, state parliamentarian and racehorse owner. He was thrust into even greater public prominence by the Big Philou doping scandal but his volatility, and tensions between himself and trainer Bart Cummings and jockey Roy Higgins, had already been a major talking point in racing circles.

In the late 1960s he was fortunate to have three excellent horses with Cummings – Big Philou, Alrello and King Pedro. However, in 1969 when Alrello was unluckily beaten in the Epsom Handicap, Gawith seized on an explanation Higgins made to the press and blamed him for the horse's defeat. 'You have cost me $26 000,' he said. Then, when Higgins was awarded the protest on Big Philou in the Caulfield Cup that year, Gawith, instead of expressing gratitude, said, 'What about the $26 000 you cost me in Sydney?'

The next year Gawith clashed with Cummings over the trainer's decision to scratch Big Philou from the Caulfield Cup because of an injury. Gawith delivered a letter to the metropolitan race clubs stipulating that none of his horses was to be scratched without his permission. A few hours later he had Big Philou removed from the Cummings stable. VATC stewards later backed the decision Cummings made on the scratching.

Vain and Pat Hyland at the line in the Golden Slipper.

Vain, glorious Vain

Few young horses have captured the imagination as Vain did in the autumn of 1969. Vain ignited the Melbourne–Sydney rivalry when, after dominating the two-year-old races in Melbourne, he was set for the rich Golden Slipper Stakes at Rosehill.

New South Wales racing followers, including some well-known commentators, scoffed at the idea of a challenge from Victoria. The NSW filly Special Girl had a huge following in Sydney after she blitzed the opposition in two-year-old races there.

So on 22 March 1969 the stage was set for a magnificent moment in racing – what many considered a match race between two outstanding horses. A huge crowd of 40 000 crammed Rosehill to watch the contest. Of huge interest would be the tactics employed by Victorian jockey Pat Hyland and Sydney supremo George Moore.

Alas, the race was a fizzer. Vain jumped to the front immediately and was never headed for the entire 1200 metres. Special Girl could not keep in touch and Moore let her walk to the line to finish fifth.

So Vain was king of the turf, but the great uncertainty of racing soon prevailed. At his next start, in the 1400-metre Sires' Produce Stakes at Randwick, Vain was considered unbeatable – and after taking a huge lead still looked to be home a few metres from the post. But the extra distance told, and he was run down by the outsider Beau Babylon.

Consequently, Vain was again written off by the Sydney experts. He again proved them wrong by coming out next start (and back to 1200 metres) and winning the Champagne Stakes at Randwick by 10 lengths. Vain went on to win the Craven 'A' Stakes and the Linlithgow Stakes during the Melbourne Spring Carnival. He was also a success at stud, siring among other good horses the exceptional speedster Sir Dapper, winner of the 1983 Golden Slipper.

TURF TOPICS

The brilliance of 'Darby' McCarthy: Aboriginal rider Richard 'Darby' McCarthy set the seal on his class when he won the AJC Derby and Epsom Handicap in successive races on Saturday, 4 October 1969. His wins – on Divide And Rule (Derby), then Broker's Tip (Epsom) – were rated two of the best performances ever seen at Randwick. The rides were a complete contrast. Divide And Rule drew barrier 16 but McCarthy had him on the rails poised behind the leaders approaching the home turn. He dashed away to win easily. Broker's Tip had a chequered run and it was only McCarthy's inspired riding nearing the post that got him the verdict over Roy Higgins on Alrello.

Amateur success: In NZ, Matamata rider Bob Autridge became just the second amateur rider to win Wellington's premier jumping race when Foxonewa saluted in the Wellington Steeplechase.

The 'remote battery' scandal: In August 1969 AJC stewards reported that a battery had been found in the saddle of Smashing Blonde at Rosehill. Sydney jockey Sammy Mezzasalma and three other men were later disqualified for life by stewards. Mazzasalma eventually served four years.

A Sydney electronics expert told the inquiry he had been asked to perfect a remote-controlled battery-saddle. When he said this would mean the jockey would have almost no control over the horse, a syndicate member replied: 'That's perfect! There's no need to put the jockey in the scheme at all.'

Mayo Gold's treble: Three-year-old filly Mayo Gold scored a memorable trio of wins at the Wellington Cup Carnival. On day one she won the Wellington Stakes, on day two the Metropolitan Handicap and on day three the Wellington Oaks, despite a slipped saddle.

1969 RESULTS

VRC MELBOURNE CUP (2m)
Rain Lover, 9.7 (J Johnson) Trained by JB Cummings; 3:21.5; Alsop, Ben Lomond
AJC SYDNEY CUP (2m)
Lowland, 8.8 (R Higgins) Trained by JB Cummings; 3:24.4; Rain Lover, Rocket Fuel
QTC BRISBANE CUP (2m)
Galleon King, 7.6 (F Marsland) Trained by EG Boland; 3:20.7; Roman Consul, Sandy's Hope
SAJC ADELAIDE CUP (2m)
Gnapur, 7.11 (H White) Trained by GM Hanlon; 3:21; Debhel Boy, Arctic Coast
WATC PERTH CUP (2m)
Jenark, 7.5 (F Treen) Trained by H Campbell; 3:20; Naupella, Polo King
VATC CAULFIELD CUP (12-f)
Big Philou, 8.2 (R Higgins) Trained by JB Cummings; 2:28.3; Nausori, Tobermory

VRC AUSTRALIAN CUP (10-f)
Dead-heat first Cyron, 8.5 (G Moore) and Yootha, 8.4 (F Reys) Cyron trained by T Hill; Yootha trained by A Smerdon; 2:2.3; Sunhaven third
MVRC WS COX PLATE (10-f)
Daryl's Joy, 7.11 (WD Skelton) Trained by SA Brown; 2:05.4; Ben Lomond, Fileur
AJC DERBY (12-f)
Divide And Rule, 8.10 (R McCarthy) Trained by N Begg; 2:33.5; Gallicus, Might Concorde
VRC VICTORIA DERBY (12-f)
Daryl's Joy, 8.10 (WD Skelton) Trained by S Brown; 2:33.3; Top Flat, Gallicus
AJC DONCASTER HANDICAP (1m)
Bye Bye, 8.4 (N Voigt) Trained by TJ Smith; 1:35.9; Foresight, Sandy's Hope
BTC DOOMBEN '10 000' (7-f less 93 yds)
Black Onyx, 8.8 (G Moore) Trained by TJ Smith; 1:18.1; Regal Hunter, Regal Vista

VRC NEWMARKET HANDICAP (6-f)
Begonia Belle, 8.6 (WA Smith) Trained by AE Elkington; 1:9.4; Black Onyx, Academy Star
AJC SIRES' PRODUCE STAKES (7-f)
Beau Babylon, 8.10 (R Higgins) Trained by F Lewis; 1:25; Vain, Grammar Lass
VRC SIRES' PRODUCE STAKES (7-f)
Vain, 8.10 (P Hyland) Trained by J Moloney; 1:23.6; Ballylachan, Lone Wolf
VRC GRAND NATIONAL STEEPLECHASE (3m 1-f)
Summer Flight, 9.13 (M Laurance) Trained by T Howe; 5:52.7; Bankstown, The Fox
STC GOLDEN SLIPPER STAKES (6-f)
Vain, 8.7 (P Hyland) Trained by J Moloney; 1:12.1; Peter's Empire, Gaelic Spirit

Big Philou pips Rain Lover in the clash of the century in the Queen Elizabeth Stakes (Age).

The clash of the century

By the autumn of 1970 the two top staying horses in the country, Rain Lover and Big Philou, had little left to prove – except, perhaps, who was the better. Rain Lover had won the previous two Melbourne Cups – the first horse since initial winner Archer to achieve the feat – while Big Philou had won a Caulfield Cup and, many believed, been robbed of certain Melbourne Cup glory in 1969 by being nobbled.

So, when at final acceptances these two titans of the turf were declared the only runners in the Queen Elizabeth Stakes, the VRC had a magnificent match race to showcase: surely a promoter's dream. Soon, it was billed as the clash of the century.

Certainly it would have been hard to script a racing duel with more piquancy. The horses were out-and-out champions. They had met four times with two victories each. They had the services of two of the best jockeys in the land (Roy Higgins on Big Philou; Pat Hyland on Rain Lover) and the race would unfold down the long straight at Flemington. It would, of course, be a classic battle of tactics. And so it proved.

The big crowd on 16 March 1970 hushed in anticipation as the horses jumped. Hyland, perhaps believing that Rain Lover's two Melbourne Cup victories meant he was the better stayer, went straight to the lead, allowing Higgins to settle Big Philou 2½ lengths behind. Hyland alternately eased and increased the pressure, but Higgins was always the same distance behind.

Then, in the straight, Hyland looked around and Big Philou was upon him. The crowd erupted as two great horses and two top jockeys raced neck and neck toward the post. The whips flailed in unison. It was a stride-for-stride battle. Suddenly it was over – and Big Philou had won by a half-head.

Baguette mystery

Baguette made racing history when he became the first horse to win the Sydney two-year-olds' Triple Crown in 1970. Baguette had already stamped himself an exceptional colt by winning the Maribyrnong Plate at Flemington and the Slipper at Rosehill. After taking out the AJC Sires' Produce and the Champagne Stakes to complete the Triple Crown, Moore announced his retirement. Baguette won more races but also recorded a number of surprise losses. However, in 1971, Moore, the only jockey who really understood Baguette, decided on a comeback in the 1971 Newmarket. The pair scored a comprehensive victory over the top filly Dual Choice.

TURF TOPICS

The courage of Black Onyx: Trainer T. J. Smith knew he had an exceptional young horse when Black Onyx won three successive races as a two-year-old. Surprisingly beaten in the Golden Slipper of 1968, Black Onyx made amends by taking out the AJC Sires the following week. Smith, never one to under-race a horse, then set Black Onyx on an ambitious campaign to which the grey responded magnificently by running second in the Newmarket in the autumn and then taking out the Doomben Ten Thousand. He demonstrated his courage by running second at the unsuitable longer distance of the 2220-metres Doomben Cup. The following autumn he won the Lightning Stakes, then lumped 57.5kg to victory over Tauto in the Newmarket. After third placings in the Doncaster and Stradbroke Handicaps, Black Onyx won a second Doomben Ten Thousand under 59kg.

He went on to win more top races before bleeding in 1970 Hill Stakes in Sydney, then in the Futurity Stakes in Melbourne. He then raced in America where he was administered drugs to prevent bleeding and won more races before fading into relative obscurity.

Sad end: Rarely has there been such widespread sadness about the death of a racehorse as there was when jumper Lots Of Time had to be put down in 1970. When in the previous year he won the Toolambool Hurdle he notched his eighth win in a row, breaking the Victorian record set nearly 50 years earlier by Le Mattan and equalling Air Fox's 21-year-old Australian record. Then at his next start he claimed the record by winning the Port Phillip Hurdle at the Sandown track. Burdened with 73kg, he came from five lengths behind at the turn to sweep past Brother Bart, who carried 11kg less. Lots Of Time was switched to steeplechasing in 1970, but fell and had to be put down, in the Hiskens Steeple.

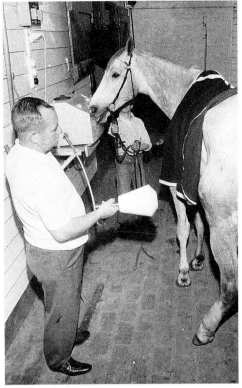

Baghdad Note gets some heat treatment (BP).

Baghdad Note is third last as the field swings out of the straight for the long Cup circuit (Age).

A forgotten grey wins the Melbourne Cup

It had been three years since he had won a Melbourne Cup, but the Bart Cummings magic still dominated pre-Cup discussions in 1970. His lightly raced stayer Voleur – another of the Le Filou progeny – was confidently expected to return his name to the winning list, particularly since Voleur had won the wfa Mackinnon Stakes on Derby day and had a 16 lb weight drop for the Cup. Many regarded Voleur a special.

Almost totally forgotten, if indeed he had ever seriously been considered, was a grey from New Zealand named Baghdad Note, who had dead-heated for third in the Caulfield Cup (Voleur was second) but who had finished fifth in a field of seven in the Mackinnon. On that performance and with a substantial weight disadvantage, there was good reason to

discard Baghdad Note from calculations. But there was also the state of the track. Baghdad Note was an exceptional wet tracker and the Flemington track on Cup day was rock hard. Baghdad Note went to the start friendless in the market at 25/1 while Voleur started favourite at 9/4.

Set alight by Jim Johnson after some bad luck in the run, Voleur led into the straight but was 'gone' 200 metres out. Caulfield Cup winner Beer Street took charge but was easily passed by Baghdad Note, whose rider 'Midge' Didham timed his run to perfection. On the post Baghdad Note won by three-quarters of a length from Vansittart and the three-year-old Clear Prince.

Baghdad Note became only the third grey to win the Cup but still there was little inter-

est in him. Major Cup coverage next day centred on his owner, wealthy Dunedin businessman Mr E. C. S. Falconer who had responded to the win by checking his pulse. He had suffered a heart attack the previous Christmas and didn't want a recurrence to spoil what he described as the greatest thrill of his life.

Baghdad Note stayed in the news. There was outrage a couple of years after the Cup when it was announced that Baghdad Note, now owned and trained in Victoria, would pursue a jumping career. However, this did not eventuate and the horse showed his toughness and durability by winning the 1973 Sandown Cup. He later became a clerk of course pony and lived out his retirement on a farm in Victoria's Western District.

1970 RESULTS

VRC MELBOURNE CUP (2m)
Baghdad Note, 8.7 (E Didham) Trained by R Heasley; 3:19.7; Vansittart, Clear Prince
AJC SYDNEY CUP (2m)
Arctic Symbol, 7.9 (N Voigt) Trained by J Moloney; 3:35.8; Lochcourt, Te Kura
QTC BRISBANE CUP (2m)
Cachondeo, 8.2 (A Erhart) Trained by J Griffiths; 3:22.9; Affectionate, Panvale
SAJC ADELAIDE CUP (2m)
Tavel, 7.10 (A Trevena) Trained by JB Cummings; 3:23.2; Romany, Bojon
WATC PERTH CUP (2m)
Fait Accompli, 7.4 (K Bradley) Trained by H Harrison; 3:21.5; Nauprius, Aubella
VATC CAULFIELD CUP (12-f)
Beer Street, 7.11 (B Gilders) Trained by D Judd; 2:31.1; Voleur, dead-heat third Baghdad Note and Royal Show

VRC AUSTRALIAN CUP (10-f)
Crewman, 8.12 (H White) Trained by A Armanasco; 2.1.9; Cyron, Nanna Tale
MVRC WS COX PLATE (10-f)
Abdul, 7.12 (P Jarman) Trained by GT Murphy; 2:05.5; Tails, Rough'N Tumble
AJC DERBY (12-f)
Silver Sharpe, 8.10 (N Voigt) Trained by TJ Smith; 2:31.9; Planet Kingdom, Gunsynd
VRC VICTORIA DERBY (12-f)
Silver Sharpe, 8.10 (P Hyland) Trained by TJ Smith; 2:30.5; Gay Icarus, Royal Show
AJC DONCASTER HANDICAP (1m)
Broker's Tip, 8.11 (H Cope) Trained by H Riley; 1:36.4; Alrello, Black Onyx
BTC DOOMBEN '10,000' (7-f less 93 yds)
Black Onyx, 9.4 (S Spinks) Trained by G Moore; 1:18.2; Cabochon, Mister Hush

VRC NEWMARKET HANDICAP (6-f)
Black Onyx, 9.1 (G Moore) Trained by TJ Smith; 1:10.3; Tauto, Mister Hush
AJC SIRES' PRODUCE STAKES (7-f)
Baguette, 8.10 (G Moore) Trained by F Allotta; 1:23.4; Fleet Royal, Royal Show
VRC SIRES' PRODUCE STAKES (7-f)
Dual Choice, 8.7 (P Gumbleton) Trained by K White; 1:24.2; Royal Show, Coalcliff
VRC GRAND NATIONAL STEEPLECHASE (3m 1-f)
Black Butt, 9.10 (T McGinley) Trained by CS Hayes; 6:2.6; Mystic Moon, Buckshot
STC GOLDEN SLIPPER STAKES (6-f)
Baguette, 8.7 (G Moore) Trained by F Allotta; 1:12.7; Royal Show, Dual Choice

Silver Knight outstays the field to win, aided by controversial interference to local favourite Gay Icarus (Age).

Silver Knight makes it 12 of 18 for NZ

New Zealand makes it 12 of 18. The grey Silver Knight's win in the 1971 Melbourne Cup was the 12th victory in 18 years by New Zealand–bred horses. And while Silver Knight was a worthy winner, few racegoers doubted that the local Gay Icarus would have figured in the finish had he not been knocked out of the race by the controversial Big Philou.

Silver Knight had a vastly different preparation from most New Zealand Cup contenders. His trainer Eric Temperton gave him a prodigious workload as a young horse, starting him nine times as a two-year-old (for one win) and 23 times as a three-year-old when his strike rate began to improve.

Flown to Melbourne in 1971, Silver Knight was distressed during the flight and ran poorly in the Cox Plate. He had recovered by the Mackinnon Stakes and recorded a slashing trial for the Melbourne Cup by finishing second to Moonee Valley Cup winner Skint Dip. Local punters, however, could not see past Gay Icarus who was a 7/4 favourite despite being asked to lump 9.7. Silver Knight, with 8.9, started at 10/1.

The 1971 Cup was one of the toughest on the competing horses in the history of the race. The track was flint-like and of the 21 runners five broke down and another lost his rider. Gay Icarus was moving up like a winner when flattened and Silver Knight, ridden superbly by 21-year-old New Zealander Bruce Marsh, outstayed the rest of the field.

The severity of the interference to Gay Icarus was reflected in the two months' suspension handed out to Big Philou's jockey, apprentice Norman Waymouth. The unlucky Ray Setches was the jockey to fall in the race. This was typical of Setches' fortunes in the Melbourne Cup – he was second in the two years before 1971 and unplaced in 1972–73.

Beginning of the Blue Diamond Stakes

By 1971 Sydney's Golden Slipper Stakes was well established as Australia's premier two-year-old event and was on the way to becoming the richest race of its type in the world. The Slipper – first won in 1957 by the brilliant Todman starting at 6/1 on – had added immensely to the prestige of two-year-old racing.

In response to that success, the Victorian Amateur Turf Club announced the inauguration of the Blue Diamond Stakes – a prestige two-year-old event to be run at Caulfield in the autumn with a $1000 diamond as a trophy. The Blue Diamond thus added still another dimension to the two-year-old calendar. Its inaugural running in 1971 created huge interest.

The Angus Armanasco–trained Tolerance was the 'boom' horse in the field and entitled to favouritism since he had won all three starts but the well-performed Lemon Twist and What's The Verdict were expected to fully extend the chestnut colt. Not too much notice was taken of a visitor from Sydney, T. J. Smith's Fairy Walk.

The race was a 'heart-stopper' for favourite-backers. Tolerance was badly interfered with as the field entered the straight and his chance looked forlorn. Fairy Walk, ridden by John Stocker, had swept to the lead and was no sooner being called the winner when the challenges came. First, What's The Verdict surged through on the rails while Tolerance was flying down the outside. Most racegoers thought What's The Verdict had lasted, but the photo gave it to Tolerance. Fairy Walk, who was to go on and give T. J. Smith the first of his Golden Slippers, was third but Lemon Twist failed badly

This was the first of many great stagings of the Blue Diamond, which Roy Higgins went on to win four times.

Mick Mallyon waves his whip to his wife as he gets up in the Caulfield Cup (Age).

The call of the card at the Victorian Club.

Gay Icarus soars for Beechey

The appellation 'character' has always been overused in racing. It should be reserved for men like Cyril Beechey, the ex-rouse-about jack-of-all-trades who first took out a trainer's licence at age 57, then won two Caulfield Cups in five years.

Beechey's first winner, when he was aged 60, was an improbable champion called Gay Icarus who might not have reached the heights he did if not trained with care and patience. Higher-profile mentors might not have persisted with a horse that was a small and weedy juvenile who placed only once in his first five starts.

But Beechey, who had bred the horse, had the quiet endurance of the bushman he had been. In his second campaign Gay Icarus won a maiden at Werribee, then ran two seconds in town followed by a win in the Burwood Handicap at Caulfield. He signalled his future greatness by then running second to Silver Sharpe in the Victoria Derby.

In the autumn of 1971 the three-year-old really blossomed, winning the Blamey Stakes, the St George Stakes and the Australian Cup. He then went to Sydney where he won the Chipping Norton Stakes, the Champion Stakes and the Queen Elizabeth Stakes. It was little wonder he was allotted the substantial impost of 9.2 (a champion horse's weight) in the Caulfield Cup. He justified the handicapper's assessment by continuing his winning ways in the spring – taking out the Underwood Stakes and the Caulfield Stakes leading up to the Caulfield Cup.

Cyril Beechey might by now have become one of racing's high flyers but he was instead being criticised by a section of the racing press for insisting he would scratch Gay Icarus from the Caulfield Cup if the track was wet. Some journalists claimed this brought the viability of early Cups doubles betting into question. Beechey's late start in racing meant he was not used to censure from outsiders and he resented it. He told racing journalists: 'Don't visit me, don't ring me up. I'm not at home to you.'

As it happened, the Caulfield Cup track was dry and Beechey let Gay Icarus do the talking. The horse started favourite in what was considered a high-class Cup field with Gunsynd, Big Philou, Igloo and the three-year-old Beau Sovereign well in contention. But they were no match for Gay Icarus, who was ridden in copybook style by Mick Mallyon. The jockey stood up in the irons and waved his whip as he passed the post a clear winner.

TURF TOPICS

Little old lady sails home: South Island breeder Joyce Edgar Jones and Sailing Home became public icons in the summer of 1971–72 as the stooped, grey-haired little woman led her 17.1-hand mare back to scale after victories in the Auckland Cup and the Waikato International Stakes. Dramatic disparity of size was nothing new for Sailing Home. When she was a foal, she used to kneel to suckle her diminutive dam, Chocolate. Not a freak of genetics; Chocolate had been born a twin and never grew beyond pony size.

A pregnant win: Princess Mellay set a bunch of records when she won the 1971 New Zealand Cup in the hands of Bob Skelton (who thus gained his 10th success in a two-mile event, with more to come). Princess Mellay, who had also won the year before, was the first horse to win two New Zealand Cups since the race was first held in 1883; she set a weight-carrying record for a mare with 8 st 12 lb and she was the first mare to win the big Riccarton race when in foal.

Princess Mellay was later found to have been carrying twins to Causeur. It was a triple dead-heat!

1971 RESULTS

VRC MELBOURNE CUP (2m)
Silver Knight, 8.9 (R Marsh) Trained by E Templeton; 3:19.5; Igloo, Tails
AJC SYDNEY CUP (2m)
Gallic Temple, 7.3 (P Cook) Trained by A Ward; 3:20.3; Bluelough, Arctic Symbol
QTC BRISBANE CUP (2m)
Royal Shah, 7.13 (R Quinton) Trained by TJ Smith; 3:22.4; Chilton, Earlmark
SAJC ADELAIDE CUP (2m)
Laelie, 7.5 (D Hillis) Trained by JB Cummings; 3:25.5; Lancelot, Scotch And Dry
WATC PERTH CUP (2m)
Artello Bay, 7.5 (WA Smith) Trained by J Wall; 3:23.7; Reodora, Kilrickle
VATC CAULFIELD CUP (12-f)
Gay Icarus, 9.2 (R Mallyon) Trained by CL Beechey; 2:28; Igloo, Big Philou

VRC AUSTRALIAN CUP (10-f)
Gay Icarus, 7.10 (R Mallyon) Trained by C Beechey; 2:2.1; Rajah Sahib, Tails
MVRC WS COX PLATE (10-f)
Tauto, 9.4 (L Hill) Trained by RM Agnew; 2:03.9; Igloo, Beau Sovereign
AJC DERBY (12-f)
Classic Mission, 8.10 (G Moore) Trained by S Brown; 2:36.1; Latin Knight, Daneson
VRC VICTORIA DERBY (12-f)
Classic Mission, 8.10 (G Moore) Trained by SA Brown; 2:32.5; Column, Altai Khan
AJC DONCASTER HANDICAP (1m)
Rajah Sahib, 8.8 (G Moore) Trained by T Hughes; 1:34.7; Tauto, King Apollo
BTC DOOMBEN '10 000' (7-f less 93 yds)
Baguette, 9.2 (G Moore) Trained by F Allotta; 1:19.2; Royal Treat, Waminda

VRC NEWMARKET HANDICAP (6-f)
Baguette, 8.12 (G Moore) Trained by F Allotta; 1:10.1; Dual Choice, Tauto
AJC SIRES' PRODUCE STAKES (7-f)
Latin Knight, 8.10 (R Selkrig) Trained by M Anderson; 1:23.8; Fairy Walk, Tolerance
VRC SIRES' PRODUCE STAKES (7-f)
Tolerance, 8.10 (R Higgins) Trained by A Armanasco; 1:23.7; Fairy Walk, Hippomedon
VRC GRAND NATIONAL STEEPLECHASE (3m 1-f)
Valgo, 9.6 (T McGinley) Trained by Ms K Smith; 5:46.8; Club Spirit, Foxonewa
STC GOLDEN SLIPPER STAKES (6-f)
Fairy Walk, 8.1 (G Moore) Trained by TJ Smith; 1:12.6; Beau Rouge, My Amazon
VATC BLUE DIAMOND STAKES (6-f) (First run 1971)
Tolerance, 8.7 (R Higgins) Trained by A Armanasco; 1:11.9; What's The Verdict, Fairy Walk

Sobar easily wins the Caulfield Cup (Age).

Regal Vista classed unsound (Age).

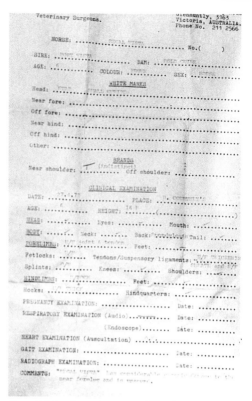

The real Regal Vista back in work (Age).

Bad day win

The great uncertainty of racing was never more graphically demonstrated than in the running of the Victoria Derby of 1972 when Sobar stepped out an odds-on favourite, and everything went wrong.

Sobar's price of 11/4 on was justified. Sobar was being compared to the mighty Tulloch and had earned the comparison by the ease with which he had won the Underwood Stakes, the Caulfield Guineas and the Caulfield Cup (in which he had eclipsed Gunsynd) over the previous four weeks.

In fact, Sobar had won the Caulfield Cup in a canter, and the Derby looked to be his for the taking. But to the dismay of his backers, Sobar was in trouble from the time the gates opened. There were gasps of disbelief as jockey Harry White wrestled with him and seemed to be trying to restrain him instead of letting him stride out freely. Worse, the colt was three wide as he pulled hard and refused to settle.

In contrast, Dayana, prepared by Bart Cummings and ridden by Roy Higgins, was having the best of runs. As the pair thundered to the post, Sobar just failed to hold Dayana, who won by a neck. At first, the large crowd was stunned, but many found their voice as Sobar returned, and shouted their disapproval of the ride. Harry White blamed himself for the horse's defeat but it was later revealed that Sobar had sprung a tendon during the race.

Regal ring-in went too royally

There was just one thing wrong with the meticulous planning that went into the notorious Royal School ring-in scam of 1972 – the horse rung in was too accomplished to be credible. That horse was Regal Vista, a top-line sprinter who had shown his class by winning the 1969 Stradbroke Handicap, the 1970 Liston Stakes (at wfa) and twice being placed in the Oakleigh Plate.

Yet Regal Vista was the horse chosen to race as Royal School in the Muntham Handicap at Casterton on 12 May. And if Regal Vista was close to being top class, Royal School could be fairly described as being a prolific non-performer who had finished last or, occasionally, second last in most of his races in 1971. When Regal Vista, racing as Royal School, won the Muntham Handicap hard held by three lengths in the slick time of 1:12.2 after being slowly away, it didn't take a racetrack genius to deduce that something above and beyond Royal School's limited ability was involved. A ring-in was obvious.

The mastermind of the ring-in, Vittorio David 'Rick' Renzella, was a former car salesman who had a deep knowledge of, and practical interest in, racing. Not only had he owned several capable racehorses, he had successfully orchestrated three or four lucrative betting coups involving these horses, in particular a good sprinter named Koda Pen. Renzella planned the Casterton ring-in affair with great foresight and attention to detail.

First, he paid $350 for Royal School – a price that must have delighted the owners considering Royal School's lack of success and with his best years behind him. Renzella then decided that Regal Vista would be the ideal horse for the ring-in. He successfully negotiated the purchase of the horse for $6000 on delivery plus $3500 from its first win.

With the ring-in in place Renzella then executed a betting plunge through Melbourne TAB agencies that involved coupling Royal School with every horse in the Casterton Cup – the main event of the day – and which saw Royal School's price tumble from 50/1 to 7/4 favourite. After the easiest of wins by 'Royal School', there were howls of disbelief, most notably from the trainer of the second horse, Apex Star, considered the best sprinter in the field.

Although the ring-in and betting plunge had been skilfully and successfully executed, Renzella's triumph was short-lived. He failed to present the horse's correct racing papers and an inquiry was opened into the event.

The case took a bizarre twist when Regal Vista went missing only to be 'found' later by Renzella. After inquiries by police and racing officials, Renzella was arrested and jailed for two years. The horse's trainer, Ross Afflick, and jockey, Stephen Wood, received suspended sentences.

Gunsynd is given a tumultuous welcome at Moonee Valley after winning the Cox Plate (BP).

The grey from Goondiwindi

He was called the Goondiwindi Grey – a name immortalised in a popular song. His exceptional courage and ability earned him the plaudits of race followers. And the gallant Gunsynd deserved them all.

His biggest win was in the Cox Plate of 1972, but many believed his greatest run was in the Melbourne Cup 10 days later when he carried 60.5 kg for a valiant third to the lightly weighted Piping Lane.

Although enjoying success as a three-year-old, Gunsynd was transferred to trainer T. J. Smith after his first start as a four-year-old. Under Smith's care, Gunsynd started 32 times for 17 wins and was unplaced once.

In 1971 he electrified the public with some great wins, and in 1972 Smith again set an ambitious program for Gunsynd, who recorded five straight wins including the Doncaster Handicap with 60.5 kg – a feat that underscored his 'iron horse' status.

A few months later Gunsynd won the Cox Plate under the expert guidance of Roy Higgins. The *Age* noted: 'Gunsynd's victory in the Cox Plate was one of those glorious moments of the turf when horse and rider combine in a thrilling, colourful triumph.'

After this win, a syndicate with an option to buy the grey to stand as a stallion made repeated attempts to scratch Gunsynd from the Melbourne Cup. Mr George Ryder said running Gunsynd in the Cup with 60.5 kg could jeopardise his stud career. However, Smith was adamant the horse should start and the owners in Goondiwindi turned a deaf ear to pleas to scratch him. His resolute third demonstrated his courage and defied his breeding.

Gunsynd's last Melbourne run was the Queen Elizabeth Stakes the next autumn. As he crossed the line the crowd gave him a thunderous reception.

TURF TOPICS

Racing goes metric: It was a sad day for traditionalists when racing turned metric on 1 August 1972. Racing clubs acceded to a request from the Metric Conversion Board, and weights and measures turned metric on that date, the first day of the new season. Metrication meant alteration to the distances of great races, and traditionalists were particularly upset by the shortening of the two-mile Melbourne Cup by 20½ yards. The Melbourne *Age* launched a spirited campaign to persuade the VRC to retain the Cup's distance of two miles and enlisted the support of many prominent racing people to bolster the case. The VRC decided to stick to its decision to run the race over 3200 metres.

Follow that hoop: Jockey John Letts faced a big assignment when he took the ride on Piping Lane in the 1972 Melbourne Cup. Letts was offered the mount by trainer George Hanlon only a few days before the race and had never ridden at Flemington. Letts had a plan. 'I decided the best way to ride Piping Lane was to follow the best jockey, so I tacked on to Roy Higgins on Gunsynd,' he said. 'I heard Roy say on television that Gunsynd needed to be taken to the outside to make his run, so I thought if I followed him there would be an opening on the inside … and that's what happened.'

Jim Ellis dies: L. J. (Jim) Ellis, the first New Zealand jockey to top 1000 winners, died in April 1972. His wins included five New Zealand Cups, two Auckland Cups and three Wellington Cups. He trained and rode Golden Souvenir to the 1945 New Zealand Cup win.

Spring in his step: Koral was the youngest winner of Riccarton's Grand National Steeple at five in 1965, and won the Homeby Steeple a week earlier. At 12, in 1972, he won it for the seventh time.

1972 RESULTS

VRC MELBOURNE CUP (3200m)
Piping Lane, 48kg (J Letts) Trained by GM Hanlon; 3:19.3; Magnifique, Gunsynd
AJC SYDNEY CUP (2m)
Dark Suit, 7.8 (J Duggan) Trained by G Hanlon; 3:20.3; Marseilles, Royal Shah
QTC BRISBANE CUP (2m)
Mode, 8.1 (G Cook) Trained by G Williams; 3:21.9, Tails, Bluelough
SAJC ADELAIDE CUP (2m)
Wine Taster, 7.7 (K Langby) Trained by CS Hayes; 3:27.2; Star Contender, Dawn Cherie
WATC PERTH CUP (2m)
Fait Accompli, 7.8 (R Oliver) Trained by H Harrison; 3:21.5; Aubella, Santa Martel
VATC CAULFIELD CUP (2400m)
Sobar, 48 (H White) Trained by K Hilton; 2:27.1; Stormy Seas, Gunsynd

VRC AUSTRALIAN CUP (10-f)
Jan's Beau, 8.8 (G Edge) Trained by T Hughes; 2:2; Sharif, Stop The Show
MVRC WS COX PLATE (2040m)
Gunsynd, 59 (R Higgins) Trained by TJ Smith; 2:01.9; All Shot, Magnifique
AJC DERBY (2400m)
Gold Brick, 55.5 (R Selkrig) Trained by T Kennedy; 2:36.5; Longfella, The Fixer
VICTORIA DERBY (2400m)
Dayana, 55.5 (R Higgins) Trained by JB Cummings; 2:29.9; Sobar, Longfella
AJC DONCASTER HANDICAP (1m)
Gunsynd, 9.7 (R Higgins) Trained by TJ Smith; 1:35.3; Triton, Big Butch
BTC DOOMBEN '10 000' (7-f less 93 yds)
Bengalla Lad, 8.3 (A Gollogly) Trained by HF Best; 1:18.1; Charlton Boy, Amberdue
VRC NEWMARKET HANDICAP (6-f)
Crown, 8.4 (R Higgins) Trained by JB Cummings; 1:9.3; Dual Choice, Tutuila

AJC SIRES' PRODUCE STAKES (7-f)
Sovereign Slipper, 8.10 (W Camer) Trained by R Guy; 1:23; Rogue River, El D'Amour
VRC SIRES' PRODUCE STAKES (7-f)
Century, 8.10 (R Higgins) Trained by JB Cummings; 1:23.7; El D'Amour, Acidity
VRC GRAND NATIONAL STEEPLECHASE (3m 1-f)
Ramleigh, 10.1 (K Bourke) Trained by T Howe; 5:47.4; Farmour, Lord Montini
STC GOLDEN SLIPPER STAKES (6-f)
John's Hope, 8.7 (K Langby) Trained by TJ Smith; 1:11.1; I'm Scarlet, Sovereign Slipper
VATC BLUE DIAMOND STAKES (6-f)
John's Hope, 8.7 (K Langby) Trained by TJ Smith; 1:10.7; Century, El D'Amour

Taj Rossi – Bart's 'best' three-year-old

Trainer Bart Cummings was more effusive than ever before when his three-year-old colt Taj Rossi won the George Adams Handicap on the final day of the 1973 Flemington Spring Carnival. 'They didn't believe me last week when I said Taj Rossi was the best three-year-old for 50 years but I reckon today proved I was not far wrong,' Cummings said.

This surely was the highest possible praise from the usually conservative trainer who would have known that some of the three-year-olds he implied were inferior to Taj Rossi included Phar Lap, Tulloch, Vain, Ajax, Spearfelt, Heroic and Manfred to name a few.

Whether Taj Rossi quite deserved that rating is arguable but certainly he blazed a mighty trail of success that Spring when he won the Cox Plate, the Victoria Derby, the Adams and finally the Sandown Guineas. Almost certainly, his record would have been even more imposing but for his habit of throwing his head about in the starting stalls and concussing himself.

This he had done in the Caulfield Guineas, after which he returned to scale sporting a lump the size of a cricket ball on his skull, after narrowly missing a place. But everything went right in the Cox Plate, even to having a pacemaker in stablemate Leica Lover, whose tearaway tactics ensured a fast pace. Taj Rossi then held off Caulfield Cup winner Swell Time, who had been expected to revel in the soft going.

Stable jockey Roy Higgins was too heavy to take the ride on Taj Rossi in the Cox Plate, but rode him in the Derby. This time Leica Lover provided his strongest opposition, but Taj Rossi collared him in the straight to give Cummings yet another big race quinella.

Stan Aitken (rails) has Taj Rossi in front of Swell Time at the finish of the Cox Plate (Age).

Harry White and his daughter's rabbit which bit him on the toe, sidelining him for two weeks.

Gunsynd has his last laugh after winning the Queen Elizabeth Stakes at 10/1 on (BP).

Frank Reys savours his greatest moment in racing – his Melbourne Cup win on Gala Supreme.

The courage of Frank Reys

When battlers figure in Cup glory there are few emotive moments in sport like it. Such was the scene after the 1973 Melbourne Cup. Jockey Frank Reys, who had battled illness and injury for years, won the Cup on the locally owned, bred and trained Gala Supreme, and the huge crowd of 103 170 acclaimed the home-town victory.

Reys, at 41 the oldest jockey in the race, was overwhelmed. He embraced his wife, his brothers and the horse, then made one of the most memorable and moving speeches at a big race presentation. He explained how just a few months earlier his wife, Noeline, begged him to retire from riding following a horror year of sickness and injury. 'But when I started to feel good again I pleaded with Noeline for one more crack at the Melbourne Cup,' he said. Then, as the crowd stayed totally silent, Reys added: 'I thank the Lord, my family and my trainer. I'll never forget this.'

Both Reys and Gala Supreme deserved the victory, but Melbourne Cup wins never come easily. Gala Supreme's chief asset was that he was set for a big Cup win as a young horse and allowed to mature, in the New Zealand tradition.

The much-vaunted New Zealander Glengowan deserved favouritism. In fact, the only doubt about Glengowan winning seemed to centre on whether young New Zealand apprentice Noel Harris, whose father trained the horse, was a seasoned enough rider for the task.

Inside the final 200 metres Glengowan ranged up to leader Daneson in what looked a winning move. But 50 metres out Reys urged Gala Supreme, who had enjoyed a dream run rarely leaving the rail, into the gap between the two leaders. Glengowan then tried to duck in and Harris momentarily lost control. In that instant Reys gave Gala Supreme one crack with the whip and the race was over.

So to Frank Reys – the spoils and his greatest moment in racing.

1973 RESULTS

VRC MELBOURNE CUP (3200m)
Gala Supreme, 49, (F Reys) Trained by R Hutchins; 3:19.5; Glengowan, Daneson
AJC SYDNEY CUP (3200m)
Apollo Eleven, 54.5 (B Andrews) Trained by M Anderson; 3:19; Dark Suit, Irish Whip
QTC BRISBANE CUP (3200m)
Irish Whip, 55 (R Higgins) Trained by M Ritchie; 3:18.5; The Developer, Baghdad Note
SAJC ADELAIDE CUP (3200m)
Tavel, 51.5 (M Goreham) Trained by ER Judd; 3:28.2; Baghdad Note, Dark Suit
WATC PERTH CUP (3200m)
Dayana, 49.5 (P Cook) Trained by JB Cummings; 3:18.2; Always Morning, Piping Lane
VATC CAULFIELD CUP (2400m)
Swell Time, 51.5 (B Andrews) Trainer WC Winder; 2:35.9; Gala Supreme, Young Ida

VRC AUSTRALIAN CUP (2000m)
Gladman, 48.5 (P Cook) Trained by JB Cummings; 2:1.6; Sharif, Sir Goglio
MVRC WS COX PLATE (2040m)
Taj Rossi, 49.5 (S Aitken) Trained by JB Cummings; 2:08.3; Swell Time, Zambari
AJC DERBY (2400m)
Imagele, 55.5 (K Langby) Trained by TJ Smith; 2:32.1; Leica Lover, Grand Cidium
VICTORIA DERBY (2500m)
Taj Rossi, 55.5 (R Higgins) Trained by JB Cummings; 2:39.4; Leica Lover, Craig Win
AJC DONCASTER HANDICAP (1600m)
Analie, 49 (R Quinton) Trained by TJ Smith; 1:34.7; Century, Lord Nelson
BTC DOOMBEN '10 000' (1350m)
Craigola, 46.5 (L Dittman) Trained by V Markey; 1:19.4; Charlton Boy, Lucky Cloud
VRC NEWMARKET HANDICAP (1200m)
Century, 55 (R Higgins) Trained by JB Cummings; 1:9; Beau Rouge, Zambari

AJC SIRES' PRODUCE STAKES (1400m)
Tontonan, 55.5 (R Higgins) Trained by JB Cummings; 1:23.8; Latin Romance, Baron Gold
VRC SIRES' PRODUCE STAKES (1400m)
Imagele, 55.5 (R Higgins) Trained by TJ Smith; 1:24; Authentic Heir, Grand Cidium
VRC GRAND NATIONAL STEEPLECHASE (5000m)
Deakin Street, 59 (J Williams) Trained by R Bones; 5:59.2; Blueholme, Transall
STC GOLDEN SLIPPER STAKES (1200m)
Tontonan, 54 (R Higgins) Trained by JB Cummings; 1:11.7; Snuff, Strong Plea
VATC BLUE DIAMOND STAKES (1200m)
New Gleam, 54 (T Finger) Trained by E Broadhurst; 1:11.6; Poppy Show, Diligent

Gary Willetts takes a walk while Roy Higgins rides Battle Heights in training (BP).

Battle Heights – a warrior

For New Zealand jockey Gary Willetts the pain was worth it. Nursing a badly bruised left hand he had just steered Battle Heights to victory in the 1974 WS Cox Plate. The injury was severe. 'I wouldn't have ridden with it on any other horse but Battle Heights,' Willetts said.

Willetts was to go on to a historic association with the great Manikato in later years but his high praise for Battle Heights underscored the great ability of that horse who raced at the top level until he was 10 (when he broke down in the 1977 Mackinnon Stakes). Although not arriving from New Zealand until he was six, Battle Heights proved to be one of the toughest and most talented stayers to race in Australia.

Given his first Australian run in the autumn of 1974, he finished a plodding fourth to Igloo and Dayana in the Autumn Stakes. Two days later he stepped out in the Sydney Cup and to the jeers of punters won at 30/1. He was forgiven when he lived up to that form by winning the AJC Queen Elizabeth

Stakes at the end of the autumn carnival, this time turning the tables on Igloo and Dayana.

His Cox Plate win, in which he swept from last to first to completely annihilate his rivals in a few strides, received a memorable ovation. Willetts did not even have to wave the whip as Battle Heights gave his younger rivals, including odds-on Derby favourite Taras Bulba, a galloping lesson.

The win saw Battle Heights installed as 3/1 Melbourne Cup favourite but Willetts' ride was not considered one of his best. Battle Heights was taken from second last to the front on the home turn – more than 400 metres from home. The effort told and he weakened to finish seventh.

Two years later he again beat Taras Bulba, this time in the Craven Plate, after carrying 56.5 kg to victory in the AJC Metropolitan. He finished second to classy mare How Now in the Caulfield Cup and was being prepared for the Melbourne Cup the following year when he broke down and was retired.

Veteran New Zealand trainer Jack Woods brought Captain Peri over to run third in the Melbourne Cup. Neither went anywhere without their travelling companion, three-year-old Silver Jubilee (BP).

Leilani seems to have the Melbourne Cup run with 100 metres to go (Age).

Leilani – lady of the turf

All the racing world loved 'sweet little Leilani' as one journalist continually referred to her. And although small and dainty, she reserved her place in racing's Hall of Fame by her effortless win in the 1974 Caulfield Cup and gallant second in the Melbourne Cup.

Owned by Liberal Cabinet Minister Andrew Peacock and Melbourne City Councillor Ian Rice, Leilani took all before her in the feature races leading up the Melbourne Cup – the Turnbull Stakes, the Toorak, Caulfield Cup and Mackinnon Stakes and hopes were high she would become only the second mare to win both Cups (Rivette had achieved the feat in 1939).

And she so nearly did. Leilani, ridden capably by Sydney jockey Peter Cook (Roy Higgins was under suspension) looked to have the race in her keeping 50 metres out, but her stablemate Think Big swept down the outside to beat her by a length.

Leilani went some way to making amends for her Cup defeat by winning the Queen's Cup (with Higgins back on board) at the end of the Carnival, then came back in the autumn of 1975 to enhance her greatness. Leilani ran track records in the Orr and St George Stakes, won the Queen's Plate and then, at the pinnacle of her career, carried a weight record of 58.5 kg to a memorable win in the Australian Cup.

In that race Higgins had to resort to using the whip on Leilani for the first time. 'She was struggling to head off Tudor Peak,' Higgins said. 'I had to pull the whip and each time I hit her it hurt me.'

Leilani suffered an injury in the Australian Cup and was to win only one more race – the St George Stakes in 1976. She broke down in the Tancred Stakes at Rosehill and was retired. But the grand little mare will never be forgotten and her record speaks for itself – 14 wins and 13 placings from 29 starts.

Regal Vista second to Natural Art at Colac.

Ring-in's chance

Top sprinter Regal Vista was centre of the ring-in case at Casterton in 1972, where he was subbed for Royal School and landed $40 000 for the ringer-in before the perpetrator was discovered and disqualified for life. But don't blame the horse. Now rising nine, Regal Vista had an excellent run behind the slick Natural Art. Connections were so impressed that thought was given to sending Regal Vista to Adelaide to contest the Goodwood Handicap.

Big Philou, withdrawn from a Caulfield race.

1974 RESULTS

VRC MELBOURNE CUP (3200m)
Think Big, 53 (H White) Trained by JB Cummings; 3:23.2; Leilani, Captain Peri
AJC SYDNEY CUP (3200m)
Battle Heights, 58.5 (G Willetts) Trained by R Douglas; 3:37.1; Grand Scale, Dayana
QTC BRISBANE CUP (3200m)
Igloo, 57 (L Dittman) Trained by TJ Smith; 3:22.1; El Karpe, Thing Big
SAJC ADELAIDE CUP (3200m)
Phar Ace, 52 (K Mitchell) Trained by R Morrissey; 3:30.2; Tallan Lad, Igloo
WATC PERTH CUP (3200m)
Allegation, 53 (L Rudland) Trained by K Williams; 3:20.8; Kabooki, Phar Ace
VATC CAULFIELD CUP (2400m)
Leilani, 52 (R Mailyon) Trained by JB Cummings; 2:38.3; Broadway Hit, Turfcutter
VRC AUSTRALIAN CUP (2000m) Bush Win, 50.5 (J Stocker) Trained by CS Hayes; 2:0.9; Grand Scale, Gala Supreme

MVRC WS COX PLATE (2040m)
Battle Heights, 59 (G Willetts) Trained by R Douglas; 2:09.9; Taras Bulba, Bellota
AJC DERBY (2400m)
Taras Bulba, 55.5 (J Stocker) Trained by GM Hanlon; 2:33.6; Definate, Stop The Music
VICTORIA DERBY (2500m)
Haymaker, 55.5 (J Miller) Trained by CS Hayes; 2:42.4; Pyramul, Fortunate
AJC DONCASTER HANDICAP (1600m)
Tontonan, 56 (R Higgins) Trained by JB Cummings; 1:39.2; Toltrice, Coolalinga
BTC DOOMBEN '10 000' (1350m)
Charlton Boy, 55.5 (M Schumacher) Trained by T Dawson; 1:19; Bengalla Lad, John's Hope
VRC NEWMARKET HANDICAP (1200m)
Coolalinga, 50.5 (P Trotter) Trained by C Beechey; 1:10.2; Tauto, Prize Lad

AJC SIRES' PRODUCE STAKES (1400m)
Gretel, 52 (K Moses) Trained by TD Brosnan; 1:26; Sydney Cove, La Grisette
VRC SIRES' PRODUCE STAKES (1400m)
Skyjack, 55.5 (R Higgins) Trained by JB Cummings; 1:23.9; Mulligatawny, Bazaari
VRC GRAND NATIONAL STEEPLECHASE (5000m)
Fire Sun, 60 (M Van Strien) Trained by ND Hoysted; 6:17.9; Bright Blue, Vernet
STC GOLDEN SLIPPER STAKES (1200m)
Hartshill, 51 (K Langby) Trained by TJ Smith; 1:13; Sufficient, Skyjack
VATC BLUE DIAMOND STAKES (1200m)
Forina, 51.5 (S Aitken) Trained by A Armanasco; 1:10.9; Eclipser, Vicenza

An unlikely Cup winner according to Cummings, but all eyes are on Think Big and Harry White.

Think Big strikes again

Trainer Bart Cummings never gave the impression he thought Think Big was worthy of greatness. His highest praise for the horse before the 1975 Melbourne Cup was, 'Well, he goes well at Flemington.'

That certainly was true. In 1974 Think Big had won the Dalgety (formerly the Hotham Handicap) and then the Melbourne Cup but by Cup time 1975 he had not won a race since. And, as in 1974, Think Big was not the stable elect in the Cup. While Leilani had that honour the previous year, in '75 it was the promising stayer Holiday Waggon. Further, the Cup was to be run on a heavy track and it was felt Think Big would not handle the conditions. Consequently, his price blew out from 16/1 to 33/1. Holiday Waggon firmed from 9s to 7s and there was also good support for Cummings' third runner Leica Lover (16s to 10s).

But handle the conditions Think Big did

and, aided by another masterly ride by 3200-metres specialist Harry White, he surged along the rails – the wettest part of the track – to hold off Holiday Waggon and give Cummings his fifth Cup and his fourth Cup quinella.

Cummings watched the race in stunned disbelief. 'Well, I've beaten myself again,' he said. 'I've got to admit I'm surprised … pleasantly surprised. I doubted Think Big's ability to win on a wet track.'

With his successive Melbourne Cup wins – only Archer and Rain Lover had achieved the feat before him – Think Big went into the racing annals. Ironically, it was only the ninth win of his career but he had proved a bargain buy for owner Dato Chin Tan, a Malaysian businessman, and Brisbane land developer Ric O'Sullivan, who paid only $10 000 for him as a yearling. Think Big's earnings were then $263 320.

Cap D'Antibes gets home ahead of Tontonan.

Sprint master

By 1975 – more than a decade after his first Melbourne Cup win – Bart Cummings had established himself as a master trainer of both stayers and sprinters. And in the flying filly Cap D'Antibes he had come up with a horse that excelled as both.

Cap D'Antibes, by Better Boy from Tereus, first demonstrated her ability by winning races in three states – at Morphettville, Randwick and Flemington – and then running second in the 2500-metres VRC Oaks behind stablemate Leica Show.

Brought back in the autumn of 1975, Cap D'Antibes brilliantly won the Lightning Stakes over 1000 metres and did not race again until the Newmarket. However, in this race she was overshadowed in pre-race assessments by the handsome 'Black Flash' from Sydney, Zephyr Bay, who had exploded to an exciting win in the Oakleigh Plate.

But the Newmarket is a race of a different character and Zephyr Bay was the first to crack under the pressure as Cap D'Antibes came with a withering run to beat the best sprinters in the land. Jockey Harry White said Cap D'Antibes was undoubtedly a champion but a congenital hip problem was to hamper her career.

After the Newmarket Cap D'Antibes won the Kewney Stakes over 1600 metres but was beaten by the brilliant but unpredictable Taras Bulba in Sydney's Spring Champion Stakes. She was then beaten at odds-on in the AJC Oaks but again proved her class in the spring of 1975 by beating the champion Tontonan in the Marlboro Cup. She retired to stud later in the year.

Terrific Tauto's last tilt

Everyone interested in racing would surely like to own a horse like Tauto. In 1975 Tauto, then nine, competed in his sixth successive VRC Newmarket Handicap and was at that time the greatest stakes-winning sprinter still racing.

Tauto always gave wonderful value. He began his career in country races but quickly ascended to the highest level. Fittingly, it was the Newmarket of 1970 in which he first displayed his class and courage in the city when he ran second to Black Onyx.

Came the spring and Tauto, who was trained by Ross Agnew, notched his first big win by taking out the Toorak Handicap. In 1971 he was second in the Lightning Stakes, third in the Newmarket to Baguette and Dual Choice and then in the spring won the Liston Stakes and the Invitation Stakes. He failed to win successive Tooraks when third behind the great gallopers Gunsynd and Sky High and went into the Cox Plate a relative outsider since 2000 metres was considered to be beyond him. However, Tauto recorded his greatest win, beating the luckless Igloo.

Again back in the Newmarket in 1974 he ran a great second to Coolalinga who was in receipt of 6.5 kg from the veteran. Even in his final tilt at the Newmarket in 1975, Tauto was competitive, running on strongly in eighth place, less than three lengths from winner Cap D'Antibes.

Trainer Wally McEwan looks relaxed, but Fury's Order is full of joy before the 1975 Cox Plate.

A conundrum at Ballarat as Turin gets himself on both sides of the fence. The horse fell before the start and then tried to jump the running rail, with this bizarre result. In a flash of genius, stewards cut the wooden rail with a saw to release the horse unscathed (BP).

1975 RESULTS

VRC MELBOURNE CUP (3200m)
Think Big, 58.5 (H White) Trained by JB Cummings; 3:29.6; Holiday Waggon, Medici
AJC SYDNEY CUP (3200m)
Gay Master, 51 (A Trevena) Trained by T Hughes; 3:22.6; Participator, High Style
QTC BRISBANE CUP (3200m)
Herminia, 50 (A Trevena) Trained by JB Cummings; 3:18.9; Participator, Dayana
SAJC ADELAIDE CUP (3200m)
Soulman, 47.5 (A Matthews) Trained by D Mack; 3:29.4; Bottled Sunshine, Dayana
WATC PERTH CUP (3200m)
Runyon, 53.5 (J Murray) Trained by JR Hawkes; 3:21.1; Taras Bulba, Think Big
VATC CAULFIELD CUP (2400m)
Analight, 50.5 (P Trotter) Trained by CL Beechey; 2:30; Leica Lover, Suleiman
VRC AUSTRALIAN CUP (2000m)
Leilani, 58.5 (R Higgins) Trained by JB Cummings; 2:2.9; Tudor Peak, St Martin

MVRC WS COX PLATE (2040m)
Fury's Order, 59 (B Thompson) Trained by W McEwan; 2:20.4; Kiwi Can, Analight
AJC DERBY (2400m)
Battle Sign, 55.5 (D Messingham) Trained by T Millard; 2:33.9; Rafique, Gold Pulse
VICTORIA DERBY (2500m)
Galena Boy, 55.5 (J Letts) Trained by JR Hawkes; 2:44.4; Romantic Archer, Gold And Black
AJC DONCASTER HANDICAP (1600m)
Dalrello, 53.5 (B Stein) Trained by JJ Atkins; 1:33.9; Sizzler, Martindale
BTC DOOMBEN '10 000' (1350m)
Spedito, 52 (G Cook) Trained by J Griffiths; 1:18.8; Dalrello, Martindale
VRC NEWMARKET HANDICAP (1200m)
Cap D'Antibes, 52 (H White) Trained by JB Cummings; 1:9.8; Aurealis, Love Aloft

AJC SIRES' PRODUCE STAKES (1400m)
Toy Show, 52 (K Langby) Trained by TJ Smith; 1:22; Lord Dudley, Dancelot
VRC SIRES' PRODUCE STAKES (1400m)
Lord Dudley, 55.5 (R Higgins) Trained by JB Cummings; 1:25.8; Warneet, Militant Road
VRC GRAND NATIONAL STEEPLECHASE (5000m)
Tossa, 63 (H Green) Trained by J McGreal; 5:58.4; Satchel, Gypsy Grey
STC GOLDEN SLIPPER STAKES (1200m)
Toy Show, 51 (K Langby) Trained by TJ Smith; 1:12; Denise's Joy, Rosie Heir
VATC BLUE DIAMOND STAKES (1200m)
Lord Dudley, 54 (R Higgins) Trained by JB Cummings; 1:11.9; Hamden, Classic Reward

Punters and brollies brave the storm (BP).

Van Der Hum wades back to scale (DB).

Owner Mrs Win Able with jockey Bob Skelton.

Van Der Hum's Cup runneth over in rain

The 1976 Melbourne Cup was among the most memorable of the century – not so much for the race itself but for the freak storm and violent downpour that almost stopped it.

The famous race was within minutes of being washed out after the storm hit half an hour before post time. Sheets of torrential rain soon flooded the Flemington betting ring and turned the track into a quagmire. Visibility was impossible. At the peak of the storm the winning post could not be seen from the stands.

The rain eased in the nick of time and after a hurried conference between VRC secretary Murray Cox, chairman of stewards Jim Ahern and racecourse manager Ron King, it was decided to go on with the Cup. But the atrocious conditions suited some – particularly the mud-loving New Zealand stayer Van Der Hum who came from mid-year obscurity to revel in the conditions and win one of the world's great races.

Van Der Hum was an unlikely Cup runner let alone a winner. The gelding, a qualified hunter in New Zealand, was twice taken to the sales as a young horse but couldn't attract a buyer. His owners, who had bred him, decided to persevere with him. It was thought he might have a future as a jumper.

But in the best New Zealand tradition Ver Der Hum matured late in his career and became something of an 'iron horse' in 1976. He became known for his love of heavy tracks. When overnight rain ensured the Flemington track would be slow, his price for the Melbourne Cup began to tumble. By post time and with the track the sloshiest in memory, Van Der Hum was favourite at 9/2.

Although barely visible to spectators, Van Der Hum staged a stirring finish with Bart Cummings' excellent stayer Gold And Black.

Tommy Smith confers with his stable foreman Darby Chester and jockey Roy Higgins (BP).

Jockeys said 'no'

Apprentice jockey Wayne Treloar was only 18 when he was asked to take a ride for trainer T. J. Smith in the Newmarket Handicap of 1976. The downside was that the ride was on the filly Toy Show and she was something of a last resort.

Toy Show, winner of the previous year's Golden Slipper, had become unpredictable as a three-year-old (it was later discovered she had a back problem that would flare intermittently). So when the filly failed in the Oakleigh Plate as a heavily backed 4/1 second favourite, a number of jockeys declined Smith's offer.

What followed was one of the great races down the Straight Six. Treloar sat off the pacemaker Plush until the 100 metres mark, then drove Toy Show to the lead. But on the opposite side of the track Bart Cummings' mare Leica Show, with Roy Higgins, looked certain to win. Only the camera could separate them. Toy Show, the 25/1 outsider, had beaten Leica Show, the 11/4 favourite, by half a head.

Surround: inaugural Horse of the Year (BP).

How Now after his Caulfield Cup win (Age).

Surround was sensational

It takes a great horse to win the weight-for-age WS Cox Plate, and it certainly takes an exceptional filly to capture the event.

Surround became the first filly to win the race and only the third of her sex to do so. (Tranquil Star and Flight each won the race twice.) Surround went on to win 10 races in succession, including the VRC Oaks, but her win in the Cox Plate was her finest.

Nevertheless, a filly beating Australia's top older horses over the gruelling 2040 metres was considered an improbable task and bookmakers bet 7/2 against her doing it (Caulfield Cup winner How Now was 7/4 favourite).

With Sydney lightweight Peter Cook aboard, Surround beat her rivals easily, winning by three lengths. Her time of 2:4.3 was a record that stood for another nine years.

After the race, trainer Geoff Murphy lamented that Surround was not entered in the Victoria Derby, since he had never prepared a Derby winner.

When the field lined up for the Oaks, Surround was 5/4 on favourite with the only possible threat being Savoir. Surround certainly settled the question of who was better by thrashing her stablemate by 2¼ lengths while Savoir beat the rest of the field by a similar margin.

The Oaks win was Surround's last for 1976. She was spelled, came back in autumn 1977 and won the Orr Stakes and the Blamey Stakes – her 10th straight – before going down to Bonfield in the Futurity. She went on to win the AJC Oaks and the QTC Queensland Oaks that year. At the end of her career, at four, she had recorded 17 wins, two seconds and two thirds from 28 starts.

TURF TOPICS

New shoes, Perhaps: Sartorial Takanini trainer Colin Jillings bought a brand-new pair of shoes for Auckland Cup Day 1976. His cup candidate, Perhaps, was not flavour of the moment when she ruined one of his new shoes. But all was forgiven when, in the hands of 18-year-old apprentice Brent Thomson, Perhaps charged to victory over the future Sydney Cup winner Oopik. It was Auckland Cup No. 3 for Jillings.

Top Dog again: Getting to the post first in the 1976 Great Northern Hurdles was the easy part for the connections of Thun, the Central Districts hurdler who had won the Top Dog hurdlers' prize the winter before. Thun appeared to interfere with Owhata Chief after the last fence. He retained the race on race day, lost it at a district committee appeal and then was finally reinstated, months later. Owhata Chief went on to take the Top Dog and the Great Northern Hurdles himself.

TJ's day of days: For trainer T. J. Smith, the passing of career milestones became a way of life. But his training triumphs on 6 March 1976 made it surely a day of days. Smith won seven races in two states – five in Sydney and two features at Flemington – the Newmarket and the Queen's Plate.

Unhappy decision: Jockey Sid Bundy decided to take one ride at Randwick rather than a handful at Moruya – but the chosen horse Storming fell on poor Sid and killed him. His son Ron saw to the family honour and rode the next week.

Darby McCarthy outed: Victorian country stewards outed gifted jockey Darby McCarthy, 32, for seven years, alleging conspiracy and dishonest practices. The harsh decision was widely disputed, and resulted in an appeal and litigation. The suspension was reduced to two years, and after 10 months the VRC lifted the ban. McCarthy's career was virtually finished.

1976 RESULTS

VRC MELBOURNE CUP (3200m)
Van Der Hum, 54.4 (R Skelton) Trainer LH Robinson; 3.34.1; Gold And Black, Kythera
AJC SYDNEY CUP (3200m)
Oopik, 57.5 (R Lang) Trained by DJ O'Sullivan; 3.23.6; Taras Bulba, Tom's Mate
QTC BRISBANE CUP (3200m)
Balmerino, 54.5 (M Campbell) Trained by BJ Smith; 3.24.2; Participator, Our Cavalier
SAJC ADELAIDE CUP (3200m)
Grand Scale, 53 (J Letts) Trained by M Willmott; 3:20.5; Storm Song, Philomel
WATC PERTH CUP (3200m)
Philomel, 49 (B Gilders) Trained by T Millard; 3:18.8; Ace Queen, Wolf City
VATC CAULFIELD CUP (2400m)
How Now, 52 (J Stocker) Trained by CS Hayes; 2:36.7; Battle Heights, Van Der Hum

VRC AUSTRALIAN CUP (2000m)
Lord Dudley, 53 (G Willetts) Trainer JB Cummings; 2:1.9; Favoured Bay, How Now
MVRC WS COX PLATE (2040m)
Surround, 47.5 (P Cook) Trained by GT Murphy; 2:04.3; Unaware, Better Draw
AJC DERBY (2400m)
Great Lover, 55.5 (K Langby) Trained by TJ Smith; 2:33.9; Chasta Bellota, Elton
VICTORIA DERBY (2500m)
Unaware, 55.5 (J Stocker) Trained by CS Hayes; 2:36.1; Salamander, Family Of Man
AJC DONCASTER HANDICAP (1600m)
Authentic Heir, 54.5 (K Moses) Trained by TJ Smith; 1:35; Leica Lover, Kingston Rose
BTC DOOMBEN '10'000' (1350m)
Burwana, 47 (R Quinton) Trained by K Hayes; 1:18.2; Ease The Squeeze, Crimson Cloud

VRC NEWMARKET HANDICAP (1200m)
Toy Show, 54 (W Treloar) Trained by TJ Smith; 1;9.5; Leica Show, Plush
AJC SIRES' PRODUCE STAKES (1400m)
Desirable, 53 (J Stocker) Trained by CS Hayes; 1:22.6; Flaunting, As You Like It
VRC SIRES' PRODUCE STAKES (1400m)
Desirable, 54 (J Stocker) Trained by CS Hayes; 1:23.3; Out Of Danger, Vivarchi
VRC GRAND NATIONAL STEEPLECHASE (5000m)
Loch Linnie, 71 (R Walsh) Trained by J Winder; 5:56.2; Lot, Aircon
STC GOLDEN SLIPPER STAKES (1200m)
Vivarchi, 51 (J Duggan) Trainer JB Cummings; 1:11.7; Romantic Dream, Desirable
VATC BLUE DIAMOND STAKES (1200m)
Out Of Danger, 51.5 (A Matthews) Trained by CS Hayes; 1:10.5; Desirable, Market Garden

The G. G. at the gee gees. Sir John Kerr looking slightly unbalanced (BP).

Luskin Star on his way to work.

Seeing red at the Cup

Apart from a few notable exceptions, trophy presentations, even after major races, are not the most stirring of events. The presentation after the 1977 Melbourne Cup was different – it generated more crowd reaction than any such ceremony in the long history of the race.

Presenting the trophy was the Governor-General, Sir John Kerr, almost two years after he had sacked Prime Minister Gough Whitlam in the historic dismissal of 1975 for which many had never forgiven him.

Sir John was under constant pressure and the target of frequent demonstrations. He was not often seen in the public domain but never before had he so discarded vice-regal restraint as to deliver verbal swipes at hecklers. It was a performance that was featured on the front pages of newspapers and made him the constant butt of cartoonists.

In a rambling, disjointed speech, Sir John urged Flemington members to 'ignore the static' coming from the vocal crowd and, as sustained booing broke out, called: 'Cheers from a small minority.' The boos did, in fact, turn to cheers when Sir John, who was due to step down, told the crowd: 'This is the last time I'll be doing this.'

Sir John said he had come to present the Melbourne Cup with the approval of Prince Charles, who had arrived at Government House in Canberra the previous day.

'I did not know when I came that an old mate of mine would turn out to be one of the owners of the winner,' he said. 'The Gages, oh well, Gage has been a mate of mine for a long time. He didn't give me the information, so I wasn't on the winner.' He concluded by promising to return to Flemington. 'I'll be back as a spectator,' he said.

Luskin stars

Luskin Star was a speed machine. His seven-length win in the 1977 Golden Slipper Stakes was the most scintillating since Todman's in the inaugural running of the classic 21 years earlier.

Luskin Star beat a top-line field including T. J. Smith's boom colt and that year's Blue Diamond winner Blazing Saddles, Bold Zest and King of the Stars from Melbourne.

Luskin Star went on to become only the second horse after Baguette to complete the Triple Crown of two-year-old classics in Sydney – the AJC Sires' Produce Stakes and the AJC Champagne Stakes. In the Sires' he smashed the Randwick track record for 1400 metres and won the Champagne by six lengths after being pressed by T. J. Smith's Marceau. Marceau's jockey Kevin Langby was moved to say: 'It was robbery under arms. He was only kidding to me.'

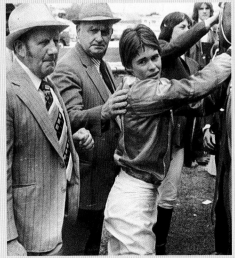

Brent Thomson after his Cox Plate win.

The rise and rise of Brent Thomson

Punters weren't amused when the unpredictable Family of Man scorched home to beat the English stallion Raffindale in the 1977 WS Cox Plate. Family of Man might have had loads of ability but he had become notoriously 'hard to catch' for form followers. But even the most affronted racegoers had to acknowledge the riding feat of 18-year-old former New Zealander Brent Thomson.

Thomson had won the race the previous year on Fury's Order but what couldn't be known was that Thomson would go on and again win in the following two years (in 1978 on So Called and in 1979 on the ill-fated Dulcify). These wins came after he replaced John Stocker as the stable jockey for the Colin Hayes establishment. Thomson then became a household name as he kicked home hundreds of winners in the next decade (among the most notable Gurner's Lane and Lord Reims in the Caulfield Cups of 1982 and 1987).

Thomson split with the Hayes camp in 1984 and later headed for racing glory overseas where he rode with great success, particularly in Great Britain and Hong Kong. He made regular trips back to Australia for the spring racing carnivals in the late 1980s and the 1990s.

A rare treat at Flemington: a young boy gets a ride on Reckless as Woodcock stands by (Age).

VRC steward Jack Purtell and Woodcock (BP).

Tommy & Reckless – sentimental favourites

What a fairytale year 1977 would have been had Reckless managed to win the Melbourne Cup. Victory would have seen him take out the Sydney, Adelaide, Brisbane and Melbourne Cups in the same calendar year – a feat unlikely ever to be matched.

As it turned out, he went very close and it took the great Bart Cummings to beat him. To be fair, Cummings's Gold And Black deserved victory after a gallant second on the bog track of 1976, but there hadn't been a horse so loved by the public since Phar Lap.

The Phar Lap link was of course valid. Reckless' trainer Tommy Woodcock had been Phar Lap's strapper and had accompanied the great horse to America as his official trainer. Woodcock had also gone into racing folklore when he shielded Phar Lap from a shooting attempt before the 1930 Melbourne Cup.

Tommy Woodcock trained many good horses in the interim and himself became one

of the most popular characters in the history of the turf. His association with Reckless was particularly appealing, both to racing and non-racing people.

He acquired Reckless, a beautifully bred stallion, in 1972 but the horse proved a duffer on the racetrack. Woodcock, however, developed a deep affection for him and persevered, only to see Reckless contest 17 races as a two and three-year-old for the miserable result of one third placing.

But in 1976 Reckless, although bred along sprinting lines, began showing staying ability. By winning the Hotham Handicap he qualified for the Melbourne Cup, Woodcock's second-only Cup since Phar Lap's failure in 1931. Despite his dislike of wet tracks, Reckless finished stoutly for fourth to Van Der Hum in the heaviest of conditions.

By the autumn Reckless had matured into a magnificent stallion. After placings at Fle-

mington and Sandown, he started in the Sydney Cup at the luxury odds of 20/1 and easily defeated Gold And Black to win the first of a remarkable treble. Came the Adelaide Cup and the Reckless bandwagon was on the roll. He won but this time at the skinny odds of 10/9. On he went to the Brisbane Cup in which he scored again, this time beating the talented gallopers Ngawini and My Good Man.

Tommy Woodcock was gracious in defeat when Reckless failed in the Melbourne Cup by a length.

Of course, the 1977 Cup was another triumph for Bart Cummings, making it his record sixth, and a well-deserved success for jockey John Duggan who had been criticised when beaten on Gold And Black by Reckless in the Sydney Cup. Duggan had also made amends for his second placings in the previous two Melbourne Cups.

1977 RESULTS

VRC MELBOURNE CUP (3200m)
Gold And Black, 57, (J Duggan) Trained by JB Cummings; 3:18.4; Reckless, Hyperno
AJC SYDNEY CUP (3200m)
Reckless, 49.5 (P Trotter) Trained by T Woodcock; 3:19.4; Gold And Black, Rhalif
QTC BRISBANE CUP (3200m)
Reckless, 55.5 (P Trotter) Trained by T Woodcock; 3:19.6; Ngawyni, My Good Man
SAJC ADELAIDE CUP (3200m)
Reckless, 52 (P Trotter) Trained by T Woodcock; 3:25.8; Straight Up, Prize Brandy
WATC PERTH CUP (3200m)
Muros, 48 (B Ryan) Trained by MS FM Gammon; 3:21.2; Valadero, So Clear
VATC CAULFIELD CUP (2400m)
Ming Dynasty, 54 (H White) Trained by JB Cummings; 2:28.5; Unaware, Salamander
VRC AUSTRALIAN CUP (2000m)
Ngawyni, 55.5 (R Higgins) Trained by JB Cummings; 2:0.9; Better Draw, Calvin

MVRC WS COX PLATE (2040m)
Family Of Man, 57 (B Thomson) Trained by GM Hanlon; 2:05.3; Raffindale, Vice Regal
AJC DERBY (2400m)
Belmura Lad, 55.5 (N Voigt) Trained by JB Cummings; 2:33; Pelican Point, Marceau
VICTORIA DERBY (2500m)
Stormy Rex, 55.5 (R Higgins) Trained by JB Cummings; 2:35.5; Jury, Lefroy
AJC DONCASTER HANDICAP (1600m)
Just Ideal, 53 (J Duggan) Trained by JB Cummings; 1:34.7; Manawapoi, Dalrello
BTC DOOMBEN '10,000' (1350m)
Maybe Mahal, 56.5 (R Higgins) Trained by JB Cummings; 1:19.2; Romantic Dream, Sir Wisp
VRC NEWMARKET HANDICAP (1200m)
Desirable, 54 (J Stocker) Trained by CS Hayes; 1:10; Maybe Mahal, Vivarchi

AJC SIRES' PRODUCE STAKES (1400m)
Luskin Star, 55.5 (J Wade) Trained by M Lees; 1:21.5; Bold Zest, Bensynd
VRC SIRES' PRODUCE STAKES (1400m)
Bold Zest, 55.5 (R Higgins) Trained by JB Cummings; 1:24.3; King Of The Stars, Princess Talaria
VRC GRAND NATIONAL STEEPLECHASE (5000m)
Strasbourg, 65 (K Bourke) Trained by JJ Houlahan; 6:3.2; The Champ, Coolgardie
STC GOLDEN SLIPPER STAKES (1200m)
Luskin Star, 54 (J Wade) Trained by M Lees; 1:10; Lloyd Boy, Blazing Saddles
VATC BLUE DIAMOND STAKES (1200m)
Blazing Saddles, 54 (R Higgins) Trained by TJ Smith; 1:1.4; Mighty General, Prince Brighton
STC MERCEDES-TANCRED CLASSIC (2400m) (first run at wfa, 1977)
Our Cavalier, 57 (L Dittman) Trained by H Davis; 2:29; Think Big, How Now

A hard-run race but Arwon is in front of Dandaleith at the moment that counts (Age).

Harry White as the celebrations begin (Age).

The Melbourne Cup winner 'TJ' let slip

The maxim goes that professionalism is dedication to the elimination of error and there has not been a more professional trainer in racing history than the legendary T.J. Smith. But Smith made one mistake he no doubt regretted acutely: he flatly rejected an offer to train a horse named Arwon who went on to win the 1978 Melbourne Cup.

Smith would not elaborate on why he refused to accept Arwon. 'I have private reasons,' was all he would say after the horse's victory. At that time Smith had trained just one Melbourne Cup winner – Toparoa in 1955 – in a long and success-studded career (he was later to prepare Just A Dash who won the Cup in 1981).

Arwon was also rejected by another Sydney trainer, Theo Green, and if the two shunned the horse because of his ordinary form and likely lack of potential, they were not alone in their thinking. Arwon had raced unflatteringly in

New Zealand as Flash Guy. (He was renamed for the NSW town of Nowra – spelt backwards – when he came to Australia and was acquired by local identity Jack Watson.) So when renowned Victorian trainer George Hanlon was asked to take over his preparation, he was far from impressed. In fact, as late as August 1978 Hanlon told the owners it would be a waste of money to embark on a Cups quest.

But under Hanlon, who conditioned his horses with frequent swimming exercise, Arwon made remarkable progress in the space of a few months, winning the Seymour Cup and running an unlucky second to Ming Dynasty in the Metropolitan. 'I knew then I had a horse with a Cup chance,' Hanlon said.

So Hanlon took Arwon into the Caulfield Cup with new-found confidence – and as the horses flashed past the post he was entitled to believe he had worked a racing miracle: Arwon looked to have just won. It wasn't to be. In a

finish that fooled everyone from jockeys to racecallers, Arwon went under by a lip to Taksan, trained by, of all people, T.J. Smith.

Hanlon was stunned by the defeat but it may have proved a blessing. Arwon escaped a severe penalty for the Melbourne Cup for which he was now set with Harry White to ride. White himself had something to prove – he had been sacked that year as Bart Cummings' stable jockey following dissatisfaction with a ride at Moonee Valley. And prove a point he did. In what was considered his best ride in a Melbourne Cup, he used his vast experience (he had won successive Cups for Cummings on Think Big in 1974–75) and peerless skill on stayers to set up a winning break and then get Arwon home by half a neck from the New Zealander Dandaleith. T.J. Smith's Caulfield Cup winner Taksan was the disappointment of the race, finishing 16th.

Arwon began to show promise with an unlucky second to Ming Dynasty in the Metropolitan at Randwick (Age).

The finish of the Caulfield Guineas with Manikato and rival Karaman wide apart (Age).

David Londregan holds on for dear life in this fall from Spearwood in the Kensington Steeple.

A champion bargain

The mighty Manikato was to thrill race-goers for five more years, but he set the scene for his future greatness in autumn 1978. Trainer Bon Hoysted knew he had a potential champion the first time he sent Manikato for a serious gallop.

Manikato had been bought for the bargain price of $3500 by Bon's brother Bob – who had nonetheless described the horse as a big, ugly, boofhead-ed colt. Clearly, not too much was expected of him. Besides, Bon Hoysted had been train-ing for 40 years and had never led in a Group 1 winner. He felt even then that Manikato had the potential to change that.

After that gallop, Hoysted took Manikato to provincial Cranbourne for an easy win. He was beaten by the outstand-ing Karaman at his next start, won at his next outing and then stepped out in the Blue Diamond Stakes of 1978. Starting at luxury odds of 12/1, Manikato, capably handled by Gary Willetts, won decisively. Bon Hoysted was against taking the high-ly strung and excitable horse to Sydney for the Golden Slipper but the will of the owners and jockey Willetts prevailed.

Manikato won the Slipper with the authority that was to mark his career. Explo-ding from the start, he allowed the speedy Black Opaque to take up the running, then with the others toiling behind them the pair settled down to a two-horse contest. Manikato appeared to be loping beside the faster action of the diminutive Black Opaque, but Manikato surged clear to win by 1 ¼ lengths in 1:10.7 – the second-fastest time record in a Slipper. Black Opaque weakened to finish fifth.

Manikato stayed in Sydney to contest the longer AJC Sires' Produce Stakes. The track was slow, Manikato was tackling 1400 metres for the first time and his great rival Karaman was in the field. Manikato weak-ened to finish fifth behind Karaman and the Sydney press was quick to label him another speedy squib from Melbourne (as they had with Vain nine years earlier).

Manikato proved in the next five years how wrong they were and what a champi-on he was.

'The Professor' slips up

Roy Higgins on a winning day (BP).

Roy Higgins, known as 'The Professor' both for having the same surname as the autocratic speech tutor in *My Fair Lady* and for his racing acumen, dominated racing in Melbourne through the 1960s and 70s during which he won 11 jockeys' premierships – equalling Billy Duncan's record set in 1933 – and rode more than 2300 winners.

Higgins' riding achievements include two Melbourne Cups (on his favourite mare Light Fingers and on Red Handed) a Caulfield Cup (on Big Philou), no fewer than six AJC Oaks, five VRC Oaks and three Victoria Derbys.

His greatest triumphs were in association with Bart Cummings (both Melbourne Cups, the Caulfield Cup, three of the Derbys, and both Higgins' Newmarkets wins). He also teamed successfully with Sydney trainer T.J. Smith to win a Metropolitan on Passetruel and a Doncaster on Gunsynd. Sydney racing, which had found many Melbourne jockeys wanting, never daunted Higgins, who won two Sydney Cups and two Golden Slippers.

But Higgins hit the headlines as never before over one incident in which he was beaten, and which caused a furore which raged for weeks. The race was the Moonee Valley Cup of 1978. Higgins was riding the well-performed but tempestuous Hyperno. Hyperno was a solid 7/4 favourite for the Moonee Valley Cup and raced accordingly, careering away to a three-lengths lead in the shadows of the post. Then, Higgins stopped riding and dropped his hands, no doubt assuming Hyperno would cruise to the post. Hyperno, who had a history of intractability, lost momentum and the 9/1 chance Clear Day, with jockey Midge Didham riding frantically, got up on the line to snatch victory.

In shock, Higgins at first tried to blame the mistake on the horse's roguish behaviour. 'He got his head up and didn't want to race,' Higgins said. 'Knowing how he dives in and out I didn't want to hit him with the whip. I tried to nurse him over the line because of his bad reputation but it failed.' On reflection Higgins admitted he had made a gross error of judgement in dropping his hands. He apologised to all concerned.

The stewards took a dim view of the incident and suspended Higgins for 10 metropolitan meetings. The boy from the bush (he was born near the Murray River town of Koondrook where his mother went into labour while riding on her husband's cart) had got to the top in racing through dedication and ability.

His career, which had included a riding stint in France when he was a young man, had been largely blemish-free. The racing public felt he was entitled to one mistake. Ironically, Hyperno continued to plague Higgins. When the horse won the Melbourne Cup, Higgins on Salamander just failed to catch him.

Former champion Samson, now a police horse, leads the winner of the eponymous Samson Handicap, Stainvita (Age).

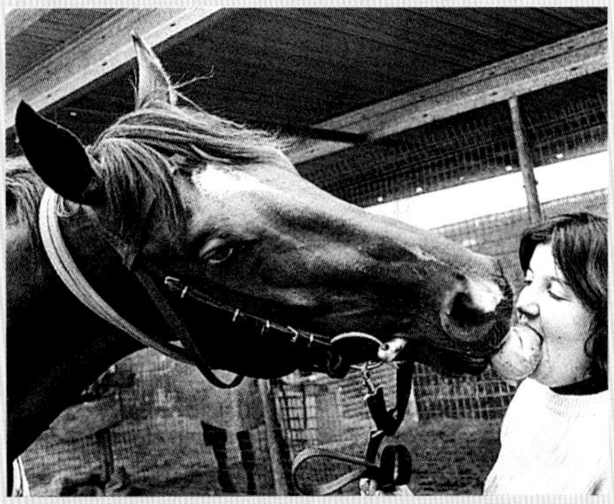

So Called takes an apple from strapper Sue Beazley's mouth in a break from training before winning the 1978 Cox Plate (BP).

1978 RESULTS

VRC MELBOURNE CUP (3200m)
Arwon, 50.5 (H White) Trained by GM Hanlon; 3:24.3; Dandaleith, Karu
AJC SYDNEY CUP (3200m)
My Good Man, 60 (D Peake) Trained by R Verner; 3:27.9: Valadero, Rhalif
QTC BRISBANE CUP (3200m)
Muros, 52.5 (D Brosnan) Trained by LB Morton; 3:22.5; Ming Dynasty, Bermudez
SAJC ADELAIDE CUP (3200m)
Hyperno, 58 (M Goreham) Trained by G Murphy; 3:32.7; Muros, Valadero
WATC PERTH CUP (3200m) Golden Centre, 46.5 (D Rudland) Trained by RH Tucker; 3:20.1; Muros, Reckless
VATC CAULFIELD CUP (2400m)
Taksan, 52 (J Duggan) Trained by TJ Smith; 2:27.5; Arwon, Father's Day
VRC AUSTRALIAN CUP (2000m)
Ming Dynasty, 58 (H White) Trained by JB Cummings; 2:2.6; Crepellox, Carl's Gift
MVRC WS COX PLATE (2040m)
So Called, 57 (B Thomson) Trained by CS Hayes; 2:08.7; Family Of Man, Karaman
AJC DERBY (2400m) (Not run in 1978)
VICTORIA DERBY (2500m)
Dulcify, 55.5 (B Thomson) Trained by CS Hayes; 2:37.5; Karaman, Turf Ruler
AJC DONCASTER HANDICAP (1600m)
Maybe Mahal, 57 (K Langby) Trained by JB Cummings; 1:39.1; Always Welcome, Avoid Island
BTC DOOMBEN '10 000' (1350m)
Blue's Finito, 54 (D Messingham) Trained by D Strong; 1:18.1; Galway Bay, Kelly's Eye
VRC NEWMARKET HANDICAP (1200m)
Maybe Mahal, 56.5 (J Stocker) Trained by JB Cummings; 1:9; Always Welcome, Bonfield
AJC SIRES' PRODUCE STAKES (1400m)
Karaman, 8.10 (B Andrews) Trained by B Ralph; 1:26.5; Jubilee Walk, Jewel Flight
VRC SIRES' PRODUCE STAKES (1400m)
Pacifica, 55.5 (J Murray) Trained by J Hall; 1:24.5; Karaman, Prunella
VRC GRAND NATIONAL STEEPLECHASE (5000m)
So And So, 64.5 (K Bourke) Trained by MA Houlahan; 6:6.9; Chocolate Royal, Lord Kamulla
STC GOLDEN SLIPPER STAKES (1200m)
Manikato, 54 (G Willetts) Trained by ND Hoysted; 1:10.7; Smokey Jack, Jewel Flight
VATC BLUE DIAMOND STAKES (1200m)
Manikato, 54 (G Willetts) Trained by ND Hoysted; 1:10.8; Toolern High, Embasadora
STC MERCEDES-TANCRED CLASSIC (2400m)
Hyperno, 57 (R McCarthy) Trained by G Murphy; 2:32.5; Lazy Pat, Our Cavalier

A Cup full of tragedy as favourite dies

If ever a horse seemed destined to win a Melbourne Cup it was the dashing Dulcify in 1979. His credentials were impeccable: undeniably a champion, he had won the Cox Plate by a record seven lengths after being set alight at the 1000-metre mark; he had gone on to win the Mackinnon Stakes before the Cup; he was trained by C. S. Hayes and was to be ridden by Brent Thomson who was so confident he had described the rest of the field as a 'jumpers' flat'.

Consequently, Dulcify was sent out 3/1 favourite. Surely only bad luck and/or injury could beat him. And they did.

Dulcify's tragic – and fatal – injury is thought to have occurred at the halfway mark of that Melbourne Cup when he was galloped on by eventual winner Hyperno. Thomson later said: 'Everything was going to plan. You can look after yourself in front, but not behind … they hit him hard and he almost sat down on his backside.'

Dulcify's courage had kept him going for another 1000 metres but he faltered near the home turn and had to be pulled up. Transported to his stable behind the course, a gathering of veterinary inspection at 6 p.m. confirmed the worst: the champion had suffered a broken pelvis and would have to be put down. It was a tragic end to what had been a marvellous Melbourne Cup with a heart-stopping finish and a myriad of ironies.

There was, for example, the irony that Hyperno should even be in the field after breaking down during the year, then 'reluctantly' being accepted into the stable of Cups King Bart Cummings.

There was also irony that Roy Higgins decided against riding Hyperno and chose instead Salamander, only to be beaten in the tightest of finishes.

And there was the irony that jockey Harry White should get a last-minute ride that would give him his fourth Melbourne Cup, equalling Bobbie Lewis' record.

Cummings, who had now made it seven Melbourne Cups, had certainly worked his magic on Hyperno. He found the key to the horse was using blinkers. 'I was trying to bring Hyperno along without them, but he wouldn't do his best and I was running out of time,' Cummings said. Hyperno wore blinkers in the Mackinnon Stakes when he ran a sound Cup trial, finishing fourth behind Dulcify.

So Hyperno, who had finished third in the Cup two years earlier, had overcome injury, waywardness and roguish behavior to win Australia's greatest race.

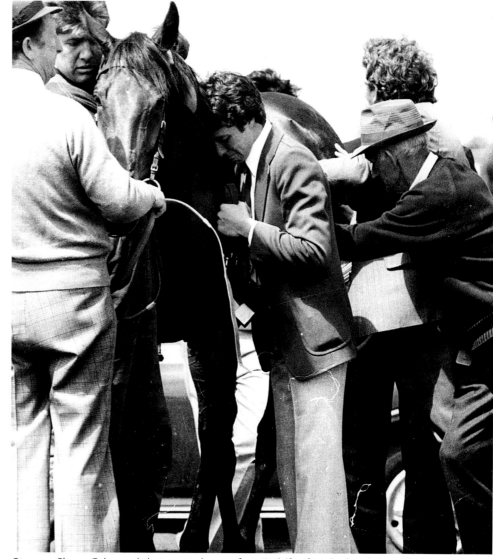

Strapper Shane Coleman is in tears as he comforts Dulcify after the breakdown (BP).

Manikato storms through heavy rain to win the William Reid Stakes from Oenjay Star (BP).

Controversy rode with Athol Mulley

The headlines were nothing new: 'Mulley to retire from riding'. The banners ran again in July 1979 but this time they were correct. Athol 'George' Mulley, one of Australia's greatest, most colourful and charismatic of jockeys, had been blinded in one eye by flying clods and there was no question this was the end.

But what a career he had had – from his illustrious association with Bernborough to his never-ending clashes with officials to his jockeys' room fistfights and his successful comebacks. Mulley was named Athol by his parents but preferred to be called George.

The son of a Grafton dairy farmer, Mulley was guided during his apprenticeship by the great Darby Munro and rode his first winner at Canterbury in July 1940. He won the Sydney jockeys' premiership in 1945–46 and in December 1945 began his partnership with Bernborough, riding him to 15 successive wins in Brisbane, Sydney and Melbourne. Then came the 1946 Caulfield Cup in which Bernborough was buffeted throughout the race and only managed fifth.

Mulley became known for his lavish spending and constant controversy. He hated routine, ignored time, and admitted to being forgetful to the extent of confusing mounts and more than once travelling to one racecourse only to find the races were being held at another. But he was hugely successful due to his horsemanship and uncanny rapport with his mounts.

He rode with distinction in India and Singapore for several years and had stints in England and France. In Australia he won the Canterbury Stakes four times and the AJC Derby, Epsom Handicap and Golden Slipper Stakes twice. After his second Slipper win – on Eskimo Prince owned by Perce Galea – he was again embroiled in a controversy when the horse failed in the AJC Derby.

Mulley was frequently before the stewards and surrounded by sensation. During the 1960s

Athol 'George' Mulley at the track.

he was lucky to escape injury when a letter bomb was sent to his house. He made national headlines when he and George Moore brawled in the jockeys' room at Canterbury and then again when he fought with Bill Wade after the Tamworth Cup. When he lost on six heavily backed horses, a punter tried to assault him.

Throughout the turbulent years Mulley continually announced his 'retirement' only to return after varying periods. He was soon back in the winning list after each comeback. In May 1974 the Sydney *Daily Mirror* paid him this tribute: 'Along with Jack Thompson, Mulley remains as the last of Sydney's great legendary jockeys – the men who, beginning with Jim Pike in the 1920s, gave us nearly 50 years of exposure to horsemen unparalleled in the world.'

Linda Jones, a trailblazer for women (BP).

Here come the women

In January, New Zealand jockey Linda Jones, already coming second in the jockeys' premiership with 36 wins, made headlines when she rode at the Wellington Cup Carnival at Trentham. After a win in her first ride, she came second in the Wellington Cup, then won the Wellington Derby the following day.

Visiting Australia in June, Jones was the first woman to win against professional male jockeys at a registered meeting when she won on Pay The Purple in the Labour Day Cup at Doomben.

New Zealand's acceptance of women riders pushed the issue in Australia and finally a full licence was granted to Brisbane's Pam O'Neill. She had been applying for years.

In June, she became the first Australian woman to win on a metropolitan course against the men in a betting race. Her biggest win was the following year when she won the Qantas–HSV-7 Handicap at Moonee Valley, beating Roy Higgins and other top men.

Another trailblazing woman rider was the Canadian jockey Joan Phipps, who stayed on in New Zealand after the Qantas Lady Riders' Series in 1977. She overcame resistance to become the first woman to ride professionally in New Zealand.

1979 RESULTS

VRC MELBOURNE CUP (3200m)
Hyperno, 56 (H White) Trained by JB Cummings; 3:21.8; Salamander, Red Nose
AJC SYDNEY CUP (3200m)
Double Century, 50 (R Mallyon) Trainer RN McDonnell; 3:20.8; Lady Dignitas, Arwon
QTC BRISBANE CUP (3200m)
Grey Affair, 50 (D Messingham) Trainer J Atkins; 3:19.6; Mr Ay Bee, Double Century
SAJC ADELAIDE CUP (3200m)
Panamint, 53 (J Miller) Trained by CJ Graves; 3:25.1; Moon Hawk, Clear Day
WATC PERTH CUP (3200m)
Meliador, 51 (J Wilson) Trained by F Castledine; 3:18.9; Arwon, Taksan
VATC CAULFIELD CUP (2400m)
Mighty Kingdom, 47 (M Johnston) Trainer TJ Smith; 2:29.9; Warri Symbol, Sonstone
VRC AUSTRALIAN CUP (2000m)
Dulcify, 52.5 (J Miller) Trained by CS Hayes; 2:1.1; Manikato, Family Of Man

MVRC WS COX PLATE (2040m)
Dulcify, 57 (B Thomson) Trained by CS Hayes; 2:04.9; Shivaree, Lawman
AJC DERBY (2400m)
Dulcify, 55.5 (B Thomson) Trainer CS Hayes; 2:30.7; Double Century, March To Glory
VICTORIA DERBY (2500m)
Big Print, 55.5 (P Jarman) Trained by A White; 2:35; Kingston Town, Runaway Kid
AJC DONCASTER HANDICAP (1600m)
Belmura Lad, 51.5 (P Cook) Trained by M Barnes; 1:33.7; Joyita, dead-heat third Manikato and Marjoleo
BTC DOOMBEN '10 000' (1350m)
Manikato, 58 (G Willetts) Trained by RE Hoysted; 1:19.2; Casca, Charmosa
VRC NEWMARKET HANDICAP (1200m)
Better Beyond, 50 (K Mitchell) Trained by JB Cummings; 1:9.7; Always Welcome, Gondolier

AJC SIRES' PRODUCE STAKES (1400m)
Zephyr Zip, 55.5 (L Masters) Trained by E Kirwan; 1:22.6; Lowan Star, Sweet Habit
VRC SIRES' PRODUCE STAKES (1400m)
Mighty Kingdom, 55.5 (W Treloar) Trainer TJ Smith; 1:23.7; Bold Diplomat, Rocky Top
VRC GRAND NATIONAL STEEPLECHASE (5000m)
Somoy, 59.5 (R Heaslip) Trained by K Thomson; 5:52.6; Young Command, Chocolate Royal
STC GOLDEN SLIPPER STAKES (1200m)
Century Miss, 51 (W Harris) Trained by JB Cummings; 1:10.7; Dawn Command, Sweet Habit
VATC BLUE DIAMOND STAKES (1200m)
Star Shower, 54 (R Higgins) Trained by A Lopes; 1:12; Stage Hit, Dawn Command
STC MERCEDES-TANCRED CLASSIC (2400m)
Shivaree, 57 (R Lang) Trained by D O'Sullivan; 2:27.7; Dulcify, Happy Union

Malcolm Johnston celebrates Kingston Town's first win, the WS Cox Plate at Moonee Valley (BP).

The King's coronation year.

Kingston Town's WS Cox Plate win was a triumph and a tragedy. Triumph because it established his champion status; tragedy because it exacerbated the leg problem that may have cost him the ranking as the mightiest Australian racehorse of them all.

Kingston Town was lame after winning the Cox Plate and he was off the scene for 10 months. But the calendar year had been a magnificent one for the almost invincible gelding. He had won 12 times and been twice placed from 14 starts.

Kingston Town was bred by prominent owner-breeder David Hains who decided to race him himself after the horse failed to reach his reserve at the 1978 yearling sales. Hains sent Kingston Town to T.J. Smith but the colt ran a long last in his first race. Kingston Town was gelded and returned three months later.

The year 1980 was a halcyon one for the 'King'. His autumn began with a sprint victory in the Freeway Stakes and ended with a superb staying triumph in the 3200-metres Sydney Cup. But in the spring his problems winning at Caulfield continued when he was beaten a neck by Hyperno in the Caulfield Stakes, then carried 60 kg for third in the Caulfield Cup to Ming Dynasty and Hyperno.

Fairytale wedding: Two prominent Sydney racing families turned on the glitz in December when Gai Smith, daughter of legendary trainer Tommy Smith, married Robbie Waterhouse, son of big doubles bookie Bill Waterhouse.

Sport of Hearts: The Brisbane racing fraternity opened its purses to help jockey Cheryl Neale, who was confined to a wheelchair after a sickening race-fall at Nanango, north-west of Brisbane. Neale, 32, was paralysed from the waist down. She made history by riding the winner of the inaugural race for women at Moonee Valley.

Country champ: Grand galloper Puramaka, trained at Warrnambool by the doyen of Victorian provincial trainers Kevin Lafferty, won the Hamilton Cup (2200m) for the fourth year in a row. He also took the Warrnambool Cup in 1977–78. To show he could handle the big time, Puramaka won the 1979 Bagot Handicap.

Back in Town: The AJC St Leger, abandoned in 1960 through lack of interest, was restored to the calendar in 1980, the winner being Shogun. First run in 1841, it numbers among its winners Windbag, Phar Lap, Peter Pan, Carbon Copy and Tulloch.

Bye, fellas: At Ascot in Perth, Irene Pateman became the first woman jockey to beat the men in a WA city race. Needless to say, she came from a horsey family, her brother, Noel, being a trainer and her nephew, Michael, a jockey.

Blood flows on: Bletchingly, a son of the speedy Biscay, and therefore a grandson of Star Kingdom, topped the Australian sires' list for the first time in 1979–80. Twenty-five of his progeny won 158 races and $876 575 in stake money. His best was Kingston Town.

Lester's quaddie: The Auckland Racing Club backed a winner when it invited crack English hoop Lester Piggott, 44, to ride at its March meeting at Ellerslie. From six rides, none of them standouts, he booted home four winners and a close second. He won the feature race, The Air New Zealand Stakes, on Arbre Chene.

Drum beats in Cup: Te Awamutu jockey Chris McNab had Drum on the bit at the home turn in the 1980 Auckland Cup and won by two-and-a-half lengths with ears pricked. With 57.5 kg, Drum carried the heaviest Auckland Cup–winning weight since Beaumaris in 1950.

Roy Higgins after Phar Lap Anniversary with Billy Duncan (r) and Tommy Woodcock (Age).

Sangster's Cup conversion

When Robert Sangster – one of the world's leading horse owners and breeders – began racing in Australia in the late 1970s, the Melbourne Cup was something of an enigma to him. In fact, he let it be known he thought it rather quaint that the sport should revolve around a two-mile handicap on the first Tuesday in November.

In November 1980 he found out why it did. His horse Beldale Ball won the Cup – and Sangster described the discovery as 'the thrill of my life'. In fact, Beldale Ball's win may have elevated Sangster into the leading owner-trainer in the world because it meant he had won the feature races on three continents for the past three years. 'This is better than Europe or Paris,' he said. 'This is a win of the heart. That's what the Melbourne Cup is all about – tradition and feeling.'

Beldale Ball was an American-bred horse bought by Sangster as a three-year-old in England 'because I thought he looked a likely type for the Melbourne Cup'. It was a piece of shrewd judgement because Beldale Ball was by no means a glamour colt. Before coming to Australia the horse had a Timeform rating of only 86, which would normally put him in the 'ordinary' class.

Sangster had horses with trainers Bart Cummings, T. J. Smith, John Hawkes and Brian Mayfield-Smith, but sent Beldale Ball to the sagacious Colin Hayes in Adelaide, who transformed him into a quality stayer.

Jockey John Letts took the lightly weighted Beldale Ball to the lead at the 1800-metre mark and the pair were never headed. For Hayes, the win eased last year's disappointment when Dulcify broke down.

Susan Sangster leads Beldale Ball & John Letts.

Midge Didham sees the courageous grey Ming Dynasty home in the Caulfield Cup (Age).

Ming the merciless

Everyone knew that Ming Dynasty had been a great stayer with an imposing record, but he had seemingly capped his career by winning the 1977 Caulfield Cup.

In 1978 he won the Australian Cup and the Metropolitan (beating subsequent Melbourne Cup winner Arwon) before running fifth in the Caulfield Cup with 61 kg. By 1979 it appeared his best was well behind him and he could finish only 15th in the Caulfield Cup to Mighty Kingdom.

So 'Ming' was friendless in the market when he again lined up for the Caulfield Cup in 1980. With most interest centred on Kingston Town and Hyperno, Ming Dynasty started at 50/1 – yet won convincingly. But it was to be his only victory from 12 starts as a seven-year-old. Retired, he continued his racetrack appearances as a clerk of the course's horse.

1980 RESULTS

VRC MELBOURNE CUP (3200m)
Beldale Ball, 49.5 (J Letts) Trained by CS Hayes; 3:19.8; My Blue Denim, Love Bandit
AJC SYDNEY CUP (3200m)
Kingston Town, 52.5 (M Johnston) Trainer TJ Smith; 3:28.2; Double Century, Marlborough
QTC BRISBANE CUP (3200m)
Love Bandit, 50.5 (G Palmer) Trainer TJ Hughes; 3:27, Calpurnicus, Pay The Purple
SAJC ADELAIDE CUP (3200m)
Yashmak, 54 (B Thomson) Trainer CS Hayes; 3:22.4; Pearl Lover, Lovelace Watkins
WATC PERTH CUP (3200m)
Rothschild, 49 (W Carson) Trained by AR White; 3:22.8; Gay Affair, Belle Talk
VATC CAULFIELD CUP (2400m)
Ming Dynasty, 58 (E Didham) Trainer JB Cummings; 2:28.5; Hyperno, Kingston Town
VRC AUSTRALIAN CUP (2000m)
Ming Dynasty, 58 (J Letts) Trainer JB Cummings; 2:2.1; Double Century, Minuetto

MVRC WS COX PLATE (2040m)
Kingston Town, 57 (M Johnston) Trained by TJ Smith; 2:07.3; Prince Ruling, Our Paddy Boy
AJC DERBY (2400m)
Kingston Town, 55.5 (M Johnston) Trained by TJ Smith; 2:34.3; Mr Independent, El Laurena
VICTORIA DERBY (2500m)
Sovereign Red, 55.5 (M Goreham) Trained by G Murphy; 2:38.4; Real Force, Our Paddy Boy
AJC DONCASTER HANDICAP (1600m)
Iko, 51 (M Johnston) Trained by TJ Smith; 1:34.3; Gypsy Kingdom, Arbogast
BTC DOOMBEN '10 000' (1350m)
Hit It Benny, 52.5 (B Thomson) Trained by N Begg; 1:18.4; Family Of Man, Bernard
VRC NEWMARKET HANDICAP (1200m)

Dor Kon, 46.5 (B Clements) Trained by N Cakebread; 1:11.6; Sportscast, Turf Ruler
AJC SIRES' PRODUCE STAKES (1400m)
Shaybisc, 53 (J Duggan) Trained by T Green; 1:22.7; Dark Eclipse, Fiancee
VRC SIRES' PRODUCE STAKES (1400m)
Outward Bound, 54 (B Thomson) Trained by CS Hayes; 1:26; Sardius, Verdi
VRC GRAND NATIONAL STEEPLECHASE (5000m)
Blue Kazan, 60.5 (N Harnett) Trained by J Winder; 6:4.3; Spycatcher, Coolgardie
STC GOLDEN SLIPPER STAKES (1200m)
Dark Eclipse, 51 (K Moses) Trained by N Begg; 1:10.4; Joy, Baglaga Miss
VATC BLUE DIAMOND STAKES (1200m)
Aare, 52.5 (L Dittman) Trained by RE Hoysted; 1:11.1; Verdi, Joy
STC MERCEDES-TANCRED CLASSIC (2400m)
Kingston Town, 52 (M Johnston) Trained by TJ Smith; 2:28.8; Double Century, Gold And Black

The two dreamers: Tommy Smith and George Moore

Arthur William Edgar O'Shaughnessy spoke of the dreamers of dreams. They were the world losers, he wrote in his 19th century ode, but then he also observed, 'They are the movers and the shakers of the world for ever, it seems.' Two losers, or more to the point two who had never been given their chance to try, played cards in the tack room of Cecil Godby's Caulfield stables in 1939.

As they played for matchsticks among the sweaty, horse-healthy smell of leather bridles and sweaty saddles, they dreamed and talked of those dreams, as dreamers have long done if someone will listen.

'He was a better dreamer than me,' one of them, George Moore, then 16, was to say. 'He was 20 or so, had seen more life, and had more to dream about.'

'I'll be the leading trainer,' the never-was rather than has-been jockey, Tommy Smith said, 'I'll train the Derby winner and George here will ride it.'

The men who were to move and shake the Australian turf as never before were both flat broke then. A permanent rather than casual condition.

Moore was down from Brisbane with a couple of Alan Cooper's horses. He was a stablehand for the sporting bon vivant really. He'd never ridden a placed horse. Smith was doing the same with a couple of Matt Sawyer's hayburners.

Ten years later the two shook hands in the mounting yard at Randwick. Sir Adolph Basser had the AJC Derby favourite, Delta, that day. Resplendent in top hat and morning suit, as any gentleman would be on Derby Day, he was the toast of a racing world then more British than the British.

Men like Smith were simply Smith, and the confounded chap seemed to make a habit of forgetting to touch his hat in respect for the committee.

Moore, the rider of the dreadfully noisy little fellow's horse, was just a jockey boy, even if, damnitall, he had been winning quite a few races. This was the Derby, and Smith's horse was a maiden, had never won a race, should not even be in it, and the arrogant little trainer had even called the horse after himself. Playboy, indeed.

They won. A first classic for Smith and Moore, a first win ever for Playboy. It was the awakening of two astounding careers.

Smith became the single most dominating factor ever in Sydney racing, or for that matter Australian racing.

At the end the dreamer had won two Melbourne Cups, four Caulfield Cups, seven WS Cox Plates, three Sydney Cups, six Brisbane Cups, seven Metrops, seven Doncasters, seven Epsoms, six Golden Slippers, and dozens of other Group 1 events.

He was a multi-millionaire, a Rolls-Royce was parked outside his magnificent harbourside home in Point Piper and he had been the confidant of princes. The world welcomed T. J. Smith.

That first Derby win with Playboy preceded no fewer than 34 more wins in Australian Derby events, in every state including Tasmania.

The lesser dreamer, George Moore, was far from a lesser mover and shaker. He was to win the NSW jockeys' premiership on 10 occasions between 1956–57 and 1968–69.

In 1966–67 he did the unbelievable. He was premier jockey in NSW and England. In

TJ and George, two winning dreamers.

the same season. He rode for the Queen. He won the English Derby on Royal Palace, the Prix de L'Arc de Triomphe on Saint Crespin, the Thousand Guineas, the 2000 Guineas, races in Europe, races in the States.

Playboy's 1949 AJC Derby win prefaced 10 more Derbys on the eastern seaboard, and his partnership with T. J. Smith was simply extraordinary. The pair, as a stable, were as formidable as they were ferocious.

With each other. It was said that no couple ever fought and forgave as they did without having the undoubted benefit of the containing bonds of holy matrimony. Their combination was forever tenuous, but always one of mutual admiration.

'The greatest jockey in the world,' Smith would say of Moore. 'But he's at his best when he's angry. Got to gee him up.' He would accuse Moore of being a prima donna, a loafer who wouldn't attend track work, and threaten to call the partnership off forever.

He never did. The fiery Moore would fight his rivals on and off the track if he thought he was being wronged. He squared off to Athol George Mulley in the stewards' room, and took Billy Camer on in the Randwick stripping sheds. He once threw his jockey's badge at the stewards and 'retired'.

He regularly accused Smith of putting him on 'the wrong one'. 'You've done it again Tommy,' he would call out openly and bitterly, sitting back typically at the base of the saddle as his horse moved into the second placegetter's stall, trailing into the winner's circle behind another and, more significantly from George's point of view, longer-priced stablemate.

'Don't know what you're talking about,' TJ would chirp in his high-pitched counterpunch, quite possibly nimbly calculating what small fortune awaited him at the serious cost of certain bookmakers who had been taken unawares by a Smith 'outsider'.

Naturally, George had been on the more fancied candidate. Hadn't Tommy told him it was a good thing? For Moore seemed forever on the favourite. The bookies would automatically form their betting around him. George Moore rode for 13 years in Sydney and punters could back his mounts on a level stake and win. Not only over the 13 years. Each year. Every year.

George, too, has always enjoyed a punt. Born in 1923 in Mackay, Queensland, the son of a sugar farmer who died when George was eight, Moore did it the hard way. His mum was a station cook and even when he was apprenticed he played bit parts to fellow apprentice Neville Sellwood's starring role in Jim Shean's stables.

Accused of backing Flying East at Hawkesbury in 1953, which he did, and owning it, which he denied, he was disqualified at the AJC Committee's pleasure. He was out for two-and-a-half years. He was 46 when he approached the AJC Easter Carnival in 1969. He rode 15 winners of the 25 races over the four days. Fourteen of them had the notation in the results 'trained by T. J. Smith'.

Smith was born in Jembaicumbene, about 10 miles out of Braidwood, on 3 September 1918, and grew up in Goolgowi. He ran away from home in 1931 to try his luck in Melbourne. He had what he stood up in and a quid. But he had dreams, and horseracing is the real field of dreams.

We cannot say his dreams came true. When he moved and shook the Australian racing world, he exceeded even the hopes of two dreamers in Cecil Godby's old tack room just before the world went to war for the second time.

by Bill Casey

Mighty Manikato: big, brave and beaut

Manikato wins the Memsie Stakes (Age).

Manikato shows the style that had him top the million-dollar stakes mark in 1982.

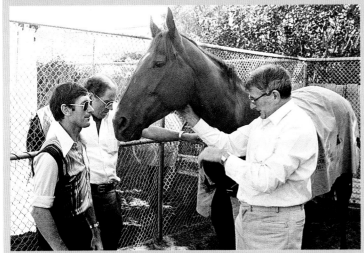

Gary Willetts, Mal Seccull and Bob Hoysted scratch Manikato (Age).

Manikato, Roy Higgins up, wins the Futurity Stakes in 1980 (Age).

Gary Willetts returns to scale on Manikato in February 1980 (Age).

'Rancher is as good a horse as I've ever put a saddle on,' said Charlie Waymouth (Age).

Cups runneth over in the Cook family.

A royal run from Rancher

Rancher gave a performance fit for the Queen in his race debut, the 2nd Balmoral Stakes at Caulfield. The striking two-year-old won the 900-metre event by eight lengths, breaking the course record set by the great Vain by 0.6 seconds. The race was part of the VATC's specially carded program for Queen Elizabeth II in September.

Rancher was ridden by Norman Waymouth whose father, trainer Charlie Waymouth, paid $5000 for the colt, by Brave Lad from the Virginia Gentleman mare Awakening, at the Victorian selected yearling sales. Charlie Waymouth liked the look of Rancher after his first win. 'If he is a genuine racehorse then he is as good a horse as I've ever put a saddle on,' he said cautiously.

On 10 October, Rancher won the Caulfield Debutant Stakes, setting another course record and defeating Grosvenor, the winner of the 1st Balmoral Stakes, by three lengths. (Grosvenor was bought by his trainer Geoff Murphy and co-owners Geoff Tobias and Tom Maltby for $40 000 at the New Zealand sales.) One week later, Rancher followed up with another course record, winning the Merson Cooper Stakes (1000 metres) at Caulfield by seven lengths. His last race for 1981 was at Flemington in the VRC Maribyrnong Plate, which he won from a demoralised Trading Post by eight lengths.

In 12 career starts before finishing as a three-year-old in 1982, Rancher won $225 750 in prize money.

Third Cook Cup

When Peter Cook rode Just A Dash across the line to win the 1981 Melbourne Cup, he was following a family tradition. His father Billy Cook won the Cup on Skipton in 1941 and Rainbird in 1945. Peter Cook acknowledged his father's influence and support with an emotional 'I love you, Dad' during his victory speech.

His father was equally forthright. 'When I won my first Melbourne Cup I thought there couldn't be a bigger thrill. Then there was the second win. But today surpasses those,' he told *Age* journalist Glen Lester.

Billy and Peter Cook are the second father-son combination to ride Cup winners. In 1894 H. Dawes rode Patron to victory. His father had won the Cup on Banker in 1863, under the assumed name of H. Chifney.

Just A Dash was trainer T. J. Smith's second Melbourne Cup winner. Just A Dash started at 15/1; the race favourite was Smith's Kingston Town who never was in the race. Afterwards the favourite's jockey, Malcom Johnston, suggested he might need a spell. Part-owner David Hains agreed he needed a rest. 'He deserves it,' he said.

Just A Dash was bought by Lloyd Williams, George Frew and Tom Pettiona for $45 000 with a Melbourne Cup win in mind.

Jockeys call it a day

Jockeys called a halt to an AJC meeting at Randwick in June when they refused to ride in the final two races. AJC officials had left the decision on whether or not to continue the eight-race meeting up to the jockeys who went to the barrier for the seventh race, the Austral Handicap. On reaching the stalls they turned their horses around and returned to the saddling paddock and the meeting was abandoned.

The Randwick track had been declared heavy before the meeting began and deteriorated as rain fell continuously throughout the afternoon. But it was visibility, rather than the condition of the track, that posed the main problem for the jockeys. According to Denis McClune, president of the NSW Jockeys' Association, 'We have not been able to see the horses racing ahead of us – that is the reason we have made the decision.'

Jockey Malcolm Johnston believed the meeting should have been called off even earlier than it was. 'It was the kids who voted to ride. In my opinion they were being silly,' he told journalists.

However, jockey Wayne Harris (pictured) said he had wanted to continue the meeting because his horse in the Austral, Folly's Prince, had 'a good winning chance'.

Seemingly impervious to the rain and the safety issues at stake, racegoers jeered when it was announced that the final two races had been cancelled.

A casual Hyperno was under guard when he returned to racing in August, thought by police to be the 'leading horse' referred to in a shooting threat. It was the champion's first start since the autumn. He finished second to Demus in the 1st Aurie's Star Handicap (Age).

Gentleman Jack Purtell looks back

When VRC steward and former champion jockey Jack Purtell retired in January, he nominated as his most cherished moment his win on Cromis in the Queen Elizabeth Stakes at Flemington in 1954.

'Never in my wildest dreams did I ever think that one day I would be shaking hands with the Queen and her actually talking to me,' Purtell told *Herald* chief racing writer Jack Elliott. 'I will never forget that day.'

Cromis won from Flying Halo with Olympic Girl third, in a field which included Wodalla, Aldershot, Hydrogen, My Hero and Peshawar.

Said Purtell: 'Everything was going to the plan I thought out before the race with Aldershot bowling out in front with the pace just right. I kept telling myself "This is the one, so do everything right" and I did until we straightened for home when Aldershot went off the course and Wodalla, on whom I won the Melbourne Cup the previous year, shot to the front.

'Wodalla never had, and never did, win a weight-for-age race, but I knew he could stay and was going as strong as a lion. As Wodalla was going like a winner, the thought flashed through my mind that I should have ridden him instead of Cromis.

'It was then I gave Cromis a cut across the

Jack checks the form.

rump with the whip and he nearly went from under me, in fact he went so quickly that we shot to the front sooner than I wanted. The Flemington straight seemed always to be the longest in the world and there I was in front with about one and a half furlongs to go.

'I had a sneak look over my shoulder thinking that Hydrogen, Gallant Archer, My Hero and Peshawar would be coming hard. But to my amazement I saw the colours of Flying Halo and further out Olympic Girl. I got my head down and whacked away with the whip, riding as hard as I could, and Cromis kept giving plenty. He was showing how good he was and eventually he went on to win. I was never so relieved to get past a winning post in my life.'

Jack Purtell rode his first winner, a horse called Bonus, at Mentone in 1937 and during his 30-year career, he rode three Melbourne Cup winners, Hiraji (1947), Wodalla (1953) and Rising Fast (1954), and the English Oaks on Long Look in 1965.

He was also a part of the triple dead-heat in the Hotham Handicap in 1956, an event which he said 'means much more to me now, for the two other jockeys, Bill Williamson who rode Pandie Sun and Reg Heather on Ark Royal, were great mates of mine and both have since died'.

The State of Excitement: Attendances were up 27 per cent on the previous year for the Perth Cup carnival, with the Perth Cup crowd of 41 124 the second biggest since 1972 when the Cup became a $100 000 race.

The end of a Lifetime: New Zealand's most valuable mare, Lifetime, was destroyed in January after breaking a shoulder while galloping at Trentham. The mare was from the imported stallion Sovereign Edition from the 1973 Caulfield Cup winner Swell Time. She had won seven races, including most of New Zealand's top 1600-metre events. One more season and she was to have retired to stud.

A winning start: John Duggan's win on Lawman in the Doncaster Handicap was a win for 'Terry', one of the assistants at the Randwick barrier. The excitable Lawman broke out in a sweat and was in danger of losing before the race had even begun, and assistant Terry calmed the horse by towelling him down. He went on to win the event, beating Ducatoon by 1¼ lengths, with Hit It Benny a half-length back in third place. Duggan, who earned $8500 for his winning ride, rewarded 'Terry' for his assistance at the start.

Payouts to dream of: Sky Castle's winnings topped $100 000 when he won the Forrest Handicap for his new trainer Eddy Laing at Caulfield in January. And some lucky punters' winnings topped that when the $1 trifecta (Sky Castle 4/1 equal favourite; Hyabusa 125/1 and In Light 33/1) paid $151 704. The $1 trifecta paid well again in April at Canterbury, when the dividend was $125 652 in the Strong Plea Handicap (Valensky 66/1; Prince Tatt 6/1 and Late Bid 100/1).

Whoops! Stewards' foul-up means no race: Jockeys in the Newminster Handicap at Caulfield in July found their way blocked near the 900-metre mark by a false rail. A gap wide enough for only two horses meant severe interference as jockeys checked their mounts. Stewards said later that workmen had believed race six was over 2000 metres rather than 1600 metres, and left the false rail used in the previous race, thinking the race was on a different track which linked up to the course proper in a different place. The chief steward Pat Lalor met with the jockeys in his room for 15 minutes following the debacle, then stewards declared the Newminster Handicap a no-race.

A rare moment of magic

Ever so rarely racing climbs above its clichés, its around-they-go-again sameness, to produce an undying moment.

Such was the 1981 Cox Plate. Magic. A race of pure theatre. The sort you bore people about by trying to re-create 10 years hence.

A race followed by a piece of mass euphoria seldom offered in such hard-nosed places as racecourses. People actually stayed to hear the speeches. They actually used binoculars to watch the presentation.

For 15 minutes, it seemed, Kingston Town was owned not by David Hains and others – but vicariously, longingly, by these thousands who usually shun the waffle for the early hustle of the ring.

Lawman was the only bad sport. He let fly a clanging kick at the stall. Why not? He tried hard, got a hiding, and nearly won. To that crowd he didn't exist.

And it was proper that Tommy Smith should invoke Tulloch in his speech. This was the most wonderful Cox Plate since Tulloch stormed to the post in 1960 as hundreds of hats flew in the air.

It was proper, too, because with this win Kingston Town carried himself to the very rim of Tulloch's pedestal. Many were claiming this at Caulfield Cup time in 1980. That was unfair to the horse. He hadn't done enough, nor had he gone fast enough, to justify the comparison. And, of course, the people who rushed him up to that mantle were the first to tear him down when he failed.

But two runs settled his greatness. The first was the George Main Stakes in Sydney when, coming back from a staying distance,

Kingston Town blazed over 1600 metres in 1:34.3, a world-class performance. The other was his 1981 WS Cox Plate win (the second of a record three successive wins) on the 'wrong-way' track at the Valley when nothing went right for him.

One of the old definitions of a champion is the horse who can win sprinting or staying, in Sydney or Melbourne or Darwin, wet or dry, from in front or behind (an American writer also adds hurricanes or volcanoes). This is a better test than stake money because the currency has been so debased. And it makes Kingston Town one of the dozen or so greats.

Something else needs saying after his Cox Plate win. One has crept up on it before only to run away at the heresy of it. The fact is the Cox Plate has become *the race*. Not just of the spring but of the Australian racing calendar. It is consistently won by champions. It is superbly relevant to the pattern of Australian racing. An internationally fashionable distance, long enough to be won by a speed horse with substance or a stayer with a big finish. It is weight-for-age and the field is all quality. And it is staged with all the professionalism that makes the Moonee Valley administration special.

The anticipation, the feeling that one was about to witness something rare, was there before the horses came down the tunnel.

David Hains preceded them and couldn't stop smiling. With him was Tommy Smith, wearing an off-white hat and a conservatively tailored suit, and carrying a walking stick he tends to wave imperiously, more in the manner of a cane.

A few minutes earlier, in the saddling

enclosure, Smith with his stick looked like a caricature of the American master trainer come to Saratoga for the 1928 season.

Such was the mood that the crowd clapped every horse. Kingston Town with his terrific girth ... Koiro Trelay with his Tetrarch-like spots ... the tough and honest Belmura Lad ... Sovereign Red still wanting to be the colt ... the Cinderella stories Binbinga who cost $1000, and Deck The Halls who shouldn't have been there at all because her dam was sold as being empty.

The effect was galvanic when Bill Collins suddenly brought that strident note into his voice to say 'only two to come in'. Form guides were stuffed away, glasses raised, voices hushed.

Then the theatre began. The first furlong was anti-climactic. Instead of a scramble down the straight, the sort of rip and tear which finished Luskin Star in 1977, the pace was steady, there was little hustling, and Kingston Town seemed in a good position, behind the leader on the rails.

But down the back the speculation began: would he get out? At the school, amid murmurs and the shaking of heads, and as the strident note came to Collins' voice again, one was reminded of the things that so often happen on the trots track inside the turf. Here was the favourite, the best horse in the race, smothered away on the rails.

Then it happened. The black came out of the pack like a great reeling drunk shouldering his way back for a refill. The whip used in the left hand sent him rolling out at Silver Bounty. Then he turned his head toward the rail.

But – and this is the uncanny part – from the instant he got clear he was going to win. This despite the reeling and rolling, despite the tendency to hang in, despite the horse being literally as unbalanced as a two-year-old having his first race around corners.

You knew he was going to win because of the way he put that head out. And tried and tried.

More than half an hour later there was still a crowd around the black's stall as a farrier with arms big enough to rip out a red gum by the roots gently rasped down the last nail. And with the horse standing there, unconcerned about his wrong-footed glory, and the sun filtering through that big elm in the top ring, it was hard to walk away and end the magic.

David Hains is a rich man, and presumably he won't be reduced to Vegemite sandwiches if, for any reason, the horse doesn't start in the 1981 Melbourne Cup. Indeed at this stage you could say the Melbourne Cup needs Kingston Town much more than he, or his owners, need it.

by Les Carlyon

So hungry I could eat a horse? My Brown Jug tries to bite Manikato in the CF Orr Stakes.

Koiro Trelay works in reverse at the Valley.

'Jug' bites 'Man', comes off second

Manikato must have wondered what struck him when My Brown Jug turned and snapped at his neck in the closing stages of the CF Orr Stakes at Sandown.

The two were fighting it out two lengths clear of the field in the straight when My Brown Jug's jockey Brent Thomson said he suddenly felt he had a chance to beat Manikato to the line. At much the same moment the stallion, who raced successfully in New Zealand as Little Brown Jug, turned his head and snapped at the champion, narrowly missing him with his teeth.

Would My Brown Jug have won had he not turned his head? You can bet Manikato doesn't think so. He didn't miss a stride, and ran on to win his third Orr Stakes in succession by a head.

My Brown Jug, taken on by trainer Tommy Smith as a four-year-old, lost to Hyperno in the Australian Cup at Flemington in March, but had his first Australian win in the Alister Stakes one week later with Roy Higgins aboard.

Koiro Trelay challenges

Koiro Trelay and trainer Eric Temperton completed the New Zealand–Wellington Cup double in January with a powerful three-quarters of a length win in Wellington from Arethusa, with Eruption a half-neck away third. The last horse to win the New Zealand–Wellington Cup double in the same season was Golden Souvenir in 1945–46.

Temperton, who won the 1971 Melbourne Cup with the grey Silver Knight, set the big grey Koiro Trelay for the Wellington Cup rather than the 1980 Melbourne Cup, preferring first to win the double in his own country. The trainer is also known in Australia for his success with his jumping horses.

Temperton brought Koiro Trelay to Melbourne in the spring of 1981, and the six-year-old ran in the Cox Plate, finishing eighth in a field of 10, and then in the Mackinnon Stakes.

But it was the Melbourne Cup Temperton had in his sights. Koiro Trelay (6/1) carried 54.5 kilograms, despite his wins in the New Zealand Cup with 53 kilograms and the Wellington Cup with 54, and the punters saw the value and made him second favourite after No Peer (4/1). The New Zealand champion finished 10th behind Just A Dash.

1981 RESULTS

VRC MELBOURNE CUP (3200m)
Just A Dash, 53.5 (P Cook) Trained by TJ Smith; 3:21.1; El Laurena, Flashing Light
AJC SYDNEY CUP (3200m)
Our Paddy Boy, 51.5 (R Mallyon) Trainer CS Hayes; 3:21.7; My Blue Denim, Gatcombe
QTC BRISBANE CUP (3200m)
Four Crowns, 52.5 (J Cassidy) Trainer D Enright; 3:24.9; Granite King, Bay Legend
SAJC ADELAIDE CUP (3200m)
Just A Dash, 48.5 (M Johnston) Trainer TJ Smith; 2:23.2; Beau Noble, Bright Halo
WATC PERTH CUP (3200m)
Magistrate, 49.5 (R Skelton) Trained by IH Steffert; 3:21, Rubicon, Yashmak
VATC CAULFIELD CUP (2400m)
Silver Bounty, 53 (E Didham) Trainer GM Carson; 2:27.1 ; No Peer, Deck The Halls
VRC AUSTRALIAN CUP (2000m)
Hyperno, 58 (H White) Trained by JB Cummings; 2:4.3; Turf Ruler, My Brown Jug

MVRC WS COX PLATE (2040m)
Kingston Town, 59 (R Quinton) Trained by TJ Smith, 2:06.7, Lawman, Binbinga
AJC DERBY (2400m)
Our Paddy Boy, 55.5 (R Mallyon) Trainer CS Hayes; 2:31.2; Ring The Bell, Deck The Halls
VICTORIA DERBY (2500m)
Brewery Boy, 55.5 (W Treloar) Trained by TJ Smith; 2:36.2; Birchwood, Binbinga
AJC DONCASTER HANDICAP (1600m)
Lawman, 51.5 (J Duggan) Trained by GM Hanlon; 1:34; Ducatoon, Hit It Benny
BTC DOOMBEN '10000' (1350m)
Sovereign Red, 53.5 (L Dittman) Trainer G Murphy; 1:19; Grey Sapphire, Atlantic Flyer
VRC NEWMARKET HANDICAP (1200m)
Elounda Bay, 49 (L Dittman) Trained by JB Cummings; 1:8.5; Turf Ruler, Misty Vain
AJC SIRES' PRODUCE STAKES (1400m)
Full On Aces, 55.5 (L Dittman) Trainer A Armanasco; 1:22.1; Allez Show, Calm Joe

VRC SIRES' PRODUCE STAKES (1400m)
Full On Aces, 55.5 (L Dittman) Trained by A Armanasco; 1:25.8; Anyone Home, Fearless Pride
VRC GRAND NATIONAL STEEPLECHASE (5000m)
Kaimoto, 64.5 (P Hely) Trained by R Hore-Lacy; 6:2.6; Mr Hickey, Suede Boy
STC GOLDEN SLIPPER STAKES (1200m)
Full On Aces, 54 (L Dittman) Trained by A Armanasco; 1:13.1; Food For Love, Rose Of Kingston
VATC BLUE DIAMOND STAKES (1200m)
Black Shoes, 51.5 (G Robson) Trained by AV McKenna; 1:11.4; Sharp Walk, Birchwood
STC MERCEDES-TANCRED CLASSIC (2400m)
My Blue Denim, 57.5 (P Cook) Trained by D O'Sullivan; 2:35.3; Red Nose, Love Bandit

Roy Higgins's reward at Moonee Valley (BP).

Bruce Postle's award-winning sports picture.

Pat Hyland: a muddy ride at Flemington (BP).

'There will be something for you': jockey

It was 'very common' for jockeys to discuss the prospects of their mounts and where they would be running in the race, leading jockey Roy Higgins told a VRC hearing into the running of the 1981 Ararat Cup.

Speaking in support of veteran jockey Bob Skelton, he said it was not uncommon for a jockey to ask not to be impeded if another horse was beaten.

Asked to interpret the comment: 'If you keep out of my way, there will be something for you', Higgins said he understood it to mean that a jockey who asked for such a favour was suggesting that in the future, the other rider should not hesitate to give him a call under similar circumstances.

The 13-day hearing into the Ararat Cup ended in June with the disqualification of jockeys Rodney Dawkins and Skelton. Dawkins, who rode the Cup winner Gary Bruce,

was disqualified for three years, and Skelton, who rode A Secret Show and admitted accepting $500 from Dawkins, for nine months. In a sensational twist, within hours of the decision an indefinite stay was put on both suspensions when it was disclosed that a member of the VRC committee had spoken to a witness soon after the Cup was run.

The 1980-metre Ararat Cup was won in course record time in November by the 7/2 favourite Gary Bruce. A VRC stewards' inquiry began in December and more than 30 people were called to give evidence. All 24 bookmakers present at Ararat submitted their betting sheets on request to the four-man panel.

In April, 10 people, including five jockeys, were charged on a total of 39 counts involving race fixing at country meetings. Most related to the Ararat Cup, though races run by Gary Bruce at Wangaratta and Seymour meet-

ings were also involved.

Six of those charged were cleared: Gary Bruce's trainer Wayne Walters, jockey Gerald Ryan who rode third placegetter Dom's Image, jockey Dale Broadfoot who rode seventh placegetter Al's Gamble, bookmaker Brian Mann, and the owners of Al's Gamble, Alan Jorgenson and Barry Long. Charges against Stephen Ridler, rider of Glenigis who came last in the Cup, and horse owner Geoff Salter were dismissed on the 11th day of the inquiry.

Ron Skelton, 47, denied riding his horse A Secret Show to anything other than the trainer's instructions or helping Dawkins during the race. He told the inquiry that he did say: 'If my horse is beaten, I'll help you,' and said this was common practice for jockeys in any race.

Miller's son outed for 'rein pulling'

The 16-year-old apprentice jockey Mark Miller (pictured), youngest son of champion jockey John Miller, was disqualified for 15 years over an incident at the Coral Park Club at Pinjarra, Western Australia in March.

Miller was found guilty of foul riding in an alleged 'rein pulling' incident. The race was won by Echoing, ridden by apprentice Jim Taylor, with Mark Miller's Lemrac second by a long neck.

The WATC stewards found that Mark Miller reached out, took hold of Echoing's rein during the race, pulled the horse's head towards his mount, then grabbed Taylor's whip. Miller was riding Lemrac for his 77-year-old grandfather John Miller Snr, who was suspended until 19 June for refusing to attend the inquiry when it was first opened.

Mark Miller, who had been riding for only 12 months, denied the accusations.

'I had my own whip in the left hand and that's the hand they claim I used to grab the reins,' he said. 'If I had done that, I would have dropped my own whip. But I continued to use it.'

The young rider had ridden three winners from 63 mounts. John Miller Snr said he could not believe such a savage penalty could be inflicted on a young boy. The Millers said an appeal would be lodged on Mark's behalf.

Two of Gurner's Lane's 39 happy owners lead Mick Dittman back to scale (Age).

Gold and Black leads Cup street parade (Age).

The breeder doesn't always know best

Gurner's Lane and the mighty Kingston Town battled it out in a Melbourne Cup finish so close that even the trainers failed to call it. Gurner's Lane looked to have the race won at the 150-metre mark, but the crowd favourite Kingston Town fought back to come within a neck of victory. Kingston Town's trainer Tommy Smith and owner David Hains set off for the winner's stall only to find that the champion had come second. Bart Cummings, the trainer of many Melbourne Cup winners, said of Gurner's Lane: 'Only once in 50 years do you see a run like that in a Melbourne Cup.'

The tight finish vindicated VRC handicapper Jim Bowler's decision to give Kingston Town 53 kg, one kilogram under weight-for-age, while penalising Gurner's Lane three kilograms for his Caulfield Cup win. In August, Kingston Town had been greeted by incessant cheering when he made his comeback to racing to win the Warwick Stakes at Warwick Farm. He went on to prove his class yet again by winning the weight-for-age WS Cox Plate at Moonee Valley for the third time.

With his Melbourne Cup win, Gurner's Lane became the first winner of the Caulfield and Melbourne Cups double since Galilee in 1966. He won the Caulfield Cup by a record five lengths from Gala Mascot in heavy going, despite his reputation as a poor mud runner. He then ran a creditable second to Mighty Kingdom in the Mackinnon Stakes. As a three-year-old he had won both the VRC and AJC St Legers and run third in the AJC Derby, and second in the Tulloch and Chelmsford Stakes.

If Gurner's Lane's New Zealand breeder, Patrick Hogan, had been given his way, the gelding would have been put down as a yearling. The young horse wounded his leg in a fence and, on top of that, Hogan noticed he was a windsucker. The vet called in to mend the leg and cure the windsucking refused Hogan's request to put the horse down, so Hogan sent the gelded Gurner's Lane to trainer Geoff Murphy in Australia with the suggestion he sell him if possible.

Murphy paid Hogan $7000 for Gurner's Lane and sold him to a 39-member syndicate. Each of the part-owners paid $360. 'That is the only money we have contributed because from the initial outlay we have kept on winning prize money,' one part-owner said. The Melbourne Cup win took Gurner's Lane's earnings to $538 000.

Magistrate gives the Perth Cup a mauling

Magistrate, a bad-tempered 10-year-old with three screws in his leg, won the $200 000 Perth Cup on New Year's Day for the second year in succession. In 1981 he won by a record 10 lengths. In his second win, he came from behind to snatch the race from Allez Bijou by a long head.

Magistrate drew attention to himself in the mounting yard when, amidst lashing out and snorting, he attempted to maul strapper Harry Armstrong's shoulder. Such behaviour was nothing new for the Kiwi stayer. New Zealand owner-trainer Ian Steffert said after the race: 'I don't like socialising very much myself and neither does the horse.'

Magistrate was ridden by 47-year-old Bob Skelton, one of the few humans Magistrate seemed to like. Skelton gave himself little chance of winning the race 300 metres from the line.

'It's just that this horse never gives up. He just keeps trying all the time,' he said.

Magistrate improved with age. As a five-year-old his racing days looked finished when he split his off-fore cannon bone. In the ensuing operation, three screws were inserted and after a long spell he returned to the track. With his second Perth Cup win, the veteran stayer's winnings totalled $470 000 – more than two-thirds of it won as a nine and 10-year-old.

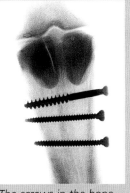
The screws in the bone.

They're still racing in winter at Flemington, waiting for the spring crowds to return (BP).

The Waymouth family go wild as Rancher wins the Blue Diamond Stakes at Caulfield (BP).

TURF TOPICS

Connections connect: Rancher's trainer Charlie Waymouth and the part-owner of Grosvenor Geoff Tobias clashed verbally and physically before the horses returned to scale after the Tatts Blue Diamond Prelude. The two men were separated by onlookers. Rancher had just defeated his on-course rival for a third time. VATC stewards later fined Waymouth and Tobias $500 after finding them guilty of 'unseemly conduct'.

Hold your horses: Jockey Garry Murphy was not in the saddle when his horse Sabotic, race favourite at 13/4, started in the Textile Handicap at Caulfield in May. The jockey was about to mount the horse when the starter David Wood released the field. Sabotic was drawn in barrier 12 of a field of 17 and so may have been unsighted. Murphy was delaying mounting the horse, which he considered nervous. Wood failed to see that the horse was riderless, and said Murphy had not indicated that he was not ready. Racecaller Bill Collins picked up the fact that the horse was riderless after about 300 metres of the 2400-metre race had been run. Wood did not call a false start so Sabotic was declared a race runner by the stewards.

Star chestnut: The eight-year-old 17½-hands chestnut Towering Inferno won the role of Phar Lap in the John Sexton/Michael Edgley feature film *Phar Lap*.

Hayes blitz: On Saturday, 23 January, the Hayes stable won a remarkable 10 races, with seven out of eight winners at Victoria Park and three winners at Caulfield.

The Adelaide winners were Open Menu, High Drifter, War Chest, Ronleigh Bisque, Frivolous Lass, Black Mandate and Supertrack. The winners at Caulfield were Mysterious Ways, McCabe and Glaisdale.

Ten days earlier, Hayes runners won four at Flemington and three at the Murray Bridge meeting in South Australia.

STC's 'phantom' race meet thwarted

The Sydney Turf Club's attempt to stage a 'phantom' race meeting at Rosehill in October was thwarted when police stopped the betting on Melbourne and Brisbane events. Seven bookmakers had taken bets on four interstate races when the axe fell at 12.59 p.m.

The scheduled Rosehill meeting had been postponed one hour before the first race, due to threatened strike action by the Australian Workers' Union. Bookmakers, working with the permission of the STC, were doing lively business on the William Clark Welter at Caulfield, which featured two Sydney gallopers Gold Noble and Holborn Court. The race was six minutes from starting time when punters were told that all bets were 'off'. One punter who had bet on the favourite and winner Synsky had a bet of $12 000 to $8000 refunded.

The AWU had refused to work on the first race at the meeting because the field contained Proud Tradition, trained by Pat Farrell of Muswellbrook. Farrell was one of eight trainers the union black-banned because they claimed the trainers had placed their horses into the barrier after barrier attendants were stood down by the Newcastle Jockey Club the previous week.

Winning women take the money

New Zealand jockey Diana Mosley became the first woman jockey to win a major race in Australia when she won Queensland's richest race, the $155 000 Fourex Cup at Doomben on Double You Em in July. It was the 24-year-old rider's 46th winner for the season. Asked how she felt about her win, she said, 'Bloody terrific.'

Before the end of the month Nerida Saunders on Scrappy Sal had come second to her brother Ben on Cheryl Maree at Eagle Farm and sisters Carlene, Ramona and Leoni Wehr had ridden the trifecta in the Stuart Handicap in Alice Springs.

At the other end of Australia, Tasmanian jockey Beverley Buckingham became the first female apprentice to win a senior jockeys' title on 31 July when she won Tasmanian premiership. Buckingham, yet to turn 18, outrode her apprentice claim with 63 winners for the season and said she doubted she would have another season to equal it. 'Trainers aren't so keen to put you up without a claim,' she said. While Bev Buckingham went from strength to strength, she had reason for concern.

Buckingham was apprenticed to her father, Ted Buckingham, the leading Tasmanian trainer and, like Buckingham, most successful women jockeys in the early 1980s had some familial connection with the racing industry. Trailblazers Pam O'Neill and Linda Jones were married to trainers. In the case of New Zealander Debbie Healey, who won the 1983 Geelong Cup on Deb's Mate, her parents had bought a promising horse to ensure their daughter a ride. (It certainly wasn't her only ride. In the 1982 season, Healey rode 57 winners in New Zealand.) The Payne sisters' father Pat was a trainer.

In the early 1980s, women riders were proving their worth all over the country, but the male-dominated racing industry remained suspicious of women jockeys.

In 1982 the racing clubs capitulated and allowed women to become full members. The VRC committee was the last to give up its male-only privileges (the Moonee Valley Race Club had seen the light in 1977), but didn't tell everyone. The wife of the Sports Minister Neil Trezise was refused admittance to a stand by a VRC commissionaire on Melbourne Cup Day and the club was publicly berated by Victorian Premier John Cain.

Bev Buckingham: won jockeys' premiership.

Bev leads the charge on Le Spectre.

Another Rose wins the AJC Derby

Rose of Kingston, 1982 Horse of the Year, became the first filly to win the AJC Derby since Tea Rose won in 1944. The Derby win was also the first for jockey Gary Willetts who had been trying to win a Derby for 20 years. 'This is the biggest thrill of my career,' Willetts told the *Age*'s Tony Bourke. 'I've finished second three times in the Victoria Derby and I don't know how many seconds I ran in New Zealand.'

Thirty-nine-year-old Willetts went on to become Victoria's first $1 million jockey when he won on General Salute at Ballarat on 30 June. A former New Zealander, Willetts settled in Victoria in 1975, and General Salute was his 1070th winner. 'It is a very satisfying target to reach,' he said.

Sydney's Malcolm Johnston was believed to have reached the $1 million mark while riding Kingston Town in his winning 1979–80 season.

Rose of Kingston won 10 of her 26 races, including the Australasian Oaks, the VRC Oaks and the Ascot Vale Stakes, before a strained suspensory ligament ended her lamentably short racing career. It concluded with a win in the Coongy Handicap at Caulfield on 13 October.

Helen Hains and Rose of Kingston (Age).

1982 RESULTS

VRC MELBOURNE CUP (3200m)
Gurner's Lane, 56 (L Dittman) Trained by GT Murphy; 3:21.2; Kingston Town, Noble Comment
AJC SYDNEY CUP (3200m)
Azawary, 50 (N Tiley) Trained by A Jones; 3:22.8; Allez Bijou, World Vision
QTC BRISBANE CUP (3200m)
Queen's Road, 48.5 (G Murphy) Trained by TJ Hughes; 3:19.7; El Laurena, Amarant
SAJC ADELAIDE CUP (3200m)
Dealer's Choice, 49 (D Coleman) Trained by RB Morgan; 3:29; Amarant, Boktisan
WATC PERTH CUP (3200m)
Magistrate, 52.5 (RJ Skelton) Trained by IH Steffert; 3:21.9; Allez Bijou, Pearl Lover
VATC CAULFIELD CUP (2400m)
Gurner's Lane, 53.5 (B Thomson) Trained by GT Murphy; 2:32.5; Gala Mascot, Veloso

VRC AUSTRALIAN CUP (2000m)
Kip, 56.5 (R Heffernan) Trained by GM Hanlon; 2:6.1; Lawman, Galleon
MVRC WS COX PLATE (2040m)
Kingston Town, 59 (P Cook) Trained by TJ Smith; 2:05.5; Grosvenor, My Axeman
AJC DERBY (2400m)
Rose Of Kingston, 54.5 (G Willetts) Trained by RE Hoysted; 2:31; Our Planet, Gurner's Lane
VICTORIA DERBY (2500m)
Grosvenor, 55.5 (L Dittman) Trained by G Murphy; 2:35.9; Cossack Prince, Veloso
AJC DONCASTER HANDICAP (1600m)
My Gold Hope, 53.5 (N Tiley) Trained by R Verner; 1:34.6; Grey Sapphire, Smileakyle
BTC DOOMBEN '10 000' (1350m)
Ideal Planet, 52 (M Johnston) Trained by TJ Smith; 1:18.5; Grey Receiver, Beach Boy

VRC NEWMARKET HANDICAP (1200m)
Razor Sharp, 53 (D Short) Trainer J Johnstone; 1:9.1; Penny Edition, Pure Of Heart
AJC SIRES' PRODUCE STAKES (1400m)
Mighty Manitou, 55.5 (W Harris) Trained by JR Hawkes; 1:23.9; Grosvenor, Marscay
VRC SIRES' PRODUCE STAKES (1400m)
Grosvenor, 55.5 (P Cook) Trained by G Murphy; 1:26.6, Cossack Prince, Sir Trout
VRC GRAND NATIONAL STEEPLECHASE (5000m)
Somoy, 68 (S Jenkins) Trained by T Hughes; 5:46; Elanora Girl, Light Horse
STC GOLDEN SLIPPER STAKES (1200m)
Marscay, 54 (R Quinton) Trained by J Denham; 1:10.6; Vaindarra, Grosvenor
VATC BLUE DIAMOND STAKES (1200m)
Rancher, 54 (N Waymouth) Trained by C Waymouth; 1:10.8; War Chest, Grosvenor
STC MERCEDES-TANCRED CLASSIC (2400m)
Prince Majestic, 57 (N Tiley) Trainer R Verner; 2:28.7; Allez Bijou, Rose Of Kingston

Snowy Lupton takes Kiwi for an early-morning stroll along Port Phillip Bay before the Cup (BP).

A happy BATC Horse of the Year (Age).

Farm horse comes from last

When Bart Cummings saw Kiwi come into the mounting yard for the 1983 Melbourne Cup, he liked what he saw. He dashed off and had a few dollars on the powerful chestnut from the Wanganui farming district in the North Island of New Zealand.

Of all the endearing tales of the turf, that of the aptly named Kiwi, ridden by 20-year-old NZ lad Jimmy Cassidy, holds a special place. For he was prepared by a quiet New Zealander, Ewen 'Snowy' Lupton, a 63-year-old farmer and hobby trainer. A shy, nevertheless engaging fellow who showed the pros a thing or two, giving hope to all those small-time trainers who dream of winning the Melbourne Cup.

The Kiwi story began in 1977. Anne Lupton was in the habit of encouraging her husband to buy and train horses who served a dual purpose, also rounding up stock on the farm. Mrs Lupton picked Kiwi from a sale catalogue. Two things influenced her. The colt was a chestnut (she liked them) and he was by the American sire Blarney Kiss, thus the ideal replacement for a Blarney Kiss colt they had lost with a broken leg.

Kiwi did not race as a two-year-old and it was not until he won the 1982 Wellington Cup as a five year-old that his owners entertained thoughts of running him in the Melbourne Cup.

When weights for the Melbourne Cup were published, Kiwi was allotted only 52 kilograms, a little less than the owners antici-

pated. After five lead-up races in NZ, including a win in the Egmont Cup at Hawera, Kiwi was flown to Melbourne a week before the Cup.

Lupton's decision not to give his six-year-old gelding a pre-Cup hit out in Melbourne puzzled the critics. All Lupton wanted for his horse was peace and quiet, which was available at Mornington, a seaside town with a fine racetrack 50 kilometres south of Melbourne. There, with Lupton in the saddle, Kiwi was given long, steady work in preparation for his first race in Australia.

Leaving the straight the first time, Kiwi, a 9/1 chance, was last of the 24 runners. He was still 22nd at the 800m, a good 25 lengths from the lead, and 20th at the 400m. No sooner had his supporters reached for a consoling gulp from their hip flasks, than Cassidy angled Kiwi to the middle of the track and set sail after the leaders.

With an unforgettable finishing burst that took racegoers by surprise, Kiwi swept to victory as though racing against draught horses, defeating Noble Comment by a length and three-quarters easing up. He ran the last 400m in 48 seconds. His time of 3:18.9 was only 1.5 sec outside Gold And Black's record.

After receiving the gold cup (and later a cheque for $195 000), a tearful Snowy Lupton told the big crowd: 'Gosh, this is the greatest thrill of my life.' He then faded into the background, where he was happiest.

Strawberry's Plate

Some horses look the part but are slow-coaches. Strawberry Road, with his distinctive mahogany-red coat and flowing mane, had presence on and off the track.

He came to attractive Moonee Valley on a warm spring day with an imposing record: wins in the AJC and QTC Derbys and in the Rosehill Guineas. And he had given an inkling of his liking for the Valley with his win in the Freeway Stakes two months before the Cox Plate. Still, he was not the popular pick on the big day, starting at 11/2.

Kingston Town, winner of the past three Cox Plates and by now retired, was given a rousing reception when he led the field out, after which Roy Higgins galloped him gently down the straight for the last time. Five minutes later his mantle had been assumed by Strawberry Road, who scooted away from his rivals as though they were novices.

Some novices! Classy colt Sir Dapper, the 7/2 equal favourite, tried his heart out but couldn't sprint when the heat was on. As for co-favourite, the leggy, erratic grey mare Emancipation, winner of the Doncaster, she decided she would rather be in her home town of Sydney and behaved churlishly, pulling and reefing and sulking. She ran out of steam before the turn. No horse could match Strawberry Road, who responded to a couple of slaps from Mick Dittman's whip, and sped down that short straight to win by 3½ lengths. Kiwi Slave, a classy plodder at 100/1, ran second.

In the Sydney way of going, big, courageous Manikato strides his stuff to another win.

Manikato the marvellous

Manikato was big in every sense of the word – in conformation, gameness, in the eyes of the racing public and, where it counted most, on the scoreboard.

For sheer pluck, his half-head win in the 1983 William Reid Stakes at the age of seven brought tears to many an eye. Astonishingly, it was his fifth win in a row in the glamour Valley race over 1200 metres (formerly 6 furlongs, less 20 yards), first run in 1925. That 18 993 people turned out in heatwave conditions to see a slice of history in the making was testimony to Manikato's greatness.

Manikato's battle-weary legs sported a cut or two after the race. Blood was streaming from one of them but trainer Bob Hoysted soon established it was superficial and required only a bandage. But Hoysted said Manikato had not pulled up too well. 'The problem is his old legs. He felt today's race.'

But you can't beat heart. Six weeks later Manikato came out and won the Futurity Stakes at Caulfield, his fourth win in that event, his 29th from 46 starts. But for running second to Galleon in 1982, he would have won five Futuritys on end too.

'I've never known a horse to have his will to win,' said Gary Willetts, who rode the powerhouse gelding in all but three of his wins. 'He was like a machine, perfect to ride, especially in weight-for-age races.'

After the '83 Futurity, Manikato, by Manihi, would have one more race, the George Ryder Stakes at Rosehill, in which he fin-

ished second to Emancipation. Within a year he was dead, the victim of a virus. The racing fraternity mourned a great sprinter. He had bowed out with $1 154 210 in stakes and was buried at Moonee Valley, his favourite racetrack.

Not since Lord won four consecutive Memsie Stakes from 1958 to 1961 had a horse so dominated not one, but two feature races as Manikato did. The Reid Stakes and the Futurity were not for slouches. Before Manikato, the Reid Stakes was won by such notables as Heroic, Tranquil Star, Flying Halo (three times), Comic Court, Winfreux and Family Of Man and the Futurity by Phar Lap, Ajax (three times in a row), High Caste, Bernborough, Royal Gem, Sky High and Gunsynd. It will be a long time before Manikato's feats, sustained over so long a period, are repeated. Only a horse called Brown Jack has won a feature race more times in a row, the Queen Alexandra Stakes at Ascot in WA six times from 1929 to 1934.

Even the losers were on Manikato's side in the '83 Reid Stakes. There was a surge of excitement when the old fellow, who was allowed to go to the post at 10/9, rounded the turn in front. Could he hang on? Fellow veteran Torbek tried hard to gather him in, but Willetts said: 'He spotted Torbek about 100 metres out and wasn't going to get beaten.' Torbek's part-owner Barry Long said: 'I'm glad we didn't bring Manikato undone; the public deserved his win.'

Robert Sangster and Brent Thomson (Age).

Ron Quinton aboard Sir Dapper (Age).

Emancipation returns to scale a winner.

Silver City ring-in

A Victorian bookie on holidays smelled 'a ring-in' when Foden won the last race, an 1100m Improvers, at the Broken Hill St Patrick's Day meeting on 19 March 1983. Foden, backed from 50/1 to 2/1 equal favourite, bolted in by a length and a half.

The bookie, John Hallam, told stewards that the winner could not be Foden, whose moderate form he was familiar with. 'He won too easily to be Foden,' said Hallam.

As a result, stewards suspended betting payouts, then disqualified Foden, amending the placings to Eastern Crisis, 1; Clear The Deck, 2; Duncan Lass, 3. Bookies sighed with relief. They had been saved a $250 000 pay-out. One of the first bets about Foden was $30 000 to $600. 'They just wanted to back it for anything,' said one bookmaker.

Foden, who turned out to be the well-performed Melbourne horse Nordica, was impounded by AJC stewards so as to examine his markings.

Just like his dad

Sir Dapper became the first son of the mighty Vain to win the Golden Slipper Stakes, and he did so in a race record 1:9.9.

Breeding was not the only link between Sir Dapper and his sire. Les Bridge, a Sydney trainer for 20 years, watched Jim Moloney prepare Vain for his successful assault on the Slipper in 1969. 'Jim stabled Vain at my place and I used the same methods with Sir Dapper,' said Bridge.

Sir Dapper, who cost his owners $17 000 as a yearling, started at 7/2 and won the $300 000 race convincingly from Been There and the 7/4 favourite Love A Show.

Five months after winning the Slipper, Sir Dapper, now three, brought off the single richest prize in Australian turf history. Revenue of $284 300 flowed from his win in the Spring Champion Stakes – $81 600 first prize plus $2700 in trophies, $100 000 for landing the spring treble and a $100 000 bonus for his breeder Don Buffier.

She is no lady

Make no mistake. Emancipation was no lady. The three-year-old grey filly, who dazzled the racing world with her easy win in the 'mile' Doncaster Handicap, had a reputation for unruly behaviour at trainer Neville Begg's Sydney stables.

'She will kick and bite you as soon as look at you,' said the trainer, adding that all good horses showed a bit of temperament.

The person mostly on the receiving end of these tantrums was Begg's son, 21-year-old Graeme, the filly's personal assistant since she entered the stables. Young Begg's labours were fruitful and painful. In the words of jockey Ron Quinton: 'Graeme is black and blue from Emancipation's bites.' Neville Begg praised his son, saying: 'A lot of credit for the filly's performances must go to Graeme. She is the sort that needs a lot of attention.'

The attention was worthwhile, as Emancipation won nine races before her impressive Doncaster win.

Just back losers

Colourfully dressed John Mort Green, one of the last great characters of Brisbane racing, told Sydney turf scribe Bert Lillye that he made his money out of losers.

'I make my money by finding losers,' he said. 'You can't pick winners all the time, but if you know your onions you can pick losers. I prefer to risk my capital opposing horses I don't think can win. There are so many ways

a good thing can get beaten. I lay these horses to lose with my bookmaker friends.

'It's natural cunning you know. You've got to learn how jockeys think and you must bet to faces, knowing who is betting for whom. That is why I'm always nosing around the betting ring. If they operated on me they'd find a stomach full of ears. And I try to keep friendly with everyone.

'One thing I learnt early is that you must study the horses in the mounting yard.

Recently a horse called Seeker's Gold, a 6/1 chance, broke out in a sweat in the yard. She was a 100/1 chance in my book. I laid her and never had an anxious moment. She was beaten on the home turn.

'That's stealing by trickery but it's a nice way to pick up easy money.'

Green said he could only succeed where there were licensed bookmakers and reckoned jockeys were poor judges, getting too enthusiastic about their mounts.

Gary Hill on Strasburg at Moonee Valley (BP).

The Hills' great hoist

When the Hill clan from Gippsland went to the races, the opposition could be forgiven for heading for the hills, so to speak.

Take the 1983 Great Eastern Steeplechase at Oakbank. The winner Venite, heavily backed at 28/10, was ridden by Gary Hill, 44, giving him his third win in the famous Easter race over 4950 metres. One of the fences, the fallen log, has been a feature of the event since its inception in 1876.

Venite was trained by Gary Hill's brother Maurie. The silks were made by Maurie's wife, Betty, and their daughters Rhonda (23), Vicky (20) and Sally (16) took it in turns to ride Venite in his lead-up work. As well, son Mark, 25, was the strapper.

Also present among the crowd of more than 65 000 were Gary Hill's wife, Fay, and their daughters Kellie (20) and Kasey (16). That made a team of 10 Hills. With such a cheer squad it's no wonder that Venite raced to an 18-length win over Light Horse, the 14/10 favourite. For good measure, the Hills provided the third placegetter, Gawkie.

The Hill brothers drove school buses in Gippsland when they were not involved with horses. Maurie had a small team, mainly jumpers. 'Today was just like a dream come true,' he said. 'Venite has been a great trier throughout her career and after Saturday's Von Doussa win, when she sprinted home beautifully, I thought she had a great chance. And to see old Gawkie, who's also one of the family, battle on for third was a great thrill.'

Spike not short on Sharp success

Not many big wins came the way of popular jockey Dale 'Spike' Short. Except in major sprint races in Melbourne's autumn. In 1983, for the second year in a row, he won the nation's premier 'dash', the Newmarket Handicap up the Flemington straight six on the same horse, the Newcastle speedster Razor Sharp.

Asked how many city winners he had ridden between Newmarkets, a smiling Short was short on words: 'About one.' This time Short had an armchair ride on Razor Sharp, who started at the liberal odds of 25/1 and won by two lengths in a slick 1:9.7.

Short's first big autumn success was on Gleaming Waters in the 1981 Oakleigh Plate. That victory broke a drought of 228 losers. His humour shone through that day. Asked what he thought when his number (18) was semaphored, he replied drolly: 'I thought it was a dead-heat between 1 and 8.'

Short's lack of success was surprising considering he was Victoria's top apprentice in 1980. Razor Sharp's trainer Jim Johnstone was a staunch supporter of Short. 'He has never done anything wrong for me.'

In winning successive Newmarkets, Razor Sharp became the first horse to do so since Gothic in 1927–28 and Correct in 1960–61. The Newmarket has been won by some dandy gallopers, notably Heroic, Aurie's Star, Ajax, Bernborough and Royal Gem. And by some grand horsemen – Billy Cook, Harold Badger, Bill Williamson, Scobie Breasley, Roy Higgins etc. So Spike is in good company.

1983 RESULTS

VRC MELBOURNE CUP (3200m)
Kiwi, 52 (J Cassidy) Trained by ES Lupton; 3:18.9; Noble Comment, Mr Jazz
AJC SYDNEY CUP (3200m)
Veloso, 51 (P Cook) Trained by MG Barnes; 3:23.4; Secured Deposit, Fountaincourt
QTC BRISBANE CUP (3200m)
Amarant, 52.5 (P Cook) Trained by GM Hanlon; 3:23; Bound To Honour, Lady Capulet
SAJC ADELAIDE CUP (3200m)
Amarant, 51 (J Letts) Trained by GM Hanlon; 3:27.5; Toujours Mio, Magistral
WATC PERTH CUP (3200m)
Bianco Lady, 52.5 (B Thomson) Trainer R Thomsen; 3:23.8; Swift Knight, Port Carling
VATC CAULFIELD CUP (2400m)
Hayai, 52.5 (N Voigt) Trained by JR Lee; 2:38.8; Cossack Prince, La Cocotte
VRC AUSTRALIAN CUP (2000m)
Spectrum, 52.5 (B Thomson) Trainer CS Hayes; 2:2.3; Noble Comment, Silver Bounty

MVRC WS COX PLATE (2040m)
Strawberry Road, 57 (L Dittman) Trainer DR Bougoure; 2:09.1; Kiwi Slave, Mr McGinty
AJC DERBY (2400m)
Strawberry Road, 55.5 (L Dittman) Trained by D Bougoure; 2:41.8; Veloso, Chiamare
VICTORIA DERBY (2500m)
Bounty Hawk, 55.5 (H White) Trainer JB Cummings; 2:38.5; Cobbobonee, Albany Bay
AJC DONCASTER HANDICAP (1600m)
Emancipation, 54.5 (R Quinton) Trainer N Begg; 1:35.9; Ringtrue, Foregone Conclusion
BTC DOOMBEN '10 000' (1350m)
My Axeman, 56.5 (W Robinson) Trained by T Griffin; 1:21.4; Lord Sambeau, Brenlaine
VRC NEWMARKET HANDICAP (1200m)
Razor Sharp, 55.5 (D Short) Trained by J Johnstone; 1:9.7; Ideal Planet, Foregone Conclusion

AJC SIRES' PRODUCE STAKES (1400m)
Keepers, 55.5 (P Cook) Trained by PC Barns; 1:23.3; Belle Tetue, Brave Show
VRC SIRES' PRODUCE STAKES (1400m)
Brave Show, 55.5 (B Thomson) Trained by CS Hayes; 1:24.7; Keepers, Dynastic
VRC GRAND NATIONAL STEEPLECHASE (5000m)
Diwali, 62.5 (G Hill) Trained by R Hore-Lacy; 5:55.8; Headford Town, A Chara's Lad
STC GOLDEN SLIPPER STAKES (1200m)
Sir Dapper, 54 (R Quinton) Trained by L Bridge; 1:9.9; Been There, Love A Show
VATC BLUE DIAMOND STAKES (1200m)
Love A Show, 52.5 (G Willetts) Trained by RE Hoysted; 1:10.7; Solo Performance, Worth
STC MERCEDES-TANCRED CLASSIC (2400m)
Trissaro, 57 (L Olsen) Trained by JB Cummings; 2:27.4; Veloso, Mr McGinty

Black Knight wins the Cup. Every horse is in the picture, except Legana, the 100/1 shot who finished 19th and last (Age).

A red-letter day for Hanlon's Black Knight

When Black Knight crossed the line to win the Melbourne Cup, trainer George Hanlon felt pangs of remorse as well as joy. The trainer had helped persuade jockey Robert Heffernan to ride Martian's Son instead of Black Knight, doubting Black Knight's ability as a stayer. Instead jockey Peter Cook won his second Melbourne Cup, on board a horse he had not heard of only a few days earlier.

Black Knight was Hanlon's third Melbourne Cup win (he won with Piping Lane in 1972 and Arwon in 1978) and he confessed that he had not backed the horse. 'I knew he was fit enough,' he said after the race. 'The big question was, could he stay well enough?'

Black Knight was originally set for the 1983 Melbourne Cup but that plan was abandoned when he was galloped on in the Geelong Cup. One year later he ran second to Chagemar in the Geelong Cup, then ran third to the same horse in the Dalgety of 2500 metres.

Jockey Peter Cook had seen the Dalgety on television and thought the run impressive enough to cancel the five rides he had lined up for Randwick on Cup Day. Cook's father, Billy Cook, the rider of two Melbourne Cup winners, watched the race from his home on the Gold Coast.

For the younger Cook, there were omens aplenty which connected his ride with those of his father. Both Skipton (1941) and Rainbird (1945) were last-minute engagements and Black Knight, like Rainbird, carried the No. 17 saddlecloth. Billy Cook died early in 1985. Black Knight was sired by the 1971 Melbourne Cup winner Silver Knight. The New Zealand–bred stallion and the dam Brenta were the foundation pair of entrepreneur Robert Holmes à Court's Heytesbury Stud in Western Australia and Black Knight was their second produce.

No expense had been spared by Holmes à Court in setting up the Heytesbury stud in the early 1980s. He hit the headlines in Easter 1981 when he paid $828 000 for a colt by Luskin Star from Visit at the Sydney Easter yearling sales and was in the headlines again in July 1981, when he paid $1 570 000 for five horses at the dispersal sale of Brian Maher's stud on the Queensland Gold Coast. He paid a Queensland record of $700 000 for the Biscay mare Shannara.

Silver Knight and Brenta were an odd pairing: the stallion was bought for $72 000 and the dam, who had a few wins on Victorian provincial tracks, none beyond 1000 metres, cost $600. Holmes à Court set out to breed a fast stayer, and Black Knight was the result.

It's all action as the jockeys desperately drive their mounts to the line at Moonee Valley (BP).

Kingston Town and Neville Pepper (Age).

Red Anchor's skew-whiff start in the Victoria Derby, which he won by four lengths (Age).

Red Anchor's away in Derby

Mick Dittman was full of praise after riding Red Anchor to a four-length victory in the Victoria Derby. 'I've never ridden a better horse,' he said. He defeated National Gallery and Clovelly Bay.

Red Anchor's win a week earlier in the WS Cox Plate gave Tommy Smith his seventh Cox Plate winner, breaking the record set by the legendary Jack Holt. The 11/8 favourite won the race in record-breaking time, clipping 0.6 seconds from the record set by the filly Surround eight years earlier with the time of 2:3.7. He defeated the pacesetter, another three-year-old from Sydney, Street Cafe, with King Delamere in third place.

Dittman, who had dropped 2.5 kg to ride Red Anchor at 48.5 kg, was distressed and required medical attention in the jockey's room after the race. 'It was one of the hardest rides of my career because he was sluggish and I had to work hard on him a long way from home,' he said.

Red Anchor was bred in New Zealand at the Millfield Stud, Matamata, by Peter Stechell. From good galloping stock, his sire was the imported Donatello 11 horse, Sea Anchor, with the dam Decoy Girl.

The owners of Red Anchor, a syndicate managed by John Gigante, had set their sights on the Victoria Derby. Gigante had bought out the chestnut's previous trainer and part-owner Paul Sutherland for $30 000 for his half-share. As a two-year-old Red Anchor had won the 1984 Champagne Stakes. In Brisbane, he won the Sires' Produce Stakes from Noble Peer, equalling the race record time of 1:23 for 1400 metres.

Gigante transferred the horse to T.J. Smith and the wins continued. Early in October his owners rejected an offer of $3 million for the horse, with Smith applauding, saying, 'I wouldn't accept $5 million.'

TURF TOPICS

Women winning: Carol Tucker, a 20-year-old apprentice from Benalla, made history when she became the first woman to win a race against male riders in Melbourne in August. Tucker won the Woodlands Handicap on Rich Fields Lad by four lengths. Jockeys Sue Cadzow and Marie Bolden rode five of the seven winners at Horsham races in January, echoing a similar feat in January 1983 when women won four of the Mt Gambier meeting's five races, and were only beaten by a short half-head in the fifth race.

Eight-horse pile-up: New Zealand jockey Tony Williams received spinal injuries and broke his neck in a spectacular fall in the Hinemoa Maiden at Rotorua in January. Eight horses fell 800 metres from the finish in one of the worst smashes in New Zealand's racing history. Williams was riding the three-year-old Blagdan in the 1400-metre race.

The pile-up occurred when Liqueeno, one of three leaders, fell. Blagdon went over the top and another six horses came down. Amazingly no horses were seriously injured, but another two jockeys, Lance O'Sullivan and Earl Harrison, were hospitalised. An inquiry by the racing club's judicial committee into Liqueeno's fall revealed that the filly stumbled for no apparent reason, and the report declared the incident 'entirely accidental'.

With only seven horses left standing after the fall, Major Tonks won from an outsider Almeric, with the favourite Amloch third.

Quinton on Sir Dapper after the Slipper (Age).

Sir Dapper explodes after bomb scare

Sir Dapper exploded to victory in the $40 000 Hobartville Stakes at Warwick Farm in March and the race meeting came to a temporary standstill due to a bomb scare. The main grandstand was evacuated and the meeting was held up for 15 minutes after what turned out to be a hoax call.

Sir Dapper, last year's Golden Slipper winner, won with such ease that trainer Les Bridge declared the Vain colt would never be beaten again. The 1/5 favourite beat Victoria Derby winner Bounty Hawk by three-and-a-half lengths with Beechcraft, who had defeated him in the Caulfield Guineas, a half-length back third. Jockey Mick Dittman took the time to peer over his shoulder in the straight to see how far back his rivals were.

Sir Dapper's connections planned to retire the three-year-old to stud after just three more races. They had already refused an offer of $4 million and he had won 12 of his 15 starts and $582 500 in stake money.

In April, Sir Dapper and Emancipation fought it out in the $100 000 wfa Ryder Stakes at Rosehill with Emancipation winning in a reverse of the horses' last meeting. Mick Dittman on Sir Dapper was trapped in the early stage of the race, and gave Emancipation a start of more than two lengths. But Sir Dapper managed to get within a half-neck in a thrilling finish.

That month Sir Dapper suffered a deep cut behind the nearside leg in the wfa AJC All-Aged Stakes and was lame after the race.

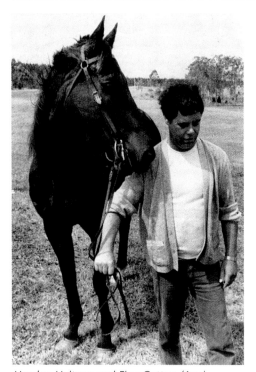

Hayden Haitana and Fine Cotton (Age).

Robbie Waterhouse fronts the inquiry (Age).

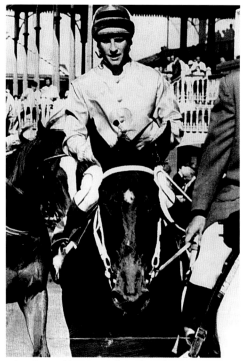

Ring-in: Bold Personality after the race (Age).

Fine Cotton's Bold Personality unmasked

It all began when Fine Cotton won the 2nd Commerce Novice at Eagle Farm on 18 August. Bookmakers on course and throughout the eastern states and Darwin had reeled as the winner's price plunged from 33/1 to 7/2 equal favourite. Punters in the interstate ring at Warwick Farm were prepared to take almost any price, and he started at 6/4. Hundreds of small punters followed the dramatic shift in the market with their dollars. Yet according to his form the eight-year-old had finished 10th in an ordinary field of 12 at Doomben at his previous start and done nothing much before that.

The Queensland Turf Club stewards summoned the Coffs Harbour trainer Hayden Haitana over the public address system to appear before them but he failed to appear. The horse was disqualified and placed under police guard.

Earlier, stewards had delayed declaring correct weight while they attempted to check the horse's registration papers. Haitana claimed that someone must have removed them from his race-day gear bag.

The race was awarded to Harbour Gold after stewards lodged an objection that Fine Cotton was not the horse he was represented to be. They ordered all bets to stand, which meant punters who had backed Fine Cotton lost their money, saving bookmakers more than $1 million in pay-outs. Of the bookmakers, Sydney's Mark Read was set to be the biggest loser, with close to a $200 000 pay-out had Fine Cotton not been disqualified.

It was soon revealed that the winning horse was, in fact, the better performed Bold Personality, a seven-year-old bay gelding clumsily dyed brown to pass for Fine Cotton, with his legs bandaged to hide the absence of Fine Cotton's white markings. Bold Personality also

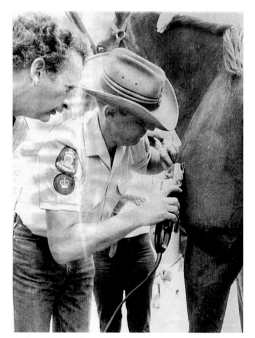

Police check for the correct brand (Age).

had a star in the middle of his forehead, along with different brandings to the horse he was impersonating.

The Queensland Racing Minister Russ Hinze jumped to the defence of the Queensland racing industry. 'Ask yourself why?' he said. 'Ask why the horse was from New South Wales … the plunge was centred in NSW and the price was shorter in Sydney. Ask these questions and if there's something wrong then perhaps we're looking in the wrong state.'

In December the AJC 'warned off' the bookmakers Bill Waterhouse and his 30-year-old son Robbie Waterhouse, a decision effectively forbidding them attending all race meetings worldwide, while at the same time revoking their bookmaking licences. The AJC committee found that Robbie Waterhouse had prior knowledge of the substitution of Bold Personality for Fine Cotton, and that he connived with others in committing a dishonourable action in connection with racing on 18 August. Canberra bookmaker Peter McCoy was also warned off, along with a bookmaker's clerk, and four punters.

The retired District Court Judge Alf Goran, the one-man Appeals Tribunal for the AJC, rejected appeals and confirmed the 'warning off'.

Trainer Hayden Haitana and the man considered the 'mastermind' behind the bungled affair, former used car salesman John 'The Phantom' Gillespie, both received jail sentences.

In 1988 the NSW District Court quashed all charges against Robbie Waterhouse in relation to the affair, Judge Smyth commenting that 'the facts, as presented, showed no criminality', but the AJC stood its ground.

Thanks for the memories, Bert

'Sing no sad songs for me. Given a chance I would do it over again, making the same mistakes but enjoying always the weird but wonderful lifestyle that is racing,' Bert Lillye wrote in his final column in the *Sydney Morning Herald* on Monday 16 July. The highly regarded sporting journalist was looking back on a career of close to 50 years of writing about horseracing.

In that time he watched racing grow from a small colourful world full of characters in which there were no starting stalls, on-course broadcasts or steward's films, to one in which the entire racing public 'has never had it so good … in racecourse amenities, race control and media communication'.

Wherever there was a story in racing, chances are Bert Lillye was there. It was a

Lillye, by Charles Altmann.

young Lillye who accompanied Phar Lap on his last journey and reported news of the horse's death back to his readers in Australia.

In his final column, Lillye named Bernborough as the best racehorse he had seen, with Rising Fast, Dalray, Peter Pan and Tulloch as 'each deserving their own peculiar pedestal'. He declared he had never seen a better rider than 'the complete horseman' Bill Cook, and nominated T. J. Smith as the best trainer. 'He has set records, the like of which will never be repeated.'

Bert Lillye himself would appear on many a racing person's list – as the best racing journalist. 'So, it's goodbye,' he concluded, 'and thanks for the memories.'

Roy Higgins, Australia's No. 1 hoop (BP).

Professor calls it a day

After battling for months to keep his weight down, the 11-times champion jockey Roy 'The Professor' Higgins finally retired from riding in March. He had been hoping to finish with a flourish. 'Just one more carnival and maybe a classic winner was what I was hoping for,' the disappointed champion told Tony Bourke of the *Age*. He retired on medical advice.

Roy Higgins remained in the public arena through his job in the sporting department at Channel Seven. Later in the year, he was appointed manager of the Hyperion Thoroughbred Syndicate. He also became the business manager for jockey Darren Gauci.

Higgins's final race was on In The Slot at Flemington in October 1983. Earlier in his 30-year career, the jockey was asked by an interviewer: 'Roy, what do you want to be when you retire?' His reply? 'Fat.'

TURF TOPICS

A battler goes down: Sprinter Sans Rival broke his near shoulder near the 500-metre mark in the Coca-Cola Bottlers Handicap at Moonee Valley in January and was put down. The galloper was considered a pet by the family of trainer Laurie Cleary who watched the sprinter's last moments. 'As long as the boy is all right,' Cleary said as he enquired after jockey Rob Scarlett's condition. The jockey had escaped with bruising.

Sans Rival was special to the Clearys, not least because he had won the 1983 Oakleigh Plate as a rank outsider. 'He was more important to us than anything … nothing compensates for these things,' he said. 'People with horses know. You have an affinity with them.'

Moving on: Peter Hayes, 34-year-old foreman for his father Colin for the last 12 years,

announced he would set up as a trainer in the 1984–85 season. Hayes's younger son David, 21, took over as assistant.

Top colt's heart fails: Frame, the 4/6 favourite in the $60 000 Sires' Produce Stakes, collapsed and died about 200 metres past the finish after running last. Frame, by Sir Tristram from the former champion mare Surround, was bought for $NZ420 000 and his part-owners included Robert Sangster's Swettenham Stud syndicate, New Zealand studmaster Patrick Hogan and trainer Colin Hayes.

On the move: The young Freedman brothers, Lee, Richard and Anthony, moved to Melbourne and set up shop at the Brackley Lodge Stables near Flemington in May.

1984 RESULTS

VRC MELBOURNE CUP (3200m)
Black Knight, 50 (P Cook) Trainer GM Hanlon; 3:18.9; Chagemar, Mapperley Heights
AJC SYDNEY CUP (3200m)
Trissaro, 56.5 (J Marshall) Trained by JB Cummings; 3:22.4; Our Shout, Alibhai
QTC BRISBANE CUP (3200m)
Chiamare, 53.5 (P Cook) Trained by TJ Smith; 3:22.5; Beaver Boy, Rose And Thistle
SAJC ADELAIDE CUP (3200m)
Moss Kingdom, 53 (J Taylor) Trained by F Maynard; 3:21.6; Affinity, Our Shout
WATC PERTH CUP (3200m)
Moss Kingdom, 46 (J Taylor) Trainer F Maynard; 3:23.1; Chiamare, Head For Space
VATC CAULFIELD CUP (2400m)
Affinity, 53 (P Hyland) Trained by JJ Moloney; 2:29.7; Bounty Hawk, Al Dwain
VRC AUSTRALIAN CUP (2000m)
Admiral Lincoln, 52 (K Forrester) Trainer G Murphy; 2:2.4; Loyal And True, Astrolin

MVRC WS COX PLATE (2040m)
Red Anchor, 48.5 (L Dittman) Trained by TJ Smith; 2:03.7; Street Cafe, King Delamere
AJC DERBY (2400m)
Prolific, 55.5 (J Marshall) Trained by JB Cummings; 2:34.8; Alibhai, Beechcraft
VICTORIA DERBY (2500m)
Red Anchor, 55.5 (L Dittman) Trainer TJ Smith; 2:35.9; National Gallery, Clovelly Bay
AJC DONCASTER HANDICAP (1600m)
Vite Cheval, 51 (K Mitchell) Trainerd by I Saunders; 1:38.9; Royal Regatta, Sovereign Chief
BTC DOOMBEN '10 000' (1350m)
Getting Closer, 54 (G Hall) Trained by H Davis; 1:18.5; Mr Magic, Prince Hervey
VRC NEWMARKET HANDICAP (1200m)
Heron Bridge, 54 (K Watson) Trained by N Donovan; 1:8.8; Nouvelle star, River Rough

AJC SIRES' PRODUCE STAKES (1400m)
Victory Prince, 55.5 (A Marney) Trained by C Conners; 1:26.2; Red Anchor, Spirit Of Kingston
VRC SIRES' PRODUCE STAKES (1400m)
Street Cafe, 55.5 (B Clements) Trained by T Green; 1:26; Tristalight, Lord Of Camelot
VRC GRAND NATIONAL STEEPLECHASE (5000m)
Gogong, 62.5 (G Julius) Trained by L Robinson; 5:48.9; Trans Yonder, Dulico
STC GOLDEN SLIPPER STAKES (1200m)
Inspired, 54 (D Beadman) Trained by T Green; 1:11.6; Love A Kiss, Royal Troubador
VATC BLUE DIAMOND STAKES (1200m)
Street Cafe, 54 (B Clements) Trained by T Green; 1:11.3; Fair Verdict, Slick Draw
STC MERCEDES-TANCRED CLASSIC (2400m)
Hayai, 57 (N Voigt) Trained by J Lee; 2:34.6; Trissaro, Beechcraft

Laurie Connell punts $65 000 on a zebra-striped colt at the Trentham sales (Age).

Connell lofts the Perth Cup (Age).

Lucky Laurie takes on the racing world

When Phizam won the $225 000 Perth Cup (3200m) in January, his owner, banking entrepreneur Laurie Connell, appeared on the members' deck at Ascot and offered to buy drinks for everyone. Champagne (French, of course) flowed.

Connell had picked up close to $1 million in a betting coup when Phizam won by three lengths from Swift Knight with Pliancy another three-quarters of a length back third. The 5/4 favourite's time was the second fastest for eight years.

Laurie Connell set out to conquer the rac-ing world in 1985. He not only had the east-ern states in his sights, but also the New Zealand breeding industry. To this end he had invested more than $4 million in some 50 yearlings in 1984, purchased a property in the Waikato district of New Zealand's north island and bought a share in the USA in one of the world's most valuable horses, a half-brother to the outstanding sire Sir Tristram.

He bought Phizam for $150 000 on the recommendation of the New Zealand blood-stock agent John Cameron and his private trainer Brian 'Buster' O'Malley with the Perth Cup in mind.

In addition to his racehorses, Connell owned a string of 50 showjumpers and was manager of the Australian showjumping team at the Los Angeles Olympics in 1984. It seemed he had the world at his feet.

With the Phizam win, Rod Kemp, 31, became the first jockey to win all of the fea-ture races at the Perth summer carnival in January. He also won the $300 000 Australian Derby on Importune and the $175 000 Railway Stakes on Eastern Temple, the carni-val's other two feature races.

Kevin Langby and Deirdre Stein (Age).

Deirdre wins Cox Plate

Bathurst's Deirdre Stein became the first woman to train a WS Cox Plate winner when Rising Prince defeated Roman Artist by two-and-a-half lengths with Drawn third. The striking chestnut with a white blaze was raced by the Exchange Racing Syndicate of 12 Lithgow men who included miners, a publican, a railwayman and a carpenter. 'All workers,' Cecil Thompson, one of the syndi-cate managers, told Glenn Lester of the Age.

Rising Prince, by Round Top, a stallion who stood at the Stein's Rockleer Stud at Bathurst for $1500, and the Capricorno mare Bonlene, was one of four of the Round Top–Bonlene progeny raced by the Lithgow syndicate, each of them trained by Deirdre Stein. The syndicate also stuck with jockey Kevin Langby, whose win brought him back to the classic winners' list.

The tough middle-distance galloper en-joyed a rural life at the Steins' Rockleer Stud: Vince Stein rode the five-year-old 'around the cows and calves' on the Friday before the race.

Deirdre Stein believed in working her horses on a mile-long hill on the property and this no doubt contributed to Rising Prince's toughness, which he demonstrated last season when he won the Villiers–Summer Cup double only four days apart at Randwick. In April at Randwick he won the wfa Queen Elizabeth Stakes.

Darren Gauci pilots River Rough home in the William Reid Stakes at Moonee Valley (Age).

Bob Hoysted has rough trot

When River Rough won the $35 000 Lightning Stakes (1000 m) at Flemington in February, his trainer Bob Hoysted announced he was thinking of moving to Sydney. The previous Friday the Epsom trainer had lost an appeal to the VRC Committee over a record $5000 fine imposed by stewards in October after he had refused to saddle River Rough for the Moir Stakes at Moonee Valley. Hoysted had been denied permission for the horse to urinate in the swabbing stalls and River Rough, the even-money favourite, was scratched from the Moir only minutes before it began.

Under the rules of racing, the swabbing stalls were closed an hour before the race began. Hoysted asked the Moonee Valley Racing Club's veterinary surgeon for permission for River Rough to urinate in the stalls but this was refused. The rule apparently related to the stewards' fear that it would make it difficult to get a urine sample after the event.

Hoysted, president of the Victorian division of the Australian Trainers' Association, threatened to hand in his licence at the time, saying, 'No one knows what effect a bladder full of urine would have on a horse during the race.'

Following River Rough's narrow win in the Lightning Stakes over the three-year-old High Signal, the trainer of Manikato, Rose of Kingston and Spirit of Kingston said he doubted if he could continue training under the Victorian system.

'If I stay here, I know I'll do something that racing will be sorry for and I don't want to do that,' he said.

Hoysted appealed again, this time to the Racing Appeals Tribunal which decided in favour of the trainer. Meanwhile, River Rough carried topweight (58 kg) in the Newmarket Handicap in March, which was won by Red Tempo with Hula Drum second and King Phoenix third, and a week earlier came second in the Futurity Stakes (1400 m) at Caulfield to Vite Cheval, with Red Tempo third.

In April, Bob Hoysted's Spirit of Kingston missed out on the three-year-old Triple Crown (and the $250 000 bonus offered by the STC and the AJC) when she failed to run on in the last 200 metres of the AJC Derby. The race was won by Tristarc. Hoysted said the filly was knocked around during the race and would be spelled.

Earlier, Spirit of Kingston had won the Canterbury Guineas and the Rosehill Guineas, which she won from Castinillia and Luck's a Lottery. Spirit of Kingston was a half-sister to Rose of Kingston, who won the AJC Derby for Hoysted and owners Mr and Mrs David Hains in 1982.

TURF TOPICS

Four out of five: Darren Gauci, 19, won four of the first five races at Sandown in January, equalling a record he set in 1982 for the most wins at a Sandown meeting. The champion apprentice came close to breaking the record when he came second on 25/1 chance Bev Rose in the last race, the Siren Handicap.

His other winners were Seiger (2/5 favourite), Flight Judge (6/4 equal favourite), Winged Keel (2/1 favourite) and Maintenon (10/1). He went on to become the first apprentice to earn $1 million in prize money.

Training records: T. J. Smith won his 33rd successive Sydney trainers' premiership, breaking his previous world record. Earlier in April, the win by three-year-old Foystaan at Warwick Farm in April took the Smith stable's earnings past $3 million for the season. Meanwhile, Colin Hayes broke his own Commonwealth record, training 265 winners in the 1984–85 season, and winning his eighth consecutive trainers' premiership in Melbourne and his 23rd in Adelaide.

Atlantis sinks: While the Golden Slipper wasn't a dream come true for Adelaide's 'galloping grandfather' 52-year-old jockey Des Coleman, his fellow South Australian, trainer Colin Hayes, won the $600 000 race at Rosehill for the first time.

Jockey Ron Quinton accepted a ride on Hayes's Rory's Jester when he drew barrier three and he made the most of it, securing the perfect run. Not so lucky was Coleman's mount, the favourite New Atlantis who drew barrier 14. Coleman was unable to manoeuvre New Atlantis toward the rail and he rounded the home turn about 10 horses deep to run fifth.

Hunterville's treble: Hunterville became the 12th double winner of New Zealand's Great Northern Steeplechase in 1984. In 1985, with regular rider Dennis Gray aboard, he became the only horse to have won the arduous race three times, despite his distinct dislike of the Ellerslie waterjump which he botched nearly every time.

Lucky all round: Canberra-trained Dorica Galaxy was lucky to be alive, let alone winning his 10th race from 16 starts at Warwick Farm in May. The four-year-old broke his pelvis during his first race as a two-year-old. The veterinary advice was to have the colt put down but his trainer, John Morrissey, and breeder and part-owner, Trevor Brogan, decided to try to save him.

Jack Thompson retires at age 62 (Age).

Thompson and Mr & Mrs W. J. Smith (Age).

Jack Thompson, a winner in 1944 (Age).

Jack Thompson: a great among the greats retires

Jack 'The Professor' Thompson, one of Australia's greatest jockeys, retired in May after a remarkable 47-year career which consisted of at least 15 000 rides and 3000 wins. Thompson, 62, was immediately granted a number one trainer's licence by the AJC.

Thompson won the Sydney jockeys' premiership five times, twice while still an apprentice. 'Jack started a new era for the apprentice rider,' according to turf authority Bert Lillye. 'Before Jack showed his great horsemanship as a youngster, apprentices received few opportunities. Jack rode with superb judgement and was one of the greats.'

A tall lad for a jockey, Thompson was apprenticed to the Randwick trainer Frank Dalton and made history in the 1940–41 season when he won the jockeys' premiership with 106 winners. He was the first apprentice to ride more than 100 winners in a season.

Jack Thompson was a great jockey in an era of great jockeys, riding alongside fellow greats like Billy Cook, Darby Munro and Athol Mulley. During his career, he won every important race in Sydney. He also rode T. J. Smith's first winner, Bragger, in a maiden welter at Rosehill in 1942.

One race in which Thompson had little luck was the Melbourne Cup. He finished second in 1945, 1948 and 1956. Known for his poker face, the jockey showed some amazement in 1948 when Dark Marne was judged to have finished second in the Cup behind a 80/1 long shot Rimfire.

'And I still think my horse won,' Thompson said 37 years after the event. 'It was the very first photo-finish and they realigned the camera at the Australian Cup meeting soon after.'

In 1951 he was on board the favourite Morse Code when it struck the heels of the horse in front at the turn into the straight, causing him to fall.

In 1967 a young apprentice, Ron Quinton, was racing alongside Thompson when his filly stumbled. Thompson leaned over and grabbed Quinton, taking the weight from the filly's back long enough for her to regain her footing. After the race, Quinton told the stewards, 'I certainly would have fallen but for Thompson's help.'

Jack Thompson, who trained at Randwick after his retirement from the saddle, died in 1992.

T. J. Smith, a winner in anyone's colours.

The big man says so

Kerry Packer rebuked the 1985 premier trainer T. J. Smith, after Easter, a horse the two men owned in partnership, won the NSW Cancer Council Handicap at Randwick in September.

Easter raced in Smith's colours, and Packer berated Smith: 'I have been trying for a long time to get a good horse; I've got one now and you don't use my colours!'

Smith responded by saying he did not care what colours Easter ran in. 'He could run in black and white so long as he could gallop. He raced in Kerry's colours last time and I can't say why he was in my colours today,' Smith said.

'Obviously there was a mistake somewhere, but in future I can assure you he will be in the green and white hoops and red cap, the Packer colours.'

The rider of Easter, Mick Dittman, was suspended for two weeks after pleading guilty to a charge of careless riding.

$65 000 of What A Nuisance's Cup winnings was donated to the Save the Children Fund (Age).

Punters queue at a suburban TAB (Age).

A couple of crocks win the Melbourne Cup

Only 18 months after his career (and shoulder) appeared shattered by a fall at Morphettville, Pat Hyland rode What a Nuisance to victory in the Melbourne Cup. The winning trainer, John Meagher, described the 44-year-old jockey's first and only Cup win, as 'the ride of the year'.

Born in the Western Victoria coastal town Port Fairy, Hyland joined Jim Moloney's stables at Warrnambool as a 15-year-old. He moved with the stables to Melbourne and in 1958 had his first Melbourne win on the Moloney-trained Saranover in the Granville Handicap at Flemington on a heavy track.

Early in his career, Hyland won 18 races on Craftsman, including the 1963 Victoria Derby and he also rode the champion Vain (by Wilkes from Elated) in all his wins, including the 1969 Golden Slipper.

After his horrific Adelaide fall, Hyland, with his shoulder pinned and wired together, made a comeback to riding against doctors' orders, and combined with Moloney to win the 1984 Caulfield Cup on Affinity. It was Hyland's 20th Caulfield Cup ride; he had finished second in 1962, 1963 and 1979, and third in 1965. He retired from racing in 1990.

What A Nuisance won the Melbourne Cup by a short head from the mare Koiro Corrie May (10/1) with Tripsacum (33/1) three-quarters of a length away in third place. Like Hyland, the seven-year-old What A Nuisance was something of a miracle, having broken down first in the 1984 Sydney Cup, and then again months later.

He recovered from the first injury, to his back, then broke down again with a strained ligament in preparation for the 1984 Melbourne Cup and had to be rested for eight months.

Trainer John Meagher nursed the seven-year-old gelding along, and the Monday rain which resulted in a soft track helped What A Nuisance sneak to a victory from Koiro Corrie May. The winner was jointly owned by Lloyd Williams and Dennis Gowing.

Despite the presence of the Prince and Princess of Wales, the first members of the royal family to visit Flemington on Cup Day, the disappointing crowd of 77 000 was the smallest since 1965.

1985 RESULTS

VRC MELBOURNE CUP (3200m)
What A Nuisance, 52.5 (P Hyland) Trainer J Meagher; 3:23; Koiro Corrie May, Tripsacum
AJC SYDNEY CUP (3200m)
Late Show, 51 (N Campton) Trained by B Mayfield-Smith; 3:26.7; Imaprince, Secured Deposit
QTC BRISBANE CUP (3200m)
Foxseal, 54 (G Hall) Trained by R Hore-Lacy; 3:24. Our Compromise, Rushcutter
SAJC ADELAIDE CUP (3200m)
Toujours Mio, 53.5 (T Dawkins) Trained by JP Courtney; 3:28.8; Nicholas John, Mapperley Heights
WATC PERTH CUP (3200m)
Phizam, 52 (R Kemp) Trained by B O'Malley; 3:20.1; Swift Kingdom, Pliancy
VATC CAULFIELD CUP (2400m)
Tristarc, 50.5 (W Treloar) Trained by R McDonald; 2:30.9; Our Sophia, Lacka Reason
VRC AUSTRALIAN CUP (2000m)

Noble Peer, 50 (H White) Trained by JB Cummings; 2:1.5; Astrolin, Ankara
MVRC WS COX PLATE (2040m)
Rising Prince, 59 (K Langby) Trained by Mrs DL Stein; 2:05.3; Roman Artist, Drawn
AJC DERBY (2400m)
Tristarc, 54.5 (W Treloar) Trained by RS McDonald; 2:31.1; Sir Zephyr, Silver Award
VICTORIA DERBY (2500m)
Handy Proverb, 55.5 (J Cassidy) Trained by B Mayfield-Smith; 2:36.4; Acumen, Born To Be Queen
AJC DONCASTER HANDICAP (1600m)
Row Of Waves, 51 (M De Montfort) Trained by L Bridge; 1:36; Foxseal, Vite Cheval
BTC DOOMBEN '10 000' (1350m)
Lord Ballina, 53 (L Dittman) Trained by TJ Smith; 1:19.8; Princess Tiber, Mr Magic
VRC NEWMARKET HANDICAP (1200m)
Red Tempo, 55.5 (D Gauci) Trained by CS Hayes; 1:9.2; Hula Drum, King Phoenix

AJC SIRES' PRODUCE STAKES (1400m)
Wonga Prince, 55.5 (M De Montfort) Trained by TJ Smith; 1:24.6; Acumen, Dream Lodge
VRC SIRES' PRODUCE STAKES (1400m)
True Version, 55.5 (G Hall) Trained by A Armanasco; 1:25.4; Jackson Square, Eminency
VRC GRAND NATIONAL STEEPLECHASE (5000m)
Gogong, 68 (P Hillis) Trained by L Robinson; 5:51.9; Region, Tengah Hari
STC GOLDEN SLIPPER STAKES (1200m) Rory's Jester, 55.5 (R Quinton) Trained by CS Hayes; 1:10.3; Speed Check, True Version
VATC BLUE DIAMOND STAKES (1200m)
Let's Get Physical, 54 (G Murphy) Trained by R Smerdon; 1:10.4; Acumen, Sudden
STC MERCEDES-TANCRED CLASSIC (2400m)
Alibhai, 57 (L Dittman) Trained by TJ Smith; 2:29.4; Hayai, Prolific

They're off in the Cox Plate, with Bonecrusher fourth from bottom (CA).

Our Waverley Star and Bonecrusher go head-to-head (Age).

Bonecrusher wins the 'greatest race of all'

In a battle well fought there is honour in defeat. But the glory of sport is winning. If the WS Cox Plate (2040m) had ended in a dead-heat between Bonecrusher and Our Waverley Star, it would have been an honourable result. Nothing more.

There had to be a winner. And in the race that only champions win, there was.

The Crusher was once an unlikely hero. Bred by a New Zealand sheep farmer, his pedigree (Pag-Asa–Imitation) suggested nothing. His sire had won three minor events in Australia. His dam had never won a race. His brother was doing stunts in a show ring.

With his chest deeply scarred after running into a fence, Bonecrusher wasn't the prettiest yearling at the Waikato sales in 1984, where stockbroker Peter Mitchell paid a paltry $NZ3250 and afterwards sent him to Ellerslie trainer Frank Ritchie, whose son Shaune became his devoted strapper.

After huge wins in the NZ Derby and Air New Zealand Stakes, Bonecrusher reached Australia in March 1986 and systematically shattered all comers in the Tancred Stakes, the AJC Derby, and the Underwood and Caulfield Stakes.

He began awkwardly in the Cox Plate, losing a length while Our Waverley Star was caught three wide. When the field settled Roman Artist was sizzling along in front, followed by Dandy Andy, Society Bay and Drought. Bonecrusher and Our Waverley Star were ahead of only three others.

Near the 1000-metre post, Gary Stewart took off on Bonecrusher. It looked like suicide, but the move flushed out Our Waverley Star, racing seventh, who was kicked into top gear by Lance O'Sullivan.

Contemptuous of 11 other high-class runners, the two geldings shot to the front. At the 600m mark Our Waverley Star held a narrow lead, with Bonecrusher at his hindquarters. As Stewart went for the whip, Frank Ritchie put down his glasses.

'We're gone,' he told Shaune.

But there was something in the Crusher that couldn't be beaten. Call it heart. Or spirit. Or just plain guts. But he had it.

At 400m, the margin was half a length. Approaching the home turn he drew almost level. The champions matched strides as 26 000 people leapt to their feet and roared.

Our Waverley Star entered the straight first. Then Bonecrusher clawed ahead. Seventy metres out, Our Waverley Star surged again and stuck his head in front.

That should have been the end. But the Crusher never said die.

Our Waverley Star had nothing left. Bruised and broken, he was staggering home when the Crusher punched past and drew away to win by a neck.

Even Bart Cummings just shook his head, enthralled. 'That's the best race I have ever seen or ever hope to see,' he said.

A win for Rising Fear, Damien Oliver up (Age).

Racing – no joke for larrikin Larry

Rising Fear's win in the STC Stayers Cup (3200m) gave trainer and cartoonist Larry Pickering his first success in a listed race. Unluckily, Pickering missed the victory, his helicopter forced to hover over Rosehill, unable to land due to turbulence.

Horses were Pickering's life when he left school at 14 to work on outback stations in Western Queensland. And he might have remained there but for a horse which threw him off, badly injuring his back and ending his droving days. So, at the age of 27, Pickering taught himself to draw.

The lavish $5 million farm and training establishment he later built at Mangrove Mountain on NSW's Central Coast owed more to his brilliance as a cartoonist than as a trainer, but that didn't worry Larry.

Something of a sentimental bloke, he once said: 'Christ mate, bein' with 'orses is bloomin' crazy, but it's magnificent. It's like havin' a different bird every night. It's like bein' out on the town with a good sort. Costs you plenty, but it's worth it.'

Kay Miller leads in Ullyatt and John Miller after winning the Perth Cup (Age).

Grandfather Miller puts family first

For veteran WA jockey J.J. Miller, the Perth Cup was the one race he always wanted to win. And when he finally came home on Ullyatt, the 53-year-old grandfather had no hesitation in declaring it the highlight of a long career that included six Australian Derbys and the 1966 Melbourne Cup.

Ullyatt was special. He was part-owned by Miller and his wife Kay, who also trained the horse. Son John rode him in track work and another son, Raymond, was the stable foreman. In early 1985 the husband-and-wife team went looking for horses in NZ, where

Miller rode more than 60 prospects before they finally settled on Ullyatt.

Under Kay's somewhat unconventional methods, her charge worked his way up through restricted ranks to become one of the fittest horses in Australia. Percy Cerutty would surely have approved of Ullyatt's long training treks on the sandy straights of Kwinana beach, where the five-year-old gelding became so tough that in the lead-up to the Perth Cup he shook off three runs in six days, and just two days before the big race he galloped over 6000 metres at Pinjarra.

End of TJ's era

When Fix the Date won the Jumbuk Racing Enterprises Handicap at Rosehill, Brian Mayfield-Smith grabbed the NSW trainers' premiership with glee.

The great T.J. Smith trailed by 7½ wins coming into the last meeting in July. He had won the premiership for a record 33 seasons. For a while it looked like being 34 when the old master camped by the post and plonked the first four winners in his tuckerbag. But to snatch the season he needed eight of the nine races on the card. That was too much.

Nobody was going to catch Mayfield-Smith alive after Fix The Date took his lead to 8½ wins. At last, TJ was beaten.

Mayfield-Smith ended season 1985–86 with 99 winners. His predecessor had passed that tally 20 times, but TJ's reign, the longest waltz in Australian turf history, was over.

Brian Mayfield-Smith wins the premiership.

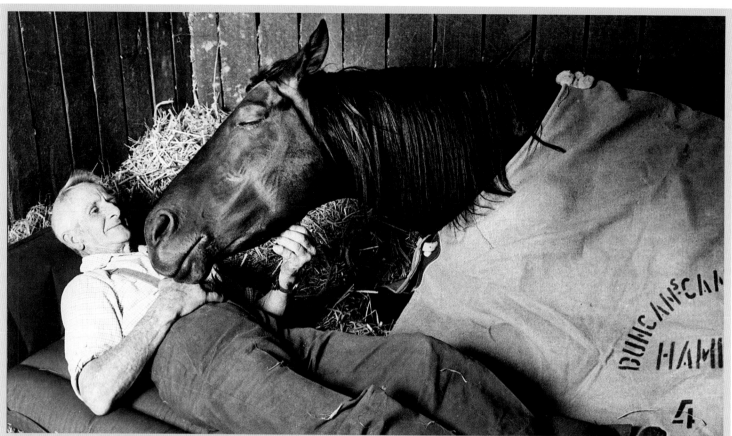

Greater love hath no horse: Bruce Postle's famous picture of Tommy Woodcock and Reckless. Reckless, who died this year, was mourned by all.

Explanations, after false false start (Age).

'No race' is a race

The final of the $60 000 Statewide Winter Championship at Flemington was noteworthy for a fine win by Gay Tulip, ridden by Chris Barrett. More remarkable was the fact it was a race at all.

The starter accidentally hit the false start button just after the horses jumped. When all the riders raced through to the winning post, VRC stewards warned punters to hold all tickets.

An inquiry revealed that every jockey had been oblivious to the false start signal. After no rider claimed any inconvenience, the race that became a 'no race' was declared a race.

The fiasco overshadowed Gay Tulip's farewell appearance on a racetrack.

Bounding Away gallops into glory

T. J. Smith said he'd rather win one Golden Slipper than two Melbourne Cups, and in 1986 a filly he owned, trained and bred presented him with the Slipper for a record fifth time.

Bounding Away, the 5/4 favourite, almost lost the race on the home turn when she tottered out three wide on the wrong leg and didn't seem to respond to Mick Dittman.

'I started to get desperate,' said Dittman, 'but she's got a ton of guts and kept on finding something.'

The powerfully built filly overhauled the pacemaker Pre Catelan in the final 50 metres and gamely held off the fast-finishers Just Blooming and Imperial Baron.

Bounding Away's time of 1:9.9 equalled the race record set by Sir Dapper in 1983, but the heart-stopping finish was in contrast to her seemingly effortless performance in the Blue Diamond Stakes a few weeks earlier at Caulfield, where her winning margin of four lengths was a record.

They couldn't wipe the smile off TJ's face then, and torrential rain couldn't wash it off three weeks after the Slipper, when Bounding Away claimed the Champagne Stakes (1600m) from the colt Myocard in a mudbath at Randwick.

Of course Smith was smiling. Between January and April 1986 his favourite filly was taking home an average of just over $100 000 every time she went to the office.

'No two-year-old in the world has won anything like $900 000!' Smith declared after the Champagne Stakes.

Bounding Away, with Dittman and TJ (Age).

Mick Clarke salutes on At Talaq (Age).

Bucks & beer shake up Cup

If anyone had the good oil on the 1986 Melbourne Cup, the Sheikh should have. To think he didn't even have a bet! Mind you, the winner At Talaq, owned by Sheikh Hamdan bin Rashid al Maktoum of the United Arab Emirates, was just one of more than 500 horses in the Maktoum stable. But a good one.

And he didn't come cheap. At Talaq (Roberto–My Nord) cost $800 000 at the yearling sales at Keeneland in Kentucky in 1981. When he won the Melbourne Cup he became the most expensive horse ever to claim the people's race.

The Sheikh's English trainers placed At Talaq under Colin Hayes for his Australian campaign. An international horse and a proven stayer, At Talaq was by an English Derby winner. He had finished fourth to Secreto in the 1984 Derby and won the Group 1 Grand Prix de Paris over 3000m.

Money talked big in the mid-1980s. Enough for the Melbourne Cup to reach a million dollars in stakes. Enough to buy another horse for an oil-rich Sheikh, and enough to tempt him away from the lush European turf.

Carlton and United Breweries put up the dollars and in return demanded the name of their 'international' product, Foster's, on the Melbourne Cup. And so, in the mounting yard where the blue bloods had passed the Cup to the battlers so many times before, there stood the beer baron in his Foster's tie, surrounded by hundreds of Foster's blue banners and emblems.

Since 1861, the three-handled Cup had crossed the Tasman many times, but NZ was almost like home. Then, in 1980, the imported horse Beldale Ball won the Cup for English owner Robert Sangster. Now, it was heading to Dubai.

1986 RESULTS

VRC MELBOURNE CUP (3200m)
At Talaq, 54.5 (M Clarke) Trained by CS Hayes; 3:21.7; Rising Fear, Sea Legend

AJC SYDNEY CUP (3200m)
Marooned, 49.5 (J Cassidy) Trained by B Mayfield-Smith; 3:27; Our Sophia, Foxseal

QTC BRISBANE CUP (3200m)
Marlon, 55.5 (D Walsh) Trained by RB Marsh; 3:21.6; Foxseal, Rising fear

SAJC ADELAIDE CUP (3200m)
Mr Lomondy, 51.5 (D Walsh) Trainer JB Cummings; 3:25.3; Late Show, Mint Master

WATC PERTH CUP (3200m)
Ullyatt, 49 (J Miller) Trained by Ms K Miller; 3:20.14; Importune, Rant And Rave

VATC CAULFIELD CUP (2400m)
Mr Lomondy, 53.5 (D Walsh) Trained by ND Eales; 2:30.1; At Talaq, Our Sophia

VRC AUSTRALIAN CUP (2000m)
Playful Princess, 53 (L Maund) Trainer S Lanyon; 2:4.5; Under Oath, Knight Of Avon

MVRC WS COX PLATE (2040m)
Bonecrusher, 57 (G Stewart) Trainer FT Richie; 2:07.2; Our Waverley Star, The Filbert

AJC DERBY (2400m)
Bonecrusher, 55.5 (G Stewart) Trained by F Ritchie; 2:35.6; Handy Proverb, Agent Provocative

VICTORIA DERBY (2500m)
Raveneux, 55.5 (R Quinton) Trained by JJ Moloney; 2:26.6; Drough, Imprimatur

AJC DONCASTER HANDICAP (1600m)
Hula Chief, 52 (G Duffy) Trained by JB Cummings; 1:36.2; King Phoenix, Heat Of The Moment

BTC DOOMBEN '10 000' (1350m)
Between Ourselves, 49 (J Marshall) Trainer C Beechey; 1:18.5; Daybreak Lover, Concrete

VRC NEWMARKET HANDICAP (1200m)
Lockley's Tradition, 54.5 (B Werner) Trained by L Armfield; 1:10.6; Hula Chief, Coal Pak

AJC SIRES' PRODUCE STAKES (1400m)
Diamond Shower, 54 (N Tiley) Trained by B Mayfield-Smith; 1:25.6; Bounding Away, Imperial Baron

VRC SIRES' PRODUCE STAKES (1400m)
Simbolico, 55.5 (C Dinn) Trained by T Hughes; 1:24.3; Military Plume, Urbane

VRC GRAND NATIONAL STEEPLECHASE (5000m)
Prince Lindal, 60 (K Wynne) Trainer Ms B Girling; 6:6.5; Arabian Myth, Norfolk Tiger

STC GOLDEN SLIPPER STAKES (1200m)
Bounding Away, 52.5 (L Dittman) Trained by TJ Smith; 1:9.9; Just Blooming, Imperial Baron

VATC BLUE DIAMOND STAKES (1200m)
Bounding Away, 52.5 (L Dittman) Trained by TJ Smith; 1:10.2; Bataan, La Zip

STC MERCEDES-TANCRED CLASSIC (2400m)
Bonecrusher, 52 (G Stewart) Trained by F Ritchie; 2:31.1; Rant And Rave, Abit Leica

Laurie Connell's Rocket Racer, on the verge of collapse after winning the Perth Cup, had to be assisted to his stall (Age).

Vo Rogue (on the rail), ridden by Cyril Small, beats Fair Sir in the Turnbull Stakes (Age).

Queensland invasion: the Vic and Vo show

In 1987 a shaggy little horse called Vo Rogue emerged from the Gold Coast, Tweed River and Sunshine Coast tracks in Queensland. He'd started 10 times for only a maiden win by Christmas 1986, but the Rogue wasn't one for lying on beaches. He liked to train on bitumen, without shoes.

As bold and unorthodox as his legendary trainer Vic Rail, Vo Rogue went on to win such big races as the Alister Clark Stakes, the William Reid Stakes, CF Orr Stakes, Blamey Stakes, St George Stakes, Futurity Stakes and the WATC Winfield Stakes. He won the Turnbull Stakes at Flemington twice, but the first time in 1987 was special. The $5000

horse left champions worth $5 million gasping in his wake. Les Carlyon captured the moment in his article, 'The Vic and Vo Show Comes to Town'.

'Victory Robert Rail, the battling trainer, had towed Vo Rogue, his one good horse, all the way from Brisbane to Melbourne in a two-horse float … He's 42, this nuggety man with the lived-in face, and he puts you in mind of a boxer gone to seed … the game has never been kind to him, but it is the only game he knows …

'Vo Rogue is a bay with no white: lean and workmanlike, no false muscles. With his high wither, he's close to 16 hands; he's long

in the rein and, from behind, looks robust enough. But, side-on, he looks weedy, unfinished almost: the point of his hip stands up; he seems light through the loins and doesn't have much of a forearm. Don't be fooled. He's as hard as ironbark, this one.

'Vo Rogue won the Turnbull by breaking hearts. He was ridden the way he should be – for speed. There he was at the 1100-metre mark, ripping along in front and with the field spread out over 30 lengths behind him … He beat them all … and here's Vic telling you: "He's not 100 per cent yet … I think he needed that run to clean his wind out, you know?"'

Our Kenny's comeback

In one of the great Melbourne Cup rides, Larry Olsen hugged the Flemington rails for 3200 metres on Kensei, and never went round any other horse in the field of 21.

Pushing along the inside, Kensei (12/1) burst from 10th on the turn to beat the big NZ mare Empire Rose (25/1) by a half-length with the imported stallion Rosedale (5/1 fav.) a short half-head away third.

If Rosedale had won, it would have been a victory for the Texas oil magnate Nelson Bunker Hunt. Five of the past seven Cups had been won by millionaires.

But Kensei brought the Cup back to the people. The gelding was purchased in NZ by Harry Lawton, a fitter and turner who syndicated him into six $3750 shares. A cleaner, a computer manager and a pensioner were

Larry Olsen victorious aboard Kensei (Age).

among the buyers, none of them wealthy.

The owners put him under Les Bridge, who had been training at Randwick for 25 years without a Melbourne Cup starter, let alone a winner, before Kensei came along.

The man who rode him into history, 39-year-old Larry Olsen, was milking cows at Kyogle in 1985. He had retired from racing to become a dairy farmer, but decided to come back, for about the 'sixth or seventh time', early in 1987.

With a diet of brown rice and plenty of exercise Olsen battled his way down from a 72kg farmer to a 49kg jockey. He struggled to find rides and it was mainly thanks to the confidence of Bridge that he broke back into metropolitan racing in Sydney.

'Kenny', as he was fondly known in the stables, did everyone proud. No wonder they were crying.

The Ark sails east, on fire

The WA sprinter Placid Ark (Arkenstone–Northern Queen) set the eastern Australian turf on fire in 1987.

In his first start outside Perth, in February, the flying three-year-old gelding scored a runaway win in the 1000m Lightning Stakes at Flemington in a near record time of 56.6. And if, seven days later, Placid Ark's huge three-lengths win in the Oakleigh Plate (1100m) had not confirmed his status as the best sprinter in the land, there was no doubt a few weeks after that, when he won the Newmarket Handicap (1200m) and became the first horse to complete Victoria's sprinting 'triple crown'.

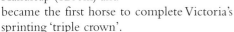

Following the Newmarket, which was Placid Ark's eighth win from 11 starts, his tearful jockey John Scorse declared: 'He's the best in Australia, a champion sprinter, and I don't think I'll ever ride a better horse.'

A fortnight later, Scorse was almost speechless when the Ark stormed home under full sail in the $100 000 Canterbury Stakes (1200m) in Sydney.

Following a five-month spell, the sprint king returned faster than ever. His new rider Brendan Clements said 'I don't know how any horse will beat him' following his cruise home in the Rupert Steele Stakes (1200m) at Flemington.

Clements couldn't believe it when he looked back at the finish of the Moir Stakes (1000m) at Moonee Valley and the rest of the field was four lengths behind. The Ark had run 56.7, unstretched. That's when Clements knew his job was superfluous.

'You don't ride a horse like Placid Ark – you steer him,' he said.

'Really, he doesn't ever need a jockey. He only needs to find the rail and he does the rest himself.'

The Ark's next passenger, jockey Rod Dawkins, was utterly astonished at his mount's performance in the Linlithgow Stakes (1400m) at Flemington, where he registered a course record 1:21.8 at weight-for-age (57 kg).

'He's unbelievable,' said Dawkins. 'I couldn't go slowly enough early and the others still had no way of keeping up. He is a machine. A running machine from the start.'

There was just one problem with this remarkable machine that cost only $5000 as a yearling. His joints gave trouble. Trainer Wally Mitchell treated him with an anti-inflammatory drug and was suspended, then fined after Placid Ark returned a positive swab.

In September 1988 the super horse was put down after an accident in training. T. J. Smith described him as possibly the best sprinter he'd ever seen.

Maree Lyndon with the Adelaide Cup (Age).

Winning woman

History was made at Morphettville when 23-year-old NZ jockey Maree Lyndon won the Adelaide Cup on Lord Reims (25/10) by three lengths from Bourbon Boy (15/10 favourite) and Enchanteur.

In winning, Lyndon became the first female jockey to land a major cup race in Australia.

Quick to congratulate her was legendary rider Scobie Breasley, who said: 'She rode a marvellous race. She settled the horse in right, and she didn't go too soon. I never would have imagined a woman jockey when I was here 50 years ago.'

The young rider was rated the best woman jockey in the world. 'As a jockey I'm thrilled to win,' she said 'Same as a man, I suppose.'

TURF TOPICS

Wife-beating at Rosehill: In a photo-finish in the Baguette Welter Hcp, John Austin's Swift Cheval beat Bellibo, a horse owned by his wife Jan.

Pablo's Pulse ... 500/1 ... 1000/1: Pablo's Pulse was beaten twice in the week before he won at official odds of 500/1 in the Warwick Stakes at Warwick Farm on 22 August. One lucky punter obtained 1000/1 in a $50 000 to $50 bet with rails bookmaker Peter Todd.

Happy birthday: The Mildura Racing Club's Centenary Cup on 26 September had been planned for over 12 months as a special event to help celebrate the local centenary. Organisers attracted a first-class field of 13 runners. Everything looked right. Then the starter went and hit the button when one horse (Talking Doll) was still riderless behind the stalls. Unfortunately, the false start signal was too late to be noticed by the leaders who ran through to the post. The race had to be abandoned.

'Bird' beats Magic Flute: There was a 'bird' in the Light Fingers Handicap at Randwick. It was a seagull, which crossed the line just ahead of Magic Flute and triggered the electronic timing apparatus, suggesting a race record (1:9.1) had been run. The hand time, however, was 1:9.2, leaving Emancipation's old record intact.

Quinton's 'time trifecta': Sydney jockey Ron Quinton won the Shannon Quality Hcp (1500m) at Rosehill on 19 September on Never Quit in 1:28.8, precisely the same time as his Dalmacia (1982) and Eastern Bay (1984). So how did he do it? 'Stopwatch in the head,' he said.

Punters' pals: Mal 'the punter's pal' Johnston lived up to his name when he rode five winners at Warwick Farm on 16 May. It was the fourth time Johnston had bagged five on a metropolitan track. Jim Cassidy rode six winners at Rosehill on 12 December.

Don't look twice: QTC Turf Club stewards declared correct weight on the wrong result in the Turf and Surf Flying Handicap at the Gold Coast when a power failure temporarily prevented use of the photo-finish print. When the print became available, the judge's decision was shown to be incorrect.

The Rosehill Grocer

It seemed he believed he was a committee of one. They called him 'The Grocer', half in compliment and half in inverted snobbery. He was the free-spending entrepreneur and the small-time retailer, in trade, rolled into one. Forces within considered he was perhaps too much of an individualist, too much of the dominator for his club's own good.

But Jim Fleming changed the face of NSW racing, and put the finishing touches to a 1200-metres flutter for juveniles to make it the Golden Slipper we know today. Vice-chairman of the Sydney Turf Club from September 1980 and elected chairman in September 1983, Jim Fleming boosted prize money for the Golden Slipper to challenge the Melbourne Cup not only as Australia's richest race, but the country's most talked-about race.

And he set in motion a hugely ambitious change to the STC's major racecourse, Rosehill. Rosehill was the 'Westies' course'. Sydney's east, harbour-side east, sneered at the Western Suburbs. Bus drivers and brigands. Randwick was for the gentry, the Silvertails, and The Grocer knew who his customers were. The West was where the city's population was exploding, and Fleming knew racing needed people past the check-in, not the check-out, chicks. He determined to make it the people's track. They would come first. He made his intentions obvious when his opening ploy in a $50 million renovations plan was to build a magnificent new public stand. 'It's for the public. The members will get theirs ... last,' announced Fleming. Retail shoppers from Balmain to Parramatta and beyond pushed prouder shopping trolleys as they rejoiced.

James Richard Fleming was born in 1932. He started work at 16 with the family chain of grocery stores. By 1960 the business had grown and had become Fleming's Food stores. 'Fabulous' Fleming's was sold to the giant Woolworths and he stayed with that company for 10 years.

After he left Woolworths he bought another 42-store grocery chain and renamed it Jewel. The year Fleming became chairman of the STC was the year Jewel was named in the top 10 retailers in Australia. Racing was always in his background.

The family had owned the Kilkee Stud at Koorawatha in the Lachlan Valley and had already bred an AJC Derby winner, Concerto. Fleming himself was later to breed the winner of the 1993 Golden Slipper, Bint Marscay, a proud achievement.

When the time came for Fleming to lose his chairmanship of the Sydney Turf Club he didn't walk away. In the vernacular of the public enclosure, he didn't spit the dummy. The numbers were counted and a new man took over. But Fleming remains one of the most influential figures in Australian racing, still a vital member of the STC board of directors and recently appointed as a Director of NSW Racing, a body with import second only to the NSW Thoroughbred Board in his state.

His most recent contribution was in the sale of the TAB, a scheme he favoured and publicly supported. An innovative man, he had wanted his own way, and as far as the STC was concerned, he made the mistake of demanding it. He was not allowed to be a committee of one.

The JR Fleming public stand at Rosehill remains evidence of his impact on racing. Even the naming of the stand has long been a point of contention. It was said a select, carefully chosen subcommittee made the naming choice. But few deny 'The Grocer' deserves his place in NSW racing history.

by Bill Casey

Rubiton rated

After winning the $100 000 WFA Memsie Stakes (1400m) at Caulfield in September, jockey Harry White rated four-year-old Rubiton the most outstanding horse to race in Australia since Tobin Bronze.

The magnificent Century–Ruby stallion had shown his class earlier in the year with placings in the Newmarket Handicap, Autumn Stakes, and Oakleigh Plate, as well as a fine Group 1 win in the Futurity Stakes.

The Memsie saw Society Bay dash clear at the 600m, but Rubiton courageously outsprinted her in the straight to win by three-quarters of a length, with Cossack Warrior running on for third.

A few weeks later White steered Rubiton to a superb win in the Underwood Stakes where he ran a course-record 2 minutes dead for the 2000 metres. That success, added to victories in the Manikato and Feehan Stakes, gave Rubiton his fourth weight-for-age win for the spring of 1987.

And it was a fabulous number five in the $1 million WS Cox Plate (2040m), where he also smashed the Moonee Valley track record, running 2:2.9, with some thanks owing to the tactics of front-runner Vo Rogue, who was 10 lengths ahead at the halfway mark, then faded for a creditable fourth.

The Cox Plate field was strung out over 30 or 40 lengths at the 1000m. White remained cool, despite being 25 lengths behind and second-last at one stage. Our Poetic Prince looked hard to beat on the home turn, but White, in the ride of his career on Rubiton, had his mount within reach and pounced in the last 50 metres to win by a long neck.

Rubiton went on to win the Mackinnon, but tragically broke down in his autumn preparation in 1988 and never raced again.

Myocard upsets 'race of the decade'

Myocard wins the Rawson Stakes (Age).

The $175 000 Rawson Stakes (2000m) at Rosehill in March was billed as the return bout between Bonecrusher and Our Waverley Star, following the pair's epic Cox Plate struggle in October 1986.

Our Waverley Star was a short-priced 11/8 chance while Bonecrusher was sent out favourite at 10/9 on. The Crusher was in scintillating form. In the Australian Cup at Flemington a few weeks earlier he was badly checked and conceded three lengths to At Talaq at the 300 m, then stormed home in typical style to win in the last stride.

But instead of Bonecrusher and Our Waverley Star dominating the Rawson, as everyone expected, Myocard, a 16/1 chance with a 4-kg weight-for-age advantage, simply exploded down the outside to swamp Our Waverley Star by three lengths, with Bonecrusher, another three away, third.

Darren Gauci pilots Scarvila to a win (Age).

Snippets takes home the Magic Millions (Age).

Bookie Eric Tymms on Cup Day (BP).

Scarvila scores

There's nothing unusual about the Darwin Cup ending in uproar, but in 1987 the aftermath was more sensational than normal.

Locally trained Scarvila, ridden by Ricky Lloyd, won the $60 000 race and took his winnings to a NT record of $145 875.

There was also another record in the race. Well, after it, anyway. David Bates, rider of Romantic Spirit, beaten a half-head by Scarvila, alleged interference to his mount by the winner over the final 200 metres.

The resulting stewards' inquiry took 48 minutes, an Australian record, before being dismissed. A full hour elapsed from the finish of the race to the presentations.

Bates fought back tears after the decision, and said: 'I can't believe it. It is just so wrong.'

The Tennant Creek trainer of Romantic Spirit, Karen Greenwood, angrily confronted chief steward Maurie Boyd and was told she had no grounds to appeal. 'That decision stinks,' she said. 'It's a home-town rort.'

The fury raged on after Greenwood claimed some jockeys were denied the chance to present evidence. Then the *NT News* published a photograph allegedly showing white paint on Romantic Spirit from hitting the running rail.

A senior committeeman said: 'This decision has scarred us forever.'

Sally's Snippets

In a brilliant all-the-way win, Snippets, by Lunchtime, made a snack of the inaugural Magic Million race at the Gold Coast.

The 2/1 favourite shot out of the stalls at Southport to run the 1200m in a snappy 1:9.9. Prince Anton (12/1) and Mother Duck (11/4), who stood flat-footed at the barrier, were four lengths behind at the post.

It was such an easy win that jockey Phillip Smith admitted he was actually laughing on the home turn. The owners were probably laughing too, especially after Snippets brought home the tasty $500 000 first prize.

The widely publicised Magic Million for two-year-olds was Queensland's first million-dollar race. In a clever marketing strategy by the promoters, only those horses sold at the Magic Millions yearling sales on the Gold Coast were eligible to enter.

Snippets' win was a personal triumph for 26-year-old trainer Sally Rogers, who temporarily left her hospital bed after a lung operation to attend the race.

She had feared that the owners might have transferred Snippets to another trainer, and with no other horse in her stable, she would have been forced to return to secretarial work. Now, there was no question of that. She had a track record.

Bookie bitten

Australia's biggest bookmaker, Bruce McHugh, announced at Rosehill in February that he was giving the game away.

When asked why he was retiring at the age of 45, McHugh told the *Sydney Morning Herald*: 'Maybe I've been in bookmaking too long. I started working for my father when I was a boy and I know better than most just how demanding it is.'

McHugh's million-dollar battles with Australia's biggest punter might have tempted him to quit while he was ahead.

'Everyone thinks I've won millions,' McHugh replied. 'You only hear about the wins, never the losses, and I can tell you that my biggest client has had his triumphs over me.' Free of the 'big fellow', who many believed was Kerry Packer, McHugh settled down to enjoy his other interests. He travelled to Caulfield to watch Voltage Peak, a horse he bred, win the Debutant Stakes for Perth millionaire Laurie Connell.

1987 RESULTS

VRC MELBOURNE CUP (3200m)
Kensei, 51.5 (L Olsen) Trained by LJ Bridge; 3.22; Empire Rose, Rosedale
AJC SYDNEY CUP (3200m)
Major Drive, 54.5 (G Hall) Trained by J Meagher; 3:21.2; Myocard, Foxseal
QTC BRISBANE CUP (3200m)
Limitless, 54.5 (G Duffy) Trained by RB Dowling; 3:30.8; Round The World, Enchanteur
SAJC ADELAIDE CUP (3200m)
Lord Reims, 51.5 (Ms M Lyndon) Trained by C Fenwick; 3:30.9; Bourbon Boy, Enchanteur
WATC PERTH CUP (3200m)
Rocket Racer, 48 (J Miller) Trainer B O'Malley; 3:18.6; Puckle Harbour, Royal Sharif
VATC CAULFIELD CUP (2400m)
Lord Reims, 52 (B Thomson) Trainer CF Fenwick; 2:36.3; Beau Zam, Cossack Warrior

VRC AUSTRALIAN CUP (2000m)
Bonecrusher, 57 (G Stewart) Trained by F Ritchie; 2:5.6; At Talaq, Ima Red Man
MVRC WS COX PLATE (2040m)
Rubiton, 57 (H White) Trained by PC Barns; 2:02.9; Our Poetic Prince, Fair Sir
AJC DERBY (2400m)
Myocard, 55.5 (M De Montfort) Trainer G Chapman; 2:32.6; My Precious Lad, Joindre
VICTORIA DERBY (2500m)
Omnicorp, 55.5 (J Cassidy) Trained by JB Cummings; All Ashore, Ascot Lane
AJC DONCASTER HANDICAP (1600m)
Magic Flute, 51 (RS Dye) Trainer B Mayfield-Smith; 1:37.6; Colour Page, Royal Sceptre
BTC DOOMBEN '10000' (1350m)
Broad Reach (J Marshall) Trainer JB Cummings; 1:18.8; Northern Copy, Lord Penn
VRC NEWMARKET HANDICAP (1200m)
Placid Ark, 55 (J Scorse) Trained by WJ Mitchell; 1:9.5; Princely Heart, Rubiton

AJC SIRES' PRODUCE STAKES (1400m)
Snippets, 55.5 (P Cook) Trained by M Lees; 1:23.5; Sky Chase, Marauding
VRC SIRES' PRODUCE STAKES (1400m)
Kaapstad, 55.5 (M Clarke) Trained by CS Hayes; 1:24.6; Rancho Ruler, Mighty Dear
VRC GRAND NATIONAL STEEPLECHASE (5000m)
Kanihi, 60 (B Constable) Trained by E Musgrove; 6:6.1; Tengah Hari, Region
STC GOLDEN SLIPPER STAKES (1200m)
Marauding, 55.5 (R Quinton) Trained by B Mayfield-Smith; 1:10.6; Lygon Arms, Boasting
VATC BLUE DIAMOND STAKES (1200m)
Midnight Fever, 52.5 (J Courtney) Trained by CS Hayes; 1:14.3; Rancho Ruler, Twining
STC MERCEDES-TANCRED CLASSIC (2400m)
Myocard, 52.5 (M De Montfort) Trainer G Chapman; 2:28; Our Waverley Star, Foxseal

What a horse. Vo Rogue thrived in the Queensland sun, and came south for rich pickings in the autumn (Age).

Australian racing's latest cult figures

On Australia Day 1988, Vo Rogue, the bold front-running Queensland horse sporting white blinkers, blew into Moonee Valley. As usual, all the way from Brisbane by float, with Vic Rail at the wheel.

Vo Rogue's 'autumn' campaign would open in a race won by some of the finest horses in the land. The $200 000 William Reid Stakes (1200m) was no contest. In a tick under 70 seconds (1:9.9) Vo Rogue celebrated the Bicentenary, running a good field off its legs and showing he was ready to assume the mantle of Rubiton, twice his conqueror in '87. Rubiton had been retired prematurely because of a leg injury.

Starting at 11/2, Vo Rogue beat the much-vaunted Colin Hayes–trained Military Plume, who cost $300 000 as a yearling, by three-quarters of a length, with Groucho (9/4 fav.) third. Campaign King was unplaced.

The magnitude of Vo Rogue's win, hailed by a crowd eager to salute a knock-about trainer and his flying machine, surprised even Rail and jockey Cyril Small. Said Rail, resplendent in reefer jacket and Cuban-heeled riding boots: 'I would have been happy if he'd run fourth. He hadn't even had a trial since

coming back.'

'Suntanned' from being out in the paddock, Vo Rogue, aged four, had thrived during his spell up north. Lots of good feed was the recipe for success, as passed on to Rail by his mentor Tommy Woodcock.

Vo Rogue's preparation for the Reid Stakes was unconventional, even for Victory Rail. On the way to Melbourne, Rail stopped the float every four hours so that horse (in particular) and trainer could stretch their legs. Topped off in Melbourne with a little jogging and cantering.

On race day, Les Carlyon noted, Vo Rogue, displaying not a false muscle, 'moved as smooth as molasses from the barrel to lead nearly all the way. Proving that a battler with a good horse can still whip the heavies on the Australian turf.'

Vo Rogue had come a long way since owner Jeff Perry bought him as an 11-month weanling. His stable name was Erky because everyone who saw him said 'Erk!' He was soon gelded. 'The ugliest thing you ever saw,' said Perry.

The Reid Stakes in the bag, Vo Rogue turned up at Sandown 12 days later and won

the weight-for-age CF Orr Stakes, beating Military Plume again and delighting the crowd of 11 245. A great roar went up as Vo Rogue accelerated in the straight, winning by six lengths. Especially from those who had taken the generous odds of 9/4. Said Military Plume's jockey Michael Clarke, alluding to the difficulty of staying with Vo Rogue: 'I was under pressure on the turn.'

A week after the Orr Stakes, lightning struck twice on Lightning Stakes day. This time Vo Rogue shattered Amiable's 1600-metre record in the Blamey Stakes, clocking 1:34.0. Amiable had run the pre-metric equivalent of 1:34.2 in 1940, beating two champions High Caste and Ajax. Vo Rogue bettered that time, seemingly with a leg in the air. Small said he could have gone faster. Asked why he had looked to his inside at the top of the straight, Small said: 'I had to. The others were only coming around the home turn.'

Before the Australian Cup, there was time for two more wins – in the wfa St George Stakes and Futurity Stakes, both at Caulfield. Those successes gave Vo Rogue five wins on end in the space of 38 days for a career total of 14 wins from 35 starts.

Brent Thomson on Dandy Andy races past Vo Rogue to win the Australian Cup (Age).

Dandy Andy is too handy

It was billed as the ultimate clash of the heavyweights. The first meeting between Vo Rogue and Bonecrusher, in the Australian Cup (2000m) on 14 March. So how come Dandy Andy from Coleraine got home?

Well, until the Flemington clocktower, just short of 200 metres from the post, everything was going to script. Then the race of the century came apart.

Vo Rogue, Vic Rail's express from Queensland, had ripped along in front. At the clocktower, Vo Rogue's mind was suddenly making appointments he couldn't keep. He began to race 'high' instead of flattening for the post. His legs were lead weights. He had gone too hard earlier. Now, he was going up and down in the one spot.

And Bonecrusher, the other wonder horse? He was six lengths behind. And here was this beast called Dandy Andy, who had been last most of the way and had never won at weight-for-age. He was coming on like the overture to Carmen.

Dandy Andy, ridden by Brent Thomson, got there by a length and a half at 125/1 after opening at 33s. Vo Rogue, even-money favourite and all courage, wobbled in second. Bonecrusher, second pick at 5/2, floundered in third, five lengths further back.

Jim Cerchi, who trained Dandy Andy, was one of those indestructible characters of the Australian turf; a 70-year-old father of 13, owner of a slightly scuffed float sighted at racetracks from Manangatang to Doomben, a battler since his first race ride in 1926.

Here was a frail-looking, white-haired old man in a grey sportscoat over a blue and grey pullover, in danger of being buried in a media avalanche. 'I thought if I could run third I'd be doing well,' he said. The only thing better would be to win the Melbourne Cup – and I'll tell you, mate, he won't get that far.'

A jockeys' ward

Nine jockeys were admitted to Inverell Hospital in NSW after a 10-horse pile-up in the $10 000 Inverell Cup on New Year's Day. It was the biggest casualty list since Grace Darling's 1885 Caulfield Cup, when 16 of the 41 runners fell.

In the Inverell Cup, won by Parraguny from Coonabarabran, all was well until the field passed the 600-metre post.

Grand Zephyr, ridden by Moree jockey Henty Cameron, was carting the field along when he lost his footing and came down. As

Dangerous: D. Gauci falls at Yarra Glen (Age).

did nine other horses.

Other than Cameron, who was seriously injured, the riders admitted to hospital were Troy Brandenburg (on the favourite Marmies Girl), Gary Baker, Julie Shephard, Jamie De Belin, Scott Norris, Bruce Powell, Darren Jones and Tommy Atkins.

Pantheon of Cup winning jockeys assembled in 1988: Standing (left to right): Larry Olsen (Kensei, 1987); Bob Skelton (Van Der Hum 1976); John Letts (Piping Lane, 1972; Beldale Ball, 1980); Bruce Marsh (Silver Knight, 1971); Midge Didham (Baghdad Note, 1970); John Miller (Galilee, 1966); Roy Higgins (Light Fingers, 1965; Red Handed, 1967); Ron Taylor (Polo Prince, 1964); Jim Johnson (Gatum Gatum, 1963; Rain Lover, 1968 & 1969); Les Coles (Even Stevens, 1962); Pat Glennon (Comic Court, 1950; Macdougal, 1959); Ray Selkrig (Lord Fury, 1961). Seated (left to right): Ossie Phillips (Wotan, 1936); Harry McCloud (Colonus, 1942); Jack Purtell (Hiraji, 1947; Wodalla, 1953; Rising Fast, 1954); Ray Neville, with Cup (Rimfire, 1948); George Podmore (Evening Peal, 1956); Mel Schumacher (Baystone, 1958); W.A. 'Billy' Smith (Hi Jinx, 1960).

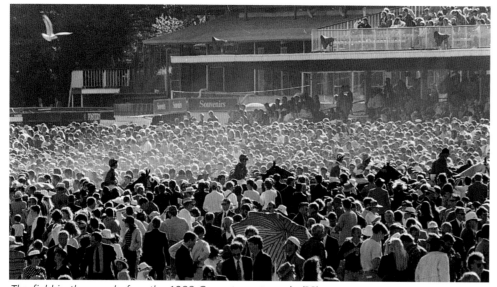
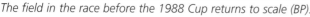

The field in the race before the 1988 Cup returns to scale (BP).

Sandown winners: Dick Merton leads Rendoo.

Roses all the way

Sport is fertile ground for howlers. 'He'll never be a Test batsman,' someone once said of cricket's highest run-scorer, Sir Jack Hobbs. When Empire Rose, popular winner of the 1988 Melbourne Cup, started out on the road to fame, her New Zealand breeder and part-owner Fred Bodle told trainer Laurie Laxon: 'She's too big to be any good.'

Wrong. 'Big Rosy', as she became known, certainly was big – about 17 hands. She wasn't beautiful either, having a thick jaw. And she had big feet, which caused her trouble. Vet Timothy Bodle, son of the owner, worked on her hooves, cutting them away and fixing them.

But Empire Rose had what mattered. Class and, in the words of Laxon, 'a good, aggressive attitude'. A female to reckon

with. Three days before the Cup, the six-year-old chestnut daughter of Sir Tristram, revealed her quality by downing Vo Rogue in the Mackinnon Stakes in record time.

Having run fifth in the 1986 Cup and second in '87, 'Big Rosy' won in '88 the hard way from barrier 20. Her courage and long frame and head won the day in a slick 3:18.9 to the delight of the crowd of 93 651. Everyone loved her.

Beau Zam: the colt that Bart bought

It was a misty day at Randwick, so not many folk were aware that Bart Cummings was close to tears after Beau Zam's win in the $1.1 million AJC Derby by 5 ½ lengths.

The trembling voice of a man never far from centre stage was the giveaway. 'My greatest moment,' Cummings managed to mouth at the presentation, at which the star turn was meant to be the Prime Minister, Bob Hawke.

Cummings' emotion was understandable. He had paid $200 000 for Beau Zam (by Zamazaan) in NZ and sold half to another admirer of the immaculate little colt, Jack Eastgate.

Not far from Cummings at the presentation, standing only 15.3 hands and bleeding from cuts on both hind legs, was Beau Zam himself, winner of the Tancred International the week before and now with a bank balance of $1 962 580.

Starting at 4/1 on, he continued the streak odds-on favourites had enjoyed since the Derby was switched to the autumn. But not even Kingston Town (9/2 on in 1980) could win with such authority.

No one argued with Cummings' assessment of Beau Zam: 'He's the best horse in this part of the world.'

Shane Dye, who rode third placegetter Hunter, all but agreed. 'On straightening, Beau Zam joined us, then in a matter of a few strides he was gone. Boy, he's something special,' he said.

Winning jockey John Marshall, splattered with mud, was his usual humble self. Though on top of the jockeys' list, the teenage boy from Perth who crossed the Nullarbor by train 13 years ago to try his luck in Sydney, was no

Beau Zam wins the Queen Elizabeth (Age).

Dye or Cassidy at the microphone or at media interviews. He said simply that Beau Zam was the best horse he had ridden.

Sydney racetrack manager Dick Roden gave an insight into Marshall's psyche. 'I've never seen one like him,' said Roden. 'Get here at dawn and watch him. No jockey works harder If he says something, and he doesn't say much, it will be fair dinkum. Straight down the line.'

For Marshall it was his fifth Group 1 win for Cummings in the autumn of '88 and second AJC Derby win (after Prolific in 1984). For Cummings it was his third AJC Derby, after Belmura Lad (1977) and Prolific.

Two weeks later Beau Zam, starting at 16/1 on, took his winnings past the $2 million mark with an easy win in the AJC St Leger.

In May, the Queen saw Beau Zam score a thrilling win by a head over Bonecrusher in the Queen Elizabeth Bicentenary Stakes at Canberra. The Queen took more than a passing interest in Beau Zam. Her daughter Princess Anne rode the colt in track work before he won the AJC Derby.

Brian York on Caulfield Cup victor Imposera.

TURF TOPICS

Mudlark: Single Endeavour set 'two records' in the mud at Rosehill in July, winning by 16 lengths and running the 2000 metres in 2:13.9, the slowest at the track for years. In his 20 years as judge, John Nicholson said he had never seen an easier win.

Gauci's day: In September, Darren Gauci rode five winners at Sandown, the fifth on Tawrrific in the last. Only three other riders have won five races on a Melbourne card – Bill Williamson (1959), Roy Higgins (1972) and Harry White (1980).

It must be me: 'It's not the race, it must be me,' NZ trainer Dave O'Sullivan lamented after top mare Horlicks ran second to Our Poetic Prince in the WS Cox Plate at Moonee Valley. O'Sullivan also finished second with Shivaree in 1979 and Our Waverley Star in 1986.

With Vo Rogue scratched because of a rain-impaired track, the John Wheeler–trained Our Poetic Prince, favourite at 5/4, had everything his own way and won easily. Bonecrusher was third.

Horlicks had no luck, almost losing her feet when checked at the first turn.

1988 RESULTS

VRC MELBOURNE CUP (3200m)
Empire Rose, 53.5 (T Allan) Trained by LK Laxon; 3:18.9; Natski, Na Botto
AJC SYDNEY CUP (3200m)
Banderol, 53.5 (P Cook) Trainer DJ O'Sullivan; 3:34.1; Round The World, Equity Girl
QTC BRISBANE CUP (3200m)
Lord Hybrow, 55.5 (K Moses) Trained by N McBurney; 3:26.2; Pakura Boy, Round The World
SAJC ADELAIDE CUP (3200m)
Lord Reims, 55.5 (B Thomson) Trained by C Fenwick; 3:28.5; Foxseal, Saratov
WATC PERTH CUP (3200m)
Linc The Leopard, 49.5 (B Clements) Trained by WJ Mitchell; 3:24.3; Buckshot Bandit, Arcolad
VATC CAULFIELD CUP (2400m)
Imposera, 51 (B York) Trained by RS McDonald; 2:29.4; Congressman, Authaal

VRC AUSTRALIAN CUP (2000m)
Dandy Andy, 57 (B Thomson) Trained by C Cerchi; 2:1.5; Vo Rogue, Bonecrusher
MVRC WS COX PLATE (2040m)
Our Poetic Prince, 57 (M Clarke) Trained by CS Hayes; 2:06.9; Horlicks, Bonecrusher
AJC DERBY (2400m)
Beau Zam, 55.5 (J Marshall) Trained by JB Cummings; 2:34.6; Brixton Town, Hunter
VICTORIA DERBY (2500m)
King's High, 55.5 (AG Clarke) Trained by CS Hayes; 2:36.1; Sir Midas, Big Grey Roo
AJC DONCASTER HANDICAP (1600m)
Lygon Arms, 50 (RS Dye) Trainer TJ Smith; 1:37.2; Sound Horizon, Our Waverley Star
BTC DOOMBEN '10 000' (1350m)
Campaign King, 58 (J Marshall) Trainer JB Cummings; 1:20.3; Rancho Ruler, Rendoo
VRC NEWMARKET HANDICAP (1200m)
Special, 56 (M Clarke) Trained by CS Hayes; 1:11.2; Franklin Drive, Rancho Ruler

AJC SIRES' PRODUCE STAKES (1400m)
Comely Girl, 54 (L Dittman) Trained by TJ Smith; 1:27.9; Full And By, Wonder Dancer
VRC SIRES' PRODUCE STAKES (1400m)
Wonder Dancer, 55.5 (H White) Trained by TJ Smith; 1:23.7; Vitalic, Glowing Tribute
VRC GRAND NATIONAL STEEPLECHASE (5000m)
Derrydonnell, 65.5 (N Harnett) Trainer B Kennedy; 6:18.3; Prince Lindal, Golden Sino
STC GOLDEN SLIPPER STAKES (1200m)
Star Watch, 55.5 (L Olsen) Trained by TJ Smith; 1:13; Comely Girl, Startling Lass
VATC BLUE DIAMOND STAKES (1200m)
Zeditave, 54 (G Hall) Trained by A Armanasco; 1:9.8; Vitalic, Startling Lass
STC MERCEDES-TANCRED CLASSIC (2400m)
Beau Zam, 52 (J Marshall) Trained by JB Cummings; 2:36.2; Highland Chieftain, Vaguely Pleasant

Mick Dittman – character, not style

Mick Dittman: the Enforcer (Age).

Making the presentation to the AJC Derby winner Research, the Prime Minister, Bob Hawke, said: 'It's worth having a couple of lengths in your pocket when Dittman is riding a horse.'

Even the reclusive trainer Jack Denham had something to say when Dittman rode his horse Flotilla to victory over Bart Cummings' Beau Zam in the Chipping Norton Stakes at Warwick Farm in February.

'When Mick took off at the 600, it won us the race,' he said. Denham had the AJC to thank for the ride. After a dispute over which horse Dittman should ride, they gave him Flotilla.

In bringing Research home in the Derby, Dittman disobeyed trainer Clarrie Conners' instructions. He let the 11/8-on favourite lead throughout, then held her in check when she wanted to duck away from the Toohey's sign on the winning post. During the race, Conners was outraged by Dittman's disregard, but it turned out the jockey knew exactly what he was doing.

Dittman snatched the 1988-89 Sydney jockeys' premiership by half a win from Shane Dye with a winning double at Rosehill in the last meeting of the season. A Little Kiss was the sixth of his seven wins in the week and 'The Enforcer' lived up to his nickname with his ardent use of the whip.

Turf writer Les Carlyon believes the nickname is not entirely appropriate. 'Dittman has the softest hands,' Carlyon wrote. 'Horses relax for him. In a finish, he intimidates rather than enforces. Figuratively, he not only stands over his horse but also the jockeys around him. He gets out of pockets other jockeys can't. He finds opening others can't. His demeanour, all that raw energy, says he has to win. He wins when he should lose … The wispy-haired Dittman, he of the cheeky smile and vice-like handshake, is as hungry as a top apprentice, as daring as when he sneaked up inside Kingston Town to snatch the 1982 Melbourne Cup on Gurner's Lane.

'There are prettier riders than Dittman, but with Mick, you can see everything he's trying to do. From 100 metres away you can taste his hunger, which is why the punters love him. His best gifts are not so much of style as of character.'

Research pays off

She may have been temperamental, but she certainly did have style. With her win in the AJC Derby, the cantankerous Research became the first filly to win the AJC Derby and Oaks double. In the same season she also won the VRC Oaks, and the Flight, Wakeful and Storm Queen Stakes.

Research showed her disposition when she bucked and objected to the winner's garland of roses that was placed around her neck. She then attempted to take a piece out of a strapper and her jockey Mick Dittman warned onlookers around the winner's stall to beware of her hind legs. 'The filly likes to kick,' he said.

By the Sir Ivor horse Imperial Prince, who ran second in the Epsom Derby, from Outing, a mare by Boucher (the winner of the English St Leger), Research was bred to stay and stay she did. Australian Horse of the Year for the 1988–89 season, she was odds-on favourite for the AJC Derby and won by two lengths from Royal Pardon.

Horlicks is history

Horlicks (r) wins NZ's first million-dollar race.

The New Zealand mare Horlicks made history when she became the first Australasian winner of the Japan Cup on 26 November, clocking 2:22.2 (2400m). Before Horlicks, the highest placegetter from this part of the world was The Filbert, who ran third in 1984.

Earlier in November, Horlicks won the VRC $301 000 Mackinnon Stakes at Flemington, giving her New Zealand trainers Dave and Paul O'Sullivan their first Melbourne win. The O'Sullivan father (Dave) and son team had come tantalisingly close in the past with two placings in the Melbourne Cup, three in the Cox Plate and another in the Mackinnon Stakes. Horlicks missed the Cox Plate due to a high temperature. She ran the Mackinnon Stakes in the fastest time recorded for the 2000m Flemington course since metrics were introduced in 1972 (just 0.3 seconds short of Sky High's 1961 record), beating King's High and Vo Rogue, with Super Impose fourth and Empire Rose fifth.

Horlicks had shown she meant business when she won the inaugural $NZ1 million DB Draught Classic (2100m) at Ellerslie in March. The mare, by Three Legs from Malt, won New Zealand's richest race in 2:7.48, breaking the course record, defeating Regal City by half a length with Westminster third. Bonecrusher and the English entries Highland Chieftain and Lapierre ran disappointing races. The winning stake of $NZ600 000 lifted the mare's career earnings to $A1.3 million, and by 1990 she had won more than $A3 million.

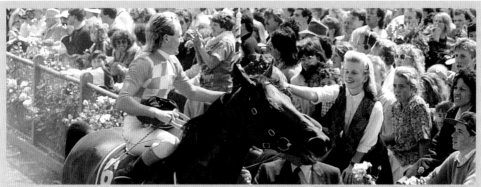

Shane Dye receives a rosy tribute on behalf of Tawrrific after the 1989 Melbourne Cup (BP).

Not all rosy for jockeys

New South Wales jockeys went out on strike in August in an effort to force the AJC to discuss their demands for legal liability insurance assistance. The demands came out of a landmark court case in which leading jockey Malcolm Johnston was ordered to pay damages to another jockey for injuries sustained during a race.

Racing was stunned in May when the NSW Supreme Court ordered Johnston to pay damages of $121 490 to jockey Glenn Frazer for injuries he received in a fall at Wyong in 1978. The jockeys wanted the AJC to pay an extra $2.70 a ride to cover the extra insurance they needed to protect themselves from the situation Malcolm Johnston found himself in. The strike was maintained for a week.

No takers when Vo Rogue is 1/10 (BP).

TURF TOPICS

NZ record: Bart and Anthony Cummings broke the New Zealand record for a yearling in January when they paid $850 000 for a Western Symphony filly related to Imposera at the NZ National yearling sale in Auckland.
Like father … Jockey John Didham won the Oakleigh Plate on Clay Hero, 12 years after his father Midge won the same race in 1977.
Hawke uncaged: The SP bookie Michael Hawke, Australia's longest-serving contempt prisoner, was freed in March after serving 11 months' gaol for refusing to answer questions at the Fitzgerald corruption inquiry.
Not such good oil: The NSW chief stipendiary steward John Schreck had made it clear that he didn't like jockeys commenting on the state of the track, so after Regal Theory badly missed the start in the Oils Ain't Oils

Handicap at Rosehill in July, jockey Craig Carmody offered two explanations.

The distressed jockey explained to the owner that Regal Theory, who made up ground to come a close fourth, was bogged at the barrier. To the stewards, with the press in attendance, he chose his words carefully, saying Regal Theory's back legs became 'fairly entrenched in the soil'.
Bunches of fives: Apprentice jockey P. Webster rode five winners at a meeting at Kalgoorlie in Western Australia in May, apprentice Frank Stockdale did the same at Traralgon in August and Darren Gauci rode five in a row at Ballarat in November.
Off the rails: The Queensland trainer Ron Noud and jockey Roxanne Wrigley were both fined $1000 for a public brawl in June

in the rails bar at Eagle Farm. The altercation was over who rode Noud's horse Blarney Queen at Caloundra two years earlier. 'I'd had a few beers,' Noud said. 'I didn't think I hit her. I was hit in the nose.'
Petty good going: With a win at Longreach, the 'Blackall Bullet', Miss Petty, broke Picnic In The Park's Australasian winning sequence record, taking her tally of consecutive wins to 22 on 21 July. She equalled the old record on 1 July, carrying 66 kg and smashing a Longreach track record.
Hot Diesel: Vo Rogue's win in the Australian Cup in March took his winnings past $2 million. The Rogue won the BMW Quality at Doomben in near-record time and was beaten by Cole Diesel at Randwick and remained a maiden in Sydney.

1989 RESULTS

VRC MELBOURNE CUP (3200m)
Tawrrific, 54 (RS Dye) Trained by DL Freedman; 3:17.1 Super Impose, Kudz
AJC SYDNEY CUP (3200m)
Palace Revolt, 48.5 (K Moses) Trained by NC Begg; 3:38.1; Coshking, Regal Chela
QTC BRISBANE CUP (3200m)
Coshking, 52.5 (B Hibberd) Trained by HW Matthews; 3:24.5; Lord Hybrow, The Brotherhood
SAJC ADELAIDE CUP (3200m)
Lord Reims, 57 (G Cooksley) Trained by C Fenwick; 3:27; True Finish, The Brotherhood
WATC PERTH CUP (3200m)
Saratov, 55 (R Jolly) Trained by J Hall; 3:16.8; Rising Fear, Muromoon
VATC CAULFIELD CUP (2400m)
Cole Diesel, 50 (M Kerr) Trained by G Mance; 2:27.2; Nayrizi, The Phantom

VRC AUSTRALIAN CUP (2000m)
Vo Rogue, 59 (C Small) Trained by V Rail; 2:1.6; Super Impose, Our Poetic Prince
MVRC WS COX PLATE (2040m)
Almaarad, 59 (M Clarke) Trained by CS Hayes; 2:03.2; Stylish Century, Empire Rose
AJC DERBY (2400m)
Research, 54.5 (L Dittman) Trainer C Conners; 2:34; Royal Pardon, Power Of Destiny
VICTORIA DERBY (2500m)
Stylish Century, 5.5 (K Moses) Trained by FW Mitchell; 2:34.2; Zamoff, Dr Grace
AJC DONCASTER HANDICAP (1600m)
Merimbula Bay, 50.5 (K Russell) Trained by Ms B Joseph; 1:34.7; Tiarra, Lygon Arms
BTC DOOMBEN '10 000' (1350m)
Potrero, 49 (RS Dye) Trained by G Chapman; 1:22.2; Robian Steel, Count Henri
VRC NEWMARKET HANDICAP (1200m)
Grandiose, 54.5 (AG Clarke) Trained by CS Hayes; 1:10.1; Clay Hero, Bowie

AJC SIRES' PRODUCE STAKES (1400m)
Reganza, 54 (J Marshall) Trained by JB Cummings; 1:27.6; Straussbrook, Tristanagh
VRC SIRES' PRODUCE STAKES (1400m)
Rechabite, 55.5 (C Dinn) Trained by T Hughes; 1:26; Ice Solid, Macwind
VRC GRAND NATIONAL STEEPLECHASE (5000m)
Bar The Shouting, 62.5 (T Wheeler) Trained by Ms D Waddell; 6:12.4; Valiant Gamble, Direct Mail
STC GOLDEN SLIPPER STAKES (1200m)
Courtza, 52.5 (RS Dye) Trained by R McDonald; 1:12.8; Paris Opera, Show County
VATC BLUE DIAMOND STAKES (1200m)
Courtza, 52.5 (RS Dye) Trained by R McDonald; 1:10.3; Sculptured Arch, Dancer's Choice
STC MERCEDES-TANCRED CLASSIC (2400m)
Our Poetic Prince, 57 (N Harris) Trained by J Wheeler; 2:32.2; Top Class, Apollo Run

Colin Hayes, the boy who could catch horses

Colin Sidney Hayes's family had no racing tradition. As a 12-year-old at Semaphore, a beachside suburb north of Adelaide, he would save 25 cents to spend an hour on a plug at a local riding school. 'I used to sit and dream about owning my own horses,' he recalled.

At 17, he fractured his spine at a rodeo when a horse fell all over him. The injury may have saved his life: it disqualified him from war service. Many of his childhood mates were killed.

By now he had acquired a reputation – as a horse psychologist. He could catch horses other people couldn't. He could think like a horse. He knew how to advance and retreat, the importance of eye contact. He was in demand. The blacksmith would knock on the door and ask Hayes's mother: 'Is Colin there? Could you get him to come and catch this horse for me?'

Every freak in sport is burdened with a question which is summed up in the cliche: What's his secret?

Here's a tiny part of the Hayes secret.

He has lovely instincts. He taught himself about horses. He had the natural intelligence to figure things. Just as important, he was unburdened by the traditions passed down in racing families.

He set out to make horses happy, to pander to their herd instincts, to let them run outside whenever possible, to remember they are creatures of habit, that they have good memories but very little reasoning power, and that some traditions, such as an hour's grooming, can turn a racehorse sour.

Lindsay Park, Hayes's Camelot world in the Barossa Valley, is a thing of beauty: vines climb the sandstone walls of barns, deer run in a paddock below the great house on the hill. Camelot indeed. But its charm can divert you. At another level, as practical as the other is aesthetic, Lindsay Park is simply about making horses happy. Everything is laid out to that end: the sole architect was C. S. Hayes.

Hayes, the media figure, is measured, cool, discreet. But in private, when he starts talking about how horses should be handled, he becomes intense. His voice rises, his speech quickens, and he leans forward. Suddenly he is the preacher at the climax of a homily:

'They want to know why you're successful – it's the sensitivity to the animal, that's what it's about! It's everything. It doesn't matter whether it's dogs or cats or horses. You've got to be sensitive to them. You spot little things in the eye or the gait. They tell you what the animal's thinking, how it's feeling. That eye contact – it's so important.'

As he says this, I'm reminded of CS after he won the 1989 Cox Plate with Sheikh Hamdan's Almaarad. Another departure from the persona. As the chestnut clawed his way to the line, CS was suffering angina pains (he had heart surgery when he was 56).

He consented to interview after interview, photo after photo. Eventually he managed to break away and find a quiet spot to sit. He was grey and breathless.

But he wanted to talk, gently, in phrases rather than complete sentences. It was almost eerie. He had announced his retirement two days earlier. Now Almaarad had given him his biggest thrill, the Moonee Valley crowd had given him three cheers and his chest hurt. It was as though his life had flashed by and he had to say the things that mattered, to sort dross from gold.

'You know,' he puffed, 'when I started, all I had was an instinctive feel for horses.' (He said it several times, sipping on tonic water, his face the colour of parchment.) 'I love horses … I love animals … that's all I started out with – a "feel" … You know, when I was a kid, I could catch horses other people couldn't … Lindsay Park – horses have built the whole place, everything … All the money has come back from horses – and we've always ploughed it back, too.'

Colin Hayes with Pat Glennon in 1952 (Age).

Colin Hayes with Moonee Valley Chief Executive Ian McEwen (BP).

Racing abounds with millionaires who build their 'showplaces', then finance their racing and breeding, their whims and vanities, with profits earned elsewhere. In terms of winners produced, Lindsay Park may be one of the most productive bits of dirt in the world.

The reason Lindsay Park works is that while Hayes is a careful financier, an enthusiast who infects others and a figure of real presence, he is first of all a horseman. The bulk of Hayes's 5300 winners have been horses an average owner could afford.

CS is unlike many of the new men who must buy the 'perfect horse', who will forgive no faults in God's engineering, and who seem to forget that the qualities that make a champion, equine or human, ultimately come not from angles of bone, or size, or even blood. They are summed up by something you cannot see or touch but can sometimes divine. It is called desire.

CS forgives a lot in youngsters and, in thrall of his own instincts, does not tow vets about to tell him what to think. He is unforgiving about only a few things: 'I place great importance on the head and eye,' he says. 'I don't like small eyes or ears, never have. I hate straight shoulders. I love a horse with a good swinging walk, a horse that's good to follow.'

In New Zealand in 1977, Hayes saw a colt who was unprepossessing, weedy even, and cursed with a parrot mouth. But the bay walked as if he was going somewhere. He teased Hayes's instincts, though obviously no one else's. Hayes bought him for around $3000. The colt was Dulcify and he turned out to be a champion.

Hayes bought Lindsay Park in 1965. From his Semaphore property of an acre or so, he had quickly become Adelaide's leading trainer, but the achiever was unfulfilled. He felt horses could be trained better in the country, as they are in England. Besides, he wanted to breed more of his own. He heard from a friend that Sir Keith Angas might be prepared to sell Lindsay Park.

The Angas family had owned it since 1842. It was more than gorgeous dirt: rolling hills of sandy loam over limestone and marble, hundreds of massive red gums to tell you the country is kind but not soft. With its chapel and English gardens, Lindsay Park was also a South Australian institution. Hayes told Sir Keith he wanted to raise good horses there, and was told: 'Colin, this place will grow anything.'

Hayes began training there in 1970, and he perhaps took another decade to lay out the place exactly as he wanted it. Until 1980, Hayes had trained 3000 winners in 30 years; in the next decade he trained another 2300. Just as Hayes had planned it, everything became better. Or as he put it on his retirement: 'This past 10 years is the vision come true.'

That vision is a large part of the legacy Hayes has left. He proved horses could be trained another way, and away from the cities. When he moved to Lindsay Park, parts of the racing establishment said he was a dreamer; now he is imitated. In a game still thick with tradition, he had vision. He loved to experiment and innovate – whether with one-eyed blinkers, or Norton bits, or floats riding on air suspension.

And, unconsciously, he argued with the stereotype. The myth is that the game is about the seedy and the hard-bitten, about rorts and spivs. So how do you account for this heavily built man with the kind eyes who smiles and looks straight at you, who is eloquent and reflective, and might briefly be mistaken for some president safely into his third term and comfortable with his world? That's of course, part of it: Hayes has created a world within a world.

Yet it is far from all of it. Beneath the Hayes benevolence is a toughness, a will to succeed, that is as hard as the red gums of Lindsay Park. And here, perhaps, is the greater part of the Hayes legacy. Racing is all about outrageous fortune: the unforeseen, the triumphs that got away, the foul luck that brought us undone again. In other words, racing is mostly about losing.

Yet, from the deep wells of his enthusiasm, Colin Hayes often seems to arrange his own luck. Like no trainer before him, he seems to eliminate an inordinate amount of chance from the game.

by Les Carlyon

Colin Hayes takes a stroll at Lindsay Park in the Barossa Valley (Age).

Colin Hayes on Cox Plate day, 1990 (BP).

Great men of the turf: Bart Cummings gives the good oil to Roy Higgins after the Cup (BP).

Another King came and conquered

The aristocratically bred Kingston Rule flashed across the Australian racing vista all too briefly in the spring of 1990. He came, he raced, he conquered – and then he was gone.

But what a great presence he exhibited – winning the Moonee Valley Cup, then giving master trainer Bart Cummings his eighth Melbourne Cup just when he needed it most. Cummings had accepted the five-year-old into his stable after he was rejected by French trainer Patrick Biancome and by T. J. Smith. The stallion's breeding was the lure: Kingston Rule was considered the best-bred horse racing in Australia.

Kingston Rule was the product of a mating between the outstanding United States racehorse and sire Secretariat and David Hains's excellent racemare Rose of Kingston. Hains arranged the mating under a long-range plan for Melbourne Cup success.

Under Cummings, Kingston Rule became only the fourth horse, and the first since Wodalla in 1953, to win the Moonee Valley Cup and Melbourne Cup. (He ran a close second in the Dalgety in between).

And T. J. Smith was not the only one to spurn Kingston Rule. Jockey Jim Cassidy had the mount in the Valley Cup but chose another in the major event. Darren Beadman, 24, took the ride and displayed the talent for which he became such a crowd favourite in coming years.

The 1990 Cup was Cummings' first in 11 years – he did not win the race throughout the 1980s – but it could not have been better timed. A huge financial burden still hung over his racing empire from the ill-fated, tax-driven scheme under which he splurged $23 million on yearlings at the Easter sales in Sydney. The scheme collapsed.

Cummings held a 'fire-sale' of 63 horses and sold his home and his champion horse Beau Zam to reduce the debt to $10 million but was being sued by major bloodstock agencies for the rest of the money.

However, the pressure did not stop him training winners and there was towering confidence about Kingston Rule's prospects in the Cup. The horse was backed from 12/1 to 7/1 and ran a course record 3:16.3 to beat two quality New Zealand contenders in The Phantom and Mr Brooker.

Kingston Rule came back in the autumn without distinguishing himself further and was subsequently retired to stud.

Champion from bush

What a great day it was for the legions of battlers in racing when the honest gelding Redelva defeated the sheikh's horse, Alquoz, in the 1990 Linlithgow Stakes at Flemington.

Redelva, prepared by hobby-trainer Greg Varcoe and ridden by dairyfarmer cum jockey Neville Wilson, had added more lustre to his reputation as a quality sprinter who had earned more than $1 million in winnings.

But such victories don't come easily. Alquoz, owned by a prominent Arab sheikh and trained by David Hayes, was ridden by top jockey Michael Clarke who fired in a protest and the contest was rejoined in the stewards' room.

Again the battlers were victorious. The protest was dismissed and Varcoe had scored a major Spring Carnival win with a dream racehorse who was a top sprinter in Adelaide and Melbourne over five years.

In Adelaide, Redelva won the Lightning Stakes, the Irwin Stakes, plus the Spring Stakes in consecutive years.

Redelva (N. Wilson) wins Lightning (Age).

In Melbourne, he won the Standish Handicap, the Rupert Steele Stakes (and was second in that race for the next three years), the Lightning Stakes, the Stanley Wootton Stakes, the Rubiton Stakes, and the Futurity Stakes. Redelva showed that he wasn't just a sprinter by winning the Memsie Stakes over the longer distance of 1400m in 1991.

Neville Wilson, who milked 70 cows at Camperdown in Western Victoria, piloted Redelva to most of the wins. Wilson was a prolific winner in the bush but more than held his own in city company. He was also associated with the great stayer Sydeston.

Bob Hoysted takes a good hard look at Sydeston after the Caulfield Cup (BP).

Mick Dittman takes Naturalism outside Silk Ali (Shane Dye) to win the Grey Smith Stakes (Age).

'The Enforcer' strikes again

Jockey Mick Dittman wasn't labelled 'The Enforcer' for nothing. No rider in Australia showed more polish and determination in getting a horse to the line. And his performance in landing four winners – half the card – at Caulfield on Toorak Handicap Day was testment to his effectiveness.

Dittman's winners included Ricochet Rosie in the Toorak Handicap and Sydeston (Caulfield Stakes), on whom he was to win the Caulfield Cup the following Saturday.

Sydeston, trained by Bob Hoysted, was originally from Tasmania where he ran second in the Derby. He showed scintillating form in the autumn of 1990, winning the BMW and Queen's Plate in Sydney before capping his career with the Caulfield Cup victory. On retirement, he had won more than $3 million in stake money.

Leonard (Mick) Dittman had won the 1982 Melbourne Cup on Gurner's Lane among hundreds of other feature race triumphs. Originally from Brisbane, he was associated with many great horses including Red Anchor, Strawberry Road and Bounding Away.

Ironically, one of his greatest rides was on a beaten horse – he did everything but carry Naturalism over the line when the horse ran a gallant second in the Japan Cup of 1992.

TURF TOPICS

Upstaged: Two 1989 Melbourne Cup placegetters, Tawrrific (winner) and Kudz (third) came down to earth in the Perth Cup. They could finish only ninth and sixth respectively.

Upstaging them were local heroes Word Of Honour and Troy Jackman. Jockey Shane Dye was unable to explain Tawrrific's poor showing while Michael Clarke said Kudz had pulled up sore.

Brother's day: Michael Clarke might have been top jockey in 1990 but his brother Gary took the spotlight at Flemington in February. While Michael chose to ride at Morphettville, Gary rode four winners at headquarters for the Colin Hayes stable. Michael had a disappointing day, landing just one first placing.

Manangatang multiple: They were racing at Manangatang in March – and bush jockey Ron Burgess was dominating. Burgess rode five winners on the program. He proved this was no fluke the following year when he landed another five winners – this time at Kerang, Victoria.

Hayes – again: Colin Hayes, who had announced he was to retire at the end of the season, won yet another big race when Mahaasin took the 1990 Blue Diamond Stakes. Hayes, producer of more race winners than any trainer in Australia, had won 170 races since the retirement announcement, including the 1989 Cox Plate with Almaarad and the Chester Manifold Stakes with Power of Destiny.

Dye's second: Jockey Shane Dye took his second Golden Slipper Stakes when he won on Canny Lad in April. The ever-confident Dye said: 'The first time I rode him last August I thought he was the best horse I'd ever been on, so when he was within two lengths of them at the furlong today, I had no worries.'

Canny Lad, trained by Rick Hore-Lacy, was suited by the heavy track at Rosehill. It was the colt's sixth win from seven starts.

History made: Jockey Alan Scourse, best known for his association with great Western Australian sprinter Placid Ark, notched a place in Canberra racing history by landing five winners from five rides in April 1990.

Maree and Miss Stamina: The 1990 DB Auckland Cup was notable because the winning rider, Maree Lyndon, on Miss Stamina, became the first female jockey to win the Auckland Cup some 14 years after women were first licensed in NZ.

'Oh no! Better Loosen Up's owners react after Shane Dye's protest in the Cox Plate. It failed (BP).

Over to you, son: Colin & David Hayes (BP).

Gritty Japan Cup winner

What a year 1990 was for Australian racing – thanks to a gritty, gutsy gelding named Better Loosen Up.

Better Loosen Up rarely won by great margins – but he generally won and his victory in the 1990 Japan Cup against the world's best (the first by an Australian horse) underscored his outstanding quality.

His win was the high point of an incredible first season for David Hayes who at 26 had just taken over the training empire of his father Colin. Better Loosen Up was one of a number of stars in the stable, but his wins in the Cox Plate and Japan Cup set him apart.

Better Loosen Up was first owned and trained by Les Theodore of Berrigan, who sold his share in the horse to Bart Cummings (as he had with his other champion Campaign King) following financial difficulties. Better Loosen Up won a few races in Sydney, but was diagnosed as suffering a hairline pelvic fracture and therefore was spelled.

Michael Clark on Better Loosen Up.

David Hayes took over his training and the bay gelding improved as he matured, winning at Flemington and in Perth before returning in the autumn to beat outstanding rivals Vo Rogue and Super Impose in the Blamey, then failing to match Vo Rogue's sustained speed in the Australian Cup. But he atoned in Sydney by beating not only Vo Rogue but Sydeston, Horlicks, Dr Grace and King's High in the Rawson Stakes.

Came the spring of 1990 and Better Loosen Up came into his own after a first-up fourth in the Liston Stakes. He won the Feehan and Turnbull Stakes and it was thought his heroic win over Sydeston in the Cox Plate would cap his career but his Japan Cup win was even more dramatic.

Seemingly too far back to figure in the finish, he unwound a surging charge under Michael Clarke's desperate riding to overpower the top international field and win narrowly. Heady moments followed as press and television reports around the world ensured fresh interest in Australian racing and breeding.

In 1991 Better Loosen Up looked even better as he thrashed Vo Rogue by five-and-a-half lengths in the Australian Cup before breaking down and being retired. Thanks to his victories in the Japan Cup (second richest race in the world) and the Cox Plate (richest wfa race in Australia), his winnings amounted to more than $4.5 million.

Instant success

Success in racing – the toughest of businesses – was instantaneous for the young David Hayes in 1990. Hayes took over the flourishing operation established by his father Colin and led in winner after big-race winner in the weeks that followed.

The highlights, of course, were Better Loosen Up's triumphs in the Cox Plate and Japan Cup just months after Hayes was granted his licence – a B class training permit. He went on to phenomenal success in both Australia and Hong Kong but 3 November 1990 – Derby Day at Flemington – stands out as a day of days.

On that afternoon Hayes set a world record of six Group race winners in one day on the eight-event card. The stable did not have a runner in the Derby and saddled up an unplaced outsider in the other race.

Hayes' winners were: Raise a Rhythm – Group 2 Maribyrnong Plate; Wrap Around – Group 3 Hilton on the Park Stakes; Beachside – Group 2 Wakeful; Planet Ruler – Group 1 Gadsden Stakes; Better Loosen Up – Group 1 Mackinnon Stakes, and Mount Olympus – Group 2 Dalgety.

In achieving the feat David surpassed his father's record of five Group winners set in February 1987.

David Hayes' built on his 1990 successes. He became the first trainer in the Commonwealth to train 300 winners in a season and had his 1000th winner in less than four years.

Notable successes, among many, were Fraar's win in the 1993 Caulfield Cup and Jeune's victory in the 1994 Melbourne Cup.

Wealthy owner Willesee with Rubiton (Age).

Ex-jockey Pat Hyland in trainer mode (Age).

Mike's squillions

By his own admission, TV current affairs host Mike Willesee put 'squillions' into racing. He bought into top horses such as Sir Dapper and Rubiton and launched into breeding from his expansive Transmedia Park Stud at Cootamundra.

He held high hopes for the Argentinian Horse of the Year, Savage Toss, but he failed dismally in three races before winning the Werribee Cup.

On the strength of his Argentinian performances, Savage Toss had been allotted top weight in the Melbourne Cup, but few liked his chances. He started at 66/1. But he ran an outstanding race, leading until well into the straight until he faded to finish seventh, only five lengths from the winner.

However, on the final day of the Cup Carnival he stylishly won the Queen's Plate and trainer Lee Freedman admitted he hadn't realised the key to the horse should have been more hard racing.

Hyland trainer

The racing world said farewell to Pat Hyland the jockey and welcome to Pat Hyland, trainer, in 1990.

Hyland had been one of Australia's top jockeys for more than three decades, winning most of the nation's big races including the 1985 Melbourne Cup (on What a Nuisance), the 1984 Caulfield Cup (on Affinity) and the 1969 Golden Slipper (on Vain).

He also won 18 races on the first-class galloper Craftsman, including the 1963 Victoria Derby, two Queen Elizabeth Stakes, two Australian Cups and a Liston Stakes. In 1964 Hyland had won the Newmarket–Australian Cup double on Rashlore and Grand Print.

Sometimes volatile, Hyland enjoyed an enduring and distinguished association with trainer Jim Moloney to whom he was apprenticed at Warrnambool (Victoria) in the late 1950s. Hyland was still riding for the trainer when he retired.

TURF TOPICS

Horse dead ahead: Following scenes of unprecedented racetrack chaos, stewards declared the Noel Mason Steeplechase at Moonee Valley in May a 'no race' after track attendants had waved the field to change course to avoid a dead horse and injured jockey. The trouble began when favourite Tippler's Oath fell heavily the first time round and had not been moved by the time the field completed the next lap. In the ensuing chaos, only six of the 12 runners completed the race, five horses fell and the leader Gun de Wyn was withdrawn.

Troubles with Gavin: Controversial jockey Gavin Eades had a sorry record by June 1990. It included three times being dealt with by stewards for easing mounts before the winning post, disqualification five times for hitting the head of a rival runner in a finish, suspension for interfering with the scales, obscene language in front of a club official, and spitting.

A jumps first: Christine Reeve became the first woman jockey to win a mainland steeplechase when she won the Springvale Steeplechase on 25/1 chance Silver Peak at Sandown in June. In 1985 the former New Zealander had become Australia's first woman jumps jockey.

A drugs first: In August, Perth's Jeremy Hurstwitt became the first jockey in Australia to be suspended for returning a positive drug test in August. The suspension was incurred after the test detected cannabis in a urine specimen at Belmont Park. Hurstwitt, 35, was suspended for three months from riding in races and trials.

A 1-2-3 treble: It was three strikes with a difference for owners Geoff and Beryl White, trainer Jack Denham and jockey Ken Russell when their horses Pipiwar, Pockets and Logogal won the first three races at Randwick in November.

1990 RESULTS

VRC MELBOURNE CUP (3200m)
Kingston Rule, 53 (D Beadman) Trainer JB Cummings; 3:16.3; The Phantom, Mr Brooker
AJC SYDNEY CUP (3200m)
King Aussie, 53 (N Harris) Trained by JF Harris; 3:36.6; Chaleyer, Palace Revolt
QTC BRISBANE CUP (3200m)
Shuzohra, 51.5 (RS Dye) Trained by E Skelton; 3:32; Lord Hybrow, King Aussie
SAJC ADELAIDE CUP (3200m)
Water Boatman, 54.5 (P Hutchinson) Trained by CS Hayes; 3:2.3; Double Gin, Ideal Centreman
WATC PERTH CUP (3200m)
Word Of Honour, 49.5 (T Jackman) Trained by AD Matthews; 3.20.5; Our King Crimson, Green Range Boy
VATC CAULFIELD CUP (2400m)
Sydeston, 50 (L Dittman) Trained by RE Hoysted; 2:31.6; Water Boatman, Shuzohra

VRC AUSTRALIAN CUP (2000m)
Vo Rogue, 58 (C Small) Trained by V Rail; 2: 0.9; Better Loosen Up, Super Impose
MVRC WS COX PLATE(2040m)
Better Loosen Up, 59 (M Clarke) Trained by DA Hayes; 2:01.5; Sydeston, Canny Lad
AJC DERBY (2400m)
Dr Grace, 55.5 (J Cassidy) Trained by G Chapman; 2:31.7; Stylish Century, Solar Circle
VICTORIA DERBY (2500m)
Fire Oak, 55.5 (B Hibberd) Trained by GD Yorke; 2:35.8; Centro, Lord Revinir
AJC DONCASTER HANDICAP (1600m)
Super Impose, 57 (B Compton) Trained by DL Freedman; 1:38.4; Shaftesbury Avenue, Our Grey Invader
BTC DOOMBEN '10,000' (1350m)
Prince Trialia, 51.5 (S Schofield) Trained by W Hailes; 1:19.9; Planet Ruler, Boasting
VRC NEWMARKET HANDICAP (1200m)

Gold Trump, 52 (H White) Trainer JB Cummings; 1:8.3; Lightning Bend, Tango Master
AJC SIRES' PRODUCE STAKES (1400m)
Rhythmic Charm, 54 (RS Dye) Trained by TJ Smith; 1:32.4; Somalia, St Jude
VRC SIRES' PRODUCE STAKES (1400m)
Canny Lad, 55.5 (J Cassidy) Trainer R Hore-Lacy; 1:24.5; Century Pike, Draw Card
VRC GRAND NATIONAL STEEPLECHASE (5000m)
Trei Gnaree, 63.5 (B Constable) Trained by J Craddock; 5:56.5; Bar The Shouting, Commission Red
STC GOLDEN SLIPPER STAKES (1200m)
Canny Lad, 55.5 (RS Dye) Trained by R Hore-Lacy; 1:15.41; With Me, Paklani
VATC BLUE DIAMOND STAKES (1200m)
Mahaasin, 52.5 (W Harris) Trained by CS Hayes; 1:9.9; Canny Lad, Triscay
STC MERCEDES-TANCRED CLASSIC (2400m)
Sydeston, 57 (L Dittman) Trained by RE Hoysted; 2:38.1; Lord Hybrow, Horlicks

Bart Cummings' new big champion Let's Elope (L. Dittman aboard) at Caulfield (BP).

Bart's back in town

Bart Cummings was back with a vengeance in the spring of 1991. He had decided to ignore, he said, the financial troubles still hanging over his stable and do what he did best – train winners.

By carnivals' end, Cummings had trained nine Group 1 and 2 races, as he had in 1974. The difference this time was that the feat was achieved with only three horses – Let's Elope, Richfield Lady and Shaftesbury Avenue (pictured).

Let's Elope won the lion's share with victories in the Turnbull Stakes, Caulfield Cup, Mackinnon and Melbourne Cup. Richfield Lady gave Cummings his seventh Oaks Stakes (in fact, he quinellaed the race with India's Dream) after winning the Edward Manifold Stakes. Shaftesbury Avenue scored a brilliant win in the Caulfield Stakes, beating Super Impose.

Shaftesbury Avenue slipped and nearly fell in the Cox Plate in which he was strongly fancied, and in the Honda Stakes carried 60.5 into second place behind Pontormo and protested unsuccessfully.

Let's Elope – another Cummings champ

The spring of 1991 belonged to Bart Cummings – and a big lump of a mare named Let's Elope.

Let's Elope seemed to come from nowhere and suddenly she was winning the major races of the carnivals. At first it was thought she was another New Zealander who had simply beaten the handicapper but when she won the weight-for-age Mackinnon Stakes it began dawning on race followers that Cummings had come up with another champion. And an outstanding champion she was.

Let's Elope was bought by Dennis Marks with the better-performed Richfield Lady and placed in Cummings' care. Cummings knew he had acquired something special but little notice was taken of her when she failed first up. Then, however, she won the Turnbull

Stakes with such authority she went into the Caulfield Cup a lightly-weighted (48.5 kg) 7/1 chance.

Popular young jockey Steven King steered her to a last-stride win to give Cummings his sixth victory in the race and the trainer said he was confident the mare would get the 'two miles of the Melbourne Cup'. As a tune-up she would run in the wfa Mackinnon Stakes on Derby day. With 54.5 kg it was expected she would run a sound trial for the Melbourne Cup. Instead, the mare fairly blitzed them, leaving top horses Super Impose and Prince Salieri in her wake. Her Melbourne Cup price was then slashed to 3/1.

Big and strong and back to only 51 kg, Let's Elope was simply too powerful in the Cup but drama was to follow. Runner-up

Shiva's Revenge (also trained by Cummings who had scored his ninth Cup win and fifth quinella) had suffered interference severe enough for jockey Shane Dye to lodge a protest – the first of its kind in 120 years.

Let's Elope survived the deliberations of the stewards, and the result stood. She became only the second mare after Rivette to complete the Cups double, but jockey Steven King's 22nd birthday was soured by a six weeks' suspension.

Let's Elope returned in the autumn of 1992 to continue her winning ways. She was scratched from the Melbourne Cup and she bled in the Japan Cup which signalled the end of her racing career in Australia.

Shaftesbury Avenue wins the Newmarket Handicap from Redelva and Century God (BP).

Shaftesbury's gallant Japan Cup run

Shaftesbury Avenue was considered one of Australia's best horses up to 2000 metres. His record spoke for itself.

In the autumn of 1991, Shaftesbury Avenue made short work of the other sprinters in the Lightning Stakes, then carried 58 kg to victory in the Newmarket. Super Impose had the better of him in the Doncaster (1600m) but Shaftesbury Avenue turned the tables in the All Aged Stakes (also 1600m).

Shaftesbury Avenue brilliantly won the Caulfied Stakes, but slipped and fell on the greasy track in the Cox Plate and probably should have won the Honda Stakes (1600m), in which he finished an unlucky second.

However, Shaftesbury Avenue ran possibly his best race over a distance considered beyond him – the 2400 metres of the 1991 Japan Cup.

Against some of the world's best stayers, he stormed home for third behind Golden Pheasant.

Shaftesbury Avenue then suffered leg problems that restricted his racing, although he came back in the spring of 1992 to defeat Super Impose in the Warwick Stakes over 1400 metres. He retired with winnings of more than $2 million.

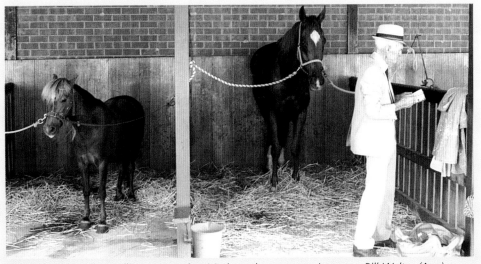

Redelva, his small travelling companion Marie and part-owner/strapper Bill Walter (Age).

TURF TOPICS

Briefest favourite: Outstanding mare Mannerism flashed in and out of the news in September. She won the Feehan Stakes at Moonee Valley by four lengths and was promoted to Caulfield Cup favouritism. But she had bled from both nostrils during the Feehan and was automatically banned for three months. Trainer Lee Freedman said next day: 'I couldn't see how they'd possibly beat her in the Caulfield Cup on yesterday's run.' Mannerism came back to win the 1992 Caulfield Cup, beating Veandercross. Whether she could have beaten the rampant Let's Elope in 1991 is a matter of turf conjecture.

Better Loosen Up stops Vo Rogue winning a third successive Australian Cup (BP).

TURF TOPICS

Beadman shines: Young jockey Darren Beadman was said to have come of age as a rider with another multiple-winning display at Rosehill. Beadman's winning mounts were all for different stables – unlike his five winners at the same track in October the previous year. That day all were for the Crown Lodge stable and the Ingham brothers. It was that performance that brought him the winning ride on Kingston Rule in the Melbourne Cup.

Record equalled: The six-furlong record of 1:07.8, established down Flemington's 'straight six' by Aurie's Star in 1940, had stood for so long few thought it would ever be broken. Indeed, many doubted its accuracy as top sprinters failed to better it over the next half century. It took a Cummings to at least equal it – not Bart but his son Anthony. His charge, Final Card, ran 1:07.8 in the Gadsden Rheem Stakes on Derby Day, 1991. Apart from that run, Final Card hardly deserved any comparison with Aurie's Star.

Unbeatable first-up: The flying mare Joanne thrilled racegoers with another scorching win in August – this time in the Premiere Stakes at Rosehill. She was to go on and win the race the following year. Joanne won numerous sprinting races in Sydney, among them the Expressway Stakes and the Theo Marks Quality, but will always hold a place in the hearts of her followers for her amazing first-up record: the mare had the perfect record of seven from seven first time in.

Denham – narrowly: It had taken a long time but Jack Denham finally won the Sydney trainers' premiership in July. He had been locked in a head-and-head battle with Vic Thompson for the title, which was only decided on the final day of the 1990–91 season. Denham horses scored a double to clinch the title.

King is dead: The end came for one of Australia's greatest racehorse in March. Kingston Town failed to recover from a leg injury suffered while frolicking in a paddock. The gelding, aged 14, was humanely put down at owner David Hains's property Kingston Park, on the Mornington Peninsula, Victoria.

Jim's triumph: Jim Houlahan had another jumping triumph when Look At Me won the Great Eastern Steeplechase over 4950 metres at Oakbank in April. Houlahan, a former builder, who had not started training until his late 50s, dominated jumping events throughout the 1990s.

Shane Dye salutes on Canny Lad (1990).

The enigmatic Peter Cook.

Tierce & Clarrie

The autumn of 1991 was dominated in Sydney by the brilliant Tierce – and his jockey Shane Dye.

Tierce won the Golden Slipper, then completed the two-year-old's triple crown of the Sires' Produce and the Champagne while Dye won his third consecutive Slipper and went on to notch more than 100 winners for the season.

Tierce, unfashionably bred but trained by the masterly and ever-exuberant Clarrie Conners, carried off a meritorious string of victories as he went from strength to strength.

Dye, who was to go on and win his fourth successive Slipper the following year, rode four winners at the 1991 Slipper meeting. Of course, his most important win had come 18 months earlier when he piloted Tawrrific to land the 1989 Melbourne Cup.

But many more big race wins – and continuing controversies – were to come.

Cook heartstopper

Jockey Peter Cook, winner of most of Australia's biggest races, looked to be at the end of his career when he suffered a heart attack during a race at Canberra in March.

The setback would at least sideline Cook, son of champion jockey Billy Cook, for many months. It was the worst of luck for the jockey, who was then only 40.

Peter Cook was always in the news. When not winning important races he was taking rebellious and often confrontationist stands. His fashionable moustache and long hair were frequent targets of criticism but his great ability was unquestioned.

Recognised as a brilliant judge of pace, Cook won two Melbourne Cups (his father also won two), three Sydney Cups and two Cox Plates as well as two AJC Metropolitans and two AJC Oaks. He was associated with some of modern racing's greatest horses, including Kingston Town, Gunsynd and Think Big.

Bob Hoysted and Sydeston (BP).

Surfers Paradise wins the Cox Plate (Age).

Super Impose completed the double double.

'Surfers' dumps top horses

Everyone, it seemed, ignored the New Zealander Surfers Paradise when assessing prospects for the 1991 Cox Plate. This was understandable: some great gallopers prepared by great trainers were lining up for the premier weight-for-age race in Australasia.

Bart Cummings' sprinting and middle-distance star Shaftesbury Avenue was there. So was his great rival, Lee Freedman's Super Impose. So was Caulfield Cup winner and the previous year's runner-up Sydeston, plus Rough Habit, and Stylish Century.

So Surfers Paradise was easy to overlook. Besides, the trainers-jockey team, O'Sullivan father and sons, had had their chances at the Cox Plate with horses such as Shivaree, Our Waverley Star and Horlicks – all runners-up.

But of course nobody told Surfers Paradise this – and a deeper look might have

established his credentials more indelibly. He had not been New Zealand's Horse of the Year for nothing, he had won the Rosehill Guineas in the autumn, heavy tracks had plagued his lead-up races and surely the O'Sullivans' luck was due to change.

And change it did. Shaftesbury Avenue slipped and nearly fell, ruining his chance, Rough Habit and Stylish Century made early runs which they could not sustain, Sydeston loomed up fleetingly, then it was left to the gallant Super Impose to hit the lead until Surfers Paradise came at him with the last run. It was too much for 'Super' and Surfers Paradise drew clear to win by a length. The no-nonsense O'Sullivans, father Dave and son Paul, and jockey Lance, praised the courage of the horse. No one begrudged their overdue change of fortune.

A super horse

They were running out of superlatives to describe Super Impose in October after he achieved a feat unlikely to be equalled. He had staged a freak performance to win the Epsom Handicap and complete an unprecedented fourth victory in the AJC's two feature 'mile' races.

After winning the previous year's Epsom, Super Impose had completed back-to-back wins in the Doncaster in the autumn of 1991. Said an ecstatic Lee Freedman: 'You know this will never, ever be done again.'

Super Impose, whose career had earlier been threatened by a bleeding attack, carried 61 kg to victory – the highest Epsom winning weight since Chatham scored in 1934. He was given a rousing five-minute standing ovation from the big Randwick crowd.

In the 20-horse field Super Impose had been a conspicuous 20th into the straight, on the outside of the other tailenders. Jockey Darren Beadman spotted a passage near the fence and the big red galloper took off. 'You've got to take your hat off to him,' he said. 'Horses were everywhere in front of him. Then I saw a bit of an opening. I had the horse to take me where I wanted to go – he just exploded.'

Super Impose had a slightly disappointing spring in 1991 – running second in the Caulfield Stakes, Cox Plate and Mackinnon Stakes but his biggest win was still to come: in the dramatic Cox Plate of 1992.

1991 RESULTS

VRC MELBOURNE CUP (3200m)
Let's Elope, 51 (S King) Trainer JB Cumming; 3:18.9; Shiva's Revenge, Magnolia Hall
AJC SYDNEY CUP (3200m)
Just A Dancer, 52 (G Cooksley) Trainer G Rogerson; 3:19; Castletown, I'm In Heaven
QTC BRISBANE CUP (3200m)
Just A Dancer, 54 (J Cassidy) Trainer G Rogerson; 3:32.8; Spring Thaw, Donegal Mist
SAJC ADELAIDE CUP (3200m)
Ideal Centreman, 53 (H White) Trained by CA Balfour; 3:22.3; Shiva's Revenge, Te Akau Pearl
WATC PERTH CUP (3200m)
Zamlight, 51.5 (M Sestich) Trained by SR Bates; 3:20.8; Word Of Honour, Ideal Centreman
VATC CAULFIELD CUP (2400m)
Let's Elope, 48 (S King) Trained by JB Cummings; 2:30.3; Ivory Way, Royal Creation

VRC AUSTRALIAN CUP (2000m)
Better Loosen Up, 58 (M Clarke) Trained by D Hayes; 2:1.6; Vo Rogue, Prince Salieri
MVRC WS COX PLATE (2040m)
Surfers Paradise, 57 (L O'Sullivan) Trainer DJ O'Sullivan; 2:03.8; Super Impose, Sydeston
AJC DERBY (2400m)
Durbridge, 55.5 (G Hall) Trained by B Murphy; 2:31.9; Cool Reception, Mountain Rule
VICTORIA DERBY (2500m)
Star of the Realm, 55.5 (S King) Trained by JF Meagher; 2:35.8; Naturalism, Ready To Explode
AJC DONCASTER HANDICAP (1600m)
Super Impose, 59.5 (D Beadman) Trained by DL Freedman; 1:36.5; Royal Creation, Shaftesbury Avenue
BTC DOOMBEN '10000' (1350m)
Prince Trialia, 52.5 (S Schofield) Trainer W Hailes; 1:20.6; Barossa Boy, Tiny's Finito

VRC NEWMARKET HANDICAP (1200m)
Shaftesbury Avenue, 58 (D Gauci) Trainer JB Cummings; 1:11; Redelva, Century God
AJC SIRES' PRODUCE STAKES (1400m)
Tierce, 55.5 (RS Dye) Trained by C Conners; 1:23.4; Shadea, Electrique
VRC SIRES' PRODUCE STAKES (1400m)
Not Related, 54 (G Hall) Trained by D Balfour; 1:23.8; Diddy Do It, Umatilla
VRC GRAND NATIONAL STEEPLECHASE (5000m)
Believable, 62.5 (S Jenkins) Trained by S Fox; 6:15.1; Vinchiam, Questland
STC GOLDEN SLIPPER STAKES (1200m)
Tierce, 55.5 (RS Dye) Trained by C Conners; 1:9.3; Canonise, Big Dreams
VATC BLUE DIAMOND STAKES (1200m)
Canonise, 54 (P Hutchinson) Trained by D Hayes; 1:10.1; Umatilla, Chief Headhunter
STC MERCEDES-TANCRED CLASSIC (2400m)
Dr Grace, 57 (RS Dye) Trained by G Chapman; 2:28.1; Shuzohra, Castletown

Burst wins a lead-up to the Golden Slipper with Shane Dye's help (Age).

That grin again: Dye's fourth Slipper (Age).

The Slipper led to a Burst of triple crowns

The outstanding filly Burst set the scene for the triple crown sequences that were the racing highlights of 1992.

Burst became the first filly to win the grand slam of Sydney two-year-old events – the Golden Slipper, the Sires' Produce and the Champagne. (To follow was Schillaci's treble of the major sprints in Melbourne and the Freedmans' annexing of the Cox Plate and Caulfield and Melbourne Cups.)

Burst's triumph was all the more remarkable because it was achieved by the charismatic team of trainer Clarrie Conners and jockey Shane Dye who had also won the triple crown the previous year with Tierce. And the Slipper win gave Dye an incredible fourth successive victory in the race – the greatest riding achievement in its history.

It was another 'swooping' win by Dye – so often the master of the perfectly timed finish. He had caught the leader, Clan O'Sullivan, within metres of the post – and that horse's trainer wasn't impressed.

'What about the four of them [the jockeys on horses who had challenged Clan O'Sullivan throughout],' fumed Frank Cleary. Then, pointing to Dye, he said: 'I'll just say this. He's done his homework and we haven't.'

But nothing could detract from Burst's great ability. Despite Conners' expressed doubt that she was as good as Tierce, the filly took out the Sires' Produce and again had to finish with a powerful surge to win the Champagne.

This time Conners criticised Dye (who had come from last on the filly), saying the ride was 'dreadful'. To which Dye laughingly replied, 'I've heard this out of Clarrie before.'

A very big year for the Freedmans

Few trainers have had as much success in a year as Lee Freedman and his brothers enjoyed in 1992. Their horses won the triple crown of autumn sprints – the Lightning Stakes, Oakleigh Plate and Newmarket Handicap – then the triple crown of spring staying races – the Cox Plate and Caulfield and Melbourne Cups.

Their three-year-old Schillaci was the star of the autumn. The powerhouse grey became only the second horse to annex all three sprints and won 13 of his first 19 starts. He completed his 1992 campaign by taking the Moir Stakes on Cox Plate Day.

The Freedmans won the Caulfield Cup with the mare Mannerism whose short-half-head victory was achieved after Shane Dye took Veandercross (second) to the centre of the wet track in one of the most controversial finishes for years. The wonder horse Super Impose gave them the Cox Plate after their main contender, Naturalism, lost his jockey. Then Subzero won the Melbourne Cup for them, after also winning the 1992 Adelaide Cup.

So the Freedmans had a great year and although all four brothers played important roles, most credit went to their principal, Lee – young, high-profile and painstakingly professional.

Racing was very much in the Freedmans' blood. Their great grandfather was the cham-

The Freedmans: Lee (Subzero) Anthony (Super Impose), Richard (Heroicity) (Age).

pion jockey Bill McLachlan who rode three Melbourne Cup winners; their grandfather Alan Freedman owned racehorses and their father Tony was an owner and trainer. Lee Freedman managed the family's breeding establishment from 1975 until 1983 when he took up training, in Sydney then Melbourne.

Damien Oliver and the big grey Schillaci, after the Newmarket Handicap win (Age).

Schillaci really scorched

When the massive grey Schillaci powered to racing fame in the autumn of 1992, he unleashed the explosive speed seen only by truly great sprinters. On his way to the triple crown of sprints – the Lightning, Oakleigh Plate and Newmarket – he broke track records in the first two events.

After duly taking the Newmarket (trainer Lee Freedman quinellaed the race with Storaia) he then went to Sydney and won the Galaxy. Freedman predicted the horse 'could be another Manikato'.

Schillaci, named after Italy's World Cup soccer star Salvatore Schillaci, couldn't match Manikato's five-year dominance of big races, but scorched the turf for a further two years.

After failing in the 1992 Stradbroke, Schillaci returned in the spring to beat Mookta (who was to win the 1994 Newmarket) in the Moir Stakes. The following year he again won the Lightning Stakes and then took the Futurity over 1400 metres.

More wins came in the Stanley Wootton Stakes at Moonee Valley and the George Ryder at Rosehill but he found the distance of the Doncaster beyond him.

The edge appeared to be coming off his scintillating speed when he ran second in the Moir Stakes of 1993 and in the 1994 Lightning. However, he came out in the spring of 1994 to take the Caulfield Sprint under 60.5 kg from All Our Mob.

A paddywhacked Doncaster

A young man with a baby face and an impeccable racing pedigree took Australian racing by storm when he became the youngest jockey to win the Doncaster Handicap in April 1992.

Sixteen-year-old Ballarat apprentice Patrick Payne showed nerves of steel to win the time-honoured race on the (then) unknown Victorian three-year-old Soho Square whose victory was labelled as one of the great anti-climaxes in the history of the event. The 5/1 favourite Kinjite (Mick Dittman) could finish only fourth – 'Slow horses kept getting in my way,' Dittman said – and the great miler Super Impose, trying for his third successive Doncaster, was also unplaced.

Payne had Soho Square (30/1) handy to the lead all the way and gained a vital 1 ½-length break coming to the 200-metre mark. He held on to win by a long neck from the fast-finishing Old Role.

Patrick, son of former New Zealand trainer and patriarch of racing's famous Payne family, Paddy Payne, was virtually unheard of in Sydney, but had been making a name for himself in Melbourne, as had his older sisters Therese and Maree.

Next month Patrick celebrated his 17th birthday by becoming the youngest apprentice to outride his allowance in Australian racing history. He beat the previous best – under the current apprenticeship system – of Simon Marshall, who was 17 years and three months when he outrode his claim.

TURF TOPICS

Gai a trainer: Gai Waterhouse finally became a trainer in January 1992. Her 2½-year battle for a licence ended unexpectedly when she was summoned before the AJC committee and told her application had been approved.

Waterhouse, daughter of veteran trainer T. J. Smith, had had her many applications denied because she was married to former bookmaker Robbie Waterhouse who had been warned off for his part in the Fine Cotton ring-in affair of 1984.

TJ meets Queen: Tommy Smith achieved a long-held ambition when he met the Queen after his horse Aquidity won the Queen's Cup in her presence at Randwick in February.

'This is one of my greatest thrills in racing,' said Smith, a trainer for more than 50 years. Winning jockey Shane Dye had to ride vigorously to land Aquidity by a long neck. 'You left it awfully late,' the Queen told him.

Mick's big dollar day: Even by his high standards, jockey Mick Dittman had a day out at Rosehill in April. He rode three winners and figured in the placings in every event on the card. He thus earned $600 700 prize money for connections and, of course, a tidy sum for himself. Dittman's day went like this: Race 1 (1st Regina Madre); Race 2 (2nd Discriminate); Race 3 (3rd Enjoy Dancing); Race 4, (2nd Aquidity); Race 5 (2nd King Marauding); Race 6 (1st Naturalism), Race 7 (1st Kinjite); Race 8 (3rd Moods).

'Losers' were winners: Punters in April were paid dividends on a 'winner' at Wyong that was later disqualified. Keen Force scored in the opening event but Queensland apprentice Lyle Finlay did not carry the correct weight.

The mistake was not discovered until after race four – long after correct weight had been declared. Keen Force lost the prize money but Finlay, who had been given incorrect information about the weight he should carry, was not penalised.

'Clan' again: Canberra two-year-old Clan O'Sullivan turned on a powerful display of speed and strength to complete the Magic Millions double by winning the $1 million Australasian Classic at Southport in May.

Jockey dies: Young apprentice Leanne Crook was killed in a horrific fall at Doomben in April. Crook, 19, died after she crashed from Spotted Dancer, 250 metres from the winning post, rolling and hitting the running rail.

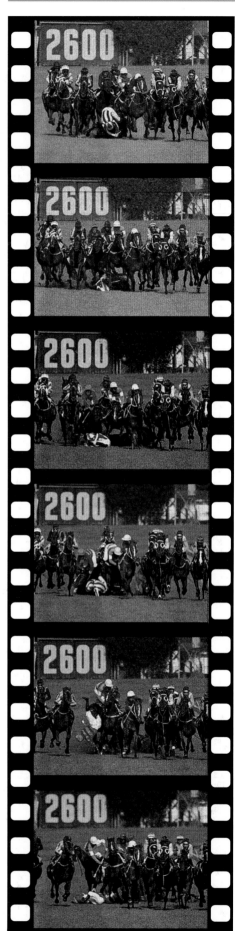

Geoff Ampt captured the Cox Plate drama as Naturalism and Sydeston crash.

Greg Hall wins – and grins

The horses were the victors, of course, but jockey Greg Hall stole the limelight after he won the 1992 Cox Plate and Melbourne Cup double.

Hall's ride on Super Impose (Cox Plate) and Subzero (Melbourne Cup) were classics of their kind and no one begrudged the one-time-larrikin rider his success.

Super Impose had been racing's favourite horse for years. He probably would not have beaten stablemate Naturalism had that horse not fallen when going like a winner, but who was to say?

And, yes, Veandercross was again unlucky in running second to Subzero on a sodden track in the Melbourne Cup but Hall was the winner – and the grinner. And grin he did, in a show of jubilation after both races that signalled that the days of poker-faced jockeys such as Bill Williamson and Jack Purtell were gone for ever.

Greg Hall was never far from controversy in his career but no one enjoyed their greatest moments in racing more than he did.

Accident-prone Stylish Century

Stylish Century was a horse rarely out of the headlines – not only because of his unquestioned ability but also for the misadventures that studded his career.

Stylish Century was a shock late scratching from the Group 2 Carlyon Cup in February 1992, when owner-trainer Dick Monaghan failed to arrive at Caulfield in time to pay the acceptance fee.

Monaghan was delayed when his car overheated and though his daughter was at the course with Stylish Century, she didn't have the necessary $500.

Earlier in the year, Stylish Century had nearly drowned in the training pool at Flemington.

A striking black horse who had been trained briefly by Bart Cummings, Stylish Century had burst into prominence in 1989 by running a mighty second in the Cox Plate, then winning the Victoria Derby by three lengths in record time.

Stylish Century then became the first three-year-old to contest the Melbourne Cup since 1974 but failed dismally. He came back in the autumn and, after a number of wins, inexplicably lost all form.

He returned better than ever in 1991 when one of his best performances was his second to mare Big Colony in the Sandown Cup. He ended up the winner of the race when Big Colony returned a positive swab.

TURF TOPICS

Repeat quinella: It was a repeat of Bart Cummings' 1991 Melbourne Cup quinella when Let's Elope beat Shiva's Revenge in the Australian Cup at Flemington in March. The consistent Prince Salieri was third – as he had been the previous year.

Naturalism's AJC Derby: Lee Freedman's Naturalism served notice of the greatness to come when he won the AJC Derby in April – but jockey Mick Dittman had to survive a protest from the rider of Veandercross. New Zealander Jim Walker accused Dittman of causing interference over the last 50 metres of the classic. Dittman admitted Naturalism had drifted out under pressure but said he had the race well won at the time.

Wrong-way Charlie: Visiting Irish jockey Charlie Swan cost Victorian punters an estimated $250 000 in winnings when he steered King Taros on the wrong course in a steeplechase at Sandown in August. King Taros, 13/8 favourite, was leading by six lengths when Swan missed the right-hand turn on to the course proper in the home straight. He was charged with carelessness and suspended for five weeks.

Crowd a record: They like their racing in the Northern Territory. A record crowd of more than 18 000 turned out to see the Darwin Cup at Fannie Bay in August. Visitors included contingents from interstate and overseas. The cup was won by Victorian galloper Clam's Comet over 1991 winner Silver Shark.

Tough times: Big-race jockey Peter Cook, who suffered a career-threatening heart attack in 1991, was finding the going hard in trying to re-establish himself. 'It's getting tougher and tougher,' he said. 'I'm getting rides in the bush but they don't want to know me in town.' Cook's career took a turn for the better when he gained the rides on New Zealander Captain Cook in his spring engagements.

Veandercross meanders across to Mannerism in the Caulfield Cup (BP).

Let's Elope and Better Loosen Up (BP).

Beaten – by the *width* of the straight?

It was the biggest controversy of a sensation-packed Spring Carnival – the Caulfield Cup defeat of Veandercross after being wide all the way then 15 deep in the straight. 'How much should he have won by?' punters asked each other after Lee Freedman's Mannerism came along the rails to score by a lip.

Veandercross goes down as one of the unluckiest horses in racing. He ran second in the 1992 Rosehill Guineas, AJC Derby, Caulfield Cup and Melbourne Cup. Some believe he should have won them all but it was his defeat in the Caulfield Cup – and the amount of extra ground he covered – which aroused

controversy that would be discussed for years.

Jockey Shane Dye remained adamant he had ridden the correct race given the heavy track but it seemed only he believed he needed to take the horse so wide. However, Dye did steer Veandercross to victory in the subsequent Mackinnon Stakes after missing the start.

Meanwhile, a jubilant Lee Freedman said Mannerism was the equal of Let's Elope and praised the young Damien Oliver as 'a mature jockey now'. Mannerism gave Freedman his first Caulfield Cup.

Match a strike-out

It rejoiced in the grandiose title of the TAB $75 000 Super Challenge: the match race between champion horses Let's Elope and Better Loosen Up and their jockeys Mick Dittman and Michael Clarke on Thousand Guineas Day at Caulfield. As a promotion it aroused great interest but as a contest it was a fizzer. The crowd saw a dawdling first 800 metres, then a sprint home in which Let's Elope proved the stronger. It was thought that Dittman won the battle of tactics over Clarke. Let's Elope started at 4/7, Better Loosen Up at 11/8.

Former winner Baghdad Note enjoying himself during the Melbourne Cup Parade (Age).

Racing's a picnic at Dunkeld (BP).

1992 RESULTS

VRC MELBOURNE CUP (3200m)
Subzero, 54.5 (G Hall) Trained by DL Freedman; 3:24.7; Veandercross, Castletown
AJC SYDNEY CUP (3200m)
My Eagle Eye, 52.5 (G Cooksley) Trained by M Baker; 3:23.8; Aquidity, Castletown
QTC BRISBANE CUP (3200m)
Grooming, 53 (C Munce) Trained by E Cameron; 3:20.1; Mr Eurostar, Mountain Rule
SAJC ADELAIDE CUP (3200m)
Subzero, 51.5 (G Hall) Trained by DL Freedman; 3:31.5; Big Barron, Mystery Adventure
WATC PERTH CUP (3200m)
Mirror Magic, 52.5 (T Jackman) Trained by AD Matthews; 3:21.7; Red Javelin, Vite Filou
VATC CAULFIELD CUP (2400m)
Mannerism, 54.5 (D Oliver) Trained by DL Freedman; 2:34.9; Veandercross, Aquidity

VRC AUSTRALIAN CUP (2000m)
Let's Elope, 55.5 (D Beadman) Trained by JB Cummings; 2:0; Shiva's Revenge, Prince Salieri
MVRC WS COX PLATE (2040m)
Super Impose, 59 (G Hall) Trained by DL Freedman; 2:05.5; Kinijite, Slight Chance
AJC DERBY (2400m)
Naturalism, 55.5 (L Dittman) Trainer DL Freedman; 2:31.2; Veandercross, Cavallieri
VICTORIA DERBY (2500m)
Redding, 55.5 (D Oliver) Trained by GJ Kelly; 2:40; Muirfield Village, Raising Kentucky
AJC DONCASTER HANDICAP (1600m)
Soho Square, 47.5 (P Payne) Trained by I Saunders; 1:35.7; Old Role, Prince Salieri
BTC DOOMBEN '10 000' (1350m)
Barrosa Boy, 53.5 (C Munce) Trained by R Taylor; 1:21.3; Rough Habit, Meg's Ego

VRC NEWMARKET HANDICAP (1200m)
Schillaci, 55.5 (D Oliver) Trained by DL Freedman; 1:9.4; Storala, Umatilla
AJC SIRES' PRODUCE STAKES (1400m)
Burst, 54 (RS Dye) Trained by C Conners; 1:23.7; Commissar, Merry Shade
VRC SIRES' PRODUCE STAKES (1400m)
King Marauding, 55.5 (L Dittman) Trained by G Marconi; 1:23.7; Just Juan, Apopka
VRC GRAND NATIONAL STEEPLECHASE (5000m)
Donnie's Chance, 61 (M Robertson) Trainer K Rogerson; 5:58; Man Of Ayr, Vim's Brother
STC GOLDEN SLIPPER STAKES (1200m)
Burst, 52.5 (RS Dye) Trained by C Conners; 1:10.2; Clan O'Sullivan, Loving Cup
VATC BLUE DIAMOND STAKES (1200m)
Riva Diva, 52.5 (G Childs) Trained by JB Cummings; 1:11.4; Yachtie, Chingquillo
STC MERCEDES-TANCRED CLASSIC (2400m)
Heroicity, 52.5 (G Hall) Trained by T Andrews; 2:29.1; Aquidity, Rough Habit

Schillaci (Damien Oliver) outside, wears down Tanjian Prince (Greg Childs) to score a record-breaking win in the Rubiton Stakes (Age).

Freedmans' winning roll continues

The all-conquering Freedmans continued on their winning roll in the autumn of 1993, initially with the unstoppable grey Schillaci. The four-year-old resumed in January to break the Sandown track record and run the fastest 1000 metres recorded in Australia in the Rubiton Stakes.

He then took out the Lightning, Futurity and Stanley Wootton and indicated he could win over more ground by winning the George Ryder over 1500 metres at Rosehill.

The Freedmans were confident he was ready for the hard 1600 metres of the Doncaster Handicap but he faded to finish 11th. Schillaci then endured a lean trot but came back in 1994 and regained form to win the 1100-metre Caulfield Sprint.

Meanwhile, the Freedmans had uncovered another record-breaker in the outstanding filly Bint Marscay who shattered the best time in winning the Golden Slipper in April.

Bint Marscay ran a stunning 1:8.88 for the Rosehill 1200 metres – almost half a second, or three lengths, faster than Tierce's 1991 Slipper record.

Lee Freedman gave the credit for Bint Marscay's success to brother Anthony who had turned her out in top condition despite her history of chronic shin soreness.

Jockey Mick Dittman partnered the filly in her success, then won the $1 million BMW on Kaaptive Edition, earning for himself around $200 000 for the afternoon.

Rough Habit: fast, not good-looking (Age).

A habit of winning

If there were any doubts that Rough Habit was one of the best horses to race in Australia in the early 1990s he dispelled them in March 1993 by taking out his third successive Doomben Cup.

Rough Habit had nothing left to prove. A New Zealander, described as the plainest of horses, he notched a marvellous record in Australia, particularly in Queensland where he also won two Stradbrokes and two Southport Cups.

He arrived in Australia in 1990, won the Queensland Derby and, at his first attempt in the Doomben Cup, finished third.

On his annual trips across the Tasman, Rough Habit proved a prolific winner in Brisbane and Sydney, then showed he could handle the Melbourne way of going by winning at Caulfield and running places in the Mackinnon and Queen Elizabeth Stakes.

In the autumn of 1993 Rough Habit defeated Naturalism in the All Aged Stakes, then received a sustained and joyous reception that visibly moved trainer John Wheeler after the Doomben Cup win.

Rough Habit won more than $1 million in Queensland in his overall total of more than $3 million.

Norman Waymouth on speedy Sequalo (Age).

A family affair

The Waymouths came up with another top sprinter in 1993: the exciting Sequalo who won his first five starts. Charlie was trainer and one of the part-owners of the horse. His wife Dawn was another part-owner. Stable jockey Norman, Charlie's son, piloted Sequalo to his wins but after the narrowest of victories in the CS Hayes Stakes, Charlie made derogatory comments to which Norman replied: 'Well, sack me then. I'll just get Mum to put me back on.'

Vale Ken Russell

The racing world was in mourning in October 1993 when popular jockey Ken Russell, 42, was killed in a fall at Rosehill.

Russell was one of the few jockeys who did not serve an apprenticeship as a jockey (he served one as a newspaper compositor) but nonetheless he

Russell on Merimbula Bay.

became a highly successful rider on the Gold Coast and in Sydney. His biggest wins included two Magic Millions, two Queensland Oaks, a Queensland Derby and a Doncaster Handicap. The previous year jockey Noel Barker, who had only recently returned to Sydney from Hong Kong, died after suffering head injuries in a fall at the Randwick barrier trials.

Kerry Packer, Greg Hall, strapper Raelene Jury, Lee Freedman and Lloyd Williams after the Derby.

Kerry Packer's rich pickings

Lee Freedman was back in the Group 1 action when the flashy Mahogany careered away with the 1993 Victoria Derby, but it was the three-year-old's owners who made the headlines.

Mahogany's win meant huge pay-outs for VRC committeeman Lloyd Williams and media magnate Kerry Packer – not only from the $¾ million prize money but from the $1 million they were estimated to have taken out of the betting ring.

Mahogany had failed at his previous start at Moonee Valley but was backed with confidence in the Derby to start 7/2 favourite.

Colourful jockey Greg Hall lived up to his reputation as the big-race jockey by setting Mahogany alight at the top of the straight. The gelding exploded away to win easing down.

Leading rails bookmakers bore the brunt of the substantial plunge. 'It was a good old-fashioned go,' lamented bagman Allen Cleary.

For Packer, it was another example of his Midas touch. Williams had only invited him to join the partnership earlier in the month.

For Freedman and his brothers, it was their first Derby. For Mahogany, it was his fourth Group 1 success.

TURF TOPICS

Winners aplenty: The Melbourne trainer–jockey combination of John Meagher and Steven King struck the most purple of patches in November 1993. On the final day of the Melbourne Cup carnival Meagher trained five winners with King riding four of them. King then landed a fifth winner – for a rival trainer.

The following week Meagher and King resumed where they left off by combining to win the feature double at Sandown. The next Saturday they took out the $50 000 Eclipse Stakes at Caulfield with Palareign, and King rode a treble.

Cutaway criticised: The controversial cutaway rail had its first big test on Derby-Doncaster Day at Randwick in April – and was roundly criticised by jockeys and trainers. The general feeling was that the rail, which cuts away 2.5 metres at the top of the straight, had dramatically affected the usual pattern of racing. The principal difference was that there was a notable lack of late finishers.

A Payne trifecta: Three members of the Payne family filled the placings in the fifth race at Bendigo. Patrick Payne rode the favourite Besta Besta to victory, beating his older sister Therese on the 16/1 chance Initial Red and another sister, Maree, on Locharn (12/1). The 'Payne' trifecta paid $160.30 on the Victorian tote.

Vale Geoff Murphy: His laconic style made him a character but few racehorse trainers were more professional than Geoff Murphy who died in 1993 aged 66. Murphy's most significant triumph was his 1982 Caulfield–Melbourne Cups double with Gurner's Lane but his best horse was Surround, the only filly to win the Cox Plate. Murphy learned his profession thoroughly. He was a strapper and jockey (with limited success) and then foreman for Basil Conaghan before setting up his own training establishment.

Drought ends: The frustrating losing streak of Melbourne's four-time premier jockey Harry White finally came to an end in April after a run of outs totalling 114. White won the last race on the card at Moonee Valley and said: 'It's fantastic; more like winning a Cup than an ordinary Saturday race.'

Jolly good win: Acupuncture helped Melbourne sprinter Jolly Old Mac's improvement to win the Goodwood Handicap at Morphettville in May. Jolly Old Mac had been laid low by pleurisy and deep-seated muscle soreness.

Peter Hutchinson gets a hug from Dad, Ron (BP).

Fraar, in blinkers, with Peter Hutchinson riding the race of his life, lands the Caulfield Cup (Age).

'Hutchy' lands a cup his Dad couldn't win

The personable Peter Hutchinson had to do something right to salvage his standing with the powerful Hayes stable after he was trenchantly criticised for his losing ride on their horse Maraakiz.

And do something right he did: he came out and won the 1993 Caulfield Cup for them on the unpredictable import Fraar.

Although only 27, Hutchinson had had a long association with the family of Colin Hayes with whom he served his apprenticeship and through whom he won the Adelaide jockeys' premiership in 1989–90 and 1990–91. He had also ridden a number of Group 1 winners for the stable.

But racing is a capricious business and jockeys are only as good as their last ride.

In the Coongy Handicap on the Wednesday before the 1993 Caulfield Cup, Hutchinson had ridden a copybook race on the lightly weighted import Maraakiz, trained by David Hayes for Sheikh Hamdan din Rashid al Maktoum.

Believing he had the race won, Hutchinson dropped his hands near the line only to be devastated when Silk Ali flashed up to snatch victory. It was Hutchinson's worst moment in racing. He did not need to be reminded of how the stable viewed his mistake. Fortunately for him, it was too late to replace him on Fraar in the Caulfield Cup,

which was only three days away.

Hutchinson didn't dare hope for victory on Fraar. Since arriving in Australia, Fraar had done little to put himself into Cup contention and he went to the post at 30/1.

Hutchinson rode the race of his life on the import who beat Air Seattle and the 5/1 equal favourite The Phantom, who had also run third back in 1989.

'Am I forgiven?' Hutchinson asked as he returned to the winner's stall. 'Tenfold,' replied Colin Hayes. In winning the Cup, Hutchinson had achieved something father Ron couldn't do in his distinguished career.

Mahogany jumps to win Victoria Derby (BP).

J. Cassidy & Rough Habit win Doomben Cup.

Super Impose (G. Hall) wins Cox Plate (Age).

Vintage Crop leads the Cup field back (BP).

Vintage Crop, Dermot Weld, David Phillips and staff at home in Ireland (Age).

Vintage Crop – a smooth Irish stayer

The freakish Irish stayer Vintage Crop did more than just win the Melbourne Cup in 1993: he engendered dire forebodings that the Cup was now lost forever as an Australian institution.

'The Cup has lost its innocence.' 'Now a hi-jacked international event.' 'The end of an era.' So ran the headlines as veteran racing figures lamented a perceived revolution in Australian racing.

Of course, the doom peddlers were proved wrong, or mostly so, anyway. The Cup had perhaps been elevated in world status but the forecast domination by stayers from Europe did not eventuate. Or at least not yet.

What had not been fully grasped was that Vintage Crop truly was a staying freak, as he was to repeatedly prove in Australia in the months to come.

The courageous gelding had more than just impeccable credentials for the Melbourne Cup (a number of imported failures have had those). He had a magnificent fighting heart and iron will-to-win. He had graduated from winning a novice hurdle at Leopardstown to taking the premier distance race in England, the 3600-metre Cesarewitch at Newmarket in 1992.

In 1993 he had won the Curragh Cup, then in September took out the Irish St Leger in what was to be his last run before tackling the Melbourne Cup.

Prepared at Melbourne's Sandown racecourse by his Irish trainer Dermot Weld, Vintage Crop was overshadowed in press reports by his travelling companion and fellow imported Cup contender Drum Taps, who had won the Ascot Gold Cup.

Given his international form, Vintage Crop had a comparative luxury weight of 55.5 kg but his unusual preparation in not contesting lead-up races for the testing 3200 metres of the Cup resulted in his starting at a generous 14/1.

Vintage Crop proved a class staying act. The Gai Waterhouse–trained rank outsider Te Akau Nick (who started at 160/1 despite having won the Metropolitan) looked to have outstayed the field well down the Flemington straight but Vintage Crop gathered him in with ease and was said to be lengthening stride on the post. To complete a rout for punters, Mercator at 125/1 was third. Drum Taps, 6/1 second favourite and ridden by Frankie Dettori, was ninth.

Vintage Crop was not the first overseas-bred horse to win the Cup (there had been several dating back to Comedy King in 1910) but he may have been the best. In 1994 he was rated the top horse in the world at 2800 metres and beyond in the International Classification of racehorse performances.

Vintage Crop's jockey Michael Kinane joined Australian Pat Glennon as the only riders to win the English Derby, the Prix de L'Arc de Triomphe and the Melbourne Cup.

1993 RESULTS

VRC MELBOURNE CUP (3200m)
Vintage Crop, 55.5 (M Kinane) Trainer Dermott Weld; 3:23.4; Te Akau Nick, Mercator
AJC SYDNEY CUP (3200m)
Azzaam, 53.5 (L Dittman) Trained by D Hayes; 3:28.3; Te Akau Nick, Subzero
QTC BRISBANE CUP (3200m)
Barbut Delcia, 52 (S Sharman) Trained by KS Cullen; 3:19.8; Cool Affair, Silk Ali
SAJC ADELAIDE CUP (3200m)
Our Pompeii (T Jackman) Trained by GM Hanlon; 3:22.6; Check That Style, Headcutter
WATC PERTH CUP (3200m)
Field Officer, 46.5 (P Knuckey) Trained by AD Matthews; 3:22.1; Red Javelin, Kawtuban
VATC CAULFIELD CUP (2400m)
Fraar, 54.5 (P Hutchinson) Trained by DA Hayes; 2:28.0; Air Seattle, The Phantom

VRC AUSTRALIAN CUP (2000m)
Veandercross, 57 (L Dittman) Trained by J Wheeler; 2:1.3; Star Of The Realm, Fraar
MVRC WS COX PLATE (2040m)
The Phantom Chance, 57 (B Vance) Trainer C Jillings; 2:02.8; Solvit, Golden Sword
AJC DERBY (2400m)
Innocent King, 55.5 (J Cassidy) Trainer K Jordan; 2:33.6; Kaaptive Edition, Air Seattle
VICTORIA DERBY (2500m)
Mahogany, 55.5 (G Hall) Trained by DL Freedman; 2:34.9; Shelved, Waikikamukau
AJC DONCASTER HANDICAP (1600m)
Skating, 52.5 (G Cooksley) Trained by G Rogerson; 1:34; Soho Square, Gifted Poet
BTC DOOMBEN '10,000' (1350m)
Unequalled, 50 (M Pelling) Trained by K Wood; 1:18.5; Buck's Pride, Meg's Ego
VRC NEWMARKET HANDICAP (1200m)
Primacy, 52 (L Dittman) Trained by D Hayes; 1:8.1; Victory Dais, Keda

AJC SIRES' PRODUCE STAKES (1400m)
Tristalove, 54 (G Cooksley) Trainer D O'Sullivan; 1:23.7; Justice Prevails, Allez Glen
VRC SIRES' PRODUCE STAKES (1400m)
Pride Of Rancho, 55.5 (D Oliver) Trained by G Marconi; 1:23.1; Taps, Staff Sergeant
VRC GRAND NATIONAL STEEPLECHASE (5000m)
Another Nugget, 66.5 (P Worthington) Trainer D Cave; 6:4.5; Yrangie, Vesper Flavour
STC GOLDEN SLIPPER STAKES (1200m)
Bint Marscay, 52.5 (L Dittman) Trained by DL Freedman; 1:8.88; Justice Prevails, Sports Works
VATC BLUE DIAMOND STAKES (1200m)
Lady Jakeo, 52.5 (G Hall) Trained by J Sadler; 1:11.1; Keltrice, Justice Prevails
STC MERCEDES–TANCRED CLASSIC (2400m)
Kaaptive Edition, 52.5 (L Dittman) Trained by G Rogerson; 2:27.13; Rough Habit, Veandercross

Lee Freedman holds the Australian Cup (Age).

Greg Hall and Danzero's Slipper (Age).

Top young trainers

Master trainer Bart Cummings took something of a back seat to the younger brigade of trainers in 1994.

Lee Freedman served notice early that his successes in 1993 were set to continue when he won a drama-filled Golden Slipper Stakes in March with Danzero. In fact, Subzero's Melbourne Cup connections (owners, trainer, jockey) completed a unique racing double with the win.

But the 1994 Slipper was marred by even more interference than usual in the helterskelter of the world's richest two-year-old event. Beaten jockeys described the race as one of the roughest in history and 'a complete disgrace'. Three protests were lodged. All were dismissed, but jockeys Damien Oliver and Steven King were suspended and Shane Dye cautioned over their rides.

Freedman, who had won back-to-back Golden Slippers, continued his excellent autumn. Mahogany won the AJC Derby, Durbridge took the Australian Cup and Freedman continued his top-level success when Paris Lane won the Caulfield Cup.

Ironically, Paris Lane had begun his training with David Hayes. The horse, described as 'plain ugly' was rewarded for his consistency, having earned prize money at each of his 17 starts since failing first-up in the country.

Gai Waterhouse, who had taken little time to establish herself at the top level of racing after her protracted battle for a trainer's licence, scored her biggest success when Pharaoh won the Doncaster in April.

'Thanks, Dad', was her tribute to father T. J. Smith after Pharaoh got the nod in the tightest of finishes. Smith had had to miss his first Doncaster in more than 60 years because he was recuperating from a knee operation.

Smith had won a record seven Doncasters but transferred Pharaoh to his daughter only 10 days earlier due to his inability to prepare the horse during his recuperation.

David Hayes tasted early success when his mercurial St Covet won the Black Opal Stakes in Canberra, but had to be satisfied with that horse's second in the rough-house Golden Slipper.

In the spring, Hayes triumphed with the win of Blevic in the Victoria Derby before capping his short career by taking the Melbourne Cup with the import Jeune. Jeune's win was a tribute to Hayes's training methods. The temperamental stallion thrived on a hard lead-up preparation that shocked the representative of owner Sheikh Hamdan bin Rashid al Maktoum. 'He would not have been prepared that way in England', said Angus Gold, the sheikh's racing manager.

Hats on for Gai Waterhouse (Age).

Pharaoh wins the Doncaster (Age).

David Hayes congratulates Jeune (Age).

Jeune relaxes before the Cup (Age).

Improved with age

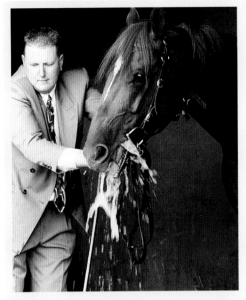

Strapper Bill Aiton gives the old man a drink.

The grand galloper Durbridge appeared to be getting better with age in 1994. He had been winning races at the highest level since 1990. Following a bleeding attack, which sidelined him for a year, he was transferred to Lee Freedman's stable. In the autumn of 1994, however, Durbridge was at his peak. He took the Chester Manifold, Blamey and St George Stakes before beating stablemate Mahogany in the Australian Cup.

Campaigning in Sydney, he failed in the Tancred but easily won the Queen Elizabeth Stakes when he led throughout to win by 2¼ lengths. It was his 16th win from 55 starts for earnings of $2 625 073. Taken to Brisbane, he won the Hollindale Cup and then the Doomben Cup from Paris Lane.

Damien Oliver drives home Paris Lane in the Caulfield Cup: another Freedman success (BP).

A study in concentration: heads up at the start of the Victoria Derby at Flemington (BP).

TURF TOPICS

Death of a racing man: Novelist, racing devotee and inveterate punter Frank Hardy died in January as he would have wished to go – at his desk with a form guide in his hand. His novel *The Four-Legged Lottery* centred on the punter's battle against racing's insuperable odds.

No drink-riding: Western Australian Turf Club officials were red-faced at the Perth Cup meeting in January when visiting Canadian jockey Mark Larsen failed a breathalyser test. Stewards ordered Larsen, 20, to forfeit four rides and stood him down for one meeting. They had been tipped off that Larsen had been drinking on New Year's Eve and might be over the legal limit allowed for WA jockeys.

Primacy's prime role: By March it appeared that the David Hayes–trained Primacy had usurped Schillaci as Australia's top sprinter. Primacy easily beat Schillaci in the Futurity Stakes at Caulfield, giving him his third Group 1 victory for the season.

Mookta's reward: The flying sprinter Mookta led throughout to win the Newmarket in March – then was retired to a life of ease at stud. 'He's been kind to us. Now it's time to return the favour,' said 31-year-old Mark Riley after landing his biggest win as a trainer. (He had won the Oakleigh Plate as a jockey.)

'Group One Gavin' strikes: Jockey Gavin Eades was on top of the racing world in April. Eades capped a fairytale week when he won his third Group 1 race in a week on dour stayer Cross Swords in the Sydney Cup. Eades had just won his first, the Doncaster on Pharaoh. Then he took the Galaxy on Jetball. Elated, Eades labelled himself 'Group One Gavin'.

And 'no' to Cook: Former champion jockey Peter Cook received another setback when his application to become a trainer was rejected by the AJC committee in June. Cook, winner of two Melbourne Cups and considered one of the best horsemen Australia has produced, had suffered a heart attack and was plagued by back problems. He had a compensation case pending against the AJC.

'Two-Whip' Woodhouse: Cairns jockey David Woodhouse surely created a first in September when he began a race with one whip and finished it with two! Rival rider Athol Ryan's whip snapped halfway down the shaft and the binding splayed out. The binding caught around Woodhouse's whip and he snatched it from Ryan's grasp.

Wayne Harris and Jeune win a damp Melbourne Cup (Age).

Owner Robert Sangster (left) and jockey Mick Dittman at Flemington (Age).

Foreign challenge fizzles out

It rarely pays to make hard and fast predictions in racing. Those who glumly forecast that international horses would dominate Melbourne Cups after Vintage Crop's win in 1993 were proved hopelessly astray in 1994.

True, an import in Jeune won the race, but he was victorious through Australian training methods. Three of the four northern-hemisphere horses were among the tailenders.

Vintage Crop did his best in running seventh – and should have finished much closer. Burdened with 60 kg and out of barrier 17, his jockey Michael Kinane embarked on a daring strategy that set the horse an impossible task. Vintage Crop was to prove the worth of the run by finishing a gallant third in 1995.

Despite the hype, Quick Ransom, River Verdon and Cliveden Gail were not good enough – and fears of an international hijack of the Melbourne Cup evaporated.

Against all odds

For 33-year-old Wayne Harris, Jeune's 1994 Melbourne Cup victory was sweeter than for other winning riders. Harris had come back from illness and injuries that would have caused most to give racing away long before.

Ten years earlier the Sydney jockey was operated on for a brain tumour and told he would never ride again. And only 12 months previously he was in hospital fighting for his life as an infection riddled his body. Twice surgeons had to amputate part of his left index finger that had become infected after being caught in a girth buckle.

His injuries had included broken ribs, smashed bones in both feet, and broken hands, wrists, hip and tailbone, vertebrae, sternum, nose, shoulder and collarbone. After each illness and injury he had thought of giving up.

Harris had only gained the ride on Jeune after Shane Dye rejected the mount (saying the horse would not settle well enough to win a Melbourne Cup) and after Rod Griffiths had been on him in a poor run in the Cox Plate (and declared the horse a hopeless Melbourne Cup proposition).

But Harris had the silky hands needed to settle the horse in the run. That – and the pacifiers fitted by trainer David Hayes – proved a decisive factor in the horse's win.

Too fast, too soon

Damien Oliver would dearly have liked to win the Perth Cup. But he lost the race because his mount Diamond Heist got such a flying start it appeared he might have broken through the barrier gates. After enjoying a good run Diamond Heist hit the lead at the top of the straight and looked the winner until Palatious lunged at him on the line to snatch victory. Stewards viewed film of the start before deciding Diamond Heist had simply anticipated the jump – quite fairly.

Oliver, who was trying to win his first Perth Cup in memory of his father Ray, who won two, was philosophical. 'I don't mind those sort of starts over 1100 metres but it's not a good thing over 3200,' he said.

Patrick Payne was king of the kids when he beat four brothers and sisters at Ballarat in November. His sisters Therese and Maree filled the placings while brother Andrew and sister Bernadette were unplaced in the field of nine. The Payne trifecta paid $52.70 for $1.

Moira Murdoch, Solvit at Mornington (Age).

'Crafty George' triumphs again

Not for nothing have they called him 'Crafty George' through most of his long and high-achieving career.

Victoria's George Hanlon earned the sobriquet through his training acumen, his ability to place horses to perfection and for his patience with them when they seemed to have exhausted their potential.

A case in point was his second Adelaide Cup win with the solid stayer Our Pompeii in 1994. The horse had been winless since winning the same race the previous year.

George Hanlon has won top races at all distances, including dual Newmarkets with Correct, but it is as a conditioner of stayers that he has excelled. His successes include three Melbourne Cups (with Piping Lane, Arwon and Black Knight) plus the Australian, Brisbane, Moonee Valley, Sandown and Sydney Cups plus four Adelaide Cups. (For good measure, his durable stayer Royal Snack won the Moe Cup four years in a row).

Among the top-class horses he has trained are Family of Man (Cox Plate), Taras Bulba (Rosehill Guineas, AJC Derby) and Lawman (Doncaster, and two Feehan Stakes).

Moira's Solvit

The 1994 Cox Plate win of New Zealander Solvit was another triumph for a woman trainer. Moira Murdoch joined Deirdre Stein, who won with Rising Prince in 1985, as the only women to train Cox Plate winners. Solvit, a bold front-runner who finished second in 1993, gave New Zealand its fifth win in the race in nine years. The large crowd desperately wanted the popular Queenslander Rough Habit to win Australia's greatest wfa event but his storming finish failed by just a half-head.

Joked trainer John Wheeler after the event: 'Just as well he didn't win. They'd have torn the stand down.' Rough Habit was also placed in the Mackinnon and Queen Elizabeth Stakes in 1994.

1994 RESULTS

VRC MELBOURNE CUP (3200m)
Jeune, 56.5 (Wayne Harris) Trained by D Hayes; 3:19.8; Paris Lane, Oompala
AJC SYDNEY CUP (3200m)
Cross Swords, 52.5 (G Eades) Trained by JR Hawkes; 3:28.8; Hear That Bell, Azzaam
QTC BRISBANE CUP (3200m)
Sky Flyer, 49.5 (B Compton) Trained by BF Deacon; 3:15.7; Cool Credit, Cross Swords
SAJC ADELAIDE CUP (3200m)
Our Pompeii, 55.5 (P Payne) Trained by GM Hanlon; 3:21.1; Sweet Glory, Top Rating
WATC PERTH CUP (3200m)
Palatious, 51.5 (D Gundry) Trained by AD Matthews; 3:22; Diamond Heist, Kathros
VATC CAULFIELD CUP (2400m)
Paris Lane, 53 (D Oliver) Trained by DL Freedman; 2:26.5; Alcove, Tenor

VRC AUSTRALIAN CUP (2000m)
Durbridge, 58 (S Marshall) Trained by DL Freedman; 2:2.2; Station Hand, Mahogany
MVRC WS COX PLATE(2040m)
Solvit, 59 (D Walsh) Trained by Ms M Murdoch; 2:02.6; Rough Habit, Redding
AJC DERBY (2400m)
Mahogany, 55.5 (G Hall) Trained by DL Freedman; 2:36.5; Waikikamukau, Fraternity
VICTORIA DERBY (2500m)
Blevic, 55.5 (R Griffiths) Trained by DA Hayes; 2:35.7; Danewin, Stony Bay
AJC DONCASTER HANDICAP (1600m)
Pharaoh, 53 (G Eades) Trained by G Waterhouse; 1:38.2; Kingston Bay, Telesto
BTC DOOMBEN '10 000' (1350m)
Flitter, 53 (J Cassidy) Trained by M Lees; 1:19.6; All Our Mob, Bint Marscay
VRC NEWMARKET HANDICAP (1200m)
Mookta, 54 (S Baster) Trained by M Riley; 1:10.2; Gatana, Let Him Ride

AJC SIRES' PRODUCE STAKES (1400m)
St Covet, 55.5 (W Harris) Trained by D Hayes; 1:25; Danzero, Blevic
VRC SIRES' PRODUCE STAKES (1400m)
Blevic, 55.5 (L Dittman) Trained by D Hayes; 1:24.5; Delsole, Racer's Edge
VRC GRAND NATIONAL STEEPLECHASE (5000m)
Outstride, 60.5 (C Hedditch) Trained by M Trinder; 5:51.8; Conramo, Squire John
STC GOLDEN SLIPPER STAKES (1200m)
Danzero, 55.5 (G Hall) Trained by DL Freedman; 1:9.81; St Covet, Racer's Edge
VATC BLUE DIAMOND STAKES (1200m)
Hurricane Sky, 54 (S King) Trained by G Ryan; 1:8.1; Mr Vitality, Renarchi
STC MERCEDES-TANCRED CLASSIC (2400m)
Miltak, 55.5 (B York) Trained by D O'Sullivan; 2:29.5; Dark Ksar, It's All In Fun

Strapper Rebecca Newman and Schillaci – the most spoiled horse in Australia (Age).

Grey power: good-looking Schillaci (Age).

Freedman up, down then back on top

Lee Freedman – the trainer who had breathed new life into racing in the 1990s – had a roller-coaster year in 1995. His fortunes rose exhilaratingly with another Golden Slipper win, crashed when he was suspended for four months, then soared when he won the Caulfield and Melbourne Cups.

Freedman and his Freedman Brothers Incorporated (the FBI) constantly made headlines in the autumn – principally because they had such exciting horses in their stable including the evergreen Schillaci, the amazing veteran Durbridge and the best filly in Australia, Northwood Plume.

But it was the sometimes-wayward colt Flying Spur that etched the trainer's name into Golden Slipper immortality. Flying Spur lasted to beat flying Octagonal who had been knocked down at the 200-metre mark.

But Freedman's world was to crash soon after when it was revealed he had substituted a horse in a blinkers trial – he admitted committing the indiscretion for what he said was a good reason – and had his trainer's licence suspended for four months.

(Freedman was found guilty of improper practice for deliberately substituting another horse from his stable, Spanish Reign, for Central Express in the blinkers trial on 14 March. As a result of the trial, Central Express was approved for blinkers and wore them in her win at Flemington on 15 March. Freedman said he had not wanted to jeopardise her chances by 'flattening' her in a trial.)

Freedman's great piece of luck was that his brother, Richard, was allowed to take over the stable during his enforced absence. Freedman found himself jobless but travelled widely and used the time to learn even more about the racing craft.

Meanwhile, most owners stuck with the Freedmans and successes continued, although Richard said in a newspaper interview he did not believe the stable had a star for the spring.

Enter the rangy chestnut Doriemus in whom Lee had always had a lot of faith and on whom he had spent an inordinate amount of time. He had always regarded the horse's chance in the big Cups highly.

That regard sprang from the day Freedman, who had recommended the purchase of the gelding after seeing him on a video taken

Lee Freedman appeals his suspension (Age).

in New Zealand, watched him win a lowly graduation race in Brisbane during a winter carnival. 'It wasn't much of a race,' he said, 'but it was the way he won it. He ran a sensational time with great sectionals. I thought then he just might be special.'

And special he proved, winning the Caulfield Cup in authoritative fashion. However, this win, while full of merit, was not enough to establish Doriemus as favourite for the Melbourne Cup (overseas invaders were

there in force and capturing most of the praise), especially when Freedman opted not to give him another lead-up race via the Mackinnon Stakes.

The more he thought about it the more he believed that would be the wrong strategy for Doriemus, who he was sure would not stand up to two demanding runs so close together, the Mackinnon being only three days before the Cup. And a poor run might well have sapped the horse's confidence.

So against what was all the tradition and most of the logic, Freedman announced Doriemus would not run in the Mackinnon and would go straight into the Melbourne Cup without another race. However, the strategy was not quite that simple. Another 'race' did not mean another 'run'.

So, on the Saturday when most Cup entrants were at Flemington lining up for the Mackinnon, and in keeping with his philosophy of giving horses outings and variety, Freedman sent Doriemus to Sandown racecourse for a 'good' working gallop.

'I just reckoned that was what he would need. It would top off his confidence. Because something has always been done one way doesn't mean it always has to be done that way,' he said.

The rest is racing history. Damien Oliver again brought Doriemus with a well-timed run to out-stay the Cup field and Freedman's strategic acumen had won him his third Melbourne Cup. Of the vaunted internationals, Vintage Crop ran a gallant third while Double Trigger failed so badly the only excuse that could be offered was that he was not 'sound'. However, many believed he was the victim of the wrong training strategy.

Damien Oliver's magnificent ride on Doriemus in the Caulfield Cup earned the horse a three-kilogram penalty, but that didn't stop him (Age).

Damien Oliver joins racing's top shelf

Jockey Damien Oliver joined the truly elite set of riders when he won the Caulfield and Melbourne Cups on Doriemus in 1995.

Oliver took his third Caulfield Cup (having won on Paris Lane the previous year and on Mannerism in 1992) and his first Melbourne Cup. Only Scobie Breasley, Neville Sellwood, Frank Dempsey and Mick Mallyon had won three or more Caulfield Cups in the 118-year history of the race.

It had been a meteoric rise to the top for Oliver, who had arrived in Melbourne as a raw-boned 18-year-old in 1990 – and only ridden his first winner at the top level that spring – Submariner in the VicHealth Cup.

But his dedication and improvement were such that he became Victoria's four-time premier rider in five seasons.

Oliver was certain Doriemus would handle the extra distance of the Melbourne Cup – and he was proved right, but in the meantime he looked certain to also annex the Cox Plate. He had secured the ride on the rampaging Danewin after other top jockeys were sacked.

And Oliver could scarcely have ridden a better race on Danewin – he had the horse coasting on the fence with 800 metres to go when he met interference so severe the horse was instantly out of the race.

No such misfortune befell him in the Melbourne Cup as he drove Doriemus to the lead to score the most convincing of wins. Oliver's youthful exuberance burst through as, almost incredulous, he told a world television audience during the horseback interview: 'I've just won the Melbourne Cup.' He said he dedicated the win to his father, killed in a race fall in Kalgoorlie 20 years ago.

Gai Waterhouse's glittering year

Gai Waterhouse was riding high as one of the most popular and successful figures in Australian racing by the spring of 1995.

She capably filled the shoes of her legendary father T. J. Smith and had had a stunning autumn, taking the Newmarket with All Our Mob, winning three races on Golden Slipper Day (including the $1 million BMW), then scoring another treble on Doncaster Day (including the main event for the second time with Pharaoh).

In fact, her achievement in preparing Pharaoh for back-to-back Doncasters was remarkable. Pharaoh had broken down badly in the near foreleg two years previously – and again after his first Doncaster win. (Waterhouse said daily swimming had kept Pharaoh off his legs and on his feet.)

Her commitment and dedication to success led to Waterhouse being dubbed the new darling of the turf and she was expected to be a star of the Melbourne spring. She duly was – via her exceptional three-year-old Nothin' Leica Dane.

The colt had 'champion' written all over him as he improved with every run – and his stunning win in the Victoria Derby confirmed his entitlement to the rating.

Part-owner T.J. Smith let it be known the horse would start in the Melbourne Cup if he won the Derby. Waterhouse at one stage appeared to differ in opinion about a start but then enthused about his chances.

Young champion that he was, Nothin' Leica Dane could not break the long hoodoo on three-year-olds winning the Melbourne

Gai gives orders during track work (BP).

Cup – a feat not achieved since Skipton in 1941. However, he ran a slashing race, finishing second to Doriemus, with the freakish Vintage Crop third.

Nothin' Leica Dane came back in the autumn to run second in the AJC Derby and was runner-up in the Sydney Cup but he was never to realise the potential expected as an older horse, again raising doubts about three-year-olds recovering from Cup assignments.

Shane Dye and the great Octagonal (Age).

He's no darling: Shane Dye (Age).

Irrepressible Dye recaptures crowds

The ever-confident Shane Dye was hardly the darling of the Melbourne race crowds in 1995.

On Cox Plate Day, Dye was jeered as he went to the start on Octagonal – a quality colt overshadowed by the other three-year-old in the field, Our Maiscay.

But the all-conquering Danewin with Damien Oliver up was expected to blow them all away, including the Lee Freedman–trained Mahogany who was attempting to win Australia's greatest wfa event on a single race preparation.

It was another magnificent Cox Plate. Our Maiscay led but compounded. Danewin was in a winning position when he was stopped dead by interference. Mahogany, ridden perfectly by Greg Hall, hit the front in the straight and looked the winner.

But Dye, who had been wide most of the way, sent Octagonal after him and the three-year-old triumphed after a short, sharp tussle.

Dye, almost choking with emotion, said as much in the horseback interview as he returned to scale. 'It was just a ride,' he said; but 'This was the one I wanted to be on all along,' he enthused. The jeers broke out at the presentation when Dye 'thanked' Danewin's owners for removing him, allowing him to ride the winner.

Jockey tapes affair rocks racing

The racing world was rocked by what became known as the Jockey Tapes Scandal in early 1995, with the consequent disqualification of two of Sydney's leading jockeys.

Jim Cassidy (three years) and Kevin Moses (pictured, one year) were banned after being found guilty by the AJC of racing offences relating to race-fixing allegations.

The race-fixing accusations proved groundless. Cassidy, as taped conversations revealed, had merely tried to profit from pretending some mounts had won by arrangement while Moses had arranged that he would, if asked … collaborate a claim that he had given a signal regarding a horse.

Both jockeys, naturally, were devastated by the disqualifications. Cassidy had at first refused to attend the AJC inquiry and for this was suspended for six months. This ban meant he lost the ride on Golden Slipper winner Flying Spur – and the winning fee of about $120 000.

Moses, then 42, predicted the ban would end the career he had spent two decades building. He had ridden more than 100 metropolitan winners in each of the past two seasons.

NZ-born Cassidy, 32, had forged an illustrious record in Australia since his storming Melbourne Cup win on Kiwi in 1983. Both jockeys were to come back to the top level of racing after serving their terms.

Finest family effort: Perth's leading racing family, the Millers, celebrated their crowning achievement when Ros Reef ran away with the Perth Cup in January 1995. Former champion jockey 'J. J.' Miller saddled the winner for his trainer wife Kay with jockey son Mark returning from suspension to ride a memorable race aboard the four-year-old stayer.

Out-thought to win: The Argentinian-bred Blue Boss was a thinking man's horse. His win in the Standish Handicap at Flemington in January was a tribute to almost Machiavellian planning by young trainer David Hall. Blue Boss had unquestioned ability, but also had a mind of his own. His heavy weights (from his successful Argentinian days) meant he had to be placed carefully, then detailed race plans devised. On Standish morning, Hall came up with the idea of popping him over a few hurdles. 'It seemed to get his mind on the job,' the successful trainer said later.

Bart bounces back: The year 1995 wasn't a vintage one for the master Bart Cummings – no Melbourne Cup, no Cox Plate (they would come next year with 'the horse from heaven', Saintly) but he was not without one major success. Cummings led in his first Group 1 winner in six months when Ivory's Irish narrowly downed favourite Danewin in the $1 million AJC Derby.

Ugly duckling maiden scores: A maiden with a 'head on him only a mother could love' gave trainer David Hayes his second Blue Diamond in five seasons in March. Principality, beaten in each of his three preparatory runs, came from last to become the first maiden winner of Victoria's premier two-year-old race. It was Hayes's eighth Group 1 win of the season.

'Peep' takes Guineas: A new staying star was hailed when the unfashionably bred Peep On The Sly brilliantly won the Sandown Guineas of 1995, defeating Saintly. Peep On The Sly, prepared by little-known Mornington trainer Bob Maxwell, had come through the classes via country tracks to win at the top level thanks to a withering finish. He was later to run third in the Australian Cup of 1996.

Dumb but dynamic: Trainer David Hall may have described Khaptingly as a 'big, dumb thing' but he was full of admiration for the horse's dynamic sprinting ability after he won the Oakleigh Plate of 1995 in February. Khaptingly gave Hall his first Group 1 success.

Jim Houlahan oversees a schooling session on his Rosebud property (Age).

Mick Dittman at the office (Age).

Houlahan hits straps – at 82

Jim Houlahan turned 82 in 1995. He celebrated by winning yet another Grand National Hurdle and embarking on an ambitious new phase of his training career.

Houlahan had long been Australia's leading trainer of jumpers, taking all the major races in Victoria including three Grand Annuals at Warrnambool, two Great Eastern Steeples at Oakbank, two Grand National Steeples and previous Grand National Hurdles with Sharp As, Fun Verdict and Tennessee Blue.

He had not begun training thoroughbreds until reaching his late 50s but had had a wealth of experiences with horses, having learned to ride about the same time he learned to walk.

Houlahan was initially a hobby owner-trainer of trotters, but a change from farming to the building trade led him to become involved with gallopers as an owner.

His first thoroughbred, Bellaron, failed to win races but when Houlahan tried to sell him the new owner returned him, saying he was unsound.

Houlahan bought him back, set him on a new preparation and won eight races with him – such was his expertise with unfashionable horses.

By 1995 Houlahan had set himself the goal of winning more flat races and by the spring his two promising gallopers, Unsolved and Toil, were on their way to qualifying for the Caulfield and Melbourne Cups.

And while they didn't take out the major events, both horses won good races (they both scored on the same program at Sandown that year) as Houlahan served notice that racing was going to hear a lot more of him yet.

TURF TOPICS

Punter's all-up coup: Sometimes it happens: a Melbourne TAB punter turned $1000 into a fortune in December 1995 and gave new impetus to the expression 'making something favourite'. He did it by having a $1000 all-up win bet at a Mornington mid-week meeting. His first selection scrambled home and paid $3.90. He thus had $3900 on his second selection, which also just managed to win. His all-up bet then required him to have $26 130 on his third selection, which firmed from $8.40 to $1.60 through the weight of his money before starting at $3.60. It bolted in and the punter collected $94 068.

Richard Cranium: How did handy NZ stayer Richard Cranium acquire the name? Said trainer Norman Wood: 'He was a fair dinkum rat when he was young. His owner told me: "I've named that horse", and that's what we called him'.

1995 RESULTS

VRC MELBOURNE CUP (3200m)
Doriemus, 54 (D Oliver) Trained by DL Freedman; 3:27.6; Nothin' Leica Dane, Vintage Crop

AJC SYDNEY CUP (3200m)
Daacha, 51 (B Prebble) Trained by J Meagher; 3:24.3; Dark Ksar, Gold Sovereign

QTC BRISBANE CUP (3200m)
Desert Chill, 50.5 (C Munce) Trained by S Laming; 3:18.8; Protara's Bay, Few Are Chosen

SAJC ADELAIDE CUP (3200m)
Scrupulous, 48 (M Carson) Trained by JD Smith; 3:23.8; Ice Doctor, Storm

WATC PERTH CUP (3200m)
Ros Reef, 52.5 (M Miller) Trained by Ms K Miller; 3:26.4; Fine Whiskey, Sweet Glory

VATC CAULFIELD CUP (2400m)
Doriemus, 52 (D Oliver) Trained by DL Freedman; 2:28.1; Count Chivas, Beaux Art

VRC AUSTRALIAN CUP (2000m)
Starstruck, 56.5 (M Miller) Trained by Ms K Miller; 2:0.4; Jeune, Station Hand

MVRC WS COX PLATE (2040m)
Octagonal, 48.5 (RS Dye) Trained by JR Hawkes; 2:06.3; Mahogany, Station Hand

AJC DERBY (2400m)
Ivory's Irish, 55.5 (L Cassidy) Trained by JB Cummings; 2:33.8; Danewin, Blevic

VICTORIA DERBY (2500m)
Nothin' Leica Dane, 55.5 (RS Dye) Trained by G Waterhouse; 2:36.5; Octagonal, Donar

AJC DONCASTER HANDICAP (1600m)
Pharaoh, 55.5 (G Eades) Trained by G Waterhouse; 1:38; Aunty Mary, Brave Warrior

BTC DOOMBEN '10 000' (1350m)
Chief De Beers, 51 (L Dittman) Trained by JW Calder; 1:17.8; All Our Mob, Cohort

VRC NEWMARKET HANDICAP (1200m)
All Our Mob, 56 (W Harris) Trained by G Waterhouse; 1:8.2; Hareeba, Moss Rocket

AJC SIRES' PRODUCE STAKES (1400m)
Octagonal, 55.5 (G Cooksley) Trained by JR Hawkes; 1:25.4; Isolda, Show Of Force

VRC SIRES' PRODUCE STAKES (1400m)
Lochrae, 55.5 (S Marshall) Trained by G Ryan; 1:23.7; Donar, Flying Spur

VRC GRAND NATIONAL STEEPLECHASE (5000m)
Ivanhoe, 60 (A Garraway) Trained by P Healey; 6:7.8; Outstride, Donegal

STC GOLDEN SLIPPER STAKES (1200m)
Flying Spur, 55.5 (G Boss) Trained by DL Freedman; 1:10.21; Octagonal, Millrich

VATC BLUE DIAMOND STAKES (1200m)
Principality, 54 (R Griffiths) Trained by D Hayes; 1:9.4; Flying Spur, Tuscany Flyer

STC MERCEDES-TANCRED CLASSIC (2400m)
Stony Bay, 52.5 (RS Dye) Trained by G Waterhouse; 2:27.2; Jeune, Turrido

Darren Beadman and Saintly make a perfect picture of style to win the easiest of Bart Cummings' 10 Cups (BP).

Saintly and Beadman: the heavenly Cup

Bart Cummings' 10th Melbourne Cup – perhaps Australian racing's greatest achievement – may well have been the easiest he had landed.

If ever a Cup was won a long way from the post it was this one. Saintly, under the confident hold of Darren Beadman, cruised throughout, was pulled out in the straight and simply glided to victory.

It was the smoothest, softest of Cup wins, in vivid contrast to most of Cummings' other stirring struggles to the post – often between his own horses.

But Saintly was saintly in every way. He had shown his class by winning the Australian Cup earlier in 1996, had demonstrated courage by taking the Cox Plate and certainly had the angelic temperament best suited to distance performers – but could he really stay the 3200 metres of the Melbourne Cup?

This was the doubt the experts continually pointed to, especially as one of Europe's finest stayers, Oscar Schindler, was in the Cup field as were last year's winner Doriemus, runner-up Nothin' Leica Dane, Sydney Cup victor Count Chivas and Perth Cup hero Crying Game – all tested at the distance.

Yet for a Melbourne Cup it was the hollowest of contests. Nothing threatened Saintly in the run to the line with Count Chivas doing best of the others and outsider Skybeau finishing well for third.

The world television audience saw something racegoers had not witnessed in 34 Melbourne Cups – Bart Cummings quietly wiped tears from his eyes as he walked from the stand through the throng of wellwishers to greet his winner.

How had Saintly done it, he was asked. 'We had to teach him to stay, that was it,' Cummings said. And his 10th Cup victory became even more meritorious because it was testimony to the long hours of walking and maturing, of patience and persistence, of building the stature of the horse – things that Cummings did better than anyone.

Darren Beadman paid due tribute to the 'genius' of the trainer in the now traditional horseback interview. He again thanked the Lord Jesus for his blessing and treated the crowd to his Frankie Dettori victory leap from the saddle.

The Victoria Racing Club had readied a special Melbourne Cup replica for Cummings in anticipation of his winning his 10th – and the crowd paid homage to perhaps racing's ultimate achievement.

Heavenly horse

He was Saintly by name, saintly by nature and he became known as the 'Horse from Heaven'.

But what was most extraordinary about Saintly's victories in Australia's two greatest races – the Cox Plate and Melbourne Cup of 1996 – was the holy link provided by jockey Darren Beadman. Beadman found God and became a born-again Christian after his life reached its lowest ebb when he was disqualified for failing to allow a horse to run on its merits in Hong Kong.

His fervent embrace of religion meant it was preordained that he would partner Saintly in the horse's greatest triumphs. Beadman spurned rides on Octagonal to complete the 'heavenly' partnership.

Darren Beadman does his thing (Age).

Octagonal: good enough to be compared with history's greatest horses (Age).

Octagonal after a Rosehill win (Age).

The big O's all-conquering autumn

Trainer John Hawkes never had been the most effusive of advocates when discussing the merits of his substantial and high-quality team owned by chicken kings Jack and Bob Ingham.

But when their greatest horse, Octagonal, won the 1996 Mercedes Benz Classic in the autumn of 1996, Hawkes uncharacteristically and unequivocally labelled him a champion.

The win meant 'the Big O' had won Australia's two premier weight-for-age events (he had taken the 1995 Cox Plate) and been desperately unlucky in the Golden Slipper and the Victoria Derby.

'He's a champion. He's the best three-year-old you've seen for a long, long time,'

Hawkes said after the colt's third straight win (he had also landed the Canterbury and Rose-hill Guineas) and his ninth win from 15 starts.

But it was the following week when the serious accolades started flowing. Octagonal – the epitome of courage in a racehorse – demonstrated hitherto-unseen will-to-win to take the AJC Derby, grinding home late to beat Saintly and Filante.

Then the comparisons with Kingston Town and Tulloch (even with Phar Lap and Carbine) began – and if the comparisons were based on courage alone they would seem fully justified.

Veteran Sydney racing writer Keith Robbins declared he had never seen a gamer horse

than Octagonal. 'When Saintly sprinted to the lead halfway down the straight (in the Derby) and Octagonal was striving wider out to match him no one thought he would have been able to do it,' Robbins wrote. 'But Octagonal never gives in.'

Trainer Hawkes had advised some time earlier that Octagonal was an autumn horse – and so it proved.

The Big O was disappointing in Melbourne in the spring. Only Darren Beadman got the best from him to win the Underwood Stakes at Caulfield but greater moments were to come. Octagonal was set to become one of the turf's true heroes.

Freedman's phenomenal fourth Slipper

Lee Freedman's training feat in capturing his fourth successive Golden Slipper Stakes in 1996 may have taken a back seat to Bart Cummings' 10th Melbourne Cup but it ranks nearly as highly.

The Slipper had grown from ambitious beginnings in 1957 to the world's richest and most prestigious juvenile event. It is one of the four top races in Australia, along with the Cox Plate and Caulfield and Melbourne Cups, and Freedman became the first trainer to win one of the quartet four years in a row.

In 1996 he did it with the outstanding filly Merlene, ridden by Greg Hall whose aggressive part in the win resulted in a $50 000 fine and suspension. Merlene produced a sizzling finish to succeed Flying Spur (1995), Danzero (1994) and Bint Marscay (1993) as Freedman-trained Golden Slipper winners.

'This is magnificent. She is such a brilliant

filly,' Freedman said after Merlene (15/4) beat the Gerald Ryan-trained Paint (13/4) by a length and a half with Flavor (7/1) a length back in third place.

But while it was certainly beer and skittles for Freedman – he won a lifetime supply of sponsor Tooheys' product – it wasn't the same for winning jockey Hall who described the fine and two-month suspension as 'tough, but winning was probably still enough for the pocket'.

For her part, Merlene went on to win the AJC Sires' Produce Stakes to complete two legs of the triple crown for two-year-olds.

For Freedman, the successes continued in the first half of 1996. He took the Sydney Cup with Count Chivas (an addition to the stable after running second to the Freedman-trained Doriemus in the 1995 Caulfield Cup when trained by New Zealander Don Sellwood),

Merlene in trackwork at Caulfield (Age).

then won his first Stradbroke Handicap with Danasinga. Freedman had recorded an unlucky second with Schillaci the previous year.

The Waterhouse clan: from left Bill, Tom, Gai, Robbie – and T.J.Smith (Age).

Shadow over Gai's triumphs

Nothing, it seemed, could dim the brilliance of Gai Waterhouse's blazing triumphs as the 90s rolled on … nothing except the AJC's refusal to reinstate her warned-off husband Robbie.

As a consequence, 1996 began badly for the Waterhouses. Just when many were conceding Robbie had served long enough for his part in the Fine Cotton ring-in of 1984 – 11 years was a fair stretch, they said – along came estranged brother David to destroy any chance of the ban being lifted.

David, 37, himself a former bookmaker, presented himself at Robbie's AJC appeal hearing. Amid headlines highlighting the family feud, David testified that Robbie had masterminded the Fine Cotton ring-in and stood to make millions of dollars from it.

Robbie's refusal to take the stand in the hearing (on, he said, his lawyer's advice) did not help his case and the AJC committee was left with little choice. It refused to lift the ban. However, Gay's disappointment was soon behind her as the winners kept coming.

By February, she was exultant as Nothin' Leica Dane looked to have come back as good as ever with a first-up win over Octagonal and Filante in the Hobartville Stakes. In April, Waterhouse won her third successive Doncaster, this one with Sprint By.

Came the spring and Waterhouse won her third Metropolitan, with Hula Flight from Nothin' Leica Dane, in the four years she had been a trainer.

Crying Game's Cup: Crying Game confirmed his status as the new star of WA racing when he scored a dashing victory in the 1996 Perth Cup in January. The three-year-old, the baby of the field, led from start to finish in one of the most authoritative wins in the state's best race.

Danewins at last: Danewin made a stunning return to racing after the disastrous interference in the 1995 Cox Plate and unplaced run in the Japan Cup. Burdened with 60 kg, Danewin displayed sizzling speed and courage to win the 1200-metres Frederick Clissold Handicap at Rosehill.

Fallen log attack: Oakbank's famous fallen log – the racecourse's best-known landmark and tough obstacle for steeplechasers – was under attack from wood borers and white ants in 1996. With the Great Eastern Steeple only days away, pest controllers were treating the log, which had not been moved for 65 years.

Trainer's fourth: New Zealand trainer John Wheeler lived up to his reputation as the uncrowned 'King of Oakbank' when he scored his fourth victory in the race, equalling Alex Fullarton's feat between 1948 and 1961. (Fullarton also won the 1934 race as a jockey, on Kenjin.) Wheeler quinellaed the 1996 event with Light Hand and Denali while jockey B. R. Scott took his third successive Great Eastern.

Peter prolific: Trainer Peter Hayes, who had taken the reins of the famous stable after David decamped to Hong Kong, trained seven winners at a Murray Bridge meeting in May, supplied the trifecta in the Group 1 South Australian Oaks later in the month and then prepared six winners from seven races at Balaklava in November.

First to Oliver: Jockey Damien Oliver became the first winner of the Scobie Breasley Medal for outstanding horsemanship in August. The award was voted for on a 3,2,1 points basis after each meeting by racing industry figures. Oliver won despite riding in Hong Kong for part of the season. Later in the year the VRC paid tribute to veteran racing writer Jack Elliott by making him an honorary life member.

A win of spirit: Brawny Spirit was bought for $3250 as a yearling, and joined the millionaire class by winning the Newmarket Handicap over Sequalo. Brawny Spirit was the smallest horse in the race. The win was also a fillip for jockey Michael Clarke whose career had plummeted after leaving the Hayes stable.

Flemington experienced its worst setback in December when 'funnel racing' forced a venue switch. Renovations to the inside section of the straight created bias and a 'fast lane' on the outside or grandstand rail to which jockeys in both straight and around-the-turn races were making beelines. The VRC reluctantly closed the track until mid-February for re-renovations.

Caulfield Cup: The Kid shows them how

Former jockey and successful trainer Pat Hyland, interviewed before the 1996 Caulfield Cup, said: 'The best horse will win the race.'

Generally true with Caulfield Cups perhaps, but racing is rarely that simple. The mare Arctic Scent, a 20/1 outsider ridden by a 17-year-old apprentice, prepared by a trainer only recently licensed and opposed to the best stayers in the country, should have had no chance.

But when conditions suit and everything goes right on the day, the horse so favoured is unstoppable. So it proved with Arctic Scent.

The mare, winner of the Queensland Oaks and placed in the Victorian fillies classic, had some staying credentials if not scintillating form. The Caulfield track was rain-affected, suiting front-runners, and apprentice Brent Stanley had her forward all the way.

Well into the straight she looked reluctant to take a split between leaders Iron Horse and Circles of Gold but Stanley, riding the most polished of races, drove her through and she surged away to win easily. Doriemus, on-track for another Melbourne Cup bid, finished better than anything else for fourth.

Jim Mason went into the record books as trainer but the real work had been done by Gerald Ryan, the trainer who was matching it with the Freedmans, Cummings and Hayes when he sensationally handed in his licence after allegations of sexual harassment.

Jockey Stanley went into the record books as the youngest to ride a Caulfield Cup winner and certainly the only apprentice not indentured to a licensed trainer. Arctic Scent's owner David Moodie, had taken over as master since Mason had not been training sufficiently long since Ryan's departure.

Caulfield Cup winning jockey Brent Stanley.

The first night meeting at Moonee Valley in January 1998. Night racing began in Australia at Toowoomba in September 1996, when locally trained Binary was the first night winner.

TURF TOPICS

Happy Birthday, Sir Tristram: 550 guests turned up at Patrick Hogan's Cambridge Stud for the birthday for the greatest sire of the era, Sir Tristram, who turned 25. He was six times Australian champion sire, and nine times head of the combined Australia/NZ list. He produced 44 Group 1 winners.

Yes, Indeed: Unfashionably bred Yes Indeed was bought for $3000 by battling trainer Danny Deegan as an unbroken two-year-old, but went on to win the 1996 Wellington Cup for Mike Moroney.

The Senator from Matamata: Jack Tims from Matamata turned up on New Year's Day 1996 at Ellerslie for the Auckland Cup with a huge bay gelding called Senator. Which he duly won – making five wins in succession.

1996 RESULTS

VRC MELBOURNE CUP (3200m)
Saintly, 55.5 (D Beadman) Trained by JB Cummings; 3:18.8; Count Chivas, Skybeau
AJC SYDNEY CUP (3200m)
Count Chivas, 55.5 (S King) Trained by DL Freedman; 3:26.3; The Bandette, Beaux Art
QTC BRISBANE CUP (3200m)
Dupain, 50.5 (K Forrester) Trained by A Bell; 3:20.6; Maxam, Super Slew
SAJC ADELAIDE CUP (3200m)
French Resort, 50 (J Holder) Trained by C Alderson; 3:22.6; Skybeau, Gaekwar
WATC PERTH CUP (3200m)
Crying Game, 49.5 (P Harvey) Trained by Ms AC Johnson; 3:23.9; Ernesto, Bullwinkle
VATC CAULFIELD CUP (2400m)
Arctic Scent, 49 (G Stanley (a)) Trained by J Mason; 2:30.2; Circles Of Gold, Iron Horse

VRC AUSTRALIAN CUP (2000m)
Saintly, 52.5 (D Beadman) Trained by JB Cummings; 2:2.1; Vialli, Peep On The Sly
MVRC WS COX PLATE (2040m)
Saintly, 57 (D Beadman) Trained by JB Cummings; 2:05.7; Filante, All Our Mob
AJC DERBY (2400m)
Octagonal, 55.5 (D Beadman) Trained by JR Hawkes; 2:28.4; Saintly, Filante
VICTORIA DERBY (2500m)
Portland Player, 55.5 (G Hall) Trained by DL Freedman; 2:35.2; Dead-heat for second Alfa and Ebony Grove
AJC DONCASTER HANDICAP (1600m)
Sprint By, 53 (G Boss) Trained by G Waterhouse; 1:35.4; Danasinga, Juggler
BTC DOOMBEN '10,000' (1350m)
Suntain, 51 (M Pelling) Trained by B Howlett; 1:21; Encores, Quick Return

VRC NEWMARKET HANDICAP (1200m)
Brawny Spirit, 54 (M Clarke) Trained by J Winks; 1:77; Sequalo, Royal Discard
AJC SIRES' PRODUCE STAKES (1400m)
Merlene, 54 (RS Dye) Trained by DL Freedman; 1:22.4; Clang, My Duke
VRC SIRES' PRODUCE STAKES (1400m)
My Duke, 55.5 (D Nikolic) Trained by G Ryan; 1:23.1; Zeya, Clang
VRC GRAND NATIONAL STEEPLECHASE (5000m)
Best Endeavours, 66 (F Stockdale) Trained by P Hyland; 6:7.7; The Hunted, Outstride
STC GOLDEN SLIPPER STAKES (1200m)
Merlene, 52.5 (G Hall) Trained by DL Freedman; 1:9.31; Paint, Flavour
VATC BLUE DIAMOND STAKES (1200m)
Paint, 54 (D Nikolic) Trained by G Ryan; 1:10.2; Flavour, Our Cashel
STC MERCEDES-TANCRED CLASSIC (2400m)
Octagonal, 52 (D Beadman) Trained by JR Hawkes; 2:27.3; Count Chivas, Saintly

Sir Tristram: the top New Zealand sire, pictured in his prime, has died at age 26 (Age).

A kiss for a saint from his jockey (Age).

The sire no one wanted

Sir Tristram, one of New Zealand's greatest sires, had to be put down after breaking a shoulder in an accident at Patrick Hogan's Cambridge Stud, the establishment he put on the map with progeny such as Empire Rose, Zabeel (sire of Octagonal and Might And Power), Dr Grace, Tristarc, Sovereign Red, Gurner's Lane and Grosvenor. And Saintly, whose dam All Grace was by Sir Tristram.

When Hogan, through a British blood-stock agent, bought Sir Tristram sight unseen from France for $144 000, the agent thought him demented. On examining Sir Tristram, the agent told Hogan he was a 'terrible beast'. Hogan, son of an Irish immigrant dairy farmer with a love of horses, took the punt and bought him. He was impressed with Sir Tristram's bloodlines (by English Derby winner Sir Ivor out of Isolt) and the fact that he had good front legs.

He didn't look like a stallion. But Sir Tristram wasn't worried about his looks. He had some potent blood in his veins and got results. So much so that his service fee mush-roomed from $1200 to $200 000 at the end of his career.

One noted NZ breeder, Fred Bodle, apologised to Hogan early on for not taking up a share in Sir Tristram on the grounds that he would never make a stallion. Some years later Bodle sent a mare called Sunny Fleur to Sir Tristram, paying $100 000 for the privilege. The result was Empire Rose.

From the start, the shrewd Hogan had a plan – for three years only his best mares would be serviced by Sir Tristram and the progeny would go to the best trainers. Before long, Hogan had a team of turf heroes.

Beadman is called

Darren Beadman was given a long and loving send off in December when he retired from racing at the age of 32 to train as an Assembly of God pastor. After massive media coverage, which included 'This Is Your Life' and '60 Minutes', he rode in his final race meeting on Boxing Day at Randwick, first winning on Igerwin, then losing on Ask the Waiter in his final race. It didn't really matter. The crowd of 20 074 had come to see their hero, and Octagonal's owner Jack Ingham presented Beadman with a huge antique Bible and told the crowd: 'The big loser is racing. The winner – God.'

Darren Beadman, nicknamed 'Tom Cruise' because of his gentle good looks, had a remarkable 17-year career.

Larry Cassidy and Secret Savings (Age).

Another Gai first

Gai Waterhouse became the first woman to win the Sydney trainers' premiership in July, completing an extraordinary season during which she quinellaed the Doncaster in March, entering the history books as the only trainer to saddle up the winner four years in a row. In April she quinellaed the Sydney Cup and, in June, took her winners' tally past 100 for the season.

The American-bred Secret Savings (8/1) overtook the Waterhouse-trained All Our Mob (9/2) in the final 200 metres of the Don-caster and won by a long neck. Secret Savings, brought to Australia by His Excellency Nasser Lootah of Dubai to stand at his Emirates Park stud, had won nine of 21 starts and more than $1 million in stakes. The race lacked glamour thanks to the absence of hot favourite Mou-awad with a leg injury.

In the Sydney Cup, Larry Cassidy rode Linesman to an easy victory, Waterhouse's Leica Lover finishing five-and-three-quarter lengths back in second place.

Mighty Might and Power, with Jim Cassidy, after their Caulfield Cup win (Age).

Mighty Might And Power

When Might And Power, cruising along at a fair clip, led the field into the straight in the Caulfield Cup, watchers around the country waited for the challengers to come. They're still waiting.

With a display of arrogance and speed that revived memories of Tulloch's devastating win in 1957, Might And Power surged to victory by a record 7 ½ lengths in 2:26.2 – a race and track record for 2400 metres.

As for Might And Power's rivals, it was left to old Doriemus, the 1995 Melbourne Cup winner, to run second. His trainer Lee Freedman said: 'The most amazing race I've ever seen. They just couldn't get near him. He was in a race of his own.' As usual, Might And Power's trainer Jack Denham didn't say much.

For jockey Jim Cassidy it was a triumphant return. Asked if Might And Power could win the Melbourne Cup, Cassidy said: 'It's certainly not beyond him. He's trained by Jack Denham and I'll be riding him.'

Sixteen days later in the big one, Cassidy soon had Might And Power, carrying a 3.5-kg penalty, in the lead. Halfway down the straight, they were two lengths in front. Once again it was left to Doriemus to issue the challenge. Neck and neck they went to the line, Might And Power getting there first by a short half-head.

Jack Denham did a bit of a jig for the crowd of 94 143. Unlike Denham, Might And Power's excited owner Nick Moraitis talked and talked. Kerry Packer reportedly cleaned up $5million on the winner, who firmed from 9/2 to 3/1 favouritism.

Time runs out

Time Frame, trained by Angela Smith from the little Western Australian town of Wagin, led throughout to win the $300 000 Perth Cup. The temperature in the mounting yard reached 45 degrees and the crowd of more than 20 000 sweltered on the hottest New Year's Day on record.

The winner, ridden by Dennis Gundry, was leased two years before from Wagin sheep and wheat farmers Jeff Ward and Greg Ball, by Smith and her shearing contractor husband Malcolm. The eight-year-old gelding won the WA Sires' Produce Stakes at Ascot in his early years, but more recently he had been best known for his unruliness.

A run in the 1996 Kalgoorlie Cup almost led to a ban from racing when he jumped out of the gates and raced towards the fence, interfering with a number of runners. Smith, a 36-year-old former jockey, persevered and, at the time of his Cup win, he had won nine races for her.

Bill Collins: Racing Personality of the Year, '87.

Farewell, Bill

Racing was in Bill Collins' blood and he became one of its stars, one of the best racecallers in the land. His keen eye and talent for picking winners in tight finishes earned him the sobriquet 'The Accurate One'. He was also the suave one, the likeable one, the unflappable one. His well-modulated voice was the stuff of show business, of vaudeville. As a singer and entertainer in TV shows such as 'Sunnyside Up' and the 'Penthouse Club', he was up to weight-for-age class. With Ron Casey, he was one of the stalwarts of HSV-7's long-running and much-watched Sunday lunchtime program, 'World Of Sport'. Away from the camera and the microphone, cards was one of his loves. So was the South Melbourne football club.

When he died on 14 June, aged 68, after a battle with cancer, Collins was mourned at the racetrack and beyond. He died on a Saturday. When the news was made public the following day, the races were at Moonee Valley. Everyone there said a silent prayer when the MVRC paid a special tribute to him on the giant TV screen.

Personal tributes flowed. 'His accuracy was dynamite,' said fellow caller Bryan Martin. Another caller, Clem Dimsey, praised his generous spirit, saying, 'He was always trying to help the younger blokes coming through.'

As a caller, Collins' fame reached beyond these shores. He called races in England and America. His coolness and clarity impressed racing folk in those countries. He once advised Bryan Martin: 'Imagine that you're calling to a blind person.'

Most of all, Collins was good at finding words to fit the occasion. 'Bonecrusher races into equine immortality', he told the Valley crowd that famous Cox Plate day.

Great lines on the spur of the moment don't come any better than that.

Octagonal's farewell appearance at Randwick, where he was a great crowd favourite (Age).

Shane Dye salutes, Big O at Doomben. (NP)

Jack and Sue Ingham with the champ (Age).

Sky's the limit for big 'O'

Shane Dye, master of all things spectacular, called for three cheers and the crowd obliged falsetto after Octagonal's win in the weight-for-age Mercedes Classic at Rosehill. Only Dye could get away with such a show of theatrics.

The win made Octagonal, one of the most popular horses to grace the Australian turf, the country's highest stakes winner, with $5 824 231 from 14 wins out of 27 starts. Even the heavens joined in the celebration, a big 'O' being written in the sky above the racecourse 30 seconds after the judge gave Octagonal the nod over Arkady in a camera finish.

As usual, Octagonal gave the punters more than their money's worth, his bulldog spirit gaining him the day by a whisker. Said chief steward Ray Murrihy: 'Half a stride before the finish, Octagonal was behind Ark-

ady. And half a stride after the post he was still behind. But on the post, he was in front.' That was Octagonal's hallmark. He knew where the line was.

For a moment, everyone seemed to forget that it was Golden Slipper Stakes day. The juvenile dash for cash was won by a good colt called Guineas, raced by Octagonal's owners, chicken kings Jack and Bob Ingham. Ridden by Darren Beadman, Guineas got home by an eyelash from Dye's mount, Encounter.

The following month, April, Octagonal bowed out of racing, not on a high but still the darling of racegoers. He ran second to Intergaze in the Queen Elizabeth Stakes. But the defeat didn't quell the enthusiasm of the 28 200 at Randwick, many of whom came with posters, banners and poems proclaiming the 'Big O'. They loved Octagonal, who always gave them a show.

TURF TOPICS

Seven of the best: John Morrissey, a trainer for 30 years, saddled up the first seven winners on the nine-race card at Canberra on 26 January. For good measure he trained the second placegetters in the last two races. Jockey Michael Cahill rode four of the winners. Morrisey's feat equalled that of Colin Hayes, who trained seven winners at Victoria Park in 1982. On the same day Hayes had three winners at Caulfield.

Some hangover! After a washout in 1996, more than 11 000 racegoers and picnickers threw off their hangovers and turned up for the 111th running of the Hanging Rock Cup on New Year's Day. To accommodate the huge crowd, the club had to use the centre of the track for the overflow. This hadn't happened since the days of horse and buggies.

Boys day: Four apprentices rode the program at Moonee Valley on 4 January. An Australia-wide strike by senior jockeys saw Eddie Cassar, Aaron Spiteri, Steven Vella and Sam Hyland each ride a double at the Valley. Senior riders withdrew their services, demanding an increase in the losing-ride fee of $65–75. After fines and squabbling, a fee of $85 was settled on.

Two more firsts: Lee Freedman chalked up his first Blue Diamond Stakes win with 20/1 shot Knowledge, his 77th Group 1 victory in 13 years as a trainer. In July, the Freedman stable won their first Melbourne trainers' title, ending a 19-year run by the Hayes dynasty.

'Big O' is back: Shane Dye was close to tears after Octagonal's game win in the Australian Cup before an emotional crowd of 21 000 at Flemington in March. Considered to be burned out last spring, Octagonal returned to the winner's circle in the Chipping Norton Stakes at Warwick Farm in February. But Dye ranked his narrow Australian Cup win over Gold City and Juggler in March as one of his gutsiest. Even trainer John Hawkes admitted he thought Octagonal might have been past his best.

Have saddle, will travel: When jockey Dale Spriggs rode at Port Macquarie in July, it was the 90th track he had ridden at in Australia — a record. He celebrated by riding four winners. Spriggs has ridden in the WA outback and at Royal Randwick, and most places in between. Last July, before being seriously injured in a fall at Canberra, he had ridden 122½ winners for the season.

A beaming Chris Munce after he won the 1997 Brisbane Cup on Desert Chill (NP).

Jim Cassidy fulfils his promise after he won the Queensland Derby at Eagle Farm on Yippio (NP).

Big smile from the lady Dane Ripper (Age).

Ripper of a lady

Dandy filly Dane Ripper gave Bart Cummings his fourth Stradbroke Handicap when she overpowered a top field in the 1400-metre race at Eagle Farm. Afterwards Cummings said he had plotted the win several months beforehand. In winning, Dane Ripper (16/1) became only the second filly to win the race in 30 years. The other was Canterbury Belle in 1985.

For Sydney jockey Chris Munce, it was his first win in the race. Cummings praised him, saying Munce had ridden the filly perfectly, keeping her back in the field and away from the fence.

Punters have short memories. Three months later Dane Ripper, having failed in the Epsom Handicap, came to Moonee Valley for the Cox Plate. This time Damien Oliver was in the saddle. 'Save her', said Cummings and that's what Oliver did. Until the turn into the straight when the mare stormed past Filante and company, giving Cummings his third Cox Plate. At 40/1, too.

1997 RESULTS

VRC MELBOURNE CUP (3200m)
Might and Power, 56 (J Cassidy) Trained by J Denham; 3:18.3; Doriemus, Markham
AJC SYDNEY CUP (3200m)
Linesman, 51.5 (L Cassidy) Trained by G Waterhouse; 3:20.5; Nothin' Leica Dane, Ebony Grove
QTC BRISBANE CUP (3200m)
Desert Chill, 52 (C Munce) Trained by S Laming; 3:24.6; Sapio, Sharscay
SAJC ADELAIDE CUP (3200m)
Cronus, 49.5 (RS Dye) Trained by R James; 3:29.4; Lord Ted, Power
WATC PERTH CUP (3200m)
Time Frame, 53 (D Gundry) Trainer AJ Smith; 3:22.8; Regimental Tattoo, Beau Heed
VATC CAULFIELD CUP (2400m)
Might and Power, 52.5 (J Cassidy) Trained by J Denham; 2:26.2; Doriemus, Catalan Opening

VRC AUSTRALIAN CUP (2000m)
Octagonal, 57 (RS Dye) Trained by JR Hawkes; 2:1; Gold City, Juggler
MVRC WS COX PLATE (2040m)
Dane Ripper, 54.5 (D Oliver) Trained by JB Cummings; 2:07.6; Filante, Vialli
AJC DERBY (2400m)
Ebony Grove, 55.5 (RS Dye) Trained by G Rogerson; 2:28.8; Danendri, Intergaze
VICTORIA DERBY (2500m)
Second Coming, 55.5 (G Childs) Trainer M Moroney; 2:36.3; Tie The Knot, Kalastaire
AJC DONCASTER HANDICAP (1600m)
Secret Savings, 57 (L Cassidy) Trainer G Waterhouse; 1:35.5; All Our Mob, Ravarda
BTC DOOMBEN '10 000' (1350m)
Accomplice, 51 (RS Dye) Trained by JR Hawkes; 1:18.5; Blazing Steel, Monopolize
VRC NEWMARKET HANDICAP (1200m)
Ruffles, 52.5 (RS Dye) Trained by M Lees; 1:8.9; Catalan Opening, All Our Mob

AJC SIRES' PRODUCE STAKES (1400m)
Encounter, 55.5 (RS Dye) Trained by C Conners; 1:22.4; Guineas, Adeewin
VRC SIRES' PRODUCE STAKES (1400m)
Millward, 55.5 (D Beadman) Trained by A Bell; 1:23.1; Cornwall Queen, Evader
VRC GRAND NATIONAL STEEPLECHASE (5000m)
Palace Symphony, 65 (R Maund) Trained by E Musgrove; 6.1.5; Best Endeavours, Burrowye Lord
STC GOLDEN SLIPPER STAKES (1200m)
Guineas, 55.5 (D Beadman) Trainer JR Hawkes; 1:8.99; Encounter, Regal Chamber
VATC BLUE DIAMOND STAKES (1200m)
Knowledge, 54 (D Brereton) Trained by DL Freedman; 1:10.2; Rose Of Danehill, Sports
STC MERCEDES-TANCRED CLASSIC (2400m)
Octagonal, 57 (RS Dye) Trained by JR Hawkes; 2:27.4; Arkady, Istidaad

Might And Power: the tick of a great heart

Jack Denham: yes, he can smile! (NP).

Jim Cassidy guides Might And Power (inside) to win the Melbourne Cup from Doriemus (Age).

Superlatives are the cut flowers of sports reporting. They look good for a few days, then they wilt and, after a week or so, they usually look limp and soggy. Facts are better. Facts are for the ages. And the 1998 Cox Plate was one for the ages – one to tuck away for the grandkids, as Paul Brettell, Moonee Valley's chief executive, said afterwards.

There were two remarkable facts about Might And Power's win.

First, when a horse knocks a couple of seconds off a track record, as Might And Power did, the race is usually set up for him. Some tearaway pours on the speed, breaks up the field, then fades on the home turn, allowing the better horses to come swooping down the outside.

That's how it was in 1960 when Tulloch broke the record in the Cox Plate: Sky High, a brilliant colt, took the field through the first half-mile in 46 seconds before fading to sixth. That's how it was in 1987 when Rubiton broke the record: Vo Rogue cleared out by 15 lengths before wobbling up the straight like a drunk. And that's how it was in 1990 when Better Loosen Up broke the record after Stylish Century had led by a dozen lengths in the middle stages.

Might And Power did it at both ends. He rushed to the lead going out of the straight. He didn't stop and start like some front runners. Rather, he kept lifting the tempo, upping the stakes, gradually making the contest unbearable, reeling off furlong after furlong in about

12 seconds so that long before the home turn, agony and panic had broken out behind him. Then, at the point of the turn, when he should have fallen down the hole that swallowed Sky High, Vo Rogue and Stylish Century, Might And Power kicked two lengths clear, galloping extravagantly, zestfully, a cruel and wonderful machine.

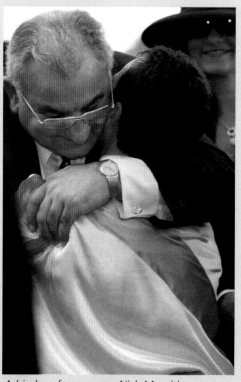

A big hug from owner Nick Moraitis.

The horse is a champion in the old-fashioned sense of the word, a freak. He does things others can't do. He is the best horse since Tulloch.

The second remarkable fact relates to this last claim. The Cox Plate was the final link in a golden chain. In 1997, Might And Power won his first Group 1 race, the Caulfield Cup. Legs flailing everywhere, he stormed away to win by seven-and-a-half lengths, breaking the track record. Between that and the 1998 Cox Plate, he won another five Group 1s: the Melbourne Cup, the Mercedes Classic, the Queen Elizabeth, the Doomben Cup and the Yalumba Stakes (formerly the Caulfield Stakes).

Other horses have won more Group 1s in a year – Tulloch won 11 as a three-year-old – but it's hard to think of a horse who has won more 'great' races in a year. And Might And Power has won the three toughest races in Australia – the Caulfield Cup, the Melbourne Cup and the Cox Plate – by leading all the way and making time. The odds are that no horse will ever do that again.

There was a third remarkable thing about the Cox Plate – the aftermath. Crowds often go wild for racehorses, particularly at Moonee Valley, a bearpit designed for theatrics. Crowds occasionally go wild for a trainer, as when Bart Cummings won his 10th Melbourne Cup, or for a jockey, as when Darren Beadman pulled 20 000 into Randwick for his farewell.

At the Cox Plate – and this is something

new – the crowd fell in love with an owner and the owner fell in love with the crowd. Nick Moraitis, the Sydney fruit and vegetable merchant, tumbled from the grandstand, smiling and sweating, to be bailed up by the media and well-wishers.

'Nick, come out on to the track,' Gary Gray, the Moonee Valley presenter, called to him.

Moraitis stepped on to the turf, looked up at the cheering and boisterous crowd, and a curious chemistry began. Moraitis raised his hands high above his head, fingers extended, black braces showing as his blue shirt bulged open. The crowd roared back at him as though he was running for president. Moraitis walked along the fence for maybe 80 metres, followed by several TV crews and a dozen or so photographers. He kept reaching out, touching hands, saying: 'Thanks Melbourne, thanks, you're all beautiful people.'

The beautiful people were mostly young men, in jeans, T-shirts and baseball caps. They chanted 'Might And Power' and 'Nick, Nick, Nick'. Some were close to delirious. They jumped the fence to hug and kiss Moraitis before clambering back. 'It was like being with Jesus,' said Gray, who, in a more sensible moment, may need to explain what he really meant to the parish priest.

'How does this compare with the Melbourne Cup win?' someone shouted at Moraitis.

'Better,' he said, still touching hands. 'This is fantastic. Money can't buy what this means to me.'

How about the prize money?

'F… the prize money.'

Moraitis was neither going out of his way to be profane nor pretending that he couldn't use $975 000. He was simply saying something obvious and important: the moment was priceless.

Up in the stand, Jack Denham, Might And Power's 74-year-old trainer, said: 'Yeah, that's the one I wanted.' Then he slung his binoculars over his left shoulder and headed for the madness below. He made a short speech in a quavering voice. The crowd cheered him for 10 seconds before he began speaking. Afterwards, looking pleased and shy and confused, he signed autographs. He is not used to being a folk hero.

Nearby, Moraitis was saying: 'He's done it all now, this horse, done it all … There were a lot of doubting Thomases today. That was the best of the lot.'

Might And Power broke into a jog every time cheering broke out during the presentation. He was still blowing a little, his flanks rising and falling under the white satin rug, his nostrils flaring gently. But he didn't have that look of exhaustion the other runners wore as they trudged back to their stalls. And watching him, you were reminded again about the mysterious nature of this thing we call sporting class.

Might And Power shouldn't be this good. His legs mock the rules about conformation. His hind legs are wide apart and his front legs are close together, so that at full gallop he moves on two tracks, one inside the other. At the slower paces, the near-side front leg flaps to the side as if on a hinge. At high speed, it comes through in a circular, paddling motion. He brings his knees up too high, as if he's trying to climb something. He also carries his head too high. And he's so full of nervous energy that he comes back from a race like a coiled spring. He did it after the Melbourne Cup and again after the Cox Plate. He doesn't seem to know about exhaustion.

He has a lovely pedigree, but a piece of paper doesn't seem adequate to explain him either. All we know is that he had the greatest thing of all, the thing you can't see, the thing an American trainer once called 'the great tick of the heart'.

Nick Moraitis knows he had been blessed. At the presentation he said: 'I would like to thank my beautiful animal, a wonderful athlete … May God keep you for many more years to come to give us the enjoyment we've seen here today.'

Amen to that.

by Les Carlyon

Might And Power, a crowd magnet (NP).

Jack Denham has a word to Might And Power before the Yalumba Stakes (Age).

Might And Power wins the Cox Plate (BP).

Nick Moraitis happy with another win (BP).

Jim Cassidy says that's three big wins (BP).

Might And Power grabs grand slam

In 1954, the legendary Rising Fast won the Caulfield Cup, Cox Plate and Melbourne Cup within the space of 17 days. No horse has matched that feat, but in 1998, Might And Power added the Cox Plate to his 1997 Caulfield and Melbourne Cups double.

Might And Power jumped to the front at the first turn in the Cox Plate. And that was it. Nothing was going to catch him as he clocked up sectional times of around 12 seconds every 200 metres. And when his giant strides came to an end, the track record for 2040 metres was smashed by a massive two seconds.

'I would like to thank my beautiful animal. He is a great athlete,' said owner Nick Moraitis as punters leapt the fence to shake his hand and congratulate the winning jockey Jim Cassidy.

'Might And Power just wouldn't slow down,' said Kenny Man, trainer of second-placed Northern Drake. Shane Dye, who rode

Tycoon Lil (third), said Might And Power had no faults. Lee Freedman, trainer of Doriemus (sixth), called Might And Power's front-running performance as good as any he'd ever seen, as did chief steward Des Gleeson: 'The best staying performance I've seen. His time was 12 to 15 lengths better than Saintly's.'

Here was a horse who had won from 1200m to 3200m and switched from handicaps to weight-for-age with ease. But not all of his wins were certainties. The 1998 Doomben Cup forced him to dig deep in the straight to resist strong challenges from Intergaze and I Like Him. There were still some knockers before the Chelmsford Stakes at Randwick, where he beat Juggler who raced on his heels all the way.

'That should shut a few people up,' chirped his normally tight-lipped trainer Jack Denham. For his training of Might And Power, Denham received the inaugural Fred

Hoysted Award. Might And Power was named Horse of the Year.

Moraitis played front-row for South Sydney and Eastern Suburbs and met Denham at a rugby match. The son of Greek parents at Townsville, Moraitis made his money as a fruit and vegetable supplier. He knew his apples well enough to select Might And Power, but admitted it was 'an act of God'. The horse was named after a hymn.

Moraitis cried after the Cox Plate, and again when Might And Power won the Queen Elizabeth Stakes. He dearly wanted to contest the $4.2 million Japan Cup, but the prospect of Might And Power travelling in a box for 24 hours was not worth the risk.

In late 1998 the VRC announced plans to stage the 1999 Australian Cup as an international race. Might And Power would be set for it. The world could come to him.

Billy Idol lights up Moonee Valley

Rock star Paul Kelly was the curtain-raiser at Moonee Valley for Australia's first metropolitan night race meeting on 26 January, but it was jockey Shane Dye, nicknamed Billy Idol, who took centre stage.

Dye had most of the 32 342 crowd on their feet when he won the historic first race on three-year-old colt Vitrinite. And everyone was jumping after he won the main event, the Group 1 Australia Stakes (1200m) on Sydney filly Stella Cadente.

In an encore performance the following year, Dye stole the limelight again in the Australia Stakes with a superb win on Grand Archway. No wonder he said: 'Every meeting should be held at night.'

Jezabeel (on the inside) is about to overtake Champagne (outside) in the Cup (Age).

Lady Herries, trainer of Taufan's Melody (Age).

Melbourne Cup winning jockley Chris Munce celebrates Jezabeel's victory with his cup (Age).

Taufan's Melody, Jezabeel, Caulfield Cup (Age).

Foreign invasion – but the locals dig in

The Aussies and Kiwis headed for the trenches when huge prize money, more flexible quarantine rules, and vigorous overseas recruiting made 1998 the year of the biggest foreign assault on the Caulfield and Melbourne Cups.

Local trainer Colin Alderson returned the first shots by threatening legal action over the exclusion of his highly fancied horse Our Unicorn from the Caulfield Cup field in favour of visiting English horse Taufan's Melody who, unlike Our Unicorn, had not met the prize-money qualification for entry.

The VATC, believing it had a moral and contractual obligation to allow Taufan's Melody to run after encouraging it to enter, decided to exercise discretionary powers to exempt it from standard eligibility conditions.

Our Unicorn, named first emergency, could only run if there was a scratching. So Alderson tried to buy rank outsider Count Chivas, with a view to scratching him in favour of Our Unicorn, but failed. Ironically,

there was a late scratching when Fayreform reared in the stalls before the race, but it was too late to allow Our Unicorn a start.

Taufan's trainer Lady Herries, wife of former English cricketer Colin Cowdrey, said her horse would do the talking. Everyone was talking when it won the cup at 66/1 and survived a protest from the rider of sixth-placed Jezabeel, Chris Munce, who alleged severe interference from Taufan's jockey Ray Cochrane near the 200-metre mark.

For such interference in England, Cochrane might have been relegated to last, but Jezabeel was too far back for a protest to stick under Australian rules. Taufan's Melody kept the race. Cochrane was fined $20 000 and suspended.

In the lead-up to the Melbourne Cup, Yorkshire, another English horse, was allowed into the field ahead of better-qualified locals Bridleman and Bulta.

'The race is not an Australian race any more. It is a joke,' said Bulta's trainer Jim

White. Neville McBurney, trainer of the eliminated Praise Indeed, condemned the VRC for turning the Melbourne Cup into an invitation race. But Bart Cummings, who opposed preferential treatment before the Caulfield Cup, was quieter this time. His horse Perpetual Check was granted discretionary inclusion.

Five English horses (Faithful Son, Persian Punch, Sheer Danzig, Taufan's Melody, and Yorkshire) and two Asian horses (Three Crowns and Peak of Perfection) contested the Melbourne Cup. With over a quarter of the field 'foreigners' it was the biggest international field in the history of the race.

The locals had the last laugh when Jezabeel won on the post from Champagne. These were the two horses who had been most inconvenienced by Taufan's Melody in the Caulfield Cup.

'This is for Australia and New Zealand,' said Jezabeel's jubilant trainer Brian Jenkins.

Who said the Anzac spirit was dead?

T. J. Smith and the Bragger

On 2 September 1998 the champion trainer T. J. Smith died in Sydney after a stroke. He was 81.

The little bloke with the twinkling blue eyes and the rosy cheeks and the air of a bantam rooster was like a man before he was 10. Had to be. He grew up on the western plains of the Riverina, a pitiless place in summer: red dust and baking clay pans and hardly a tree and, back then, no irrigation.

Tommy Smith, TJ as everyone came to know him, was the eldest boy in a family of seven kids. As a youngster, he worked the

ing belief in himself, he took a job as work rider and unofficial trainer for a grazier at Bethungra, near Cootamundra, NSW.

Running wild on the property was a three-year-old horse, a big bay lump with a plain head. He must have been handled at least once because he had been gelded. Although regarded as an outlaw, he was no brumby. His sire was Windbag, the 1925 Melbourne Cup winner. TJ liked him and decided to break him in.

Everyone said he was mad to persist, but several months later, TJ managed to get a saddle on. He swung a leg over and the horse

two-metre fence and disappeared. The police later found him grazing at La Perouse, about 10 kilometres away.

At the next trial, TJ put a rodeo rider on Bragger. The horse bucked but the rider stayed on. So TJ gave Bragger a start at Canterbury early in 1942, backed him, and watched him run last. Then, at Randwick, Bragger ran second at 100/1. TJ was so broke he was living on biscuits. He took Bragger to Newcastle, where he ran third.

At Rosehill on 14 March 1942, Bragger gave TJ his first (official) win as a trainer.

Tommy Smith as a 13-year-old winner.

The successful trainer of the 50s.

Hats off, a salute by a winner in the 1990s.

scoop behind a team of draught horses, killed sheep for the butcher's shop, broke in rough horses, carted water and waited for his old man outside the pub. He briefly attended a convent in Narrandera. Later, TJ would sigh: 'All I wanted to do was get away from home.'

A poddy calf became his escape. At 13, he swapped his stockwhip for a calf whose mother had died. He collected spilled wheat from the railyards and boiled it for the calf. He sold the fatted calf for a pound, enough for a train fare to Melbourne and the stables of 'Battling' Bill McLaughlin at Mordialloc.

He was sorry to leave his mother, who, he would later say, had a 'cruel life', but he had to get on with his own. He was going to be a great jockey. By the time he broke his hip in a fall from a hurdler, TJ knew he wouldn't be even a moderate jockey. He hadn't ridden one city winner. With little more than an unswerv-

bucked furiously. 'By Jeez, he used to tickle me up,' TJ recalled, but he wasn't thrown.

After the grazier died, TJ headed for Sydney with his ratbag horse. He took him off the goods train at Darling Harbour and led him to Todman Avenue, Kensington, where he'd rented a stable. TJ lived in the box next door.

It was 1941. TJ went to the Australian Jockey Club to register blue and green racing colours and take out a permit to train at Kensington, opposite Randwick. He also filed a name for his horse – Bragger. Bragger became the most important horse TJ trained, more important than Tulloch or Kingston Town or Gunsynd.

Bragger still bucked so keenly that TJ had to ride him in a stock saddle at track work. Eventually, he entered him for a barrier trial. Bragger jumped out, threw the jockey, leapt a

Bragger then won his next three. TJ kept backing him. He admitted winning $140 000, probably the equivalent of several million in today's money.

While Bragger was out spelling, TJ blew his hoard on nightclubs, hire cars, travel, gambling and a wardrobe of suits and hats that George Raft would have envied. When Bragger came back, he won at 14/1. TJ had money again. As he often said, that was a turning point in his life. 'I was never broke again,' he'd smile.

Bragger won 13 races. He was put down after being horribly burned in a horse float fire. TJ never said so, but you always figured that Bragger, that wild spirit from the Cootamundra hills, was the horse he loved best.

by Les Carlyon

Bart Cummings and Saintly

Saintly was pretty much Bart Cummings' creation. He bred him, raised him, trained him, sorted out his quirks and ruffled his forelock, taught him how to relax and how to eat and part-owned him through a brief career, just 23 starts, that brought in $3.8 million. Then Saintly broke down.

'You've got to be philosophical about these things … they happen,' Cummings begins. A pause. He isn't given to theatrics – he's won 10 Melbourne Cups and seen too much – yet something is teasing at him.

'But he was something special,' he finally says. 'He was still growing up, still putting it together. We'd only seen half his potential. When he was winning early on, he was only half a horse. This year [1998] would have been his best. If he'd raced for another season, I think he would have been the equal of Galilee.' Another pause. 'Equal if not better.'

His voice raises slightly. 'He had a stride like Phar Lap. He's the longest strider I've ever had. I reckon he would have gone 18 feet.'

That's just the way we'll all remember

Darren Beadman does his thing (BP).

Saintly was born in 1992, the worst of times for Cummings, who was then carrying $20 million in debts after schemes to market yearlings as tax shelters collapsed during the 1990 recession. Cummings didn't know how much of his world he was going to keep but he still had his mare All Grace, who traced to the champion Taj Rossi. Cummings decided to send her to Sky Chase. Saintly, the foal, was slabby like his father, more bone than flesh. 'Just another foal,' says Cummings, 'nothing special.' He won only one of his four minor races as a two-year old.

In the spring of his three-year-old season, Cummings brought Saintly to Flemington. Saintly won in a sparkling time. Cummings knew he had a good one.

Then it was back to Sydney for that unforgettable autumn of 1996 when four cracking youngsters – Saintly, Nothin' Leica Dane, Octagonal and Filante – ran their hearts out, race after race, week after week.

When Saintly returned as a four-year-old in 1996, his second place in the Metropolitan

The classic picture of perfect poise in action (BP).

Reflections of a glorious win, Beadman and Saintly (BP).

Saintly. He just flowed along, stretchy and rubbery, like a goods train that had been coupled up carelessly, a washy chestnut gelding who tended to roll around a lot because, even at four, he was still trying to work out how to use his body.

And then he'd let go. His hind legs would drive far underneath him and he'd flatten his ears into his mane. And he'd try so extravagantly, sometimes turning his head on the side or changing his leading leg.

He bowed the tendon in his off-leg at Caulfield in 1997. On the dirt track at Eagle Farm in 1998, he wrecked his other leg. Cummings admits it was always even money to happen. Saintly didn't hold anything back: he went too freely to be careful.

Bart Cummings after winning the Cup (BP).

at Randwick taught Cummings and jockey Darren Beadman two things: Saintly didn't like being hit with the whip and, second, because of his slabby build, the saddle was shifting on him.

Saintly was to have only three more starts: the Cox Plate, the Melbourne Cup and the Orr Stakes. He won them all and they called him the horse from heaven. 'Have you ever seen as easier Cup win?' Cummings asks. 'I haven't. None of mine have won the Cup that easily.' Saintly always had kind ways. 'He'd just cuddle up to you and nudge you,' Beadman says.

Saintly is now back at Cummings' farm. In the meantime, there's a void in the stable.

by Les Carlyon

Tide's out, they're off at Ocean Grove (Age).

Racing's a beach

The weather was fine and the track was wet for the Ocean Grove Cup, held annually in February on Victoria's surfcoast.

Running a race meeting on a public beach also proved the usual challenge for officials, who had to contend with wayward surfers, toddlers building sandcastles, and people trying to walk their dogs down the main straight. The straight itself almost had to be moved when the tide came in.

The 5000 punters were a fashionable lot, hats on, thongs off, all comfortably perched on eskies for the big race. Leading dunes bookie, Bill Tenner, was holding about $600 on each event on the six-race program. The race that doesn't stop the nation, but sure stops Ocean Grove, was won by Pog Hunter.

Bart's other Cup

The big bay mare Dane Ripper gave Bart Cummings his 12th Australian Cup (2000m) at Flemington in March. Ridden patiently by Steven King, Dane Ripper (7/4 fav.) settled in fourth and eased out in the straight to sizzle home over the last 600m in 33.4 seconds. Cummings' other entrant, Delinquent (14/1), was 4½ lengths behind, with Marble Halls (4/1) a neck away, third.

When asked to rate Dane Ripper's performance against his previous 11 Australian Cups, especially Let's Elope's win in 1992, Cummings refused. 'They're all my little mates. I wouldn't like to put one down and compare them like that.'

Asked whether Dane Ripper would have beaten Might And Power, out injured, Cummings said: 'I think we would have beaten him'. Cummings himself was injured, limping with a broken ankle thanks to another little mate who jumped on his foot in the stables. 'If I was a horse, they'd put me down,' he said.

The Sundance Kid (B. Scott) clears a fence (Age).

Rough dreams

Ex-NZ jockey Brett Scott rode a typically patient race at Moonee Valley on Maybe Rough to win the AV Hiskens Steeplechase and clinch the Melbourne jumping jockeys' premiership. Scott, riding for trainer John Wheeler, had won four consecutive Great Eastern Steeplechases (Wheeler won five on end) and the last two Grand Annuals.

They triumphed with The Sundance Kid in one of the great races of the year, the Grand Annual Steeplechase at Warrnambool, where in a 33-fence showdown The Sundance Kid and Jim Houlahan's Usurper were level at the last before Usurper crashed heavily. Usurper lay motionless but despite the hessian screen going up, was only winded. The Sundance Kid raced on to victory.

Robbie Waterhouse leaves the hearing (Age).

End of exile

In late 1998, the NSW Thoroughbred Racing Board allowed former bookmakers Robbie and Bill Waterhouse to return to racecourses after a 14-year ban. Both men were originally warned off for life in 1984 following the Fine Cotton ring-in affair.

Several other ring-in identities were also readmitted in 1998. As for Fine Cotton, he was living the good life near Brisbane, preparing to make his film debut at the age of 22. A film of the fix was being produced by his new owner John Stainton. Even Fine Cotton's former leading man, Hayden Haitana, had been tempted to talk. He said: 'Some have a weakness for drink, some for women, some for the punt, and some for the con. I got the lot.'

Into the limelight: Cathy Payne became the seventh member of her family to ride a metropolitan winner when George On Broadway grabbed the Flying Halo Handicap at Sandown.

Two great straights: Queensland three-year-old Al Mansour, a son of 1986 Melbourne Cup winner At Talaq, scored his seventh win on end (from 11 starts) in the Rubiton Stakes at Caulfield. When NZ sensation Zonda burst home in the Alister Clark Stakes, his record was five out of five.

Cup fever: The 1913 Melbourne Cup trophy, won by Posinatus, fetched $68 500 at auction in March. A story that Phar Lap's 1930 Cup was lying in a Port Macquarie car yard was not so easy to sell. It was believed to be a replica.

Cheviot keeps Force at bay: Former SA Derby winner Cheviot was due to be retired to become a police horse after the Sandown Cup. His win at 33/1 kept him off the beat for a little longer.

Unlucky miss: When Juggler lost by a short head to Catalan Opening, trainer Gai Waterhouse missed out on winning a record fifth consecutive Doncaster Hcp.

Clean sweep at Werribee: A cleaning company and an art dealer sponsored a race on Werribee Cup day and offered the winning owners a $2500 credit towards a painting purchase. The winning filly was owned by a syndicate of 3000 owners.

Perpetual bridesmaid: Doriemus just failed to hold off Tie The Knot in the Sydney Cup in scenes reminiscent of the 1997 Melbourne Cup when Might And Power found the altar first.

A legend in his own lifetime: Trainer Angus Armanasco, who announced his retirement at the age of 86 in November, already had a race named after him and a wall in his honour at Caulfield. 'They were sick of waiting for me to die,' he said.

Top trifecta: Colin Hayes, trainer of 5333 winners in his 42-year career, joined Bart Cummings and T. J. Smith in the Australian Sports Hall of Fame.

Oliver keeps getting more: Damien Oliver rode winner no. 999 in the NZ Derby at Ellerslie in December. After beginning as a Perth apprentice 10 years ago, his average was 100 winners a year.

Big China coup: In a $500m deal prematurely announced on 31 December, a Victorian syndicate was set to develop a horseracing complex for the Chinese city of Dalian, supplying everything.

Women 'at the barrier'

Australian racing has long been a conservative, masculine industry. In the 1980s the 'lady jockeys' room' arrived, but it remains a lonely place while old prejudices survive and women do not receive the opportunities they deserve.

In 1998 there were 31 females among Victoria's 274 professional jockeys. Sally Wynne had ridden over 200 winners. Maree Payne's tally was more than 300. A woman trained the Caulfield Cup winner. There was even a woman on the VRC Committee. Women were winning more than the 'fashion stakes'.

Sadly, 1998 was a tragic year for two women jockey pioneers. Australia's first female Aboriginal jockey, Leigh-Anne Goodwin, died on 7 December from injuries sustained in a race fall at Roma in Queensland. A single mother with a nine-year-old son, Goodwin had ridden most of the bush tracks in Queensland. She had dreamed of making enough money from racing to support her son, perhaps enough to buy a small home, and she had dreamed of winning in the city.

Beverley Buckingham-Smith was named 1998 Personality of the Year by the VRC and Victorian Racing Media Association (Age).

In the springtime before her death, Goodwin rode Getelion to victory at Eagle Farm. It was the first time an Aboriginal woman had ridden a metropolitan winner.

Leading Brisbane jockey Mike Pelling said statistics showed riding horses was the most dangerous job on earth. He said he would never encourage anyone to take it up, especially not a woman because he believed their bodies were less suited than men to withstanding the kinds of injuries that could be incurred.

That may, or may not, be so. Since 1933, 58 Australian jockeys have been killed in race falls. Hundreds more have been seriously hurt, most recently the champion Tasmanian jockey Beverley Buckingham-King who sustained multiple spinal fractures in a horrific four-horse fall at Elwick on 30 May 1998.

When her mount Theutelle clipped another horse's heels and crashed, Buckingham-King was catapulted into the air and landed on her back. It was the kind of accident where a jockey's gender could not have made any difference.

Buckingham-King was Australia's most successful woman rider, with over 1000 winners and the Hobart, Launceston and Devonport Cups resting on her mantelpiece. As a teenager in 1982, while still an apprentice in Tasmania, she became the first female jockey in the world to win a senior jockeys' premiership. In 1994–95 she was the first woman anywhere to ride over 100 winners.

Bravely, Buckingham-King vowed to overcome her terrible injuries and has since made remarkable progress. The fall changed her life, but her will to win remained.

That's racing. For all the pain and effort, and the risks, the struggles and setbacks, there's a home straight somewhere up ahead and a winning post at the end.

Down the straight in the Ipswich Cup (NP).

Insecure (M. Pelling) wins Queensland Guineas.

1998 RESULTS

VRC MELBOURNE CUP (3200m)
Jezabeel, 51 (C Munce) Trained by B Jenkins; 3:18.6; Champagne, Persian Punch
AJC SYDNEY CUP (3200m)
Tie The Knot, 50.5 (RS Dye) Trained by G Walter; 3:25.7; Doriemus, Praise Indeed
QTC BRISBANE CUP (3200m)
Praise Indeed, 52 (RS Dye) Trained by N McBurney; 3:22.3; Yobro, Star Covet
SAJC ADELAIDE CUP (3200m)
The Hind, 50.5 (RS Dye) Trained by PC Hayes; 3:22.4; Bohemiath, Kristalero
WATC PERTH CUP (3200m)
Heed The Toll, 50.5 (N Rudland) Trained by M Pateman; 3:25.52; Old Cobber, In Name Only
VATC CAULFIELD CUP (2400m)
Taufan's Melody, 535 (R Cochrane) Trained by Lady Herries; 2:30.16; Lisa's Game, Tie The Knot

VRC AUSTRALIAN CUP (2000m)
Dane Ripper, 55.5 (S King) Trained by JB Cummings; 2:2.4; Delinquent, Marble Halls
MVRC WS COX PLATE (2040m)
Might And Power, 56 (J Cassidy) Trained by J Denham; 2:03.54; Northern Drake, Tycoon Lil
AJC DERBY (2400m)
Gold Guru, 55.5 (G Childs) Trained by L MacDonald; 2:33.49; Tie The Knot, Northern Drake
VICTORIA DERBY (2500m)
Arena, 55.5 (L Cassidy) Trained by JR Hawkes; 2:35.16; Sky Heights, Lawyer
AJC DONCASTER HANDICAP (1600m)
Catalan Opening, 56.5 (L Beasley) Trainer JB Cummings; 1:38; Juggler, Iron Horse
BTC DOOMBEN '10000' (1350m)
Chief De Beers, 57 (K Waller) Trained by JW Calder; 1:19.8; Staging, General Nediym

VRC NEWMARKET HANDICAP (1200m)
General Nediym, 55 (B York) Trained by FW Mitchell; 1:9.2; Toledo, Scandinavia
AJC SIRES' PRODUCE STAKES (1400m)
Alf, 55.5 (G Childs) Trained by D O'Sullivan; 1;24.5; Mossman, Shovhog
VRC SIRES' PRODUCE STAKES (1400m)
Coup De Grace, 55.5 (G Hall) Trainer DL Freedman; 1:26.1; Special Edition, Admired
VRC GRAND NATIONAL STEEPLECHASE (5000m)
Burrowye Lord, 66.5 (WD Smith) Trained by D Brideoake; 6:6.8; Off Again, Paxtino
STC GOLDEN SLIPPER STAKES (1200m)
Prowl, 55.5 (C Munce) Trained by C Conners; 1:9.5; Shovhog, Glammis
VATC BLUE DIAMOND STAKES (1200m)
Danelagh, 54 (G Hall) Trained by DL Freedman; 1:10.1; Danari, Piccadilly Circus
STC MERCEDES-TANCRED CLASSIC (2400m)
Might And Power, 57 (B York) Trained by J Denham; 2:27.2; Gold Guru, Doriemus

Bernborough

Columnist

Flight

Windbag

igh Castle

Gloaming

Beauford

Gothic

H

Amounis

Phar Lap

Phar Lap

Peter Pan

Chatham

Carbine

Poitrel

Tranquil Star

Heroic

Royal Gem

Bernborough

Columnist